HOLMAN

ILLUSTRATED GUIDE TO BIBLICAL GEOGRAPHY

HOLMAN

ILLUSTRATED GUIDE TO BIBLICAL GEOGRAPHY

READING THE LAND

PAUL H. WRIGHT

Holman Illustrated Guide to Biblical Geography

B&H Publishing Group
Brentwood, Tennessee

ISBN: 978-0-8054-9483-9

Dewey Decimal Classification: 220.91
Subject Heading: BIBLE—GEOGRAPHY/
HISTORICAL GEOGRAPHY/BIBLE—ATLASES

The interior of the *Holman Illustrated Guide to Biblical Geography* was designed and typeset by 2K/DENMARK, using Bible Serif created by 2K/DENMARK, Højbjerg, Denmark.

Printed in China
4 5 6 7 8 9 10 • 29 28 27 26 25
RRD

For Benjamin

Go up this way to the Negev,
then go up into the hill country.
See what the land is like.
Num 13:17–18

WITH GRATITUDE

Land is a gift—all land, really, although most of the time we use the phrase theologically in connection with "the land that I will show you" (Gen 12:1). The land of ancient Israel was entrusted to Abraham, grazed by Jacob, anticipated by Moses, settled by Joshua, ruled by David, tilled by Naboth, evoked by the psalmists, embraced by Isaiah, wept over by Jeremiah, left but not forsaken by Daniel and restored by Ezra and Nehemiah. In the biblical world, as in much of the modern one, people were so tightly identified with *place* that to speak of a person was to speak of the land that he or she called home. Biblically, land (*eretz*) is not just soil, rock, and water, but encompasses everything that belongs within its boundaries, that draws strength from its substance, and that allows its people to develop a sense of identity and belonging. Jesus redeems people, but not in isolation from their contexts, and this includes the places in which they live. To speak of land is to speak of the human-divine encounter of this life within the context of real places, real experiences, real blessings, and real needs.

The chance to explore the land of ancient Israel is also a gift, one that I and my family have been privileged to receive for a quarter century. With that gift comes obligations, willingly accepted. One is to pause and reflect on the impact that the events of the Bible, grounded in time and place, have in our here and now. Another is to strive to see the land in its fullness, to recognize the breadth and depth of all of its living things. A third is to view the land through the eyes of its former inhabitants—all of them, not just those fronted in the biblical story. And a fourth is to think and act in ways that take redemption holistically—of the soul, of the heart, of the mind, and of the hands.

This book, an excursion into the geography of the Bible, has been a long time a-making. It was born amidst a community of students and scholars living and working together in Jerusalem, on Mount Zion, who were drawn to the vibrant possibility of coming alive to the Bible by immersing themselves in its historical, geographical, and cultural contexts. It was honed over time as I journeyed again and again into corners of the land both familiar and unfamiliar, throughout Israel, the Palestinian territories, Jordan, Egypt, and the Sinai. "How many times have you been to these sites?" I am often asked. "Don't you get tired of them?" Then I remember Carl Ortwin Sauer, whom you will meet on the pages that follow and whose advice to his colleagues was that "locomotion should be slow, the slower the better, and be often interrupted by leisurely halts to sit on vantage points and stop at question marks." Historical geography is by nature a cross-discipline endeavor. It allows us to see broadly, to "read the land" in its fullness, and to know that even if we visit a place over a hundred times, there are still new ways of relating to things found there, new connections to make, and much more to be seen.

I am indebted first to the late G. Douglas Young and the school that he founded in Jerusalem in the 1950s, the Institute of Holy Land Studies, now Jerusalem University College. Over the years its board of directors, faculty, and leadership teams have fueled a desire for serious, on-site study of the landed context of the Bible. The text and land approach to biblical studies that Anson Rainey (of blessed memory), Jim Monson, and Carl Rasmussen developed at "the Institute" has secured a place for historical geography in the curriculum of biblical studies. Generations of students and colleagues have followed their lead in revolutionizing the way people engage God's word around the world today. David Weisberg and John Sailhamer, both of blessed memory, taught me how to read texts; it was Lawson Stone who awakened me to the construct of "reading the land."

I mentioned that this book is an excursion into the geography of the Bible. There is double entendre here. Much of the information found on the following pages is about the geography of the land on which the people of the Bible lived. This is the physicality of their story, and it interests us on an academic level, perhaps also out of curiosity, and certainly to lay the groundwork for our own Bible reading. But this book is also an introduction to the way that the writers of the Bible used geography to strengthen the messages they shared with their contemporaries, and with us. Soil, rock, and water are physical things, but also things that easily reflect enduring qualities of human life. Physical geography and literary geography both are elements of historical geography; one is concerned about the land in which the biblical writers lived, the other is a window into how these authors saw their own experiences there. For the sensitivity of this excursion, I am grateful to Jack Beck.

Pride of place also belongs to the thousands of students, undergraduate, graduate, and adult learners—far too many to name individually—with whom I have had the privilege of exploring the lands of the Bible. They come from all backgrounds and stages of life, nearly all of them wide-eyed and eager. Many bring years of experience in fields outside of the humanities or biblical studies—engineering, architecture, agriculture, geology, medicine, construction, military science, astrophysics—and have helped me to see the land through eyes that I myself will never possess. Some whom I first knew as students are now teachers at universities, colleges, study centers, churches, and secondary schools around the world. Each is invested in the pages that you are about to read. Writing on paper is fulfilling; writing on human hearts is more so.

The vision, guidance, and counsel of gifted editors is crucial to any writing project. For the talent and good graces of Steve Bond and David Stabnow, editors at B&H Publishing Group, a division of LifeWay Christian Resources, I am forever obliged. Steve launched this project as a short study guide, then quickly realized the need for a new, full length monograph that could introduce the Christian world to biblical geography. His persistent vision was decisive for steering the manuscript through the initial stages of publication. Dave's editorial finesse, which melds precision with fluency, has brought it to completion. Genuine thanks is due to both, not only for the professional side of things, but for the character, integrity, and grace that has shaped their work. Of the many others on their publishing team whom I wish to mention specifically are Trevin Wax, director of the

Bible and Reference section at LifeWay, who was able to link the maps created for this book with other editorial projects, and Dustin Curtis, assistant project editor at LifeWay, who oversaw the print version of this book, as well as Matthew Byrd, who created the ePub version. I am grateful that the team at LifeWay has grasped the vision of the need to introduce persons who are already fluent in the literatures and theologies of the Bible to the landed context in which the authors of the Bible, and the persons whose stories they told, actually lived. Geographical information is not incidental to the biblical story. Rather, it is foundational to our shared task of living, learning, and communicating the Word of Life.

I offer tremendous gratitude as well to Thomas Frogh and the cartographic team at International Mapping, who strove to make the maps that you will read on the pages that follow both accurate and useful. A good map is pleasant to behold, a feast for the eyes and nutrition for the mind and soul. A really good map is also evocative, using art to represent both precision and possibilities about the world, or, more correctly, about how we (or our ancestors) see (or saw) our world. Biophysicists use the term "map" to describe the spatial arrangement of genes on a chromosome and are able to identify fine details of a person's genetic identity in the process. But of course they have borrowed both the term and the method from geographers. Being "on the map" gives each of us an identity, a heritage, a place in time. Social historians can debate the pros and cons of our rush to become citizens of the world; in practical terms, we all identify ourselves by sets of local geographical labels.

At the same time, the more focused an image, the less we see its context or how we relate to the reality it depicts. Hand-held devices, for instance, are usually very good at getting us to where we want to go, but less effective in telling us where we are as we get there. When a map's orientation is "me and straight in front of me," we tend not to think broadly, and certainly not collectively. So bring on printed maps, the larger the better! Once we learn to read maps and think by them, we realize that they can tell us stories as readily as can a text—and stories not just of events, but of situations of life and points of view. At the very least, maps set the stage by which stories make sense. In doing so, maps that depict the lands of the Bible enable us to enter into the world of our biblical ancestors. For readers of the Bible who also have a working understanding of the all-encompassing role that *place* plays in the consciousness of the modern Middle East, they also help us to identify issues of belonging and identity that have persisted throughout millennia. And that, if nothing else, allows the Bible to stand front and center in a world that badly needs to ponder its claims today.

Learning to read takes time. Perceiving what we read takes a lifetime, even more so if what we read is the text of the Bible and the land from which it arose. Joshua and Caleb followed the instruction of Moses. So can we: "See what the land is like . . ." (Num 13:18).

LIST OF ABBREVIATIONS

ABD	Anchor Bible Dictionary
AfO	Archiv für Orientforschung
AJBA	Australian Journal of Biblical Archaeology
ANET	Ancient Near Eastern Texts
ASOR	American Schools of Oriental Research
BA	Biblical Archaeologist
BAR	Biblical Archaeology Review
BASOR	Bulletin of the American Schools of Oriental Research
CAD	Chicago Assyrian Dictionary
CSB	Christian Standard Bible
EA	El-Amarna Texts
ESV	English Standard Version
HTR	Harvard Theological Review
HUC	Hebrew Union College
IAA	Israel Antiquities Authority
IEJ	Israel Exploration Journal
IES	Israel Exploration Society
ISBE	International Standard Bible Encyclopedia
JBQ	Jewish Bible Quarterly
JETS	Journal of the Evangelical Theological Society
JNES	Journal of Near Eastern Studies
JP	Jerusalem Perspective
JRA	Journal of Roman Archaeology
KJV	King James Version
LCL	Loeb Classical Library
NASB	New American Standard Bible
NEAEHL	New Encyclopedia of Archaeological Excavations in the Holy Land
NIV	New International Version
OA	Oriens Antiquus
PEF	Palestine Exploration Fund
PEQ	Palestine Exploration Quarterly
RB	Revue Biblique
RIMA	Royal Inscriptions of Mesopotamia, Assyrian Periods
SBL	Society of Biblical Literature
TA	Tel Aviv

1 EXPLORING THE WORLD OF THE BIBLE

We read the Bible for many reasons. For many of us, it is inspiring literature. For others, it is a window to events of the past or a witness to the hopes and dreams of our ethnic or spiritual ancestors. Some of us read the Bible because of its curiosities. Most of us likely read it as a guide to faith and right living. Whether we read the Bible through the lens of literature, history, theology, or ethics, we cannot help but encounter its record of how God has interacted with the world over the course of the ages. The Bible's claims that God chose to create and then interact with people on planet Earth is an awesome thought. God entered the world of flesh and blood—a land of rocks, some soil, and not enough water; a place bound by time and marked by celebrations of life; an arena squeezed between empires. He used natural elements such as these to reveal things about himself. Over the course of millennia, God spoke to a small band of eager yet stubborn folk dug into this narrow, arid land on the southeastern bend of the Mediterranean Sea. Abraham, Moses, Ruth, David, Isaiah, Jeremiah, Anna—signposts in the narrative—marked God's words well. They also looked forward to a point "*when the time [would come] to completion*" (Gal 4.4) and, as Jesus, God would immerse himself in the daily hustle and bustle of a small, dynamic, and very needy portion of the Roman Empire called Galilee (Phil 2:5–8).

The Bible is jam-packed with accounts of real people living in specific places at specific times. This attribute sets it apart from all other sacred texts. God's decision to communicate eternal truths through the mundane things of human life—through normal happenings in fields, at threshing floors, along wave-lapped seashores, in village houses, or along crowded streets—is as compelling as it is humbling. It also suggests that we can better understand God's revelation if we take the time to learn and better appreciate something about the physical context in which the Bible was given.

The physical and cultural world of the Bible was, in many ways, quite different from our own. For most of the people who walked through what we read about in the pages of Scripture, everyday life was rooted in small agricultural villages made mostly of rock and mud or in goat-hair tent encampments scattered along steppe lands facing open desert. Economic resources were limited, with patterns of communication and trade taking place within narrowly circumscribed locations. Society was communal and stable, exhibiting a regular life rhythm year in and year out, generation after generation. Multigenerational families lived within the same tent or house, on small plots of ancestral land in close proximity to other members of their extended family. Grazing patterns for livestock were mutually recognized and rarely changed. People were born, lived their entire lives, and were buried on their family's land (e.g., Gen 3:19; Ps 90:3; Eccl 12:6–7). Throughout biblical history, carefully preserved social forces preferred the known over the unknown, helping ensure that a family's limited resources remained intact (the practice of arranged marriage to one's cousin, e.g., reflects this value; Gen 24:2–4,15,67; 29:10–13,28; Judg 14:3).

> For millennia, village and shepherding lifestyles in the Middle East have fostered endogamous marriage in which the bride and groom are members of the same extended family. The male head of a family finds wives for his eligible sons within the family village or tent encampment or from one nearby, where resources (water, fields, or grazing land) are shared. The custom is time-honored because it is practical: it strengthens existing social and economic relationships in a land where resources are scarce and must be protected.

Within this slowly turning cycle of events was found the good life, the best to which a typical Israelite or Judean might hope to aspire. In day-to-day affairs, security sprang from the soil, the substance from which Adam, the father of mankind, was created and for which he was named (from *adāmāh*, "ground;" cp. Gen 2:7). "Throughout Solomon's reign, Judah and Israel lived in safety from Dan to Beer-sheba," on ancestral land, we read, "each person under his own vine and his own fig tree" (1 Kgs 4:25). This was *shalom* in its most practical sense. Peace was defined not just by an absence of hostilities but as life lived the way it was supposed to be—quiet, secure, faithful, and full—in a special place that came to be called the Holy Land (cp. Ps 78:54). It is no accident that the fifth most frequently used noun in the Hebrew Bible (after "Lord," "son," "God," and "king") is *eretz*, "land," a term that often appears in the phrase *eretz Yisrael*, "the land of Israel," the place specially chosen and prepared by God as a home for his chosen people (cp. Gen 12:1–9; Deut 32:8–14; Ps 78:1–72). Throughout, the people of the Bible were reminded that a lifestyle as earthy as theirs was not complete without the full realization that God had fashioned their land and placed them on it for his purposes. Medieval rabbis such as Ibn Ezra and Rashi took this concept so seriously that they saw ancient Israel's journey to the land of Canaan—first as Abraham their father and then with Moses and Joshua—as a kind of return to the garden of Eden.[1] We can almost speak of the "completion of place" (to paraphrase Gal 4:4, which speaks of the completion of time) in reference to the soil on which the story of redemption would unfold. A land can't be more promised, or full of promise, than that!

> This is my Father's world,
> and to my listening ears
> all nature sings, and round me rings
> the music of the spheres.
> This is my Father's world;
> I rest me in the thought
> Of rocks and trees, of skies and seas;
> His hand the wonders wrought.
> —Maltbie Babcock, 1902

1 For a basic discussion, see John H. Sailhamer, *The Pentateuch as Narrative* (Grand Rapids: Zondervan, 1992), 101.

This house and garden, in Dana village in the Highlands of Edom, preserves age-old living patterns of rural life in the lands of the Bible. The walls of the house are mud-washed while the garden is fenced by tumble-down stone. Vines trained as an awning provide shade and a ready source of food in the summertime; fatted sheep and an attentive goat graze nearby. Neighbors are always welcome. *"In that day," declares the LORD of hosts, "every one of you will invite his neighbor to sit under his vine and under his fig tree"* (Zech 3:10, NASB).

The line between biblical geography and biblical theology blurs easily in a land that is holy. The writers of the Bible (certainly those who composed the Old Testament, but even the authors of the New) saw an intimate connection between God, his people, and the land Israel called home. Israel was God's people; their land was his land. This was a kind of sacred trinity (small *s*, small *t*), a tight triad through which the writers and characters of the Bible sought to understand their place in the world. "*LORD, you showed favor to your land; you restored the fortunes of Jacob*" (Ps 85:1). The fortunes of one, then, rose and fell with the other. When the people of Israel sinned, it was as if the most productive parts of their land had been cursed: "*The land mourns and withers; Lebanon is ashamed and wilted. Sharon is like a desert; Bashan and Carmel shake off leaves*" (Isa 33:9; cp. Deut 28:23–24; 38–40). But when, by the grace of God his people were restored, then . . .

the wilderness and the dry
land [would] be glad;
the desert [would] rejoice and
blossom like a wildflower.
It [would] blossom abundantly
and [would] also rejoice
with joy and singing.
The glory of Lebanon [would]
be given to it,
the splendor of Carmel and
Sharon. (Isa 35:1–2)

Read the land; see the text; live the Book. The Jezreel Valley is full of historic and prophetic associations that fairly leap off the pages of Scripture. Deborah, Barak, Gideon, Saul, Elijah, Elisha, Josiah, and Jesus all passed through this pivotal locale. The view here is from the fields surrounding Endor, home of the medium (1 Sam 28:7), toward Mount Tabor, where Deborah and Barak deployed their troops (Judg 4:6) and atop which, according to an early church tradition, Jesus was transfigured in the presence of three of his disciples. Looking from the present into the past requires that the student of biblical historical geography maintain an attentive gaze. While the general shape of the land of ancient Israel remained essentially unchanged throughout time, the imprint of human activity on it varied, sometimes greatly. The tasks of reading the text and reading its landed context are intertwined, prompting skills of fluency in both.

Understandably, the biblical authors took the reality of place seriously—not only as a theological concept rooted in God's choice for ancient Israel (Gen 12:1–9) but also in its most utilitarian sense, for the land of the biblical story was their home.[1] As would be expected, the human writers of the Bible (and the characters in the stories they told) were intimately familiar with the rugged terrain of Judah (Isa 41:15), with cold winter rain and scorching desert heat (Ezra 10:9,13; Isa 4:6; 49:10). They had seen the fields and hills surrounding their towns and villages ripe with crops (Ruth 2:2–3; 1 Kgs 4:25), or full of enemy troops ravaging everything held dear (2 Kgs 6:13–15,24–29). They had experienced the relief offered by a small spring of water or by the shelter of a crevasse in a mighty rock (1 Sam 23:25; 24:3; 2 Sam 23:15–17; Isa 58:11). Aspects of their home—of *geography*—were not only a vital part of the story they had to tell (references to place in the text of the Bible abound); they shaped the way the story was told. Isaac's paternal blessing, for instance, not only carries the satisfaction of a life well lived, but speaks of the land *on which* he lived: *"Ah, the smell of my son is like the smell of a field that the Lord has blessed"* (Gen 27:27). On virtually every page of the Bible, the divine message is infused with geographical information; its writers assumed that their readers knew even more.

The Bible's preoccupation with place prompts us, as readers, to pay attention to the grounded contexts where the events recorded on its pages occurred. In our rush for relevance, we would do well not to forget the points of geographical reference that the text already had for its original readers. When the Bible's authors made the effort to include specific geographical information in their work, with items as minute as single place names, they intended these bits of data to be an important part of what they had to say. As a result, knowing something of the landed context of the Bible is a necessary prelude for recognizing, interpreting, and applying the other, more "practical" aspects of the biblical text to our lives. It was perhaps Saint Jerome, who lived the last thirty-two years of his life in Bethlehem where he had moved to immerse himself in the context

1 In recent decades, the rubric "theology of the land" has largely been limited to discussions about rights of ownership or use of the land of ancient Israel. For some implications, see Paul H. Wright, *Understanding the Ecology of the Bible: An Introductory Atlas* (Jerusalem: Carta, 2018): 6: "Although *eretz* is most often used in the Hebrew Bible in connection with a particular, bounded area that became the homeland of the people of ancient Israel (e.g., Gen 12:1; 15:18; Deut 1:21), its sweep of territory was much larger, encompassing that of 'all the nations of the earth' (*eretz*) (Gen 18:18; Jer 25:26; Zech 4:10, 14). Thinking inclusively, this prompts readers of the Bible to consider how principles of the ecology of place, understood first within the context of the land of ancient Israel, can be expanded to include the whole of the created order. We might argue, in fact, that a full-orbed theology of land should take into account concepts of place that apply wherever a Bible reader's own locality might be, whether it is a place that is owned, used, or simply visited by oneself or by others. The Bible's own emphasis on the created order as the locus of the divine-human encounter shows us that place—whether it is the land of ancient Israel or somewhere else—gives order to human existence, providing a sense of connectedness and belonging. When land is reduced to political concepts of ownership, rights or control, the result is a conversation that ignores or overrides the more essential aspects of what land, as a God-made place for human fulfillment, can be, and the interconnected relationship of all living things (the eco- of ecology) on it."

of Scripture, who said it best: "Just as those who have seen Athens understand Greek history better, and just as those who have seen Troy understand the words of the poet Virgil . . . thus one will comprehend the Holy Scriptures with a clearer understanding who has seen the land of Judah with his own eyes."[1] He had, and he did.

In the middle of the last century the great American geographer Carl Ortwin Sauer spoke about the essence of the discipline of historical geography, which is the study of communities within cultural areas over time. Essential to the task is the need to define just what any given cultural-geographical area is, or, more properly, was. Sauer's methodology remains our starting point:

> The reconstruction of critical cultural landscapes of the past [by the historical geographer] requires (a) knowledge of the functioning of the given culture as a whole, (b) a control of all the contemporary evidences . . . and (c) the most intimate familiarity with the terrain which the given culture occupied. . . .
>
> One might say that [the historical geographer] needs **the ability to see the land with the eyes of its former occupants**, from the standpoint of their needs and capacities. This is about the most difficult task in all human geography: to evaluate site and situation, not from the standpoint of an educated American [for instance], but to place oneself in the position of a member of the cultural group at the time being studied.[2]

The observation that every biblical event took place somewhere is as obvious as it is underappreciated. Once we become familiar with the Bible's own maps (i.e., its internal systems of geographical information) and learn to relate these maps to the shape of its land as well as the human endeavors described in the Bible on that land, we can start to develop a coherent and meaningful set of pegs on which to hang what are otherwise often seen as a long and confusing series of events that march across the open pages of Scripture. For many readers (and teachers!) of the Bible, one king, one battle, one story of everyday life blurs into the next. A geographical grid provides an objective structure by which we can begin to make sense of the flow of the pieces of the biblical narrative. Moreover, an understanding of place becomes an indispensable tool to help us recognize a whole range of factors (policy decisions, economic forces, political and military realities, and the like) that were just as much a part of human activity in the past as they are today.

More than that, biblical authors, as well as characters within the biblical story, frequently used geographical imagery to talk about matters of the heart or of things eternal. *"The LORD is my rock,"* the psalmist intoned repeatedly (Ps 18:2,31; 31:1–2; 42:9; 62:6; 71:3; 78:35; 89:26; 92:15; 94:22), and it behooves a careful reader of the Bible to know something about the rocks of the land of

This image of St. Jerome adorns the left-side panel of the main doorway of the Church of St. Catherine in Bethlehem. Jerome came to Bethlehem first as a pilgrim in AD 386 when he was about forty years old, then settled in the town two years later, remaining there until he died in AD 420. The lower level of the Church of St. Catherine contains a grotto which tradition holds was the cell in which Jerome lived when he translated the Old Testament from Hebrew into Latin (the Vulgate). One of Jerome's primary motives for moving to the Holy Land was to better learn biblical Hebrew; his working knowledge of the landed context of the Bible was enriched immeasurably in the process.

1 From the preface to Jerome's translation of Chronicles, *Pref. Chron.* (LXX), cited in G. S. P. Freeman-Grenville, Rupert L. Chapman III, and Joan E. Taylor, *The Onomasticon by Eusebius of Caesarea* (Jerusalem: Carta, 2003), 2–3.

2 Carl Ortwin Sauer, "Forward to Historical Geography," in *Land and Life: A Selection from the Writings of Carl Ortwin Sauer*, ed. John Leighly (Berkeley: University of California Press, 1963), 362; emphasis added.

ancient Israel, and those around the city of Jerusalem in particular, to begin to understand why he dared compare God to what is otherwise a hard, inanimate object. Isaiah's heraldic call, *"Prepare ye the way of the Lord, make straight in the desert a highway for our God"* (Isa 40:3 KJV), familiar as a tenor *recitative* in Handel's *Messiah*, takes on heightened significance after the reader (or concert-goer) has acquired a first-hand appreciation of the topography of the wilderness that rises from Jericho to Jerusalem, the direction from which Jesus typically approached the city. Jesus announced that *"streams of living water [would] flow from deep within"* those who believe in him (John 7:38). The image was aptly spoken within the courtyards of the Jerusalem temple on the last day of the fall Festival of Tabernacles (John 7:2,10,14,37), but is more fully grasped when the reader understands the nature of Jerusalem's normal water supply in the first century AD and something about the cycle of seasons in that land in the process. Of course, recognizing that Jesus was also drawing on a rich collection of earlier uses of water as an idiom found in nearly all of the books of the Old Testament and Jewish writings of the intertestamental period heightens the image—but not without prompting the reader to become familiar with grounded details of those instances as well in order to see why there is such a fixation on water in the Bible in the first place.

Traditional Arab poetry, nearly always oral, offers an instructive analogy. For the Bedouin, desert-dwellers in much of the Middle East and conservators of Arab traditions from hoary antiquity, the world of nature offers an unending host of metaphors that reveal not only their abiding and intimate relationship with the land but also the varied interpersonal relationships that define the tribal realities of everyday life.[1] So, for instance, one's homeland is likened to a fair maiden: "A homeland in Najd that was once a haven, a refuge sought by those burdened by hard times. She resembles a fair, chaste maiden; In her beauty my homeland outshines all fair maidens." Homelands might also be likened to wild animals or to persons of valor in battle: "A wild falcon took off, followed by horsemen and cameleers, seeking to despoil the enemy and attack him unawares. . . . Hail, you rider on a speedy mount that runs like a terrified ostrich on level plains." And, of course, the beauty of women was always a popular theme: "Her neck, O 'Agab, O neck of the gazelle! The neck of the timid female antelope in the desert land. . . . You are the perfume of a sweet basil growing by the rain pool; wherever the wind blows, it carries your fragrance."[2] Parallels to biblical texts such as the Song of Songs and Ezekiel 19 are obvious.

All of this gives Bible readers a double-edged geographical task. One is to understand aspects of geography that inform events recorded in the Bible. The other is to come to appreciate how a geographical reality can become a metaphor of a heightened reality, one of the spirit or the heart. The former task is properly the subject of historical geography, while the latter is a gateway into literary geography.[3] Biblical geography properly encompasses both disciplines, and careful readers need to be cognizant of each, reading, as it were, land and text in tandem.[4]

Perhaps a word about fluency is in order. Becoming fluent is something that is usually associated with learning a language. A person is said to be fluent if he or she can speak and write as skillfully as someone who is native-born to that language group. To be *really* fluent, though, is to be able to understand shades of meaning with all the intimations that are second-nature for someone who learned a language at his mother's knee. Fluency is a goal of geographers who are intent on "reading" a land as well.[5] A few parallels are instructive:

- The investigation of a written language often begins with learning the graphic symbols that represent the sounds of that language, then by studying the formation of words and patterns of syntax. Similarly, for the student of biblical geography, the characteristics of a region's rocks and soils, the location of its available water resources, the patterns of landforms, climate, and the like are not random introductory details but essential building blocks in the process of understanding the "syntax" and eventually the "genre" of a land. In both cases, the whole is much greater than the sum of its parts.
- Units of a text, whether they be individual sounds, words, or phrases, gain context when they interact with one another and reflect or anticipate similar units in portions of texts that precede or follow them. In much the same way, the context of a geographical region is found in the interaction of its natural features and their relationship, individually or collectively, with regions they border.
- When we read a text fluently, we notice how meaning is embedded in literary structures and how the repetition of words or the development of themes provides texture to a paragraph or a pericope. Similarly, the texture of a geographical region is shaped by the location and structure of resources, strategic points, natural routes, and patterns of land use. For the historical geographer, the "meaning" of a region is found in a set of real-life opportunities that the texture of a land provides for its inhabitants.
- In short, just as readers of texts do well to understand details of literary genre, so an effective historical geographer pays attention to aspects

1 Eveline van der Steen, *Near Eastern Tribal Societies during the Nineteenth Century: Economy, Society and Politics between Tent and Town* (Sheffield: Equinox, 2013): 71.

2 Eveline van der Steen, "Bedouin Poetry and Landscape," pg. 424–428 in Jacques van Ruiten and J. Cornelis de Vos, eds., *The Land of Israel in Bible, History and Theology: Studies in Honor of Ed Noort* (Leiden, Brill, 2009).

3 Note in particular the works of John A. Beck: *God as Storyteller: Seeking Meaning in Biblical Narrative* (St. Louis: Chalice Press, 2008); *Zondervan Dictionary of Biblical Imagery* (Grand Rapids: Zondervan, 2011); and *Discovery House Bible Atlas* (Grand Rapids: Discovery House, 2015).

4 See Paul H. Wright, "Introduction to Historical Geography," in Jonathan S. Greer, John W. Hilber, and John H. Walton, eds., *Behind the Scenes of the Old Testament: Cultural, Social, and Historical Contexts* (Grand Rapids: Baker, 2018), 5–11.

5 I am dependent on wordsmith Lawson Stone, who suggested to me the idiom of reading the land.

of geographical "genre" that define how any particular region should be "read." And, in the same way that reading one text helps us become sufficiently fluent so as to tackle another, so learning to read one particular landscape helps the biblical geographer roam meaningfully over the horizon to the next.[1]

Once we gain a skill set that allows us to read the land of the Bible with fluency, we will not only be able to understand more fully the significance of the divine-human events that transpired within its pages, but will see something of the full-orbed beauty of the text and the event that quick-journeyers, like tourists or speed readers, might miss. One of the best readers of the land of ancient Israel was the Scottish clergyman and Bible scholar George Adam Smith. Smith's *The Historical Geography of the Holy Land*, first published in 1894,[2] remains unsurpassed in its eloquent grasp of the dynamic of the land and, in spite of its age, remains a must-read for any budding biblical historical geographer. The lands of the Bible, like the Bible itself, deserve to be read and re-read slowly. Perhaps the best advice comes from Sauer, who, at the end of a brilliantly productive career in both classroom and field geography, reminded his colleagues that "locomotion should be slow, the slower the better, and be often interrupted by leisurely halts to sit on vantage points and stop at question marks."[3] Sauer's words were intended for apprentices in field study, but work equally well amid the terrain of a library or an individual book. Fluency in matters related to the context of land cannot be gained by short, touristic experiences, as profitable or moving as they may otherwise be.

Studying the geography of the Bible, then, allows us to take a book that in its extraordinary details might otherwise seem opaque or disconnected from our own realities and make it our own. It becomes possible to follow Joshua's army into the hill country of Canaan (Josh 6–11) or to crest the rise on which David's Jerusalem stood and experience a bit of the energy of the Songs of Ascent (Pss 121–134). We are able to see Rehoboam plot a line of defense against the Egyptian Pharaoh Shishak, then witness his desperation in circling the wagons around his hill country home (2 Chr 11:5–12; 12:1–13). Jesus must have climbed the hills above Capernaum often in the early mornings to gaze over the Sea of Galilee (cp. Mark 1:35). By doing the same today, we can better appreciate his call to ministry or our own place in the kingdom of God. It has been said that the best way to get to know someone is to spend time in his or her home. The land of the Gospels was the earthly home of Jesus. We can be sure that an intentional look at his land doesn't so much make the Bible come alive (since the Bible already *is* alive; cp. Heb 4:12) as much as it makes us come alive to the Bible.

A careful study of the geographical information of the Bible also has apologetic value. The biblical writers had to be accurate when presenting geographical material since their assertions about the realities of landforms and climate, or the relative position of cities or the use of strategic routes (to give just a few examples), could easily be verified by anyone—then and now—who took time to go out into the land and see things for themselves. Verifiable geographical information provides a solid foundation (of bedrock, to use an analogy at hand) on which to place and evaluate the veracity of the other truth claims in the Bible.

This book is an illustrated guide to biblical geography. As a discipline, geography focuses on details of geology, landforms, soils, water resources, climate, and the like. Because the lands lying along the eastern Mediterranean seaboard are not only characterized by a highly dissected topography but are wedged between the encroaching desert and a restless sea, aspects of their geography are interesting in their own right. Indeed, the modern state of Israel, for example, is only a little larger than the state of New Jersey plus Long Island; nevertheless, it contains the same variety of landforms and climate as does all of California. Historically, this wide dissimilarity of geographical features has played a major role in settlement patterns and land use in the area since the dawn of time. That the region is also a land bridge linking the continents of Europe, Asia, and Africa as well as the Arabian Peninsula only adds to the geographical uniqueness and special dynamic of the place.

The modern state of Israel, plus the West Bank, covers approximately 10,700 square miles (27,713 km sq), an area that is slightly larger than New Jersey including Long Island. The distance from Dan to Beer-sheba, the historic northern and southern extremities of ancient Israel (1 Sam 3:20; 2 Sam 3:9–10; 1 Kgs 4:25; 2 Chr 30:5), is 110 miles (177 km), the same as the highway mileage between New York City and Philadelphia. That drive can be made quickly by automobile, over ground that is topographically uniform. To walk the rugged and difficult terrain from Dan to Beer-sheba in biblical times, by contrast, took at least a week. Indeed, the variety of landforms in Israel, from snowy Mount Hermon to the cut of the Dead Sea at 1,312 feet (400 m) below sea level, more closely resembles the contours of California—though squeezed into an area the size of New Jersey.

Details of geography, however, are just so much data if we fail to view them through the prism of human activity, specifically the historical events of the biblical period. While this book is organized along traditional geographical lines (chapter headings refer to natural resources and settlement regions), the underlying premise posits a two-way flow of information: geographical data informs our understanding of human (and God-moved) activity in the land of the Bible, while the Bible's own description of these events, rooted deeply in the realia of the land itself, helps us to better understand

1 Conversely, geography can also serve as an analogy for language: "Language is the landmass that is continuous under our feet and the feet of others and allows us to get to each other's places." Sven Birkerts, *The Gutenberg Elegies: The Fate of Reading in an Electronic Age* (New York: Fawcett Columbine, 1994), 82.

2 George Adam Smith, *The Historical Geography of the Holy Land* (London: Hodder and Stoughton, 1894); thirtieth edition reprinted by Ariel Publishing House, Jerusalem, 1966.

3 Carl Ortwin Sauer, "The Education of a Geographer," in *Land and Life: A Selection from the Writings of Carl Ortwin Sauer*, ed. John Leighly (Berkeley: University of California Press, 1963), 400.

Parable imagery abounds in the broad valleys of Lower Galilee, places where Jesus often walked in those silent years between his birth and the beginning of his public ministry. An appreciation of the living spaces of Galilee helps give voice to those intervening years, presenting the Gospels to us in high definition.

the geographical stage on which these events took place. In essence, our work is an exercise in *historical*, *cultural*, and *literary* geography, practical aspects of the discipline that give hue and texture to what are otherwise seen as rather flat, black-and-white pages of the biblical text.

So how do we gain a working knowledge of the places in which the events—and the theological message—of the biblical text are grounded? Our first task is to read (or, reread) the Bible with geographical data in mind. Texts contemporary to the Bible such as letters, tales, or annals from ancient Egypt or Mesopotamia, victory stela touting local military campaigns (e.g., the Moabite Stone or Tel Dan Stela), or the histories of Josephus (*Antiquities of the Jews* and *The Jewish War*) provide a wealth of additional geographical data related to the biblical story that can be mined by interested and energetic readers. As we read, we need to pay particular attention to place names, to movements of people from here to there, and to the reality of places and events mentioned in the text. Geographical information is found in the Bible's historical books, poetry, prophetic oracles, and wisdom literature, and even in the didactic portions of the Epistles.

> *The Amorites forced the Danites into the hill country and did not allow them to go down into the valley.* (Judg 1:34)
>
> *He is like a tree planted beside flowing streams . . . they are like chaff that the wind blows away.* (Ps 1:3–4)
>
> *The one I love had a vineyard on a very fertile hill.* (Isa 5:1)
>
> *My brothers are as treacherous as a wadi, as seasonal streams that overflow.* (Job 6:15)
>
> *When he heard that John had been arrested, he withdrew into Galilee.* (Matt 4:12)
>
> *They wandered in deserts and on mountains, hiding in caves and holes in the ground.* (Heb 11:38)
>
> *Consider how a small fire sets ablaze a large forest.* (Jas 3:5)

Even if many of these referents are used creatively, as literary images, the pictures they produce are grounded in a geographical reality that can be known and which, to a large extent, can still be verified. A prerequisite for understanding a biblical image is first to know the tangible reality of the actual object behind the image. This is the case whether we want to understand the intent of the image in the text itself or the significance of the image for the modern reader.

As we learn to read both text and land, patterns begin to emerge. For instance, notices of rainfall (2 Sam 21:10), the advent of the barley and wheat harvests (Deut 16:9–10; Judg 15:1; Ruth 2:23; 2 Sam 21:9), or the onset of military maneuvers (1 Sam 23:1; 2 Sam 11:1) were used as a kind of calendar by the biblical writers, signaling the time of year an event took place. Notations within the biblical narrative of fortified towns strung along natural routes serve to indicate strategic gateways into and out of regions (e.g., the route passing through the towns of Beth-horon; 1 Kgs 9:17; 2 Chr 8:5). Jesus's visits to places such as Nazareth, Nain, Caesarea Philippi, and Jerusalem raise the memory of earlier biblical or other historical events that took place in the same regions and that surely impacted his own messianic self-awareness. When plotting and organizing the flow of biblical history this way, it is helpful to consult an atlas that shows some detail of landforms and topography—hopefully one that has large enough pages for note-taking!

Beth-horon was the name of two towns lying northwest of Jerusalem during the biblical period, one Upper Beth-horon and the other Lower Beth-horon (Josh 16:5; 18:13; 2 Chr 8:5). These twin towns still occupy upper and lower positions on a natural ridge route connecting Jerusalem to Gezer and the Mediterranean coast. This route has always been Jerusalem's best access to the west, serving as the economic lifeline for the Judean capital. Not surprisingly, the Beth-horon ridge route has seen its share of military activity throughout history. Many battles described in the Bible were fought for control of this route and the resources it represented (Josh 10:10–11; 1 Sam 7:5–12; 13:15–18; 14:31,46; 2 Sam 5:17–25; 1 Kgs 9:17; and 1 Macc 3:13–26).

Second, it is helpful to work regionally. Despite the justified tendency of faith traditions to hallow plots of ground and the eagerness of many Holy Land visitors who want to walk where Jesus walked, X almost never marks the spot. More importantly, if we focus only on bits of geographical data or limit our investigation to individual sites or events, our view becomes a series of isolated, disjointed snapshots, perhaps good for touring but inadequate for recognizing, appraising, and interpreting the multi dimensional *Bible + land* equation set before us.[1] The biblical world was a complex place, where no site, event, or natural feature stood alone, any more than a word or phrase stands alone in a text.

A regional approach starts with defining what makes any given region a region. This presupposes an understanding of how to define a region in the first place. The least helpful method is to start with political borders. A political border typically represents a particular set of historical circumstances due more to the successful efforts of victorious armies or charismatic politicians than anything inherent on the ground itself, as a glance at borders drawn just about anywhere on the face of a modern (or ancient) globe reveals. More helpful is the method of the great German biblical scholar Albrecht Alt, who advocated a *territorial Geschichte* (territorial history) that examined geographical units as they appeared, or were described, in ancient sources such as the Bible.[2] A good example is Joshua 10:40: "*So Joshua conquered the whole region—the hill country, the Negev, the Judean foothills, and the slopes—with all their kings.*"

The territory that was to become the heartland of ancient Israel included four distinct regions that can easily be distinguished by differences in geographical features and terrain—a fact that was as obvious to the writer of the book of Joshua as it is to any diligent observer of the land today. Another example is the borders of Canaan described in Numbers 34:1–12, the only ancient source that delineates Canaan as a bounded territory. Here Canaan neatly fit between several natural topographical features: the Rift Valley to the east, the Sinai Desert to the south, and the Mediterranean Sea on the west.

But because not all geographical regions are described or even named in ancient texts, perhaps the most helpful methodology is to first delineate a region based on natural geographical features, then strive to determine what makes that region unique in terms of its own set of geographical realities regardless of the period of time under study. In this way geographical realities become an important context for understanding historical data drawn from texts or even from archaeology. Sometimes it becomes difficult to define exactly which geographical factors best constitute a region, and where one region ends and another begins. Regional boundaries tend to be rather indistinct; for instance, a mountain range drops to a plain or arable land gives way to steppe land and then desert. On the other hand, unlike political boundaries that, as we have seen, are sharp on the ground but shift over time, boundaries defined by geographical features are quite stable over time, blurred as they may be on the ground. The regional boundaries indicated by white lines on the maps in the chapters that follow are not meant to mark clear geographical lines on the ground, for rarely do sharp lines exist in the physical world; instead, the white lines acknowledge the place where the characteristics of one region, as defined in the text, give way to those of its neighbors. To return to the analogy of fluency, biblical scholars often debate how prose should be divided into paragraphs or poetry into stanzas. An effective reader knows how to group words, sentences, or paragraphs into meaningful units and, by doing so, to read with intent. The same holds true for the process of defining regions and understanding (or reading) the relationship of each region in the context of its neighbors. It is important to keep in mind that each region will, by definition, differ geographically from every other, and sometimes widely so. The many microenvironments blanketing our "California squeezed into the size of New Jersey" area add to the complexity—and interest—of the biblical narrative. What quickly complicates the discussion is that often the name of a geographical region can also be the name of a political unit located in roughly the same place. The biblical text provides many examples, such as "Moab," "Israel," and the names of each of the Israelite tribes that received a bounded inheritance upon entering the land with Joshua. "Judah,"

1 Not so incidentally, this is reason enough for the student of historical geography to cultivate the habit of consulting maps that are significantly larger and considerably more detailed than those commonly displayed by hand-held electronic devices!

2 Albrecht Alt, *Die Landnahme der Israeliten in Palästina* (Leipzig: Reformations Program der Universität Leipzig, 1925), 2; *Essays on Old Testament History and Religion*, trans. by R. A. Wilson (Oxford: Basil Blackwell, 1966), 136.

One hundred years ago, the Scottish geographer and Bible scholar George Adam Smith likened the gaze into the barren wilderness of Judah from the hill country high above to the view of a sailor on the narrow deck of a ship, peering at rolling sea waves below.[1] But unlike the oceans, the wilderness above the Dead Sea is utterly devoid of water. Here tumbled brown swells sear into an eternal jumble of nothingness; even shepherds take great care when making it their seasonal home. This stark springtime view lies only fifty miles from the churning Mediterranean Sea, yet seems a world away.

for instance, is a person, a tribe, a political kingdom, and a bounded territory; we sometimes need to read carefully to make the proper associations. Studying changes in political boundaries is a critical element in the historical geographer's craft, but that process must begin with a prior understanding of what makes a meaningful geographical unit in the first place.[2]

A regional approach pays particular attention to the network of natural routes that connect a region's towns and villages to one another, as well as the longer-distance routes leading to the resources of neighboring regions and more distant regions beyond. Particular attention should be paid to the seams—borders, buffer zones, and gateway cities connecting one region to the next. It is these areas, rather than the heartlands themselves, that were the scene of so much of the political, military, and economic activity of the events recorded in the Bible and its contemporary ancient literature.

In spite of the great regional diversity of the lands of the Bible, it is possible, based on overall geographical similarities, to group certain regions together into larger districts. For the land of ancient Israel, these include a southern district (Judah and the Negev), a central district (Samaria), and a northern district (Galilee). To the east lies Transjordan, a string of regions joined to one another like beads on a chain. Of course, the lands of the Bible take in a much larger sweep than just these: ever-widening circles encompass the Sinai, Egypt, Phoenicia (Lebanon) and north Syria, Mesopotamia, Anatolia (modern Turkey), Cyprus, the Aegean, and lands beyond. From Abraham's day to Paul's, the world of the Bible was large and interconnected—even though most biblical events took place in the tiny sliver of land hugging the southeastern bend of the Mediterranean Sea.

Third, it is possible to gain important insights into the ancient nexus of people + land by examining indigenous people groups in the cultural present who in various ways preserve or reflect ways of life held in the same region during the time of the Bible. Although traditional ways are fast disappearing as even the more remote parts of the modern Middle East enter the age of high tech, a careful look at Bedouin in the Sinai or Jordan, in particular,[3] or at peasant farmers (*fellahin*) living in villages distant from the larger cities of Jordan, Syria, and Lebanon,[4] can reveal timeless and relevant cultural patterns of how to shape societies within a largely unchanging set of natural resources. Here a strong note of caution is in order, however, since the natural tendency of readers is to oversimplify or romanticize connections that might look anthropologically interesting at first glance. At the same time, much can be gained from sensitive work in ethnography, especially from studies of data taken prior to the rise of nationalism and industrialized technology in the Middle East.

And fourth, even though we have access to a wonderful number of printed or electronic study tools today, the best way to understand the geography of the Bible is to travel to its lands personally. While it is impossible to visit the actual world of the Bible (time machines remain tools of science fiction), all of us have ready access to a "place machine," that is, an airplane or other means of transport that can carry modern man to the places of the biblical story. Once we have done our textual and anthropological homework, a series of informed visits to the lands of the Bible can revolutionize our understanding of God's work in the world, both then and now.

1 Smith, *The Historical Geography of the Holy Land* (London: Hodder and Stoughton, 1894), 261–62.

2 The opposite tendency is illustrated by the comment of the old Polish farmer who, upon hearing that the border between Poland and Russia had once again shifted, thus leaving him under the control of a government based in Warsaw, exclaimed, "Good! I can't stand another cold Russian winter!"

3 See, for instance, Ghazi bin Muhammad, *The Tribes of Jordan at the Beginning of the Twenty-First Century* (Amman: Atalla Design, 1999); Joseph J. Hobbs, *Bedouin Life in the Egyptian Wilderness* (Cairo: American University Press, 1989); and Ze'ev Meshel, "Wilderness Wanderings: Ethnographic Lessons from Modern Bedouin," *BAR* 34/4 (2008): 32–39.

4 Carol Palmer, "'Following the Plough:' The Agricultural Environment of Northern Jordan," *Levant* 30 (1998): 129–65.

Israel's King Ahab brought his armies here, to the flats of Ramoth-gilead where, in 853 BC, he engaged the superior chariot forces of Ben-hadad in a pitched battle for control over Transjordan's international highway. He lost his life in the process (1 Kgs 22:29–40). Twelve years later, the sun set on Ahab's dynasty when his general, Jehu, emerged from another battle at Ramoth-gilead to seize the Israelite throne (2 Kgs 9:1–26). When we look at the lands of the Bible regionally, the horizons for connected study are endless.

The Bible contains a record of how God encountered people in particular places and at particular times. But while the Bible is rooted in time and place, its eternal truths are transcendent. As we read with one eye focused on the earth, the other on the eternal, and in our living in between we do well to consider how the people of the Bible did the same.

> We, too, are people of place. Each has a special spot where he feels most secure, most at peace, most "at home." For some, it's the old homestead. For others, it's a particular town or city, or a view of a mountain or lake. Even if it's just a particular room or spot within a room (that favorite chair), individuals tend to gravitate to place. We who live in societies that are highly mobile and transient haven't given up on the reality of that special place in which to escape, to regroup, to recover, to reenergize—to find *shalom* and become whole again.

SUMMARY

The biblical writers were intensely aware of their own physical environment. Not surprisingly, nearly every aspect of the biblical story is infused with geographical information of one kind or another. A student of the Bible is best able to appreciate the landed context on which the events of the Bible took place by pursuing a regional approach to biblical geography. In doing so, he or she is able to better understand the impact of geographical realities on patterns of human settlement, communication, economy, and defense during the biblical period, thereby gaining a more complete appreciation of the geographical, historical, and theological perspectives from which the biblical authors wrote.

QUESTIONS

1. Is a life lived *"under his own vine and his own fig tree"* (1 Kgs 4:25) appealing, or quaint, for a post-modern, urban, mobile Westerner? Which of its values are most important (or most elusive) for you?
2. Jerome asserted that people who visit the lands of the Bible have a clearer understanding of the Bible's message than those who don't. Is this assertion reasonable? If so, why?
3. What specific geographical images do the biblical writers use to characterize God? Which did Jesus use of himself? How are these images both powerful and mundane?
4. How might a study of the biblical geography enhance our understanding of God's on-going participation in events of the world?
5. Highlight the geographical data mentioned in Deuteronomy 32 or Psalm 78. How many of these images seem familiar to you based on the living conditions of your own home? Which are most different or cannot be accurately visualized without either studying biblical geography or visiting the lands of the Bible?
6. In what ways might reading a text be a helpful metaphor for "reading the land"?

2 BUILDING BLOCKS OF BIBLICAL GEOGRAPHY

A study of biblical geography needs to start from the ground up—or, more accurately, from *underground* up. The material substances of earth—rocks, soil, and water, together with their sources and present conditions for human use—are not incidentals to the biblical story; they are the practical stuff of life. Just as a builder must know how to use the tools and materials at his or her disposal before starting to put up a house, so we must become familiar with the basic building blocks of human and historical geography prior to examining the specific regions in which episodes of the biblical story took place. We start with a word on terms and place names, the essential points of geographical identification.

A. UNDERSTANDING GEOGRAPHICAL TERMS AND PLACE NAMES

First-time visitors to the lands of the Bible typically comment, "This isn't at all how I imagined it would look!" They're not alone. Medieval artists from the time of the Renaissance typically depicted biblical life in the full context of their own world, defining a scene by the costumes, architecture, plant life, and physical environment of Europe rather than the ancient Near East. We, too, quite naturally approach the subject of biblical geography—both what is described in the text and the realities of what must be on the ground—with mental images based on landforms and patterns of climate we have experienced personally. The issue is both obvious and subtle: the geographical terms we encounter in the biblical text—and some of them are quite technical—should be understood within the range of actual geographical options found in the lands of the Bible, not those from our own hometowns. Moreover, Hebrew, the language of most of the Old Testament, has a much smaller number of words than does English; thus, some geographical terms must do double duty. The biblical Hebrew term *har*, for instance, refers to true mountains (parts of Mount Hermon are snow-capped much of the year), as well as hills that are significantly lower. The Hebrew word *yam*, "sea," designates both the salt water Mediterranean and the fresh water Sea of Galilee; in the vocabularies of much of the rest of the world, the latter would qualify as a smallish lake. The local inhabitants of a land as rocky as ancient Israel naturally used several words for "rock," and the biblical terms *tsur* ("cliff"), *sela* ("crag"), and *even* ("stone," large or small), though sometimes all appearing as "rock" in our English Bibles, should be distinguished—especially when one or another is used to describe God himself (as in Ps 18:2: "*The* LORD *is my* sela . . . *my God, my* tsur"). For that matter, we should not liken the wilderness of Judah to the dense woods of the Great American Wilderness. It is, rather, *midbar*, "steppe grazing land," and *yeshimon*, "empty wasteland." Rainfall (*matar*) in ancient Israel was and is seasonal, occurring cyclically as "early rain" (*yoreh*, NASB) and "latter rain" (*malqosh*, KJV) in the autumn and spring, thereby signaling the turn of the year (Deut 11:11–14). Such distinctions, and many more, are grounded in the geographical realities of the Middle East and help us connect to ways its ancient inhabitants perceived and organized the physical and, by extension, spiritual aspects of their universe.

Many geographical terms found in the Hebrew Bible come from parts of the human body. The summit of a hill is its *rosh*, lit. "head" (2 Sam 15:32). A slope dropping from a flat area is a *keteph*, lit. "shoulder" (Josh 18:19)—at least within the tribal inheritance of Benjamin, for the term occurs only in connection with that narrow territory. A bumpy ridgeline is sometimes called *tsela'ot*, lit. "ribs" (2 Sam 16:13), while the upper tributaries of a wadi form its *yad*, lit. "hand," with crooked tributary fingers outstretched (Deut 2:37). A *shen*, lit. "tooth," is a rocky crag (1 Sam 14:4). Both a well and a spring are an *ayin*, lit. "eye," a hole from which water flows (Gen 24:16,20; Ezek 47:10). The rim of a canyon, the bank of a wadi, or the shore of a sea are all a *saphah*, lit. "lip," the edge of something wet (Gen 22:17; Josh 12:2). Today's geographers call the dry peninsula that projects into the Dead Sea from the east the *Lashon* (*Lisan* in Arabic), lit. "Tongue." The writers of the Hebrew Bible, though, did exactly the opposite: they used the term *lashon* to refer to an elongated bay or gulf of the sea (Josh 18:19; Isa 11:15); a tongue is, after all, a wet appendage. Language used this way may seem fanciful or quaint, but it is quite natural. It also reflects the tendency of the ancient Israelites to personalize the land on which they lived.

Of all the geographical terms found in the Bible, those that are usually the most underappreciated are the place names. The study of place names (toponymy) plays an important, although usually overlooked, role in biblical studies. What people in the ancient world called the places where they lived, including the hills, valleys, water sources, and other topographical features nearby, tells us something about who these people were, about their language, history, and patterns of settlement, about the characteristics of their natural environment, and about how they related to the world.

> Place names appearing on maps of US states or Canadian provinces suggest wonderful tales about indigenous populations that once inhabited those lands, as well as the first foreigners who made their homes there. All place names, in fact, hold local interest. Most are matter-of-fact; some are curious or amusing. For instance, Greeley County, in far western Kansas, is home to towns named Horace and Tribune. (Clearly some of its settlers took that news publisher's well-known charge "Go West, young man!" to heart.) Comparing place names across regions allows historians to map population movements and settlement patterns over time. In principle, the same is done by biblical historical geographers who, by combining information found in texts with that unearthed by archaeology, seek to track the ebb and flow of people groups in the lands of the Bible during ancient times.

In the biblical world, a clan or tribe typically took its name from an eponymous (i.e., "name-related," or founding) ancestor, with such names often attaching themselves to the portion of ground where each clan or

A number of written sources from the ancient world preserve the names of cities and towns in Canaan during the biblical period. Among the more helpful are lists of dozens of cities conquered by the Egyptian pharaohs Thutmose III (ca. 1479–1425 BC) and Shishak (ca. 945–924 BC; cp. 1 Kgs 14:25–28; 2 Chr 12:1–8).[1] Both city lists can still be seen in all their pharaonic glory on the walls of the Karnak temple in Luxor, Egypt. This portion of the Thutmose III city list depicts three places also known from the Bible: Rabbah (Josh 15:60, left), Gezer (1- Kg 9:15–17, center), and Gibbethon (1 Kgs 15:27, right). Each place name, written in hieroglyphics, is shown as the body of a conquered city, personified with Semitic facial features and arms tied in subjugation. Shishak's list is important because the artists who produced it showed the conquered cities in geographical order, thus providing a kind of "map" that helps historical geographers identify unknown sites on the ground.

tribe lived. The best-known examples for Bible readers are the names of the sons of Jacob, which came to designate the specific bounded territories in which the tribes of Israel settled. On a larger scale, the spread of people groups across the earth after the flood is depicted in Genesis 10 as a process by which individuals became tribes in their own lands. Towns and cities, too, often bore the name of a founding father or other early resident of the place. For example, Shechem (Gen 33:18–19), Samaria (from Shemer; 1 Kgs 16:24), Anathoth (1 Chr 7:8), and Keilah and Eshtemoa (1 Chr 4:19) were all names of people first. Sometimes, too, a town took the name of one of its more recent residents when the flow of events moved that direction. For instance, Gibeah in the tribe of Benjamin became known as Gibeah of Saul after Saul exerted his kingship over Israel (1 Sam 15:34; Isa 10:29).

Sometimes topographical features or landforms took the names of persons who lived in their vicinity. One example is the Valley of the Sons of Hinnom, apparently the location of the Hinnom clan's ancestral land. This valley came to demarcate the settled limits of the city of Jerusalem on the west and south (Josh 18:16; 2 Kgs 23:10). Another example is the "palm tree of Deborah," a spot between Ramah and Bethel that apparently boasted a prominent palm where the prophetess Deborah made herself readily available for consultation (Judg 4:4–5). Interestingly, the elevation of the region between Ramah and Bethel, the heartland of the tribal inheritance of Benjamin, is a bit high for palm trees to grow naturally; this one likely gained special notice when Deborah made it hers.

A different kind of example of how a place name can indicate settlement patterns is Mahaneh-dan, "the camping place of Dan," Samson's hometown. Judges 13:25 places Mahaneh-dan between Zorah and Eshtaol, where the foothills of the Shephelah meet the Judean hill country. Judges 18:12 places it higher in the Judean hills to the east, by Kiriath-jearim. In fact, the name suggests that Samson was raised in a temporary tent settlement that probably moved around. In any case, Mahaneh-dan seems to have been a place that wouldn't leave archaeologically recoverable material. Its location between the established Judean towns of the hill country and an encroaching Philistine presence in the foothills to the west suggests that Samson's exploits should be read with the social, political, and economic

1 Yohanan Aharoni, *The Land of the Bible: A Historical Geography*, rev. and enlarged edition, trans. and ed. by A. F. Rainey (Philadelphia: The Westminster Press, 1979), 152–66; 323–30; Anson F. Rainey and R. Steven Notley, *The Sacred Bridge: Carta's Atlas of the Biblical World*, 2d. Emended & Enhanced Ed. (Jerusalem: Carta, 2014), 72–75; 186–89.

uncertainty that is typically characteristic of frontiers between expanding people groups.

The Table of Nations offers the following genealogical note explaining the origin and spread of populations in the land of Canaan: *"Canaan fathered Sidon his firstborn and Heth, as well as the Jebusites, the Amorites, the Girgashites, the Hivites, the Arkites, the Sinites, the Arvadites, the Zemarites, and the Hamathites"* (Gen 10:15–18). That Sidon was listed as the firstborn of Canaan is poignant in light of ancient Israel's subsequent history. The Sidonians, Israel's economically successful neighbor to the north, were among the most persistent cultural thorns in Israel's side throughout the biblical story.

Many place names mentioned in the Bible were formed from the lexical element *beth* ("house of"), plus the name of a local Semitic or Canaanite deity. Hence, Beth-anath (Judg 1:33), Beth-baal-meon (Josh 13:17), Beth-dagon (Josh 15:41; 19:27), Beth-horon (1 Kgs 9:17), Beth-shemesh (Josh 15:10; Judg 1:33), and others (probably including Beth-lehem; 1 Sam 17:12): all reflect the active polytheistic environment of Canaan into which Israel entered. Other place names highlight the pervasive presence of Baal in the region (Baal-gad, Josh 11:17; Baal-hazor, 2 Sam 13:23; Baal-hermon, 1 Chr 5:23; Baal-meon, Num 32:38; Baal-perazim, 2 Sam 5:20; Baal-shalishah, 2 Kgs 4:42; Baalath, 1 Kgs 9:18; and the like). Baal, "lord" or "master," was the primary nickname of Hadad, the chief male deity in the Levant; by appellation, he was localized in many places throughout the land. The town of Ashtaroth (Deut 1:4) in Bashan probably was a regional center of worship for Ashtoreth, the popular Canaanite goddess of fertility and oft-times consort of the Baals. It is interesting to note that when the Israelites settled in Canaan, they did not give these cities new names reflecting the divine name YHWH. Indeed, no place name mentioned in the Bible contains the name YHWH.

On the other hand, we do have many place names formed from *-el*, the generic Semitic word for god/God. During the days of Israel's earliest history, the patriarchs gave names to spots where they sensed God's special presence dwelt, sometimes erecting altars to his name. These include Beth-el ("the house of God," a name that eventually replaced Luz as the name of the nearby city; Gen 28:19), Peni-el ("the face of God"; Gen 32:30), and El-Elohe-Israel ("God, the God of Israel"; Gen 33:20). Of this type is also the place name Beer-lahai-roi ("A Well of the Living One Who Sees Me"; Gen 16:14). Note also the later name Jezreel, "God sows" (1 Kgs 18:46).

Perhaps Israel's reticence to name places after YHWH (often pronounced "Yahweh" today) stemmed from an understanding that even though the land belonged to the Lord, he, unlike the Canaanite deities, was neither to be identified with it in substance (the Lord is transcendent over, not coextensive with, creation) nor to be localized (and hence limited) to specific spots within. In contrast, many Israelite *personal* names were built from the divine name YHWH. Examples are numerous and include Jehoshaphat ("YHWH has judged"), Isaiah ("YHWH is salvation"), Joel ("YHWH is God"), Jehoiakim ("YHWH will establish"), Elijah ("My God is YHWH"), and so on. The practice of using the divine name for personal but not geographical names might indicate an understanding among the ancient Israelites that the most proper locus for God and his actions was not in places but with people:

> *When the Most High gave the*
> *nations their inheritance*
> *and divided the human race,*
> *he set the boundaries of the peoples*
> *according to the number*
> *of the people of Israel.*
> *But the* LORD*'s portion is his people,*
> *Jacob, his own inheritance.* (Deut 32:8–9)

The Bible gives only a few examples of cities that were given new names of any kind when Israel entered Canaan (e.g., Laish/Leshem was changed to Dan—Judg 18:29; Josh 19:47, and the villages of Bashan became Havvoth-jair, "Jair's Villages," after a clan of the tribe of Manasseh—Deut 3:14; Kiriath-arba was renamed Hebron earlier—Gen 23:2; Josh 14:15). Taken as a whole, these instances seem to be exceptional rather than the rule. They support the maxim that in the ancient Near East as in the modern Middle East, where indigenous populations are stable and conservative, place names are conservative as well. Once established, place names tend to resist change even in the face of population shifts. This basic principle will come into play in our discussion of how to identify the location of ancient sites, below.

"For I tell you, concerning the names of villages and rivers written in the sacred writings, both written and oral, that little has changed of their names among the [Arabs] . . . for the land stands forever, together with most of its names, and the change in names is very slight." So commented the Jewish geographer Estori ha-Parhi, who in the fourteenth century AD wrote the first book in Hebrew on the geography and place names of the land of ancient Israel.[1]

The exception that proves the rule took place in the centuries immediately preceding the New Testament days, when the surge tide of Hellenism and then the Latin cultures of Rome washed over the lands of ancient Israel. In their wake, important cities were elevated to the status of a *polis* and given Greek or Latin names, signaling the coming of a new world order. Hence Acco became Ptolemais (after the Hellenistic Egyptian pharaoh Ptolemy II, who controlled the east Mediterranean coast in the mid-third century BC); Paneas was renamed Caesarea Philippi in honor of both Caesar Augustus and his dutiful client Philip the Tetrarch; Herod the Great built Caesarea Maritima for Caesar Augustus, his emperor and patron, on the site of a ruined Mediterranean fishing village called Strato's Tower; Bethsaida, the city of Jesus's disciples, became Bethsaida-Julias after the

1 Pages 245 and 632 of *Sefer Kaftor veFerech*, written in 1322 but not published until 1549 in Venice, quoted in Yoel Elitzur, *Ancient Place Names in the Holy Land: Preservation and History* (Jerusalem: The Hebrew University Magnes Press, 2004), 1.

wife of Augustus; Ahab's capital, Samaria, was renamed Sebaste, the Greek form of Augustus; Shechem was re-founded as Neapolis, "New City;" Beth-shean became Scythopolis; Rabbah-bene-Ammon, the ancient Ammonite capital, was given the name Philadelphia, and so on. As a result, a New Testament map of ancient Israel reads very differently from its Old Testament counterpart.

But this Greco-Roman intrusion, at least in regard to place names, was not to last. Even though these intrusive names remained in place in official documents for over a millennium, until after the Arab conquest in the seventh century AD, the local folk typically just kept calling their hometowns by the old Semitic names they were used to using. Most of the original Semitic place names then simply resurfaced, with minor linguistic changes, once the forces of Hellenism subsided. So the name Paneas returned as Baniyas (as spoken in Arabic); Beth-shean survived as Beisan; Acco again became Acco. Caesarea Maritima had so overshadowed little Strato's Tower that its name was preserved even after the Arab conquest, as was Neapolis, modern Nablus, and Sebaste, modern Sebastieh. But even with these exceptions, the basic principle of name preservation remains intact.

Most place names in ancient Israel, however, were less politically sensitive, having been derived from notable topographic features, regional flora or fauna, or local human activity. Examples are numerous; a few familiar place names will suffice: Geba and Gibeah ("hill"), Ramah ("height"), Mizpah ("lookout spot"), Mahanaim ("twin camps"), Hazor ("settlement"), Ai ("ruin"), Sorek ("finest vine"), Socoh ("thorn bush"), En-gedi ("spring of the kid"), Aijalon ("deer field"), Gath-rimmon ("pomegranate press"), Gethsemane ("olive press"), and Taricheae ("salted fish").[1] Together these names provide an earthy witness to details of everyday life in ancient Israel, including landforms and natural resources, which would otherwise escape casual readers of the past. Such names, however, should not be over-read. Popular etymologies, midrashic allusions, and fanciful interpretations not grounded in the biblical text abound and should be avoided, such as finding anything more than casual significance in that Jesus, "the Bread of Life" (as mentioned by John), was born in Bethlehem, "the house of bread" (as mentioned by Matthew and Luke).

The discipline of toponymy is the careful study of place names and the principles that govern their preservation over time. For historical geographers, toponymy is an important tool in identifying the location of cities and towns mentioned in ancient texts. This was first understood in a practical way by Edward Robinson, an American Bible scholar who visited Ottoman Palestine in 1838 and again in 1852. Having first gleaned all available topographical and toponymic (i.e., place name) information from primary sources known in his day (the Bible and classical texts written in Hebrew, Greek, and Latin), Robinson traveled the length and breadth of the land of ancient Israel, from

Eusebius (ca. AD 260–340), Bishop of Caesarea and Metropolitan of the Holy Land in the early fourth century, is usually remembered for his extensive writings on church history, apologetics, and dogmatics (doctrine). Yet his *Onomasticon*,[2] written in Greek, is the best surviving early work on the land of ancient Israel during the Roman period. Eusebius identified and commented on the location of biblical cities, towns, and villages as they (or their ruins) were known in his day, arranging them alphabetically by site in his work. When possible, Eusebius also gave the distance in miles that each site lay from key urban centers of Late Roman Palestine, according to the established system of Roman roads that networked the land in the third century AD. Jerome translated the *Onomasticon* into Latin seventy years later. Although Eusebius's conclusions are sometimes more dependent on tradition than fact, his *Onomasticon* remains an invaluable primary source for biblical site identification. This likeness of Eusebius is found on the right-side door panel of the Church of St. Catherine in Bethlehem.

1 For a more complete discussion, see Yohanan Aharoni, *The Land of the Bible: A Historical Geography*, rev. and enlarged ed, trans. by Anson Rainey (Philadelphia: Westminster Press, 1979), 107–11.

2 There are two English translations of the Onomasticon: G. S. P. Freeman-Grenville, Rupert L. Chapman III, and Joan E. Taylor, *The Onomasticon by Eusebius of Caesarea* (Jerusalem: Carta, 2003), and R. Steven Notley and Ze'ev Safrai, *Eusebius, Onomasticon: A Triglot Edition with Notes and Commentary* (Leiden: Brill, 2005).

Edward Robinson matched the location of the ancient city of Beth-shean (Judg 1:27; 1 Sam 31:10; 1 Kgs 4:12) with extensive ruins lying just north of the Arab village of Beisan, in the northern Jordan Valley. Linguistically, the toponymic connection Beisan = Beth-shean is perfect; what Robinson didn't know is that the particular ruins he saw belonged to Scythopolis, the Greco-Roman-Byzantine city that replaced Beth-shean in the centuries following the Old Testament era. The majesty of Scythopolis, raised back to life and shown here with columns that once lined the city's main street, has been uncovered by archaeologists from the Hebrew University of Jerusalem. The Old Testament site of Beth-shean actually dominated the tell above (left). Although archaeology has determined that the exact spot of ancient Beth-shean was the tell rather than the columned ruins at its base, Robinson nevertheless gets credit for correctly identifying the site.

the Mediterranean to Transjordan and from southern Sinai to Lebanon and Syria, looking for evidence of the location of biblical sites. He was assisted by Eli Smith, a Beirut-based missionary who possessed a working knowledge of practical linguistics. With an eye for the lay of the land and an ear for place names preserved through the tongues of local inhabitants, Robinson and Smith were able to match 1,712 sites with their biblical counterparts, many through the principles of name preservation mentioned above.

Robinson and Smith identified biblical Gibeon, for instance, with the Arab village of el-Jib; Geba with Jeba'; Michmash with Mukmas; Lydda with Ludd, and so on. The name Jericho, Robinson correctly reasoned, was preserved in the name of the Arab village Eriha (it's a good linguistic match), near the spring and tell (Tell es-Sultan) that we now know to be the exact site of the Old Testament city. When we take into account that they were working prior to the origins of scientific archaeology and without a proper understanding of tells (i.e., mounds of destruction debris built up from a sequence of layers from destroyed cities), Robinson and Smith did remarkably well in defining the principles of biblical site identification. In the process, they established the discipline of toponymics as a credible academic endeavor. Their published record, *Biblical Researches in Palestine*,[1] is a gold mine of toponymic and ethnographic data interspersed with tales of courage, raw adventure, and derring-do; it makes for fascinating reading of early scientific exploration in the Holy Land.

In the 1870s, teams from the British Royal Engineers working for the Survey of Western Palestine (the SWP) were able to produce the first complete, modern map of the land of ancient Israel west of the Jordan River, from the Litani River in south Lebanon to the Beer-sheba wadi in the Negev. Most of the work of the survey was done by C. R. Conder and H. H. Kitchener; the latter would go on to become Britain's Secretary

1 Edward Robinson and Eli Smith, *Biblical Researches in Palestine, Mount Sinai and Arabia Petraea: A Journal of Travels in the Year 1838 by E. Robinson and E. Smith Undertaken in Reference to Biblical Geography*, 2 vols. (Boston: Crocker and Brewster, 1841); and *Later Biblical Researches in Palestine and in the Adjacent Regions: A Journal of Travels in the Year 1852, Drawn up from the Original Diaries, with Historical Illustrations, with New Maps and Plans* (Boston: Crocker and Brewster, 1856). Reprinted as Edward Robinson, *Biblical Researches in Palestine and the Adjacent Regions: A Journal of Travels in the Years 1838 & 1852*, 3 vols. (Jerusalem: The Universitas Booksellers, 1970).

of War during the First World War. The SWP labeled over ten thousand sites (every hill and valley, wadi, spring, well, and cistern, village, old structure, ruin, and grave they saw). Then they published six volumes of field notes, drawings, analyses, and indices, with twenty-six large map sheets at a scale of one inch to one mile.[1] A survey of eastern Palestine (Transjordan) was started but not completed due to political unrest in the region at the time. Nevertheless, through the work of the SWP and the efforts in the decades since by historical geographers from France, Germany, England, America, and Israel, together with the careful work of dozens of archaeological missions in the land of ancient Israel from around the globe, many (though certainly not all) of the ancient sites mentioned in the Bible have now been identified with absolute or reasonable certainty.

Ultimately, the most persistent problem in site identification is that there just aren't enough pieces of matching data to go around. Most archaeological sites do not maintain a toponymic connection with an ancient place name; those that do were identified long ago. Rather, most are known today only by modern (Arabic or Hebrew) names which bear no linguistic resemblance to the names of any known ancient site. Additionally, many places mentioned in the Bible or other ancient documents don't appear with enough context to narrow down their exact locations (e.g., Beer-lahai-roi; Gen 16:14). Others appear in the sources with variant spellings or in multiple contexts, either of which suggests the possibility of more than one place of the same name (e.g., Geba/Gibeah/Gibeon). Or sometimes a place mentioned in an ancient text was of such a nature that archaeologically attestable material simply can't be found to pinpoint its location. Such is the case for most of the named spots where Israel camped during their years of wilderness wandering (Num 33:5–49). Many important place names such as Libnah (2 Kgs 8:22; 19:8; 23:31), Eglon (Josh 10:3), Gilgal (there were at least three—Josh 4:19; 12:23; 2 Kgs 2:1; 4:38), and Elath/Eloth/Ezion-geber (Deut 2:8; 1 Kgs 9:26; 22:48; 2 Chr 26:2) are notorious for having several reasonable site location options. In such cases, matching name to site can seem like a grand game of musical chairs. And, if an event is mentioned in the Bible without a specific notation regarding its exact location (such as the Sermon on the Mount), we are left to the whims of tradition and scholarly guesswork as to where it might have taken place—however fine a particular suggestion might seem otherwise.

"Jerusalem" is an ancient place name that predates the arrival of Israel in Canaan. The name appears as [U]rusalimum in the Egyptian Execration Texts of the late nineteenth century BC,[2] and as Urusalim in the mid-fourteenth century BC Amarna letters, also found in Egypt.[3] The city of Jerusalem was called Jebus when David sent his opportunistic general, Joab, through a shaft in its bedrock that had been hewn to allow its residents access to the fresh waters of the Gihon spring. Climbing from bottom to top, Joab entered, then conquered, the city (1 Chr 11:4–9; cp. Judg 19:10). When David dislodged the Jebusites from the region, the city's original name, Jerusalem, was easily restored. There have been numerous creative attempts to explain the origin of the name Jerusalem: most connect the element *salem* with the Hebrew word for peace, *shalom*, or with Shalem, a local Canaanite deity (see Gen 14:18). In spite of the appeal of these or other suggestions, the original meaning of the name Jerusalem, a word beloved by people of faith for millennia, remains unknown.

One final point regarding place names needs to be mentioned, and this is the most tendentious dilemma of all, for here the ideals of dispassionate scholarship crash headlong into the convictions and realities of modern life. What should the lands of the Bible be called, either in the time of the Bible or today? The earliest name mentioned in the Bible for what became the land of ancient Israel is "Canaan" (Gen 12:5). This designation, which can be traced to Late Bronze Age Egyptian sources,[4] refers to a region that seems to include much of what is now Israel, southern Lebanon and the West Bank/Palestinian territories, but not Transjordan. The Egyptians assumed everyone knew where the borders of Canaan were and saw no reason to mention them. The only ancient texts that do are Genesis 10:19 and Numbers 34:1–12, enclosing a territory that was consistent with the Egyptian use of the term. Many Bible readers, for obvious reasons, prefer to use the name Israel rather than Canaan, although as a political term Israel referred to the land "from Dan to Beer-sheba" only during the short-lived united monarchy of David and Solomon (1 Kgs 4:25), then to the smaller region of the Northern Kingdom for the two centuries following. The collocation "land of Israel" (*eretz Yisrael*), which occurs frequently in the Old Testament (2 Kgs 5:2, etc.), has persisted primarily in Jewish religious texts and historical texts of a religious nature up to the present, having been resurrected as an active political term with the rise of Zionism only in the last 140 years or so. The Southern Kingdom in the time of the Old Testament was, of course, called Judah; and it is this name that survived as a political term after the Babylonian captivity, first as the Persian province *Yehud*, then as the Hasmonean *Judea*, and finally as the Roman Imperial Province *Judaea* during the time of the New Testament. Its most frequently used derivative is the word "Jew" (*Yehudi*); i.e., someone from Judea.

1 C. R. Conder and H. H. Kitchener, *The Survey of Western Palestine: Memoirs of the Topography, Orography, Hydrography and Archaeology*, in 3 vols: *Galilee, Samaria, Judaea* (London: The Committee of the Palestine Exploration Fund, 1881–1883); Sir Charles Warren and Claude Reignier Conder, *The Survey of Western Palestine: Jerusalem* (London: The Committee of the Palestine Exploration Fund, 1884); Henry C. Stewardson, compiler, *The Survey of Western Palestine: A General Index* (London: The Committee of the Palestine Exploration Fund, 1888).

2 Yohanan Aharoni, Michael Avi-Yonah, Anson F. Rainey, Ze'ev Safrai, and R. Steven Notley, *The Carta Bible Atlas*, 5th ed. (Jerusalem: Carta, 2011), 29.

3 Anson F. Rainey, *Canaanite in the Amarna Tablets: A Linguistic Analysis of the Mixed Dialect Used by the Scribes from Canaan*, vol. 1, *Orthography, Phonology, Morphosyntactic Analysis of the Pronouns, Nouns, Numerals* (Leiden: Brill, 1996), 16, 21, 29.

4 Rainey and Notley, *The Sacred Bridge*, 33–36.

Other Bible readers favor the name Palestine, from the Greek toponym *Palaistina* first used by Herodotus in the late fifth century BC to refer to the southern coastal plain around Gaza.[2] Herodotus clearly derived the term Palaistina from Philistia (Hb *pelešet*; Isa 14:29, etc.), homeland of the Philistines, long-time inhabitants of the region. Assyrian texts first mention Philistia (*palaštu*) in the eighth century BC,[3] distinguishing it from Israel and Judah and always limiting the name to the southern coastal regions. By contrast, the Assyrians called Israel *Mat-Humri* or *Bit-Humria*,[4] "the land" or "house of Omri," father of Ahab (1 Kgs 16:23–29), even after the fall of Omri's dynasty. Palestina became the official political designation of the entire area, including the interior hills and valleys of Judea, Samaria, and Galilee, only after Rome put down the Second Jewish Revolt of AD 132–135.[5] The Romans were motivated to change the official name of the province of Judaea to Palestina in part by the need to legitimize a new, non-Jewish identity in the region, though on geographical grounds alone it makes sense that a power based on the sea would use the name of a coastal plain to reference its hilly hinterland. The Roman name of the province was actually Syria Palaestina, to indicate that Palestina was a subdivision of the larger province of Syria governed through Damascus. In any case, references to Palestine in the context of the Gospels, though frequent and typically accepted by scholars and generalists alike, are

One identification that Robinson got wrong was Megiddo. Standing on the flat top of Tell el-Mutesellim, what we now know to be the correct site, Robinson noted that the tell "would indeed present a splendid site for a city, but there is no trace of any kind to show that a city ever stood there."[1] Robinson instead suggested that the ruins of the nearby site of Lejjun—which preserved the name of the Roman city Legio—must have also been the location of the earlier city of Megiddo. Robinson's textual work lacked a toponymic connection to Megiddo. Without the aid of the discipline of archaeology to tell him that twenty-five layers of destroyed cities lay beneath his feet, he literally missed the site by a mile. The view here is through the great cut in the northeastern side, excavated by the University of Chicago in the late 1930s, with the Jezreel Valley beyond.

1 Robinson, *Biblical Researches in Palestine and the Adjacent Regions*, vol. 3, (Jerusalem: The Universitas Booksellers, 1970), 117.

2 Herodotus, *Histories* 1:105: "Thence [the Persians] marched against Egypt; and when they were in the part of Syria called Palestine, Psammetichus king of Egypt met them and persuaded them with gifts and prayers to come no further. So they turned back [north] and . . . came on their way to the city of Ascalon in Syria."

3 James B. Pritchard, ed., *Ancient Near Eastern Texts Relating to the Old Testament* (*ANET*) (Princeton: Princeton University Press, 1955), 281–82, 287, 294, 301.

4 *ANET*, 284–285; William W. Hallo, ed., *The Context of Scripture*, vol. II: *Monumental Inscriptions from the Biblical World* (Leiden: Brill, 2000), 288, 297–98.

5 Fergus Miller, *The Roman Near East, 31 B.C.–A.D. 337* (Cambridge: Harvard University Press, 1993), 107–8.

We read in Matthew 2:20–21 that when Mary, Joseph, and Jesus came out of Egypt, they returned to *"the land of Israel"* (Gk *gē Israel* = Hb *eretz Yisrael*). This is the only place in the Gospels where the place name "land of Israel" appears. Matthew used the term *Judea*, the official name of the land in the first century AD, in the very next sentence, when he mentioned that Herod the Great's son, Archelaus, had inherited the throne (Matt 2:22). So why "the land of Israel" here? Matthew pictures Jesus's return from Egypt as a reenactment, or fulfillment, of the journey Moses and the Israelites took from Egypt to their proper home in Canaan, a place that they came to call the land of Israel during the time of the Old Testament. By choosing his words carefully and citing Hos 11:1, *"Out of Egypt I called my Son"* (Matt 2:14–15), Matthew intended to show that Jesus embodied Israel, now faithful and renewed. Matthew's account of Jesus's return to Judea is a reminder that when we ask about the accuracy of place names, we also need to ask, "Accurate for what purpose?" and remember that accuracy and neutrality are not always the same thing.

anachronistic and not technically correct. It is also important to note that the Roman derivation of Palestina from "Philistine" is of linguistic and historical but *not* theological significance.

Modern political events clearly heighten the urgency (and sensitivity) of a reader's preference for either "Israel" or "Palestine" in discussions of the historical geography of the land of the Bible. Some scholars even prefer the term "The Levant" (from the French phrase *soleil levant*, "rising sun"), although this use of the word, which originated in the context of nineteenth century Western expansionism, is both Eurocentric and largely antiquated. The term *Morgenland*, "Morning-land," for speakers of German is similar. Others have resurrected the name Syro-Palestine, a popular scholarly convention that seeks to recognize a common cultural sphere in the southern Levant composed of the territory of ancient Israel and its near neighbors. The Near East, the Orient, or Turkish Asia (this last one was proper prior to the First World War) are also all either too ill-defined or too limiting. Without intending to make any statement regarding the modern political realm, it is perhaps easiest to simply refer to the land where the majority of events described in the Bible took place as "the land of ancient Israel," making further refinements in nomenclature as the topic of discussion warrants.

The term *ancient Near East* refers to the landmass encompassing Egypt, Anatolia (Turkey), Persia (Iran), the northern part of the Arabian Peninsula, and, at its center, the Fertile Crescent including the land of ancient Israel. *Middle East*, on the other hand, refers to the same region plus outlying areas in modern times. The latter term is actually quite new, first appearing in an article by the American Navy Captain Alfred Thayer Mahan that was published in the British monthly, *The National Review*, in September 1902.[1] It is proper to use the term *Middle East* for the region when speaking of current events or recent history, or when referencing the unchanging geographical realities of the region, but not in connection with events or peoples of the ancient past.

The lowest level of the rock sandwich underlies all regions of the central Middle East. Composed of metamorphic rock (formed when parts of the earth's crust are super-heated by contact with molten magma), this basement complex can be seen wherever severe uplifting has thrust the rock to the earth's surface. This view takes in the time-worn granite mountains of southern Sinai from Jebel Musa, the traditional location of Mount Sinai. Far from areas of permanent human settlement and bearing the wrinkles of hoary antiquity, the setting is perfectly appropriate for God's awe-filled revelation to Moses (Exod 19:1–20:21).

B. GEOLOGICAL STRUCTURE AND LANDFORMS

The land of ancient Israel is dominated by vast expanses of exposed bedrock. Various geological processes have shaped the complex surface pattern and underlying substructure of the "foundations of the earth" since creation (Ps 104:5; cp. Job 14:18–19; 38:1–11; Ps 90:2; Prov 8:29). The entire mass can be pictured as a gigantic rock sandwich made of three different kinds, or layers, of rock. Each of the so-called sandwich layers is visible on the surface of the ground somewhere in or adjacent to the land of ancient Israel.

The massive bottom layer, the crust of the rock sandwich, is composed **of granite, diorite, crystalline schist**, and other **igneous rocks**. Its largest exposed expanse is in the southern Sinai, where massive granite mountains, worn and weathered, dominate the landscape. Relatively small outcroppings of granite and schist also dot the edges of the southern part of the Rift Valley between the Dead Sea and the Gulf of Aqaba/Eilat.

The middle layer of the rock sandwich, thousands of feet thick, is composed primarily of **Nubian**

1 Karl E. Meyer and Shareen Blair Brysac, *Kingmakers: The Invention of the Modern Middle East* (New York: W. W. Norton & Company, 2008), 37–8.

Two types of Nubian sandstone, red (above) and white (below), are clearly visible in the rugged terrain of Wadi Dana in the Edomite highlands. Sandstone can be either durable or friable, depending on the composition of the material cementing its grains together. Areas of sandstone lie on the desert fringes of the settled lands of the Bible, offering landscapes reminiscent of those described in the book of Job.

Herman Melville, author of *Moby-Dick*, visited Judea in January of 1857. He was not impressed by what he saw, letting a cursory look at the rocks that seemed to be everywhere obscure his view of the larger landscape. "We read a good deal about stones in the Scriptures," he observed. "Monuments & memorials are set up of stones; men are stoned to death; the figurative seed falls in stony places; and no wonder stones should so largely figure in the Bible. Judea is one accumulation of stones—stony mountains & stony plains; stony forests & stony roads; stony walls & stony fields; stony homes & stony tombs; stony eyes & stony hearts. Before you and behind you are stones. Stones to the right & stones to the left. The removal of one stone only serves to reveal those stones still lying below it."[1]

sandstone, a sedimentary rock. Highly granular in structure, Nubian sandstone is easily recognized by its vivid colors, which are caused by varying amounts of minerals: silica and calcite have produced sandstones that are light tan and bright white; iron oxide yields red, rose, pink, and purple sandstones; brown and yellow sandstones are tinted by sulphur; and black sandstones have a high manganese dioxide content. White and red sandstones dominate, giving the middle of the rock sandwich a kind of peanut butter and jelly look. Huge blocks of uplifted sandstone can be seen in areas immediately south and east of the land of ancient Israel, specifically in Wadi Rum (southern Jordan and northwestern Saudi Arabia), along the eastern scarp of the Rift Valley between the Dead Sea

1 Herman Melville, *Journals*, ed. by Howard C. Horsford with Lynn Horth (Evanston and Chicago: Northwestern University Press and Newberry Library, 1989), 90. Note as well Hilton Obenzinger, *American Palestine: Melville, Twain, and the Holy Land* (Princeton: Princeton University Press, 1999), 61–158.

and the Gulf of Aqaba/Eilat, and edging the towering granite mountains of southern Sinai.

The top crust of the rock sandwich is composed of **limestones.** Limestone is a sedimentary rock of calcium carbonate formed from the detritus of marine plant and animal life that was deposited as strata in the region by successive inundations of the ancient forerunner of the Mediterranean Sea, a body of water that geologists call the Tethys Sea. Because the Tethys Sea moved into the region from the northwest, the limestone is thicker in the northern and western parts of the land (Galilee, the Carmel Range, and Gilead) and thinner as it runs up against areas of uplifted Nubian sandstone in the south and east.

This upper layer of limestone, visible as bedrock across most of the land of ancient Israel, is far from uniform in its composition. For the sake of convenience, geologists divide it into three basic types, each named with the term that corresponds with the geological period in which the limestone was deposited at the bottom of the Tethys Sea. The lowest layer (and hence oldest in the stratified sequence) is a hard limestone of the **Cenomanian** and **Turonian** periods. Above this was deposited a relatively thin layer of very soft **Senonian** limestone, or chalk. The uppermost and hence most recent layer in the sequence is **Eocene** limestone, which varies from a chalk-like to a relatively hard consistency. We should note that an even older fourth layer, **Jurassic** limestone, underlays the limestone of the Cenomanian and Turonian periods everywhere except in the southeast. Jurassic limestone is visible only in deep surface cuts such as the Jabbok Canyon, or on the Lebanese ranges due to severe uplifting. Thin, dark layers of hard, fine-grained **chert**, a form

Psalm 104 tells the story of creation poetically, yet in a way that reflects the geological processes that formed the foundations of the earth:

He established the earth on its foundations;
it will never be shaken.
You covered it with the deep as if it were a garment;
the water stood above the mountains.
At your rebuke the water fled;
at the sound of your thunder they hurried away—
mountains rose and valleys sank—
to the place you established for them. (Ps 104:5–8)

We can easily recognize Cenomanian-Turonian limestone by its brown-red tint and horizontal, stratified lines. It was deposited in beds, typically ranging from one to four feet (0.3 to 1.2 m) thick and each separated from the next by a thin layer of hard marl or chert. As a result, Cenomanian-Turonian limestone is easy to quarry. Its hardness allowed this type of limestone to become the building material of choice in hill country towns and villages throughout ancient Israel. Skeletal remains of quarry sites, scarring the bedrock at right angles, can be seen in areas where flat stretches of the rock are exposed on the surface of the ground. As an added advantage, Cenomanian-Turonian limestone holds water well and produces fertile terra rosa ("red earth") soil that is excellent for growing grapes and orchard crops. The result? Areas of Cenomanian-Turonian limestone such as the Hill Country of Judah, the Hill Country of Ephraim, Galilee, and Gilead were all well suited for human settlement.

Formed from the sediment of microscopic organisms, a relatively thin band of crumbly Senonian chalk was deposited above the Cenomanian-Turonian strata in the upper layer of the rock sandwich. Senonian chalk does not absorb water well (rather, its powdery structure tends to repel water), and when cut into building blocks, it cracks and crumbles easily (Isa 27:9 speaks of "*crushed bits of chalk*" that are useless for building). Here in the Judean Wilderness east of the Mount of Olives, the Senonian chalk has eroded into a jumble of smoothly rounded, egg-shaped hills devoid of vegetation, all cascading like powdery rapids into the Rift Valley. Areas of exposed Senonian chalk can support permanent human settlement only if other factors are present to override these otherwise negative qualities.

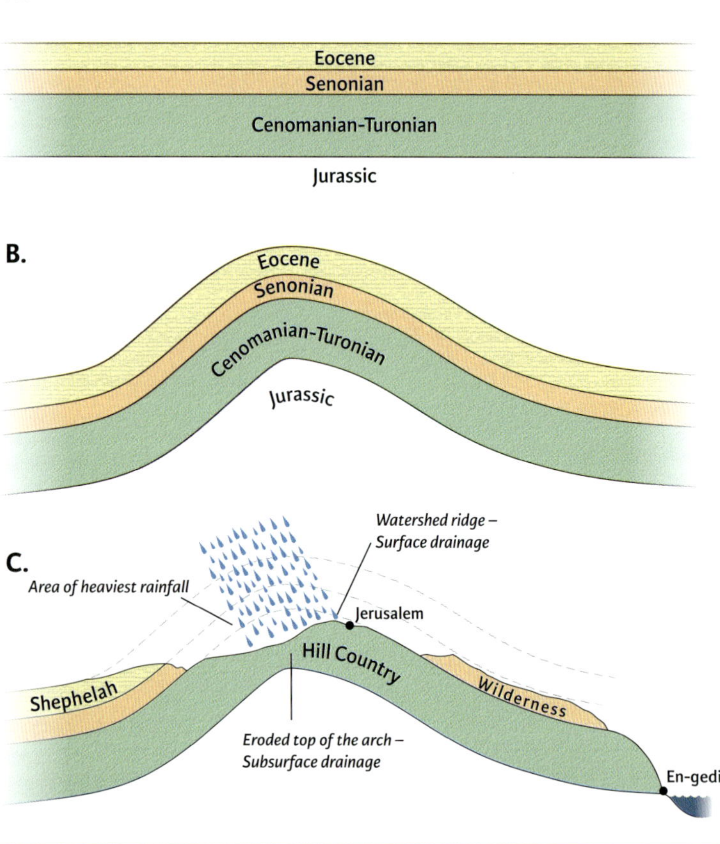

This diagram shows the geological sequence of mountain-building in the region of Judah:
A—Limestone was deposited in stratified layers, with the oldest limestones at the bottom and the youngest on top.
B—The stratified limestone layers were folded (uplifted) into an arch.
C—Faulting and erosion have given the land its present shape.
Much of the heavy rainfall west of Jerusalem seeps into the limestone strata below ground, where it follows the angle of stratification downward and eastward to emerge along the Dead Sea as some of the most powerful springs in the land.

of quartz, are found throughout these limestones. The harder, black varieties of chert are flint stones (Deut 8:15; 32:13; Ps 114:8; cp. Isa 50:7). The most useful types of flint keep a hard, sharp edge and have been shaped into cutting, boring, piercing, and scraping tools for millennia (e.g., Josh 5:2).

Due largely to movements of the plates of the earth's crust, the entire rock sandwich was compressed in some places, stretched in others. A violent upheaval on a NNE–SSW axis raised the top layers of the sandwich into a series of closely related arches (an arch is a massive geological rise, or ripple, in the underlying rock structure). These arches form the spiny limestone backbone of the land of ancient Israel. Their line parallels the shore of the Mediterranean Sea, determining the smoothly contoured shape of Israel's coastline from Mount Carmel to the Sinai.

A series of violent fractures, slippages, and displacements dramatically altered this relatively simple geological structure. It is possible to trace an intricate network of fault lines on a detailed geological map of Israel. The most pronounced are the parallel north-south faults that mark both sides of the section of the Great Rift Valley that lies between the Sea of Galilee and the southern end of the Dead Sea. Several smaller fault lines run parallel to the NNE–SSW line of the limestone arch. Others have bisected the arch, causing the ground between to drop into broad, low valleys that function as corridors that allow travel access deep into the hills (e.g., the Wadi Farah [Fari'a], the Harod and Jezreel Valleys, and the eastern, upper end of the Aijalon Valley). Extensive fracturing throughout Galilee has produced a highly complex surface topography, providing a unique mix of tight spaces and open passageways throughout the region.

We might correctly suppose that a land as marked by faulting as this would lie prone to earthquakes, and indeed the effects of many earthquakes are seen in the

White Eocene limestone, shown here on a hollowed-out cliff face at Beth Guvrin in the Shephelah of Judah, has a low water-carrying capacity and is generally too soft to be cut and used as building blocks. It can, however, be hollowed out into cave dwellings or harvested, as it was here, as soft limestone for plaster, leaving a gaping cave behind. Wherever it is exposed to the surface of the ground, Eocene limestone tends to be covered by a three-to-five-foot (1 to 1.5 m) thick layer of Nari crust, a hard, limey covering that is durable enough to be used as building blocks. Cities found in Eocene areas such as Megiddo and Gezer were largely built out of local Nari. Nari is rough and ashen gray in color, with the underlying Eocene light brown to white; this gives patches of exposed bedrock of the Shephelah a pallid look when viewed under a blinding summer sun.

archaeological and literary record of the land of ancient Israel.[1] Some have been quite severe; among the most catastrophic were those in AD 749, 1034, 1546, 1759, 1837, and 1927 (this last one killed more than 500 people). As would be expected, the epicenter for most earthquakes has been somewhere in the Rift Valley, often close to Jericho. Most have registered between 6.5 and 6.8 on the Richter scale. Still, the author can personally attest that even in a relatively minor earthquake in the Judean hill country, *"the foundations of the mountains [of Jerusalem] trembled"* (Ps 18:7). Biblical writers, in fact, sometimes used a severe earthquake to date an important event (Amos 1:1; Zech 14:5) or to describe an appearance of God (Pss 18:7; 68:8; 114:4,6–7; Hab 3:10; cp. Matt 27:51).

Volcanic eruptions, another result of seismic activity, also provide a reservoir of images for the biblical writers who sought to reach beyond the norm to illustrate the power of God (Pss 18:7; 104:32; 144:5). These occurred most recently in the geological sequence of mountain building. Volcanic activity has deposited a thick layer of black **basalt** (lava) across the limestone core of Bashan and in the eastern part of Lower Galilee, with smaller patches appearing in the Mishor (Medeba Plateau), Moab, and Edom. While none of the volcanic cones or fissures responsible for this flow of lava are still active, a line of hot springs in the Rift Valley offers living evidence of this earlier age in ancient Israel's geological past.

The landforms of ancient Israel also take their shape from the ongoing effects of erosion due to wind, rain, and fluctuations in temperature. Because the prevailing rains come from the northwest, erosion is most pronounced on the westward slopes of the limestone hills. Here large expanses of the upper, softer Eocene and Senonian strata of the rock sandwich have completely

Job described the forces of erosion to illustrate a life come apart:

But as a mountain collapses and crumbles
and a rock is dislodged from its place,
as water wears away stones
and torrents wash away the soil from the land,
so you destroy a man's hope. (Job 14:18–19)

1 D. H. Kallner-Amiran, "A Revised Earthquake-Catalogue of Palestine," *IEJ* 1 (1950–51): 223–46; D. H. K.Amiran, "A Revised Earthquake-Catalogue of Palestine," *IEJ* 2 (1952): 48–62.

Black volcanic basalt once flowed over the Eocene limestone strata of the northeastern part of the land of ancient Israel, then cooled into many thousands of crystalline (often hexagonal) columns. In places such as the Yehudiya Canyon on the Golan (shown here), the basalt has collapsed to expose fragments of these columns; elsewhere it has eroded into a thin layer of rich, black topsoil. Basalt rock is very hard and so makes for durable building stones even though it is difficult to cut and carve. Regions of basalt are generally sparsely populated because of the challenging living conditions in which it is found, although in areas where the basaltic soil collects into open fields, farming can be quite profitable.

worn away, exposing the harder and more favorable Cenomanian-Turonian layers beneath. As a result, the higher hills of the area, including most of the spiny NNE–SSW backbone that so defines the lay of the land of ancient Israel, are all typically composed of badly weathered Cenomanian-Turonian limestone.

The differing characteristics of these rock types were noticed by the biblical writers, who generally referred to areas of Cenomanian-Turonian limestone as "hill country," regions of Eocene limestone as "lowland" or "foothills" (*shephelah*), and to the exposed mass of Senonian chalk lying west of the Dead Sea as "slopes" (Josh 10:40). Because the specific characteristics of each of these rock types differ significantly from the others, each of the geological regions of the land of ancient Israel tends to have a distinctive topography, water supply, vegetation cover, economic basis, network of routes, and pattern of human settlement. In short, the "foundations of the earth" (Ps 104:5) underlying each particular region strongly influenced ("determined" would perhaps be too strong a word) ancient—and to a large extent also modern—living conditions there. Indeed, it would not be too much to say that our entry into biblical geography must begin with, and constantly return to, rocks, because geology plays such a formative role in setting the parameters for the possibilities and qualities of life on the surface of the ground above. In the same way that scholars or students of the Bible who pursue literary or grammatical-historical approaches to the text must keep returning to aspects of phonetics, morphology, and syntax when constructing meaningful and coherent understandings of the text, those who attempt to recover the geographical context of the Bible must continually return to the "grammar" of the building blocks of the land.

C. CLIMATE

The lands lying along the southeastern shore of the Mediterranean Sea sit somewhat north of the Tropic of Cancer, in a portion of the subtropical zone that experiences hot, dry summers (in May through October) and cool (though seldom cold), wet winters (in November through April). Compared to the bracing climate of the Taurus and Caucasus Mountains further north and the blistering conditions of the Arabian and Sahara Deserts to the south, the Mediterranean climate is, on the whole, relatively mild. Still, we who are blessed with warm clothing and buildings of modern construction must note the daily trials of living largely out-of-doors, or surrounded by a shelter of, at most, goat-hair, mud brick, or stone. *"There I was" [protested Jacob]—"the heat consumed me by day and the frost by night"* (Gen 31:40). And Job gave this insight: *"Without clothing, they spend the night naked, having no covering against the cold. Drenched by mountain rains, they huddle against the rocks, shelterless"* (Job 24:7–8).

The climate of the land of ancient Israel is affected in part by larger weather patterns that surround the region, and in part by the effects of local topography. Moreover, because the land of ancient Israel is so narrow and pinched tightly between the humid Mediterranean Sea and the arid North Arabian Desert—regions with opposite climatic tendencies—any slight variation in global weather patterns can result in extreme fluctuations in temperature and rainfall from one year to the next. This interplay of desert, sea, and elevation on such a tiny stage causes the climate to vary greatly on the micro level, and it is difficult to speak of overall averages except in relation to specific regions.

Probably the most important climatic element in the land of ancient Israel—and certainly one that is directly

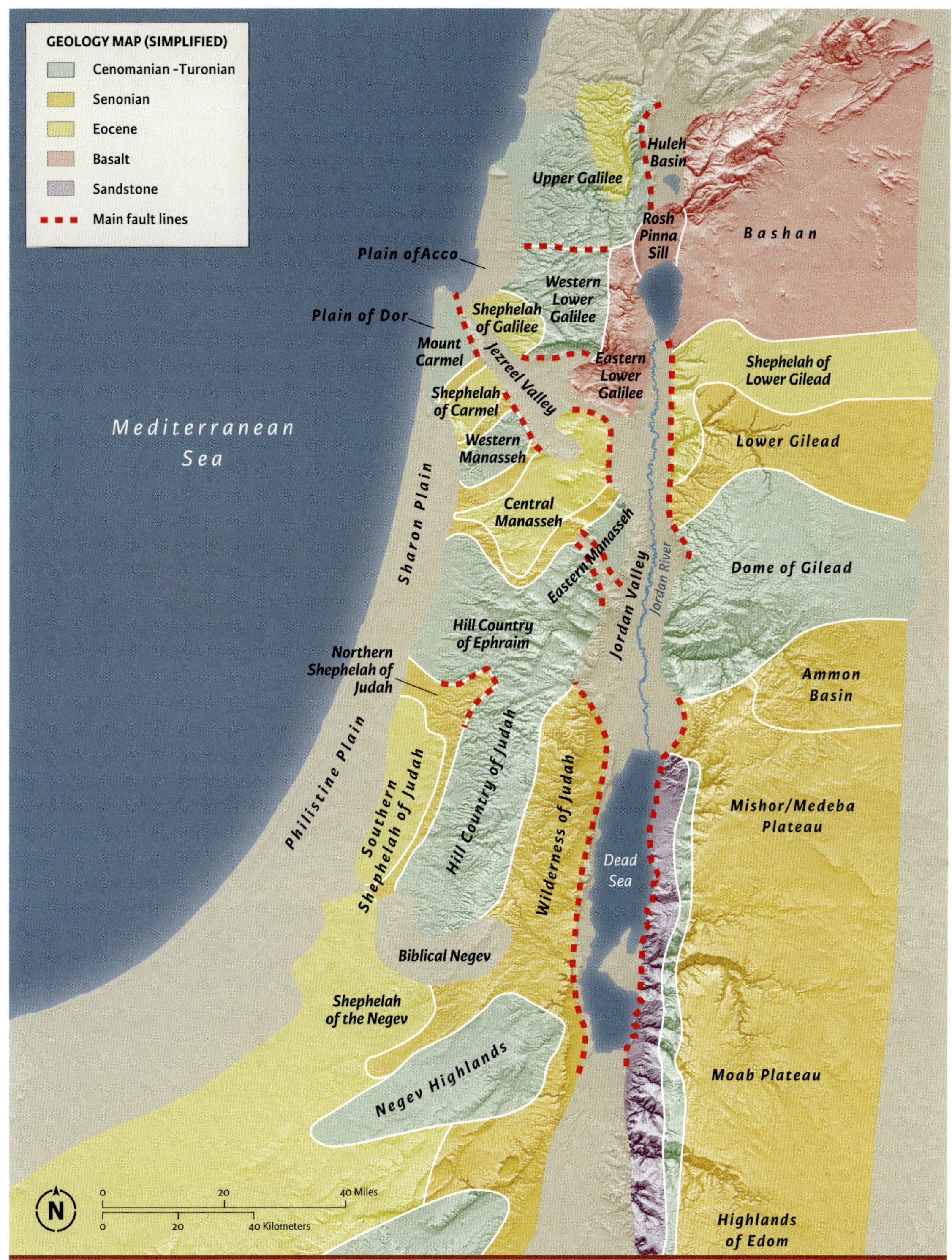

This simplified geology map shows the placement of the major rock types within the land of ancient Israel. The main line of hills running NNE–SSW of the Rift Valley is composed of hard Cenomanian-Turonian limestone, framed in places by softer Eocene limestone and Senonian chalk. A large area of basalt dominates the northeast, with the area of Transjordan dominated by Senonian chalk. The overall surface pattern of these rock types reflects various economic tendencies—and, often, historic political divisions—within the land.

affected by elevation, desert, and sea—is rainfall. The main line of mountains defining the overall topography of the land lies NNE–SSW, parallel to the coast but perpendicular to the direction of the prevailing rains, which typically blow in off the Mediterranean from the northwest. Because the mountains block the rain, the amount of moisture that reaches the Rift Valley and eastern regions beyond is dramatically reduced. The spiny line of hills that form the backbone of the land of ancient Israel acts as a watershed, trapping moisture on its western side and preventing significant rainfall from falling onto its eastward-facing slopes. The Judean Wilderness's desert conditions are largely due to the rain shadow that forms between the top of this watershed ridge and the hills of Transjordan. It is not unusual in the wintertime to see a large gap of blue

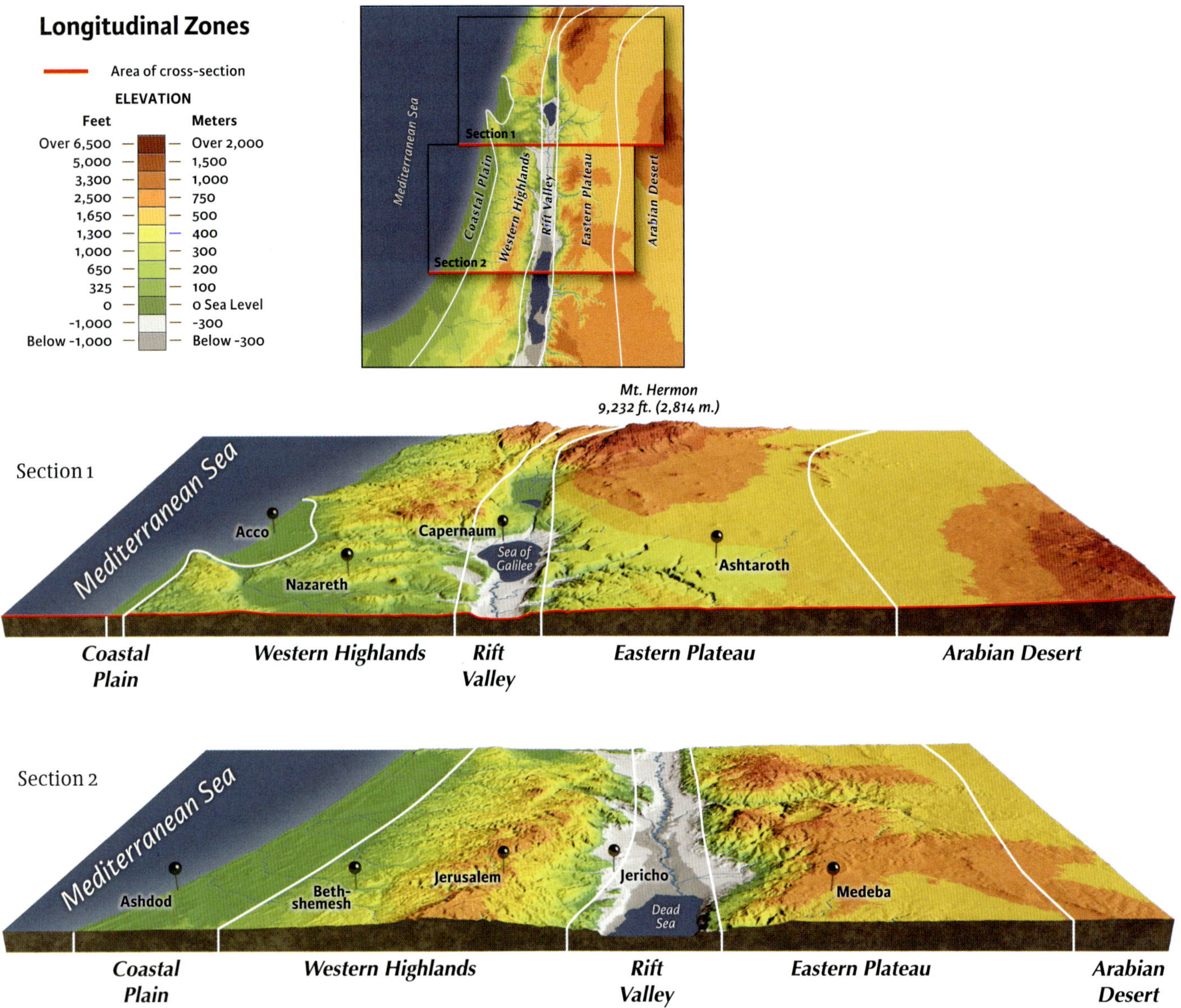

The traditional way of viewing the structure of the land of ancient Israel is to emphasize its longitudinal zones. From west to east, these are the Coastal Plain, the Western Highlands, the Rift Valley, the Eastern (Transjordanian) Plateau, and the Arabian Desert. It is easy to appreciate the effect of rainfall on the western slopes, the impact of the rise of hills that blocks the ready movement of traffic, and the dominance of the eastward-facing deserts. Note that in the Galilee cross-section (Section 1), the Jezreel Valley creates a broad corridor through the hills, connecting the coast with the rift.

sky exactly over the wilderness and southern Jordan Valley as the clouds of the Hill Country of Judah and Ephraim dissipate, then reform over the hills of Gilead, the Mishor, and Moab further east.

It is possible to speak in terms of three basic rules of rainfall for the land of ancient Israel:

1. higher elevations generally receive more rainfall than lower elevations;
2. the regions in the north tend to be wetter than those in the south; and
3. rainfall amounts decrease significantly from west to east.

For example, it is not uncommon for Mount Carmel (with an elevation of 1,790 ft/545 m), which rises abruptly out of the Mediterranean Sea in the northwest, to receive 40 inches (1,016 mm) of rain during the course of a year, while the region of Masada, only one hundred miles (160 km) to the southeast yet lying 1,200 feet (366 m) below sea level, typically sees only 1 to 2 inches (25 to 50 mm) annually. The rainfall of Jerusalem (with an elevation of 2,600 ft/792 m), midway between Mount Carmel and Masada, averages 21 to 24 inches (533 to 610 mm) per year, about the same as Abilene, Texas, Sioux Falls, South Dakota, or London, England—although in London precipitation is spread out over 170 days per year while Jerusalem has on average 50 rainy days annually.

Bible readers often wonder whether the climate in Israel has changed significantly since ancient times; after all, it is hard to imagine a "*land flowing with milk and honey*" (Exod 3:17; Deut 6:3; Jer 11:5) among the sun-bleached, rocky hillsides that dominate much of the landscape today. All available evidence, including that gained by tracing patterns of human settlement or the presence or absence of plant and animal species over time, or from rock weathering and soil formation, suggests that the climate of the land of ancient Israel has been essentially stable for the last four millennia.[1] The centuries between 2300 and 2000 BC were a little hotter and drier than today, but over the last four thousand years the influence of human activity in the region (e.g., improved farming techniques) has tended to level out any minor long-term variations in climate that might have occurred. Of course, there are always yearly fluctuations (drought one year followed by ample rainfall the next, or a few dry years in a row followed by a single wet one; Gen 41:29–30; 2 Sam 21:1), but these do little to change the long-term average.[2] Scientific evidence for overall climate stability since ancient times is confirmed by numerous biblical statements about the weather, all of which ring as true today as they did when they were written millennia ago (Deut 32:2; Job 38:22-38; Ps 65:12–13; Prov 25:14; Jer 4:11; 14:1–6; Matt 16:2–3; Mark 4:37; and Acts 27:14–15).

Perhaps the most helpful way to view the climate of the land of ancient Israel is to journey through the yearly cycle with an Israelite farming family, folk who were the economic backbone of the biblical world. Theirs was an agricultural society, deeply dependent on rainfall and on the "*Lord your God . . . [who] is always watching over [your land], from the beginning to the end of the year*" (Deut 11:12). Even people who lived in larger cities such as Jerusalem during the time of the Bible maintained close ties to the resources of their ancestral lands (Jer 32:6–12). The cycle of life for everyone was wrapped tightly in the land and its seasons. The earthy realities of moisture and soil are present on nearly every page of the biblical text.

The agricultural year begins with the onset of the **early rains** (Hb *yoreh*), a technical term that English Bibles sometimes translate "autumn rains" (Deut 11:14; Ps 84:6; Joel 2:23). With them, rock-hard, sun-parched ground is transformed to the promise of simple mud. Almost always the early rains are preceded by a change in the air that beckons moisture but doesn't quite deliver. "*Like clouds and wind without rain is a man who boasts of his gifts falsely*" ran the proverb (Prov 25:14 NASB), and those who spoke it knew the edgy anticipation of waiting for the heavy cloud that would finally burst its contents onto the land (Job 36:27–28; 37:11; 38:37–38). Timely rains have always been a great blessing (Deut 28:12; Matt 5:45; Acts 14:17); when they are late and the summer drought refuses to loosen its raspy grasp, it is as if both people and land are shamed:

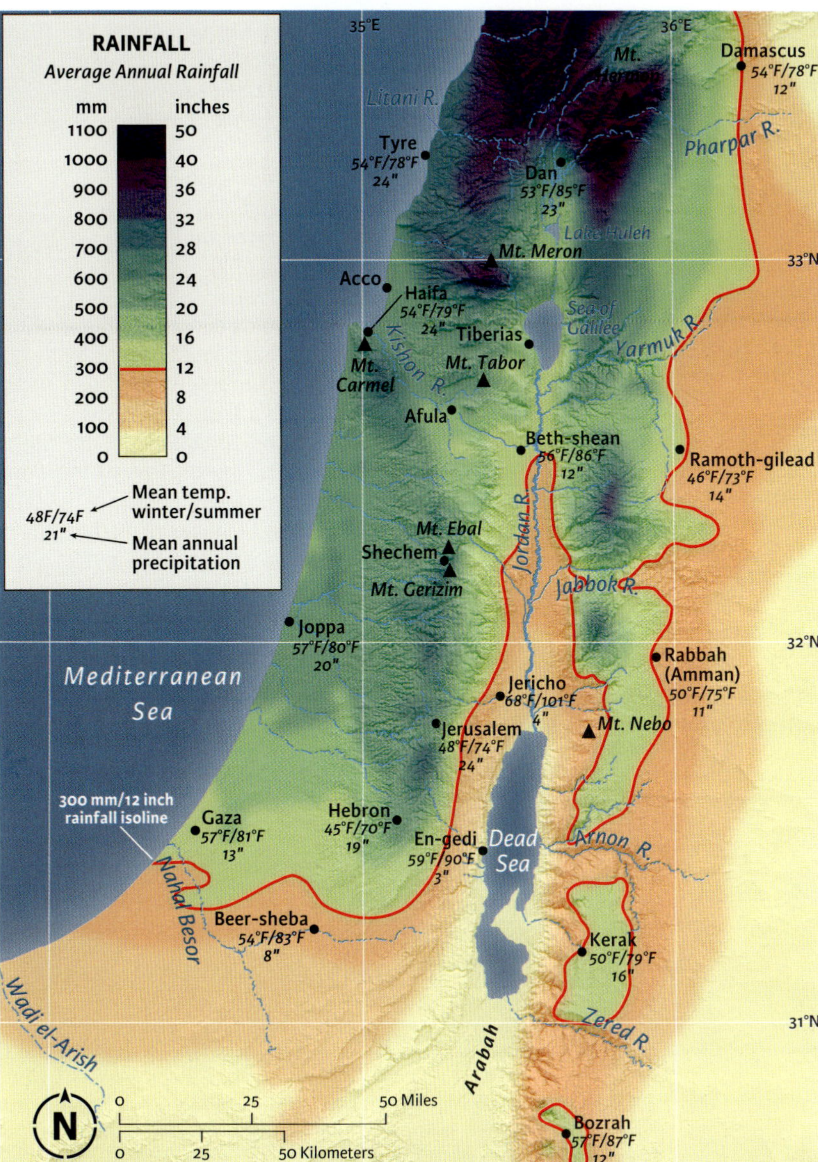

The land of ancient Israel can be divided into two subsistence zones based on yearly rainfall averages. Regions in which twelve or more inches (300 mm+) of rain fall every year are able to support farming villages and other permanent settlements, while areas that see less than twelve inches annually (as indicated by areas that are shades of orange on the map) are better suited to semi-nomadic, sheep-herding lifestyles. This twelve-inch (300 mm) rainfall line has played a significant role in population density levels over time. It has also influenced the location of the borders of viable regional nation-states.

The onset of heavy winter rains adds an amusing touch to the setting of Ezra's fiery sermon in which he chastised the people of Judah and Benjamin for their sins. Ezra called everyone to Jerusalem for the somber occasion and made them sit in the open square before the temple. It was late December. The dark clouds moving overhead burst open, dumping their contents on the recalcitrant people who were listening to Ezra's sermon, "*trembling because of this matter and because of the heavy rain*" (Ezra 10:9). It didn't take long before the people came around: "*Yes, we will do what you say! But . . . it is the rainy season. We don't have the stamina to stay out in the open*" (Ezra 10:12–13). Ezra relented, though only for the moment. He was a good teacher, planning his sermon for just the right time of year to show his congregation that before God, everyone is chilled to the bone.

1 Denis Baly, *The Geography of the Bible*, new and rev. ed. (New York: Harper & Row, 1974), 64–8; Nili Lipschitz and Yoav Waisel, "Dendroarchaeological Investigations in Israel (Taanach)," *IEJ* 30 (1980): 132–36; Avinoam Denin, "Paleoclimates in Israel: Evidence from Weathering Patterns of Stones in and near Archaeological Sites," *BASOR* 259 (1985): 33–43.

2 An example of yearly variations in rainfall can be found in *Atlas of Israel: Cartography, Physical and Human Geography*, 3rd ed. (Tel Aviv, The Survey of Israel, 1985), sheet 13 (ed. Naftali Rosenan and Mordechai H. Gilead), which includes individual maps for the years 1932–1976. Of the 44 years shown, 11 might be considered wet years; these fell at irregular intervals (only once, 1963–1964, back-to-back).

A dark Mediterranean sky portends the coming of rain, always a blessing for the desert lands along its eastern shore. To the Canaanites, the sea was Yam, a god of chaos and death. The ancients maintained a healthy respect for the forces beyond their control that the sea represented (Jonah 1:4–5). The people of ancient Israel largely inherited this fear of the sea from their Canaanite neighbors and were hesitant to venture onto its waters, especially during the unpredictable winter season (Pss 93:3–4; 107:25–27; Acts 27:9–44; cp. Isa 57:20–21). Not surprisingly, biblical writers pictured the sea as chaos, noting that at creation it was pushed aside so that dry land, a place where people could actually live, would appear (Gen 1:9–10; cp. Gen 8:13–17; Exod 14:21–22; Rev 21:1). Making things personal, the prophet Isaiah compared wicked people to *"the storm-tossed sea [which] cannot be still, and its water churns up mire and muck"* continually (Isa 57:20).

Their nobles send their servants for water.
They go to the cisterns; they find no water;
their containers return empty.
They are ashamed and humiliated;
they cover their heads.
The ground is cracked since no
rain has fallen on the land.
The farmers are ashamed; they
cover their heads. (Jer 14:3–4)

But the early rains always do come, usually gently at first so that the Israelite farmer could scratch-plow his field and catch the runoff into the furrows (Isa 28:24; 1 Cor 9:10), but sometimes as a great downpour sending everyone scurrying and suddenly filling the dry wadis with torrents of living water (Ps 126:4). Everything is unpredictable when it comes to rainfall: the timing, the daily amount, and the total, though in most years the cycle is reasonable enough to ensure a decent crop. The most practical definition of drought is when it doesn't.

By the onset of winter (late November or December), a deep trough of low pressure usually forms over the eastern Mediterranean, squeezed between high pressure areas lying over the Russian steppe and the Arabian Peninsula. This trough sucks in great gulps of moisture from the humid air of the Mediterranean Sea and Atlantic Ocean which, when mixed with warm air from north Africa and the cooler air of Europe, brews the perfect potion for storms. Wintertime storms typically take four days to sweep across the eastern half of the Mediterranean, slamming into the Lebanese and Israeli coastlines and dumping heavy sheets of rain, especially onto the higher elevations in the north and west (Matt 7:27). Each storm system typically pummels the land for two to four days in alternating waves of cloudburst, then blue sky, then cloudburst. These **winter rains** (Hb *geshem* or *matar;* Ezra 10:9,13; cp. Deut 11:14; Jer 5:24; Hos 6:3) fill the underground aquifers and prepare the land for its springtime growth. When the storms come in quick succession (every week or so), then the land and its people feel blessed, but when they were sporadic or separated by endless weeks of dry skies, everyone in the biblical world knew that a year of emptiness and drought lay ahead (1 Kgs 17:1,7; 18:2). Barley, a grain that is rather coarse for bread, needs a minimum of eight inches (200 mm) of rainfall per year to mature, and wheat, the staple of life, twelve inches (300 mm). In years when crops withered in the fields for lack of rain, the region's economy was wrecked for at least the next twelve months, and everyone's belly was gnarled and empty:

I also withheld the rain from you
while there were still three
months until harvest.
I sent rain on one city but no rain on another.
One field received rain while a
field with no rain withered.
Two or three cities staggered to
another city to drink water
but were not satisfied. (Amos 4:7–8)

Ample rain *"in the proper time"* (Deut 11:14) was critical for the Israelite farmer. The prospect of several years of below-average rainfall meant the inevitable desperation of famine and then death (Jer 14:1–6; Hag 1:10–11), when even *"wild donkeys stand on the barren heights panting for air like jackals"* (Jer 14:6). In times such as this, Abraham, Isaac, Elimelech and Naomi, and the Shunammite couple all chose to leave their homes for the hope of wetter climes elsewhere, rather than face the slow, dry death of starvation (Gen 12:10; 26:1; Ruth 1:1–5; 2 Kgs 8:1–2; cp. 1 Kgs 17:8–12).

As for wintertime temperatures, January is the coldest month at all weather recording stations throughout modern Israel, with overnight temperatures in the hills often slipping into the 30s Fahrenheit (0–4° C) and sometimes below. Winter temperatures range from the upper 40s to the low 60s Fahrenheit (8-17° C) during the day. Throughout the biblical period and up until quite recently, everyone in the land of ancient Israel (and certainly our typical farmer) lived in mud brick or stone houses—many of which were extensions of caves. Once the cold weather penetrated a building (1 Kgs 1:1), it was more comfortable to be out of doors on sunny wintertime days than remain inside. *"Who can withstand [God's] cold?"* the psalmist asked (Ps 147:17).

It doesn't snow often in the land of ancient Israel, certainly not every year. When it does, the snow typically

The writer of 2 Samuel tells us that *"Benaiah son of Jehoiada was the son of a brave man from Kabzeel, a man of many exploits . . . he [even] went down into a pit on a snowy day and killed a lion"* (2 Sam 23:20). It was a noteworthy event, even more so because of the snow. So, too, when the Seleucid general Trypho was prevented from marching his army against Jerusalem during the winter of 142 BC because heavy snow clogged the hills (1 Macc 13:22). Heavy snow typically falls in the Judean hill country when temperatures dip below freezing overnight. The sudden whiteness of the landscape, visible at the first light of dawn, is striking—as is this view of the David's Citadel area of the modern Old City of Jerusalem. David asked God to whiten his soul even more so (Ps 51:7).

falls during the nighttime at elevations over 1,600 feet (500 m). The snow usually melts the day after it falls, filling the wadis with powerful, rushing water. That's when things can become dangerous. Job noted this: "*My brothers are as treacherous as a wadi, as seasonal streams that overflow and become darkened because of ice, and the snow melts into them*" (Job 6:15–16).

The rains taper off in March and April. These **latter** or **spring rains** (Hb *malqosh*; Deut 11:14) swell the heads of grain for harvest. Jesus's parable gave the sequence of growth: *"first the blade, then the head, and then the full grain on the head"* (Mark 4:28). By now both the temperature and carpets of grasses have risen everywhere, and wildflowers of every color fill hillside and plain:

> *The wilderness pastures overflow,*
> *and the hills are robed with joy.*
> *The pastures are clothed with flocks*
> *and the valleys covered with grain.*
> *They shout in triumph; in-*
> *deed, they sing.* (Ps 65:12–13)

Barley is harvested in March and April,[1] wheat in May and early June. Boaz stayed at his threshing floor throughout the harvest period, guarding his crop and making sure everything was done correctly at this most critical time of the growing season (Ruth 1:22; 2:23); he reaped a wife in the process. Although August is the hottest month by average, the late harvest season of May and early June usually seems hotter because the transition from rain to summer drought happens so quickly. Even before the fields are bare, the temperatures spike to scorch all of the green from the land (Ps 90:5–6): *"For the sun rises and, together with the scorching wind, dries up the grass; its flower falls off, and its beautiful appearance perishes"* (Jas 1:11). This natural phenomenon is likely behind this verse too: *"The grass withers, the flowers fade, but the word of our God remains forever"* (Isa 40:8; cp. vv. 6–7). And as with the land, so with the people of the land: *"My strength was drained as in the summer's heat"* (Ps 32:4).

It was apparently at such a time as this that the young Shunammite boy died of sunstroke and dehydration after spending a day in his father's fields (2 Kgs 4:18–20). Contrary to the advice given to modern travelers in the same land, he probably hadn't taken his water bottle along!

Unlike the climate of winter, summertime conditions in the land of ancient Israel are almost completely predictable. Throughout the summer months, a huge high-pressure system in the stratosphere stabilizes the air below, minimizing the effects of a massive surface low pressure system that tends to hang over India, Iran, and Iraq to the east and a smaller low positioned

1 Alex Strashny, "Modern Searches for Aviv Barley in the Context of the Hebrew Calendar: A First Description of the Israeli Barley Observation Data," *JBQ* 45:3 (2017): 179–87.

Sections of the Wilderness of Judah, barren and brown for most of the year, are covered by a lush blanket of purple and green for a scant few weeks in late winter. Biblical writers relished the view.

Spring seems always the time that young hearts turn to love:

Arise, my darling.
Come away, my beautiful one.
For now the winter is past;
the rain has ended and gone away.
The blossoms appear in the countryside.
The time of singing has come,
and the turtledove's cooing is heard in our land. (Song 2:10–12)

between central Turkey and Cyprus to the northwest. Skies are almost always cloudless, and the high angle of the sun, when felt directly, adds intensity to the summer heat. While temperatures in the higher elevations rarely reach the century mark in degrees Fahrenheit (38° C), the summer heat in regions to the south and east can be insufferable, reaching 120 degrees Fahrenheit (49° C) or more. A little shade goes a long way in the middle of the day (Gen 18:1; Ps 121:5; Isa 25:4; Ezek 31:6; Hos 14:7; Jonah 4:6). Relief is also brought by the Mediterranean's Etesian winds, which blow constantly over the Aegean during the summer months from north to south, then sweep counterclockwise around the Turkish-Cypriot low toward the east. The morning air of a typical Israeli summer day hangs still, but the cooler Etesian winds usually blow ashore by a little after noon, bringing air-conditioned relief far inland. In the early summer months, these winds serve the farmer well by blowing away winnowed chaff (Job 21:18; Pss 1:4; 35:5; Isa 17:13). Boaz, for instance, winnowed in the evening when the winds were the strongest (Ruth 3:2). The westerly summer winds never bring rain, but they do cool the air sufficiently so that summer evenings are quite pleasant, especially in the hills. In this regard note Genesis 3:8, which presupposes a Mediterranean climate for the garden of Eden, and Luke 2:8, in which shepherds in the fields were surely *"keeping watch over their flock by night"* (NASB) in the summertime rather than during the icy cold evening hours of December.

Not one drop of rain typically falls on the land during the annual five-month summer drought from late May to early October, although once every few years there may be a surprise sprinkle out of season. This dryness is moderated by **dew** that forms when warmer sea air from the west encounters ground surfaces cooled by inland nighttime air. Greater quantities of dew accumulate at the higher elevations on the western hill country slopes and in high desert regions such as Arad, the Ramon crater, and the Highlands of Edom in the south. On heavy dew nights, moisture drips from leaves onto the ground exactly under each plant. The moisture content

The religious worldview of Canaan was wrapped up entirely in issues of rainfall and fertility. The activities of Baal and his consort Ashtoreth, Canaanite fertility deities, represented the annual cycle of seasons that culminated in Baal, "Rider of the Clouds,"[1] throwing his thunderbolt to the earth and impregnating the ground with the fluid of life-giving rain. Baal and Ashtoreth were earthy and capricious, and their devotees had to entreat them through ecstatic rituals (1 Kgs 18:26–29). Israel faced the same harsh cycle of seasons as did the Canaanites, yet Moses reminded his people that theirs was *"a land the LORD your God cares for. He is always watching over it from the beginning to the end of the year"* (Deut 11:12). The psalmist added, *"Sing to God! Sing praises to his name. Exalt him who rides on the clouds—his name is the LORD—and celebrate before him"* (Ps 68:4).

1 Note the various texts from Ugarit which refer to Baal by his most common epithet, Rider of the Clouds; *ANET*, 130–31, 134, 137–38, 142, 153; William W. Hallo, ed., *The Context of Scripture*, vol. I: *Canonical Compositions from the Biblical World* (Leiden: Brill, 1997), 248–49, 251–52, 258, 261.

of summer dew can reach the equivalent of another seven inches (180 mm) of rainfall annually, which is sufficient to allow plants bearing summer fruit (olives, grapes, pomegranates, figs, dates, and almonds; Deut 8:8) to thrive throughout the months of Mediterranean heat. Biblical writers pictured dew as God's gentle blessing: quiet, refreshing, and always welcome (Gen 27:28; Deut 32:2; 33:13,28; Ps 133:3; Prov 19:12; Isa 26:19; Hos 14:5; Mic 5:7; cp. Ps 110:3).

The presence of dew completes the agricultural cycle, carrying summer fruit to its plump fullness. From plowing after the early rains to harvesting the fruit of summer dew, the Israelite village farmer could dwell secure, content that he was living in *"a land that the Lord [his] God cares for. He is always watching over it from the beginning to the end of the year"* (Deut 11:12). *"They will sow in peace,"* Zechariah 8:12 points out. *"[T]he vine will yield its fruit, the land will yield its produce, and the skies will yield their dew. [God] will give the remnant of this people all these things as an inheritance."*

This regular winter-summer cycle is broken twice a year by the uncertainty of the transitional seasons, when the heat of summer turns to winter and the wet of winter gives way to the long, hot months of summer. During these in-between seasons, the wintertime high pressure system over the Arabian Peninsula is either not yet established or begins to break down, and the climate of the land of ancient Israel switches face with little notice. The early days of spring and the waning days of summer can be unpredictable, as when a sudden storm catches those on land and sea off guard. Such was the storm that drove the ship on which the apostle Paul was prisoner across the Mediterranean shortly after "the Fast" (the Day of Atonement, Yom Kippur in late September or early October; Acts 27:9–44). Similarly, one spring *"a high wind arose, and the sea began to churn"* as Jesus and his disciples tried to make their way across the Sea of Galilee by boat (John 6:18; cp. v. 4). Farming is also risky during the transitional seasons. A heavy rainstorm during the early summer wheat harvest can quickly ruin a crop (1 Sam 12:17).

More notable is the opposite, when in fall or spring the **sirocco** (Hb *qadim*; Arabic *khamsin*) blows off the desert from the east or southeast. This hot, sultry wind is typically either drawn across the land by the counterclockwise movement of air around an area of low pressure over Libya or Egypt, or brought in by a low pressure area moving up from the Red Sea. During a sirocco, temperatures rise suddenly—as much as twenty to thirty degrees Fahrenheit (10°–17° C)—to what are normally the hottest days of the year, while the relative humidity drops as much as forty percent.[1] The east winds fill the air with fine particles of dust and sand, color the sky brown, and turn the sun to a dull blob of yellow ochre. *"The LORD will turn the rain of your land into falling dust,"* says Deut 28:24, and a person can taste it seeping around the edges of windows when the same happens today. When these hot, intensely dry winds last for days and raise the air temperature above that of the human body, they can actually sap the life from people, animals, and plants alike. The young are most at risk: *"Even though*

The higher elevations west of Jerusalem receive dew on many summer nights, and it is this blessing that both signals and represents the pleasantness of being out of doors during the evening hours in Judea. Morning mist hangs in the wadis but doesn't last long, quickly disappearing with the smile of the rising sun. Warming to the metaphor, Hosea likened a cloud of fog to those who persist in sin: *"They will be like the morning mist, like the early dew that vanishes"* (Hos 13:3; cp. 6:4)—vaporous, ephemeral, and gone.

1 Baly, *Geography of the Bible*, 51–53.

This mid-September sirocco (*khamsin*) blew in from northeast Syria, then settled over the modern states of Jordan and Israel for several days. The view is at mid-day. Locals called it the worst sirocco in recent memory. Fine, sandy dust covered everything, penetrating every room and living space. With the air absolutely still and temperatures in the high 90s Fahrenheit (mid-30s C) even in the normally cooler hills of Jerusalem, residents were advised to stay indoors and restrict their activities.

it is planted, will it flourish? Won't it completely wither when the east wind strikes it? It will wither on the plot where it sprouted" (Ezek 17:10).

A similar phenomenon can happen any time of the year whenever an area of high pressure settles over the region, compressing and quickly heating the air below and allowing more hot air to move in from the east. Israeli meteorologists typically label both this condition and the sirocco with the term *sharav*, borrowing from a biblical Hebrew term that means *"parched ground"* or *"scorching heat"* (Isa 35:7; 49:10).

The reality of *"the searing wind [blowing] from the barren heights in the wilderness on the way to my dear people"* was all too present for the prophets to ignore (Jer 4:11; cp. Ps 48:7; Isa 27:8; Hos 12:1; 13:15; Hab 1:11). Facing an east wind, Jonah wanted to die (Jonah 4:8). Jeremiah, who grew up in the Benjaminite village of Anathoth facing the open eastern wilderness, punctuated his prophetic speech by including raw desert imagery: *"I will scatter [Israel] before the enemy like the east wind . . . on the day of their calamity"* (Jer 18:17).

When the area of low pressure causing the east wind to blow finally moves out over the North Arabian Desert, it brings behind it wonderfully cool air from the Mediterranean Sea, and sometimes rain that, when passing through the remnants of the dust-laden sky, falls as drops of mud.

The men, women, and children of ancient Israel celebrated the yearly agricultural cycle with three harvest festivals: a Festival of Unleavened Bread (*Matsot*) at the beginning of the barley harvest (in late March or early April), a Festival of Harvest (*Qatsir*) at the end of the wheat harvest (in late May or early June), and a Festival of Ingathering (*Asiph*) when summer fruit was picked in September-October (Exod 23:14–16; 34:22). The Canaanites certainly celebrated similar festivals at the same times of the year, since their calendar was quite naturally based on the same agricultural cycle as the Israelite calendar. As the tribes of Israel settled in the land of Canaan, these festivals took on the double role of also commemorating events in the great Israelite national epic of redemption. This was a gradual process, beginning already with Moses's commands in the Torah (Lev 23:4–44; Num 28:16–31; Deut 16:1–17) and continuing throughout the biblical and post-biblical periods. So the Festival of Unleavened Bread became connected to Israel's celebration of the exodus—the first taste of redemption remembered, appropriately, at the beginning of spring (*Pesach*, or Passover). The next great act in Israel's redemption story, when Moses received the Torah on Mount Sinai, was connected with the harvest festival of *Shavuot* or Weeks. And Israel naturally came to remember their forty years of wilderness wandering at the fall Festival of Ingathering, since the annual summer drought echoed their years in the Sinai wasteland (at *Succot*, or Shelters/Booths/Tabernacles). Even though many Jews live outside of the land of Israel today (and the vast majority everywhere no longer gain their living from the soil), all recognize the inherent and vibrant

The Gezer Calendar, found at Tel Gezer in the northern Shephelah by archaeologist R. A. S. Macalister in 1908, is a small slab of soft limestone inscribed with eight short lines of old Hebrew script (below). The text seems to date to the middle or end of the tenth century BC, the time of Solomon and Rehoboam. It divides the year into eight periods of one or two months each, beginning in the fall. The activities mentioned in connection with each month reflect the normal Canaanite and Israelite agricultural cycle in the land. Interestingly, the Jewish celebration of Rosh Hashanah (New Year's Day) occurs in the fall, which is consistent with the sequence of the Canaanite Gezer Calendar, rather than in the spring in connection with Passover.

Translation:

His two months: Ingathering (olives)	[mid-Sept—mid-Nov]
His two months: Sowing (grain)	[mid-Nov—mid-Jan]
His two months: Late sowing	[mid-Jan—mid-Mar]
His month: Chopping flax (or, grass)	[mid-Mar—mid-Apr]
His month: Barley harvest	[mid-Apr—mid-May]
His month: (Wheat) harvest and measuring (grain)	[mid-May—mid-June]
His two months: Vine harvest	[mid-June—mid—Aug]
His month: Summer fruit	[mid-Aug—mid-Sept][1]

connection between God's great acts of redemptive history that are celebrated faithfully every year at these High Holy Days, and his common blessing that *"as long as the earth endures: seedtime and harvest, cold and heat, summer and winter, and day and night will not cease"* (Gen 8:22).

D. WATER RESOURCES, SOILS, AND FERTILITY

Camped on the Plains of Moab opposite their promised land, Moses took the opportunity to remind the people of Israel that the land where they were going was different from the place from which they had come: *"The land you are entering to possess is not like the land of Egypt,"* Moses explained, *"where you sowed your seed and irrigated it by hand* [lit. 'by foot,' *regel*] *as in a vegetable garden"* (Deut 11:10). Given the opportunity, he could have described the land of Babylon, the Ur of the Chaldeans which Abraham had left behind, the same way. Though they lie on the opposite ends of the Fertile Crescent, Egypt and Babylonia resemble each other in broad geographical outline. Both are centered on wide, open expanses of barren land made fertile by the benefit of a mighty river (or, in the case of Babylon, two rivers) running through them. The Nile, Tigris, and Euphrates bring life to the lands lining their long banks, offering not only the promise of annual inundations of dark, rich silt, but by serving as channels of transport and communication. As a result, the Nile and the Mesopotamian river valleys provided just the right conditions for the world's first cities to emerge, as well as for the origin and development of writing, massive public works (including irrigation systems that prompted further growth), and, eventually, the rise of empires. On every criterion of what normally makes for a definition of civilization, life in Mesopotamia and Egypt was bountiful. The writer of Genesis even favorably compared Egypt to Eden, calling it "the LORD's

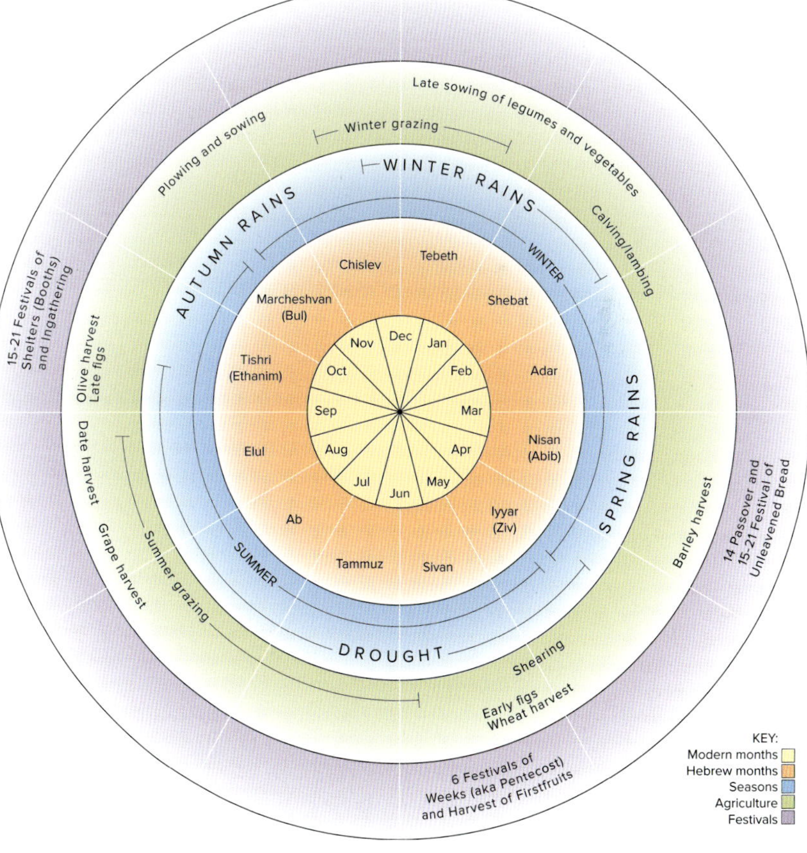

The ancient Israelite calendar was divided into twelve months, each beginning with the new moon (*chodesh*). Harvest festivals were fixed to specific lunar months, even though the actual agricultural season corresponds to the solar year. As a result, the lunar calendar was off by about ten days every year. In order to keep the two in sync, the Israelites adopted the practice of periodically adding a month to their calendar. The modern Jewish calendar does the same, placing a second month of Adar (Adar II) before the Passover month of Nisan every three or four years.

1 Picture from Briscoe, *Holman Bible Atlas*, 27; trans. from Rainey and Notley, *The Sacred Bridge*, 42.

"I have placed my bow in the clouds," God told Noah, *"and it will be a sign of the covenant between me and the earth"* (Gen 9:13). God loves his earth and wants only the best for it and its people. Here a late winter rain washes over the perpetually thirsty hills of the Judean Wilderness north of Jericho. It was at these stark folds that Joshua and all Israel stared prior to crossing the Jordan River to receive their land of promise. The writers of the Bible forged a clear connection between human obedience and God's blessing: *"If you carefully obey my commands I am giving you today . . . I will provide rain for your land in the proper time, the autumn and spring rains, and you will harvest your grain, new wine, and fresh oil. I will provide grass in your fields for your livestock. You will eat and be satisfied"* (Deut 11:13–15).

garden" (Gen 13:10). But it was precisely *away from* these lands that God pulled Abraham, then Moses and all Israel, to journey *"to the land that [he would] show [them]"* (Gen 12:1).

As the people of Israel stood at the eastern doorstep of Canaan, Moses made clear that his people—God's people—were headed for a very different kind of homeland than Egypt: *"The land you are entering to possess is a land of mountains and valleys, watered by rain from the sky* [*shamayim*, the heavens]*"* (Deut 11:11). With rainfall totally absent nearly half of the year and unpredictable when it finally does fall and the only real river the Jordan (hardly world class!), Israel was entering a land where adequate water sources were scattered and scarce. To heighten the urgency, it has been estimated that of the total amount of water brought to the land of ancient Israel by rainfall, only 10 to 25 percent ends up being available for the local needs of the people.[1] This calculation assumes that 50–60 percent of rainwater evaporates on contact with ground surfaces (by comparison, countries with tropical summer rains lose up to 95 percent to evaporation), while another 10 percent is lost through later evaporation (for instance, from the surface of the Sea of Galilee) and from 5–15 percent more flows into the Mediterranean or Rift Valley by surface runoff. What's left is not much in a land where precipitation is marginal to begin with! Estimates suggest that prior to the introduction of modern farming techniques, the best average wheat yields in the land of ancient Israel were less than one-third those of the Nile Valley.

In the days of the Bible, the Sea of Galilee (Hb *kinneret*) and the Jordan River met the water needs of people living along its shore, but virtually no one else's.[2] Today, the Sea of Galilee is the most plentiful source of water for the entire State of Israel. Since 1964, water from the Kinneret has been pumped via Israel's National Water Carrier to the Eshkol Reservoir in Western Lower Galilee, treated, and then piped to cities as far away as Tel Aviv, Jerusalem, and Beer-sheba. Up until then, the most widespread source of "living water" throughout the land was **springs** (Hb

1 Efraim Orni and Elisha Efrat, *Geography of Israel*, 4th ed. (Jerusalem: Israel Universities Press, 1980), 148.
2 Yigal Levin, "The Jordan River in Biblical Geography: From Boundary to Allegory," *ARAM* 29/1-2 (2017); 222.

Psalm 104 is a nature psalm that portrays, in sequence, the first four days of Creation (Day 1 = vv. 2a; Day 2 = vv. 2b–4; Day 3 = vv. 5–18; Day 4 = vv. 19–23). But rather than continuing in sequence with days five and six of Creation to complete the psalm, the psalmist instead interwove mention of creatures that God made on days five and six—birds, animals, and people—with the events of days 1 through 4:

He causes the springs to gush into the valleys;
they flow between the mountains.
They supply water for every wild beast;
the wild donkeys quench their thirst.
The birds of the sky live beside the springs;
they make their voices heard among the foliage.
He waters the mountains from his palace;
the earth is satisfied by the fruit of your labor.
(Ps 104:10–13)

The implication? The world was made in such a way that it is perfectly suited for the benefit of its living creatures. Interestingly, the world described in Psalm 104 matches exactly the landscape of ancient Israel, not Mesopotamia where atlases often locate the garden of Eden.

ayin), with the best dotting the Cenomanian-Turonian limestone hills of Judah, Ephraim, Galilee, and Gilead. Most of these are not particularly strong, producing little more than a trickling brook easily lost among the rugged, dry hills in the vicinity. Today, virtually all of the springs have been harnessed by *Mekorot*, Israel's national water authority, and by the Water Authority of Jordan. Yet throughout recorded history, each was adequate for the needs of a family or small group of families who lived in the area, providing clean drinking water for them and the village flocks (cp. Judg 1:15).

Springs are scarce in areas that are lower in elevation—such as the Judean Shephelah, the coastal plain, and the Negev. In these regions, it has been possible for local populations to tap into the underground water table by digging a **well** (Hb *be'er*). Digging one is an arduous and unpredictable task, but well worth the effort if successful. The people of Israel even composed a song about a well they had dug on their journey to Canaan: "*Spring up, well—sing to it!*" (Num 21:17).

A well can supply unlimited amounts of fresh water from the same aquifer that in other places pushes through a crack in the surface of the ground as a spring. Like a spring, a well offers a place for villagers or country folk to meet. Drawing water from a well was hard work, typically done in the cool hours of the morning or evening, before and/or after the flocks had grazed

Irrigation techniques developed as early as six thousand years ago in Mesopotamia and Egypt (left) have been adapted on a small scale in the hillside terraces at Sataf (below), site of a Roman and Palestinian-era agricultural village west of Jerusalem, now maintained by the Jewish National Fund (*Keren Kayemet Lisrael*). Water from the Nile is channeled through a series of canals to the endless line of fields that line the river's length, then to small plots within each field bounded by mounds of soil. At Sataf, the water is channeled from the village spring. In both instances, a quick pull of the hoe or drag of the foot allows the water to be directed from one plot to the next, allowing the farmer to literally *"irrigate by your foot as in a vegetable garden"* (Deut 11:10).

for the day (Gen 24:11; 29:7; John 4:6–7). Access to springs and wells is still guarded jealously in the Middle East, where the struggle to obtain and protect water rights remains an important part of the political and social dynamic of the region (Gen 21:25–34; 26:15–22; Exod 2:16–22; Judg 1:11–15).

Most ancient Israelites, however, drank **cistern** water. Plastered cisterns (Hb *bor*) appear frequently in the archaeological record just about the same time that Israel entered the land of Canaan (toward the end of the Late Bronze Age and during Iron Age I; ca. 1200–1000 BC). They seem to have been a technology that allowed Israel to settle the dry hillsides above the better-watered areas that were already dotted by large Canaanite cities when they arrived (Judg 1:27–36). Hewn into bedrock beneath a house or under a courtyard, a cistern collects runoff water throughout the rainy season. If used sparingly, this water can keep a family and its livestock alive during the rainless summer months. By the end of the dry season, most cisterns run low and a dipped bucket picks up both water and sludge. Most of the residents of the old walled city of Jerusalem drank cistern water for centuries, right up to the introduction of municipal plumbing in modern times. In the nineteenth and early twentieth centuries, European visitors to the Holy Land sometimes spoke of deplorable living conditions within the walls of cities such as Jerusalem, due in large measure to the filth of the streets that too often washed into the cisterns every rainy season[1] (cp. 2 Sam 22:43; Isa 10:6; Jer 38:6; Mic 7:10). A good cistern allows a family to meet its own water needs. If kept in good repair and sealed tightly so that no sunlight would cause things in the water to grow, the quality of human life, with all reasonable expectations, could remain fairly high. Interestingly, Jeremiah, a resident of Jerusalem, used the example of water sources to comment on his people's attitude toward God, from whom all blessings flowed: *"They have abandoned me, the fountain of living water, and dug cisterns for themselves—cracked cisterns that cannot hold water"* (Jer 2:13).

This *"spring whose water never runs dry"* (Isa 58:11) spills from a crevice in the rock in the upper reaches of the Wadi Qelt, east of Gibeah at the edge of the Judean Wilderness. It is one of several that make up the Fara springs (En Prat) which, in the time of the New Testament, were channeled by a Herodian aqueduct to Jericho, ten miles to the east. The flow is constant and strong, more than enough to have supplied the needs of villages and shepherds in the vicinity. It is estimated that a pre-modern Middle Eastern family of six, together with their donkey and a small flock of sheep and goats, could subsist on 5,300 gallons (20 cubic meters) of water for the entire year, or less than 15 gallons (56 liters) per day. Unencumbered by social pressures fostered by modern bathroom conveniences, it was enough!

One autumn, Jesus spoke about water when he was celebrating the fall festival of *Succot* (the Feast of Tabernacles) in Jerusalem. This eight-day Jewish festival is celebrated every year in early to mid-October. It was during *Succot* that the Jews of Jesus's day prayed earnestly for rain—rain to end the drought of the dry season, to replenish the fields, and to refill the cisterns. It was also at this time of year, in anticipation of the renewal of the early rains, that the people of ancient Judea were most aware of their thirst. The Gospel of John tells us that *"on the last and most important day of the festival [when prayers for rain were most intense], Jesus stood up and cried out, 'If anyone is thirsty, let him come to me and drink! The one who believes in me, as the Scripture has said, will have streams of living water flow from deep within him'"* (John 7:37–38). Not stale, unsanitary cistern water. Not standing well water. Not even a little brook of spring water. But rivers of living water, flowing from Jesus and the hearts of those who believe in him. Fully quenching. Healthy. Invigorating. And able to empower people to truly live.

Unlike *"the land of Egypt"* that enjoys the Nile's benefits (Deut 11:10), the fertility of the land of ancient Israel is directly connected to rainfall, to the soil base produced by its underlying bedrock, and to the efforts of local inhabitants at collecting both into usable places. There was something inherently unpromising about

1 Yehoshua Ben-Arieh, *Jerusalem in the 19th Century: The Old City* (Jerusalem: Yad Izhak Ben Zvi Institute, 1984), 90–101. As one example among many, Ben-Arieh supplies a lengthy quote from Dr. Chaplin, a British physician in Jerusalem in 1864. A few phrases of it will suffice here: "Jerusalem is one of the most unhealthy of cities, and fever is its principal disease. . . . All kinds of animals and vegetable matter are allowed to lie and rot in the streets. If a dog or cat dies, it putrefies in the roadway, or is eaten by one of its companions. . . . The air during the long dry season becomes filled with the loathsome dust and odour which results from so much impurity. . . . With proper care in cleaning cisterns, water may be kept sweet and good for many months, but if such care is not taken, it becomes loaded with organic matter and acquires a bad smell and taste. The water of the best wells, indeed, usually contains [an] abundance of animalculae toward the end of the summer. . . . On the whole, it may be safely affirmed that after the month of July no water in the city is fit to be drunk without being previously filtered or boiled." We must wonder to what extent the living conditions of walled cities in the ancient Near East, including biblical Jerusalem, were any different.

Functioning cisterns still dot the landscape of Israel, the West Bank, and Jordan. This one is in the dry hills of eastern Benjamin, northeast of Jerusalem. The cistern was cut into surface bedrock. It is several feet deep, with an interior diameter of perhaps 20 feet (more than 6 m). The opening is protected today by a square, rusted metal cover. Two ropes enter the left side of the opening, a sure indication of buckets below. To the left is a large stone that has been hollowed to serve as a watering trough. Here area shepherds are able to find water for their flocks—and themselves—throughout much of the year, just as shepherds have done for millennia.

the resource base of Canaan, and Moses compensated by reminding Israel that theirs was *"a land the Lord your God cares for"* (Deut 11:12). The implication is that the Lord's care was required because human effort alone would never quite be enough (lessons of dependency and trust were ever at hand). This is a land where heat and dryness work overtime to destroy the small addition of organic material that is added to the soil yearly (no annual inundation of dark, rich silt brought down by the Nile floods here!). Rather, erosion by rain and wind scours the hills, displacing its scant soil cover as alluvium in valley bottoms far below. The archaeological record shows that like cisterns, agricultural terracing became popular in Canaan during Iron Age I, about the time that Israel was transitioning from tent encampments to permanent stone villages. By trapping and holding both water and soil, these terraces—long, narrow plots of arable land—allowed the otherwise rocky mountain hillsides of Judah, Ephraim, Galilee, and Gilead to become agriculturally productive.

The various rock types found in the land of ancient Israel erode to produce different types of soils. While all of the soils are enriched annually by organic material from plants that grow in each region, clearly those that are found where vegetation is thicker will be richer and more productive than those in desert areas. The best soils in the land of ancient Israel are red-brown **terra rosa soils** produced in areas of Cenomanian-Turonian limestone. These soils are heavy and clayey in composition and hold water well, quickly becoming slippery and clingy when wet. This is one reason the time *"when kings march out to war"* was in the spring, after the ground dried out and travel was easier (2 Sam 11:1). Terra rosa soils fill terraces and narrow wadi bottoms throughout the Hill Country of Judah, Ephraim, Galilee, and Gilead. They are particularly well suited for vineyards and orchards of summer fruit, where "my roots will have access to water, and the dew will rest on my branches all night" (Job 29:19). Isaiah pictured a terrace filled with terra rosa soil when he sang, *"The one I love had a vineyard on a very fertile hill. He broke up the soil, cleared it of stones, and planted it with the finest vines"* (Isa 5:1–2; cp. Ezek 17:8). The Hebrew word *sorek*, "finest vine," is also the name of the wadi system immediately west of Jerusalem, the slopes of which are filled with the horizontal lines of ancient and modern terraces.

Where not terraced, the hard limestone hills of the land of ancient Israel are either devoid of anything but the scrubbiest vegetation or covered with thickets of bushes (many of which are thorny) and small trees

It takes generations of effort to shape a hillside with terraces, and constant attention to holding back the forces of erosion to ensure they remain standing. Even so, terraced crops of summer fruit remain susceptible to the ravages of drought. Here terraces that are centuries old support the Palestinian village of Batir, southwest of Jerusalem; its old stone houses themselves rise like terrace walls out of the ground. Batir sits in the Rephaim wadi, a large branch of the Sorek, the rugged wadi draining Jerusalem to the west. This is a late summer morning view: only the olive and almond trees remain green; the rest is given to scrub brush, thorns, and a wisp of smoke—all eager competitors for the moisture that yet remains behind each terrace wall.

clinging to the rocks. This scrub forest, or *maquis*[1] (Hb *ya'ar* refers to both scrub forests and larger stands of trees), offers a nice habitat for wildlife (Gen 49:21; 1 Kgs 4:23; 2 Kgs 2:24; Isa 56:9; Jer 5:6; Amos 3:4) and protection in which people can hide (1 Sam 22:5; 2 Sam 18:6–9; Matt 24:16).

The Eocene limestone of the Shephelah, softer and more granular in composition than the hard limestone of the hill country, forms **brown forest soils** that are lighter in color and weight and not quite as fertile as the terra rosa soils. But when mixed with terra rosa soils that have washed down from the higher hills above, the brown forest soils filling the valleys of the Shephelah become excellent producers of grain. Judah's King Uzziah established royal estates in the valleys of the Shephelah, *"since he was a lover of the soil"* (2 Chr 26:10). The Shephelah is also well suited for sycamore fig trees; Solomon even placed one of his government officials there to oversee their production (1 Chr 27:28; 1 Kgs 10:27). Because the exposed Eocene slopes of the Shephelah are covered with a hard Nari crust, they are too rocky for grain farming; nevertheless, they do provide excellent grazing land for sheep, goats, and cattle (2 Chr 26:10).

1 Baly, *Geography of the Bible*, 80–81.

Large areas of the coastal plain are covered with brightly colored **brown-red sands** (*hamra*) formed by the mixture of alluvium with shoreline sand. Under favorable conditions, this composite soil provides almost perfect moisture conditions. Unfortunately, in ancient times much of the coastal plain was poorly drained and as a result consigned to sandy marshes and a dense scrub forest. Isaiah called the northern part of the coastal plain *"the splendor of . . . Sharon"* (Isa 35:2). Today much of the region that is not covered by urban sprawl is dominated by Israel's modern citrus industry.

Whitish to light brown **rendzina soils** are produced in areas of Senonian chalk. Rich in lime, low in clay, and generally poor in organic materials, rendzina soils are not particularly fertile—especially in the Judean Wilderness where the surface of the ground is sun-bleached, powdery, and strewn with stones. Yet rendzina plows easily and with adequate rainfall can be suitable for grains, such as on the fields of Moab where Elimelech and Naomi fled to escape the Bethlehem drought (Ruth 1:1). The westward-facing Aijalon Valley, lined with hills of Senonian chalk, is especially fertile since the rendzina there is well mixed with richer terra rosa soils washed down from the Judean hills above.

Dark brown to black **basaltic soils** are found throughout Israel's northeastern regions, including the plains that line the Sea of Galilee. Though basaltic soils are quite fertile (the black topsoil of the Midwest United States has a high basaltic content), many of the areas in which they are found are strewn with large boulders, making farming difficult. Many of Jesus's hearers around the Sea of Galilee quite naturally would have had basaltic soil in mind as he spoke the parable about seed that fell *"on rocky ground,"* then *"on good ground and it grew up, producing fruit that increased thirty, sixty, and a hundred times"* (Mark 4:5,8).

Yellowish brown in color, wind-blown aeolian **loess soils** fill the arid Negev basin, immediately south of the Judean hills and the Shephelah. Loess is composed of very fine silt that has blown into the region from the Sahara, Sinai, and Arabian Deserts. When it rains—and in the Negev rainfall amounts are generally less

This stately olive tree is firmly rooted to the terraced slope of the Sorek wadi west of Jerusalem. The soil here is all terra rosa. For millennia, it has faithfully supported the residents of the high hill country villages surrounding Jerusalem. Olive trees are wonderfully suited for the Mediterranean climate and do well just about anywhere in the region as long as the moisture is sufficient. (Writing with his normal irreverent flair, Mark Twain, who visited the region in 1867, called them the "fast friend of worthless soil").[1] Noted for their stout trunks, twisted branches, gnarled bark, and evergreen, ageless beauty, olive trees can survive for centuries. Olives (Hb *zayit*) are a staple in the Mediterranean diet—and it's a good thing: theirs is the only oil that actually helps fight cholesterol.

1 Mark Twain, *The Innocents Abroad* (New York: New American Library Signet Classic, 1966), 401.

A flock of sheep and goats graze the Nari-covered hill of Azekah in the central Shephelah after the winter rains. While the broad valleys of the Shephelah are well suited for growing grain, the hard-crusted hills that make up the bulk of the acreage in the area are practically useless for agriculture. They do provide good grazing land, however, for all kinds of livestock. The Judean King Uzziah, a *"lover of the soil,"* kept herds of royal livestock in the Shephelah and on the coastal plain (2 Chr 26:10; note Hb *miqneh*, a generic word for possessions of livestock that could include cattle, sheep, goats, donkeys, and even camels). We might wonder how often he wandered the hills to inspect his holdings.

than what is needed for agriculture—the upper layer of the loess soils swells into a crust that repels water, leaving the ground beneath powdery and dry. The seasonal watercourses of the Negev, though, are lined with desert shrubs, offering enough vegetation there for flocks of sheep and goats (Gen 12:9). In the eastern parts of the Negev basin, agriculture is possible only with irrigation—a thoroughly modern introduction into the region.

Unproductive **Lisan marls** and **desert soils** are found in the southern Jordan Valley, in the region around the Dead Sea, and throughout vast tracts of arid to hyper-arid wilderness to the south. These soils are thin, stony, and immature, and because they carry a substantial lime content are almost totally unproductive. The badland desert soils around the Dead Sea have become especially salty, leading the prophet Jeremiah to comment that a person who does not trust in the Lord *"dwells in the parched places in the wilderness, in a salt land where no one lives"* (Jer 17:6; cp. 2:6).

Sitting at the juncture of Asia, Europe, Africa, and the Arabian Peninsula, the land of ancient Israel is a

As is the case everywhere, soil cover in the land of ancient Israel has been enriched and depleted by the best—and worst—of human efforts.[1] When the men of Ephraim and Manasseh complained that their inherited land was not suitable for settlement because it was covered with forests, Joshua simply replied, *"Clear it and its outlying areas will be yours"* (Josh 17:18). The farmers of ancient Israel, then, quickly learned that deforestation had to be offset by productive techniques of land management. The practice of building terraces and constructing low dams to collect rainwater and prevent soil erosion has been used in the land for millennia. Modern Israelis are especially adept at reforestation, restoring the *"splendor of Carmel"* (Isa 35:2) to vast areas of Judah and Galilee through the tree planting efforts of the Jewish National Fund (*Keren Kayemet Lisrael*). Warfare, poor management, and general neglect quickly return the land to thorns and stones (cp. Ps 80:12–13; Isa 5:5–6). Campaigning in Moab, Israel's King Jehoram sentenced the land to death: *"You will cut down every good tree and stop up every spring. You will ruin every good piece of land with stones"* (2 Kgs 3:19). That which is destroyed quickly takes generations to recover.

1 Paul H. Wright, *Understanding the Ecology of the Bible: An Introductory Atlas* (Jerusalem: Carta, 2018), 40–44.

botanist's and zoologist's paradise. While many other places in the world are home to a larger number of plant and animal species, no place has a larger variety per capita: plants and animals from three continents converge to find their homes here. In addition, a large number of species of birds find the corridor that is the land of ancient Israel to be the preferred migratory route between Europe and Africa. Of the total varieties of plants that grow in the land, the "seven species" are most prominent, a fact to which Deuteronomy 8:7-8 (emphases added) alludes: *"For the LORD your God is bringing you into a good land, a land with streams, springs, and deep water sources, flowing in both valleys and hills; a land of* wheat, barley, vines, figs, *and* pomegranates*; a land of* olive oil *and* honey." So also the testimony of *The Story of Sinuhe*, an ancient Egyptian historical novel dating to the eighteenth century BC, which describes the land of Canaan this way: "It was a good land. . . . *Figs* were in it, and *grapes*. It had more wine than water. Plentiful was its *honey*, abundant its *olives*. Every kind of fruit was on its trees. *Barley* was there, and emmer *wheat*. There was no limit to any kind of cattle."[1]

Both writers called the land "good," an echo, intentional or not, of the Edenic refrain of Genesis 1: *"and God saw that it was good."* It seems as though both texts had the land's western-facing, agriculturally-blessed valleys and slopes in mind. The Deuteronomy passage lists the seven species generally in harvest order (first winter grain, then summer fruit), beginning with wheat, the better of the grains, and ending with the best of the fruit if honey, following recent interpretations, is date jam, the sweetest of the land's native products.[2] (Traditional Arab families still offer a piece of fruit as an after-meal dessert.) Together these seven species offer a healthy, varied diet to the villager: *"wine to gladden the heart of man, oil to make his face shine and bread to strengthen man's heart"* (Ps 104:15; cp. Hos 2:22). The writer of the apocryphal book Ecclesiasticus (or Sirach) gives a slightly longer list of the land's essential commodities: "Basic to all the needs of man's life are water and fire and iron and salt and wheat flour and milk and honey, the blood of the grape, and oil and clothing" (Sir 39:26).

A list of more exotic goods appears in connection with the caravan of traders who took Joseph to Egypt: balsam, honey, aromatic gum and resin, pistachios, and almonds (Gen 43:11). Of these, the first two and last two listed are common to the land of ancient Israel, while aromatic gum and resin (of which frankincense and myrrh are examples) are native to the south Arabian

Winter wheat, the staff of life, was the foundation of the economy in the ancient Near East. Here, in Lower Galilee's Beth-netophah Valley adjacent to what was once the city of Cana (Khirbet Qana), rich alluvial soil produces crop after crop of edible gold. *"He endows your territory with prosperity; he satisfies you with the finest wheat,"* sang the psalmist (Ps 147:14), whose own patrilineal estate must have included similarly productive land. Jesus surely walked this valley often, yet he knew that the harvest that really counted was the one of human souls: *"Open your eyes and look at the fields, because they are ready for harvest"* (John 4:35).

1 *ANET*, 19.

2 John A. Beck, gen. ed., "Honey" in *Zondervan Dictionary of Biblical Imagery* (Grand Rapids: Zondervan, 2011), 126–28. The words for honey in Hebrew (*dbaš*), Arabic (*dibs*), and Akkadian (*dišpu*) all refer to the sticky product of the bee (e.g., Judg 14:8) as well as to a kind of thick, sweet syrup made out of grapes or dates (Gen 43:11). In support of the traditional view that *dbaš* refers to bee honey, recent excavations at Tel Rehov in the Beth-shean Valley have uncovered a number of bee hives dating to the Israelite monarchy (Iron Age II). DNA analysis of the remains indicates that the bees were imported from Anatolia (Turkey) and produced a superior kind of honey. See Amihai Mazar, Dvory Namdar, Nava Panitz-Cohen, Ronny Neumann, and Steve Weiner, "The Iron Age II Beehives at Tel Rehov in the Jordan Valley: Archaeological and Analytical Aspects," *Antiquity* 82 (2008): 629–39.

An Israelite farmer typically planted vines along terraces. Some, certainly, were planted close to his stone-built house (1 Kgs 4:25) where the tendrils of the plant could be trained to climb upright on a wall. These were indeed fruitful vines, an apt image for Joseph, Jacob's favorite son (Gen 49:22). But out in the open field, the most common way to grow vines in ancient Israel was to allow the tendrils to just spread along the ground as pictured. Ezekiel 17:6 compares a *"spreading vine, low in height"* (Hb *gefen sorachat*) to the way his people filled their land. The first-century BC Latin writer Varro mentioned that this method of tending vines was common in the eastern Mediterranean in his day as well, while vines in the western Mediterranean tended to be grown on trellises (Varro, *On Agriculture* I.viii.46). In any case, the same method can still be found in the fields around Hebron. When the fruit on a spreading vine begins to form, the branch is lifted up and propped on a rock so that the grapes (Hb *anavim*) can hang unhindered. This practice may lie behind Jesus's statement about vine tending in John 15:2 (ESV): *"Every branch in me that does not [yet] bear fruit he takes away,"* that is, he takes it away from the ground (lifts it up) so that it can be given a chance to become productive.

Peninsula. In contrast, a list of foodstuffs recorded in 1 Kings 4:22–23 reveals the eating habits of Solomon and his courtiers, a diet heavy in range-fed livestock and wild game (fattened oxen, range oxen, deer, gazelles, roebucks, and pen-fed poultry are mentioned in particular). The point here is that Solomon, following the prerogative of kings, was able to import foodstuffs not typically found in the Judean hill country (1 Kgs 4:24). But for the average Israelite who depended directly on the fertility of the soil of his own ancestral land, life was simple and complete, lived quietly under one's own vine and fig tree (cp. 1 Kgs 4:25).

The fertility of the rainy parts of the land of ancient Israel stands in sharp contrast to a thin band of steppe land (Hb *midbar*) that lies between the hill country and open desert, receiving on average between four and twelve inches (100–300 mm) of rainfall each year. This band follows the seam of the Fertile Crescent from Mesopotamia to Egypt wherever the desert meets arable land, and includes regions such as the Judean Wilderness, the Negev, and parts of eastern and southern Transjordan. Here, mixed flocks of sheep and goats graze on the thin fuzz of grass that covers its northern slopes in late winter or on hardy desert shrubs lining the wadi bottoms throughout the year (cp. 1 Kgs 18:5; Isa 15:6; 40:6–8; Jas 1:10–11).

Perhaps the best known moniker for the land of ancient Israel is *"the land of milk and honey,"* or, more properly, *"the land flowing with milk and honey"* (Exod 3:8,17; 13:5; 33:3; Lev 20:24; Num 13:27; 14:8; 16:13–14; Deut 6:3; 11:9; 26:9,15; 27:3; 31:20; Josh 5:6; Jer 11:5; 32:22; Ezek 20:6,15). After using the phrase, Ezekiel added that this was *"the most beautiful of all lands"* (Ezek 20:6). Many Bible interpreters, imagining only the best for ancient Israel, often equate milk and honey conceptually with abundant material blessings. A modern paraphrase might be "gold and silver," "stocks and bonds," "health and wealth," or something similar. In fact, the land of ancient Israel was full of milk and honey because it was divided between steppe land and arable land, between the milk-based products of the shepherd and the honey-like products of the farmer, between a lifestyle that was harsh and difficult and one that was relatively predictable. It was a land well-suited for a full-orbed human experience, one that was both green—and dry.

Grazing is a tough job for these sheep in the stony desert flats above Jericho. Unlike the scrub hills of the Shephelah, the Judean Wilderness's soil cover is virtually nil: only tubers and sparse clumps of thin grass find roots between the rocks. No lying down in green pastures here (cp. Ps 23:2)! Biblical writers often pictured their leaders as shepherds (Num 27:15–17; 1 Kgs 22:17; Pss 23:1–6; 78:70–72; 80:1; Isa 40:11; 63:11; Ezek 34:1–31; Matt 9:36; 15:24; John 10:11–16; 21:15–17) rather than farmers or city folk, perhaps as a way to come to terms with the reality that life more often mirrors harsh landscapes than lush pastures or busy thoroughfares.

Goats were an important source of protein in the ancient Israelite diet, also supplying milk, cheese, and yogurt to hungry families. Meat on the hoof, one's economic capital, was eaten only on special occasions (cp. Gen 18:7–8; Luke 15:22–23). Shepherd and sheep are hardy souls, but they need constant care and are not immune to the ravages of the desert clime (Gen 33:13).

Lying south and east of this steppe land is *yeshimon*, the *"barren, howling wilderness"* (Deut 32:10) beyond the limits of normal human lifestyle and endurance. In such a land God himself intervened to keep his people alive during their journey to the land of milk (where shepherds can live) and honey (the homeland of the farmer; cp. Exod 16:1–21; 17:1–7; Num 11:31–34; 20:8–13; 21:16–18; Hos 2:14–15).

E. SETTLEMENT AND ROUTES

It is clear that some parts of the land of ancient Israel were more favorable for permanent settlement than others. The Israelites felt most at home in the hard limestone Hill Country of Judah, Benjamin, Ephraim, and Gilead, where sources of water and food were adequate if not plentiful and the rugged terrain served as a measure of protection against enemies. There *"each person [could] sit under his grapevine and under his fig tree with no one to frighten him"* (Mic 4:4; cp. 1 Kgs 4:25).

On the other hand, Israel's founding experiences were tied to the desert (Abraham, Moses, and David were all shepherds), and the wilderness (*midbar*) lying east and south of the Hill Country of Judah continued to play an important role in the national economy even after Israel settled down in Canaan. The differing needs and on-site demands of the farmer and the shepherd ensured that their interrelationship was both competitive and symbiotic.

Some shepherds were permanent residents of a village and took care of their family's flocks, grazing them on nearby hills or on the post-harvest stubble in the fields. David (the youngest son was often sent out with the sheep; cp.1 Sam 16:11; 17:18,34–35) and the shepherds of Bethlehem who visited the infant Jesus (Luke 2:8) are examples. Nabal, a successful though hard-nosed shepherd from the village of Maon southeast of Hebron, had large flocks of sheep and goats and a crew of hired men (1 Sam 25:2,11). King Mesha of Moab and Amos of Tekoa took things up a notch by breeding and dealing in sheep (the Hb term for "shepherd" here is *noqed*, sheep-breeder; 2 Kgs 3:4; Amos 1:1), though Amos supplemented his income from orchards of sycamore-fig trees (Amos 7:14–15). Amos's business success at the local level qualified him—in spite of self-reservations—to pinpoint the socio-economic woes of the Northern Kingdom of Israel (Amos 2:6–8; 5:10–15; 8:4–6).

Other shepherds, somewhat akin to modern Bedouin, were nonresidents of villages, living in tents some distance into the wilderness. These shepherds came into town periodically for market days in order to renew their resources. They also approached settled areas in the summertime to find seasonal grazing land after the grass in the wilderness had burned off with the early summer heat. The best biblical example of a nonresident shepherd is Abraham, who moved his family and flocks throughout a fairly well-defined zone of grazing land in response to the needs of the seasons, showing up in established cities such as Gerar, Hebron, or Bethel during the drier times of the year (Gen 13:3,18; 20:1; 26:1). David became a nonresident shepherd when he was on the run from Saul. Villagers tend to treat nonresident shepherds warily, extending to them grazing and water rights only after carefully assessing the potential threat (and benefit!) that the newcomer might pose to village resources (cp. Gen 21:22–34; 26:12–22; 1 Sam 25:10–11). Over time, economic patterns become established between certain towns and families of shepherds, ensuring that each could benefit from the other. We can assume, for instance, that the kings of Gerar, Hebron, and Bethel were willing to allow Abraham to use their resources to graze his flocks because they saw in him an important ally who could help to protect their steppe land frontier from the incursions of other, less friendly shepherds.

Date palms thrive in areas of brackish water and saline soil, forming oases across the desert landscape of the ancient Near East. The Jericho oasis was appropriately nicknamed *"the City of Palms"* (Deut 34:3; Judg 3:13; cp. Exod 15:27). Standing strong and tall in the most inhospitable of conditions and producing the sweetest of all fruits in the process, the palm (Hb *tamar*) naturally became a symbol of righteousness and victory in Israelite and Jewish thought:

The righteous thrive like a palm tree
and grow like a cedar tree in Lebanon.
Planted in the house of the Lord,
they thrive in the courts of our God.
They will still bear fruit in old age,
healthy and green.
(Ps 92:12–14)

The line of cities that traces the top of the watershed ridge lay close to the seam between the land of the farmer and the land of the shepherd; thus, places such as Hebron, Tekoa, Bethlehem, Jerusalem, and Bethel, as well as Gerar in the western Negev, became major market towns where farm products could be exchanged for those of the shepherd. We find that the towns lining the seam between the desert and the arable land in Transjordan, such as Rabbah, Dibon, Kir-hareseth, and Bozrah, played a similar role east of the Rift Valley. Jerusalem's Sheep Gate, on the northeastern side of the city (the corner facing the road to the wilderness), for instance, was an active market place for millennia (cp. Neh 3:1,32; 12:39; John 5:2). *"Come, buy wine and milk"* Isaiah intoned to the residents of Jerusalem (Isa 55:1), a city where the best products of the farmer and the shepherd were readily available. Indeed, a proper diet included foods from both economic zones: "*Curds from the herd and milk from the flock, with the fat of lambs, rams from Bashan, and goats, with the choicest grains of wheat; you drank wine from the finest grapes*" (Deut 32:14).

It was watershed ridge cities such as these that played the primary role in the mixed economy of ancient Israel.

In the historic pattern of shepherding in the land of ancient Israel, shepherds in search of pasture and water sometimes left the security of their own grazing lands and set of symbiotic villages for the land of strangers who usually considered them to be spies, tricksters, or thieves. Each was naturally suspicious of the others' lifestyle, and for good reasons: animals ate crops, and farmers restricted access to sources of fresh water. Prejudices of each, aimed at the other, ran deep in the ancient Near East. "All shepherds are abhorrent to Egyptians" intoned the proverb, and it was pretty well believed (cp. Gen 46:34). A Sumerian composition from the second millennium BC relates a dialogue between Dumuzi, the shepherd-god, and Enkimdu, the farmer-god, as to the relative merits of each and faults of the other.[1] After lengthy banter, friendly but pointed, the two were reconciled—a necessity on the cosmic level if real shepherds and farmers had any hope for cooperation back down on earth.

Israel was most at home in places where both kinds of goods could be produced, and never lasted long politically in other ecosystems such as the deep Negev, the high eastern flats of Transjordan, or along the

1 *ANET*, 41–42; see also Hallo, *The Context of Scripture* I, 575–78.

Built from the mud of the fields from which it arose, the mound of the ancient city of Hannathon dominates the fertile Beth-netophah Valley in Western Lower Galilee. The city once controlled a major regional intersection, receiving profits from traffic running between international and local markets. Now all that remains is the classic profile of a tel enclosing scant remains of a once-thriving metropolis. The Bible mentions the place only once, in an oft-ignored list of cities belonging to the tribal inheritance of Zebulun (Josh 19:14). With the help of the twin witnesses of archaeology and geography as well as two references in the Amarna letters dating to the fourteenth century BC (*EA* 8, 245),[1] we can reconstruct something of the city's glorious past. Yet the relative lack of reference to the place in ancient documents—important though it must have been—is a humbling reminder that our understanding of the world of the Bible remains largely incomplete.

Mediterranean coast. "*Their gods are gods of the hill country,*" reasoned the king of Aram-Damascus in an attempt to explain Israel's success in their own hilly homeland; 1 Kgs 20:23). Israel also had a harder time settling on the coast and in the larger valleys such as the Jezreel Valley because there, where the climate and resources were more favorable, large Canaanite cities had already sunk their roots deep into the soil (Judg 1:27–36). Indeed, not just the Canaanites had done this: the textual and archaeological record shows that Israelites in the hill country were under a constant competitive threat from whomever settled on the coast (Egyptians, Philistines, Phoenicians, Assyrians, Babylonians, Persians, Greeks, and Romans, to name a few), and they enjoyed only brief periods of success there when they were strong enough to call the economic shots in the region.

Archaeological evidence attests to several periods of urbanization in the land of ancient Israel. The Early Bronze Age II–III (ca. 3200–2300 BC), Middle Bronze Age II (ca. 2000–1550 BC), Iron Age II (ca. 1000–586 BC), and Roman-Byzantine period (37 BC–AD 638) in particular were characterized by large urban centers and a thriving, interconnected economy. Cities in the land of ancient Israel varied greatly in size, although the largest (with the exception of Hazor at 200 acres/80 ha. during the Middle Bronze II Age) tended to be 20 to 30 acres (8–12 ha.), quite small by today's standards. Population estimates are notoriously difficult to determine, but a large city could have been home to a few thousand people. The larger cities were usually located on the coast or in the inland through-valleys, where greater concentrations of natural resources and better highway access fostered growth. Those at strategic points on the highway network (e.g., at main junctions or passes) tended to be surrounded by a wall. During the time of the Israelite monarchy, walled cities included Lachish, Azekah, Gezer, Megiddo, Hazor, Beer-sheba, Mizpah, and Jerusalem, among others. Some, such as Beer-sheba, seem to have been a product of careful urban planning, while others grew more haphazardly. The same seems to have held for villages, some of which took the shape of a protective ring while others show no discernable overall plan—although the villagers in each certainly knew their way around. Every ancient city can be understood in terms of its own spatial syntax, that is, how the various areas (i.e., the industrial, governmental, religious, and/or economic zones, as well as public versus private space in general) functioned. Public areas (e.g., the city gate and square) were the focus of everyday hustle and bustle; they were the places where travelers could be encountered and goods exchanged (Judg 19:15; Job 31:31–32).

When considering the settlement dynamic of the land of ancient Israel, we should resist the tendency to view its cities and towns in isolation from one another, as artifacts confined to specific times or places. Rather, an intricate network of ancient routes—both bypaths and highways—tied village to village, city to city, region to region, and land to land. By identifying and tracing these routes, we gain an important tool to help us reconstruct the social and economic fabric of the peoples who inhabited the land of ancient Israel.

The task of reconstructing the highway network of ancient Israel is complex, though the basic premise is clear enough: main cities were connected by main routes. Yet the location of the main routes changed over time, partly in response to the political or economic fortunes of individual cities (i.e., as their role as regional magnets or anchor points rose and fell) and partly as a result of overall regional security conditions. Moreover, the technological processes of road building also changed over time, allowing highways to be constructed along routes that were once prohibitive to travel, or the reverse, if dire economic or political conditions weakened the regional infrastructure.

The first step in mapping the network of highways in ancient Israel is to locate the major cities during

1 William L. Moran, *The Amarna Letters* (Baltimore: Johns Hopkins University Press, 1992), 16; 299.

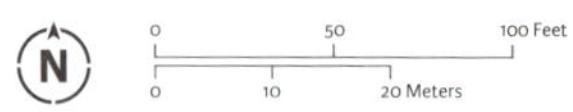

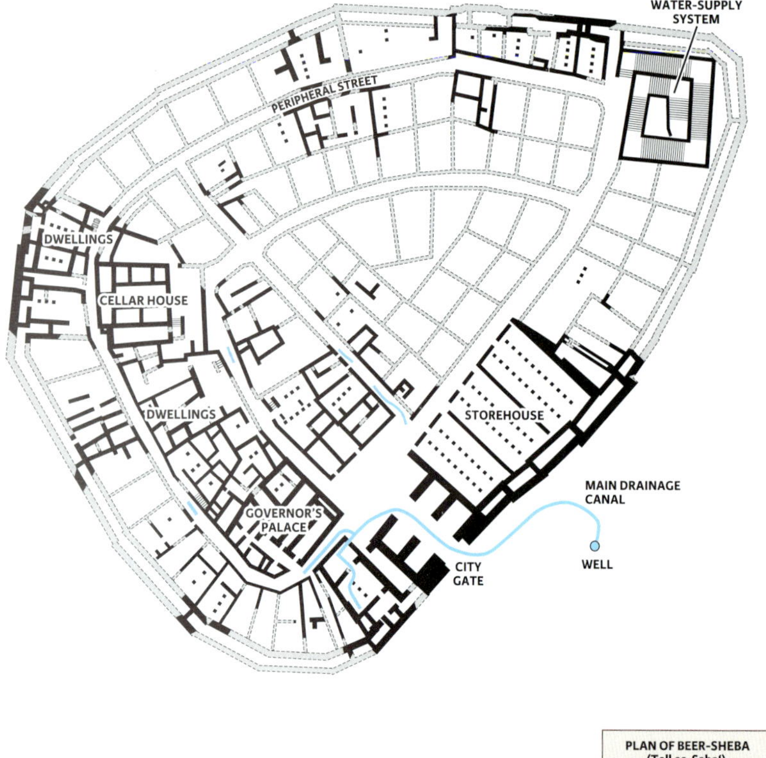

This diagram reveals the city plan of Beer-sheba, provincial capital of the Negev in the eighth century BC. Excavated remains are shown as solid black lines, while conjectured remains appear as hollow lines. The city's organized shape suggests it was built according to a predetermined plan. The casemate (i.e., double) wall, roughly oval in shape, provided a safe perimeter for Beer-sheba's inhabitants. The city's single, controlled entrance (a strong, four-chambered gate facing east) opened into a large square, which was the focus of public activity. To the immediate right (north) of the city gate were three large, pillared storehouses, providing strong corroborative evidence for the idea that Beer-sheba was the economic center of the region. Fronting the left (southern) side of the city square was a large-roomed building, likely the home of the provincial governor, who could easily keep an eye on all the comings and goings. All streets radiated out from the town square. Fronting them were narrow row houses for city residents, mostly of a repeated four-room plan. The city's well was just outside the gate, close enough so that the water supply could be protected yet remain easily accessible to flocks and travelers. Though located in an arid land, Beer-sheba was on a major T-junction linking the international highway running between Transjordan and the coast with Jerusalem. The care with which the city was built testifies to its importance for the political and economic priorities of Iron Age Judah.

A satirical letter from the time of Egypt's New Kingdom (ca. thirteenth century BC) gives a first-hand account of the dangers of travel in the ancient world. The sender, an Egyptian scribe, takes the opportunity to impress upon the recipient, his pupil, the difficulties that await him once he gets a real job that involves travel into Canaan: "the narrow valley is dangerous with Bedouin hidden under the bushes. . . . You are alone; there is no messenger with you, no army host behind you. You cannot find a scout to show you how to cross . . . shuddering seizes you, the hair on your head stands up, your soul is faint . . . the path is filled with rocks and boulders, without a toe hold for passing by, overgrown with reeds, thorns, and brambles. On one side is a ravine, on the other the steep mountain. You go jolting along, the chariot almost tipping, afraid to press your horse too hard. . . . In the middle of the narrow valley you unfasten the yoke because the collar piece is broken, but you don't know how to fix it. . . . Your horse is exhausted by the time you find a place to stay for the night."[2]

any given period of time. The next involves tracing the most natural routes between them, linking as many smaller villages on the way as possible.[1] This method combines data from archaeology with realities of geography, mainly topography. Generally speaking, natural routes in the high hill country of Israel (areas of Cenomanian-Turonian limestone) followed the tops of ridges, connecting villages that were almost always located on them for reasons of security. In the process, they tended to avoid dropping to the precipitous valleys below. For instance, the most important route in the Hill Country of Judah ran NNE/SSW along the top of the watershed ridge, from north of Bethel to south of Hebron (the so-called Central Ridge Route or "Patriarchal Highway;" cp. Gen 12:6–9; 13:2–4; 37:14; Judg 21:19). From it, routes extended westward to the coast and eastward into the Rift Valley and Transjordan. Of these radial routes, the busiest followed the tops of the continuous ridges that separated major wadi systems from each other (e.g., the Beth-horon Ridge Route tracked the ridge between the Aijalon and Dilb wadi systems, or the Husan Ridge Route, a name of modern convenience, which followed the ridge separating the Sorek and Elah wadi systems).

Persons traveling on routes in the lowlands (the Shephelah) through larger inland valleys such as the Jezreel and Beth-netophah Valleys in Galilee or along the coast had more freedom of movement. Routes in these lower regions had to avoid areas of poor drainage and usually did so by hugging higher elevations along the edge of the hills where travel was easier during the rainy season. Other obstacles to be avoided (or crossed with difficulty) included the sand dunes that line the Mediterranean coast, steep ascents and descents, sheer cliffs, and rivers or streams. Some rivers, such as the Jordan, the Kishon (draining the Jezreel Valley), and the Yarkon (on the coast north of Joppa), had to be forded, a difficult task in the winter and spring when the water flow was strong (cp. Gen 32:22–23; Josh 3:1–17; Judg 3:28; 5:21; 2 Sam 19:15–18; Ezek 47:3–5; 2 Cor 11:26).

There is no archaeological evidence to confirm the exact location of any of the roads that traversed the land of ancient Israel until Roman times, so precise routes can only be estimated. In the late first and early second centuries AD, routes that connected some of the larger cities on the coastal plain to urban centers

1 David Dorsey, *The Roads and Highways of Ancient Israel* (Baltimore: Johns Hopkins University Press, 1991), provides the methodology and reconstructs an extensive network of highways in the land of ancient Israel for the time of the Old Testament.

2 *ANET*, 477–78.

Because the empires of the day were in Mesopotamia and Egypt, the major traffic pattern through the land of ancient Israel during the time of the Old Testament was longitudinal. The International Coastal Highway carried traffic between the inland desert city of Damascus on the one hand, and cities on the Mediterranean coast such as Gezer, Ashkelon, and Gaza—the gateway to Egypt—on the other. It threaded its way through various obstacles in Galilee in the process. The main international highway in Transjordan, the King's Highway, also ran north-south. By the time of the New Testament era, when international priorities had swung to the Mediterranean under the rising influence of Greece and Rome, the major traffic patterns in the land shifted to east-west, connecting inland routes to ports such as Acco/Ptolemais and Caesarea and Gaza. Throughout, important spurs angled toward Jerusalem, the primary locus of the biblical story.

A thin ribbon of asphalt pushes its way through the low hills of the Shephelah, a diagonal connector following the track of the ancient route linking the six east-west valley systems of the region. This was part of the longer *"road that goes down from Jerusalem to Gaza"* on which Philip encountered the Ethiopian eunuch (Acts 8:26–28). Sections of the modern roadbed lie exactly over paving stones from the Late Roman Period, following the path of the natural route that served traffic in the region for millennia. Typical of routes in the relaxed topography of the Eocene lowlands, this highway follows in part the rise along the edge of the valleys, saving the fields for agriculture.

inland were graded, paved, and curbed, thus integrating them into a growing network of Roman roads encircling the Mediterranean.[1] This became a "fact on the ground" as much as anything that linked the province of Palestine to the rest of the Roman Empire. For our purposes, such archaeological evidence allows us to trace the line of several of these roads. Some certainly followed the courses of the natural routes of earlier periods, but others conquered the terrain and went more directly between major cities. Also helpful in reconstructing the road network of ancient Israel are maps of nineteenth-century Palestine that show routes connecting Ottoman Turkish-era cities and villages of the day.[2] Because these roads tended to follow the paths of least resistance rather than the more sophisticated Roman road network, they, too, provide a reasonable witness to the location of many of the natural routes of the biblical period.

It is also possible to assume the general location of important routes from lists of cities mentioned in connection with the march of armies to battle, or their flight afterward. Examples are numerous and include 1 Samuel 14:31; 1 Chronicles 14:16; 1 Maccabees 3:38–40,46; and also Egyptian records listing cities in Canaan conquered by Pharaohs Thutmose III and Shishak[3]; as well as accounts of battles in Assyrian records or Josephus's *Wars of the Jews*. Similarly, we should assume that the cities built by King Rehoboam *"for the defense of Judah"* (2 Chr 11:5–12 (ESV)) were located at strategic points or junctures on the network of natural routes leading to Jerusalem, thus serving to confirm the active military routes of his day.

In 1916, British Prime Minister David Lloyd George gave his personal copy of George Adam Smith's seminal work *The Historical Geography of the Holy Land* to Field Marshall Allenby, who was preparing the British offensive against the Ottoman Turks in Palestine. Allenby kept the book in his saddlebag so he would have constant reference to Smith's understanding of the natural routes and strategic positions of the land. In the preface of the twenty-fifth edition of his book, published in 1931, George Adam Smith paid due homage to Allenby by tracing in detail the British advances toward Jerusalem in 1917 with reference to the ancient routes. Noted Smith, "I have been much encouraged by the generous tributes from Field Marshall Viscount Allenby and many of his officers in Palestine to the real usefulness of my volume in framing the strategy and tactics of their campaign."[4]

It should be kept in mind that there was no formal highway planning system in the land of ancient Israel until its major cities began to be linked by Roman roads. In earlier periods, road networks developed primarily in response to the expediency of local needs. Throughout the biblical period such roads were essentially footpaths worn bare by the passage of people and donkeys. The latter were the most common means of transport anywhere within the land, and because donkeys can easily negotiate rough pathways even in the hills, there was no need to construct formal, paved highways for normal needs of transport. Camels played an important role with heavy cartage and were indispensable in desert areas until quite modern times. The heavier the traffic, the easier it was to fol-

1 Israel Roll, "The Roman Road System in Judea," in *The Jerusalem Cathedra*, vol. 3, ed. Lee I. Levine (Jerusalem: Yad Izhak Ben-Zvi Institute, 1983), 136–61; Israel Roll, "Roman Roads in Western Samaria," *PEQ* 118 (1986): 113–43; David Graf, Benjamin Isaac, and Israel Roll, "Roads and Highways (Roman)," pp. 782–87 in David Noel Freedman, ed., *AB* vol. 5 (New York: Doubleday, 1992).

2 See, for instance, the maps produced by the Survey of Western Palestine. C. R. Conder and H. H. Kitchener, *The Survey of Western Palestine: Memoirs of the Topography, Orography, Hydrography and Archaeology*, in 3 vols.: Galilee, Samaria, Judaea (London: The Committee of the Palestine Exploration Fund, 1881–1883).

3 Aharoni, *The Land of the Bible*, 152–66, 323–30; Rainey, *The Sacred Bridge*, 72–75, 186–89.

4 George Adam Smith, *The Historical Geography of the Holy Land*, 30th ed., reprint (Jerusalem: Ariel Publishing House, 1966), 23.

low a route due to the surface of the ground becoming hard packed or rutted.[1] Wheeled carts and chariots needed wide, flat roads and were better suited to the valleys and plains than they were to the hill country, but even on these valley roads, most traffic moved by foot (Josh 17:16; Judg 1:19; 1 Sam 6:7–14; 2 Kgs 9:16–21). One of the signs of a strong, centralized government during the biblical period was road maintenance, which essentially consisted of imposing forced labor on the population (cp. 1 Kgs 4:6) to remove large stones and thorn-bushes that cluttered the roads and also leveling rough places where needed (Isa 40:4; 62:10). When the national economy languished and the fabric of society was torn, *"the main ways were deserted because travelers kept to the side roads"* (Judg 5:6), where there were *"thorns and snares on the way of the crooked"* (Prov 22:5).

It is difficult to estimate how often common people actually traveled in the ancient world or how far, under normal circumstances, they would venture from home. When the Bible makes note of someone traveling, the purpose of the journey is usually rather mundane: to attend a banquet or religious festival (Gen 35:28; Judg 21:19; 1 Sam 16:1–3; 25:12; Luke 3:41; John 7:10), to attend a funeral (2 Sam 13:23–29), to shop for food (Prov 31:14), to check on business interests (1 Sam 25:2), or to visit one's kin (Gen 37:12–17; 1 Sam 2:19; 17:15–20; Matt 12:46–47; Luke 1:39–40). A typical full day's journey by foot probably carried someone no more than twenty to twenty-five miles (32–40 km)—more or less depending on the location of water sources or way stations. Since the location of water sources doesn't change much over time, the line of routes—especially in the desert—must have been constant as well. Armies on the march, with full equipment, or loaded caravans would probably cover about half that distance (Josh 10:9), while people in a hurry, such as the Shunammite woman frantically searching for Elisha (2 Kgs 4:22–25,29), could cover longer distances in a shorter time. It is reasonable to suppose that long-distance travel for purposes of commerce, diplomacy, or war was also relatively common, and it is occasions such as these that tended to make headlines in the stories that have come down to us (2 Sam 10:2–5; 1 Kgs 4:27; Esth 7:10; Prov 25:25; Isa 18:2; 30:2; 52:7; Hab 2:2; etc.). Much more typical, however, must have been the example of Hannah, who visited her boy Samuel just once a year (1 Sam 2:19) even though he lived only fifteen miles away in Shiloh. Largely self-sufficient at home, folks just didn't tend to get around much.

Routes mentioned in the Bible are almost always named after their point of destination, a practice common throughout the ancient (and much of the modern) world. Examples are numerous, including "the way to Shur" (Gen 16:7), *"the road to the land of the Philistines"* (Exod 13:17), *"the way to the hill country of the Amorites"* (Deut 1:19), *"the road to the Wilderness of Moab"* (Deut 2:8), *"the border road that looks out over the valley of Zeboim toward the wilderness"* (1 Sam 13:18), *"the way to the wilderness of Gibeon"* (2 Sam 2:24), and *"the road to Horonaim"* (Isa 15:5). These designations aren't proper names *per se*, but referents that were clear enough within specific contexts of ancient travel. Therefore, roads named *"the Arabah road"* (Deut 2:8),

A Roman milestone was made of two large stones: an upper rounded column with a squared-off bottom, and a wide, stout base into which the column was set (the milestone on the right is complete). Each column contained an inscription mentioning the highway distance, in Roman miles (1 mile = 4,862 ft/1,480 m), from the milestone to (usually) the center of the largest nearby city and, of course, the name of the reigning emperor. These particular milestones date to the second and third centuries AD: the one on the left mentions Emperor Septimius Severus. The earliest milestone found in the land of ancient Israel dates to AD 56. It belonged to the coastal road connecting Antioch with Ptolemais, the first Roman road marked by milestones in the southern Levant. A milestone dating to AD 69 mentions the road connecting Legio (near the ruins of Megiddo) with Scythopolis (Beth-shean), the earliest evidence of the Roman road network penetrating inland. The earliest milestone from the hill country of Judaea dates to AD 120, well after the destruction of the Jerusalem temple. The discovery location of each Roman milestone, together with information garnered from the inscription, enables historical geographers to reconstruct much of the official highway network of the Roman Empire.

1 Travelers along the Hajj pilgrim route to Mecca in the eighteenth and nineteenth centuries report that the road was rutted by a number of parallel paths, each three to four meters distance from the next, made by camels that walked as they pleased. Eveline van der Steen, *Near Eastern Tribal Societies during the Nineteenth Century: Economy, Society, Politics between Tent and Town* (Sheffield: Equinox, 2013): 99–100.

"Some seed fell along the path, and the birds came and devoured it. Other seed fell on rocky ground where it didn't have much soil . . . [or] among thorns, and the thorns came up and choked it" (Mark 4:4–7). Jesus's parable of the Sower tells us of the condition of fields in first-century Galilee, but also something about the condition of the roads that ran alongside. It's no wonder that the first act of common hospitality offered by a host was to wash his traveling guest's feet. This act has developed deep spiritual symbolism today, but once was a very practical necessity (cp. 2 Sam 11:8; Song 5:3; Luke 7:38; 9:5; John 13:5–14; 1 Tim 5:10). On a related note, scholars have long debated the meaning of Paul's *"thorn in the flesh"* (2 Cor 12:7). Maybe it was just something he picked up while walking![1]

Most visitors to Israel today zip along the countryside in air-conditioned motor coaches, largely oblivious to the challenges and adventures that those traveling the land faced prior to modern times. Persons we meet on the pages of the Bible faced many obstacles when they traveled: rough terrain, swampy ground, sand dunes, a lack of adequate drinking water, insufferable heat, and unbearable cold. The ever-present danger of brigands, roadside thieves, and wild animals eagerly awaited unsuspecting travelers at every turn. Perhaps because difficult travel conditions were such an everyday part of life in the ancient world, biblical writers never tired of using travel imagery to speak about a larger journey, the journey each of us takes through life (e.g., Gen 17:1; Deut 8:6; Ps 119:1,105; John 14:6; Acts 9:2):

This is what the LORD says:
Stand by the roadways and look.
Ask about the ancient paths:
"Which is the way to what is good?"
Then take it and find rest for yourselves" (Jer 6:16)

Unfortunately, it has become so cliché to speak about "walking with God along life's way" that we rarely pause to reflect on the enormity of the task. Life's journey is seldom easy; it's often an arduous experience. How good to know that followers of Jesus can trek with one who has walked life's paths before, showing where to step along the way.

"the Beth-horon road" (1 Sam 13:18), or *"the way of the sea"*[2] (Isa 9:1) should be understood as leading toward the Arabah, Beth-horon, and the Mediterranean Sea, respectively. On this principle, all roads would have had at least two names: one for outgoing traffic, another for incoming. For example, the road connecting Jerusalem with Jericho would have been called "the Jericho road" for those descending into the Rift Valley and "the Jerusalem road" for those heading back up into the hills. And sometimes more than one route would have had the same name. The road from Ramah to Jericho and the road from Jerusalem to Jericho are both called *"the way to the wilderness"* in the Bible (1 Sam 13:18; 2 Sam 15:23), referents that of course made sense for residents of both towns since both roads entered the Wilderness of Judah. Indeed, it is likely that any route heading to the wilderness from any point would have carried that name, with the mention of only a few finding their way into ancient texts. The only known exception to this directional rule is the King's Highway (Num 20:17; 21:22), perhaps so named because it connected the capital cities of Syria, Ammon, Moab, and Edom, but more likely named idiomatically to indicate the "main" or "public" highway through Transjordan (cp. the Vulgate's translation of "Kings Highway" in Num 20:17 as *via publica*).[3]

Because the names of the vast majority of the roads that made up the highway network in the land of ancient Israel are directionally variable, we tend to reference many of them by modern terminology. For instance, "the Beth-horon Ridge Route," "the Husan Ridge Route," "the Ascent of Adummim," and "the Patriarchal Highway" are all modern names of convenience that allow us to speak accurately of the track and location of ancient routes, irrespective of which direction any given traveler may have been going.

1 This is the immensely practical suggestion of Linford Stutzman, *Sailing Acts: Following an Ancient Voyage* (Intercourse, PA: Good Books, 2006), 199–200.

2 Rainey and Notley, *The Sacred Bridge*, 230, suggest that the Way of the Sea was the direct route from Abel-beth-maacah in the upper Huleh Valley to Tyre on the Phoenician coast, following a line of Iron Age II sites in Upper Galilee. A similar view has been advocated by Barry J. Beitzel, "The Via Maris in Literary and Cartographic Sources," *Biblical Archaeologist* 54 (June 1991): 65–75, who suggests that the name referenced a route from Capernaum to Acco. A more traditional view holds that the way of the sea was the line of the international highway as it headed toward the Mediterranean through the Jezreel Valley from points north (cp. Isa 9:1).

3 Dorsey, *Roads and Highways of Ancient Israel*, 50.

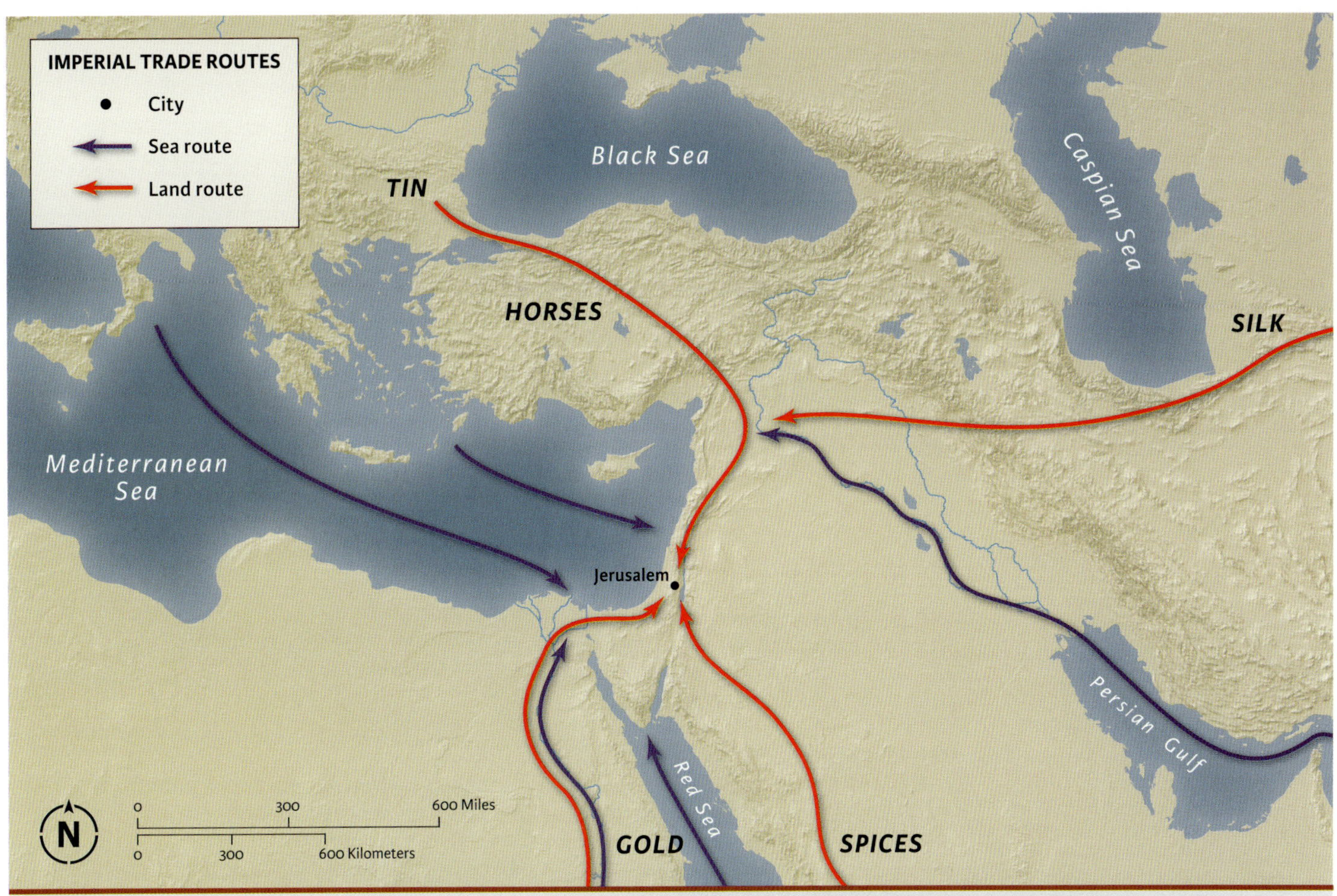

The great imperial routes of the ancient Near East flow through the Levant, a true "Land Between," as they tie the corners of the world's economy together. The routes marked red represent the main flow of land-based traffic, while those that are blue track major water routes. Archaeological and textual data suggest trade was brisk when nation states and empires were strong, though most of the traffic was in commodities less expensive than those noted here.

F. GEOPOLITICS

We have gathered enough building blocks of historical geography to allow us to begin to ask larger questions about how people groups interacted with one another in the land of ancient Israel. It should be expected that in a place as compact yet environmentally diverse as this, the ways that the various inhabitants of the land adapted to their own living spaces varied. Moreover, the unequal distribution of basic resources such as water and arable soil forced a competitive balance that on the whole prompted cooperative relations among the various peoples of the land. Yet this tenuous balance was poised to swing to open conflict with little warning. Such has been the case for millennia. A sweep through history reveals that there is nothing new under the Middle Eastern sun. A few preliminary comments are in order to describe some of the larger geopolitical principles that characterize the land of ancient Israel as a whole. Specifics related to biblical events will be mentioned in connection with our discussion of individual geographical regions below.

As an initial analogy, magnets attract. Peoples are drawn toward resources—or at least toward access points where resources might be acquired (e.g., highways or ports). The more important the resource, the stronger the pull—the wheat fields of the Nile Delta or the spices of south Arabia proving the point. On balance, the strongest magnets of the biblical world were not found in the land of ancient Israel itself, but in territory controlled by its larger, somewhat distant neighbors. As a result, issues related to human settlement in the lands bordering the eastern coastline of the Mediterranean Sea are nearly all ultimately tied to the region's primary role as a land bridge joining Asia, Europe, Africa, and the Arabian Peninsula. In perhaps the classic instance of "location, location, location," this was the ancient world's busiest highway intersection, where not only people but diverse species of plant and

> It is impossible to overestimate the role that competition for basic resources played in the land of ancient Israel during biblical times. One of the more striking examples is the context of the story of Gideon, in which the author of the book of Judges likened the scourge of desert raiders that swept across the land to a plague of hungry locusts: *"Whenever the Israelites planted crops, the Midianites, Amalekites, and the Qedemites [i.e., 'eastern peoples'] came and attacked them. They encamped against them and destroyed the produce of the land, even as far as Gaza. They left nothing for Israel to eat, as well as no sheep, ox, or donkey. For the Midianites came with their cattle and their tents like a great swarm of locusts"* (Judg 6:3-5; cp. Joel 1:4). Issues of security were paramount in a place where feast could turn to famine in an instant.

The land of ancient Israel has become home to a wide variety of plant species that originated elsewhere yet thrive in the climatic conditions of the land bridge connecting Asia, Europe, Africa, and the Arabian Peninsula. Nile Delta papyrus (right), for instance, found a second home in the rich, wet soil of the Huleh Basin north of the Sea of Galilee. In the first century AD, the Jewish historian Josephus, a native of Galilee, reported the hearsay that the Jordan River, which connects the Huleh Basin with the Sea of Galilee, must have somehow been a branch of the Nile since fish swimming in the sea resembled fish of the Nile (*War* 3.520–521). Coming the other way was the pomegranate (below), a tree so identified with the land of ancient Israel that by the time of the Bible it made the list of seven species characterizing the *"good land into which the Lord your God is bringing you"* (Deut 8:7–8). Current evidence suggests the pomegranate actually originated in the highlands of Persia (Iran) or northern India, then spread throughout southwest Asia.

animal life moved from the exit ramp of one continent to the entrance ramp of another. Migratory patterns converge here, as do overland trade routes extending as far as China (the Tea and Silk Road), Yemen (the Spice Route), East Africa (the Gold Route), and Spain and England (the Horse and Tin Route), where they merged into an intricate network of economic arteries. These great international routes traverse the Levant in generally a north-south direction, following the line of the mountain ranges that parallel the coast. It was on these imperial highways that King Solomon made a healthy living moving warhorses and chariots between Egypt and Kue (Cilicia in southern Turkey; 1 Kgs 10:28–29). His ability to dominate these routes by fortifying the cities of Hazor, Megiddo, and Gezer (1 Kgs 9:15) highlights the singular importance of the land of Israel to the economy of the ancient world.

Equally significant, at least for human geography, is that this land bridge also connects bodies of water—the Mediterranean Sea to the west, the Red Sea and Nile River to the south, and, to the east, the Persian Gulf via the Euphrates. The Euphrates is the more navigable of Mesopotamia's great rivers and the one that, in north Syria, reaches to within just a hundred miles (160 km) of the Mediterranean. Here the primary movement is east to west, with the land between a beachhead sending off or receiving large quantities of goods both exotic and unreachable to those whose customary means of transport were hoofed. During the time of the New Testament, the major city connecting the Mediterranean with the Euphrates was Antioch, a bustling, cosmopolitan place well situated to become the first center of Gentile Christianity (Acts 11:19–26). Further south, the port of Acco/Ptolemais and then Caesarea were the primary seaborne gateways into the land of ancient Israel from the west.

Together, these movements best resemble those of a complex traffic interchange, with a constant swirl of activity binding lands to seas and vice versa. Alternatively, the whole can be seen as a huge continental-sized fulcrum, polygonal in function if not in form, on which the lands and seas of the ancient world hung in an uneasy competitive balance. Because this was *the* place to control trade routes, it quite naturally yet all too often became the battleground for an endless march of empire builders who swept in from one corner of the world, then went off to conquer another.

But the land of ancient Israel also reverberated with the clash of cultures. Here, in an endlessly turning cycle, any given way of life—with a set of traits as minute as the style of one's hair, as large as one's relationship to the world of the divine, or as pervasive as language—touched, blended with, and eventually overtook another. It would not be correct to call a setting such as this a melting pot, where the cultural soup cooks to blandness and the traits of newcomers blur like the edges of a watercolor. Historic identity in the Holy Land is much more persistent than that. The peoples and cultures of the Middle East, in fact, have always more closely resembled a mosaic, in which each person or people group, like a mosaic cube (or *tessera*), maintains its own color, consistency, and sharp edge, yet—when viewed from a distance—blends into an integrated whole. The constituent parts of ancient Israel—geographically, politically, and economically—were distinct from, yet part of, the worlds of the ancient Near East and Mediterranean Basin. The cultures of the men and women of the Bible shared some of the colors and shapes of those variegated mosaics while resisting others. It is because this swirl of activity took place within the bounded sieve of the Levant, a place in which one's identity was susceptible to insecurity and accommodation yet worth fighting for, that Jim Monson was prompted to call the entire region "the Land Between."[1]

In a related dynamic, this land between served not only as a buffer between the great empires of the ancient Near East but also as a corridor between, and a connection point to, the powers of the Eastern Mediterranean. The Assyrians, for instance, necessarily crossed the land of ancient Israel in their attempts to conquer Egypt, and they found it expedient to convert the smaller nation states lying in their path into imperial provinces that would act as a barrier should an Egyptian attack come the opposite way (2 Kgs 17:5–6,24–26). During the time of the New Testament, Rome controlled

Irrespective of our understanding of its prophetic associations, the role of the modern state of Israel within the Middle East remains somewhat of an anomaly in regard to historic patterns of nation-state interaction in the region. Like the kingdom of Solomon, land controlled by Israel today extends from the Mediterranean to the Red Sea, making it the only country in the Middle East besides Egypt to have ports on both bodies of water and hence direct access to the Atlantic and Indian Oceans. This current political situation has sliced through the major natural land routes through the Levant, severing the historic highway between Egypt and Mesopotamia (i.e., between Egypt and Syria, Iraq and Iran) and forcing the ends of the Fertile Crescent to connect with each other via deep-sea and air routes instead—an option that Pharaoh in all his glory could never have foreseen.

monumental tombs in the Kidron Valley opposite Jerusalem's Temple Mount are among the most interesting architectural forms of ancient Israel. The pyramid-topped structure ight, hewn out of the living rock, is the memorial pillar (Hb *nefesh*, lit. "soul" or "living being") of an elaborate tomb belonging to the Hazir family, a wealthy family of high priests hroughout the intertestamental and New Testament periods. Local tradition incorrectly identifies it as the tomb of Zechariah. This *nefesh* is adorned by half-round and squared Ionic s. Two fully rounded columns of the Doric order stand to the left, in front the of tomb itself. The smoothed surface on the far left shows Nabatean influences. The entire complex es Egyptian, Greek (in two orders), and Nabatean forms in a matrix flaunting all rules of classical architecture. A confluence such as this was possible only in a land considered the of more proper ways of life elsewhere, where creativity flourished without need for classical restraint and imported forms were free to meld in directions as diverse as the flow of isscrossing the land.

1 James M. Monson, *The Land Between: A Regional Study Guide to the Land of the Bible* (Jerusalem: James M. Monson, 1983); *Regions on the Run* (Rockford, IL: Biblical Backgrounds, 2014), 6.

Syria, Judaea, and Arabia not only to access the wealth of the desert trade routes, but also to protect their far-flung frontier against incursions from the Parthians, Nabateans, and other eastern foes.

If location is everything, then product is a distant second—especially for the southern third of the Levant, the heartland of the biblical story. Indeed, whichever way the sum of data is totaled, acre for acre the land of ancient Israel remains among the least resourced areas of the settled parts of the Fertile Crescent. It is a place where, except for pockets such as the edges of the Jezreel Valley, the interplay of water and soil is so marginal that only local populations who have learned the secrets of the rhythm of the seasons can thrive off what the land itself has to offer. Today the Middle East is the focus of the world's appetite for oil,[1] but the petroleum reserves of the modern state of Israel are such a tiny sliver of the region's total that that land's importance on the world's geopolitical stage still is more closely tied to location than product. The only products that the land of Israel had to contribute to the regional economy in ancient times were its basic foodstuffs, just staples enough to survive. In the sixth century BC, while the rest of the world was moving exotic goods through the port of Tyre, Judah and Israel *"exchanged wheat from Minnith* [a city on the Mishor/Medeba Plateau], *meal, honey, [olive] oil, and balm for [their] goods"* (Ezek 27:17; cp. 27:12–27; Acts 12:20). It was an important role: like the grocery stores of Wall Street, food from Judah and Israel fed the Tyrians, who in turn kept the economic apparatus of the ancient world running during the centuries when the land routes of the Fertile Crescent opened up to the sea routes of the Mediterranean.

In sorting out the various players on the multileveled stage where the biblical drama took place, it can be helpful to view the actors through an analogy drawn from the familiar world of cats and mice, another illustration that belongs to Jim Monson.[2] Simple observation (and children's books) confirms that the behavior of cats differs widely from that of mice, especially when both

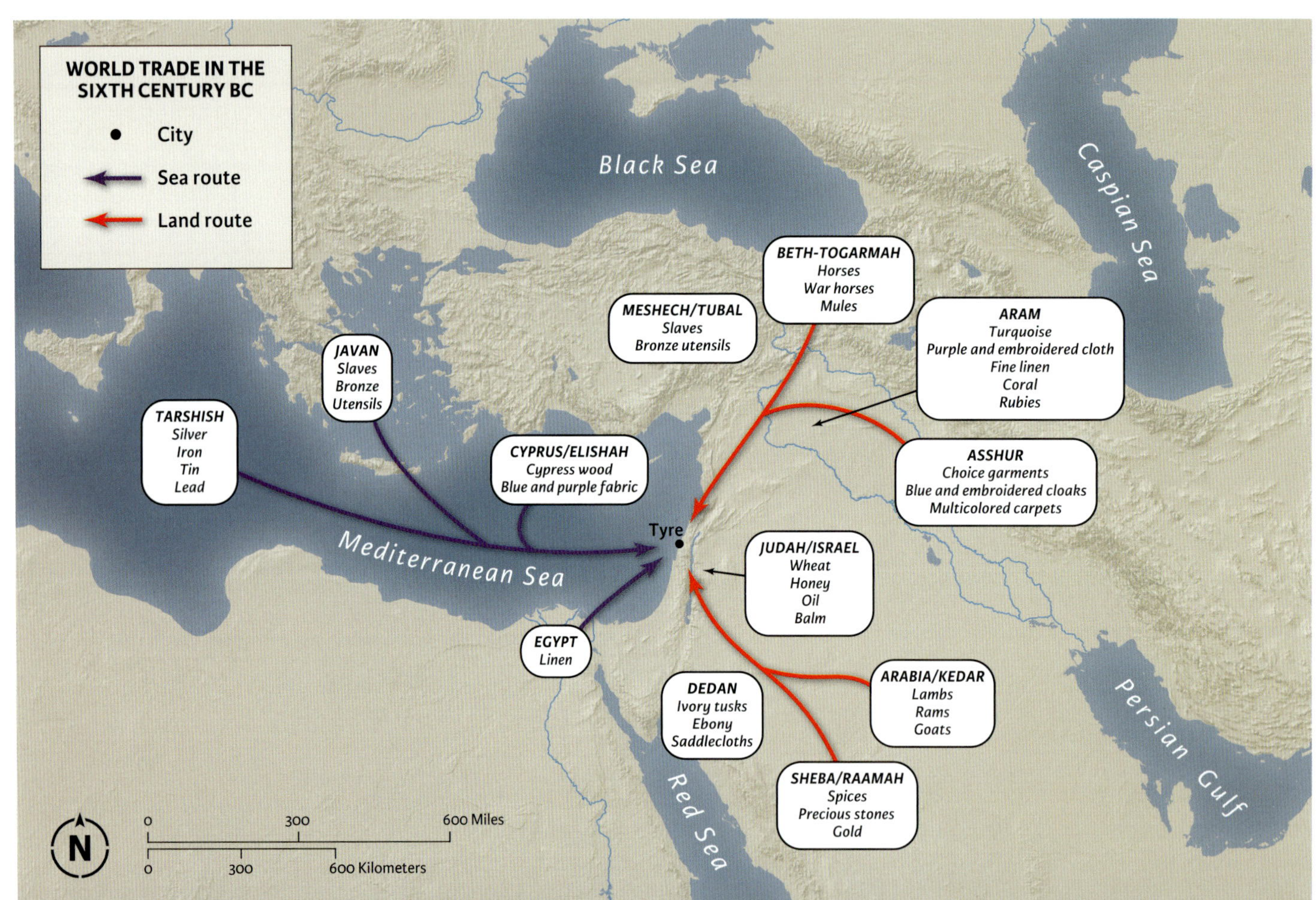

One of our most complete maps regarding economy of the ancient world is drawn from Ezekiel's lament against Tyre, a city *"located at the entrance of the sea, the merchant of the peoples to many coasts and islands"* (Ezek 27:3). In the mid-sixth century BC, all roads led to the port of Tyre, a perfectly positioned fulcrum on which the world's trade hung in symmetrical balance. A trip through the city's markets must have been enchanting: there sights, sounds, and scents from distant lands mingled in a kaleidoscope of wares. *"When your merchandise was unloaded from the seas you satisfied many peoples,"* noted Ezekiel matter-of-factly; then he looked beneath the racks of consumer goods to a system that was self-sufficient in its materialism. *"Now you are wrecked by the sea in the depths of the waters; your goods and the people within you have gone down"* (Ezek 27:33–34). The biblical prophets were never impressed with lines of credit.

1 Golda Meir, the fourth Prime Minister of the state of Israel, is oft-reported to have said, "Let me tell you something that we Israelis have against Moses. He took us forty years through the desert in order to bring us to the one spot in the Middle East that has no oil!"

2 Monson, *The Land Between*, 26.

Empires of the ancient Near East rose and fell, but in the process all had designs on the highway corridor lining the eastern seaboard of the Mediterranean. During the second half of the second millennium BC (the Late Bronze Age), Mitanni and then the Hittites pushed into Canaan from the north where they met imperialistic Pharaohs such as Thutmose III and Rameses II coming the other way. Egyptian interests on Israel's coastal plain persisted into the first millennium BC but were finally checked by the advance of Assyria in the eighth and seventh centuries. Babylon then Persia followed on the Assyrian heels. In the closing centuries of the first millennium BC, the overall movement of large armies swung ninety degrees as the Persian kings Darius, Xerxes, and Artaxerxes pushed all the way to the Aegean; then Alexander the Great and the Caesars swept in with a vengeance from the west. With large cats on the prowl, small mice-states such as Israel and Judah didn't have much of a choice: they could either keep quiet in their mountain holes or, like King Josiah of Judah, come out and risk being eaten (2 Chr 35:20–27).

The role of the Middle East as a producer of petroleum is a wholly modern phenomenon and should not color our understanding of the resource value of the land of ancient Israel in ancient times. The note about Asher *"dip[ping] his foot in oil"* certainly refers to olive oil production in western Galilee and Mount Carmel (Deut 33:24 NASB), while the *"blessings of the deep that lies below"* cannot be anything other than spring water (Gen 49:25).

are living in the same place at the same time—such as in a house with a foundation as full of holes as the land of ancient Israel was sieved. Cats are territorial (though they enjoy a good prowl), are never shy about wanting their own way, devour smaller creatures with relish, and lie down just about anywhere they please—pretty much like the great empires of the ancient Near East. Moreover, they are never really tamed, which is bad news for those mice lulled into thinking they have made an alliance that a cat might actually keep. The cats in the biblical story were the imperial powers of Egypt, Assyria, Babylon, Persia, Greece, and Rome. None were native to the eastern Mediterranean seaboard, though all proudly walked through—mostly sticking to its flatland international highways but climbing into the hills whenever a tasty morsel moved around a bit too much. Sennacherib's devastation of Judah, Neco's defeat of Josiah, and Nebuchadnezzar's sack of Jerusalem are classic examples (2 Kgs 18:13–19:37; 23:29–30; 25:1–21). These catlike empires were not particularly interested in the products of the Levant except as a resource to feed their marching armies. They did, however, very much need to control the land's strategic highways and gateway cities such as Gaza, Megiddo, Beth-shean, and Hazor as a staging ground to attack whatever cat-empire lay beyond. From the twelfth to seventh centuries BC, Assyria's goal was domination of Egypt; by the late eighth century BC, their road to pillage and slaughter necessarily led down the international highway skirting the heartland of Israel and Judah. Assyrian kings such as Tiglath-pileser III (2 Kgs 15:29), Shalmaneser V (2 Kgs 17:3), Sargon II (Isa 20:1), and Sennacherib (2 Kgs 18:13) became important players on the biblical stage in the process. During the time of the New Testament, Rome's empire was expanding into the Fertile Crescent. In the process, Judaea, Samaria, and Galilee became the beachhead that the Caesars had to conquer and hold—at any cost—to secure their eastern frontier. In every case, the value of the land between was strictly utilitarian. It was a mere buffer and bridge to something more valuable beyond.

Mice like to scamper about, too. But they make a lot less noise in the process. Mice can live on the scraps that cats leave behind or didn't want in the first place. They prefer hidden spaces under furniture, or they run along the line where the floor meets the wall, coming out into the open only when the cat's away. The hills and desert regions of the land of ancient Israel are chock full of such mouse holes, where smaller people groups (clans and tribes becoming nation-states) can settle and wrest a living from what the land itself has to offer as long as they stay out of the way of the cat-empires passing by. During the time of the Old Testament, the mice of the land included the Philistines, Phoenicians, Arameans (Syrians), Ammonites, Moabites, Edomites, and Israelites, as well as a host of other smaller players that called the region home. And this is the key—unlike the region's cat-empires, the mice-states weren't just passing through or squatting as an occupier looking to push further afield. Rather, the mice wanted a homeland in which to settle down.[1]

Historically, these smaller nation-states were most successful only when the cats were away. For instance, independent nation-states emerged and then thrived in the land of ancient Israel during the five-hundred-year window between 1200 and 740 BC, after Egypt's military presence on the coastal plain had been weakened and before the Assyrians from the north ripped and chewed their way into the land. This was the heyday of the Old Testament biblical story: the time of the judges, the united monarchy of David and Solomon, and the centuries of jostling for position between the Northern Kingdom of Israel, the Southern Kingdom of Judah, and their neighbors. In such a time, these mice could even have a go at playing on the exposed coastal plain (the Philistines made it their home) precisely *because* the cats were away. By the time of the New Testament, when Judaea, Samaria, and Galilee were Roman-occupied lands, most local folks had learned to accommodate their foreign overlords, although a few stuck their heads out as leaders of messianic political movements and promptly got them bitten off (Acts 5:3–37; 21:38; Josephus, *Ant.* 17.278–284; 20.97–104,168–172,185–188). It is a land of survivors—and road kill.

Here the concept of "center" versus "periphery" comes into play. Briefly put, the southern Levant functioned simultaneously as both heartland and frontier, depending on whether the point of view was that of a cat or a mouse. The Land Between, by definition, has always been a periphery for cat-empire centers, whether they be located in Egypt, Mesopotamia, or across the Mediterranean Sea. For them, this was a buffeted frontier of military endeavors, a place not yet properly civilized, an opportunistic edge of ebb and flow.[2] But the very same Land Between, at the exact same time, is also the conglomeration of a number of heartlands, irreducible mouse-state centers lying fully astride cat-frontiers. For the cats, these lands are buffer states at the beck and call of the empire center. For the mice, they are independent entities far enough away and civilized plenty well enough, thank you, to be left alone.

The main goal for mice-states was to secure a territory with a large enough center and secure enough frontier for everyone to live in safety. This could be either *"each person under his own vine and his own fig tree"*—a village image (1 Kgs 4:25), or each man in *"the entrance of his tent during the heat of the day"*—a shepherding image (Gen 18:1). Both are characteristic of mouse-holes. Of course, even without the threat of invading empires on the horizon, each of the mousy nation-states of the southern Levant expended plenty of restless energy trying to ensure their own security against the advances of the neighboring mice. In this context, there was ample opportunity for the pendulum to swing from cooperation to conflict as alliances were made and then broken according to the expediency of the moment (cp. 1 Kgs 15:18–20). The dynamic was based on land resources: nation-state versus nation-state, but also farmer versus herder; lowlander versus highlander; village folk versus city-dweller. Everyone knew about the strategic areas: the mountain passes, the most inviting ridge routes, the better river fords, the road junctions joining key population centers, the gateways into and out of a region or sub-region of the land. Jerusalem's best access to the Coastal Highway, for instance, followed the Beth-horon Ridge Route to Gezer. Solomon would not have been able to share in the wealth of the imperial highways on the coast had he not been able to gain and then fortify that city (1 Kgs 9:15,17). "Share" is the right verb: Solomon's control of Gezer was a joint effort with Pharaoh Siamun of Egypt (1 Kgs 9:16),[3] and this weak-cat and strong-mouse alliance, sealed by royal marriage, ensured that both nations' interests were protected along this most important corridor of the Levant. The

The rugged terrain and dissected topography of the eastern seaboard of the Mediterranean has always fostered territorial division, with small city- or nation-states jockeying for position among the region's scant resources. During the time of the Old Testament, this was home to the Phoenicians, Philistines, Ammonites, Moabites, Edomites, Israelites, and Judeans, as well as several Aramean nation-states. Similarly, today the region is divided among the states of Lebanon, Syria, Jordan, Israel, and the Palestinian Territories. On the other hand, the topographical features of the Nile and the Tigris and Euphrates river valleys foster political unification. This ancient pattern, in spite of persistent tribal infighting, gives some credence to the territorial integrity of the modern states of Egypt and Iraq.

1 For a survey of the dance between the cats and the mice in the land of ancient Israel, see Paul H. Wright, *Understanding Biblical Kingdoms & Empires: An Introductory Atlas & Comparative View* (Jerusalem: Carta, 2010).

2 Nili Wazana, *All the Boundaries of the Land: The Promised Land in Biblical Thought in Light of the Ancient Near East*, trans. by Liat Qeren (Winona Lake, IN. Eisenbrauns, 2013), 11–57.

3 Though Siamun's name is not mentioned in the biblical account, he is the most likely candidate for the Pharaoh who destroyed Gezer in the days of Solomon; see K. A. Kitchen, *On the Reliability of the Old Testament* (Grand Rapids, MI: William B. Eerdmans Publishing Company, 2003), 108–9.

strategic importance of specific areas such as this can often be traced in the historic and archaeological record. Geopolitical realities are a strong undercurrent in the biblical story, and learning to identify and trace them helps the reader appreciate the credible whys and wherefores of the events they describe.

G. THE HOLY LAND

All other associations, characteristics, and identities aside, the land of the Bible is first and foremost *Terra Sancta*, the Holy Land. The term itself, most properly in Hebrew either *eretz haqodesh* or *haaretz haqadoshah*, appears nowhere in the biblical text, though two related phrases do: *"He brought them to his holy* territory"[1] (Ps 78:54; Hb *gevul qodsho*) and *"the LORD will possess Judah as His portion in the holy [*ground*]"* (Zech 2:12 NASB, note that nearly all English translations choose to render the Hebrew in this verse, *admat haqodesh*, "holy land"). In a strict sense, the adjective "holy" applies to God alone, but by virtue of his choice of a *"place to have his name dwell"* (Deut 12:11), the biblical writers freely called the temple, the city of Jerusalem, and the Judean hill country holy as well (2 Chr 29:5; Pss 5:7; 87:1; Isa 52:1; Joel 2:1). By extension, the term *Holy Land* has been claimed for the entire land of the Bible, both west and east of the rift, as encompassing the place God chose as a special inheritance for his equally special people to live (Deut 32:49). Over time its associations have grown, becoming as much a concept of pilgrim tradition as it is biblical confession.[2]

Particulars of lexicon aside, the term *Holy Land* implies an essential unity of God + people + place, a threefold cord not easily broken (cp. Eccl 4:12). This was, after all, *"a land the Lord your God cares for"* (Deut 11:12), where *"he will bless you in the land [he] is giving you"* and "establish you as his holy people" (Deut 28:8–9). It was to here that God called Abram (Gen 12:1–9), then brought Moses and all Israel *"with a strong hand and an outstretched arm"* (Deut 26:8), driving out the nations and planting them like a vine on its terraced hillsides:

> *You cleared a place for it;*
> *it took root and filled the land.*
> *The mountains were covered by its shade,*
> *and the mighty cedars with its branches.*
> *It sent out sprouts toward the Sea*
> *and shoots toward the River.* (Ps 80:9–11)

The psalmist's reference is, of course, to Israel's expansive kingdom under Solomon, which stretched northward to the great bend of the Euphrates and southwest beyond the point where the Mediterranean shore bends toward Egypt. Solomon's reality was a concretization of future hopes when *"the kingdom [would] be the LORD's"* (Obad 21). And it was in this land that God himself walked in flesh and blood to redeem not just the times but all mankind (John 1:10–14). The Holy Land is a vine-wrapped land, with God as its vinedresser (John 15:1).

By the sixth century AD, the land of Palestine had become a magnet for pilgrims who carried relics (pious souvenirs) of their journeys back home. One city in Pontus (northern Asia Minor), Amaseia, boasted a collection of sacred relics housed in a building bearing the Greek inscription "Here are many tokens [i.e., relics] of the 'God-trodden' land" (*Supplementum Epigraphicum Graecum* 13, no. 538).[3] While the land of ancient Israel was called holy by biblical writers because it was the place God chose *"to have his name dwell"* (Deut 12:11), for many Christian pilgrims its holiness is grounded first and foremost in the touch of the feet of Jesus.

But when viewed by a dispassionate outsider, the thought surely arises: What's so holy about *that* place? If measured by gallons of blood shed and grief bled, the land is anything but holy—unless, in the justification of both Crusaders and jihadists, it is worth fighting for precisely *because* it is so. If measured in terms of resources, the land of ancient Israel also falls far short of perfection. Moses's view from Mount Nebo took in the sweep of the promised land (Deut 34:1–4), but all that everyone else saw from the Israelite camp on the Plains of Moab was the awful ascent of the Judean Wilderness rising in barren waves before them, a treeless landscape (except for the oasis of Jericho) of sun-bleached rock that looked very much like the *"great and terrible wilderness"* (Deut 1:19) in which they had just spent the past forty years. For *this* you hauled us out of Egypt?—the thought must have crossed the mind of more than one Israelite in spite of the glowing, though dimly remembered, report of the spies (Num 13:26–27). That Moses had earlier likened the resource base of Egypt to Eden, *"the LORD's garden"* (Gen 13:10), only heightened the contrast to what lay beyond the Jericho Valley. Indeed, we might consider that from the beginning, people-directed holiness had more to do with entering the fullness of "the bare immensities of God" (in the words of Amy Blank[4]) than filling a land of plenty.

In any case, the borders of the Holy Land are as difficult to define as is its name. While lands from Persia to Italy rightly qualify as hosting part of the biblical story—and hence could make a claim on the sacred name—it is the southern end of the Land Between in particular, the place to which Abraham came, Moses approached, and the Israelites and Jews called (indeed, still call) home, that is most often regarded as the Holy Land. But precisely where was this? Abram received the

---

1 For *gevul* as both territory and border, see Wazana, *All the Boundaries of the Land*, 12–13.

2 Rabbinic tradition in Judaism speaks of ten levels of holiness in regard to space, or place, with each place in sequence smaller, yet more holy, than the one prior. "There are ten degrees of holiness. The Land of Israel is holier than any other land. . . . The walled cities [of the Land of Israel] are still more holy. . . . Within the wall [of Jerusalem] is still more holy. . . . The Temple Mount is still more holy. . . . The Rampart is still more holy . . . The Court of the Women is still more holy. . . . The Court of the Israelites is still more holy. . . . The Court of the Priests is still more holy. . . . Between the Porch and the Altar is still more holy. . . .The Sanctuary is still more holy. . . . The Holy of Holies is still more holy, for none may enter therein save only the High Priest on the Day of Atonement at the time of the [Temple] service" (Mishnah Kelim 1:6–89).

3 Robert L. Wilken, *The Land Called Holy: Palestine in Christian History and Thought* (New Haven: Yale University Press, 1992), 192.

4 Amy K. Blank, "Moses Speaks," in *The Spoken Choice* (Cincinnati: HUC Press, 1959), 33.

Spires of holiness adorn the rooftops of the Old City of Jerusalem, beckoning belief in the city's sanctity if not in the faith of its residents. Here the bell tower of Mt. Zion's Dormition Abbey, center left, competes for skyline honors against the Tower of David, the minaret of a mosque built by the Ottoman Turk Muhammad Pasha in 1655. "Tower of David" is a popular misnomer, carrying the late tradition that the Israelites' King David was associated with the place. Jewish, Christian, and Muslim claims of holiness soar heavenward. At least there's no denying the beauty of the buildings erected in their wake.

first—and largest—map from God: "*I give this land to your offspring, from the Brook [lit. river] of Egypt to the great river, the Euphrates River: the land of the Kenites, Kenizzites, Kadmonites, Hittites, Perizzites, Rephaim, Amorites, Canaanites, Girgashites, and Jebusites*" (Gen 15:18–21).

While reference to the Euphrates surely means that the land promised to Abram would reach the point of that river's great bend in north Syria[1] rather than what is today southern Iraq, identification of the river (Hb *nahar*) of Egypt is problematic. The obvious (and popular) choice might be the Pelusiac branch of the Nile, the line of water and green fields that defines the eastern Delta (likely edging the land of Goshen; Gen 45:10). This was the entryway of Egypt according to both Herodotus (*Histories*, 2.141) and ancient Egyptian sources generally,[2] though with the underlying premise that because Egypt proper was confined to the Nile floodplain the entryway was, so to speak, exactly at Egypt's front door. The identification of the river of Egypt with the Pelusiac branch of the Nile[3] works in the context of Genesis 15 only if we consider that the relevant descendants of Abraham included both Ishmael, the eponymous father of desert-dwelling Arab tribes, and Isaac, the father of Jacob/Israel. But if we want to consider the maximal extent of the Holy Land in reference to the land of ancient Israel that was the home of the descendants of Jacob, then it is more helpful to consult the map of the Solomonic kingdom: "*Solomon ruled all the kingdoms from the Euphrates River to the land of the Philistines and as far as the border of Egypt*" (1 Kgs 4:21).

While the great bend of the Euphrates was the recognized western border of Assyria, the Nile River (including its Delta branches) was functionally the heartland of ancient Egypt and as such could not also be Egypt's border or, by implication, the border of the land of ancient Israel. Rather, the border of Egypt in this context was more likely the Wadi el-Arish, the water channel that drains the Sinai Plateau into the Mediterranean Sea about forty miles southwest of Gaza.[4] When the Egyptian armies crossed the Wadi el-Arish, they knew they were out of Egypt and within striking range of Gaza, hence in Asia. Coming the other way, for residents of the Philistine Coastal Plain, the Wadi el-Arish marked the furthest extent of their normal zone of control. Indeed, a map that is parallel to that of 1 Kings 4:21 mentions that Solomon's influence extended "*from the entrance of Hamath* [north Syria] *to the Brook* (Hb *nahal*; Arabic *wadi*) *of Egypt*" (1 Kgs 8:65); in this case, "the brook of Egypt" seems to have been the Wadi el-Arish—not the Nile River.

We don't know precisely where on the map of Genesis 15:18–21 all of the people groups that inhabited the land between the Euphrates and the River of Egypt actually lived at the time of Abram,[1] but certainly none were native

1 Assyrian kings of the first century BC routinely began the accounts of their campaigns into the Levant with the phrase, "I crossed the Euphrates for the X*th* time" (*ANET*, 278–82), with the part of the river crossed being the great bend that marks the westernmost frontier of the Assyrian homeland.

2 Rainey and Notley, *The Sacred Bridge*, 30.

3 So, for instance, H. Bar-Deroma, "The River of Egypt (Nahal Mizraim)," *PEQ* 92 (1960), 37–56.

4 Rainey and Notley, *The Sacred Bridge*, 31.

The kingdom of David and Solomon reached *"from the Euphrates River to the land of the Philistines and as far as the border of Egypt"* (1 Kgs 4:21). Its heartland was the older territory controlled by Saul, especially that west of the Jordan River. Control over the all-important Philistine coast remained elusive. Under David and Solomon, for the first and only time, a kingdom of Israelites controlled territory that approached the extent of God's land promise to Abram.

This schematic shows the heartlands of various mice-states of the southern Levant during the tenth through sixth centuries BC, in relation to the trunk-route highways and areas of adequate rainfall (at 12 in/300 mm minimum) in the region. In a land where resources are scarce, local states could bolster their economies if they controlled territory through which the international highways ran. As long as the cat-empires (Egypt, Assyria, and Babylon) were away, the risk-benefit ratio of seizing these imperial routes favored the commercial interests of the mice. Note that Judah is the only mouse-state in the area whose territorial heartland lay off a main trade route, a reality compounded by its proximity to the line of desert. Though Judah's was a land that by itself had little to offer, it became the bull's eye of the Holy Land, the center of God's target to redeem the world. *"God has chosen what is insignificant and despised in the world—what is viewed as nothing—to bring to nothing what is viewed as something, so that no one may boast in his presence"* (1 Cor 1:28–29). The apostle Paul spoke of people, but his words reflect equally well the land Judah and the Jews called home.

to the waterless Sinai west of the Wadi el-Arish. Of the ten people groups named in Genesis 15:18–21, "Canaanite" and "Amorite" eventually became umbrella terms for all of the indigenous people groups of the southern half of the Levant prior to the arrival of Moses (everything south of Kadesh on the Orontes). The Canaanites were typically identified with cities on the coastal plain, and the Amorites were associated with peoples up in the hills (cp. Gen 12:5–6; Num 13:29; Deut 1:19). By the time of Solomon, the roster of peoples that filled the land had changed.

The term Canaan deserves some additional mention. This was one of several terms used by the Egyptians of the 18th and 19th dynasties (New Kingdom Egypt from the mid-sixteenth through mid-twelfth centuries BC) to refer to the portion of the Levant that lies south of the Orontes River and west of the Rift Valley. (Note that according to Gen 33:17–18, Shechem was in the land of Canaan while Succoth, lying just east of the Jordan River, was not.) An actual designation of the borders of Canaan is found in ancient texts only in Numbers 34:1–12, never in ancient Egyptian sources. The Egyptian term "province of Canaan" is rare, found only in the Armana letters (EA 36:15), though nowhere do the Egyptians speak of a governor of Canaan. The term, then, seems to be one of regional convenience rather than a formal one designating a unified political sphere. Owing to the role of the cities of the southern Levant in funneling the wealth of Asia to Egypt, some scholars have suggested that the origin of the term *Canaan* was a designation for merchants. This would explain its use in particular with cities along the coast.[2]

Up to and including the present, the maximal boundaries of the land described in Genesis 15:18–21 and 1 Kings 4:21 fit only God's promise to Abram and the short-lived kingdom of Solomon. For the rest of the biblical period, the Israelites (and, later, the Jews) made do with a territory that was quite a bit smaller. The actual area of land that Joshua allotted to the twelve tribes of Israel, in fact, reached only from Dan to Beer-sheba (Josh 13–19; 1 Kgs 4:25), with the Jordan River more often than not the functional eastern boundary even though the inheritance of Reuben, Gad, and half of Manasseh lay in Transjordan.[3] Even here the landmass that actually fell under the control of any specific Israelite or Judean king varied with local political conditions, and "official" boundaries were drawn and redrawn at will. More often than not, the better-resourced areas (primarily the coast and the Jezreel Valley) lay in the hands of the Canaanites, Philistines, and/or Assyrians (Judg 1:27–36; 1 Sam 6:4,17; 2 Kgs 17:6,24), with Israel and Judah getting pushed into the high rocky hills and desert fringe above (cp. Judg 1:34). The Judean-oriented biblical writers of the late monarchy developed a special affinity for this heartland of their homeland, singing its praises in imagery and song while gazing longingly into the fertile fields round about that someday, they believed, would fall under Jerusalem's control (Ps 83:9–12; Isa 11:14; 30:23–26; Obad 19). During most of the period between the Testaments, Jewish territorial aspirations were again largely confined to the upper hill country around Jerusalem (i.e., the Persian province of Yehud). They received a boost during the Hasmonean (Maccabean) Kingdom, when control extended to the ancient boundaries of Dan to Beer-sheba. The Judaea-Samaria-Galilee division of Roman-occupied Palestine in the time of the New Testament reflects the same. Indeed, if the weight of history carries any sway, the Holy Land in its most natural sense falls between Dan and Beer-sheba (the northern half

1 Ibid., 30–31, 33–36.
2 Benjamin Maisler [Mazar], "Canaan and the Canaanites," *BASOR* 102 (April 1946): 7–12. In this light, the term *Canaan* is often used to designate merchants or traders in biblical Hebrew; Job 41:6; Prov 31:24; Isa 23:8; Ezek 16:29; 17:4; Hos 12:7; Zeph 1:11; and Zech 14:21.
3 Levin, "The Jordan River in Biblical Geography," 221–34.

From the shore of Capernaum, a rough-and-tumble band of fishermen pulled life from living waters in the first century AD. In its cycle of life, the place was as everyday-real as anywhere could possibly be. And it was precisely here that *"God with us"* (cp. Isa 7:14) pressed his indelible footprint into the rocky soil hearts of his people. Millennia of Christian memory has hallowed the site, though the accretions of tradition sometimes just have to give way to the stillness of the divine touch.

of the modern State of Israel plus the West Bank), with Jerusalem and its hills (for many Jews) plus the shore of the Sea of Galilee (for most Christians) its essence.

So why here of all places? Why a land prone to earthquake, drought, and heat (these are just its natural aspects) and overrun by the "trampling boot of battle and the bloodied garments of war" (Isa 9:5)? The writers of the Bible spoke of the great potential that lay somewhere deep within their land, when

> *the wilderness and the dry land will be glad;*
> *the desert will rejoice and*
> *blossom like a wildflower.*
> *It will blossom abundantly*
> *and will also rejoice with joy and singing. . . .*
> *For water will gush in the wilderness,*
> *and streams in the desert;*
> *the parched ground will become a pool,*
> *and the thirsty land springs.*
> *In the haunt of jackals, in their lairs,*
> *there will be grass, reeds, and papyrus. . . .*
> *And the ransomed of the Lord will return*
> *and come to Zion with singing,*
> *crowned with unending joy.*
> *Joy and gladness will overtake them,*
> *and sorrow and sighing will*
> *flee.* (Isa 35:1–2,6–7,10)

The longing of these words makes sense only because the reality in which they were first uttered—in both its environmental and its human aspects—was harsh. Theologically, if not practically, it is fair to ask the question of *place*. Given all possible options of location, why did Canaan end up being *"the land that I will show you"* (Gen 12:1,5–6)?

Without claiming that this was the best of all possible places where God *could* have first broken into the connected chain of human history, it was, certainly, in the context of the ancient Near East, a place where, due to aspects of geography, the most essential issues of life were exposed and at hand. Primary was the need for safety and security, a cultural universal if there ever was one. In the land of ancient (and modern) Israel, aspects of security cannot be taken for granted: here it's mice versus mice, mice versus cats, and mice versus the natural environment, all tumbled together into narrow confines and tight living spaces. The biblical writers did not describe the secure life in terms of amassed wealth—that option didn't really exist for the majority of the people in their world anyway. Instead, they spoke of families quietly living off their own land, specifically off of hill country land where summer fruit abounds. Again, *"Throughout Solomon's reign, Judah and Israel lived in safety from Dan to Beer-sheba, each person under his own vine and his own fig tree"* (1 Kgs 4:25). And as God said through the prophet Amos,

> *I will restore the fortunes of my people Israel.*
> *They will rebuild and occupy ruined cities,*
> *plant vineyards and drink their wine,*
> *make gardens and eat their produce.*
> *I will plant them on their land,*
> *and they will never again be uprooted*
> *from the land I have given them.*

The LORD your God has spoken.
(Amos 9:14–15)

As a result, the land of ancient Israel is a place where lessons of trust in God, rather than in the man-made strengths of economy, government, or army lay readily at hand. In the Edenic land of Egypt, human effort was enough to secure the basic commodities of life ("*where you* [all by yourself] *sowed your seed and irrigated by hand as in a vegetable garden*"; Deut 11:10). But the land of ancient Israel, by geographical definition, was a place that taught lessons of trust and dependence on God: it is "*a land of mountains and valleys, watered by rain from the sky*" (Deut 11:11), where the only reservoirs of the most essential commodity for life are God-controlled. Again, Jim Monson has summarized it best: this Land Between is "God's testing-ground of faith where saint and sinner struggled against internal upheaval and external threats. Personal and national existence could never be taken for granted, and the people of Israel were called upon to live by faith."[1]

All told, our interest in the land of ancient Israel is not found in its unique mix of rock, water, and routes *per se*, but because it is the land of the Bible, the Holy Land, and as such it is part of *our* story, wherever we may call home. Writing at the end of the nineteenth century, the pious historical geographer George Adam Smith wrestled with the relationship of land and faith. His questions had nothing to do with biblical prophecy. Writing five decades before the founding of the modern State of Israel, he instead was focused on the immediacy of the land of ancient Israel as it could be experienced in his day—and in ours. "To what degree does the geography of the land bear witness to the truth and authenticity of the Bible?" Smith asked. And as Christians, to what extent does a knowledge of biblical geography assist our faith in the Bible and in Jesus Christ?[2] Struck by the reality of the descriptions of the land offered by the biblical writers, Smith declared that, based on the geographical information they relayed, nothing in the biblical accounts was impossible. Geography, we maintain, can be an effective apologetic tool for those who wish to defend the veracity of the Scriptures.

But for George Adam Smith, the connection between the geographical shape of the land of ancient Israel and faith was deeper, rooted in the events of the Bible themselves. God, he suggested, brought Abram, Moses, and all Israel to this particular place for three reasons: the land afforded its inhabitants a unique opportunity to be preserved as a people group in spite of the forces of change that swept through history; it offered a place suitable for lessons in the revealed character and will of God; and it supplied connections and routes from which apostles could be sent out to reach all mankind.[3] He said,

> There is no land which is so much a sanctuary and an observatory as Palestine: no land which, till its office was fulfilled, was so swept by the great forces of history, and was yet so capable of preserving one tribe in national continuity and growth: one tribe learning and suffering and rising superior to the successive problems these forces presented to her, till upon the opportunity afforded by the last of them she launched with her results upon the world.[4]

And so, in spite of its vagaries of resource—or perhaps precisely because of them—the land of ancient Israel is a God-chosen, God-trodden land, one that is a particularly apt location for teaching and learning lessons of life and faith. It is also the stage of the greatest drama of redemption ever told. Though specific in its particulars, the land has become a window into the hearts and minds not just of the human authors and audience of the Bible, but of God himself. As such, it is the homeland of us all.[5]

SUMMARY

Biblical historical geography is a study of places—their names, their natural characteristics, and their connections to one another. It is also a study of events, of how the biblical story was shaped by the physical environment in which it took place and how a knowledge of that context can be an important tool in biblical interpretation. Each of the basic building blocks of biblical historical geography is an academic discipline in and of itself. When combined, these disciplines provide a holistic look at the physical settings of the Bible.

1. *Toponymy.* Biblical place names are a window into the natural and cultural environment of the land of ancient Israel. The process of identifying a biblical place name with a known archaeological site can be aided by carefully comparing geographical information mentioned in ancient texts with the actual lay of the land where the site is thought to be and, if possible, matching the ancient name with its modern counterpart.
2. *Geology.* The land of ancient Israel is primarily a land of various types of limestone. The specific characteristics of each, including the soils produced and the bedrock's suitability for water storage and building materials, shape overall settlement conditions in the land. Moreover, a highly variegated topography dissects the land into many smaller districts, each of which is a unique settlement region in its own right.
3. *Climate.* The Mediterranean climate of the land of ancient Israel is characterized by hot, dry summers and cool, wet winters. Rainfall amounts vary significantly from region to region, based largely on local topography but also on larger climatic conditions from year to year. The biblical writers were keenly aware that the land they called home was wholly dependent on rainfall, the open-handed blessing of God.
4. *Water resources, soils, and fertility.* Based on topography, soils, and rainfall, the land of ancient Israel can be divided into two subsistence zones: one where conditions allow for sustained agri-

1 Monson, *Regions on the Run*, 5.
2 Smith, *The Historical Geography of the Holy Land*, 107–16.
3 Smith, *The Historical Geography of the Holy Land*, 111.
4 Ibid., 112.
5 Wright, *Understanding the Ecology of the Bible*, 5–9, 45–47.

culture and permanent settlement, and the other that supports a semi-nomadic, shepherding lifestyle. The seven main plant species (Deut 8:8) produced in the former and the milk products of the latter sustain a well-rounded diet in this land of literal milk and honey.

5. *Settlement and routes.* The geographical diversity of the land of ancient Israel has created an intricate pattern of settlement and routes. By mapping areas of settlement and the road networks connecting them, it is possible to create a dynamic of human social, political, and economic interaction. Throughout the biblical period, the relatively isolated, local conditions of the hill country fostered connections that were socially and economically conservative, while the open plains and valleys encouraged new opportunities and growth.
6. *Geopolitics.* The overall position of the land of ancient Israel as part of the land bridge connecting Asia, Europe, Africa, and the Arabian Peninsula ensured it would also be the focus of attention of the political, military, and economic priorities of the empires of the ancient world. The small nation-states that called the place home (Israel and its neighbors) were able to participate in the economic opportunities offered by the land's imperial routes, yet they had to remain mindful of the challenges to their security and well-being that ensued by virtue of having a home in the middle of the highway.
7. *The Holy Land.* In spite of the opportunities and challenges that adhered to the land of ancient Israel, this was also the Holy Land, a place specially chosen by God as the setting for his divine encounter with humankind. The biblical writers were well-attuned to ways that the land itself reflected characteristics of both people and God, and they infused every aspect of their writings with geographical information that filled out, and illustrated, the grand story of redemption told in the Bible.

QUESTIONS

1. How might tracing the occurrences of a specific place name through Scripture help you understand each of the stories in which that name is mentioned? How might the repetition of a place name in various stories be significant?
2. What can we learn about the understanding that Abraham, Isaac, and Jacob had of God from the names by which they called the places in which they visited or settled?
3. To what extent can the use of the terms *Israel* or *Palestine* in reference to the land of the Bible be helped or hindered by modern political events?
4. Which aspects of the geography of the land of ancient Israel (rock, soil, water, elevation, rainfall) provided the most striking imagery for the biblical psalmists? Prophets?
5. How could the land of ancient Israel have been a "land flowing with milk and honey," given its overall irregularity of resources?
6. How can the priority given to water and agriculture in the biblical world become significant for Bible readers in modern, urban times?
7. Given the better resource base of the Nile Delta, why do you think that God didn't just leave Israel in Egypt and orchestrate the events of history so that Moses became Pharaoh?
8. Which is the more meaningful aspect of the term *promised land*: "the land that I promise to give you" (see Exod 12:25) or "the land in which I promise to take care of you" (see Deut 11:12)? Explain.
9. How does the cycle of the Israelite/Jewish pilgrimage festivals reflect the cycle of the seasons? Are Christian festivals better or lacking for not being tied to the seasons the same way?
10. Which holds more appeal for a long-term lifestyle, the situation of the biblical shepherd (e.g., Abraham) or that of the biblical village farmer (e.g., Elisha)? Of what advantage was it to be, like David, a resident of Bethlehem, a town situated between grainfields and grazing land?
11. How might David's life as a village shepherd, geographically speaking, have prepared him for his life as king over an emerging nation-state? How might he have felt "out of place" in the city of Jerusalem after spending years in non-urban settings?
12. What factors related to geography do modern city planners, real estate developers, or businesses take into account when expanding their interests into new areas? To what extent might Solomon have held similar discussions as he sought to push Israel's economic borders to their limits (1 Kgs 4–5; 9–10)?
13. What topographical and travel realities lay behind Jeremiah's plea to *"stand by the roadways and look. Ask about the ancient paths, 'Which is the way to what is good?'"* (Jer 6:16).
14. What is more significant for those who live on a highway: that they are well positioned to seize new opportunities, or that they might be run over? Which was more significant for the kings of the kingdom of Israel? For the Jews of Judaea and Galilee in the time of the New Testament?
15. Comment on this statement: "Jerusalem is the only world-class capital city that is not on a major land or sea route."
16. Why, in God's plan for the nations, was Israel a "mouse" and not a "cat"?

3 THE LAND OF ANCIENT ISRAEL: THE SOUTHERN REGIONS (JUDAH/JUDEA)

It is common to divide the land of ancient Israel into separate geographical units based on elevation and landforms. The typical approach views the land as a series of narrow longitudinal zones: from west to east, these are the coastal plain, the Western Highlands, the Rift Valley, and the Eastern (Transjordanian) Plateau. This division appears natural, given the landscape's rise, fall, and then rise again in four parallel lines pressed tightly between the Mediterranean Sea and the Arabian Desert.

Yet for all of this straight-line beauty, a picture like this tends to obscure significant differences in physical and human geography that distinguish south from north. That is to say, subdivisions within the longitudinal zones in the north (i.e., within Galilee or Bashan) exhibit a very different set of characteristics than do their southern (i.e., Judean or Edomite) counterparts. Similarly, the midsection of the land of ancient Israel—particularly the tribal inheritances of Ephraim and Manasseh, the heartland of Samaria—is unique in its own right, but shares important characteristics with Gilead, the corresponding central region of Transjordan. Indeed, a look at actual human settlement patterns in the land over time suggests that the essential character of the land of ancient Israel—its "living dynamic" as it were—is probably better understood with a latitudinal, rather than longitudinal, division in mind.[1]

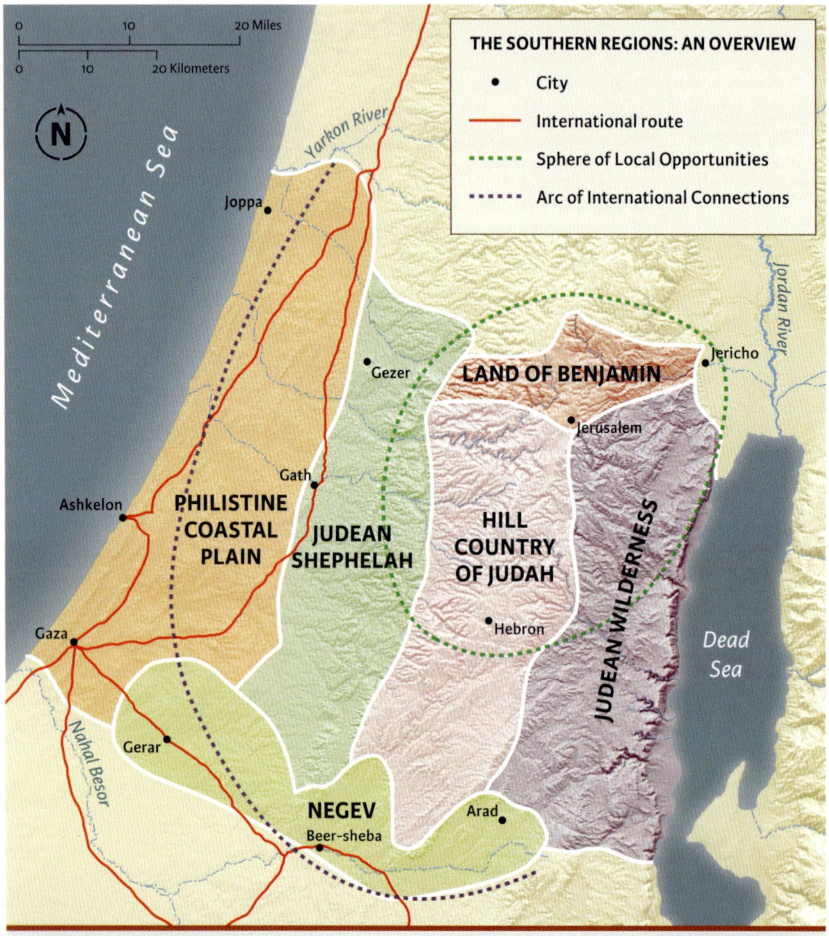

This schematic map shows the relative positions of the six regions that make up the southern arena of the land of ancient Israel. Notice Jerusalem is not in the geographical center; nevertheless, its historic and spiritual role over the ages has prompted the entire region to swing around its fortunes. The inner circle (green) represents the orbit of local opportunities afforded the residents of Jerusalem, while the outer arc (blue) scores the importance of the coastal plain and Negev for Jerusalem's connections to the world beyond. The space between the blue and the green was an active zone of opportunity and conflict between local and regional priorities in the region.

The southern regions of the land of ancient Israel include the Hill Country of Judah, the Judean Shephelah, the coastal plain, the Negev, the Judean Wilderness, and the land of Benjamin (cp. Deut 1:7; Josh 9:1; 10:40; Jer 17:26; 32:44). Viewed together, these regions form concentric rings around Jerusalem, with an inner circle (the hill country, Shephelah, Judean Wilderness, and land of Benjamin) providing a frame of local opportunities and an outer arc (the Negev and the coast) offering connections to the world beyond. Geographically, the biblical story focuses on the city of Jerusalem. Its six surrounding regions form the immediate context of the hopes and aspirations of Jerusalem's residents—royal, priestly, and common—as they sought to come to terms with their place in the world. This southernmost portion of the Levant is generally drier and its landscapes harsher than the regions further north. Routes in the south tend to be more constricted and less open to penetration from the outside. With a relatively limited population base and a horizon line that is circumscribed by rugged wilderness further south and east as well as a straight-lined coast to the west, the southern regions tended to be more isolated from international traffic and hence more limited in opportunity and provincial in outlook than their northerly neighbors.

A. THE HILL COUNTRY OF JUDAH

Defined geologically, the Hill Country of Judah is a massive block of Cenomanian-Turonian limestone lying between Jerusalem and the Negev; it's forty miles (65 km) north-south by approximately twelve miles (20 km) east-west in size and thrust upward to sustained heights of 2,800 to more than 3,200 feet (850 to 975 m) in elevation. When viewed from some distance to the west, the Judean hills rise over the foothills of the Shephelah like a gray-green wall, largely uniform in height and relatively monotonous in form, with rounded ribs and ridges throwing a bulwark[2] against anyone trying to approach from the direction of the coast. The highest point is Halhul, north of Hebron (Josh 15:58); it's 3,345 feet (1,020 m) above sea level.

1 The basic idea of defining the natural regions of the land of ancient Israel by latitudinal rather than longitudinal lines is found in James M. Monson and Steven P. Lancaster, *Regions on the Run* (Rockford, IL: Biblical Backgrounds, 2014). Monson and Lancaster define a Southern Arena, a Central Arena, and a Northern Arena, each of which spans the Rift Valley.

2 The image is that of George Adam Smith, *The Historical Geography of the Holy Land* (London: Hodder & Stoughton, 1894), 259, 286–87.

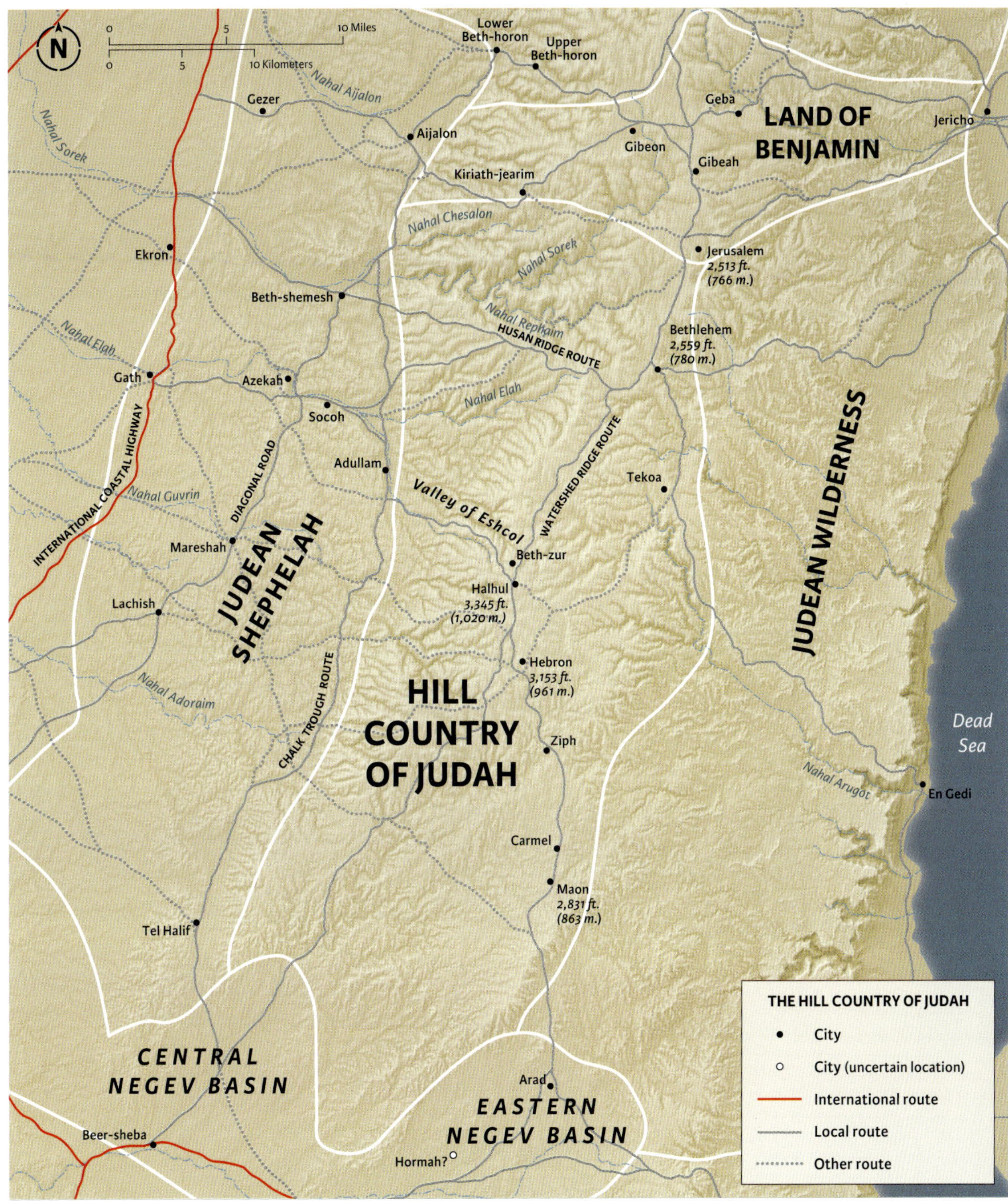

Rainfall amounts throughout the higher elevations of the Judean hill country typically reach twenty-four to twenty-eight inches (610 to 710 mm) annually, with snow, sometimes heavy, expected every two to three years. Summertime temperatures rarely exceed the low-90s in degrees Fahrenheit (mid-30s C), though the high angle of the sun often makes conditions feel hotter than they actually are. There is no hiding from the elements on top of the high and exposed watershed ridge, and any kind of cave or canopy becomes a welcome *"shelter for shade from heat by day, and a refuge and shelter from storm and rain"* (Isa 4:6). Adam's curse, *"You will eat bread by the sweat of your brow"* (Gen 3:19), seems particularly apt in this nevertheless-holy land.

With terraced hillsides lining the lower elevations of nearly every wadi that lies within walking distance of Judah's many towns and villages, this is a land where summer fruit thrives. Indeed, there are estimates that up to half the land of the Judean hills was terraced in ancient times. Grape vines and olive trees do especially well in its rocky terra rosa soil; the higher elevations around Hebron are particularly well suited to grapes. To the south and east, as the hills flatten out around Ziph, Carmel, and Maon then descend into the Negev, rainfall amounts taper off so as to favor grains and then grazing (1 Sam 25:2–4). Throughout the region, grain can be grown wherever deeper soil has collected in the bottoms of the valleys.

Without the constant, careful attention of the village farmer, the searing summer heat and the forces of water and wind erosion quickly revert the Judean highlands to a landscape of thorns and bare stones: *"I will make it a wasteland. It will not be pruned or weeded; thorns and briers will grow up. I will also give orders to the clouds that rain should not fall on it"* (Isa 5:6).

This was the condition of portions of the Hill Country of Judah in the first decades of the twentieth century AD, and early photographs betray a bleak Judean landscape with little to relieve the monotonous glare of the sun except for heavily dressed laborers stooping low in the fields (Gen 3:17–18). During the last eighty years, many of Judah's western slopes have been reforested with pine, cypress, cedar, and fir (primarily through efforts of the Jewish National Fund; Isa 60:13), giving a welcome carpet of green to the hills and providing visible testimony to the inherent fertility of its brown-red Cenomanian-Turonian base. Jacob's blessing to his fourth-born son Judah reflects the same, depicting a land where vines have the potential to grow strong and are plentiful enough to double as hitching posts: "*He ties his donkey to a vine, and the colt of his donkey to the choice vine. He washes his clothes in wine and his robes in the blood of grapes*" (Gen 49:11).

The highest reaches of the Judean hill country are its most heavily populated areas. We can trace a line of cities and villages along the watershed from earliest times, especially where the high ground broadens out around Hebron in the center of the Judean hills. Residents of the Hebron Plateau, which at more than 3,300 feet (1,005 m) is the highest part of this southern hill country (Judg 16:3), have always claimed pride of place among their fellow Judeans, and perhaps rightly so. Here resources combine to form the economic hub of the region. The natural route tracing the watershed southward from Bethlehem divides at Hebron, with the main branch dropping to Beer-sheba on a line running parallel to the Mediterranean shore. A second branch runs southeastward at a forty-five-degree angle following the high, dry ridge of Ziph, Carmel, and Maon to Arad. This confluence of routes has helped to assure Hebron's place as a regional center of trade. Here goods from the hills are most readily exchanged with the products of the shepherd. In times of an expanding national economy, even exotic wares coming off the international routes beyond the Negev, such as spices and precious materials from Arabia and the Red Sea area, have penetrated Judah through the highland port of Hebron (1 Kgs 10:11–15,22).

A little to the north of the Hebron Plateau, just beyond the rise of Halhul, the watershed cups into a broad, shallow basin usually identified with the biblical Valley of Beracah ("blessing"; 2 Chr 20:26) or the Valley of Eshcol ("grape cluster"; Num 13:23). It was perhaps in this pleasant vale that Joshua and Caleb spied out their promised land and "*cut down a branch with a single cluster of grapes, which was carried on a pole by two men. They also took some pomegranates and figs*"—worthy homecoming souvenirs for these early visitors to the Holy Land (Num 13:23).

A few miles north of the Beracah Valley and slightly east of the watershed, nestled among hills a little lower than those of both Hebron and Jerusalem, lie the fields and houses of Bethlehem. Bethlehem is backed to the west by the 3,000-foot (915 m) Beit Jala Ridge and faces

The Hill Country of Judah rises as a bulwark of hard limestone from the foothills of the Shephelah. This view takes in the serrated edge of the Elah wadi system, but it could be just about anywhere along Judah's entire western flank. This was Judah's natural defense to the west, though it was not without weak spots that could be breached by a determined foe (2 Sam 5:18,22).

the yawning chasm of the Wilderness of Judah to the east. The climate here is a bit more moderate than in Hebron, with the region's terraces and wadi bottoms having been cultivated intensely for millennia.[1] But in spite of its pleasant position, the population of Bethlehem has always lagged behind that of Hebron, its more robust and resourced neighbor to the south. The assessment of the prophet Micah, *"Bethlehem Ephrathah, you are small among the clans of Judah"* (Mic 5:2), is not without geographic merit.

The large Iron Age village of Tekoa, hometown of the prophet Amos, lay among the drier hills lining the Judean Wilderness to the east, closer to Bethlehem than Hebron (note the phrase *"wilderness of Tekoa"* in 2 Chr 20:20). Amos's life work was to breed sheep (Amos 1:1) and grow sycamore fig trees (Amos 7:14). To this day the sycamore fig thrives in the lower elevations of the Shephelah and the coastal plain (1 Kgs 10:27), and Amos apparently had land holdings there as well as in the vicinity of Tekoa. Like many residents of Judah's more marginal eastern regions, Amos spread his assets among the products of the shepherd and the yield of the farmer. His skills in providing an honest living in a difficult land stood him well when God called him to point out the social and moral failings of those living in the more economically blessed Samarian hills further north (Joel 2:6–7; 4:1,7–9; 8:4–27). Similarly, the towns of Ziph, Carmel, and Maon, all described as wilderness or shepherding towns in the biblical text (1 Sam 23:14,24–25; 25:2,4–5), clung to the high southeastern fringe of the Judean hills, representing well the uneasy seam between shepherding and farming economies.

The Judean highlands drop off sharply eastward into the Rift Valley. To the west, they plunge into a narrow chalk trough that separates its hard limestone ridges from the softer Eocene foothills of the Shephelah. Flowing both directions, wadis have scored and scoured the hills, leaving deep, V-shaped canyons separated by narrow, twisted ridges on either side of the watershed. The tangle of wadis that drain the Judean watershed to the west merges into five grand drainage systems: from north to south, these are the Sorek (with two large branches, the Chesalon and the Rephaim), the Elah, the Guvrin, the Lachish, and the Adoraim wadi systems. A sixth, the Aijalon wadi system, drains the hills of Benjamin to the north. The word *sorek* refers primarily to a choice species of vine that produces dark red grapes; the vines are particularly suited to the valley that carries their name. The *sorek* vine also became an image of the people of Judah, who were at home in the Sorek Valley's folds west of Jerusalem:

I will sing a song about the one I love,
a song about my loved one's vineyard:
The one I love had a vineyard

With his usual rhetorical flair, George Adam Smith described the shape of the wadis dropping through the western defiles of the Hill Country of Judah this way: "Few are straight, most sharply curve. The sides are steep, and often precipitous, frequently with no path between save the torrent bed, in rapids of loose shingle or level steps of the strata, which at the mouth of the defile are often tilted almost perpendicularly into easily defended obstacles of passage. The sun beats down upon the limestone; springs are few, although sometimes generous; a thick bush fringes the brows, and caves abound and tumbled rocks. Everything conspires to give the few inhabitants means of defense against large armies. It is a country of ambushes, entanglements, surprises, where armies have no room to fight, and the defenders can remain hidden; where the essentials for war are nimbleness and the sure foot, power of scramble and of rush."[2]

It's springtime in the Beracah Valley, the Vale of Blessing, where summer fruit ripens a little later than around Bethlehem but is larger and plumper for the effort. These old grape vines, thickened by years of productivity in a rich bed of terra rosa soil, are held up by a makeshift trellis, their new spring growth just starting to appear. *"All these blessings will come and overtake you,"* promised Moses in Deuteronomy 28:2, *"because you obey the LORD your God. . . . Your offspring will be blessed, as well as your land's produce."* For the Old Testament writers, the sum of people + land was inviolable. A quiet highland valley such as this provided the best of all possible homes.

1 Kay Prag, "Bethlehem: A Site Assessment," *Palestine Exploration Quarterly* 132 (2000): 169–81.

2 George Adam Smith, *The Historical Geography of the Holy Land* (London: Hodder & Stoughton, 1894), 287.

on a very fertile hill.
He broke up the soil, cleared it of stones,
and planted it with the finest vines
(Hb *sorek*). (Isa 5:1–2)

This imagery also appears in the book of Jeremiah:

"*I planted you, a choice vine (sorek) from the very best seed. How then could you turn into a degenerate, foreign vine?*" (Jer 2:21).

Judah's westward ravines are dotted by small springs and scattered villages, together fostering the kind of independence and conservatism that characterizes similar hoots and hollows around the world. Because groups of villages within a wadi system share a common set of resources, the living spaces within boundaries demarcated by drainage patterns provide a good place to forge first-level political and economic alliances (including social networks for finding marriage partners; Judg 14:3; cp. Gen 24:4; 28:2; 29:19; Tob 4:12).[1] The priority of local loyalties is illustrated by an episode in the Samson story. Somewhere in the western folds of the Sorek or Elah wadi systems, at the Iron Age village of Ramath-lehi and its spring En-hakkore (neither site has been positively identified), the Danite Samson drove the Philistines from the Judean hill country. This took place after the men of Judah had thrown Samson out of Etam, a place further up slope (Judg 15:9–19). Clearly, the Judeans wanted nothing of the Danite-Philistine struggle!

Indeed, the cities and villages lining the watershed of Judah lie in rugged isolation from population centers elsewhere, due primarily to their natural defenses east and west. The Philistine attempt to reach Jerusalem by pushing through the tangled bottom of the Rephaim wadi, hoping to catch David by surprise early in his reign as Israel's king, is the proverbial exception that proves the rule (2 Sam 5:17–25).

Yet approach from the west wasn't totally closed. Judah's natural connections with the Shephelah follow two narrow ridges, one tracking the rise that separates the Sorek from the Elah wadi systems and the other running the heights between the Elah and the Guvrin (recall that natural routes in the Cenomanian-Turoni-

A stone wall defines the perimeter of this ancient threshing floor east of Bethlehem. Grain fields in the valley below are partitioned along family lines, bearing witness to the communal nature of the harvest experience. Though modern agricultural implements have almost completely replaced traditional methods of farming in the area, the memory of threshing sledges and winnowing forks still lingers in the air (Isa 41:15; Jer 15:7). The setting evokes images of Boaz winnowing barley in the evening on the public threshing floor of Bethlehem, his portion of cultivated land somewhere nearby (cp. Ruth 2:3; 3:2). Houses of today's city approach in the distance from the left, while the blocky mass of white apartments of Har Homa, a modern Israeli settlement town marking the southernmost extent of Jerusalem, dominate the distant center above.

1 Gunnar Lehmann, "The United Monarchy in the Countryside: Jerusalem, Judah and the Shephelah during the Tenth Century B.C.E.," in Andrew G. Vaughn and Ann E. Killebrew, eds., *Jerusalem in Bible and Archaeology: The First Temple Period* (Atlanta: SBL, 2003), 136–56. Arranged marriages between close family members (cousins or second cousins) is still valued in Palestinian villages as a way to guard a family's land-based resources.

an hill country follow the tops of continuous ridges between wadi systems). The former, the Husan Ridge Route, carries traffic from the region of Etam south of Bethlehem into both the Sorek and Elah Valleys, to the Judean cities of Beth-shemesh and Socoh (spelled Soco in 2 Chr 11:7; 28:18) respectively. The latter, the Beth-zur Ridge Route, connects the Hebron Plateau at Halhul and Beth-zur to Adullam and Socoh below. The branch of the Husan Ridge Route that drops into the Elah Valley carried the Roman Road connecting Jerusalem with Gaza in the second century AD.[1] If we look carefully, we can see Philip going that way for his evangelistic meeting with the Ethiopian eunuch (Acts 8:26–28), and, much earlier, the shepherd boy David carrying bread and cheese (the products of Bethlehem's mixed economy) as he picks his way among rocks and thorns down to the Philistine line (1 Sam 17:17–19). A paved highway (Route 375) traces this natural line of the Husan Ridge Route today.

In noticeable contrast to its eastern and western defiles, the watershed ridge is approached relatively easily from the south, via Beer-sheba and Arad. As noted above, these routes were a favorite for long-distance trade, though they rarely witnessed military invasion; Israel's failed attempt to conquer the land from the direction of Hormah and Arad in the Negev is indication enough of that (Num 14:39–45; 21:1–3; 33:40).[2] More important are the natural routes that enter the Judean hills from the north, via the land of Benjamin and the city of Jerusalem. Historically, Jerusalem's economic lifeline and military priorities ran through Benjamin. As went the capital, so went its dependent cities and villages round about. This reality defines Benjamin as the primary gateway into and out of northern Judah (see Section F below).

The historic associations of the Hill Country of Judah reach back to Abraham, who traversed its length from north to south as he *"journeyed by stages to the Negev"* (Gen 12:9). Abraham frequented the vicinity of Hebron; seasonal migration patterns likely put him there in the summertime and down in the Negev at Beer-sheba during the winter. In every case he represents the timeless historic reality of necessary, though uneasy, economic interaction which takes place on the seam between "the desert and the sown."[3] It was likely high in the Hebron hills that God showed Abraham the vast expanse of stars that fill the nighttime skies, daring him to limit through counting the number of descendants that would flow from his loins. With no artificial light to temper the view, Abraham's night sky was boundless, the starry host at the same time distant yet penetratingly close. (The Middle Eastern nighttime skies, especially in its more arid climes, are among the most powerful sights on earth.) Eventually Abraham purchased a family burial cave at Machpelah, near the oaks of Mamre on the outskirts of Hebron (Gen 13:18; 23:2–20; 35:27; 37:14). In a tussle for priority of memory, both Jews and Muslims claim the city as ancestral land today. As various Israelite clans began to settle the Judean hills sometime after the conquest of Joshua, the Hebron Plateau and points south became home to descendants of Caleb (Josh 14:6–15; Judg 1:11–15; 1 Chr 2:42–50), while the region of Bethlehem was settled by the Hur branch of the Ephrathah clan (1 Chr 2:50–51; 4:4–8).

Bethlehem, of course, has gained fame beyond its expected due because of its associations with the house and lineage of David (cp. Luke 2:4). The city that faces the open wilderness was the scene of the story of Ruth, David's Moabite great-grandmother, heroine of a pastoral narrative of land rights set in a town ravaged by famine,

A couple days of heavy winter rain and the wadis flow with swollen banks in the Judean hills. This is the upper Sorek Valley west of Jerusalem, enjoying an after-storm haze of moisture. *"He waters the mountains from his palace,"* the psalmist sang; *"the earth is satisfied by the fruit of your labor"* (Ps 104:13). The downside for local village farmers is betrayed by the color of the water: the brown-red tint comes from terra rosa soil, slowly eroding the upper Judean hills into rocky heights but depositing the mud as alluvium in the Shephelah foothills down below. Spring growth abounds, the promise of renewal as sure as the moisture in the air.

1 Zecharia Kallai, "Remains of the Roman Road along the Mevo-Beitar Highway," *IEJ* 15 (1985): 195–203.

2 In preparation for their assault on Jerusalem in 1917, the British under Allenby captured Beer-sheba, the spot in the central Negev that controlled access to the watershed ridge route from the south, from the Ottoman Turks. Allenby's route of attack on Jerusalem, however, did not proceed up the watershed but circled around to the coastal plain on the west, then climbed into the hills via the Beth-horon Ridge Route. See George Adam Smith, *The Historical Geography of the Holy Land*, 30th ed. (Jerusalem: Ariel Publishing House, 1966), 196–97.

3 The phrase "the desert and the sown," popularized by the iconic English adventure traveler Gertrude Bell more than a hundred years ago, recognizes the close proximity of arable to nonarable zones of land in the Middle East and the symbiotic relationships of persons dwelling in each with the other. Gertrude Bell, *The Desert and the Sown* (London: William Heinemann, 1907).

then restored by the rainfall blessings of God. Though a native of Bethlehem, David chose to lay the groundwork for his kingdom among Judah's more established power structures in and around Hebron (1 Sam 30:31; 2 Sam 2:3–4; 3:2–5,19). His base of operations stretched from the shepherd land southeast of Hebron (Ziph, Carmel, and Maon; 1 Sam 23:14; 25:2–42) to the western hills above Keilah and Adullam (1 Sam 23:1–13; 22:1; 2 Sam 23:13). David eventually moved his capital north to Jerusalem, but the old power base at Hebron continued to pull political strings in the royal family (2 Sam 15:7–10).

After the division of the united kingdom, the borders of Judah encompassed land *"from Geba to Beer-sheba"* (2 Kgs 23:8), a tacit realization that the heartland of the truncated Southern Kingdom clung to the rocky length of the Judean watershed ridge. Attempts to push outward, especially into the lower elevations of the coastal plain and to the trade routes of the wilderness beyond the Negev, met with limited success. There is archaeological evidence that the Judean kings erected a series of watchtowers on vantage points throughout the high Hill Country of Judah in order to maintain line-of-sight communication between Jerusalem and points below.[2] Seizing the reality of the image, the Judean prophets Isaiah, Ezekiel, and Habakkuk all pictured themselves as watchmen on the wall (Isa 21:6–9; Ezek 3:17; 33:7; Hab 2:1). It takes but little imagination to hear them sound the alarm as their land—its natural and manmade fortifications encircling the high Cenomanian-Turonian hills breached—was overrun by enemies. It's only fitting that the Prince of Peace was a Judean from Bethlehem, a village squeezed between Hebron and Jerusalem yet representing the potential promise of this most essential region of the land of ancient Israel.

Numerous storage jars bearing stamped seal impressions showing two- or four-winged scarabs have been found at sites throughout Judah dating to the end of the eighth century BC. Each seal bears the Hebrew inscription *lmlk*, "belonging to the king," and the name of one of four cities: Hebron, Ziph, Socoh, and *mmšt*, the latter perhaps a reference to the center of government in Jerusalem. These jars, apparently part of Hezekiah's war effort against the Assyrians, carried commodities (perhaps wine or oil) that had either originated on royal lands or were destined for government (i.e., troop) use. In any case, the cities mentioned on the seals likely represent four different ecosystems of Judah, three in the high hill country (north—*mmšt*; south—Hebron; southeast—Ziph) and one in the upper central Shephelah (Socoh), together attesting to the economic unity of the region.[1]

Terraces, both ancient and modern, trace Cenomanian-Turonian angles in a tight wadi near the Palestinian village of Husan, southwest of Bethlehem. Though wholly dependent on runoff rainfall (Deut 11:11), local farmers have coaxed life from these rocks for millennia, giving persistent testimony to Isaiah's image of *"a vineyard on a very fertile hill"* (Isa 5:1). Terrace walls are crucial to the whole endeavor: they hold onto moisture and soil and keep passers-by away (cp. Song 2:15; Isa 5:5). The scene speaks of the immense effort to build and maintain a quiet life to enjoy.

B. THE JUDEAN SHEPHELAH

The biblical Hebrew word *shephelah*, "low[land]" or "foothills," is a technical geographical term that almost always refers to the contiguous zone of Eocene limestone and Senonian chalk foothills separating the Judean hill country from the coastal plain.[3] Because the Shephelah lies west of the Hill Country of

1 Illustrator photo, British Museum, London (31/20/62).

2 Amihai Mazar, "Iron Age Fortresses in the Judean Hills," *PEQ* 114 (July-December 1982): 87–109.

3 The Bible identifies another region by the same term, namely the area of low Eocene limestone in the vicinity of Mount Carmel and Galilee (Josh 11:2, 16). That Shephelah, located in the north, will be discussed in connection with the Carmel Range and Lower Galilee, chapters 4.D and 5.C below.

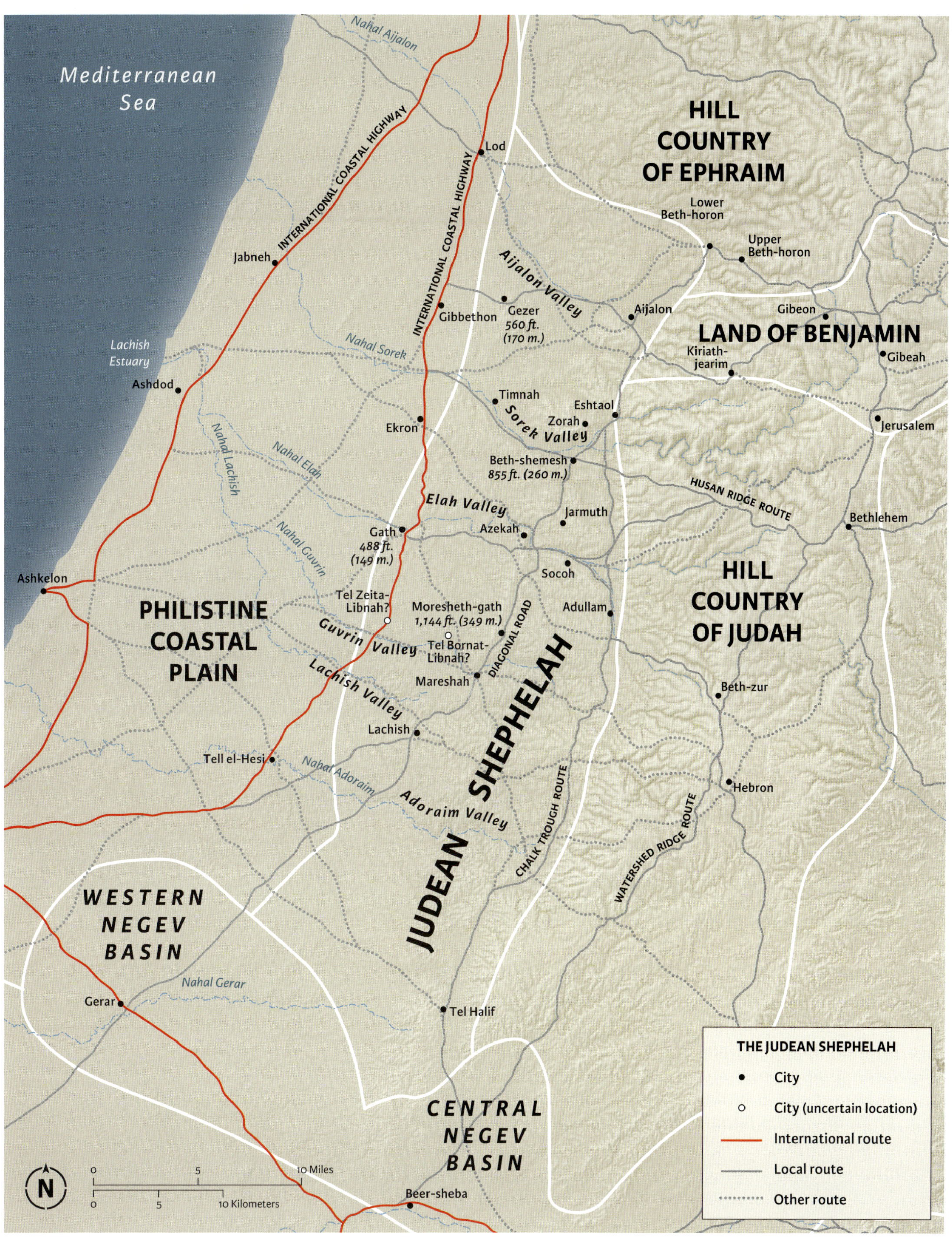
Mediterranean Sea
Nahal Aijalon
HILL COUNTRY OF EPHRAIM
INTERNATIONAL COASTAL HIGHWAY
Lod
INTERNATIONAL COASTAL HIGHWAY
Lower Beth-horon
Upper Beth-horon
Jabneh
Aijalon Valley
Aijalon
Gibeon
Gibbethon
Gezer 560 ft. (170 m.)
LAND OF BENJAMIN
Lachish Estuary
Nahal Sorek
Kiriath-jearim
Gibeah
Ashdod
Timnah
Eshtaol
Zorah
Jerusalem
Sorek Valley
Ekron
Nahal Lachish
Nahal Elah
Beth-shemesh 855 ft. (260 m.)
HUSAN RIDGE ROUTE
Elah Valley
Jarmuth
Bethlehem
Nahal Guvrin
Gath 488 ft. (149 m.)
Azekah
Socoh
HILL COUNTRY OF JUDAH
Ashkelon
Tel Zeita-Libnah?
Moresheth-gath 1,144 ft. (349 m.)
Adullam
PHILISTINE COASTAL PLAIN
DIAGONAL ROAD
Guvrin Valley
Tel Bornat-Libnah?
Lachish Valley
Mareshah
Beth-zur
JUDEAN SHEPHELAH
Lachish
Tell el-Hesi
Nahal Adoraim
Hebron
Adoraim Valley
CHALK TROUGH ROUTE
WATERSHED RIDGE ROUTE
WESTERN NEGEV BASIN
Nahal Gerar
Gerar
Tel Halif
CENTRAL NEGEV BASIN
Beer-sheba
0 5 10 Miles
0 5 10 Kilometers
N
THE JUDEAN SHEPHELAH
City
City (uncertain location)
International route
Local route
Other route

A time-worn Muslim grave atop Gath of the Philistines (Tell es-Safi) overlooks the Shephelah with a view to the east. In the foreground are the lower hills of the western, coast-oriented section of the Shephelah. The dark mid-level horizon line marks the rise to the higher, eastern part of the Shephelah, while the crest of the Hill Country of Judea rises in the distance beyond. Goliath was at home in the flatter foreground; David was so on the rise of the far horizon. Line of sight tends to draw people from the coast upward toward the hills or from the hill country back down, climbing or descending through the Shephelah as on a broad staircase.

Judah, some English Bibles render the term "*western* foothills" (e.g., Josh 10:40, NIV) or even "*Judean* foothills" (CSB). These adjectives are helpful, though not integral to the meaning of the word *shephelah per se*. A more poetic translation might be "humble hills,"[1] especially when we compare their slumped form to the Judean hills rising majestically to the east, though the modifier "humble" should stand aside to the strategic role that the Shephelah played in the geopolitics of ancient Judah.

The foothills making up the Judean Shephelah descend from the western edge of the Hill Country of Judah, where elevations hang at approximately 1,500 feet (460 m), to the inner edge of the coastal plain ten miles (16 km) west and less than 500 feet (150 m) above sea level. The descent is gradual except for a rather sharp drop on a line drawn diagonally between the Shephelah's northeastern and southwestern corners. This rather prominent change in elevation tends to associate the inner, higher, eastern half of the Shep-

1 James C. Martin, John A. Beck, and David G. Hansen, *A Visual Guide to Bible Events* (Grand Rapids: Baker Books, 2009), 72.

helah with the towns and villages of the hill country, and the outer, lower, western half of the Shephelah with cities on the coastal plain. So, for instance, we would expect the phrase *"Socoh which belongs to Judah"* (1 Sam 17:1 NASB), inasmuch as Socoh was in the eastern, upper half of the Shephelah's Elah Valley, or the note *"Samson went down to Timnah and saw a young Philistine woman there"* (Judg 14:1), since Timnah was in the outer and hence Philistine section of the Sorek Valley.

Geologically, a thin seam of Senonian chalk can be traced along the entire length of the line where the hard Cenomanian-Turonian limestone of the Judean hill country meets the weaker Eocene foothills of the Shephelah. This seam of soft chalk has eroded into a long, narrow trough stretching from the city of Aijalon in the north down to Tel Halif, above Beer-sheba, in the south. The trough is most noticeable in the area of the Sorek and Elah wadi systems, where it has formed a line of north-south valleys leveling out at approximately 800 feet (245 m) in elevation, noticeably lower than the elevation of the hills on either side. This chalk trough served as a natural moat providing an important line of defense for the cities and villages of Judah during the biblical period.

The most prominent landforms of the Shephelah, however, are the six valleys that transverse its width, east to west, and serve as connectors between the Judean hill country and the coastal plain. From north to south these are the Aijalon (Wadi Selman), Sorek (Wadi es-Surar), Elah (Wadi es-Sunt), Guvrin (Wadi el-Afranj), Lachish (Wadi Qubeibah), and Adoraim (Wadi el-Hesi). Five will be recognized as the wadi systems that drain the Hill Country of Judah (see Section A above). The northernmost, the Aijalon, carries runoff from the western hills of Benjamin. Each was formed as water flowing out of the deep, V-shaped ravines of the hard limestone hill country eroded the softer limestone mass of the Shephelah into more relaxed forms. Unlike the deep, V-shaped valleys of the hard limestone Judean hills, the valleys of the Shephelah are shallow, broad, and filled with rich expanses of mixed alluvial soil. Proceeding southward, each valley in turn is slightly narrower than the one lying immediately to its north.

The northernmost of the Shephelah's valleys, the Aijalon, is the most favored in terms of resources. It is also the only valley of the six that was formed not just as a result of water runoff, but in part as a down-faulted basin. The long sides of the inner section of the

This valley is the chalk trough that separates the strong rise of the Hill Country of Judah (right) from the softer hills of the Shephelah (left). Two tall towers carrying high voltage power lines cross the scene left to right in the distance, bringing electrical current from a substation near Tell es-Safi, ancient Gath of the Philistines, to metropolitan Jerusalem. The towers march straight up the ridge between the Sorek and Elah wadi systems—a modern version of the age-old reality of coastal resources penetrating the hills.

Thousands of caves pock-mark the hills of the southern Judean Shephelah. Here a square door was cut into the soft Eocene limestone beneath a sturdy cap of nari, opening a snug living space behind. Scrub-covered Moresheth-gath (Tell el-Judeida), the likely location of the hometown of the prophet Micah (Mic 1:1,14), rises beyond.

Aijalon Valley were formed when three parallel fault lines ripped northeastward into the hill country from the northeastern corner of the Shephelah, causing the mass of bedrock between to collapse. As a result, the Aijalon Valley penetrates into the hill country more deeply than do the other five valleys of the Shephelah; it does so on a fairly direct line connecting Jerusalem with the port of Joppa. In terms of human settlement, the practical advantage of this geographical reality is obvious: the Aijalon has always served as the main transportation corridor between Jerusalem and the coast (Josh 10:12–13; 1 Sam 14:31; 1 Kgs 9:15–17; 1 Macc 3:13; Josephus *War* 2.521).

The northern third of the Judean Shephelah, the hills surrounding the Aijalon Valley and those lining the northern side of the Sorek Valley, is actually composed of a relatively hard variety of Senonian chalk, while the southern two thirds is composed of a weak Eocene limestone that becomes softer and chalkier the further south we go. Even so, from anywhere within the Shephelah the close horizon line is rather monotonous, filled by low, featureless hills covered by a limey nari crust that is ashen gray in color and rough to the touch. The entire region is pocked with caves, especially in the south; many of these are natural, but others are the result of human activity in mining chalk for plaster—a practice common since at least the late centuries BC.

The rocky hills of the Shephelah are nearly useless for agriculture due to their nari covering (terraced agriculture is absent here). However, a natural growth of scrub brush, low oaks, terebinth (Hb *elah*, the name of the central valley of the Shephelah), poplar, carob, and seasonal grasses allow grazing. Judah's King Uzziah recognized the suitability of the hills of the Shephelah for his royal herds, and *"had many cattle both in the Judean foothills and the plain"* (2 Chr 26:10). The redeeming factor of nari is that it can be cut into durable stone blocks, thus making it the building material of choice in the Shephelah in ancient times. Cities such as Gezer, Beth-shemesh, Azekah, and Lachish were all built from this local stone, giving them a rough, grayish look that contrasted with the more angular, tan-to-golden building stones of structures made of Cenomanian-Turonian limestone in the hill country. Many of the prominent towns of the Shephelah were located on rocky rises adjacent to the fertile valley floors, sustained mostly by wells (such as at Lachish) or cisterns since springs are scarce in the Shephelah and none are comparable in flow to the springs of the hill country above.

The transversal valleys of the Shephelah and those that form the chalk trough defining the Shephelah's eastern edge are the most fertile parts of the region. Their potential for life provided more than enough incentive to draw the Judeans out of the hill country and into the lowlands below. Soils here are a mixture of the dark rendzina and brown forest types which, when combined with the alluvial downwash of terra rosa from the Cenomanian-Turonian hills above, produces a fertile base especially suitable for grain (Judg 15:5). Orchard crops, too, do well in the Judean Shephelah, so much so that the region was famed for groves of sycamore fig trees (likely *Ficus sycomorus*) during the biblical period (Judg 15:5; 1 Kgs 10:27). Good King Uzziah was, we read, *"a lover of the soil"* (2 Chr 26:10). David even found it expedient to appoint an official in charge of royal olive and sycamore orchards in the Shephelah (a man named Baal-hanan from Geder, a town not yet identified but probably located in the southern part of the region; 1 Chr 27:28; cp. Josh 12:11–14). On a modern note, the valleys surrounding the Israeli town of Lachish, adjacent to the ancient site, continue to produce some of the finest grapes grown in the country.

Barley and wheat, long staples of the Judean Shephelah, thrive during the region's mild winters. The cycle of seasons turns valley fields to harvest gold by late spring, then all too quickly to thistly brown for summer days that are just plain hot. Television weather reports announce summertime temperatures in the Judean Shephelah that are typically warmer than those of both the coastal plain and the hill country. Fortunately, cooler air from the Judean hills slides down

A look west from the top of Mareshah (Tell Sandahannah) takes in the flow of the low-slung Guvrin Valley, its soil alternately plowed or sprouting carpets of green that will become fields of grain. A nearly imperceptible rise of low, rocky hills lines the valley's snaked form, boasting only weedy grasses and sparse shrubs on their nari-encrusted slopes.

"The king [Solomon] made silver as common in Jerusalem as stones, and he made cedar as abundant as sycamore in the Judean foothills" (1 Kgs 10:27). Solomon apparently dealt in costly metals and wood rather than the everyday stuff of Judah. While the sycamore isn't exactly a scrub tree—it can attain to heights of more than thirty feet (9 m)—it does look a bit ratty, filled with short twigs poking every direction from every spot on its trunk and branches. Attached to each twig are clusters of small, soft globs of fruit—a kind of poor man's fig—first light green in color, then ripening to yellow and red-pink as pictured. Single sycamore trees can be found standing in many isolated spots in the southern Shephelah and coastal plain today; they are remnants of what must have been large stands at the time of the Bible. A note of spelling is in order: it is more accurate to refer to these trees as *sycomores* (reflecting their Latin nomenclature *Ficus sycomorus*), leaving the name *sycamore* for *Platanus occidentalis*, the species better known in North America.

onto the upper (eastern) Shephelah many summer nights, providing a welcome touch of dew that helps sustain its summer fruit. It was during the heat of a late spring harvest that Samson, in a fit of righteous rage, set fire to the standing grain that filled the fields of the Philistines around Timnah, burning nearby olive groves and vineyards in the process (Judg 15:3–5). One spring a generation or so later, David drove the Philistines out of the threshing floors of Keilah. This was in response to Judah's coastal nemesis making a deep incursion into the fertile Elah Valley section of the chalk trough, nearly crippling the local economy (1 Sam 23:1–13).

Though the fields of the Judean Shephelah easily support its local population, natural and man-made disasters—drought, plague, and invasion—always seem to lurk close at hand. This living dynamic ensures that the residents of the Shephelah have faced more than their fair share of risk. The region is both a bridge and a buffer; it links and yet separates peoples living in the hills and those on the coast. Its story is not its own, but is inherently tied to persistent neighbors to the east or west. Although the resources of the Shephelah have always supported many large cities and "countless small villages in their vicinity" (to borrow a line from an interested Assyrian king, Sennacherib),[1] the whole never formed a unified government in the way the peoples of the Judean hill country or the coastal plain were able to do. Instead, the fortunes of the Shephelah have tended to fall to the reach of whomever was stronger on either side, and often were carved up between the two.[2] As such, they evidence the true character of a "land between" within the Land Between.

It is helpful to envision the six transversal valleys of the Judean Shephelah as busy corridors or hallways carrying traffic between the hill country and the coast. Cities spaced along the length of each acted somewhat like saloon doors of the old American Wild West, swinging back and forth as traffic burst on through, first one way and then the other. Of course, in times of peace all of this signaled brisk economic and cultural activity (we should not think that Samson's romp in Timnah was his first visit to the city; Judg 14:1), and everyone benefited by the comings and goings of all.[3] But when national aspirations in the hills were strong, or when peoples on the coastal plain sought to expand their influence politically or militarily, the corridors and doorways of the Shephelah became the focus of a prolonged struggle for control. *"Philistia from the west [has] consumed Israel with open mouths"* (Isa 9:12), we read, just as Judah would *"swoop down on the Philistine flank to the west"* (Isa 11:14). It seemed natural for the Philistines or the coastal dwelling Hellenists to penetrate into the Shephelah since they viewed the wide-open western ends of its transversal valleys as extensions of the coastal plain. For the rocky top Judeans who gazed over the hills of the upper Shephelah from across the chalk moat, on the other hand, these broad valleys were a risky yet necessary frontier to be seized.

Two well-known stories from the Old Testament have this exact setting. Samson's struggles against the Philistines saw him trying to force open doorways in the upper and mid-Sorek Valley (at Zorah and Timnah, respectively) in favor of Danite penetration to the west (Judg 14:1–16:31). That ended in a draw. A generation or two later, the thrust by Goliath of Gath and his Philistine compatriots to Azekah and then *"Socoh in Judah"* was a nearly successful attempt to swing open the doorways of the Elah Valley the other direction (1 Sam 17:1–52). Because the Sorek and Elah Valleys control branches of the Husan Ridge Route leading directly to Bethlehem,

1 James B. Pritchard, ed., *Ancient Near Eastern Texts relating to the Old Testament (ANET)* (Princeton: Princeton University Press, 1955), 288.

2 Anson Rainey, "The Biblical Shephelah of Judah," *BASOR* 251 (1983): 1–10.

3 Ron E. Tappy, "East of Ashkelon: The Setting and Settling of the Judean Lowlands in the Iron Age IIA," in J. David Schloen, ed., *Exploring the Longue Durée: Essays in Honor of Lawrence E. Stager* (Winona Lake, IN: Eisenbrauns, 2009), 449–61 speaks of a "riverine network" of natural routes that follow the east-west valleys of the Shephelah and function as corridors for trade and economic cooperation.

Rich alluvial soil surrounds the level Sorek Valley plain around the low mound of Tel Batash (Tell el-Batashi), site of biblical Timnah. With a strong resource base and easy highway connections, this Philistine city offered an attractive alternative for hill country folk trying to scratch a living in the tight places above. The Danite Samson was drawn to its possibilities (Judg 14:1–4; cp. 19:40–46). As would be expected for a city in the outer Shephelah, the archaeological record shows that Timnah's fortunes rose whenever stable political conditions held sway, but fell under threat from either the coast or the hills.

trouble in either of the two valleys down below was a cause for immediate concern by residents of the hill country above.

Archaeological evidence tells essentially the same story.[1] Dozens of sites in the Shephelah have been excavated, including many of the larger ones. A comparative analysis of their material culture allows archaeologists and historical geographers to track the settlement patterns of people groups in the Shephelah over time. The big picture revealed by archaeology attests to an incursion of coastal people (likely the Philistines) eastward into the Shephelah during Iron Age I, followed by a countermove from the Judean hills westward through the valleys of the Shephelah during the first half of Iron Age II. This has every appearance of corroborating, at least in outline, the movement of Judeans into the Shephelah during the monarchy that is described in the Old Testament. The archaeological evidence then shows massive destruction throughout the region in the late eighth century BC, indication enough of another move from the coast, this time by Assyrian King Sennacherib. The confluence of textual and archaeological evidence for this back and forth dynamic in the valleys of the Shephelah supports its characterization as a liminal zone[2] connecting two larger yet diverse entities (the hill country and the coast).

1 Note especially the essays in Oded Lipschitz and Aren M. Maeir, eds., *The Shephelah during the Iron Age: Recent Archaeological Studies* (Winona Lake, IN: Eisenbrauns, 2017); and Avraham Faust, "The Shephelah in the Iron Age: A New Look on the Settlement of Judah," *PEQ* 145/3 (2013): 203–19.

2 For the characterization of the outer Shephelah as a liminal zone, see Ron E. Tappy, "The Archaeology and History of Tel Zayit: A Record of Liminal Life," in Oded Lipschitz and Aren M. Maeir, eds., *The Shephelah during the Iron Age: Recent Archaeological Studies* (Winona Lake, IN: Eisenbrauns, 2017), 155–79.

Throughout, the chalk trough played an important (though not unassailable) defensive role for Judah, supporting the maxim that taking the lowland was no guarantee of taking the hills. The trough's eastern edge is defined by the strong, closed line of the Judean hill country, while its western side lies open to the transversal valleys of the Shephelah. Geographical common sense would suggest it was in the trough that *"the Philistines were standing on one hill, and the Israelites [under Saul] were standing on another hill with a ravine* [Hb *gai*, "steep valley," i.e., the trough functioning as a moat] *between them"* (1 Sam 17:3).[1] Saul would not have wanted to expose his hill country forces in the open terrain of the Philistine-controlled Shephelah, while the flat-lander Philistines must have been wary of the threat of ambush in the closed-in ravines of the hill country. Jesse of Bethlehem sent his oldest sons down to hold the line (1 Sam 17:13). Should the Philistines break through, Jesse's ancestral homeland lay just a quick run up the Husan Ridge, with Gibeah, hometown of Saul, a short hook to the left.[2] A similar situation unfolded in the mid-eighth century BC when, in the days of Judah's King Ahaz, the Philistines *"raided the cities of the Judean foothills . . . and captured Beth-shemesh, Aijalon, Gederoth, Socoh and its villages, Timnah and its villages, Gimzo and its villages, and they lived there"* (2 Chr 28:18). These were places up to, but not across, the chalk trough. In modern times, the trough was roughly the 1948 armistice line between the State of Israel and the West Bank of the Hashemite Kingdom of Jordan.

A second important line of defense for Judah can be drawn a little further out, along the diagonal that indicates the drop in elevation separating the upper (inner) from the lower (outer) Shephelah. During the

Students of biblical geography explore remains of the six-chambered Solomonic city gate of Gezer, part of the Israelite king's efforts to draw that city into the socio-economic orbit of Jerusalem. The gate opened eastward into the broad Aijalon Valley where it received the route from Lower Beth-horon and Jerusalem, high in the hills above. Solomon's rights to Gezer, a city that was conquered during his lifetime by Egypt's Pharaoh Siamun, were sealed by a marriage alliance involving an Egyptian princess. By it, the two kingdoms shared in the work and rewards of protecting long-distance commercial activities on the coast (1 Kgs 9:15–17).

1 James M. Monson, *The Land Between* (Jerusalem: James M. Monson, 1983), 202. Reconstructions of the story that give a prominent role to the site of Khirbet Qeiyafa, a Judean fortress close to Azekah that dates to the time of the early Judean monarchy, need to place the battle somewhere out in the more exposed contours of the Shephelah instead. See, for example, Yigal Levin, "The Identification of Khirbet Qeiyafa: A New Suggestion," *BASOR* 367 (2012): 73–86.

2 Jerusalem, between Bethlehem and Gibeah, would not have been a threat to the Philistines since it was still Jebusite and not yet a part of the expanding Israelite kingdom.

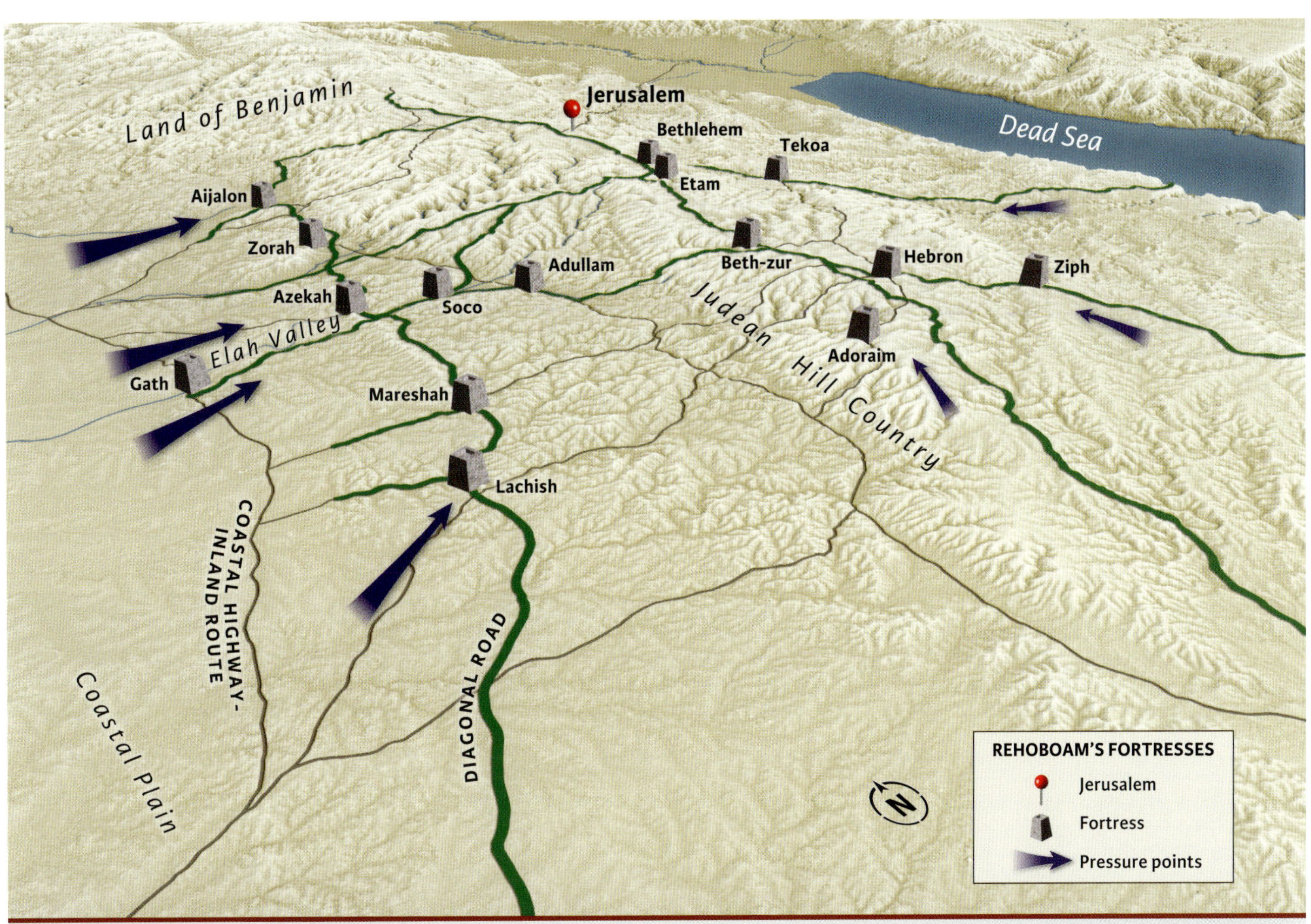

Placed on a map of the road system of the kingdom of Judah, Rehoboam's fortresses (2 Chr 11:5–12) make perfect strategic sense. Each guarded an important juncture on the network of natural routes leading to Jerusalem. The blue arrows indicate pressure points on Jerusalem from the outside. From the confluence of fortresses in and around the Elah Valley, we can conclude that Rehoboam knew all too well that that valley held the key to routes entering Judah's vulnerable midsection (Hebron to Bethlehem), and it appears he most feared an Egyptian attack that way. Rehoboam failed to fortify points north, in the allotment of Benjamin. Perhaps he felt that by doing so, he would be admitting that anything that lay beyond Benjamin no longer fell under his rightful control—a difficult pill for the son of Solomon, monarch of the great united kingdom of Israel, to swallow. In the end, Shishak attacked precisely as feared, coming through Aijalon and the land of Benjamin, as we can infer from Shishak's list of conquered cities preserved on the outer wall of the great hypostyle courtyard at the Karnak Temple in Egypt.[1] Rehoboam quickly capitulated (2 Chr 12:1–12), and the united kingdom's days were forever over.

Judean monarchy, a string of cities marked this natural boundary: Aijalon in the Aijalon Valley, Beth-shemesh in the Sorek Valley, Azekah in the Elah Valley, Mareshah in the Guvrin Valley, and Lachish in the Lachish Valley. An ancient natural route joined these cities on the diagonal (the approximate line of modern highway 38), making use of angled branches of the Shephelah's transversal valleys to join one to the next. The northern end of this diagonal road joins the natural route that runs up the Beth-horon Ridge to Gibeon and Jerusalem. This was the front line of the fortification system built by Rehoboam *"for defense in Judah"* (2 Chr 11:5–12 NASB). Rehoboam drew his shrinking kingdom back up into the hills and out of the easy reach of Pharaoh Shishak, who attacked Judah after the death of Rehoboam's father, Solomon, and the inevitable collapse of Judah's royal marriage alliance with Egypt (2 Chr 12:1–4). Rehoboam was all

The first century AD historian Flavius Josephus knew well the difficulties of establishing a harbor at Joppa. He wrote,

"Nature has not provided Joppa with a port. It terminates in a rugged shore, which runs for nearly its whole length in a straight line, but is slightly curved at its two extremities in crescent fashion; these horns consist of steep cliffs and reefs jutting far out into the deep; here are still shown the impressions of Andromeda's chains [an off-shore rock formation], to attest to the antiquity of the legend. The north wind, beating full force upon the coast, dashes the waves high against the face of the rocks and renders this roadstead more perilous to sailors than the watery waste" (*War* 3.419–422).

In spite of Josephus's negative assessment, the "slight curve" of the Joppa coast offered better protection than could be found for other coastal cities in the vicinity, giving its port at least some hope for natural viability.

1 Yohanan Aharoni, *The Land of the Bible: A Historical Geography*, Revised and Enlarged Edition trans. and ed. by A. F. Rainey (Philadelphia: The Westminster Press, 1979), 323–30; and Anson F. Rainey and R. Steven Notley, *The Sacred Bridge: Carta's Atlas of the Biblical World*, 2d. Emended & Enhanced Ed. (Jerusalem: Carta, 2014), 186–89.

about hunkering down in mouse-holes and letting the cat-lands go to the cats.

Egyptian power waned after Shishak's attack in the late tenth century BC, but the subsequent struggle for political and economic control of the Shephelah by the Philistines, Israel, and Judah ("mouse" vs. "mouse" vs. "mouse") kept everyone on their toes for the next two centuries. Things heated up in the mid-eighth century BC as Assyria, a sharp-clawed "cat," reached Israel and then Judah on its bare fanged prowl to Egypt. Judah's King Hezekiah took a stand by fortifying many of the cities of the Shephelah, including those on Rehoboam's old diagonal road, in an attempt to protect the direct routes leading from the coast to Jerusalem. Assyria's King Sennacherib boasts to have "laid siege to forty-six of [Hezekiah's] strong cities, walled forts, and to countless small villages in their vicinity,"[1] a large portion of which must have been in the Shephelah. But Hezekiah's strategy was all for naught. In 701 BC Sennacherib's war machine blew the doorways of the Shephelah's valleys inward and marched all the way to the Judean capital, trapping Hezekiah, the Assyrian king would later boast, "like a bird in a cage."[2] The prophet Isaiah summed it up this way: "*Your best valleys were full of chariots, and horsemen were positioned at the gates. He removed the defenses of Judah*" (Isa 22:7–8).

The Babylonian army under Nebuchadnezzar did the same just more than a century later, ripping through the Judean Shephelah and this time taking Jerusalem as well (Jer 34:6–7; 39:1–10). With Nebuchadnezzar's conquest, the balance of power in the Shephelah tipped away from Judah and toward the coast for the long haul. In the centuries between the Testaments, points in the southern Shephelah as close as Mareshah were overrun and settled by Idumeans, descendants of the Edomites. Following Alexander the Great's march down the coast in 332 BC, the entire region was easily penetrated by the tentacles of Hellenism. In response, the Hasmoneans (Maccabees), a Jewish family from the village of Modi'in in the far northwestern corner of the Shephelah, waged

Foundation and wall remains of a once-formidable Judean royal palace dominate the broad rise of Tell ed-Duweir, ancient Lachish. Overgrown remains of the city gate lie below (left). Located at the outer end of the next-to-southernmost of the Shephelah's valleys, Lachish held the tail of the so-called Diagonal Road, Judah's western line of defense. Hezekiah's fortifications at Lachish were strong (two walls circled the site) and protected a crack chariot corps aimed at controlling the flatlands of the southern coast. Note Micah 1:13: *"Harness the horses to the chariot, you residents of Lachish."* When Judah was able to hold Lachish, as in the days of Hezekiah, we can assume that all of the gateways of the Shephelah further north and east also lay securely in Jerusalem's hand. Assyria's King Sennacherib apparently knew this as well; he responded by first attacking key doorway cities in the Sorek and Elah Valleys (Timnah, Ekron, Azekah, and Gath) to isolate Lachish, before laying siege to the then-doomed city itself.

1 *ANET*, 288; William W. Hallo, gen. ed., *The Context of Scripture*, Vol. II: *Monumental Inscriptions from the Biblical World* (Leiden: Brill, 2000), 303.

2 Ibid.

a successful war against the Seleucids, cultural and political heirs of Alexander's empire, in the second century BC (1 Macc 2). But with Pompey's sack of Jerusalem in 63 BC and the advent of Roman imperial might in Judaea, the doorways of the Shephelah quickly and permanently opened to the interests of the West. Unable to stem the tide, Jews living in the Shephelah during the time of the New Testament either tended to accommodate the new ways of the world or headed to the relative safety of the hills surrounding Jerusalem.

This was the all-too-often reality of the Judean Shephelah. Gazing down from his caged hill country home at the end of the Old Testament period, the prophet Obadiah voiced the simple yet elusive hope of the residents of Judah: "*[Someday, people from] the Judean foothills will possess the land of the Philistines*" (Obad 19). And whenever Jerusalem was able to control even a part of the Shephelah, this realization actually seemed possible.

C. THE PHILISTINE COASTAL PLAIN

The Philistine Coastal Plain stretches fifty miles (80 km) north-south, from the short and swampy Yarkon River north of Joppa to the great bend of the Nahal Besor south of Gaza, the border of Sinai (cp. 1 Sam 30:9–10). The plain is ten miles (16 km) wide in the north but broadens to a width of twenty-five miles (40 km) in the south as the coastline of the Mediterranean sweeps away gradually to the west. Though this section of Israel's coast had its own regional integrity as the homeland of the Philistines during the days of the Israelite monarchy, it is perhaps better viewed as a wide-open through route, an international corridor connecting Egypt with Mesopotamia and the Judean hill country with the sea.

Though gently bowed, this Philistine portion of Israel's coastline is considered straight-line in the sense that, with the exception of a small rounded hook at Joppa and the narrow openings of two estuaries as the outlets of the Sorek and Lachish wadis, no natural harbor can be found along its entire length—and these barely suffice. No island lies off shore; no mountains rising from the edge of the sea offer enclosed bays to protect ships seeking anchorage from storm. Given the strong line of natural ports from Acco to Byblos in the north, nothing obvious prompts a ship that is large enough to ply the waters of the Mediterranean to want to put ashore here; neither does it compel a highland villager to venture past the shoreline dunes to the sea. On this criterion alone, the difference between the worlds of Judah and Phoenicia could not have been greater. Nevertheless, the infrastructure requirements of international trade overrode these geographical

The modern city of Ashdod, rising in white blocks on the edge of the Mediterranean Sea, backs up onto the scrub-covered sand dunes that line the water-washed shore. The view here is from atop Tel Ashdod, where the ancient equivalent to today's urban life at Ashdod once thrived. The marvels of modern infrastructure have allowed the dunes lining the Mediterranean to be tamed; in ancient times, the residents of Ashdod just let them lie. They were a barrier to cross on the way to their own small port at Tel Mor in the mouth of the Lachish estuary closer to water's edge.

Fishing boats and pleasure craft, modern vessels about the size of many of the commercial ships of the ancient world, tie up at the harbor of Jaffa (Yafo, ancient Joppa) in south Tel Aviv. All of the harbors of the Philistine Coastal Plain, both ancient and modern, including this one, were built with their entrances facing northwest—into the winter storms but away from the push of currents that would otherwise clog their openings with sand. The salmon-colored minaret on the right marks the traditional home of Simon the Tanner, where Peter stayed on his journey to the coast (Acts 9:43). In the first century AD, Joppa was a bit of a Jewish enclave between a Hellenized plain and a Gentile sea, a setting suited to illustrate God's call: *"What [I have] made clean, do not call impure"* (Acts 10:15).

THE PHILISTINE COASTAL PLAIN

- City
- City (uncertain location)
- International route
- Local route
- Other route

Mediterranean Sea
Yarkon River
Aphek
HILL COUNTRY OF EPHRAIM
Joppa
Ono
Nahal Aijalon
Valley of the Craftsmen
220 ft. (35 m.)
Lod
Brown-red Sands
Sand Dunes
Jabneh
Gezer
Gibbethon
Nahal Sorek
Lachish Estuary
Tel Mor
Ashdod
262 ft. (80 m.)
Ekron
Timnah
Nahal Lachish
Nahal Elah
JUDEAN SHEPHELAH
Gath 410 ft. (125 m.)
Jarmuth
Elah Valley
Azekah
Alluvial Soil
Nahal Guvrin
Ashkelon
PHILISTINE COASTAL PLAIN
INTERNATIONAL COASTAL HIGHWAY
Tel Bornat-Libnah?
Tel Zeita-Libnah?
DIAGONAL ROAD
Mareshah
Sand Dunes
INTERNATIONAL COASTAL HIGHWAY
384 ft. (117 m.)
Lachish
Tell el-Hesi
Nahal Adoraim
CHALK TROUGH ROUTE
Gaza
Steppe
HILL COUNTRY OF JUDAH
Tell al-Ajjul
Nahal Shiqma
Deir al-Balah
Nahal Gerar
Ziklag
Gerar
Nahal Besor
WESTERN NEGEV BASIN
HORUS ROAD
SINAI
CENTRAL NEGEV BASIN
N
Tell el-Farah
0 5 10 Miles
0 5 10 Kilometers
Beer-sheba

Philistia—where the tall corn grows. Maize was introduced to the Middle East from the New World relatively recently. Though tough and lacking in flavor compared to varieties of specialty sweet corn favored by North Americans, corn has quickly become a popular food for Arabs and Israeli Jews alike. This flat and fertile field belongs to Kibbutz Revadim, founded on the outskirts of Tel Miqne, biblical Ekron, a thriving Philistine city of the Iron Age (1 Sam 5:10). The Old English term *corn* is used in many older Bible translations (e.g., Job 24:6 KJV) and companion textbooks in its European sense, that is, to refer to wheat and barley, grains grown in these fields in ancient times; it should not be confused with the modern crop, native to North America, of the same name.

limitations as early as the third millennium BC, as Egyptian ships sought overnight harbors on their way to the ports of Phoenicia. In the process, Gaza, Ashkelon, Ashdod, and Joppa became sea terminals for the land routes of the southern Levant. Even so, the kings of Jerusalem were rarely able to control these ports, and for Judah the coastline was less a gateway to new worlds than a clear border enclosing theirs. We note that in Numbers 34:6 and Joshua 15:11–12 the western border of Judah was drawn at the edge of the sea; it is unlikely the Phoenicians would have considered the sea theirs!

Most of the Philistine seacoast is lined by sand dunes reaching up to three miles (5 km) inland, which serve as impediments to travel. The finest of the dune sand originates in the Sudan and Upper Egypt, from where it is carried by the Nile into the Mediterranean and mixed with other, coarser material. The prevailing currents then push this sand eastward toward the Levantine coast. The dunes are largest in Philistia, where the sand is driven ashore at the Mediterranean's southeastern bend; they taper off north of Joppa once the currents, directed northward by the sweeping angle of the shoreline, run parallel to the coast. Older, stabilized dunes lying inland from the Philistine shore have become covered by a scattering of grasses, brush, and scrub. Until recently, all of these dunes were largely devoid of permanent human settlement (recreational beach activities were totally foreign to people in the ancient Judean world). The only true cities located right on the water, Joppa and Ashkelon, clung to the shore at breaks in the dunes.

Behind the coastal dunes the broad plain backing the Philistine shore is relatively flat, rising slowly but surely eastward to meet the hills of the Shephelah. The mid-section of the Philistine Coastal Plain, land lying between Ashdod, Jabneh, Ekron, and Gath, is its lowest point, with sustained elevations of only 200 feet (60 m) above sea level. To the north, behind Joppa and modern Tel Aviv, the ground rises to elevations of more than 300 feet (90 m), while further south, between Gaza and Lachish, low rolling hills can exceed 600 feet (180 m). The wadis of the Shephelah merge into a few slow-moving drainage channels once out on the plain. Flowing northwestward, most of these wadis slump due north behind the coastal dunes, then bend west to cut their way through the dunes to the sea. The Aijalon wadi thus joins the Yarkon above Joppa, while the Elah and Guvrin wadis flow into the Lachish wadi in the plain's low point behind Ashdod. Except where they enter the Mediterranean as estuaries, these water channels are too narrow and silted to properly qualify as rivers; thus, shipping traffic penetrated the coastline primarily via land routes historically. Absent decent anchorage and lacking the real possibility of inland river traffic, the land rather than the sea is the focus of the Philistine Coastal Plain. It's a corridor blessed not only with a double line of the international trunk route but with near ideal conditions for agriculture.

In the third millennium BC, the Egyptians called the region of the Philistine Coastal Plain "the sand-dweller's land,"[1] a pejorative clearly intended to convey images of an open wasteland inhabited by desert savages. In contrast, the term they used for their own homeland was *kemet*, "the black land," a reference to the dark, rich soil of the Nile Valley where people were civilized and life was predictable. In spite of its clear Pharaoh-centrism, this view from ancient Egypt was not unfounded: be it in the form of dunes or mixed with alluvial soil, the entire southern coastal plain is indeed dominated by sand.

1 *ANET*, 228..

The northern third of the Philistine Coastal Plain, land lying between the Yarkon River and the outflow of the Sorek, is dominated by brown-red sands (*hamra*), a mixture of dune sand and alluvium. Rainfall amounts here average twenty inches (500 mm) annually. These soils drain well and are excellent for most crops, making the region prized for its fertility since ancient times. Today, this part of the coastal plain is famed for growing all kinds of citrus. While the Bible contains no direct references to citrus, an early rabbinic tradition (fourth–fifth c. AD) identifies the "majestic tree" of Leviticus 23:40, one of the four species Israelites were commanded to bring to the fall harvest festival of *Succot* (Tabernacles), as the citron (the *ethrog*).[1] How and when citrus first arrived in the lands of the Bible is unknown, though two popular suggestions credit either Jewish returnees from the Babylonian exile in the late sixth century BC or Alexander the Great two hundred years later for importing the plants from India. What is certain is that the orchards of Jaffa oranges and other commercially viable citrus that dominate the northern part of the Philistine Coastal Plain today were introduced to Ottoman Palestine only in the mid-nineteenth century AD.[2]

The immensely rich, flat alluvial basin in the mid-Philistine plain, behind Ashdod, is even better for agriculture than the area of red *hamra* to the north. Here in the lowest and flattest part of the plain, a deep mass of dark soil has accumulated from the runoff of the Sorek, Elah, Guvrin and Lachish wadi systems, much to the loss of the bare-boned Judean hill country above. Under other geographical circumstances all this rich alluvial soil would form a river delta and then wash out to sea, but here the soil is trapped inland behind the sand dunes lining the shore—much to the gain of coastal people such as the Philistines. Bounded by the thriving cities of Jabneh, Ekron, Gath, and Ashdod, this was the heartland of the Philistine confederacy, a massive, open bank vault in an age when wealth was measured in grain and wars were fought to feed a nation's belly (2 Kgs 8:2–3; note that Dagon, the Philistine national deity, was the local god of grain; Judg 15:1,5; 16:23; 1 Sam 5:1–5). This most fertile part of Philistia lies just southwest of, and well within sight of, Gezer, Jerusalem's gateway to the

Summertime settles over the steppe land of the southern Philistine plain. The gentle course of the Nahal Shiqma (*Wadi el-Hesi*), July-dry, promises life in wintertime, but for now even the sky takes on a thirsty haze. Modern technology can coax a crop of wheat from these sandy hills, but in ancient times this was indeed marginal land, where the shepherds of the Negev were more at home than farmers from the plain.

1 Jerusalem Talmud Sukkah 3:5.

2 Harold N. Moldenke and Alma L. Moldenke, *Plants of the Bible* (New York: Dover Publications, 1952), 185–86, 290–91; Michael Zohary, *Plants of the Bible* (Cambridge: Cambridge University Press, 1982), 123; Yehuda Karmon, *Israel: A Regional Geography* (London: Wiley-Interscience, 1971), 108–10.

The heights of Tell el-Hesi rise in two levels from the reedy banks of Nahal Shiqma (the name of the lower course of the Adoraim wadi; Wadi el-Hesi): a lower tell of 25 acres (10 ha.) and a 4 acre (1.6 ha.) acropolis covered with scrub growth. The city's spring lies nearby. The site is one of dozens of tells, large and small, that dot the southern Philistine Coastal Plain. This one proudly carries the distinction of being the first tell ever excavated in the land of ancient Israel, dug by Sir William Matthew Flinders Petrie in 1890. Petrie was the first to recognize that such mounds are composed of stratified layers of debris left from the destruction of sequential cities built one on top of the other, and that the layers can be dated by pottery found within. Petrie incorrectly thought that the site was biblical Lachish (now known to be at Tell ed-Duweir in the outer Judean Shephelah); its proper identification remains unknown.

coast. It was reason enough for the kings of Judah to *"covet anything [or, everything] that belong[ed] to [their] neighbor"* (Exod 20:17) and helped draw Judean interests westward.

Further south, from Ashkelon and Lachish to Gaza and Gerar, flat farmland gives way to wide, open spaces amid low rolling hills, where both sand and alluvium mix with the fine, wind-blown loess soils of the Negev. The result is a steppe land better suited for grazing than agriculture. In this southern part of the Philistine Coastal Plain, rainfall amounts drop to a relatively dry sixteen inches (400 mm) per year, which, though sufficient for grain, lay the entire region open to occasional drought. At least the higher elevations in the south receive an additional boost of moisture through dew, which appears more than 200 nights per year. Isaac's activities as a shepherd and a grain farmer near Gerar, a city located on the seam between the coastal plain and the Negev, reflect the character and potential of the region (Gen 26:12–17).

Groundwater levels are fairly high on the coastal plain, and because the soil cover is easily penetrated by rainwater, wells are abundant throughout the region (fifteen ancient wells have been identified around Gaza alone). People have been able to settle and build almost anywhere out here due to the generally level ground, although the larger cities naturally tended to be located at or near the courses of the major water channels. Indeed, while towns and villages in the hill country never seemed to have had enough water, their counterparts out on the coastal plain seldom lacked. Flax, a fiber crop that needs wet soil to thrive, was grown in the wetter areas of the coastal plain just as it was in the Nile Delta and at oases in the Jordan Valley (cp. Lev 16:23,32; 1 Chr 4:21; Prov 31:13,24; Ezek 16:10,13; and line 4 of the Gezer Calendar: "His month—chopping flax"[1]). Linen, made from flax, was the cloth of choice for fine and priestly textiles in ancient Israel; its presence and production out on the coast reflect well the region's cosmopolitan character.

All of this is a recipe for large cities, dense settlement, and easy connections over routes that can run just about anywhere. The major local building material on the Philistine Coastal Plain is the region's inexhaustible supply of soil; historically, structures both large and small on the plain were constructed out of mud brick on stone foundations. Numerous tells dot the landscape, each rising inexorably as one mostly mud city collapsed to provide higher ground for its successor to be built atop its ruins. Because the openness of the plain prompted the need for defense, the larger cities were not only walled but, during the Middle Bronze Age (ca. 2000–1550 BC), surrounded by earthen ramparts. Such defensive works have given tells their classic trapezoid

1 Rainey and Notley, *The Sacred Bridge*, 42.

In the early thirteenth century BC, the Egyptian Pharaoh Seti I, father of Rameses II, launched a successful military campaign to defeat a coalition of rebel Canaanite cities that had besieged Egyptian garrisons at Beth-shean and nearby Rehov, south of the Sea of Galilee. To do so, Seti marched his army across the northern Sinai to Gaza, then north along the coastal plain toward the Jezreel Valley and the rebellious Canaanites. In Seti's day, the Egyptian military route across the northern Sinai was guarded by up to two dozen well-supplied and strongly armed forts, each one day's march from the next. Egyptian texts call this the Horus Road, after the falcon-headed god Horus, patron of Egyptian kingship. The Bible calls the route *"the road to the land of the Philistines"* (Exod 13:17) and warns of the difficulty for anyone trying to sneak through. Seti returned to Egypt in triumph, then had his scribes and artisans immortalize his march against the Canaanites in full relief, with diagrams, on the northern outside wall of the great hypostyle hall of the Temple of Amun at Karnak (modern Luxor, Egypt). The text is a kind of map of the route across the northern Sinai and offers wonderful commentary on the doorway between Egypt and Asia during the period of the judges.

shape. The Philistine Coastal Plain was the southern Levant's best answer to the fertile river valleys of Egypt and Mesopotamia; the noisy, busy texture of its sophisticated urban life flourished during ancient times, as it does today.

But these local benefits, abundant as they may be, played only a bit part to the region's primary role as the imperial north-south connector, the "cat route" on which the economic and political empires of the ancient Near East and Mediterranean basin collided. From Egypt, the main line of the international highway crossed the northern Sinai to Gaza, a place the ancient Egyptians called Pa-Canaan, "the city of Canaan."[1] Sitting just above the hollow of the great sweep of the Mediterranean's southeastern corner, in the zone where the rock and sand of the Sinai first touches the arable land of Asia, Gaza was the gateway of Africa to Asia, the launch pad of Asia to Africa, and the terminus of choice for traders coming off the southern and eastern deserts. George Adam Smith commented that like Damascus, Gaza is one of those cities that has just always been there, a place whose role is proven by its history: "Gaza is the outpost of Africa, the door of Asia."[2] The tell of Gaza, nestled behind the line of coastal dunes three miles from the sea, lies entirely beneath the concrete and asphalt growth of the modern city and has barely been excavated. The location of its ancient seaport remains unknown, but following the pattern of the late second and early first millenniums BC, in which ports were typically established within the protection of wadi estuaries rather than on the shoreline itself, it is possible that Gaza's port was in the vicinity of the mouth of the Nahal Besor five miles (8 km) to the south.

The historic line of the international highway split into two routes north of Gaza. The westernmost of these routes tracked just behind the coastal dunes and linked Gaza with Ashkelon, Ashdod, Jabneh, and Joppa before

The outlet of the Nahal Lachish, bolstered by water flow from its main tributaries (the Elah and Guvrin wadis), washes into the Mediterranean Sea. The shoreline has been altered in recent years to provide a sand beach for modern Ashdodites, impeding the free flow of the wadi. In the ancient world, estuaries such as this were a welcome site for ship captains plying an otherwise straight-line coast. Mediterranean ships of the Bronze and Iron Ages—small craft by today's standard—could navigate this estuary for about a mile inland, where they tied up next to Tel Mor, the port of ancient Ashdod.

1 Note in particular the Karnak inscription of Pharaoh Seti I, who campaigned in the Levant in the early thirteenth century BC; *ANET*, 254; Hallo, *Context of Scripture* II, 24.

2 Smith, *Historical Geography of the Holy Land*, 184.

The open fields of Philistia help to feed the modern state of Israel, a population that sits squarely on the strategic juncture between Europe, Africa, and Asia. For millennia, the living gold harvested across stretches like this one near Gath of the Philistines (*Tell es-Safi*) was free game for invading armies; by it, men bent on conquest could march another day; without it, the locals were starved into submission. The Philistine Coastal Plain, a region blessed for its routes and resources, has seen more than its share of forays in the survival game of snatch-and-run. It's a high-risk enterprise, one that eventually caught the Philistines short. Whenever the Judeans, secure in the hill country above, left affairs on the coastal plain alone, they increased their chances for national survival. Not all Judean kings were content to do so.

bending inland to Aphek. This is the approximate line of Israel Highway 4 today. These cities were relatively equidistant from one another (10–12 mi./16–19 km apart), and certainly functioned as overnight way stations for both land and sea traffic.

The Philistines' presence on the coast—Philistia was a mouse in the international clothing of a cat—was so pervasive during the formative years of ancient Israel that their name stuck to the place. Even though the Philistines lost their identity as a people group sometime after the Assyrian invasion in the eighth and seventh centuries BC (cp. Ezek 25:16; Zeph 2:4–5; Zech 9:5–7), their name lives on in the early second-century Roman geographical designation *Palestina* and the modern geographic and ethnic term *Palestine*. It should be noted that the modern Palestinians, who are Arabs, bear no blood tie to the ancient Philistines.

Ashkelon is unique among them in that it was located right on the water due to a convenient break in the dunes. This, bolstered by abundant archaeological evidence that Ashkelon was a bustling economic center throughout the biblical period, suggests the city was a "favored port"[1] that dominated the Philistine coast. Archaeologists have found the remains of more than sixty wells within the city, each tapping into an underground river flowing sixty-five feet (20 m) below the surface that carries fresh water from the hills of the Shephelah to the coast. Together these waters have made the Ashkelon region a green oasis drawing traffic from both land and sea. The city's weakness was that it had no natural defenses. Remains of strong Crusader walls perched atop massive Middle Bronze Age II ramparts, cradling the site like a crescent moon to compensate for the city's vulnerability, are clearly visible today. The city was able to maintain its strength throughout antiquity by means of the right of trade. Despite extensive searching along the shore and underwater for remains of Ashkelon's port, no material evidence of a harbor has been found. It is likely cargo ships anchored in open water, their wares brought to Ashkelon by small ships that beached on the sand.[2] This, at least, was the typical way of linking ships to shore in the region during Ottoman Turkish times.

When the Assyrian kings captured the coast on their march to Egypt in the late eighth and early seventh centuries BC, they allowed the southern Philistine port cities of Gaza, Ashkelon, and Ashdod to remain quasi-independent rather than destroying them like they had the inland cities of Judah. It seems the Assyrians needed a friendly buffer against Egypt or, more likely, an ongoing local source of wealth to refuel their war effort just at the point where their armies, with supply lines from Nineveh already stretched precariously thin, had to cross the barren Sinai.[3] The writer of 2 Samuel characterized Ashkelon by its "marketplaces" (*chutzot*, lit. "outside spaces," 2 Sam 1:20), likely a reference to outdoor public bazaars near the streets or gateways of the city. References to the markets and opulent gardens of Ashkelon also appear in the Talmud (e.g., Qiddushin 31a; Jer. Talmud Shevi'it 6:1; Sifre Deut. 51). Taken together, the flash and color of oriental souks easily come to mind, as does the image of a city with a persistent tradition of producing wealth.

Next up heading north is the tell of ancient Ashdod, which, like Gaza, sits just behind the coastal dunes. Apparently, Ashdod's port from the Middle Bronze through Iron Ages was Tel Mor, a small rise five miles northwest of the city on the outer bank of the Nahal Lachish, adjacent to the bustling seaport of modern Ashdod.[4] Jabneh (Yavneh) also sat just behind the dunes further north, on the bank of the Sorek wadi. Its port was likely close to the mouth of the Sorek. The seaward side of the northern end of the Philistine Coastal Plain was marked by

1 Ron E. Tappy, "East of Ashkelon: The Setting and Settling of the Judean Lowlands in the Iron Age IIA," in J. David Schloen, ed., *Exploring the Longue Durée: Essays in Honor of Lawrence E. Stager* (Winona Lake, IN: Eisenbrauns, 2009), 450.

2 Lawrence E. Stager, J. David Schloen, and Daniel M. Master, eds., *Ashkelon 1: Introduction and Overview (1985–2006)* (Winona Lake, IN: Eisenbrauns, 2008): 94, 163.

3 For a discussion of possibilities, see Daniel M. Master, "Trade and Politics: Ashkelon's Balancing Act in the Seventh Century B.C.E.," *BASOR* 330 (2003): 49–51.

4 Protected by modern breakwaters, Ashdod and Haifa are Israel's only deep-water ports on the Mediterranean today.

Zephaniah's prophetic vision for Philistia was not that Judah would gain access to the wealth, routes, and seaports of the region, but that the entire coastal plain—cities, fields, people, and all—would revert to a sandy shepherd land that allowed the same kind of quiet, pastoral lifestyle that Judah enjoyed in the hill country and wilderness to the east. Zephaniah spoke on the eve of the Babylonian invasion, when the cry for rest from military invasion overrode any commercial benefit the international highway might bring. For the prophet, Judah's profits lay elsewhere:

For Gaza will be abandoned,
and Ashkelon will become a ruin.
Ashdod will be driven out at noon,
and Ekron will be uprooted. . . .
The seacoast will become pasturelands
with caves for shepherds and folds for sheep.
The coastland will belong to the remnant of
the house of Judah;
they will find pasture there.
They will lie down in the evening among
the [ruined] houses of Ashkelon,
for the LORD their God will return to them
and restore their fortunes. (Zeph 2:4,6–7)

the port of Joppa and, close to the mouth of the Yarkon River, Tell Qasila, a richly excavated site whose ancient name is unknown. Joppa had the double advantage of being located behind a slight protective coastline hook on the most direct line inland from the Aijalon Valley. For this reason, it was Jerusalem's favored port from the earliest times,[1] even though only a few Judean kings were able to hold enough of the coast to maintain and protect hill country interests there in Old Testament times (Solomon and Josiah are good examples).

The international highway's inland route ran along the eastern edge of the Philistine Coastal Plain, near or through cities guarding the outer end of each of the Shephelah's transversal valleys. From south to north, these cities include Lachish, Tel Zeita (possibly to be identified with biblical Libnah), Gath, Ekron, Gezer, and Lod, on the approximate line of Israel's Highway 40 today. This strategic route felt the sideways tug and pull of hill country versus plain, with Lachish, Libnah, and Gezer more often than not associated with Judah (1 Kgs 9:15; 2 Kgs 8:22; 14:19; 18:14; 19:8; 23:31; 1 Chr 6:57,67; 7:28; 20:4; Neh 11:25,30; Jer 34:7; Mic 1:13) and Gath and Ekron usually in Philistine hands (1 Sam 5:8,10; 6:16–17; 7:14; 17:4,52; 1 Kgs 2:39; 2 Kgs 1:2; 12:17; Joel 1:8; 6:2; Zeph 2:4). Since travel was relatively easy almost anywhere out on the plain, it is probably best to trace the network of routes joining the eastern and western branches of the international highway on the simple principle that main routes connected main cities—and that on as straight or nearly straight a line as possible.

All roads met at Aphek (1 Sam 4:1; New Testament Antipatris; Acts 23:31), the northern terminus of the Philistine Coastal Plain; it was a city of enormous strategic importance. Aphek lay squarely in a mile-wide bottleneck between the powerful Yarkon springs and the rise of the Ephraim hills, near the modern Israeli city of Rosh haAyin (lit. "head of the spring"). Any real force—military, political, or commercial—tramping the highway connecting the continents had to pass this way, and Aphek's role as a plug or a springboard, depending on the conditions of the moment, cannot be overestimated. The northern edge of the Philistine Coastal Plain—a triangle defined by the bottleneck at Aphek, the port of Joppa, and Gezer—the outermost doorway of the Aijalon Valley, has long seen a swirl of human activity. Jerusalem's interests on the coast most naturally have fallen here. The eastern portion of this triangle, that facing Jerusalem near Ono and Lod, was the Valley of Craftsmen (Neh 11:35); it was apparently an ancient center of both raw material and skilled human resources. Today the entire area is overrun by metropolitan Tel Aviv.

All of this makes for a truly international region and an appropriate setting for a story (or series of stories) of cats and mice. Egyptian texts from the second millennium BC, as well as the Bible, called the indigenous inhabitants of the region "Canaanites" (as opposed to "Amorites," who lived in the more conservative hill country; Deut 1:7) and tended to associate the term "Canaan" with the maritime commerce of the coast (Gen 10:19; cp. Zeph 1:11; and el-Amarna texts 8, 131, 137, 148, 367). Archaeological excavations up and down the coast reveal an indigenous material culture with clear ties to both Egypt and the Aegean. During the Late Bronze Age (fifteenth to thirteenth centuries BC), the Pharaohs of Egypt's Late Kingdom burst into Asia in full imperialistic force, establishing military posts and trading centers throughout the region and leaving monumental inscriptions of conquest in their wake. This Egyptian presence is well attested in archaeological strata at a number of coastal sites (e.g., Deir el-Balah, Tell el-Ajjul, Gaza, Ashkelon, Ashdod, Tel Mor, Joppa, Aphek, and Gath), though the Bible itself is silent on the effort.

Egyptian influence waned with the arrival of the Philistines, one of several Sea Peoples from Crete (i.e., Caphtor; cp. Deut 2:23; Jer 47:4; Joel 9:7), and other islands of the Aegean who settled on the south Levantine coast in the thirteenth and twelfth centuries BC. Remarkably, the prophet Amos made clear that just as Israel entered the hills of Canaan, so God had brought the Philistines to the coast: "*This is the LORD's declaration. Didn't I bring Israel from the land of Egypt [and] the Philistines from Caphtor. . .?*" (Amos 9:7).

With the Egyptian cat away, mice such as the Philistines found ample ground to play among the remains of Egypt's Ramasside empire (the Nineteenth Dynasty). A Philistine presence can be found archaeologically at sites throughout the coastal plain. Five cities in particular, Ashdod, Ashkelon, Gaza, Ekron, and Gath—the so-called Philistine Pentapolis of Joshua 13:3 and 1 Samuel 6:17—hassled the emerging Israelite state taking shape in the hill country above.

From Ekron and Gath the Philistines were repeatedly able to penetrate the transversal valleys of the Shephelah, then have a run up into the hill country of Benjamin and Judah (1 Sam 4:1; 7:7–14; 13:15–14:1; 17:1–2; 2 Sam 5:17–25). Redoubling their efforts to eviscerate Israel, the Philistines finally pushed north through the

1 As noted by the Greek geographer Strabo early in the first century AD (*Geography*, 16.2.28), "Indeed, the Judeans have used this place [Iope, i.e., Jaffa] as a seaport when they have gone down as far as the sea."

The most pronounced landforms of the Levant, i.e., its mountain ranges and the Rift Valley, run on roughly parallel north-south lines. Four evenly spaced geological troughs interrupt these lines at right angles, where collapsed elevations provide convenient corridors for international traffic to pierce the north-south flow. The northernmost trough, the "Euphrates-Antioch Gap," provides bee-line passage between Mesopotamia and the Mediterranean city of Antioch, gateway to Europe and the place where they *"were first called Christians"* (cp. Acts 11:26; 13:1–3). The next trough south, the "Tadmor-Byblos Corridor," carries the route tracing the arch of the Fertile Crescent to bind Mesopotamia to the Levant. The third trough, the "Galilee-Bashan Depression," produced the broad valleys and passes of Galilee as well as the water-filled hollow called the Sea of Galilee (the Kinneret). The fourth shaped the chain of basins of the biblical Negev. Historically, the open landscapes formed by these four geological troughs have carried the international highways across the ranges and rift that otherwise define the north-south character of the Levant. They also provide crossroads of international opportunities for local folk living nearby. It was only natural that Judah's kings turned to face the traffic that flowed through the one closest to them, the Negev to their south.

Aphek bottleneck all the way to Beth-shean, where they defeated Israel's first king, Saul, and put a divide-and-conquer choke-hold on the emerging kingdom (1 Sam 29:1; 31:1–6).

While the entire southern coastal plain had been assigned to the tribe of Judah according to the border descriptions in the book of Joshua (Josh 15:11–12), neither the Judeans as a people group nor the Southern Kingdom of Judah as a nation-state were ever successful in running the Philistines out and occupying the region. At best, with Egypt's help, David and Solomon were able to contain the Philistines on the coast (2 Sam 8:1; 21:15–22; 1 Kgs 9:16–17; 1 Chr 18:1) and gain some control over the port of Joppa in the process. Solomon thus used Joppa to bring Phoenician cedar and cypress logs up to Jerusalem to build the temple (2 Chr 2:16; cp. 1 Kgs 5:10); Sheshbazzar did the same when the Jews returned from exile in the late sixth century BC (Ezra 3:7). In the mid-eighth century BC, Judah's King Uzziah was able to take control of the most fertile part of the plain (the portion lying between Gath, Jabneh, and Ashdod, just beyond Gezer and the Aijalon Valley); he reaped its economic benefits as a result. His successors could not hold the region for long (2 Chr 26:6; 28:18). For their part, the Philistines found necessary allies in both the Edomites and the Arabs[1] who could ensure that they, rather than the Judeans, would control the long-distance desert trade routes that ended at the sea (2 Chr 21:16–17; 26:7–8; Joel 3:4–8; Amos 1:6). Of course, any of the ports along the coast could be used by anyone who was able to control the import and export revenues that passed through.

In the end, the cats returned—first the Assyrians (Tiglath-Pileser III, Sargon II, and Sennacherib in the late eighth century BC), then the Babylonians, Persians, and Greeks (thanks to Alexander the Great), and finally, for the biblical period at least, the Romans. These were all military conquests, but each shared the goal of exploiting the markets and resources of the southeastern Mediterranean Sea by controlling the international routes that traversed the coastal plain. Through it all, Judean interests in Philistia were largely curtailed. There was a brief resurgence from the not-yet-identified village of Modein in the far northeastern corner of the Philistine plain; a family of conservative Jews known as the Maccabees launched a rebellion in 167 BC that for a century forged an independent Jewish kingdom in most of the land that had once been conquered by David. But by the time of the New Testament, Jews living out on the coast had, on the whole, become quite Hellenized, with their identities split between the conservative tug of the hills and the boundless opportunities of the sea. This was the world that Simon Peter entered as he made his way down from the safety and security of Jerusalem to Lydda (Lod), then across the exposed expanse to Joppa, unsure if he should rest content by the sea with Simon the Tanner or push beyond the boundary of his homeland to the world of Cornelius beyond (Acts 9:32–10:48). By divine nudge, he chose the latter, and the world has never been the same for his efforts.

D. THE NEGEV

The term *negev* (sometimes spelled *negeb*), as it is used in the Old Testament, designates the geological trough of wind-deposited loess soil that lies just south of the Hill Country of Judah and the Shephelah (Gen 20:1; Judg 1:9; 1 Sam 27:10; Zech 7:7). The Semitic root *n-g-b* has as its root meaning "dry or parched [land]," an appropriate connotation for this portion of the land of ancient Israel which was well known and oft-traveled in biblical times by people at home in the wetter and more habitable regions immediately north. Through association, the term *negev* also came to indicate the direction "south,"[2]

1 The term "Arab" in the Bible and contemporary texts designated desert tribes from the Negev and points south.

2 This is against the suggestion of Rainey, who argues that the basic meaning of the Semitic nominative root *n-g-b* is "south," as preserved in the Arabic root *j-n-b* (the Hb root underwent metathesis). The root developed the verbal sense of "to be dry" later, as attested in Aramaic and late Hebrew. Anson F. Rainey, "Early Historical Geography of the Negeb," in Ze'ev Herzog, *Beer-sheba II: The Early Iron Age Settlements* (Tel Aviv: Institute of Archaeology, 1984): 88.

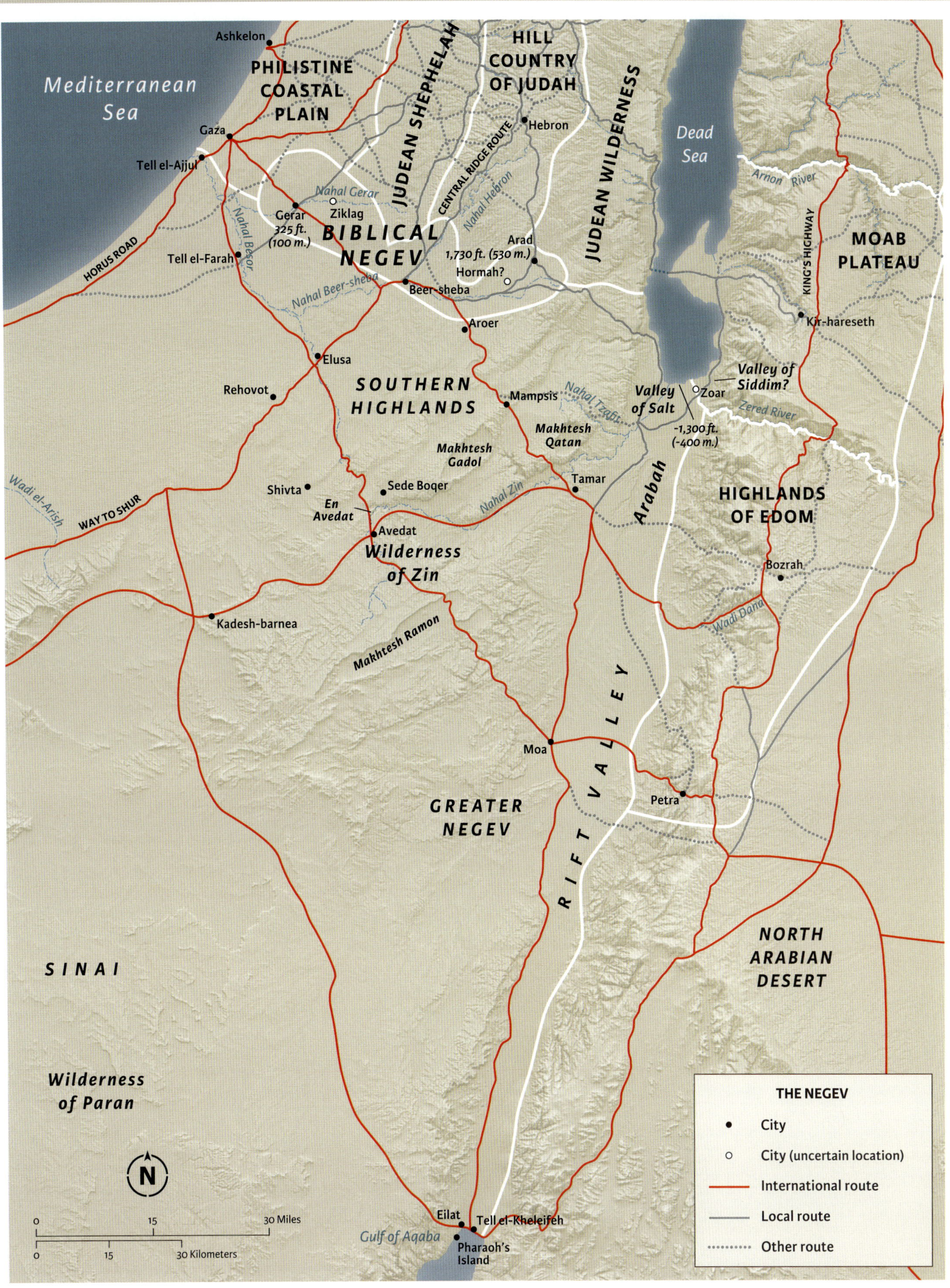
Mediterranean Sea
Ashkelon
PHILISTINE COASTAL PLAIN
JUDEAN SHEPHELAH
HILL COUNTRY OF JUDAH
JUDEAN WILDERNESS
Dead Sea
Gaza
Tell el-Ajjul
Hebron
CENTRAL RIDGE ROUTE
Nahal Hebron
Nahal Gerar
Ziklag
Gerar
325 ft. (100 m.)
BIBLICAL NEGEV
Arad
1,730 ft. (530 m.)
Hormah?
Tell el-Farah
Nahal Besor
HORUS ROAD
Nahal Beer-sheba
Beer-sheba
Aroer
Arnon River
KING'S HIGHWAY
MOAB PLATEAU
Kir-hareseth
Elusa
Rehovot
SOUTHERN HIGHLANDS
Mampsis
Nahal Trafit
Valley of Salt
Zoar
Valley of Siddim?
Zered River
-1,300 ft. (-400 m.)
Makhtesh Qatan
Makhtesh Gadol
Tamar
Wadi el-Arish
Shivta
Sede Boqer
En Avedat
Nahal Zin
Arabah
HIGHLANDS OF EDOM
WAY TO SHUR
Avedat
Wilderness of Zin
Bozrah
Wadi Dana
Kadesh-barnea
Makhtesh Ramon
RIFT VALLEY
Moa
Petra
GREATER NEGEV
NORTH ARABIAN DESERT
SINAI
Wilderness of Paran
N
0 15 30 Miles
0 15 30 Kilometers
Eilat
Tell el-Kheleifeh
Gulf of Aqaba
Pharaoh's Island
THE NEGEV
City
City (uncertain location)
International route
Local route
Other route

After settling for a while near Gerar, Isaac "sowed seed in that land and . . . reaped a hundred times what was sown" (Gen 26:12). This was a yield similar to irrigation-boosted farms in the region today. This modern temporary encampment, replete with tents and sheep, sits on the northwestern slope of the mound of ancient Gerar. The fields of the Israeli moshav (collective agricultural community) Melilot, "bundle of ripe wheat," lie in the distance.

just as the biblical Hebrew word *yammah*, "toward the sea," means "westward," and *mizrachah*, "to the place of sunrise," denotes "eastward" (1 Kgs 7:25; cp. Joel 2:20). Each of these directionals works best in reference to someone standing in the Judean hills, the heartland of the biblical narrative. In any case, after Abram entered the land of Canaan from the north and passed through the vicinity of Shechem and Bethel, he *"continued toward the Negev"* (Gen 12:9 NIV), that is, both southward and into the arid basin below the Hebron plateau where he would one day dig a well, plant a tree, and call his home Beer-sheba (Gen 21:25–34). Similarly, while at Kadesh-barnea in the northeastern Sinai, Moses told the twelve spies to *"go up this way to the Negev, then [continue on] into the hill country"* (Num 13:17), clear indication that the Negev was a distinct region between the Sinai and the Judean hills. In this case, the spies traveled north-northeastward to get to the Negev, not south like Abraham, requiring the primary meaning of the term to be geographical rather than directional.

In today's usage, "Negev" designates the entire southern half of the modern State of Israel, from south of Beer-sheba—now a sprawling industrial and supply city with a host of Bedouin settlement towns on its perimeter—all the way to Eilat, Israel's glitzy port on the Red Sea and southernmost city. The geological richness of this larger, modern Negev, geographically a slice of the Sinai Peninsula and not a part of the biblical Negev at all, is a magnet for hikers and four-wheelers who prefer to bypass the drab grit-scape around Beer-sheba in favor of eco-adventures beyond. If a modern Israeli says, "Let's go to the Negev," he or she certainly does not mean, "Let's go to Beer-sheva!" As a concession to modern parlance, it may be best to designate the part of the Negev south of Beer-sheba, which biblically was part of the *"great and terrible wilderness"* of Israel's desert wanderings (Deut 1:19; 8:15), with the term Greater Negev to distinguish it from the Negev of the Bible. Yet both regions were part of the biblical story and played a related though nuanced role in the interface between the local priorities of the hill country and the international powers that traversed the south.

Defined geologically, the biblical Negev is a wide, down-warped trough forming three connected basins which together extend eastward from the southern Philistine Coastal Plain to a point within twelve miles (19 km) of the Dead Sea. The westernmost basin doubles as the southernmost part of the coastal plain,[1] where elevations swell gently to around 500–600 feet (150–180 m) and rainfall, dew, and ground water resources are adequate, though not abundant, for agriculture. Centered on the ancient city-states of Gerar and Ziklag (Gen 20:1; 1 Sam 30:1), the expansive **western biblical Negev basin** lies open to international influences all around.

The **central biblical Negev basin**, the smallest of the three basins, is encircled by hills forming a square-ish loop three to seven miles (5 to 11 km) distant around Beer-sheba. Here the basin floor levels out at approximately 1,000 feet (300 m) above sea level and receives, on average, not more than six inches (150 mm) of rainfall annually. This is below the minimum needed even for barley, the hardiest of native grains. From the tell of Beer-sheba, it is easy to scan the Eocene hills of the Judean Shephelah rising gently to the northwest. The tail of the watershed ridge pulls up gradually to the northeast, and the rise of the highlands of the Greater Negev—the first approach into the "great and terrible wilderness"—marks the horizon line to the south. The view to the south encompasses the entrance to the wilderness (*midbar*) of Beer-sheba, into which Abraham

The Iron Age store city of Beer-sheba, here partially reconstructed following archaeological excavations by Yohanan Aharoni and Ze'ev Herzog in the 1970s, dominates the central biblical Negev basin. The Beer-sheba wadi (Nahal Beersheva), in the center of the photo, approaches from the east. Late winter rains puddle the wadi and carpet the outlying flats with a transient field of green. Three large storehouses stand in a neat row just inside the city gate, easily identified by their long, tripartite design and rows of dividing columns. These storerooms likely warehoused commodities that supplied Beer-sheba and its dependent forts and villages throughout the Negev. The modern city of Beer Sheva plays a similar role in the economy of the region today.

1 Rainey defines the biblical Negev as comprising only what are here called the central and eastern basins. Rainey, "Early Historical Geography of the Negeb," 90.

The northeastern corner of the eastern biblical Negev basin, filled with powdery loess soil, sits hard against the strong shoulder of the Judean hill country, seen here as the rise in the distance. The view is from atop the Israelite citadel of Arad. The twelve spies whom Moses sent into Canaan climbed this ridge on their way to Hebron. Reporting back, ten said they felt like grasshoppers—then acted like it, jumping up into the hills to try to take the land anyway, and scattering back down when the Amalekites and Canaanites attacked (Num 13:17–22,33; 14:44–45).

and Sarah banished Hagar (Gen 21:14; cf. 1 Kgs 19:3–4), and a portion of the wilderness of Israel's wanderings prior to entering the land. Ancient Beer-sheba is connected to Judah through the chalk trough that runs due north, and a natural route northeastward up to the hill country watershed. Broad passes connect Beer-sheba to the western and eastern biblical Negev basins as well, making the city a crossroads for the entire region.

The **eastern biblical Negev basin**, its floor elongated in shape and rising from 1,300 to 1,900 feet (400 to 580 m) in elevation, is the driest and most isolated of the three biblical Negev basins. Rainfall here averages but four to six inches (100 to 150 mm) annually. The back shoulder of Judah's Cenomanian-Turonian hill country rises dramatically to the north, neatly separating the flats of the basin from the tableland of the Hebron plateau above. The eastern basin's eastern horizon forms the watershed that divides the wadis flowing into the Mediterranean Sea sixty miles (100 km) west, from those dropping into the Dead Sea just ten miles (16 km) east. The Israelite fortress of Arad (Tel Arad), which commands the eastern Negev basin from a slight rise in its far northeastern corner, provides tangible evidence of an Iron Age reality that saw military and political priorities in Judah override the natural limitations of the land.

A lack of productive resources conspires against permanent settlement throughout the biblical Negev. All three basins are filled with fine, wind-blown particles of loess that have settled to a depth of up to fifty feet (15 m), providing a somewhat fertile soil base that, unlike the soils of the hill country, is almost completely free of stones. Unfortunately, the powdery texture of loess forms a hardpan crust when wet, leaving the soil dry and unproductive just one inch (2 cm) below the surface. After a winter storm, it is not unusual to see vast stretches of rainwater sitting on the Negev basin floor like puddles on pavement, draining off slowly into badland formations. With little warning the wadis sometimes flash flood (Ps 126:4), then quickly subside into cracked mud and quiet pools. Drowning, in fact, is more frequent in the Negev than would be supposed. We can be sure that the patriarchs of old, like the modern Bedouin who eke out an existence on the biblical Negev's dusty flats, knew every seasonal watering hole in the region. Temperatures there fluctuate as wildly as would be expected in the desert: the summer sun is intense, while strong winds scour the higher elevations throughout the year, making summers a blast furnace and winters uncomfortably cold. Even the color of the landscape is harsh: a drab tan-grey except following the winter rains, with skies seldom clear of dust and sand. Though only twenty miles (32 km) from the green fields of the Hebron plateau, the biblical Negev evokes the grim reality that people "*sow in tears*" (Ps 126:5), fully expecting the rains to fail and the seed that could have been made into bread to shrivel in the dust.

Area settlements—either permanent or of the Bedouin-encampment variety—tend to be found along the "*watercourses of the Negev*" (Ps 126:4) where the water table is high and seasonal flows are supplemented by well water. There are only a few perennial springs in the region due to the relative flatness of the land. The eastern basin is drained to the west by the Nahal (or, wadi) Beer-sheba. Two important sites lie along its banks: Tel Malhata (likely the Arad of Moses's first conquest; Num 21:1) and Tel Masos (perhaps Hormah, where Israel's southern penetration into Canaan was repulsed; Num 14:45). In the central biblical Negev basin, the Nahal Beer-sheba is joined by the Nahal Hebron, which drops out of the Judean hills from the northeast and carries what's left of the Central Ridge Route (the so-called Patriarchal Highway) with it. The tell of Beer-sheba sits exactly in the point of the "V" where these two wadis meet, directly below the tail of the chalk moat that separates the hill country from the Judean Shephelah. On the principle that in dry flatlands such as these, foot traffic tends to follow water courses, the ancient site of Beer-sheba was the ideal location to control the region's commercial flow.

These eastern and central Negev basins are marginal lands, best suited for seminomadic herders like Abraham, Isaac, and Jacob, whose wealth was of the hoofed variety and for whom agriculture played only a supplementary role (cp. Gen 13:2; 24:35; 26:12). The Hebrew term for regions such as this is *midbar*, which is not wilderness *per se* but a steppe land of the kind that supports pasturage for sheep and goats (Gen 21:14; Ps 65:12–13; Isa 5:17; Joel 2:22). A thin blanket of grasses covers the entire region from midwinter to the time of spring lambing, when life in tents is worth celebrating and economic and social obligations are renewed for another year. But everything quickly burns off by late spring. The landscape supports virtually no trees except in low spots where runoff rainwater collects in pools, or in or along the bottoms of the larger wadis. When Abraham planted a tamarisk tree by the well that he had dug near the spot where the Hebron and

This aerial view shows Tel Beer-sheba during excavations in the 1970s; these were directed by Yohanan Aharoni and Ze'ev Herzog of Tel Aviv University. Nahal Beer-sheba passes to the left, while Nahal Hebron enters from the right. The water table in the region is high and the soil soft, making well-digging a relatively reliable effort. A rail line also crosses the scene (top), a modern version of the wadi-style transportation arteries that meet at the site.

Without a significant and prolonged influx of supplies from the outside, the resources of the central and eastern biblical Negev basins are suited only for a harsh Abrahamic lifestyle, remaining largely beyond the reach of farmers and city-dwellers who need annual harvests to survive. Knowing its reputation for unpredictability, the psalmist likened the Negev's potential for sustaining settled life to the chances that God would restore the post-exile political fortunes of Israel: impossible without divine intervention. He said, *"Restore our fortunes, LORD, like the watercourses of the Negev [i.e., suddenly, and with full force]. Those who sow in tears will reap with shouts of joy!"* (Ps 126:4–5).

Beer-sheba wadis flow into a single channel, he claimed rights to a portion of ground that held enough promise to support his patriarchy—at least in good years (Gen 21:22–34).

Farther west, the region of Gerar is drained by a completely different wadi system, the Nahal Gerar. This western basin is the only one of the three where the rainfall is predictably sufficient (over 12 in/300 mm annually) so as to allow large-scale agriculture and hence urban settlement. Both Abraham and Isaac migrated into Gerar's economic zone when rainfall failed around Beer-sheba. Though only twenty miles (32 km) apart, the line of arable viability lies exactly between the two sites (Gen 20:1; 26:1). The king of Gerar, Abimelech, gave Abraham the right to dig his own wells in the region, a privilege that recognized the patriarch's relative standing and strength. Abimelech would have needed a loyal strongman to protect his exposed eastern flank anyway. Nevertheless, this right was not renewed in the next generation when Isaac planted fields near Gerar, having the apparent intent to stay in the region rather than return to the harsher climes of Beer-sheba (Gen 26:6–17). Acting out of loyalty to their king, the herdsmen of Gerar allowed Isaac to live in peace only after he moved back into the folds (and separate water resources) of the Nahal Beer-sheba wadi system, hence restoring the competitive balance in the region (Gen 26:18–25).

The Nahal Beer-sheba and Nahal Gerar wadi systems both flow into the Nahal Besor, which outlines the southern extremity of the coastal plain. Nahal Besor also drains the northwestern rise of the Greater Negev. Its wide, deeply scarred course marked the functional southern boundary of the land of ancient Israel. Beyond, the desert-dwelling Amalekites felt safe in a region where David's partisan band was largely unwilling or unable to travel (1 Sam 30:10). Several tells, including Tell el-Farah, Tell Gamma, and Tell el-Ajjul—none of which have been positively matched with known ancient names—mark the outer line of the Nahal Besor as it makes its final push to the sea. These sites define the seam between the settled area of the Philistine Coastal Plain and the shepherd land of the northeastern Sinai. As such, they served as terminals for the international routes penetrating the Negev from Egypt. It will be recalled that the maximal border between the Philistine Coastal Plain and Egypt was at the wadi el-Arish, forty miles further west into the Sinai (1 Kgs 4:21; 8:65).

The political dynamic of the biblical Negev, then, is grounded in the paradox that while most of the land does not support permanent settlement without the influx of resources from the outside, the region is a funnel for lucrative trade routes connecting the Mediterranean with the Arabian Peninsula and the Red Sea. These routes needed to be maintained and supplied on a permanent basis. The history of the Negev basin can thus be traced on two levels: first, in the spotty pattern of settlement by seminomadic clans and tribes who sought to eke out a living from the meager resources the land itself had to offer; and second, in the ebb and flow of strong, resourced, and interested governments on its perimeter. These include Judah and the Philistines to the north, Edom and the Nabateans to the east, and Egypt and eventually Rome to the west—each of which sought to control the biblical Negev's highways at the expense of the other.

First, the tribal dynamic. Throughout its history, the biblical Negev has been home to a number of Bedouin-type people groups who, by virtue of lifestyle, strength, circumstance, or mere fact of presence, claimed the right to encamp along its watercourses. The Bible mentions several tribes who called the region home in Iron Age I, the time that Israel started to settle Canaan: the Jerachmeelites (1 Sam 27:10), Cherethites (1 Sam 30:14), and Calebites (1 Sam 30:14) in the western biblical Negev; the Simeonites in the central basin (Josh 19:1–9); and the Kenites in the east (Judg 1:16; 1 Sam 15:6; 27:10). Each of these tribes maintained lifestyle patterns similar to those of Abraham, the head of the patriarchal clan that had dominated the central part of the region centuries before. Each was seminomadic, driving its flocks and herds in established grazing patterns along the seam between the settled lands of the farmer on the one hand and the open wilderness on the other. (True nomadism, where a group wanders without a recognized home-base, is rare in both the ancient and modern worlds.[1]) So, for instance, we find Heber, a Kenite from the eastern Negev basin, traveling all the way up the Rift Valley to pitch his tent by the oak of Zaanannim near the Sea of Galilee, having won the right to do so from Jabin king of Hazor, who controlled Galilee at the time (Judg 4:11,17; cp. Judg 5:24). And, of course, Abraham, Isaac, and Jacob, who journeyed to Bethel and Hebron, likely in the summertime when the harvested fields would be open for grazing and the hill country temperatures were more moderate than those of the Negev (Gen 12:8; 13:3,18; 18:1; 23:2; 35:1,27). Abraham also crossed the Nahal Besor down to Kadesh-barnea and Shur during what must have been wet winters (Gen 20:1; but cp. Gen 16:6–7). Sometimes Abraham's family traveled over to Gerar or even to Egypt, where conditions offered a hedge

1 Michael B. Rowton, following O. Lattimore, speaks of "enclosed nomadism" to describe pastoral nomads whose patterns of movement are "enclosed" within blocks of desert, semidesert, and highland country that include areas of urban settlement. Enclosed nomadism is based on a symbiotic (or dimorphic) model of social and economic interaction in which urban and pastoral elements benefit from each other, and open conflict is the exception rather than the rule. Rowton's model provides a helpful grid by which to understand the movement of the patriarchs in and around the biblical Negev basin. M. B. Rowton, "Autonomy and Nomadism in Western Asia," *Orientalis* NS 42 (1973): 247–58; "Dimorphic Structure and Topology," *OA* 15 (1976): 17–31.

against famine (Gen 12:10; 20:1; 26:1; 42:1–3). However, they always returned to the vicinity of Beer-sheba (Gen 21:32, 24:62; 26:23–25; 46:1), their recognized home base, where their patriarchal roots had sunk deeply into the flock-friendly soil. Boundaries in tribal society are fluid and defined by both social and geographical criteria, such as when Abraham separated from Lot after their joined flocks had exceeded the carrying capacity of the land (Gen 13:2–18). For his part, we should assume that Lot *"lived in the cities on the plain and set up his tent near Sodom"* not because of personal moral failings but because *"the entire plain of the Jordan as far as Zoar was well watered everywhere like the* LORD*'s garden and the land of Egypt"* and so offered the best symbiotic opportunities for him to provide for his growing family (Gen 13:10,12). What he did once he got to Sodom is another issue.

Turning to the effect of interested governments from the outside, the biblical Negev was drawn into the political orbit of the Judean hill country when Samuel of Ramah (in the land of Benjamin) appointed his two sons, Joel and Abijah, governors of Beer-sheba (1 Sam 8:1–2). About the same time, David of Bethlehem recognized the value of securing the loyalty of the seminomadic tribes who roamed the Negev basin on behalf of his emerging kingdom by incorporating key members of the Cherethites into his personal bodyguard (2 Sam 8:18). By doing so, David sought to protect Judah's southern border against tribal incursions from across the Nahal Besor (1 Sam 30:1–31; cp. Exod 17:8–16; 1 Sam 15:1–9). All of this set the stage for Beer-sheba to become the southern terminus of both the united kingdom of Israel (cp. 1 Kgs 4:25; *"from Dan to Beer-sheba"*) and the Southern Kingdom of Judah (2 Kgs 23:8; *"from Geba to Beer-sheba"*). Archaeological remains at Tel Beer-sheba date from Iron age I (ca. 1150 BC) through the Roman Period, though the city's heyday matched the period of Judah's strongest kings, Jehoshaphat to Hezekiah (the mid-ninth to late eighth centuries BC). From Beer-sheba, kings of Judah were able to siphon revenue from the international routes connecting Arabia with the Mediterranean coast and direct them up to Hebron and Jerusalem instead. The city naturally became a hub of warehousing and trade. To safeguard that role, Beer-sheba also developed into a formal administrative and military center. At the same time, the Iron Age II fortress at Tel Arad secured Judah's interests facing Edom. Neither Beer-sheba nor Arad would have been able to survive as permanent settlements without the constant influx of resources

Nahal Besor cuts a green path through the table-flat loess lands of the western Negev basin, seen here from the top of Tell el-Farah. Its crumbly banks have eroded to a width of 300–450 feet (90–140 m), producing distinct badlands topography throughout. Though not difficult to cross, Nahal Besor functioned as a marked southern border for ancient Israel, following the general line beyond which sustained agriculture and permanent settlement are no longer viable except at a few scattered oases beyond.

from a strong, centralized government on the outside, one whose foreign policy included conscious attempts to push through the gateways of the Negev to points beyond.

Both archaeological and textual data, in fact, reveal a tug-of-war over the Negev basin throughout the biblical period, as strong kings from Egypt, Edom, or Judah successively gained and then lost the upper hand in the ongoing struggle to control the region's lucrative trade routes (cp. Josh 15:21–32; 1 Kgs 22:47; 2 Kgs 3:4–9).[1] With the fall of Jerusalem to the Babylonians in the sixth century BC, the Edomites pushed through the Negev basin all the way to the southern Shephelah, thereby cutting Jerusalem from its flow of revenues from the south. The move had both real and symbolic consequences:

> *Say to the king and the queen*
> *mother [in Jerusalem]:*
> *Take a humble seat,*
> *for your glorious crowns have*
> *fallen from your heads."*
> *[That is, the store] cities of the*
> *Negev are under siege;*
> *no one can help them.*
> *All Judah has been taken into*
> *exile.* (Jer 13:18–19)

Entrenching themselves in the region, the Edomites appear in New Testament-era texts as Idumeans (1 Macc 4:61; 5:3; Mark 3:8; Josephus *Ant.* 5.81–82; 13.257–258, 396; 14.74–76; 15.254–259; 17.319). Herod the Great, who had Idumean roots on his father's side and Nabatean blood on his mother's, helped Rome secure its own southern border by establishing a fortress at Malhata (Tel Malhata in the eastern Negev; Josephus *Ant.* 18.147). Remains of forts from the Roman Period have been found at both Beer-sheba and Arad. But if we look carefully, we can see that even when the Negev was controlled by governments from the outside, the seminomadic tribes who called the basin home continued to live there throughout. They reasserted their presence whenever these outside forces—Judah included—invariably swallowed by its fine dust and sand, withdrew.

A similar dynamic holds true for the **Greater Negev** into which the doorways of the biblical Negev open southward, but here both risks and rewards are greater. The barren expanse beyond the biblical Negev was the northeastern extremity of the land of Israel's wilderness wanderings; it was "*a land of deserts and of ravines, . . . of drought and darkness, a land that no one traveled through and where no one lived*" (Jer 2:6). It was "*a great and terrible wilderness with its poisonous*

An impressive enclosure wall encircles the large Early Bronze Age city of Arad, a twenty-five-acre site in the eastern biblical Negev basin. The fortifications were bolstered with semicircular towers projecting from the wall at regular intervals. Excavations reveal careful city planning, including a primitive, though effective, water system that collected runoff from the surface within the walls. The walled city was occupied from 3100 to 2650 BC, a period contemporary with the first two Egyptian dynasties. Indeed, a potsherd inscribed in hieroglyphs with the name Narmer, the pharaoh who first united Upper and Lower Egypt around 3100 BC, was found on site. A number of Canaanite storage jars have been discovered in Egyptian tombs from the same period. Such evidence suggests that Egypt had established trade connections through the eastern Negev basin from the earliest times. Since the eastern basin is a kind of cul-de-sac off the normal line of international traffic, it is possible that Egypt may have used Arad as a terminal to import bitumen and salt from the Dead Sea, located at the bottom of the Rift Valley ten miles east.

1 Note as well cities in the Biblical and Greater Negevs that were conquered by Shishak of Egypt in the tenth century BC (numbers 66–150 in his list), as well as notices in the Arad Inscriptions of Edomite incursions into the eastern and central Negev basins in the late seventh and early sixth centuries BC. Rainey and Notley, *The Sacred Bridge*, 187–88; Yohanan Aharoni, *Arad Inscriptions* (Jerusalem: IES, 1981), inscriptions 21 and 24.

Hikers pause to consider the difficulty of passage through the easier part of Nahal Tzafit, one of the wadis draining the Greater Negev into the Rift Valley. This descent is part of the Israel Trail, which connects Dan with Eilat and exposes foot travelers to more natural and historic wonders for the distance traveled than any similar trail elsewhere in the world. With good maps and proper preparation, these hikers don't need to fear the warning of the psalmist: *"Some wandered in the desolate wilderness, finding no way to a city where they could live"* (Ps 107:4).

snakes and scorpions, a thirsty land where there was no water" (Deut 8:15).

Israel's collective memory of the wilderness south of Beer-sheba and Arad was not favorable, for obvious reasons, though the biblical writers' assessments are a bit overstated in the sense that with the right incentive and preparation, the land could be, if not tamed, at least exploited to the advantage of interested powers on the outside.

Pushing southward, the northern half of the wilderness beyond the biblical Negev is best termed the **Negev Highlands**, or the **Southern Highlands**.[1] Here are the wilderness (*midbar*) of Beer-sheba and, to its south and west, the wilderness of Shur (Gen 20:1; 21:14; 25:18; 1 Sam 15:7). The region is dominated by four parallel ridges of Cenomanian-Turonian limestone, each oriented northeast-southwest. The compass direction of these mountain ridges forms the backbone of the Greater Negev and bends in line with the shore of the Mediterranean as it starts its broad sweep toward Egypt. As a result, they cut perpendicularly across the Arabian-Mediterranean trade routes. The elevation of each ridge rises successively in turn from north to south, with the fourth, halfway between Beer-sheba and Eilat, peaking at 3,389 feet (1,033 m), somewhat higher than the Hebron plateau. All four ridges were formed by geological folding that was so severe that the tops of the second, third, and fourth ridges cracked open. The forces of erosion then scoured these cracks into large cirques, or craters (Hb *makhteshim*), called the Makhtesh Qatan ("small cirque"), Makhtesh Gadol ("large cirque"), and Makhtesh Ramon respectively. The name Ramon is probably derived from the Arabic name *Ruman*, "Roman," likely carrying the memory of Roman activity in the area, rather than from the Semitic root *r-w-m*, "high." The Ramon Crater, as the latter is most commonly called, is twenty-three miles (37 km) long and 1,200 feet (366 m) deep; it's the largest erosion crater on earth. The floor of each cirque reveals outcroppings of the colorful sandstone core that underlies all of the limestone of the region, the middle layer of the granite-sandstone-limestone "rock sandwich" described in chapter 2.B. Each cirque is drained by a wadi that has pierced its southeastern end and flows into the Rift Valley south of the Dead Sea.

The gradual rise in these stair-step ridges from Gaza to the northern rim of the Ramon Crater is an area of mixed Eocene and Cenomanian-Turonian limestone that has a plausibly fertile soil base in the bottoms of

1 James M. Monson, *Regions on the Run* (Rockford, IL: Biblical Backgrounds, 1998), 18–19.

the larger wadis, all of which drain into the Nahal Besor. Temperatures and rainfall amounts fluctuate wildly throughout these Negev highlands, with any shift in weather patterns over the Mediterranean Sea or Arabian Peninsula quickly tipping the balance from a season of possible growth to outright famine. On average, the region receives half the number of annual rainfall days as Beer-sheba, yet snow is not unexpected on the heights above the Ramon Crater.

A hiker finds her way along the wadi bed of Makhtesh Qatan, the smallest of the craters in the Greater Negev's southern highlands. Red sandstone protrudes below the limestone strata, offering an up-close look at the geologic data. Small amounts of copper, manganese, and iron have been found in the bottom of the Negev highland's three cirques, as well as quantities of silica sand and ceramic clays sufficient to make glass and high-quality ceramics.

During their forty years in the wilderness, Moses and all Israel reverted, for a generation, to the lifestyle of Bedouin (Exod 15:22–23,27; 16:1; 17:1; 19:1–2; Num 10:12; 11:3,34–35; 12:16; 13:26; 14:25; 20:1,22; 33:5–49; Deut 1:19). The Bible mentions many place names that lay on their itinerary. Many of these reference local geographical features (oases, wadis, wells, rocks, mountains, etc.) where the travelers camped for a time. Examples include this line of campsites visited in sequence: Hazeroth ("grassy places"), Ritmah ("place of broom-trees"), Rimmon-perez ("breaking out of pomegranates"), Libnah ("white place"), and Rissah ("moist spot;" Num 33:18–21). Unsurprisingly, the majority of these place names, erased by the sands of time, can no longer be identified, although church and local Bedouin traditions help to keep some of the memories alive. Several of the names designate regions, though only a few can be located with any precision. Examples are the Wilderness of Zin around Kadesh-barnea, now in Egypt (Num 33:36), and the Wilderness of Paran, the endless, featureless expanse of the mid-Sinai now called et-Tih, literally "the one who is lost" (see Num 13:26). The majestic desert tracts in southern Israel that bear the names Wilderness of Zin and Wilderness of Paran today are likely misnamed, though in a noble attempt to enclose a portion of the ground of ancient Israel's founding epic within the borders of the modern state of Israel.

This expansive region naturally fell under the eye of the stronger Judean kings for its value in controlling trade routes into and out of the biblical Negev basins. Springs and wells in the open desert invite invasion and have to be protected, either by disguising them with rocks or, when the effort is supported by outside powers, fortifications. Archaeological evidence suggests that the entire area was dotted by small ring-formation fortresses (square, rectangular, or circular in shape) during the early Iron Age.[1] Their "circling the wagons" outlines clearly indicate their function as protective enclosures, either as forts or settlement villages. Bedouin are known to pitch their tents in similarly-shaped encampments. These fortified sites attest to the difficulty of holding a frontier that is without a strong resource base of its own, and is far from easy supply lines. The prophet Jeremiah speaks of this very thing: "*The cities of the Negev are under siege; no one can help them*" (Jer 13:19).

The Ramon Crater marks the southern edge of the Greater Negev's southern highlands. South of that, the landscape takes on even more rugged forms. Crystalline rocks, those forming the middle and bottom of the limestone-sandstone-granite rock sandwich, appear in the far south, where the Greater Negev approaches the Gulf of Eilat (Gulf of Aqaba). Mineral deposits of copper and iron can be found in this area, and the Egyptians in particular mined copper at Timnah during the fourteenth through twelfth centuries BC (the 19th and 20th Egyptian dynasties). This region receives just one to two inches of rainfall per year, and that erratically; thus, normal human activity is confined to scattered known sources of water and the trade routes connecting them.

1 Yohanan Aharoni, "Forerunners of the Limes: Iron Age Fortresses in the Negev," *IEJ* 17 (1967): 1–17; Rudolph Cohen, "The Iron Age Fortresses in the Central Negev," *BASOR* 236 (1979): 61–79.

The bare, rock strewn hills of the Greater Negev's southern highlands offer a landscape that, for the untrained eye, easily hides the stark beauty of the land. Few landmarks break the monotony of the scene, and an inexperienced hiker can quickly succumb to disorientation and a lack of water. With scant rainfall, the soils here are immature, though the underlying limestone base holds potential for life. Small runoff spots like this one collect what little moisture falls during the winter season, providing brief watering holes for ibex, gazelles, or hyenas; it's alive with wildflowers for a few short days, bone-dry for months on end. *"He blossoms like a flower, then withers,"* Job commented on the frailty of human life in a sun-beaten land. *"He flees like a shadow and does not last"* (Job 14:2).

The eastern border of the Greater Negev wilderness is formed by the portion of the Rift Valley that lies between the Dead Sea and the Red Sea. Today this great cut is called the Arabah (Aravah), "desert plain" or "arid steppe land," although during the time of the Bible that name was most often reserved for the portion of the Rift Valley surrounding the Dead Sea (Deut 1:1; 2:8; 4:49; Josh 18:18; 2 Kgs 25:4; Joel 6:14, etc.).[1] The harshest section of the Arabah is "*Salt Valley*" (2 Kgs 14:7), near to if not the same place as "*Siddim Valley*" mentioned in Genesis 14:3. That region, which extends twenty-five miles (40 km) south of the Dead Sea ("the Sea of Arabah"; Deut 3:17), is not only 1,300 feet (400 m) below sea level but is composed of

1 Ze'ev Meshel, "Defining the Biblical 'Arabah," in Sidney White Crawford, ed., *"Up to the Gates of Ekron": Essays on the Archaeology and History of the Eastern Mediterranean in Honor of Seymour Gitin* (Jerusalem: IES, 2007): 423–35.

A low acacia tree and scattered bushes of oleander line the rocky floor of a small wadi flowing into the Arabah between the Dead Sea and the Gulf of Eilat. Hills of granite, exposed evidence of the lowest layer of the "rock sandwich," rise beyond. All desert plants are experts at collecting and conserving even the tiniest drops of moisture. The spindly acacia, providing the only wood readily available to Israel in the wilderness, was used to construct the ark of the covenant (Exod 25:10).

unproductive salt formations and Lisan marls. Like the wilderness south of the Ramon Crater, the greater Arabah (in its modern designation) is a hyper-arid land that receives at best one to two inches (25 to 50 mm) of rain per year. Summertime temperatures regularly reach between 100 and 110 degrees Fahrenheit (38°–43° C), or more, and the plants that survive here—such as the acacia—are extremely efficient consumers of moisture.

A massive break in the hills of the Greater Negev south of the Dead Sea has allowed the floor of the Arabah to push westward in a great sideways V shape. At the westernmost point of the V, thirty miles west of the Rift Valley, water from the Avedat spring (En Avedat) has worn the soft limestone surface into a majestic canyon. Labeled on modern maps as the Nahal Zin, this great opening has historically invited caravan routes from the east to penetrate deeply into the Negev wilderness. The En Hatzevah oasis, ancient Tamar, the largest of the Arabah watering holes, sits exactly at the midpoint of its eastern opening.

As for routes, the main international corridors through the Greater Negev ran generally east-west. The Arabian Peninsula's historic connection with Egypt traverses the mid-Sinai on a line skirting the top of the Gulf of Eilat (Gulf of Aqaba)[1] and the top of the Gulf of Suez. This is the *Darb el-Hajj*, the pilgrim route that still carries the Muslim faithful from Cairo to Mecca and for millennia has been worn by the feet of camel caravans bringing spices of the East to eager Egyptian markets. A second east-west route from Arabia climbed over, through, and around the four parallel ridges of the Greater Negev's southern highlands to Gaza, where waiting ships set sail for markets in the Aegean and Rome. The relative power of the recipient dictated which of these two routes was dominant at any given time. With the emergence of Rome and the West, Gaza rather than Egypt became

The great cut of the Nahal Zin has pirated smaller wadis as it erodes the soft limestone bed of the eastern and central portions of the Greater Negev's southern highlands. This view is from the plateau of kibbutz Sede Boqer, adjacent to the gravesites of David Ben Gurion, founding Prime Minister of the State of Israel, and his wife, Paula. Believing firmly in the spirit of collective manual labor, Ben Gurion felt it his duty to make the desert bloom, to fulfill in real time the prophecies of Isaiah that under a righteous king whose rule would be *"like flowing streams in a dry land"* (Isa 32:2), the wilderness someday would live. To the end of his days, Ben Gurion was disappointed that not enough Israelis cared enough about his vision to follow him out into the desert.

1 Israelis call the northeastern arm of the Red Sea the Gulf of Eilat after their modern seaport on its northwestern corner, while Jordanians call the same body of water the Gulf of Aqaba after the name of their seaport on the northeastern corner of the same.

The port of Ezion-geber may have been at Tell el-Kheleifeh, a low site halfway between modern Aqaba and Eilat, just inside the border of the Hashemite Kingdom of Jordan. The tell is a little more than a quarter mile (one-half km) from the current northern shore of the Red Sea (Gulf of Eilat), but was closer to the water in the past. Corroborative archaeological evidence for Israel's presence at Tell el-Kheleifeh during the time of Solomon, however, is lacking. An intriguing alternative site for Ezion-geber is Pharaoh's Island (Jezirat Feiroun), shown here, a rocky islet lying in the Gulf of Eilat just off the northeastern corner of the Egyptian Sinai. The mountains of Arabia are in the distance. While the remains of the picturesque castle gracing the site today date no earlier than the time of the Crusades, the choice of an offshore island to serve as the port for deep sea vessels is consistent with the Phoenician practice of locating ports on islands close to the Mediterranean shore (e.g., Tyre), or on rocky promontories jutting into the sea (e.g., Sidon). It is reasonable to suppose that since Solomon employed Phoenicians to build and launch his Red Sea fleet, they would have built a port similar to ones that they knew.

the primary terminus in the region. Arabia met Africa and Europe here.

At right angles (and cross-purposes, economically) lies a north-south route that runs the length of the Arabah and links Arabia and the Red Sea to Jerusalem via the oasis of Tamar (appropriately, Tamar is the Hb word for "palm tree"). This parched route is the Arabah Road up which Moses considered leading Israel on their final approach toward Canaan, before he turned eastward through Transjordan (Deut 2:8). It is also a route that interested the stronger kings of Judah. By fortifying Arad and then Tamar (1 Kgs 9:17–18), Solomon gained the main freshwater source south of the Dead Sea and hence could control the route to Ezion-geber and Eilat.[1] With the help of the big-timbered, sea-faring Phoenicians, Solomon was able to launch ships from Ezion-geber onto the Red Sea. The effort at supplying the Ezion-geber port required unimaginable energy, creativity, and skill (1 Kgs 9:26–28). One major hurdle was the logistical difficulties of hauling massive timbers down the Arabah all the way from Phoenicia. Once the ships were built, the tricky currents, reefs, and winds of the Gulf of Eilat had to be navigated. All of this was accomplished under oppressive heat and without adequate fresh drinking water. But in doing so, Solomon the mouse shut Egypt the cat, a country that was quite successful in building and navigating large ships, out of the endeavor. It is from these southern routes that he was able to import exotic goods to Jerusalem, commodities such as frankincense and myrrh via the Arabian Spice Route, or gold from Nubia (northern Sudan; 1 Kgs 10:2,10; 14–15; cp. Isa 60:6)—not to mention almug wood, ivory, apes, and peacocks for the enjoyment of the royal court (1 Kgs 10:11–12,22). Historically, Egypt had controlled the trade in many of these commodities—especially gold; but by tapping into the Red Sea trade directly, Solomon was able to siphon the products to Jerusalem right from their source (cp. 1 Kgs 9:16–18). Isaiah would later describe a similar situation but in a different context: "*Through a land of trouble and distress, of lioness and lion, of viper and flying serpent, they carry their wealth on the backs of donkeys and their treasures on the humps of camels*" (Isa 30:6).

Indeed, Solomon's efforts were so noted that the Queen of Sheba came up the same way in full exotic regalia (1 Kgs 10:1–13), echoing a similar visit in the fifteenth century BC by the Queen of Punt to Hatshep-

1 The place names Ezion-geber and Eilat both are used in connection with a port and/or settlement at the northern end of the Gulf of Eilat (Gulf of Aqaba) in the Bible. Whether there were two separate sites or these are two names for the same site remains uncertain. See P. H. Wright, "Ezion-geber," in Bill T. Arnold and H. G. M. Williamson, eds., *Dictionary of the Old Testament: Historical Books* (Downers Grove, IL: InterVarsity Press, 2005), 274–77.

sut, the first female Pharaoh of Egypt.[1] Jehoshaphat tried—and failed—at a similar attempt to sail down the Gulf of Eilat in the mid-ninth century BC (1 Kgs 22:47–48).

The Bible notes Edom's interest in the same region (1 Kgs 9:26; 22:47). Indeed, the route around the southern end of the Dead Sea through the Tamar oasis bustled with Judean-Edomite commercial and military activity. It was not, however, without real risk. Jehoshaphat's army ran out of water here, nearly succumbing to its extreme climatic conditions on a circuitous march to Moab by way of the ascent to Edom (2 Kgs 3:4–20).

Ancient Israel was never at home in the deserts of the Greater Negev, especially the region beyond the southern highlands. This was a *"great and terrible wilderness with its poisonous snakes and scorpions, a thirsty land where there was no water"* (Deut 8:15), a "barren, howling wilderness" (Deut 32:10), *"a land no one traveled through and where no one lived"* (Jer 2:6). (Here Moses had to rely on God to provide manna and quail and water out of the rock.) The prophets perhaps described it best in images that threatened to return the people of Judah to the wasteland of their wanderings should they not remain faithful to the Lord: *"I will make her like a desert and like a parched land, and I will let her die of thirst"* (Hos 2:3). Or in images of desert overwhelming the good land he had given them in Canaan: *"Like storms that pass over the Negev, [judgment] comes from the desert, from the land of terror"* (Isa 21:1).

The success of Solomon's endeavors aside, the prophets warned that Israel's efforts to siphon the wealth from the highways of the world would invariably supplant their efforts to walk on the pathways of God. Yet it was in the very worst landscape that the wilderness beyond the biblical Negev had to offer, the Arabah, where Jehoshaphat's army had run out of water (2 Kgs 3), that Isaiah came to understand the reality of renewal. In an image that speaks of God's ultimate trump card—the power of new life—Isaiah saw that the desert could indeed bloom:

The wilderness and the dry land
will be glad;
the desert will rejoice and blossom
like a wildflower.

The ibex—a type of big-horned desert goat—find their homes among the cliffs that line sources of perennial water in the Negev and Judean Wilderness. *"The high mountains are for the wild goats,"* intoned the psalmist (Ps 104:18). Habakkuk spoke in similar imagery, though of the deer, in concluding his prophetic oracles: *"The LORD . . . is my strength; he makes my feet like those of a deer and enables me to walk on mountain heights!"* (Hab 3:19). Both writers sensed that the rocky wilderness was more suitable for sure-footed, four-legged creatures than people, yet used the image to speak of God's wonderful provision in even the rocky places of life.

1 Hatshepsut left a colorful record of her visitors and the tribute they brought on the wall of her funerary temple at Deir el-Bahari on the west bank of ancient Thebes, in Upper Egypt. For a quick and colorful reference, see Alberto Siliotti, *Guide to the Valley of the Kings and to the Thebian Necropolises and Temples* (Vercelli, Italy: White Star Publishers, 2000), 100–111.

It will blossom abundantly
and will also rejoice with joy and singing.
The glory of Lebanon [rain and tall
trees!] will be given to it;
the splendor of Carmel and Sharon
[full of green and new growth!]
They will see the glory of the Lord,
the splendor of our God. (Isa 35:1–2)

E. THE JUDEAN WILDERNESS AND THE DEAD SEA

Though the desert that lies south of the biblical Negev is, by its sheer size, far more unforgiving than the Judean Wilderness, it is the latter that pressed its mark more firmly on the day-to-day affairs of ancient Israel. The reason, clearly, is the immediate proximity of the Judean Wilderness to the line of cities that trace the

The Nabateans, hardy denizens of the desert, controlled the Spice Route joining Yemen with the world of the Mediterranean during the late first millennium BC and the early first millennium AD. When Rome took away Nabatean independence in AD 106, their monopoly on trade revenue went with it, forcing the Nabateans to find alternative sources of income. Many eventually settled down at various way-stations along the Spice Route, including six in the Greater Negev's southern highlands: Avedat, Mampsis, Shivta, Nissana, Elusa, and Rehovot. Here they became masters at conserving runoff rainwater by constructing low dams at periodic intervals across the beds of shallow wadis, with wings of stone extending up the slopes to enlarge the catchment area. It is estimated that the Nabateans were able to channel runoff rainfall over an area of a half million acres (200,000 ha.) between Mampsis and Shivta. The result? They were able to increase the water content in focused areas sixfold, to up to twenty-four inches (610 mm) per year; that's equal to the rainfall amount of Jerusalem. Modern attempts to replicate the moisture efficiency of this method of farming, such as that at the Avedat field school shown here, have been less successful.

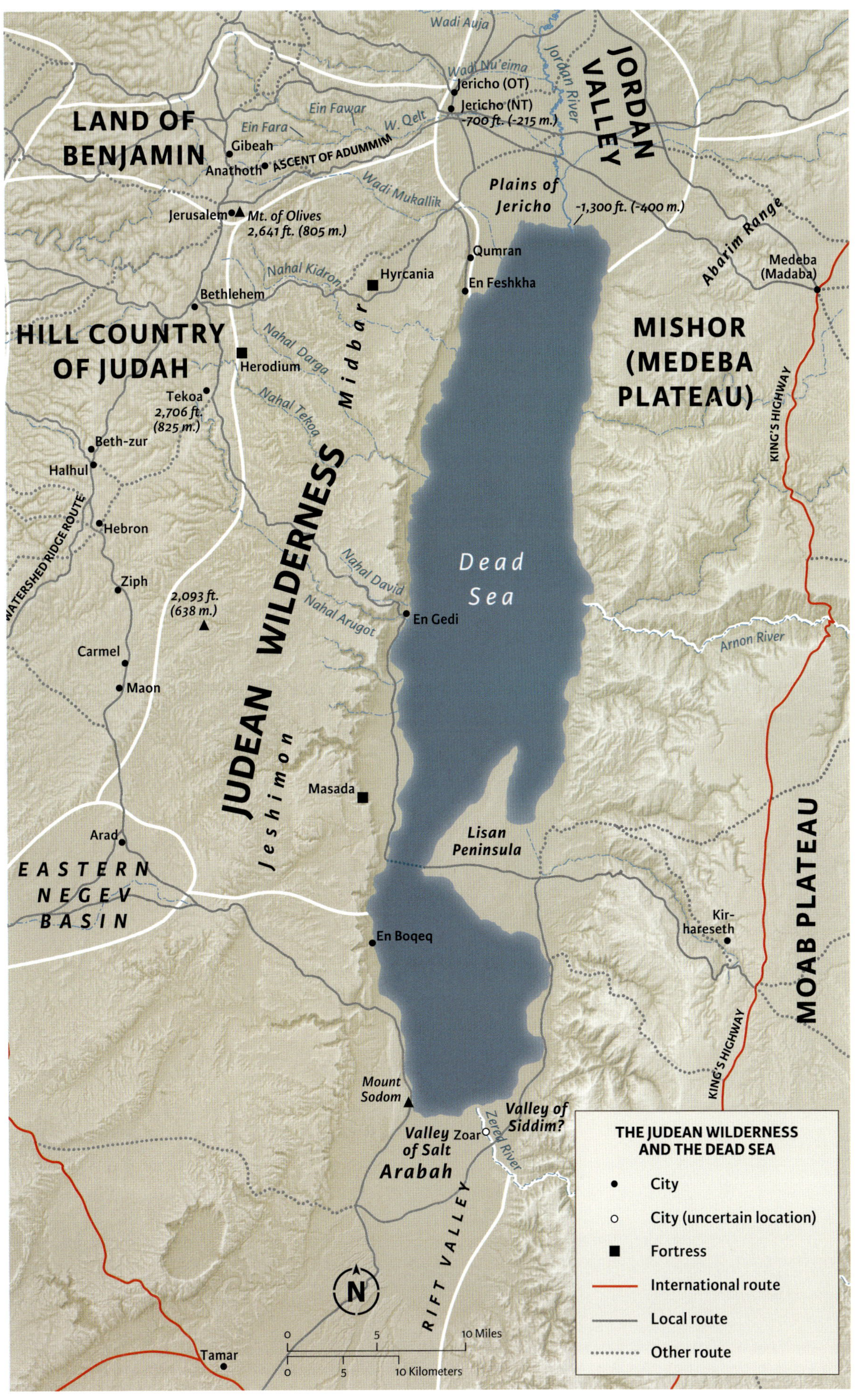

THE JUDEAN WILDERNESS AND THE DEAD SEA
City
City (uncertain location)
Fortress
International route
Local route
Other route
LAND OF BENJAMIN
HILL COUNTRY OF JUDAH
JUDEAN WILDERNESS
JORDAN VALLEY
MISHOR (MEDEBA PLATEAU)
MOAB PLATEAU
EASTERN NEGEV BASIN
RIFT VALLEY
Dead Sea
Wadi Auja
Wadi Nu'eima
Jordan River
Jericho (OT)
Jericho (NT)
-700 ft. (-215 m.)
Ein Fawar
Ein Fara
W. Qelt
Gibeah
Anathoth
ASCENT OF ADUMMIM
Wadi Mukallik
Plains of Jericho
-1,300 ft. (-400 m.)
Jerusalem
Mt. of Olives
2,641 ft. (805 m.)
Qumran
Abarim Range
Medeba (Madaba)
Nahal Kidron
Hyrcania
En Feshkha
Bethlehem
Midbar
Nahal Darga
Herodium
Nahal Tekoa
Tekoa
2,706 ft. (825 m.)
KING'S HIGHWAY
Beth-zur
Halhul
WATERSHED RIDGE ROUTE
Hebron
Nahal David
Ziph
2,093 ft. (638 m.)
Nahal Arugot
En Gedi
Arnon River
Carmel
Maon
Jeshimon
Masada
Lisan Peninsula
Arad
Kir-hareseth
En Boqeq
Mount Sodom
Valley of Siddim?
Zered River
Valley of Salt
Zoar
Arabah
N
0 5 10 Miles
0 5 10 Kilometers
Tamar

watershed—cities like Bethel, Jerusalem, Bethlehem, and Hebron, which are so prominent in the narrative of the biblical story. Like a wolf at the door (cp. Jer 5:6), the Judean Wilderness crawls out of the Rift Valley and up the backside of the Mount of Olives and to the edge of the Hebron plateau, holding its distance—though just barely—and reminding folks snug in their hill country homes that economic security is illusory whenever the hordes of the desert are driven by the whims of climate into the land of the farmer, just to survive. This may be the reality behind Jeremiah 12:10: "*Many shepherds have destroyed my vineyard; they have trampled my plot of land. They have turned my desirable plot into a desolate wasteland.*"

George Adam Smith called the Judean Wilderness the "awful deep." He likened the view from the edge of the Judean hills into the yawning chasm at his feet to that of a sailor standing on the narrow deck of a ship, watching the sea rise and fall away in endless swells below[1]—only here the billows are a jumbled mass of lifeless hills, churning in waves of white-to-pallid chalk. The writer of the book of Joshua called these chalky hills "*the slopes*" (*ashedot*; Josh 10:40; but cp. 12:8), literally the "lower part" or "foundation" of the land conquered by Joshua. In the distance, the heavy flatness of the Dead Sea fills the far side of the Rift Valley, and further to the east, the higher, dark purple-grey hills of the Mishor and Moab plateaus rise beyond in a horizon that for Judah was distant, flat, and strong (that range was called Abarim, "Over Yonder," in Num 33:47–48). The view prompts images of the earth as it was described at the opening moments of creation: "*formless and empty* (Hb *tohu wavohu*) *watery depths*" (Gen 1:2); such words are used otherwise by the author of Deuteronomy to describe the "*barren* (Hb *tohu*), *howling wilderness*" through which Israel passed on the way to their promised land (Deut 32:10). Too much water or not enough—the endlessly wide Mediterranean bordering Judah on one side or the cataclysmic drop of the rift on the other—neither was a landscape suitable for human habitation, at least from the point of view of Israelite villagers safe in the folds of their hill country homes.

The drop from the Hebron plateau (4,300 ft /1,300 m) to the surface of the Dead Sea (-1,300 ft /-400 m) is 5,600 feet (1,700 m) in less than twelve miles (19 km). Overall, the gradient is 7 percent; it's a route considered steep by modern road building standards and made even more strenuous by the constant gaining and losing of elevation over each billow on the way. The soft Senonian chalk that dominates the surface of the Judean Wilderness erodes easily, as rainfall beads up on its powdery surface and gully-washes away. The result is a

The line demarcating the change from the fertile living conditions of the Hill Country of Judah to the pallid nothingness of the Judean Wilderness is sharp and decisive. The terra rosa soils produced by Cenomanian-Turonian limestone easily support village life; the chalky, billowing hills of the wilderness don't. Here the wilderness is framed by the village of Za'tara and the Dead Sea. The view is from atop the Herodium, Herod the Great's palace-fortress southeast of Bethlehem.

1 Smith, *Historical Geography of the Holy Land*, 261–62.

Searching for greener pastures (cp. Ps 23:2), sheep graze among rocks and gravel above the Buqei'a Valley in the Judean Wilderness. This view is in March, when the spring grass is at its most lush. Later in the season, shepherds are forced to drive their flocks higher into the hills in search of more persistent pastures. Dangers abound at every turn. *"What man among you, who has a hundred sheep and loses one of them, does not leave the ninety-nine in the open field and go after the lost one until he finds it?"* Jesus asked an audience too often more interested in personal comfort than the bare necessities of life (Luke 15:4). In the harsh wilderness, duty and care are essential values.

jangled mass of smooth, egg-shaped hills, with exposed Cenomanian-Turonian limestone cliffs wherever the fast-flowing water has cut deeply through the surface covering of chalk. The final plunge is straight down the hard limestone cliffs that line the western shore of the Dead Sea; it's a sheer drop of from 400 to 1,300 feet (120 to 400 m). Here narrow, steep canyons open to the rift, their majestic bowels impassable to any but the hardiest of hikers.

The entire Judean Wilderness lies in the rain shadow on the lee side of the watershed ridge, where annual rainfall drops as precipitously as does the elevation: from twenty-four inches (610 mm) in Jerusalem to sixteen inches (400 mm) at Herodium and only four inches (100 mm) on the plains of Jericho. Further south at Masada, rainfall amounts average only a hyper-arid two inches (50 mm)—and that in a good year. With cool westerly breezes blocked by the watershed ridge, summer temperatures easily exceed 100 degrees Fahrenheit (38° C) in the bright, treeless open spaces around the Dead Sea. This heat rises to envelop the Hill Country of Judah when a withering wind blows in from the east (cp. Jer 13:24).

The result is a local desert where shepherding lifestyles lie in close proximity to the cities and towns that ring its perimeter. The southern extremity of the wilderness can be drawn on a line extending westward from the southern end of the Dead Sea to the southern bend of the biblical Negev. The northern end is usually marked just beyond the wadi Auja north of Jericho, where the Senonian chalk starts to give way to the hard limestone of the eastern Hill Country of Ephraim. This northern section of the Judean Wilderness is also the eastern extremity of the land of Benjamin, with Jericho, the largest oasis anywhere in the vicinity, a resource base for both.

Although Senonian chalk can produce somewhat fertile Rendzina soils (the Aijalon Valley is rimmed by Senonian hills), the profound lack of sustained rainfall in the Judean Wilderness means that the soils here have not been bolstered with sufficient organic materials to mature. Nothing of agricultural merit grows on the slopes of the wilderness hills, though the higher elevations do sprout a thin blanket of green grass in the brief months of late winter and early spring. This grass cover persists a little longer on slopes with a northern exposure, out of the direct rays of the sun. After it has withered and dried, the grass of the wilderness continues to provide nourishment for scattered flocks of sheep and goats, thin-eaters who don't need much. All-in-all, the carrying capacity of the Judean Wilderness is pretty low.

Yet the psalmist sings in praise of God's seasonal care for his land:

> *You soften [the earth] with showers*
> *and bless its growth . . .*
> *The wilderness pastures overflow . . .*
> *The pastures are clothed with flocks,*
> *and the valleys covered with grain.*
> *They shout in triumph; indeed, they*
> *sing.* (Ps 65:10–13; cp. 23:2)

In a moment of concern for all God's creatures, the prophet Joel adds, *"Don't be afraid, wild animals, for the wilderness pastures have turned green"* (Joel 2:22).

Perennial desert shrubs and even some larger trees manage to hold root in the wadi bottoms of the Judean Wilderness, especially where the flow has broken through the chalk into the layers of water-rich Cenomanian-Turonian limestone below. Large amounts of rain and even snow that fall west of the watershed high in the Judean hills above seep underground, then flow through the eastward-tipped strata beneath the chalky surface of the wilderness and exit as springs deep in

This playful waterfall, the "David Falls," is one of several in the David and Arugot wadis that feed the oasis of En Gedi, mid-way down the western side of the Dead Sea. The fresh waters of En Gedi, "spring of the [wild goat] kid," attract numerous ibex, or mountain goats, and hyrax, a kind of large rodent covered in fur (Ps 104:18). The region is a popular tourist destination, supported by the fond notion that David, who fled from Saul to the *"strongholds of En-gedi"* and to the *"wilderness near En-gedi"* (1 Sam 23:29; 24:1), enjoyed himself beneath the spray of this, the most majestic of its waterfalls.

the canyoned wadis facing the Rift Valley. The largest springs are Ein Fara and Ein Fawar in the wadi Qelt, as well as several in the Arugot and David wadis at En Gedi. Their green oases are stunning, even more so when set off by the sudden line of lifeless brown all around. In contrast, the spring at En Feshkha south of Qumran is brackish, supporting only hardy desert shrubs and palms, while En Boqeq south of Masada is warmed by hot sulfur springs.

The reality and reputation of the Judean Wilderness is enhanced by the Dead Sea. This body of water has several names in the ancient sources, all descriptive of its geographical situation: the Eastern Sea (Ezek 47:18; Joel 2:20; Zech 14:8), the Sea of the Arabah (Deut 3:17; 4:49; Josh 3:16; 12:3; 2 Kgs 14:25), the Salt Sea (Gen 14:3; Num 34:3,12; Deut 3:17; Josh 3:16), and Lake Asphaltites (Josephus, *War* 4.438). The flat areas that front most of the circumference of the Dead Sea together carry the name Arabah (or Aravah), which is best translated "desert plain" or "arid steppe land."[2] The two long, cliffy sides of the Dead Sea—in some places set back a bit from the water and in other places dropping right into the sea—were formed by parallel fault lines, causing the surface of the ground between literally to drop into the bowels of the earth. The shore of the Dead Sea, in fact, is the lowest spot on earth not covered by water or ice, measuring in at 1,300 feet (400 m) below sea level—over five times the depth of California's Death Valley. The sea itself is also the saltiest body of water by far, having a mineral content of 33 to 38 percent by weight, twice that of Utah's Great Salt Lake and ten times saltier than the oceans.[3] The Lisan ("Tongue") Peninsula divides the sea into two unequal sections. The

"Perhaps there is no region of our earth [other than the Dead Sea] where Nature and History have more cruelly conspired, where so tragic a drama has obtained so awful a theatre. In many other parts of the world the effect of historical catastrophes has been heightened by their occurrence amid scenes of beauty and peace. It is otherwise here. Nature, when she has not herself been, by some volcanic convulsion, the executioner of God's judgments, has added every aggravation of horror to the cruelty of the human avenger or the exhaustion of the doomed. The history of the Dead Sea opens with Sodom and Gomorrah, and may be said to close with the Massacre of Masada."—George Adam Smith[1]

Long beyond the reach of the West, the Dead Sea beckoned early travelers to the Holy Land with images of the fantastic. Wanting to check the reliability of the reports, the Irish explorer Christopher Costigan and his servant from the island of Malta rowed a boat to the southern end of the Dead Sea under oppressive heat in July 1835, then fought their way back to its northern shore having run out of fresh water. Suffering severely, the unfortunate explorers were reduced to making coffee with salt water before collapsing on the beach for an entire day. The servant survived, though just barely; Costigan expired while being hauled back to Jerusalem on horseback. The tip of the Lisan Peninsula that penetrates into the sea from the east was christened Cape Costigan in his honor. Thirteen years later, an expedition led by Lieutenant William F. Lynch of the United States Navy redoubled Costigan's efforts and was able to make scientific observations of the Dead Sea and its environs. Driven ashore by a bad storm on his first day out, Lynch, too, despaired of his life, but recovered enough to continue exploring for twenty-two more days. He capped his work by hoisting an American flag on a buoy, which he left to float on the water.[4]

1 Smith, *Historical Geography of the Holy Land*, 499.

2 For the location of the Arabah as the hyper-arid plains adjacent to the Dead Sea, see Ze'ev Meshel, "Defining the Biblical 'Arabah," in Sidney White Crawford, ed., *"Up to the Gates of Ekron": Essays on the Archaeology and History of the Eastern Mediterranean in Honor of Seymour Gitin* (Jerusalem: IES, 2007): 423–35.

3 For a fun comparison of the Dead Sea and the Great Salt Lake, see David S. Boyer, "Geographical Twins a World Apart," *The National Geographic Magazine* (114/6: December 1958): 848–59.

4 Yehoshua Ben-Arieh, *The Rediscovery of the Holy Land in the Nineteenth Century*, 2nd ed. (Jerusalem: The Magnes Press, 1983), 76, 123–33.

floor of the longer, northern section drops another 1,300 feet (400 m) beneath the surface of the water, while the smaller, bulbous southern end, now nearly completely dried up, is only twenty-five feet (7.6 m) deep. In total, the Dead Sea is sixty miles (96 km) long and ten miles (16 km) wide.

The Dead Sea is a true geographical marvel, and one that has attracted a reputation for the bizarre. One old local tradition holds that no one can venture out on the sea and live; another says that birds that fly over the sea die because of its fumes. We can let the first-century historian Josephus, a man never at a loss for words or shy about passing on a local legend, be our guide:

> The natural properties of the Lake Asphaltites also merit remark. Its waters are . . . bitter and unproductive, but owing to their buoyancy send up to the surface the very heaviest of objects cast into them, and it is difficult, even of set purpose, to sink to the bottom. Thus, when [the Roman general] Vespasian came to explore the lake, he ordered certain persons who were unable to swim to be flung into the deep water with their hands tied behind them, with the result that all rose to the surface and floated, as if impelled upward by a current of air. Another remarkable feature is its change of color: three times a day it alters its appearance and throws off a different reflection of the solar rays. Again, in many parts it casts up black masses of bitumen, which float on the surface in their shape and size resembling decapitated bulls. The laborers of the lake row up to these and, catching hold of the lumps, haul them into their boats; but when they have filled them it is no easy task to detach their cargo which, owing to its tenacious and glutinous character, clings to the boat until it is loosened by the monthly secretions of women, to which it alone yields [how Josephus knew that is anyone's guess]. It is useful not only for caulking ships, but also for the healing of the body, forming an ingredient in many medicines. (*War*, iv.476–480)

A place without rivals, the Dead Sea is both beautiful and awesome to behold. Seductively clear when still, the waters hold death for anyone or anything that tries to swim across or ingest its salty content. There is an exception—a few kinds of algae and bacteria, unique to this environment, manage to live in briny eddies and sink holes that have opened up in the marl banks as the water levels recede. Temporarily turning the otherwise azure water bright green, yellow, or sometimes red, these microorganisms provide a dash of visual spice to an already flavored sea.

Badlands of Lisan marl surround the perimeter of the Dead Sea but are most pronounced on its southern shore, such as here in the vicinity of Masada. It would be difficult to find a greater wasteland anywhere on the face of the earth. Soft, extremely friable and highly saline in composition, this marl was deposited in strata by successive inundations of the Dead Sea. It is useless for building material, water storage, or the development of soil, and as such has contributed to, and visually represents, the near impossible living conditions of the area.

Josephus's colorful assessment is not without merit. The Dead Sea is without an outlet save for intense evaporation, and its extremely high salt content is bolstered by mineral springs that issue from cracks on its floor. The chemical composition of the Dead Sea gives the water a heavy, metallic look; it's clear yet reflective when viewed from a distance. The American cleric Henry Van Dyke offered this description: "a mirror of burnished steel."[1] Indeed, because the mineral content of the human body is some percentage points less than that of the Dead Sea, buoyancy is assured for everyone who enters its waters (the feeling is something like being wrapped in a liquid moon,[2] without much gravity). Up close, the water is oily to the touch, nauseating to taste, and leaves a thick, white salty crust behind. Minerals found in the sea include sodium, magnesium, calcium chloride, bromide, sulfur, potassium, potash, and—Josephus was quite correct—bitumen, valuable as a water sealant in the ancient world (Gen 14:10).

Historically, salt has been mined at Mount Sodom, a large dome of solid salt with veins of gypsum, shale, and sands in it that rises above the southwestern end of the sea. The commercial value of the mineral content of the Dead Sea numbers many billions of dollars, making it the most valuable natural resource for both Israel and Jordan today. Many of these minerals, in solution, provide a therapeutic affect for certain skin diseases. When combined with its very low pollen count and dense atmosphere that screens out ultraviolet rays, the region of the Dead Sea offers a climate sought out for its curative properties. In a story amusing for the effect on its well-deserved subject, Josephus relates that just before Herod the Great died, he was bathed in oil at the hot springs at Callirrhoe on the eastern shore of the Dead Sea and almost succumbed to the treatment, his already rotting body apparently overcome by the ordeal (Josephus, *Ant.* 17.171–72).

The level of the Dead Sea has fluctuated over time and in recent years has been dropping at the rate of more than three feet (1 m) per year. This poses an ecological dilemma. On the one hand, salts released by natural evaporation are slowly poisoning the surrounding landscape, including fields fed by local freshwater springs that could otherwise be used for agriculture. On the other hand, with the waters so low, the minerals are more easily harvested in evaporation pans in the southern part of the sea for commercial purposes.

Even though the biblical writers often portrayed both desert and sea as places unsuitable for human

1 Henry Van Dyke, *Out-of-Doors in the Holy Land* (New York: Charles Scribner's Sons, 1908), 136.

2 The phrase comes from Timothy Yoder, one of the author's students in Jerusalem in October of 1999.

habitation, at least part of the Judean Wilderness could be tamed. Permanent settlements hugged its perimeter in places adjacent to sources of sweet water. Because the wilderness served as the eastern bulwark of Judah, many of these were fortified. One line of settlements can be traced along the base of the cliffs edging the western shore of the Dead Sea: the more important of these are Jericho, En Feshkha, En Gedi, Masada, and En Boqeq. Beth-arabah and the City of Salt (likely Qumran) mentioned in Joshua 15:61–62 certainly belong to this line as well. Of these, Jericho seems to have been settled almost continuously. Others were occupied at various times, and the line of these settlements seems to have been bolstered for strategic reasons during the Judean monarchy as well as at the time of Herod the Great. Certainly, there was money to be made in the region by anyone who controlled the lateral routes running through the wilderness: salt, bitumen, and balsam were all important exports in the ancient world. Herod the Great controlled the Roman world's supply of balsam, grown at En Feshkha and En Gedi, through his winter palace in Jericho. Archaeological evidence suggests several of the sites along the western shore of the Dead Sea, including En Gedi and Masada, had anchorages for boats that sailed between them or to any of several ports on the sea's eastern shore. These ports were active for trade and transportation generally during the time of the Judean monarchy, Hasmonean kingdom, and Roman period.[1]

The prophet Jeremiah spent his formative years in Anathoth, a hill country village just behind the watershed ridge that opened into the Judean Wilderness (Jer 1:1). The view from his home eastward, toward the salt lands surrounding the Jericho oasis, must have informed his prophetic vision (Jer 3:2–3,21; 18:15–17; 22:6; 25:34–38):

This is what the Lord says:
"Cursed is the person who trusts in mankind.
He makes human flesh his strength,
and his heart turns from the Lord.
He will be like a juniper in the Arabah;
he cannot see when good comes
but dwells in the parched places in the wilderness,
in a salt land where no one lives.
[But] the person who trusts in the Lord,
whose confidence indeed is the Lord, is blessed.
He will be like a tree planted by water.
It sends it roots out toward a stream,
it doesn't fear when heat comes,
and its foliage remains green.
It will not worry in a year of drought
or cease producing fruit." (Jer 17:5–8; cp. Ps 1:3)

The modern city of Jericho spreads into the Jordan Valley from the edge of the limestone cliffs that define the rise of the Judean Wilderness (left). Fed by springs issuing from Wadi Qelt (the cut in the foreground, left), from Wadi Nu'eima at Na'aran (below the rise of hills in the back center), and from beside Tell es-Sultan, site of the Old Testament city (hidden in the green between), Jericho is the largest oasis in the region. The spring at Tell es-Sultan, Elisha's Spring (cp. 2 Kgs 2:19–22), puts forth 1,000 gallons (3.8 m3) of water every minute. The Roman geographer Strabo described the scene this way: "Jericho is a plain surrounded by a kind of mountainous country which, in a way, slopes toward it like a theatre. Here is the palm-grove, which is mixed with other kinds of cultivated and fruitful trees . . . and is everywhere watered with streams and full of dwellings" (Strabo, *Geography*, 16.2.41). The water of these springs flowed freely into streams that crisscrossed the Jericho oasis up until recent times. Their flow is now regulated by governmental control.

1 Gideon Hadas, "Dead Sea Anchorages," *RB* 118/2 (2011): 161–79.

One of the less visited desert fortresses of Herod the Great is Hyrcania, built on a rounded mountain on the edge of the Buqei'a in the northeastern corner of the Judean Wilderness. Named after the Hasmonean king John Hyrcanus (134–104 BC), Hyrcania is one of several palace-fortresses originally constructed by the Hasmoneans in the decades prior to Herod's reign. Access is by a winding footpath up the mountain's southwestern side. The view from badly preserved remains on the summit takes in the entire Buqei'a and its longitudinal road to Jericho. Herod enclosed a prison within the bowels of the fortress where he detained, executed, and buried some of his most persistent political opponents, including his son Antipater (Josephus, *War*, 1.364, 664; *Ant.* 15.365–367). By carrying out such deeds in the middle of nowhere, Herod ensured that no one would break his code of silence.

A second line of permanent settlement hung on the upper heights of the Judean Wilderness, just east of the crest of the watershed. These towns include Jeremiah's Anathoth northeast of Jerusalem, Tekoa southeast of Bethlehem, and Ziph, Carmel, and Maon southeast of Hebron. The phrases "*wilderness of Tekoa*" (2 Chr 20:20), "*Wilderness of Ziph*," and "*wilderness near Maon*" (1 Sam 23:14–15,24) all indicate transitional zones where local shepherds grazed their flocks. All were border towns lying on the seam where shepherds met villagers and goods were exchanged. Throughout history, daily interaction such as this has allayed mutual suspicions on both the economic and political levels.

A middle line of sites is found in the Buqei'a, a small (6 by 2 miles; 9.5 by 3 km), flattened basin three miles above the northwestern corner of the Dead Sea. The Buqei'a ("Little Valley") is sometimes identified as the biblical Valley of Achor (Josh 7:26; Hos 2:15). For a short period during the late Judean monarchy, perhaps during the reign of Uzziah or Josiah, several wadis in the region were dammed by low lines of stone to contain their flow; this bolstered seasonal water resources in the area. This simple yet elegant attempt at securing water for agricultural purposes was adequate to support three small, walled settlements, possibly the Middin, Secacah, and Nibshan of Joshua 15:61–62.[1] These settlements may also have been the "*towers in the desert*" erected by Uzziah, a "*lover of the soil*" (2 Chr 26:10) who fostered agricultural initiatives in the wilderness, the Shephelah, and the coastal plain. Uzziah was also patron of a well-equipped army (2 Chr 26:11–15) and so must have appreciated the strategic value of the region. So did Herod the Great, who maintained a palace-fortress in the Buqei'a at Hyrcania, a second at Herodium on the line of settlement above the wilderness, and three more at Masada, Cypros, and Dok on the cliffs above the Dead Sea and Jericho. The fortress at Masada is, by all accounts (and certainly by popular opinion), the most dramatic of all. It's built atop a large block of Cenomanian limestone that refused to drop into the rift when the cataclysmic forces of nature shaped the cliff line along what was to become the western shore of the Dead Sea—and thereby set the tone for the resistance of the Jewish defenders of the site against the Romans in 73 BC.

For obvious reasons, the natural routes connecting the lines of settlement that track through the Judean Wilderness tend to take the high ground, on the tops of continuous ridges between wadi systems. The most heavily traveled natural route connecting Jerusalem with Jericho dips first into an upper finger of the Wadi Mukallik (Nahal Og), then climbs onto the ridge defining the southern rim of the Wadi Qelt. A portion of this Jericho Road is called the Ascent of Adummim (the "Red" or "Blood Ascent") in Joshua 15:7, apparently because of patches of exposed red clay and sandstone in the vicinity. Today this red-tinted spot boasts the

1 Lawrence Stager, "Farming in the Judean Desert during the Iron Age," *BASOR* 221 (1976): 145–58.

remains of a Turkish-era caravanserai that is popularly remembered to be the Inn of the Good Samaritan, the ultimate concretization of a parable (Luke 10:34). In any case, the setting is well suited for lone travelers to "fall into the hands of robbers . . . and be left half dead" (cp. Luke 10:30). This natural route was the path of David's flight from Absalom (2 Sam 15:23,30; 16:1,5) and Jesus's ascent to Jerusalem (Matt 20:29; 21:1). Meanwhile, Zedekiah, the last king of Judah, escaped from Jerusalem down "*the route to the Arabah*" (2 Kgs 25:4–5). This was likely not the same route, which surely would have been watched by Nebuchadnezzar's army, but probably a more difficult path via the Nahal Kidron and Buqei'a to Jericho.

A second natural route traces the ridge between the Tekoa and Arugot wadi systems, connecting Jerusalem to En Gedi (Hazazon-tamar) via Bethlehem, the Herodium, and Tekoa. The steepest section of this route, the climb up the cliffs above En Gedi, was called "*the Ascent of Ziz*" in 2 Chronicles 20:16. This was the location of Jehoshaphat's choir-led victory against a force of Moabites, Ammonites, and Meunites from beyond the Dead Sea. The invaders may have crossed the sea on the Lisan Peninsula, a sloppy, salty route that is passable when water levels are low. This Tekoa Ridge Route may have also been the "other route" that the magi took to return to their own country after visiting the Christ child (Matt 2:12).

The soft, chalky base and scant rainfall of the Judean Wilderness have placed its interior beyond the pale of the farmer. The northern half of the wilderness is *midbar* (Ps 65:12; Jer 9:10; 23:10; Joel 1:19–20; 2:22), a kind of steppe-land that can support the activities of shepherds who reside in close symbiotic (cooperative) relationships with cities and villages up in the hills. Further south is *jeshimon*, "desolation" (see Ps 107:4; Deut 32:10), a place where even shepherds won't normally go. It was here, though, that David fled from Saul (1 Sam 23:19,24; 26:1–5), and in desperation voiced the words:

> *God, you are my God;*
> *I eagerly seek you.*
> *I thirst for you;*
> *my body faints for you*
> *in a land that is dry, desolate,*
> *and without water.* (Ps 63:1)

Due to its proximity to population centers in the hill country, the Judean Wilderness has tended to be a place where those needing a safe haven could hide—distant enough for sanctuary yet sufficiently close to settled life to keep an eye on things. Herod the Great's palace-fortresses in or on the edge of the Judean Wilderness (Herodium, Hyrcania, Cypros, and Masada) served as quick escape hatches should things turn sour up in Jerusalem, but also as garrison posts should he have to fight his way back. Members of the Qumran sect (the Essenes) physically separated themselves from temple affairs in Jerusalem in order to create a kind of purified temple-replacement community on the shore of the Dead Sea. It was in the same region that John the Baptist preached a baptism of repentance for the forgiveness of sins, a countercultural message aimed not only at the temple priesthood but anyone else who was crossing the Jordan River on the road connecting Jericho with Transjordan (Matt 3:1–12; Luke 3:1–14). Tradition remembers Elijah's flight to the brook Cherith as having been within the folds of the Wadi Qelt above Jericho (the name Qelt preserves the word *Cherith*, even though 1 Kgs 17:5 locates the Cherith east of the Jordan River; a probable location in western Lower Gilead, nearer Elijah's home, is more reasonable). And Jesus himself was driven by the Spirit into the wilderness—tradition places his steps in the cliffs above Jericho—where he faced a hunger and thirst greater even than the reputation that the *jeshimon* allowed (Matt 4:1–4; Mark 1:12–13; Luke 4:1–4). Perhaps in part to replay Jesus's own wilderness wanderings, the Judean Wilderness became the go-to place for cloistered seclusion during the Byzantine period. At its height, numerous monastic communities maintained approximately sixty-five monasteries and laurae (hermitages surrounding monasteries) throughout the wilderness; these were linked by an intricate series of rocky sheep-and-goat trails. The monastery of Mar Saba, built into the rock face of the recesses of the Kidron wadi, and the monastery of St. George of Choziba, which clings to the canyon wall of the Wadi Qelt, preserve living elements of an ancient life of ascetic devotion to God. It is not by accident that the

Hermits' huts cling to crevices in the hard limestone wall of the Wadi Qelt near the monastery of St. George of Choziba, a mile and a half (2.5 km) above Jericho as the crow flies. Founded in the fifth century AD and reaching its most influential period under the direction of George of Choziba a century and a half later, the monastery has from the earliest of times provided welcome hospitality to all travelers, including women. The Desert Fathers sought to enhance spirituality through the quiet rigors of the contemplative life. Yet it would be a mistake to think they were avoiding responsibility or enjoyed a life devoid of real physical activity by doing so. On the contrary: during his probationary period, an initiate had to prove physical toughness and exhibit all the requisite survival skills to literally live off the land (note that John the Baptist ate locusts, insects the Mosaic law conveniently had declared kosher; Lev 11:21–22).

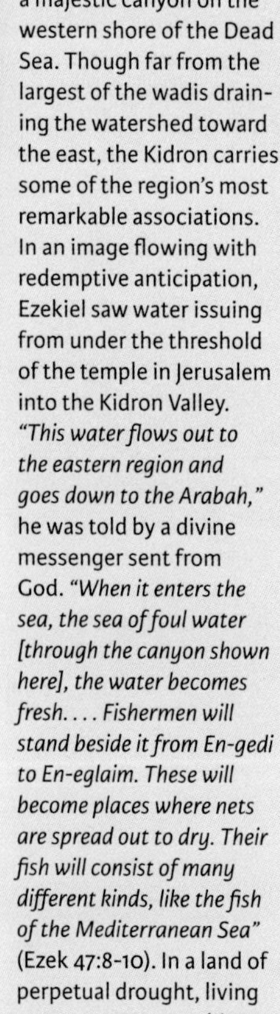

The Nahal Kidron (Wadi en-Nar) exits the limestone cliffs below the Judean Wilderness in a majestic canyon on the western shore of the Dead Sea. Though far from the largest of the wadis draining the watershed toward the east, the Kidron carries some of the region's most remarkable associations. In an image flowing with redemptive anticipation, Ezekiel saw water issuing from under the threshold of the temple in Jerusalem into the Kidron Valley. *"This water flows out to the eastern region and goes down to the Arabah,"* he was told by a divine messenger sent from God. *"When it enters the sea, the sea of foul water [through the canyon shown here], the water becomes fresh. . . . Fishermen will stand beside it from En-gedi to En-eglaim. These will become places where nets are spread out to dry. Their fish will consist of many different kinds, like the fish of the Mediterranean Sea"* (Ezek 47:8-10). In a land of perpetual drought, living water means everything.

world's three great monotheistic religions—Judaism, Christianity, and Islam—all had their founding experiences in the desert. There is something refreshingly uncluttered about monotheism.

The Judean Wilderness, then, is a place of great contrast. Adopting the words of Walter Brueggemann it was, for ancient Israel, a place of "having nothing yet lacking nothing,"[1] where life was at the same time thin but incredibly deep. When we view it from a distance, our eyes take in nothing but valleys of the shadow of death across the Judean Wilderness (cp. Ps 23:4). It is not hard to imagine Joshua and all Israel looking up at the wilderness from across the Jordan River, the only green in sight being the small Jericho oasis at its base and a vast expanse of hyper-salty water on their left, thinking: "For *this* we came out of Egypt?" Yet this wilderness, no less than the hill country, the Shephelah, and the coastal plain, was part of their own promised land. Here life was fragile, with the double punch of desert raiders (Jer 6:3; 10:22; Joel 1:4) and scorching wind remaining eager to sap life out of secure villagers living above (Jer 18:17). This reality was not lost on the biblical prophets, who constantly reminded Israel that just as they had once come off the desert, so they could be thrown back into a dry exile that reflected their moral and spiritual condition, should they so choose (Deut 28:15–68; Jer 9:16; 13:24; 18:16–17; Ezek 5:2).

But when viewed up close, through the careful eye of a Good Shepherd, the Judean Wilderness springs with life. "*I cared for you in the wilderness, in the land of drought,*" God reminded his people (Hos 13:5 NASB; cp. Deut 11:12; 32:10–11), with constant nudges that the wilderness could indeed someday bloom (cp. Isa 43:19–20;

1 Walter Brueggemann, *The Land* (Philadelphia: Fortress Press, 1977), 28.

51:3). Moreover, with language of creation, the prophet Ezekiel saw a river of life flowing from the temple in Jerusalem down through the heart of the Judean Wilderness to the Dead Sea, where everything that it touched lived (Ezek 47:1–12; cp. Gen 1:9–13,20–23,28–31). And with an eye toward travel conditions fitting the arrival of a king, Isaiah envisioned a radical change in its punishing topography:

> *A voice of one crying out:*
> *Prepare the way of the LORD in the wilderness;*
> *make a straight highway for*
> *our God in the desert!*
> *Every valley will be lifted up,*
> *and every mountain and hill will be leveled;*
> *the uneven ground will become smooth*
> *and the rough places, a plain.*
> *And the glory of the LORD will appear,*
> *and all humanity together will see it,*
> *for the mouth of the LORD has spoken.*
> (Isa 40:3–5; cp. Ezek 43:1–5;
> Matt 3:3; Luke 3:4–6)

It is no accident that whenever the Gospel writers provide geographical clues allowing us to track Jesus's travels to Jerusalem, he comes from the east, through a wilderness of death-being-transformed-to-life (Lk 18:35; 19:1,28–45; John 10:40–11:1,18; 12:1,12–15).

F. THE LAND OF BENJAMIN

The land of Benjamin is a region defined more by the events of history than its distinct geographical make-up. As a tribal territory, Benjamin was a horizontal wedge driven into the seam separating Judah from Ephraim and Manasseh, the southern from the central hills. Of the border descriptions of the tribal territories recorded in the book of Joshua, that of Benjamin is among the most detailed (Josh 18:11–20; cp. Josh 15:1–12; 16:1–3), even more so for the part of the boundary drawn around Jerusalem (Josh 15:7–9; 18:15–16). This special care in ancient record-keeping suggests that even though the tribe of Benjamin maintained its own geographical identity, it did so in particular in its relationship to Jerusalem. Indeed, the events of history bear out the maxim that the land of Benjamin is a kind of miniature Land Between on the pattern of all Israel; it's a place pinched by larger powers north and south and whose primary function was as a highway and buffer between.

The borders of the territory assigned to the tribe of Benjamin in the biblical account enclose an elongated land mass marked by the Jordan River and Jericho on the east, Bethel on the north, Kiriath-jearim on the west, and Jerusalem on the south. The maximum distance covered is approximately twenty-seven miles (43 km) east-west by ten miles (16 km) north-south. The territory is, in essence, a neat geological cross-section of Judah: the western half is uplifted Cenomanian-Turonian limestone; the eastern half is Senonian chalk and Lisan marl. As is the case with the hills to the south, the limestone heights of Benjamin receive up to twenty-five inches (635 mm) of rain annually, which tapers off behind the watershed to an average of four inches (100 mm) at Jericho. The terra rosa soil of western Benjamin provides rich farmland that supports a nice sprinkling of cities and villages, while the chalky wilderness slopes to the east sustain a shepherding lifestyle. Little Benjamin, Jerusalem's necessary neighbor, is a land of both milk and honey.

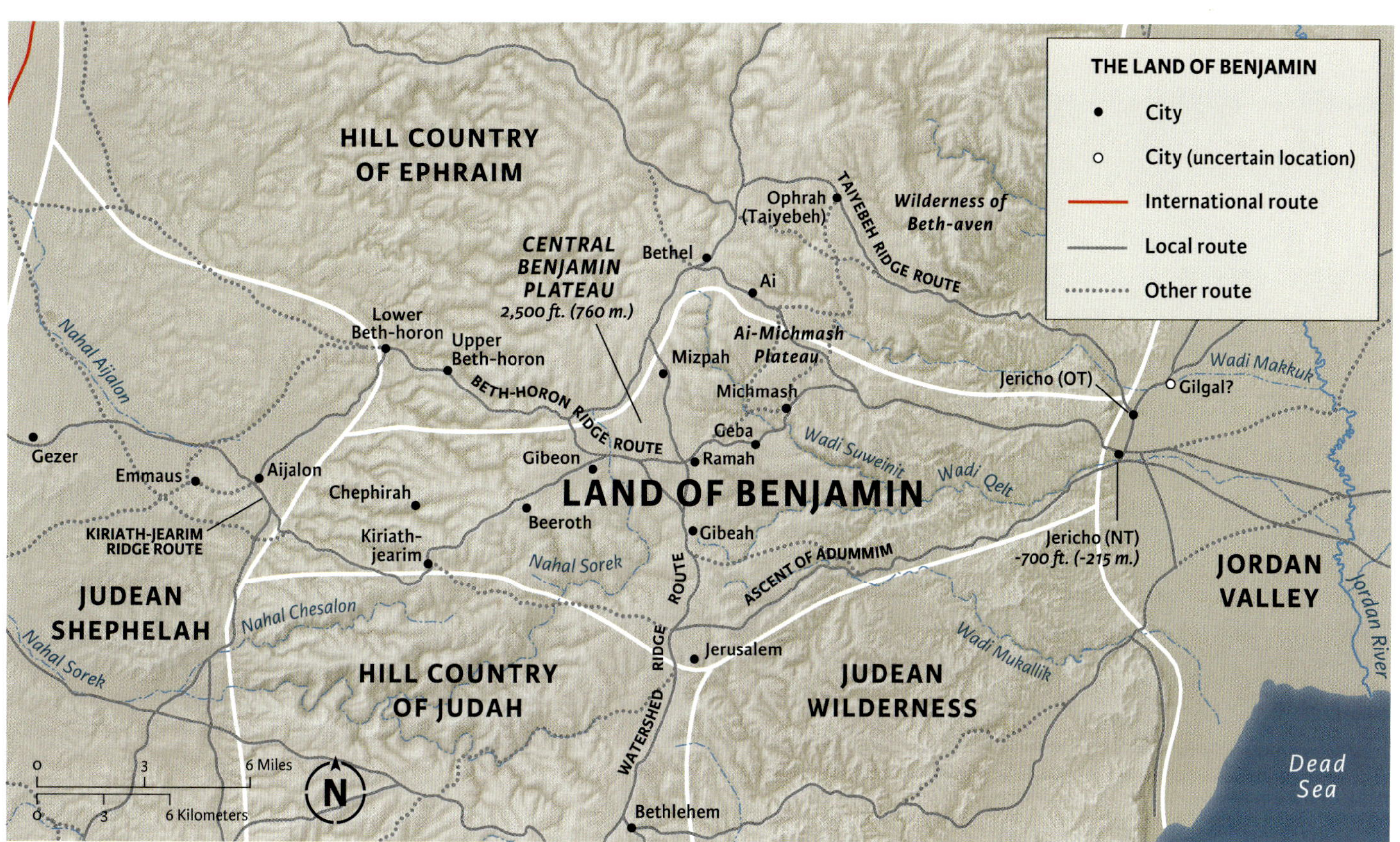

Taking a north-south view, the hills of Benjamin form a bit of a saddle in the watershed, with elevations topping out at 2,600 feet (790 m). This is somewhat lower than the hills north of Bethel and those south of Jerusalem, each of which reaches 3,000 feet (915 m) or more. This saddle is nicely positioned adjacent to the deep penetration of the Shephelah's Aijalon Valley and thus makes the land of Benjamin a natural pass over the watershed. Indeed, it is this very combination of geographical details that spurred Jerusalem's interest in the region. Given its somewhat isolated position behind the rugged Sorek wadi system, Jerusalem needed unencumbered use of Benjamin's routes to access the coast (e.g., 1 Kgs 15:17).

The heartland of the territory of Benjamin centers on three plateaus and the groups of cities and villages located on each. These are the Bethel Plateau, the Central Benjamin Plateau, and the Ai-Michmash Plateau, all names of modern convenience.[1]

The Bethel Plateau is the farthest north of the three. This is a small, relatively flat rise dominated by the old Canaanite city-state of Bethel, "house of God." Bethel was formerly called Luz, "almond tree," a name aptly reflecting the site's suitability for orchards (Gen 28:19; Judg 1:23). Archaeological excavations and surveys have revealed a number of small villages from most periods scattered on and around the Bethel Plateau, indicating the pleasant viability of the region. Today the large Arab city of Ramallah ("height of God") spills over the Bethel Plateau in all directions.

A second, larger plateau dominates the middle section of Benjamin's limestone hill country. Like the Bethel Plateau, this Central Benjamin Plateau is a wide spot on the watershed ridge, with gently rolling rather than angular topography. The settlement density of the Central Benjamin Plateau has been relatively high over the centuries, with four cities in particular playing a significant role in the biblical story: Gibeon (el-Jib), the large Canaanite city-state that first feared, then joined Joshua (Josh 9:1–10:15); Gibeah (Tell el-Ful), home of King Saul (1 Sam 1:16; 7:17; 15:34); Ramah (er-Ram), hometown of Samuel the prophet (1 Sam 19:1; 15:34); and Mizpah (Tell en-Nasbeh), the local seat of government during the Babylonian period (2 Kgs 25:22–24; Jer 40:7–12). Each of these cities has a topographically appropriate name: Gibeon and Gibeah mean "low hill"; Ramah means "height"; and Mizpah means "lookout point." In fact, all are located on gentle rises adjacent to flat, fertile fields backed by more low rises beyond which lie the fields of the next city. These four cities are relatively equidistant from one another and shared, though uneasily, the routes and resources of the plateau. Mizpah, Ramah, and Gibeah lay on the watershed ridge route in a line running from north to south, linking Bethel with Jerusalem. Gibeon, the largest of the four, dominated the more fertile west-

Here in the upper reaches of the Wadi Qelt, shepherds have transformed the upper two caves into a miniature barn fronted by a stone wall-enclosed corral. A narrow doorway can be seen at the midpoint of the wall, marking the place where a shepherd could sit or lie down at night (cp. John 10:1–9). The lower cave also once functioned as a sheepfold; its corral wall is largely broken down now. The prophet Micah likened a restored Israel to bleating sheep in a fold:

I will indeed gather all of you, Jacob;
I will collect the remnant of Israel.
I will bring them together like sheep in a pen,
like a flock in the middle of its pasture.
It will be noisy with people. (Mic 2:12)

Jesus elaborated on the image when he spoke of sheep enclosed with the Good Shepherd: *"I have come so that they may have life and have it in abundance"* (John 10:1–10).

1 The names "Bethel Plateau" and "Central Benjamin Plateau" are borrowed from Monson, *The Land Between*, 165.

The hills of western Benjamin break into traditional hard limestone forms. The main lines of communication have always stuck to the ridges above, though modern hikers prefer to blaze trails along the wadi slope. These would be analogous to the "*side roads*" (Judg 5:6) that served local farmsteads in the region from time immemorial. This is the Flute wadi (Nahal Halilim), a small finger of the Sorek beneath the modern Israeli town of Mevasseret Zion, west of Jerusalem. It is just south of the region of the four Gibeonite cities (Josh 9:17) that, having made peace with Joshua, allowed Israel access to the Shephelah. The valleys here are tight, easy to ambush, and breed a kind of loyal independence that Joshua would have preferred to have on his side rather than working against him.

ern side of the plateau. During the Late Bronze Age, Gibeon was in league with Chephirah, Beeroth, and Kiriath-jearim, three cities in the Aijalon and Sorek wadi systems which drain the plateau's western flank (Josh 9:17). Together, this Gibeonite federation controlled the all-important westward access of the Central Benjamin Plateau and, by implication, Jerusalem. It all made for an interesting dynamic as first one then another of the cities of the plateau gained ascendancy over the others throughout the biblical period—all under the watchful eye of Jerusalem just five miles (8 km) south.[1]

A third plateau, the Ai-Michmash Plateau, sits three miles (5 km) east of the watershed where the slope facing the Rift Valley flattens out a bit in the Wadi Suweinit, one of the upper tributaries of the Wadi Qelt. Here the line marking the division between the Cenomanian-Turonian limestone of the hill country and the Senonian chalk of the wilderness veers off northeastward, with the result that this plateau better resembles the fertile living spaces of the Central Benjamin Plateau than the drier expanses of the Judean Wilderness due south. At an average of eighteen inches (460 mm) per year, the rainfall of the Ai-Michmash Plateau is adequate for agriculture and supports the last line of permanent settlement in the hill country before the open drop into the land of the shepherd further east. The Bible calls the northern part of the plateau the *Emeq*, "broad valley," in connection with the narrative of Joshua's advance on Ai (Josh 8:13). Three towns of note are Ai (et-Tell), located on a ridge running up to Bethel; Geba (Jaba); and Michmash (Mukmas) further south. These latter two are closely associated with the cities of the Central Benjamin

1 As an example, Gibeon was the dominant city on the Central Benjamin Plateau during the days of the Judges (Josh 10:2). Ramah gained ascendancy as Samuel took on leadership of the Israelite tribal confederation (1 Sam 7:15–17). Saul, in turn, began to forge the instruments of kingship over all Israel from his home at Gibeah (1 Sam 10:26; 11:4); his purge of the leading men of Gibeon should probably be seen as an attempt to curtail Gibeonite influence on the plateau (2 Sam 21:2). Mizpah became an important fortified border city for Judah during the reign of Asa (1 Kgs 15:22) and served as the Babylonian administrative center of the region after the Judean exile to Babylon (2 Kgs 25:22–25).

The view here takes in the western side of the Central Benjamin Plateau from the south. The city of Gibeon once dominated the terraced hill in the center of the picture, while the modern Arab village of el-Jib, preserving its name, drops off the back left (northern) side of the hill today. The modern city of Ramallah and the rise to the Bethel Plateau mark the far horizon on the right. Gibeon's location was the most favored of all the cities on the Central Benjamin Plateau, enjoying a large expanse of fertile fields, a protective horizon line, and close connections to routes to the coast. Remains of the ancient city can be found among the terraced orchards on the site. These include city walls, numerous wine presses, and a rock-cut water system with a massive pool that may be the one by which the mighty men of Abner fell in hand-to-hand combat with the mighty men of Joab (2 Sam 2:12–16).

Plateau (e.g., 1 Sam 13:15–16), while Ai lay in association with Bethel. A fourth site is Beth-aven, which played a prominent role in the early days of Israel's settlement in the region (Josh 7:2; 1 Sam 13:5; 14:23). The location of Beth-aven, as well as the character of the site, remains disputed, though the wilderness of Beth-aven (Josh 18:12) seems to have been on the northern end of the Ai-Michmash Plateau.[1] In terms of its function, the Ai-Michmash Plateau is not only Benjamin's last bastion of viable settlement to the east, but a staging ground for invaders from the east who seek to push up and over the watershed ridge.

Benjamin's three plateaus are drained by several wadi systems. The Aijalon and Sorek wadis drain the land of Benjamin to the west and southwest respectively. Behind the watershed ridge, the main flow is to the southeast, into the Wadi Suweinit (Nahal Michmash), an upper tributary of the Wadi Qelt. The far eastern edge of the Ai-Michmash Plateau drains into the broad, gentle course of the Zeboim Valley (Wadi el-Jatta; 1 Sam 13:18). Further north, the Bethel Plateau is drained eastward by the Wadi Makkuk. With the exception of the Zeboim, all of these wadis are quite rugged once they drop off the edges of their respective plateaus and preclude easy travel anywhere except on the continuous ridges that divide them.

The tops of these continuous ridges carry the natural routes into and out of Benjamin. From the west, the

1 Beth-aven, "house of iniquity," is oddly named and seems to be a pejorative nickname for Bethel, "house of God," in Hos 4:15; 5:8; and 10:5. As an independent site in Josh 7:1 and 1 Sam 14:23, it may have been a village or, more likely, a regional religious center.

best route joins Gibeon with the Shephelah via Upper and Lower Beth-horon, two ancient villages perched on the narrow ridge overlooking the Aijalon wadi from the north. The Beth-horon Ridge Route is a name of modern convenience; the Bible calls the route either the "ascent" or the "descent" of Beth-horon depending on the direction of traffic (Josh 10:10–11). By weight of history, this route has proven to be Jerusalem's lifeline to the coast. It is not the most direct line west but does follow the shortest path of least resistance by circling the northern perimeter of the Aijalon wadi system, and it has the most agreeable slope. On the other hand, the Beth-horon Ridge Route is quite narrow at its upper end, though not quite as tight as the Babylonian Talmud makes it seem: "Two camels who meet each other in the steps of Beth-horon, if they both ascend at the same time, both may tumble down, but if they ascend after each other, they can go safely" (Bab. Talmud, Sanhedrin 32b). The narrowness of the route aids the defender, and its shortness favors the attacker; thus, everything conspires to focus Benjamin-oriented events at Beth-horon.

A second natural route westward traces the ridge dividing the Aijalon and Sorek wadi systems through the Gibeonite city of Kiriath-jearim. This Kiriath-jearim Ridge Route provides an important, though slightly more rugged, alternative to the route through Upper and Lower Beth-horon. Both the Beth-horon and Kiriath-jearim routes lead to the Shephelah's Aijalon Valley and Gezer, Jerusalem's wide and open front door to the coast.

As the Holy Land opened to the West in the nineteenth century AD, travelers of all sorts flocked to Jerusalem. Some came to stay. Those who immigrated typically landed by ship at the port of Jaffa. From there they made their way overland to Ramle on the outer edge of the Judean Shephelah. Having rested a bit or overnighted there, they continued on to Jerusalem by the most direct route, into and out of the wadis of the Sorek system on horse or donkey back, along the approximate line of the modern Tel Aviv–Jerusalem highway (Route 1). Their household goods, however, were strapped to the backs of camels for the longer, though less punishing, trek up the Beth-horon Ridge, a route better suited for the heavy truck traffic of the day.

Jerusalem's back door is Jericho, a place of travel options. From the Jericho oasis, three routes climb back up through the wilderness and into the Benjaminite hill country. From south to north, these are the Ascent of Adummim (Jerusalem's "Jericho Road"); the Zeboim Valley Route, heading due west to Geba, Michmash, and Ramah (1 Sam 13:18); and the Taiyebeh Ridge Route, which tracks the twisted ridge separating the Makkuk and Auja wadi systems and approaches the Bethel Plateau from the northwest via biblical Ophrah and Ephraim (1 Sam 13:17; John 11:54), the modern Arab village of Taiyebeh. As the first point of viable settlement north of

The rocky canyon of the Wadi Makkuk gouges its way through the Cenomanian-Turonian section of the Judean Wilderness in eastern Benjamin. Views like this one are typical throughout the region; it's a land of shepherds and hardy souls who developed a set of life-skills that villagers could never quite match. The tribe of Benjamin (lit., "son of the right hand") gained a reputation for having tough, highly skilled warriors, the kind who could even use their left hands to *"sling a stone at a hair and not miss"* (Judg 20:16). Their tribal hero, Ehud—a lefty—had the courage and craftiness (locals call it being clever) to assassinate Eglon, king of Moab, in an inner room of the king's own Jericho palace (Judg 3:12–30). It is a land like this that hones survival skills and creates people as rugged as the cliff-lands they call home.

The depiction of Byzantine Jericho on the Madaba Map, which covers a portion of the floor of the Greek Orthodox Church of St. George in Madaba, Jordan, captures the essential character of the oasis as "*the City of Palms*" (Deut 34:3; Judg 3:13; 2 Chr 28:15).[1] The map, made of colorful mosaic stones (tesserae) in the sixth century AD, depicts cities and natural features of the entire Holy Land. Only a small portion remains. Fortunately, much of the map's portrayal of the land of Benjamin and Judah is preserved. Josephus, writing in the first century AD, adds to the picture: "Of the date-palms watered by [Jericho's] spring there are numerous varieties differing in flavor and in medicinal properties. The richer species of this fruit when pressed under foot emit copious honey, not much inferior to that of bees, which are also abundant in the region. Here, too, grow the juicy balsam, the most precious of all the local products, the cypress, and the myrobalanus (ben-nut?), so that it would be no misnomer to describe as 'divine' this spot in which the rarest and choicest plants are produced in abundance" (*War* 5.467–69).

the Dead Sea, the oasis of Jericho collects traffic for all of these routes from the hills of Transjordan. Going the other way, whichever city in the Benjamin hills is able to control Jericho gains the natural advantage of being best positioned to push into Transjordan beyond. When Hiel of Bethel rebuilt Jericho in the days of Ahab, it allowed the Israelite king free access into Transjordan in a kind of reverse-Joshua move of conquest (cp. 1 Kgs 16:34).

It should be noted that each of the route names just mentioned is a designation of modern convenience rather than one that appears in the ancient sources. Ancient names, it will be recalled, are directional, hence "the way to Beth-horon" could refer either to a road across the Central Benjamin Plateau westward (1 Sam 13:18) or one through the Aijalon Valley eastward. The "*border road that looks out . . . toward the wilderness*" is also a directional term that the writer of 1 Samuel used specifically for the route through the Zeboim Valley (1 Sam 13:18; cp. Josh 8:15; Judg 20:42). Its terminology could justifiably be used for any of the routes that descend into the rift from the watershed ridge (2 Sam 15:23).

As in the Judean hill country to the south, longitudinal traffic through the land of Benjamin is largely limited to the ridge that tracks the watershed ridge, although in Benjamin that ridge widens into plateaus. When Abraham traveled from Shechem to Beer-sheba, for instance, he necessarily passed in the vicinity of Bethel and, certainly, Jerusalem (Salem); these were convenient way stations along the so-called Patriarchal Highway[2] (Gen 12:6–9; 14:17–18; cp. Judg 19:10–13). For reasons already mentioned, the Central Benjamin Plateau also carries the best regional routes connecting the watershed with the coastal plain and the Rift Valley. This made the land of Benjamin in general, and the Central Benjamin Plateau in particular, a popular assembly point throughout the biblical period. People tended to gather there for both productive and strategic reasons (Judg 4:5; 20:1; 1 Sam 7:5; 9:12; 10:3,17; 1 Kgs 3:4; 1 Chr 16:37–42; 21:29).

Of all of the biblical events that can be put on a map, more took place in the territory of Benjamin than in any other region of the land of ancient Israel. Mention of a few will help illustrate the strategic importance of the area.

The narrative of Israel's penetration into the land under Joshua's leadership provides the best sequence of events to aid understanding of the east-west dynamic of the region. Even if a Bible reader holds to a view that discounts the historicity of the Joshua narrative, the story line still portrays a geographic logic that fits the lay of the land perfectly. The conquest of Jericho gave Joshua several early strategic advantages in his push to conquer Canaan. By taking the oasis, he secured not only a foothold in Canaan but also gained an abundant source of water and fertile fields to support his advance into the hills. It is significant that Joshua destroyed the city, not its resource base (Josh 6:1–21). Conquering Jericho also allowed Joshua to seize the crossroads of the southern Jordan Valley, particularly the eastern terminus of the three routes entering the saddle of Benjamin. Taking Jericho provided Joshua the means to launch a thrust that cut the Watershed Ridge Route, the lifeline of the hill country, in half. At the same time, he ensured that the Canaanites would not have a base of operations to circle around behind his advancing troops.

Further up, the conquest of Ai on the Ai-Michmash Plateau gave Joshua a foothold on the first line of permanent settlement beyond the wilderness as well as the ability to scoot up the ridge to Bethel, then make his

When Mark Twain visited Jerusalem in 1867, he approached the city by horseback from the north, through the land of Benjamin. In those days, many parts of Palestine suffered under mismanagement by the ruling Ottoman Turks, and Twain's observations make the most of the disconsolate situation: "The further we went, the hotter the sun got, and the more rocky and bare, repulsive and dreary the landscape became. There could not have been more fragments of stone strewn broadcast over this part of the world if every ten square feet of the land had been occupied by a separate and distinct stonecutter's establishment for an age. There was hardly a tree or a shrub anywhere. Even the olive and the cactus, those fast friends of a worthless soil, had almost deserted the country. No landscape exists that is more tiresome to the eye than that which bounds the approaches to Jerusalem [from the north]. The only difference between the roads and the surrounding countryside, perhaps, is that there are rather more rocks in the roads than in the surrounding country."[3]

1 Important studies on the Madaba Map include Michael Avi-Yonah, *The Madaba Mosaic Map* (Jerusalem: IES, 1954), and Michele Piccirillo and Eugenio Alliata, eds., *The Madaba Map Centenary, 1897–1997* (Jerusalem: Studium Biblicum Franciscanum, 1998).

2 This is another name used by Monson; *The Land Between*, 94.

3 Mark Twain, *The Innocents Abroad* (New York: New American Library Signet Classic, 1966), 401.

way to Mounts Ebal and Gerizim where he renewed the Sinai covenant (Josh 7:1–8:35). This left the all-important Central Benjamin Plateau hanging. Joshua subsequently was able to conquer, though peacefully through a covenant with Gibeon, the strongest of the city states in the region (Josh 9:1–27).

By becoming an ally with the king of Gibeon, Joshua also necessarily made peace with the cities of the Gibeonite league which controlled the plateau's western approaches (Chephirah, Beeroth, and Kiriath-jearim; Josh 9:17). This was obviously too much for Adoni-zedek, king of Jerusalem, whose most essential region had just been taken from him. In response, Adonai-zedek gathered together a coalition of cities that were all potentially threatened by Joshua's cutting of the watershed ridge. These were Hebron in the southern hill country, Jarmuth in the northern Shephelah, Lachish in the southern Shephelah, and Eglon, a place not yet identified but somewhere down toward the Negev (perhaps Tel Eton or Tell el-Hesi). By defeating this coalition, Joshua secured the western approaches to both Benjamin and the Hill Country of Judah (Josh 10:1–43). He chased the enemy coalition's forces down the descent of Beth-horon to Azekah via the Shephelah's "Diagonal Road" and on to Makkedah (Khirbet el-Qom), deep into the chalk moat, securing rights to the upper, eastern Shephelah in the process.

As the various Israelite tribes began to settle the land of Canaan after Joshua's conquest, residents of Benjamin immediately began to feel pressure from all sides. Bethel quickly fell to Ephraim, its larger and stronger neighbor to the north (Judg 1:22–26). Eglon, Moab's king, took the Jericho oasis (Judg 3:12–30). Recognizing the importance of this eastern gateway into Benjamin, Eglon apparently tried to mimic Joshua's success in Canaan. However, Ehud, a Benjaminite partisan, prevented Eglon from advancing beyond Jericho. Meanwhile, Jerusalem, the southern gateway into Benjamin, remained a Jebusite (Canaanite) enclave (Judg 1:21). Data gleaned from the genealogical tables in Chronicles suggests that Benjamin and Ephraim pressured each other for economic advantage in villages and fields out west (1 Chr 8:1–14; cp. 7:20–28), bolstered, likely, by the temporary presence of the ark of the covenant in Kiriath-jearim (1 Sam 7:1).

The interior of Benjamin was also a victim of struggles for land and control. As the influential family of Saul gained strength around Gibeah, the old, established power structures of Gibeon, which had dominated the Central Benjamin Plateau since the Middle Bronze Age, certainly felt threatened. Saul's purge of the leadership of Gibeon in a kind of ethnic cleansing on behalf of Israel carries a clear subtext of economic advantage for his own family (2 Sam 21:1–2). The Philistines, too, got involved, pushing first to Mizpah (1 Sam 7:7–11), then all the way to Geba and Michmash on the Ai-Michmash Plateau, cutting the watershed ridge in another reverse-Joshua move and isolating Saul at Gibeah. The emerging Israelite kingdom was very nearly stillborn until Jonathan had the wherewithal to force the Philistines back down the Beth-horon Ridge (1 Sam 13:3–14:31). It is no wonder Samuel made a regular circuit

This small Bedouin encampment rests on a patch of terra rosa soil in Benjamin's Ai-Michmash Plateau. A four-wheel drive vehicle and heavy wagon, modern versions of the camel and pack donkeys, complement a small flock of sheep. The eastern edge of the Central Benjamin Plateau can be seen on the rise in the distance. Largely devoid of a permanent Canaanite presence in the Late Bronze and Iron I Ages, the eastern slopes of Benjamin were fertile ground for Israelite settlement in the decades following their emergence in the land. Very gradually, throughout the early Iron Age, tent encampments gave way to rude stone structures reminiscent of modern shantytowns, which eventually grew into sophisticated villages. The land was largely unforgiving, but its settlers were persistent, with the men and women of eastern Benjamin playing an important role in ancient Israel's formative years.

between Bethel, Mizpah, Ramah, and Gilgal in order to bring a sense of social stability to the region (1 Sam 7:15–17).

David and Solomon integrated the region of Benjamin into the united kingdom of Israel, with the Central Benjamin Plateau serving as a crucial junction on the corridor linking Jerusalem via the descent of Beth-horon to Gezer and the coast (1 Kgs 9:17). After the division of the kingdom, Rehoboam of Judah fortified all routes into Jerusalem except those from the north (1 Chr 11:5–12), apparently not wanting to concede to Jeroboam's rebellion and hoping to reclaim Benjamin at least by diplomatic means. His efforts failed, and a lengthy battle for Benjamin ensued. This series of events, in which the plateaus of Benjamin were ripped and torn like so many pieces of fresh meat in the jaws of ravenous wolves, best illustrates the north-south dynamic of the hill country (but cp. the blessing of Gen 49:27 in which Benjamin was supposed to be the wolf). Rehoboam's son Abijah temporarily pushed the border of Judah north of Bethel (2 Chr 13:1–20), but his son Asa lost both the Bethel and the Central Benjamin plateaus when Israel's King Baasha fortified Ramah "*in order to keep anyone from leaving or coming to King Asa of Judah*" (1 Kgs 15:16–17). Through a well-placed bribe to Aram-Damascus in the north, Asa was able to push Judah's border back up to Mizpah (Tell en-Nasbeh)[1] and Geba, leaving Bethel, Michmash, and Jericho in the hands of the king of Israel but reopening for Jerusalem the route via Upper and Lower Beth-horon to the coast (1 Kgs 15:18–22). Hiel of Bethel then quickly claimed and then rebuilt Jericho in the mid-ninth century BC (1 Kgs 16:34), allowing Israel's King Ahab use of the Bethel-Jericho axis (the Taiyebeh Ridge Route) to cut Judah's access to Transjordan and press Moab off of the Medeba Plateau. By such means the border between Israel and Judah stabilized on a horizontal line through Benjamin; the tribe's already small territory ripped in two with the wolf's share belonging to Judah.

True to its historic form, the land of Benjamin is divided today—this time between the State of Israel and the Palestinian Territories. Replete with a double fence and fresh asphalt, the border follows the contour of hills in the Chesalon wadi, a northern branch of the Sorek. The Kiriath-jearim Ridge Route tracks the far horizon line. Political aspects aside, this modern border also marks two approaches to land use. On the Israeli side (left), the hills have been reforested and are open for public recreation. Opposite (right), Arab villagers maintain traditional methods of farming on individual plots of family land.

The rest of the military history of the land of Benjamin supplies variations on the theme, mostly a loop of bad reruns for the residents of Jerusalem for whom Benjamin was the most essential region. A fast-forward look will suffice. Squashed by powerful interests on all sides, the residents of Benjamin (including Jerusalem) typically did not control their own destiny, or even Gezer, their necessary front door. Ancient Jerusalem was nearly always attacked from the north, through the Central Benjamin Plateau, either by armies marching from the coast through Beth-horon or coming up from Jericho. (The odd line of march recorded in Isa 10:28–34, in which a string of villages between the Ai-Michmash Plateau and Jerusalem were warned of an Assyrian attack, stands in marked contrast.) Moreover, the Seleucid commander Seron was driven back down the ascent of Beth-horon by Judas Maccabeus in 166 BC (1 Macc 3:13–24). In 63 BC, Pompey approached Jerusalem from Jericho, setting up his camp just north of the city (Josephus, *War* i.139–145). Herod the Great made his triumphal entry into Jerusalem in 37 BC from the north, straight down the Central Benjamin Plateau after a three-year campaign subduing Hasmonean loyalists throughout Galilee, Judea, and Samaria (*War* i.343–345). In AD 66, Jewish partisans ambushed the Roman governor of Syria, Cestus Gallus, on the descent of Beth-horon as he withdrew the Twelfth Legion Fulminata ("the Thundering One") from Jerusalem; with this rout, the Jewish Revolt kicked into high gear (*War* ii.499–500, 515–528). Four years later, Titus brought four legions to Jerusalem: one through the Sorek wadi from Emmaus, one up the Ascent of Adummim from Jericho and two, accompanied by himself, from the north. Josephus adds the detail that Titus left his army in a valley close to "Gabath Saul, which means 'Saul's hill,'" site of the old village of Gibeah (1 Sam 15:34) just five miles north of Jerusalem. "With six hundred picked horsemen, he rode forward to reconnoiter the city's strength and to test the mettle of the Jews" (*War* v.47–53). Jerusalem was, of course, destroyed by Titus. It was destroyed again in AD 1099 by the Crusaders, who reached the city via the ascent of Beth-horon. The British attacked the same way in 1917,[1] as did the Israelis fifty years later, on the third day of the Six-Day War: June 7, 1967 (the twenty-eighth day of the month of *Iyyar* in the Hebrew calendar).

No region of the hill country of ancient Israel has seen as much coming and going as has the corridor that is

1 Smith, *Historical Geography of the Holy Land*, 30th ed., 200–202.

Benjamin, a fate ensured by its geographical links to the coast and to Jericho, and heightened by its necessary connection to Jerusalem. This, the smallest of tribal territories, was assigned to a people descended from Benjamin, the youngest of Jacob's sons, a child who, his doting father knew, would have to scrap to survive. Jacob's blessing on him bespoke of a difficult future: "*Benjamin is a wolf; he tears his prey. In the morning he devours the prey, and in the evening he divides the plunder*" (Gen 49:27).

As it turned out, the *land* of Benjamin was ripped and skewered by just about everyone, from all sides. This irony is not lost on modern Israelis, who have named a pair of large Jewish towns on the northern approaches to Jerusalem Givat Ze'ev ("Wolf Height," near ancient Gibeon) and Pisgat Ze'ev ("Wolf Peak," behind ancient Gibeah). In his blessing, though, Moses looked beyond all the trouble and saw a day when Benjamin would be protected by its neighbors, as a lamb sitting safely on the shoulders of a shepherd: "*He said about Benjamin: The LORD's beloved rests securely on him. He shields him all day long, and he rests on his shoulders*" (Deut 33:12).

Indeed, all of Israel's future embraces a time and place when the wolf will lie down with the lamb (Isa 11:6), a detail embraced by the apostle Paul, a Benjaminite who saw beyond the tussle of regional geography to a world redeemed in Jesus (Phil 3:4–7).

G. JERUSALEM

And then there is Jerusalem. No place on earth evokes greater feelings of passion than does this eternal city, a locale both otherworldly and here at home. Biblical writers held a special fondness for the city, each speaking of it almost as he would a member of his own family. Their relationship with Jerusalem was personal and intense, and it infused all aspects of the biblical story. In spite of the city's many troubles—or perhaps precisely because of them—the psalmist longed that Jerusalem would not only survive, but thrive: "*Pray for the well-being* [Hb *shalom*] *of Jerusalem: 'May those who love you be secure; may there be peace within your walls, security within your fortresses'*" (Ps 122:6–7).

The Babylonian Talmud summarizes the living spaces of Jerusalem this way: "Whoever has not seen Jerusalem in its splendor has never seen a lovely city" (Sukkah 51b), and "Of the ten measures of beauty that came down to the world, Jerusalem took nine" (Qiddushin 49b). Yet for all of the hopeful associations cradling the very place where life can be lived the way it is supposed to be, Jerusalem boasts no natural features that would normally define or sustain a major place of settlement: it has no harbor, no river, not even a decent view. There's no major trunk route running through it, no on-hand supply of natural resources for production and export, and it has barely enough water to supply its own daily needs. Even the closest local route, the Patriarchal Highway tracing the cusp of the watershed ridge to the west, tracked a path that lay on the other side of the valley edging the New Testament city, or with two valleys between it and the older City of David. Jerusalem was, in the astute assessment of George Adam Smith, "on the road to nowhere."[1]

Other than its own historic associations—and these in the end have overridden all else—Jerusalem is indeed cramped by its tight geographical setting and is relatively cut off from the larger flow of events moving along the international highways of the Levant. Looking eastward, the city is isolated not only by the drop of the Judean Wilderness but by the ridge of the Mount of Olives,[2] which, at 2,661 feet (811 m), is 224 feet (68 m) higher than the hill on which the temple was built and completely blocks our view to the east. To the west, beyond the watershed, Jerusalem sits behind the deepest part of the ragged Sorek wadi system. The roughness of the Sorek is due to geological weakness in the limestone strata exactly at this point, where the ends of two parallel geological arches, one approaching from the northeast, the other from the southwest, don't quite meet. Under intense stress, this gapped joint allowed water to tear into its cracks and fissures, scouring out deep and twisted canyons in the process. Through-routes avoid the Sorek, and settlements and villages within its folds have remained isolated and small throughout all historic periods. Jerusalem lay just beyond the reach of the Sorek's uppermost fingers, with access from the coast having to circle around the wadi and enter the city either via the Central Benjamin Plateau to the north or by way of Bethlehem from the south.

The Cenomanian-Turonian limestone in the immediate vicinity of Jerusalem comes in several varieties, graded like hues on the color wheel. The limestone of the Mount of Olives and under the Temple Mount is of the type called *mizzi hilu* ("the sweet rock"). This is a whitish, relatively soft limestone of lesser overall quality, though it's useful for digging caves or tombs and suitable for making vessels out of stone (John 2:6).[3] The limestone on which most of the current walled Old City of Jerusalem is built is *mizzi meleke* ("the king's rock"). This type of limestone is relatively soft in its natural state and so can be quarried easily; it hardens somewhat over time when exposed to the air. This was the building stone of choice in the historic, biblical city of Jerusalem. Josephus sometimes called *mizzi meleke* "white marble," a pleasant misnomer worthy of the stones that Solomon and Herod quarried immediately northwest of Jerusalem to build their temples (*Ant.* 8.64; 15.392; 20.219–223). Its tinted color, when viewed under the early morning or setting sun, has prompted the reputation "Jerusalem of Gold." A very hard layer of *mizzi ahmar* ("the red rock") is exposed in the lowest part of the ancient access tunnel leading to the Gihon Spring, the city's historic water source,

---

1 Smith, *Historical Geography of the Holy Land* (1897), 319

2 The ridge separating the walled city of Jerusalem from the Judean Wilderness has several low peaks, each of which is a "mount" in its own right. In its strictest sense, the Mount of Olives is only the middle peak, the one that is opposite the northern end of the eastern hill (the Temple Mount). The northernmost peak, the location of the Hebrew University of Jerusalem, is Mount Scopus (*War* 2.528; 5.106), while the southernmost extension of the ridge, opposite the southern end of the eastern hill (the City of David), is the hill of the Silwan Village.

3 A quarry and workshop for manufacturing stone vessels during the time of the New Testament has been found at Hizma, north of the Mount of Olives ridge. See Yitzhak Magen, *The Stone Vessel Industry in the Second Temple Period: Excavations at Hizma and the Jerusalem Temple Mount* (Jerusalem: IES, 2002).

and in Hezekiah's Tunnel beneath David's City. The limestone of the watershed ridge west of the Old City of Jerusalem is *mizzi yehudi* ("the Jewish rock"). This very hard variety of Cenomanian limestone is grayish in color and abundant in the hills of the western part of the modern city. The first modern neighborhood in Jewish West Jerusalem, Rehavia, was quarried out of *mizzi yehudi* in the early twentieth century—but only with the use of dynamite.

All of these varieties of limestone hold water well and produce fertile terra rosa soil, the basic stuff for secure village life in the Judean hill country. Jerusalem receives on average twenty-four inches (610 mm) of rain per year, plenty enough to sustain productive agriculture. It is not unusual for summertime temperatures to push into the 90s Fahrenheit (mid-30s C); but by nearly every late afternoon, the Mediterranean breezes arrive. With them comes the "cool of the day" (cp. Gen 3:8). All of this is a recipe for pleasant living conditions in and around the city.

Up close, Jerusalem is a city of hills and valleys. Its local topography is determined by the course of the upper reaches of the Nahal Kidron, which splits into three fingers between the Mount of Olives and the watershed ridge. The main line of the Kidron (2 Sam 15:23; 1 Kgs 2:37; John 18:1) traces the western slope of the Mount of Olives. The top of the western scarp of this valley has always served as the eastern topographical line for Jerusalem's city walls. Today the floor of the Kidron Valley is about sixty feet (18 m) higher and somewhat east of its ancient line due to rubble toppling or being dumped into it from the city above. The Bible preserves several alternate names for the part (or parts) of the Kidron Valley closest to Jerusalem: The Valley of Shaveh[1] (Gen 14:17), the King's Valley (Gen 14:17), the Valley of Jehoshaphat (Joel 3:2,12), and the Valley of Decision (Joel 3:14).

The short upper branch of the Kidron wadi system that cradles Jerusalem on the south and west is called the Valley of the Sons of Hinnom (Josh 18:16), or, more

From earliest times the valleys adjacent to the city of Jerusalem have been cultivated by vines and fruit trees common to the Judean hills. The Kidron Valley was Jerusalem's most important breadbasket, and both archaeological and textual evidence suggest it was terraced, dammed, and irrigated by water from the Gihon Spring (note 2 Kgs 23:4 and Jer 31:39, which mention fields in the Kidron). Families who owned land in the valley were fortunate and protected their ancestral investment by stone enclosure walls. The Hebrew word for garden, *gan*, means, literally, "enclosure" or "protected space." In the time of the New Testament, one particular garden in the Kidron Valley had the name Gethsemane, "Olive Press," a witness to the type of products grown and produced there. Jesus and his disciples visited the garden often (Matt 26:36; John 18:1–2). Two enclosed compounds remember the location today: one is under the custody of the Catholic Church (the Franciscans); the other belongs to the Russian Orthodox Church. The olive trees shown here, in the very bottom of the Kidron Valley, are close to both and don't seem to be bothered by the mixed tradition. In the background is a Greek Orthodox church dedicated to the martyrdom of St. Stephen (Acts 7:54–60).

1 A tradition of the Dead Sea Scrolls community held that the Valley of Shaveh and the King's Valley were alternate names for the Valley of Beth-haccherem, which itself was likely another name for the Valley of Rephaim, the large branch of the Sorek wadi that drains to the southwest the part of modern Jerusalem lying west of the watershed ridge (1 QapGen 23:14). Michael Wise, Martin Abegg Jr. and Edward Cook, *The Dead Sea Scrolls: A New Translation* (San Francisco: Harper, 1996), 83.

conveniently, the Hinnom Valley. This valley probably takes its name from a clan whose ancestral land lay within its folds, likely somewhere toward its juncture with the Kidron Valley south of the City of David. By the time of the late Judean monarchy, the Hinnom Valley was better known as a place where fires occasionally burned in idolatrous rituals to Baal and the Ammonite god Molech (2 Kgs 23:10; Jer 7:31–32). Seizing the image, Jesus called the eschatological place of divine judgment *Gehenna*, a Greek form of the Hebrew *gai-Hinnom*, "the Valley of Hinnom" (see Matt 5:22; 18:9).

The middle, or Central, valley is the shortest and shallowest of the three. Today it is nearly completely filled in by the debris of the ages and is difficult to pick out among the modern buildings of the city. Zephaniah called this central valley the *makhtesh*, "crater" or "hollow," identifying it with the city's market district (Zeph 1:11). In the time of the New Testament, the valley carried the name the Tyropoeon ("Cheesemakers") Valley, apparently in reference to industrial activity that took place within its basin (*War* 5.140). Today the Central Valley is marked by the line of the el-Wad ("valley") Street that bisects the Old City's Muslim Quarter and connects Jerusalem's Western Wall Plaza with the Damascus Gate.

These three valleys define two intermediate hills, or ridges, on which the city of Jerusalem is built. While the oft-quoted description of Jerusalem by Josephus (*War* 5.136–137) took into account the buildings and infrastructure of the city in his day, his depiction of the topography is accurate enough for all periods of the city's history: "[Jerusalem] was built, in portions facing each other, on two hills separated by a central valley. . . . Of these hills that on which the upper city lay was far higher and had a straighter ridge than the other. . . . The second hill, which . . . supported the lower city, was [shaped] like the moon in its third quarter."

The easternmost of the two hills on which the walled city of Jerusalem is built, that which Josephus called the "second hill," is located between the Kidron and Central Valleys. This narrow, elongated hill is slightly bowed from the east, "like the moon in its third quarter" and angles downward from 2,440 feet (743 m) in elevation in the north (under the Dome of the Rock) to 2,020 feet (615 m) in elevation where the Kidron, Hinnom, and Central Valleys conjoin south of the city. The western hill, rising between the Central and Hinnom Valleys, is significantly higher than the eastern hill and quite broad, just as Josephus said, with a relatively level, rather than sloping, crest that reaches 2,540 feet (774 m) in elevation in the vicinity of today's Jaffa Gate.

Remains of the earliest settlement in Jerusalem dating to the end of the fourth millennium BC, as well as the Canaanite and Jebusite cities from the Middle and Late Bronze Ages, can be found on the lower, southern slope of the eastern hill, in the vicinity of the city's natural source of water, the Gihon Spring (1 Kgs 1:38). This is nearly the lowest place along the entire central hilly spine of the Hill Country of Judah. The walled part of the ancient city was extended northward when Solomon built the temple on the highest point of the eastern hill in the tenth century BC. The city expanded across the Central Valley onto the western hill at least as early as the late eighth century BC, during the reign of Hezekiah. The inhabited part of Jerusalem likely fell back to just the eastern hill in the days of Ezra and Nehemiah, though it certainly grew again in the centuries between the Testaments. The city of Jesus's day also stretched from the Kidron to the Hinnom Valleys, covering both the eastern and the western hills. The Jerusalem of the New Testament era was, from all available archaeological and textual evidence, one of the most magnificent cities around the Mediterranean at the time.

The earliest settlement in Jerusalem was on the sloping southern end of the eastern hill, adjacent to the outflow of the Gihon Spring in the Kidron Valley. Today the hill is once again called Ir David, "The City of David" (cp. 2 Sam 5:7), and is covered mostly by residences. The houses of the City of David slope downward from the southern wall of the Temple Mount; the golden Dome of the Rock marks the most likely spot of the temple, which had been the place of the city's threshing floor prior to Solomon's reign (2 Sam 24:18; 1 Chr 21:18–26). The Kidron Valley lies to the east (right), with the Mount of Olives beyond (far right). The Central Valley is nearly completely filled in today; its line extends outward and down from just to the right of the sunlit corner of the modern city wall (left of the golden dome).

The prophet Zephaniah also described the hills and valleys of the city of Jerusalem with precision, as only a native familiar with its topographical face could do:

> *On that day—this is the* LORD's *declaration—*
> *there will be an outcry from the Fish Gate [facing west from the temple compound],*
> *a wailing from the Second District [the newer part of the city on the western hill],*
> *and a loud crashing from the hills [those lying outside of the city to the north and west].*
> *Wail, you residents of the Hollow [the Central Valley],*
> *for all the merchants [conducting business in the center of town] will be silenced;*
> *all those loaded with silver will be cut off.* (Zeph 1:10–11; explanatory comments added)

With great drama, a cry of warning issued from high atop the temple plaza on the northwestern corner of the eastern hill, westward in the direction of Jerusalem's complacent residents. It echoed off the distant hills north and west of the western hill, then reverberated back into the middle of town, striking fear into those who were going about their daily business as if nothing out of the ordinary were happening (cp. Zeph 1:12). Both the cry and its consequences were as real as the shape of the urban landscape that energized Zephaniah's words.

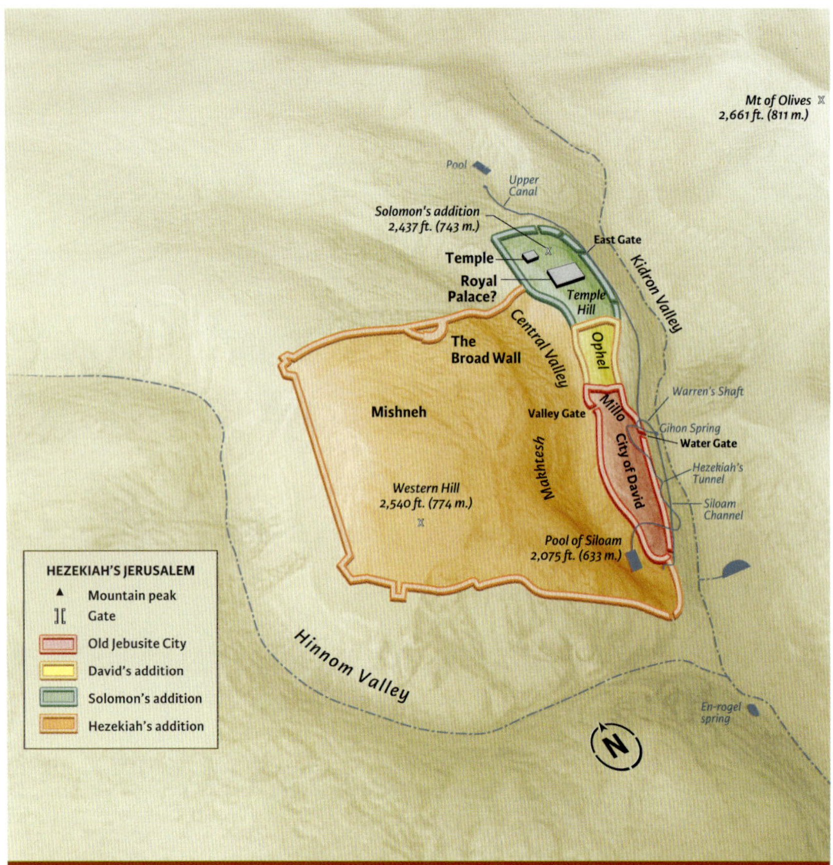

It is possible to place walls and buildings from the biblical periods on a map of Jerusalem based on the relationship of archaeological finds to natural topographical features, together with clues given in descriptions of the city found in written sources like the works of Josephus and the Bible. Some of the markings on any map of ancient Jerusalem are speculative, though most are likely and only a few are certain. In any case, all evidence points to a process by which the city's material form grew with its population while adapting to the topographical limitations underfoot. The map above shows the likely position of the city walls of Jerusalem during the late eighth century BC, the time of Hezekiah. The map on the next page depicts the shape of the city at the time of its destruction by the Romans in AD 70.

The valleys of Jerusalem drain to the southeast, around the southern end of the Mount of Olives and into the Judean Wilderness. The steepness of the valleys made for good defensive lines everywhere except on the north-northwest, where the hills of Jerusalem continue to rise, eventually joining to form a single wide ridge that merges into the watershed ridge about a half mile (1 km) beyond. For this reason, attacks have almost always come from the north. Fortunately, there are slight lateral depressions running west-northwestward off of the Kidron and Central Valleys on the northern edge of the settled area of ancient Jerusalem, which prompted the northern wall of the city to be built along these lines. The lateral valley running westward from the Central Valley follows today's David Street up to Jaffa Gate, leaving what is now the Armenian Quarter inside the walls of the ancient city and the modern Christian Quarter (including, certainly, the location of the Church of the Holy Sepulchre) largely outside. Perhaps as early as the time of Solomon, but certainly by the late Old Testament period, stone was quarried from these depressions, turning them into artificial moats that helped to defend the city from attacks from the north.[1]

The hills enclosed by the walls of Jerusalem are lower than those that surround the city. From anywhere within the city, we look up to a tight horizon line all around, as if standing in the middle of a shallow bowl. Thus, the image of the writer of the books of Kings: "*I will wipe Jerusalem clean as one wipes a bowl—wiping it and turning it upside down*" (2 Kgs 21:13).

The Mount of Olives rises closely to the east, while to the west the watershed ridge forms the horizon beyond the city's western hill. The gradual but persistent rise of the hills beyond the Temple Mount seals the view northward. To the south, at some distance yet within easy sight of anyone in the city, the view is blocked by a ridge (Jebel Mukaber) that runs perpendicularly off the watershed ridge, neatly separating Jerusalem from the hills of Bethlehem (today it is crowned by *Armon haNatziv*, the regional headquarters of the United Nations). Of the hills that rim Jerusalem, the Mount of Olives lies closest to the original southeastern core of the city, providing a sense of protection, or vulnerability, depending on the conditions of the moment. This is likely the reality behind Ps 121:1–2: "*I lift my eyes toward the mountains. Where will my help come from? My help comes from the LORD, the Maker of heaven and earth.*" In any event, being fully aware of the precarious situation of his hometown, the psalmist sensed God's care even though he sat under threatening shadows all around. After all, the "Maker of heaven and earth" had made the topography of Jerusalem to be the way it was. As Psalm 125 states, "*The mountains surround Jerusalem and the LORD surrounds his people, both now and forever*" (Ps 125:2). Here the psalmist's image is reversed, with the closeness of the mountains forming a protective barrier, a kind of natural wall around the city. The picture is reminiscent of the aviary imagery found in the Song of Moses: "*He watches over his nest like an eagle and hovers over his young*" (Deut 32:11). Or, in a tender version of the same, that of Jesus, who compared himself to a mother chicken and the topography of Jerusalem to a nest: "*Jerusalem, who kills the prophets and stones those who are sent to her. How often I wanted to gather your children together, as a hen gathers her chicks under her wings, yet you were not willing!*" (Matt 23:37).

One might note that this geographical setting was not unique to ancient Jerusalem but typical of most of the other capital cities of the region. Israel's Samaria (Sebastiyeh), Ammon's Rabbah (the Amman Citadel), Moab's Kir-hareseth (Kerak) and Dibon (Dibhan), and Edom's Bozrah (Buseira) were all located on defensible rises; each was partially or completely surrounded by higher hills. And in every case except for Jerusalem, the hills surrounding these capitals were far enough away so that an attacking army would not feel as though they could look (and maybe even shoot) directly down into the besieged city's streets. Jerusalem's situation was clearly the most vulnerable, and its royal neighbors—

1 The bibliography on the historical geography and archaeology of Jerusalem is immense. Four helpful volumes are Nahman Avigad, *Discovering Jerusalem* (Nashville: Thomas Nelson, 1983); Hillel Geva, ed., *Ancient Jerusalem Revealed* (Jerusalem: IES, 2000); Dan Bahat, *The Carta Jerusalem Atlas*, 3rd rev. (Jerusalem: Carta, 2011); and Ronny Reich, *Excavating the City of David: Where Jerusalem's History Began* (Jerusalem: IES, 2011).

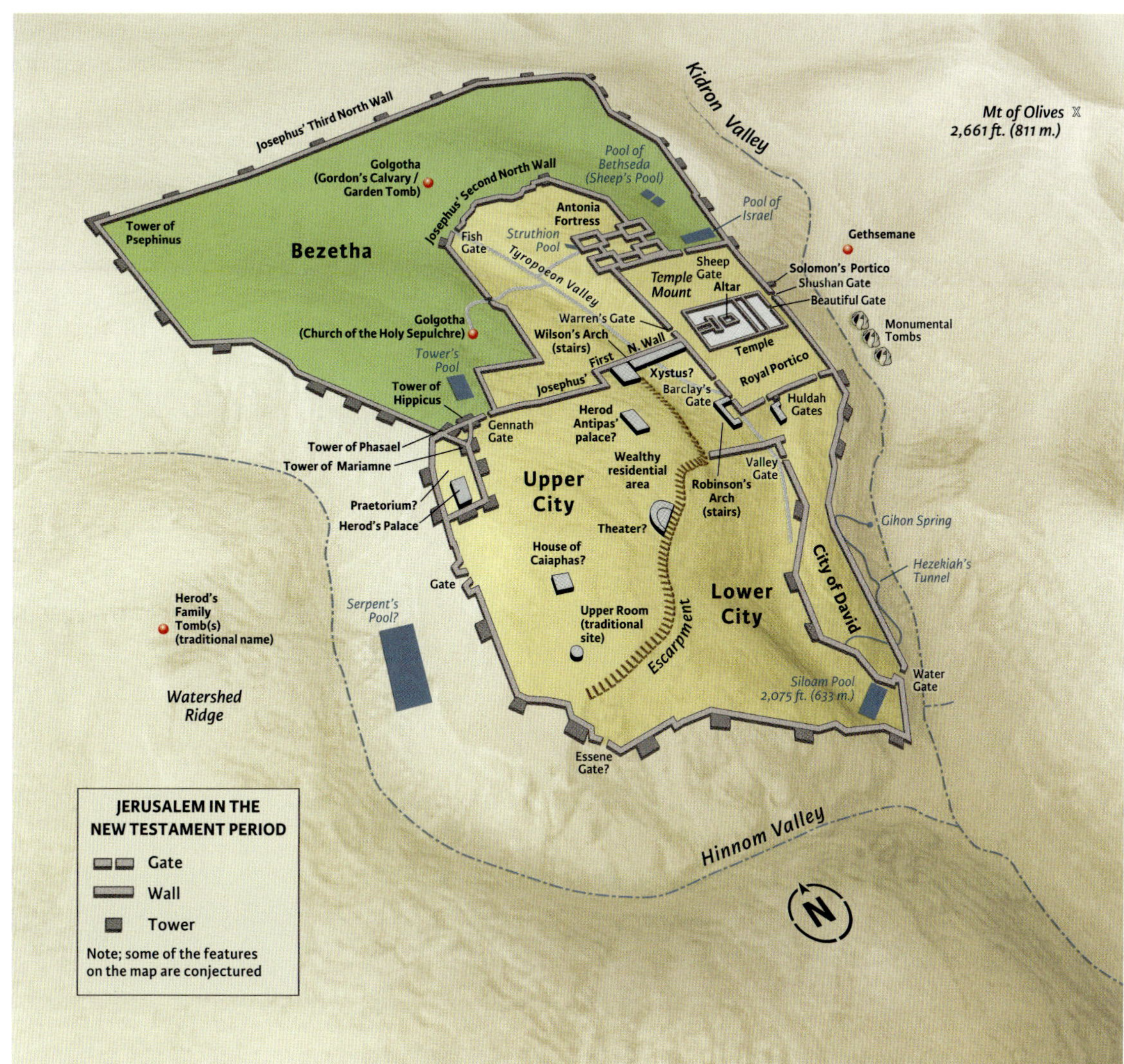

all of whom were more secure than those who lived in the capital of Judah—must have crowed with the thought. Isaiah's vision of the geographical future of Jerusalem, its connection to a divine mountains theology aside, was a justified response:

In the last days
the mountain of the LORD's house
will be established
at the top of the mountains
and will be raised above the hills.
All nations will stream to it,
and many peoples will come and say,
"Come, let us go up to the mountain of the LORD,
to the house of the God of Jacob.
He will teach us about his ways
so that we may walk in his paths."
(Isa 2:2–3; cp. Mic 4:1–2)

One would be correct to ask why, given these geographical limitations of Jerusalem, David chose it to be the capital of his kingdom. The choice of the location of Jerusalem as the place "*the LORD your God will choose . . . to have his name dwell*" (Deut 12:11) is not at all obvious from the records of Israel's earliest history. Abraham's visit to Melchizedek king of Salem (Gen 14:17–24; cp. Ps 76:1–2) and his journey to the land (note: not Mount) of Moriah[1] to offer up Isaac "*on one of the mountains I will tell you about*" (Gen 22:2; cp. 2 Chr 3:1) are at best anticipatory. After all, the Samaritans, whose Bible is only the books of the Pentateuch and whose holy mountain is Gerizim (Deut 11:29–30; cp.

1 The sole mention of the place name Mount Moriah in the Bible is in 2 Chr 3:1, where it designates the location of the threshing floor of Ornan the Jebusite over which Solomon built the temple. The place where Abraham offered Isaac as a sacrifice to God is described only as being in "*the land of Moriah . . . on one of the mountains I will tell you about*" (Gen 22:2). Although there are abundant theological reasons to connect the two locations, the historical geographical evidence to do so is far from conclusive. One of the difficulties is that the tenor of the story in Genesis 22 suggests that the journey of Abraham and Isaac took them to a place distant from witnesses (cp. vv. 4–5), while archaeological evidence shows that Jerusalem was a thriving Middle Bronze Age city at the time. Indeed, on topographical grounds, the location of the Mount Moriah of 2 Chr 3:1 would have been adjacent to the major route leading into the city, an odd place for an event as awesome (and troubling) as that of a potential human sacrifice by a stranger in town. It is more likely that the term "land of Moriah" referred to an area of the northern Judean Wilderness somewhat adjacent to the back side of the ridge of the Mount of Olives. This would be an area on Jerusalem's hinterland, a place associated with the city by proximity yet far enough away to allow the story to unfold without interference by onlookers. We should add that in Samaritan tradition, Mount Moriah was their holy mountain, Gerizim.

Josh 8:33; John 4:20), dismiss Jerusalem in part because the city is not mentioned by that name anywhere in the Torah (Gen through Deut). The choice of the city was clearly God's (Ps 78:68), yet the decision to locate the capital of Israel in Jerusalem also made perfect sense to David on geopolitical grounds. Similar to the location of Washington, D.C., Jerusalem is on the seam between northern and southern power bases, and its selection allowed David to govern both regions without seeming to favor either. Hebron, his first capital, was too deep into the territory of Judah to be taken seriously by the northern tribes as the capital of all Israel (2 Sam 5:1–9). Moreover, as an unconquered Jebusite city, Jerusalem was neutral ground that David could transform into the City of David (2 Sam 5:9),[1] a place belonging both to the royal dynasty and, by extension, to all of the people of Israel. Jerusalem was actually within the borders of Benjamin (Josh 15:7–8; 18:21,28), a northern tribe, but had remained a Jebusite enclave even though the hometown of David's kingly predecessor, the Benjaminite Saul, lay just five miles north. As a result, David, a southerner, didn't conquer Benjaminite land *per se* when he took Jerusalem (*that* would have been a divisive move). Rather, he restored

The western wall of the Old City of Jerusalem today follows the north-south line of the Hinnom Valley, a naturally fortified position on the western edge of the western hill. The modern wall, with strongly formed towers (top left), was built in the sixteenth century AD by the Ottoman Turkish sultan Suleiman the Magnificent. Remains of earlier walls can be seen at various places along the foundation of Suleiman's wall, confirming the idea that the western hill was walled as early as the reign of Hezekiah (late eighth century BC). Whenever the city wall followed this topographical line in the biblical period, it continued to trace the curve of the hill, bending eastward to David's City. The portion of the western hill in the right of the photo, which is now (incorrectly) called Mt. Zion, lies outside Suleiman's walls. Evidence of the earlier walls can be seen in the bedrock behind the Greek Orthodox seminary (center, partially hidden behind trees) and as the foundation of the angular campus of Jerusalem University College, residence of the author, right.

1 The name "City of David" appears secondarily in connection with Bethlehem, the town of David's birth; Luke 2:4,11.

The eastern wall of the Temple Mount reflects the first light of dawn over the Old City of Jerusalem. This view is from the northern end of the Mount of Olives ridge (Mt. Scopus), looking southwestward into the Kidron Valley.

With a wonderful burst of local pride, the psalmist described Mount Zion as *"Beautiful in elevation . . . in the far [lit. 'the extreme parts of'] north"* (Ps 48:2 NASB), using language that evokes images of the greatest of all mountains in the land of ancient Israel, Mount Hermon. The comparison is heightened by the two mountains' ancient names: Zion and Sion. Both are Canaanite names; the former was the nickname of the Jebusite city of Jerusalem prior to David's conquest (2 Sam 5:7). The latter was a shortened form of Sirion, the Phoenician name for Hermon, a mountain held to be divine in Canaanite myth (Deut 4:48; cp. 3:9). While the original meaning of both names is lost, the similarity in the sound of the two names (though they are spelled differently in Hebrew) was perhaps not overlooked by the psalmist who, with the force of a geographical pun, prompted his readers to embrace the divine activity on Mount Zion rather than that of pagan Hermon.

a recalcitrant piece of Benjamin's inheritance to the Israelite fold—and that in Saul's backyard. It was all quite convenient and likely calculated to bolster David's support in the north.

The location of ancient Jerusalem's walls, towers, public buildings, water pools, gates, streets, and cemeteries was suited to the contours of its topography. This is typical of any city that is built across hills and valleys. Thanks to official records as well as incidental comments recorded in the Bible, the Talmud, the works of Josephus, and other sources related to ancient Israel, we actually know the names of more of these structures than we do for any other contemporary city except perhaps ancient Rome. The city of Jerusalem had a complicated and well-planned infrastructure in all of its ancient phases, a point corroborated by archaeological excavations. It is possible to suggest where certain types of structures would most likely have been located in ancient Jerusalem based on the logic of the city's topography and archaeological remains.

- As we have seen, Jerusalem's walls tended to follow the natural fortification line of the city, namely, the upper edges of its valley's slopes. One exception was the city wall of the Middle and Late Bronze Ages (the "Jebusite Wall"), which traced the edge of the narrow eastern hill about one-third of the way down slope, apparently in order to provide adequate living space on the narrow hill above. The natural location of the northern wall of the city is more problematic, though it seemed to follow the edges of the transversal valleys that veered off westward from both the Kidron and Central Valleys. The area of the city that was walled at any given time tended to expand and contract with the city's fortunes. That is, the city's western wall sometimes followed the western scarp of the eastern hill (following the Central Valley), while at other times as the city expanded, such as in the Late

The Gihon Spring is Jerusalem's source of fresh water. Aptly named (*gihon* means "a bursting forth"), the Gihon is a siphon spring, gushing out large amounts of water at fairly regular intervals. Over the course of millennia, water from the Gihon has been diverted into a number of channels and pools in order to better meet the needs of the city's inhabitants. The earliest of these channels dates to the Middle Bronze Age II (eighteenth century BC), while the best known is Hezekiah's Tunnel, hewn by the Judean king's workers in the late eighth century BC to divert water into the city in hope of withstanding the Assyrian siege (2 Kgs 20:20; 2 Chr 32:2–4,30). This tunnel, 1,750 feet (533 m) long, was hewn from both ends simultaneously as two gangs of workmen enlarged a natural seepage fissure in the tough *mizzi ahmar* limestone to improve the water flow. In medieval times the spring was called "the Virgin's Fountain"; according to a medieval tradition, it was the place where Mary washed Jesus's diapers. The water flow is now regulated so that it no longer gushes, and walking through Hezekiah's Tunnel has become a "must do" activity for visitors to Jerusalem.

The only side of the ancient city of Jerusalem left unprotected by a deep valley was on the north, where the gradual slope of the eastern, Temple Mount hill extends from the northern city wall. To compensate, an artificial moat was dug into the bedrock adjacent to the northern wall sometime during the late Judean monarchy, in part to quarry stones for building construction and in part to strengthen the city's northern defenses. The face of "Skull Hill," Gordon's Calvary, is part of the cutting for this moat. Josephus mentions that when Pompey attacked the city from the north, he had his soldiers work on the Sabbath to fill in the moat, calculating correctly that the city's Jewish defenders would be idle on that day (*War* 1.145–147).

Iron Age II and during the time of the New Testament, it traced the western scarp of the western hill (the Hinnom Valley).

- The strongest sections of the wall of Jerusalem, as well as the city's fortresses and major palaces, were on the northern side of the city, facing the likely direction of attack. So the Antonia Fortress, which guarded the Temple Mount during the time of the New Testament, was on the crest of the eastern hill north-northwest of the temple platform. Similarly, remains of a palatial structure from the early Iron Age II (possibly David's palace) have been found on the northern edge of the Jebusite city. We might expect that the elaborate palaces and government buildings built by Solomon (1 Kgs 7:1–8) as well as many of those constructed by later Judean kings (e.g., Jer 22:13–14) were located in the same district (the neighborhood between the Jebusite city and the Temple Mount, perhaps the location of the biblical Ophel; 2 Chr 27:3; 33:14; Neh 3:26–27).
- Jerusalem's temple was built on the highest spot of the eastern hill, where the Dome of the Rock now stands. The patch of exposed bedrock that likely was under the Holy of Holies had been one of the threshing floors of the Jebusite city (2 Sam 24:18–25; 1 Chr 21:18–27). The threshing floor was located close enough to the city gate to safeguard harvest activities (cp. Jer 15:7) yet high enough to catch the late afternoon wind needed to blow away the chaff. During the Judean monarchy, this temple hill was also called Mt. Zion (Ps 78:68; Isa 31:4). The higher hill east of the City of David (the southernmost extension of the Mount of Olives) was the location of the sacred site that Solomon built to the Moabite deity Chemosh (1 Kgs 11:7).
- As might be expected, remains of Jerusalem's pools and water systems have been found in places on the perimeter of the city where spring water or rainwater naturally flows. The most extensive set of water installations was located in and along the lower extremities of the eastern hill, a downward flow from the Gihon Spring, Jerusalem's natural source of water. These include Hezekiah's Tunnel, the Pool of Siloam, and a series of other tunnels and pools dating from as early as the Middle Bronze Age II (2 Kgs 20:20;

As Jerusalem grew, so did its fields and orchards. At the height of the Old Testament kingdom of Judah, the upper slopes of the Rephaim Valley—the branch of the Sorek that drains the hills southwest of Jerusalem—were intensively cultivated. Here lines of ancient terraces mark the slope of the Rephaim above En Yael (Yael's spring), site of a farming village of the late Iron Age two miles (3.2 km) west of the walled city. Such farmsteads helped to satisfy the appetite of Hezekiah's Jerusalem. The prophet Isaiah compared the damage done to the land by an invading army to the emptiness of the post-harvest fields in the Rephaim Valley:

On that day the splendor of Jacob will fade,
and his healthy body will become emaciated.
It will be as if a reaper has gathered standing grain—
his arm harvesting the heads of grain—
and as if one had gleaned heads of grain
in the valley of Rephaim.
Only gleanings will be left in Israel,
as if an olive tree had been beaten—
two or three berries at the very top of the tree,
four or five on its fruitful branches. (Isa 17:4–6)

John 9:7; cp. Isa 7:3; 22:9,11; Neh 3:16). Other large water pools from the time of the New Testament were adjacent to the city's northern wall, which acted as a kind of dam slowing the natural flow of rainwater that would otherwise drain into the Kidron or Central Valleys. These include the Pool of Bethesda or Sheep's Pool (John 5:2), the Pool of Israel,[1] and the Struthion Pool (*War* 5.467). Note should also be made of the Sultan's Pool (Birkat es-Sultan) in the Hinnom Valley at the base of the walled city's western hill, which may be the Serpent's Pool of Josephus (*War* 5.108).

- Royal palaces and homes of the wealthy were typically located on the higher elevations of the city, out of the stench of the streets below and allowing noble residents to catch the evening breeze. Remains of the Jerusalem palace of Herod the Great and several spacious priestly mansions from the time of Jesus have been found on the crest and upper slopes of the western hill. A larger concentration of houses for the common people was likely further down slope in the Central Valley; they were "*closely compacted together*" (Ps 122:3 NIV) as huddled masses tend to be. In the time of the Old Testament, buildings constructed on the Kidron slope were protected from the forces of erosion by revetment walls and terraces called the millo, structures which themselves had to be reinforced periodically (2 Sam 5:9; 1 Kgs 9:15; 11:27; 2 Chr 32:5).
- The agricultural land adjacent to the lowest, southern part of the city that lay within reach of the municipal water system was also royal land during the time of the Judean monarchy; it was called the King's Garden (2 Kgs 25:4; Neh 3:15). This lush area, likely protected by a wall, provides an appropriate setting for the various romantic rendezvous recorded in the Song of Songs (cp. Song 2:2–15; 4:12–5:1; 7:11–13; 8:13).
- While it is difficult to reconstruct the street plan of any era for biblical Jerusalem, it is reasonable to assume that one of the main streets followed the line of the Central Valley, as it still does today (modern el-Wad, "the wadi" street). Indeed, paving stones from the first century AD and the time of the Crusaders have been found along part of the line of the Central Valley. This valley would have carried the natural runoff of the city out through a postern or other gate in the lowest point of the wall, a gate appropriately called the Dung Gate in the time of Nehemiah as well as today (Neh 2:13; 3:13–14). The lines of other interior streets can be guessed by comparing the topography to the known location of some of Jerusalem's ancient gates.
- With the exception of the place of the burial of King David, which was apparently inside the city itself (1 Kgs 2:10; Neh 3:16), Jerusalem's cemeteries are found on the perimeter of the city outside its walls—primarily on the slopes opposite the Kidron and Hinnom Valleys. Archaeological excavations confirm that Jerusalem's oldest tombs were located on the very southern extremity of the Mount of Olives in and below the modern Silwan Village. Its necropolis spread in all directions as the city expanded outward.

It seems unusual that the ancient city of Jerusalem had so many gates. The book of Nehemiah gives the names of twelve gates in the line of the wall that was rebuilt after the return from exile; indeed, it's a very high number if Nehemiah's Jerusalem was restricted to the eastern hill as most scholars traditionally have thought (Neh 3:1–32; 12:38–39). A gate is often named after something outside the city wall that is accessible by exiting the city at that point. So in Nehemiah's Jerusalem, the Water Gate led to the Gihon Spring, the Fountain Gate gave access to a pool at the southeastern corner of the city, the East Gate obviously faced east, the Valley Gate opened into the Central Valley, the Dung Gate dumped into the lowest part of the surrounding valleys (near the juncture of the Central and Kidron Valleys), and the Sheep Gate was located on the northern or northeastern side of the city where Jerusalem's sheep market has been found for millennia, up to the AD 1980s. We can locate a fish market, a horse market (or stables), and a guard house near the Fish Gate, the Horse Gate, and the Gate of the Guard, respectively—this latter one is in the northern wall, where we would expect a fortress. Most, if not all, of the gate names mentioned in the third chapter of Nehemiah were preserved from the city that had been destroyed by Nebuchadnezzar (e.g., 2 Kgs 14:13; 2 Chr 23:15; Zeph 1:10), and some certainly remained in use until Roman times if not beyond (note John 5:2, which mentions the Sheep Gate).

The psalmist expected that Jerusalem's residents and others interested in the city's fortunes would know their city well:

> *Go around Zion, encircle it;*
> *count its towers,*
> *note its ramparts, tour its citadels*
> *so that you can tell a future generation:*
> *"This God, our God forever and ever—*
> *He will always lead us."* (Ps 48:12–14)

In one sense Jerusalem's off-route setting helped to isolate the city from the larger flow of events sweeping the ancient Near East and the Mediterranean worlds. In another sense, the largest of the world's events happened right here, within the city's walls and around its perimeter, especially at a place somewhere just beyond the northern wall where there was once a cross near a slightly used tomb. For the biblical writers, Jerusalem was not only a flesh and blood reality but a window that revealed what it meant for all of

---

1 The name "Pool of Israel" (*Birkat Isra'il*) or "Pool of the Sons of Israel" (*Birkat bani-Isra'il*) occurs in early Christian and Arabic sources but not in texts from the time of the New Testament. The pool's original name is unknown, even though archaeological evidence suggests it may have been the largest standing source of water in Jerusalem in the Hasmonean and Herodian periods.

God's people to live in community with one another and with him, a home "*built as a city should be, solidly united*" (Ps 122:3).

SUMMARY

The six southern regions of the land of ancient Israel focus on the city of Jerusalem and the interrelationship of local and international powers in its vicinity. All told, these regions are not particularly well resourced, but they were of great interest for powers making their way between Egypt, Asia, and the Arabian Peninsula. Surrounded by foes and living in an environmentally precarious land, the people of Jerusalem had to learn lessons of dependence and trust in order to thrive in the place God had promised would be their home.

1. *The Hill Country of Judah.* The high, hard limestone hill country was the heartland of ancient Judah. An abundance of springs, fertile though not plentiful soil, small villages, and tight horizon lines made for a quiet and secure life there. Everyone could live "*in safety under his own vine and his own fig tree*" (1 Kgs 4:25).
2. *The Judean Shephelah.* The low foothills and wide valleys of the Judean Shephelah create a transition zone between the hill country and the coastal plain. With ample possibilities for agriculture, the Shephelah typically boasted a larger population than did the hills—though it was never unified politically under its own flag. The routes and resources of the Shephelah were coveted by peoples living in both the hill country and the plain, and each pushed into the region's transversal valleys in an attempt to gain an advantage over the other.
3. *The Philistine Coastal Plain.* The Philistine plain is that portion of the coast that lies between the Yarkon River and the Nahal Besor. Largely lacking decent spots for anchorage, this part of the coast was primarily a land route connecting Asia with Africa and a terminal for trade coming off the Arabian Peninsula. Residents of the Judean hill country were only rarely able to establish a long-term presence out on the coast, though conditions sometimes allowed cooperative efforts with international powers that controlled its routes and ports.
4. *The Negev.* The arid basin of the biblical Negev acts as a southern beltline separating permanent settlement in the hill country and the Shephelah from open desert beyond. This is a zone where seminomadic shepherds feel at home and can develop cooperative relationships with nearby cities and villages. Conditions in the "*great and terrible wilderness*" (Deut 1:19) to the south limit agricultural and even shepherding possibilities, though interested powers on the perimeter have always sought to establish a presence there in order to control the lucrative international trade routes moving through.
5. *The Judean Wilderness.* The chalky Judean Wilderness drops off of the watershed ridge into the Rift Valley, where rainfall quickly falls below the minimum needed to support permanent settlement. The result is a local desert inhabited mainly by shepherds moving their flocks of sheep and goats from one spot of available grass to another. Because of its proximity to the cities of the watershed ridge, the wilderness is a good place to find quick refuge should conditions warrant; it was a constant reminder to the people of Jerusalem of the vulnerability of life and the incessant need to rely on the provisions of God.
6. *The Land of Benjamin.* A neat cross-section of the hill country geologically, the small land of Benjamin functioned as the most important east-west natural corridor in the southern hills. Benjamin was also Jerusalem's most essential region, providing its best access to the coast. Because the flow of biblical events focuses on Jerusalem, the role of people and places in Benjamin takes on a greater significance than a land this size would otherwise warrant.
7. *Jerusalem.* Tucked just behind the watershed ridge on the cusp of the Judean Wilderness, the city of Jerusalem possesses none of the natural advantages by which we might predict greatness. The city is dependent on developing good relations with inhabitants of regions on its perimeter in order to thrive—or, failing that, in trying to dominate its regional neighbors in order to gain resources lacking in the hills. The adage "God has chosen the world's weak things to shame the strong" (see 1 Cor 1:27) speaks well of the situation of the city and the world-changing events that have happened there.

QUESTIONS

1. What factors made the Hill Country of Judah a particularly apt place for "*each man to live in safety under his own vine and his own fig tree*" (1 Kgs 4:25)?
2. With geographical considerations in mind, why do you think David chose to build a power base first among the clans and tribes of southern Judah and the Negev, rather than around Jerusalem and the land of Benjamin?
3. What did the Shephelah have to offer residents of the Hill Country of Judah in general or the king of Jerusalem in particular?
4. Compare and contrast the motives of Samson (a Danite) and Goliath (a Philistine) in wanting to establish a presence for their people in the Shephelah.
5. Explain how the valleys of the Shephelah function as swinging doorways between the hill country and the coast.
6. Describe and illustrate the function of the Shephelah's chalk trough.
7. What advantages did the Philistines have that Judah didn't, related to the geography of their own homelands?
8. Why is the Philistine coast more of a north-south land route than an east-west port route?
9. What is the most fertile part of the Philistine Coastal Plain? What cities are associated with

this region? What is the role of these cities in the biblical story?

10. Discuss the significance of Peter's move to Joppa in light of a long history of interaction between the hill country and the coastal plain.
11. Describe the importance of the location of Beer-sheba, first as a city in the biblical Negev and then as a city that belonged to the kingdom of Judah.
12. How might geographical realities explain the movements of the patriarchs from one place to another, as described in the book of Genesis?
13. In terms of its geography, connectedness, and possibilities for life, how does the biblical Negev differ from the Greater Negev to its south?
14. Choose ten adjectives that describe either the biblical Negev or the Greater Negev and explain how those words illustrate the flow of biblical history in the region.
15. Compare and contrast the efforts of Solomon, Uzziah, and Herod to control the Negev and the Judean Wilderness.
16. What geographical factors (rocks, soil, water, topography, and the like) combine to make the Judean Wilderness a local desert?
17. Describe the relationship between the shepherd and the villager in the Judean Wilderness. Where did each live? Why?
18. Why was the wilderness such an appropriate image for the biblical prophets when they spoke of God's judgment on Jerusalem?
19. How do images of the wilderness help to explain and emphasize personal and social renewal?
20. In a desert land, water is both helpful and terrifying. Give examples of both from Scripture.
21. Imagine you are the king of Moab, a kingdom of equal strength to Judah lying east of the Dead Sea. Which routes and cities would you instruct your general to attack in order to conquer Judah? What might have prompted Moab to attack Jehoshaphat by way of the Ascent of Ziz (2 Chr 20:20–30)?
22. What geographical factors combined to make the land of Benjamin a favored corridor for traffic moving east-west over the hills? North-south within the hills?
23. Describe the relationship between Jerusalem and the Central Benjamin Plateau. Why was the plateau so important for Jerusalem?
24. "*I will wipe Jerusalem clean as one wipes a bowl—wiping it and turning it upside down*" (2 Kgs 21:13). How does this statement reflect the geographical shape of Jerusalem?
25. If you are king of ancient Jerusalem, what routes and/or cities are most important for you to hold in order to protect your own interests? To expand your interests?
26. Compare the advantages and disadvantages of Hebron as opposed to Jerusalem for a capital city.
27. Why might Jerusalem be better thought of as a provincial capital than an international capital? What happened in history to change that?
28. Give some examples of how Jerusalem's topography might have influenced the location of some of its buildings or construction projects.

Flowing water in a thirsty land. This aqueduct, built by the Hasmoneans in the late second century BC and improved by Herod the Great in the first, carried water to New Testament Jericho from the springs of Prat (Fara), Mabo'a (Fawar), and Qelt. Edging the cliffy southern bank of the Wadi Qelt, the aqueduct crosses several bridges and penetrates several tunnels on its nine mile (14 km) run. Reinforced by concrete in the early twentieth century, the aqueduct provides water for people living in the southern Jordan Valley today.

4 THE LAND OF ANCIENT ISRAEL: THE CENTRAL REGIONS (ISRAEL/SAMARIA)

The view from atop Mount Gerizim, the peak from which half of the tribes of ancient Israel shouted out the blessings of the covenant (Deut 11:29–32; Josh 8:30–35), takes in a sweep of territory that encompasses the heartland of much of the biblical story. To the south lies the Hill Country of Ephraim, a jumbled mass of hard limestone hills punctuated on a clear day by the bump of Nebi Samwil hovering over the Central Benjamin Plateau. To the east, the strong rise of the Manasseh hills drops sharply out of view into the Jordan Valley. The western approaches, toward the coast, settle down more gently, like the angle of a landing jet, onto the Mediterranean's Sharon Plain. Although much of the view north is blocked by Mount Ebal, the higher twin of Gerizim, a portion of the open sweep of the Jezreel Valley is visible beyond its western crest while the highlands of Bashan running up toward Mount Hermon can be seen off to the northeast. Below, nestled between Mounts Gerizim and Ebal, lies the ancient site of Shechem (Tel Balata), now surrounded by the urban sprawl of modern Nablus. It was here, with Abram [Abraham], that the landed story of the Old Testament began: "*So Abram went, as the LORD had told him . . . [and] passed through the land to the site of Shechem, at the oak of Moreh. (At that time, the Canaanites were in the land.) The LORD appeared to Abram and said, 'To your offspring I will give this land.' So he built an altar there to the LORD who had appeared to him*" (Gen 12:4–7).

Though the terrain and living conditions in these central hills resemble the vistas and venues found in Judah and the Shephelah, their overall shape is more complex—and living conditions more favorable—than are those of the neighboring regions to the south. "Halves of the same range, how opposite in disposition and history," intoned George Adam Smith a century ago, in a literary sound bite not far off the mark.[1] These central regions formed the heartland of the Northern Kingdom of Israel and, during the time of the New Testament, the political district of Samaria. Those who lived here—and especially the Samaritans—took pride that their ancestral homeland somehow seemed superior to the parched Judean hills and desert slopes down south (e.g., Gen 49:22–26; Deut 33:13–17). Given the region's better patterns of rainfall and easier access to international highways all around, the ancient residents of the region can perhaps be excused for feeling this way.[2] While the geographical differences that distinguish the central from the southern regions are of degree rather than kind, they are significant enough to allow us to trace a pattern of historical events that seem more often than not to have been centered on growth and expansion rather than conservatism and defense. In any

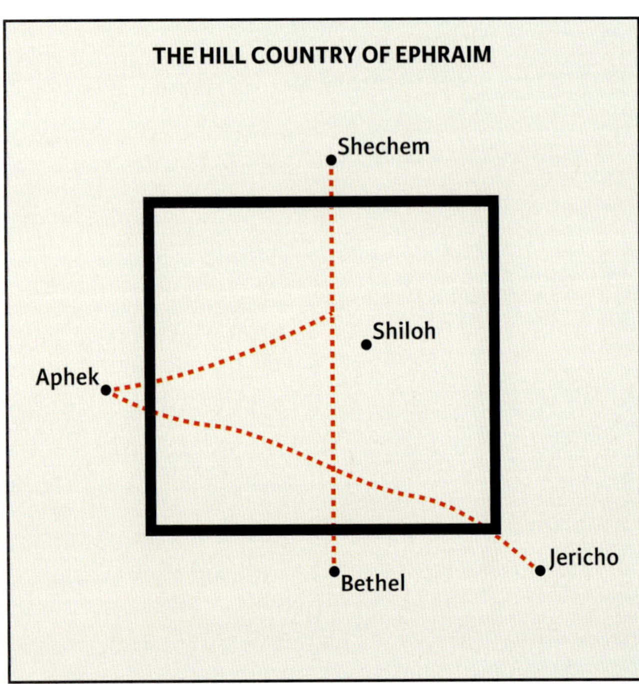

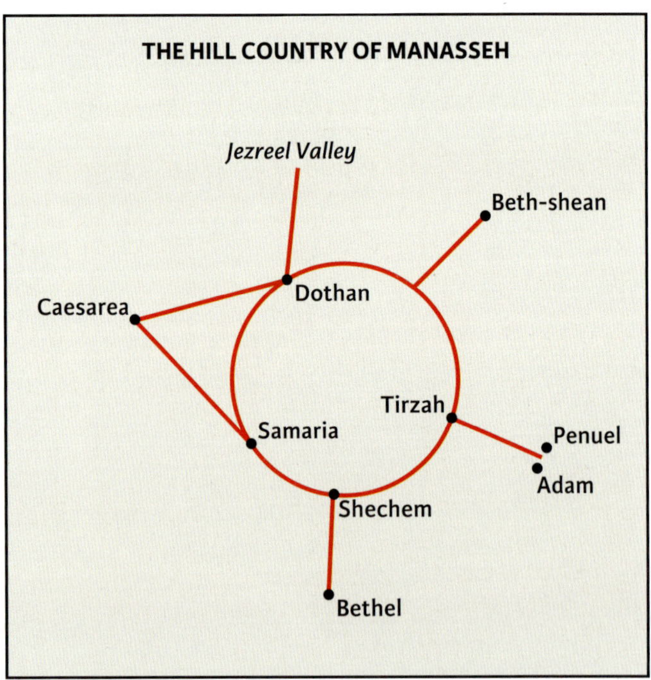

These two diagrams provide a schematic overview of the basic character of the Hill Country of Ephraim and Manasseh. The heavy box around the highlands of Ephraim shows that its land is relatively closed to traffic; the natural routes, here dotted, follow twisted ridges or snake along tight wadi bottoms. The main population center, Shiloh, lies off-route. The hills of Manasseh, on the other hand, are pierced by a number of broad, flat valleys that support large cities linked by a highway network resembling a large traffic circle. Open and expansive, the Manasseh hills formed the real heartland of ancient Israel's central regions.

1 George Adam Smith, *The Historical Geography of the Holy Land* (London: Hodder and Stoughton, 1894), 323.

2 A common Jewish blessing for children at the weekly *Shabbat* (Sabbath) meal still invokes the favored status of Jacob's prized grandsons, whose tribal descendants settled in these central hills: "*May God make you like Ephraim and Manasseh*" (cp. Gen 48:20).

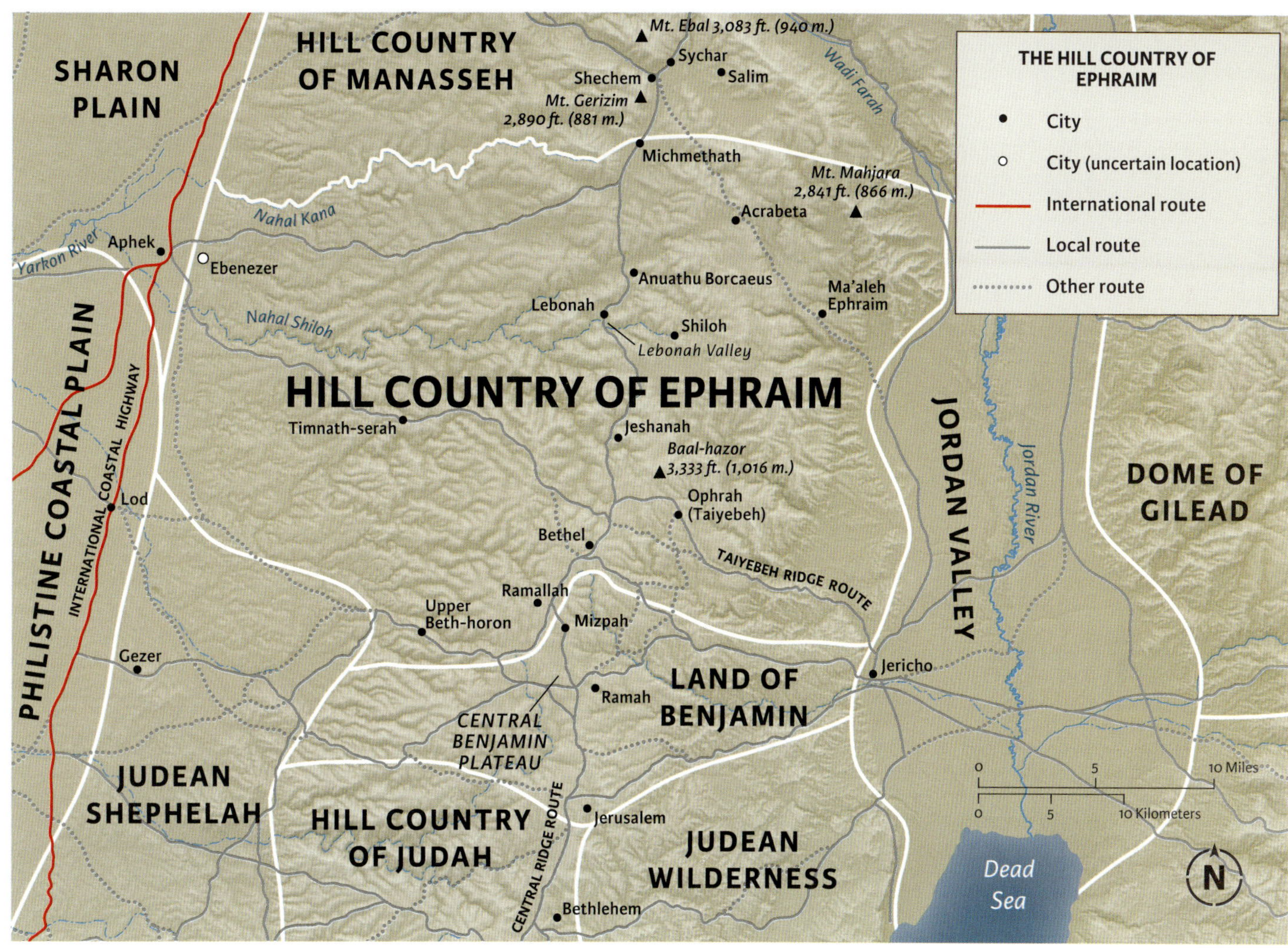

case, the story of Samaria's residents—those who were fortunate for the land on which they lived—begins, as it does for Judah, with the basic elements of rock, soil, and water. It is to these we now turn.

A. THE HILL COUNTRY OF EPHRAIM

Like the names Judah and Benjamin, Ephraim is a term that refers both to a people group and its tribal land. In this case, it's the ancestral home of the descendants of the younger son of Joseph (Josh 16:1–10; cp. Gen 48:14). The Hill Country of Ephraim was, in many ways, the idealized homeland of the Northern Kingdom of Israel, just as the Hill Country of Judah was the homeland of the Southern Kingdom of Judah. The stories of these two peoples are, in many ways, similar, as are the shapes and resources of their living spaces.

Geologically, the territory of Ephraim is a dome of Cenomanian-Turonian limestone that has been eroded on the west by the action of prevailing rainfall, pushing the watershed far to the east. The dome is shaped somewhat like a rough ball of clay that has been pressed down on one side; its western slopes are a relatively gentle angle and its eastern edge is tipped up, then sharply down. Structurally, the Ephraimite dome is an extension of the hard limestone Hill Country of Benjamin and Judah; it falls on the same north-northeast/south-southwest line. Yet Ephraim must be considered a distinct geological entity because of the absence of a band of softer Eocene limestone to the west, and only a very thin wedge of Senonian chalk to the east. Lacking a proper Shephelah or wilderness like those that embrace the Hill Country of Judah, the hard limestone hills of Ephraim run right out to the edge of the coastal plain and nearly down into the Jordan Valley. For residents of towns and villages dotting this "*remote part of the hill country of Ephraim*" (Judg 19:1), this aspect of their landscape carried both benefits and disadvantages. Lacking wide access valleys that a Shephelah would supply toward the west, the Ephraimite hills were relatively isolated and somewhat safe from attack. At the same time, its residents were not particularly well connected to the commercial opportunities that lay at their door.

According to the boundary descriptions provided in the book of Joshua, the territory of Ephraim filled these hard limestone hills between a line connecting Bethel, Upper Beth-horon, and Gezer in the south and an angle formed by the run of the Wadi Kana from Michmethath in the north (Josh 16:5–10; 17:9–10). It is important to note that each of these places lay west of the watershed, in the more fertile regions of the tribal territory. The sharper, eastern slopes of Ephraim, those dropping into the Rift Valley, were largely empty of permanent settlement. In size, Ephraim is approximately fifteen miles (24 km) north-south by twenty-seven miles (43 km) east-west; it's a space somewhat smaller than the Hill Country of Judah. No clear topographical features separate

The drop to the Jordan Valley in the eastern Hill Country of Ephraim falls about 3,000 feet (900 m) in five miles (8 km), or twice the angle of slope of the Judean Wilderness east of Jerusalem. Travel here was infrequent, and no army is known to have climbed this way to attack the interior of Ephraim. Yet the rock base is Cenomanian-Turonian limestone, with the promise of resources conducive to settled life. Archaeological surveys have revealed a pattern of small villages in eastern Ephraim dating to Iron Age I (1200–1000 BC), evidence of some of Israel's earliest settlement processes during the time of the judges.

the Cenomanian-Turonian highlands of Ephraim from the tribal territory of Benjamin. This continuity on the ground perhaps reflects the two tribes' shared historical bond through Rachel, their matriarchal ancestor (cp. Gen 30:22–24; 35:16–20; 46:19–22; cp. Num 1:32–37; Judg 5:14; Ps 80:2). Indeed, the biblical authors sometimes used the term "hill country of Ephraim" generically to refer to all points between Jerusalem (including those in Benjamin) and Shechem (a city of Manasseh to the north; cp. Josh 21:21; 24:33; Judg 4:5; 1 Sam 1:1; 1 Kgs 12:25; 1 Chr 6:67).

The higher elevations of Ephraim generally push to between 1,900 and 3,200 feet (580 and 975 m) above sea level. At 3,333 feet (1,016 m), the summit of Baal-hazor northeast of Bethel (2 Sam 13:23) is the highest point, nearly matching the crest of the Hebron hills. The region's primary drainage is to the west, through the Shiloh wadi system and its long, winding tributaries. These have created a tangled land of hills and hollows, justifying its "*remote interior of Ephraim*" name (Hb *yarketē har ephraim*; Judg 19:1, my translation). Small interior valleys of terra rosa soil such as those adjacent to the towns of Lebonah and Shiloh provide rich agricultural bases within the heart of the Ephraim highlands. "*Is not the gleaning of Ephraim better than the grape harvest of [my Manassite clan] Abiezer?*" Gideon asked in deference to a delegation of affronted Ephraimites after the battle of Midian (Judg 8:2), acknowledging by way of inference the natural productivity of the Ephraim highlands.

Annual rainfall throughout the Ephraim hills is more dependable than that in Judah, to the point that over time erosion has pushed the watershed ridge far to the east. Travelers on their way to Shechem (modern Nablus), the largest ancient city-state north of Bethel, must choose to follow either the watershed ridge on its long eastward loop behind Shiloh, or drop into the upper reaches of the Shiloh wadi system. The more direct and preferred route did the latter. This was "*the highway that goes up from Bethel to Shechem*" along which the Benjaminite bachelors traveled to snatch dancing girls from the vineyards during the fall harvest festival at Shiloh (Judg 21:19–23). It was over this familiar ground that Hannah trod to the sanctuary at Shiloh to receive the promise of a son, then made annual motherly visits to the young boy Samuel (1 Sam 1:1–28; 2:18–20). The distance between Hannah's home in Ramah (*er-Ram*) on the Central Benjamin Plateau and

A look over the Lebonah Valley reveals living conditions that pattern life as it has been lived in the Ephraim highlands for millennia. The valley floor laced with the narrow, elongated fields of ancestrally held lands, divided and then subdivided among the sons of sons for generations. The need for socialization and mutual protection prompts everyone to live together in a nearby village (Luban; ancient Lebonah, on the back slope; Judg 21:19) rather than on individual homesteads. Resources are spread among winter crops on the valley floor (wheat and barley), summer fruit lining the terraces on the lower slopes of the perimeter hills (olives, grapes, figs, pomegranates, and almonds), and herd animals (sheep and goats) grazing the rocky tops above. In the biblical world, most people likely were born, lived, died, and were buried within tight horizons such as this. It was, in fact, the biblical ideal: security within *"the bounty of the eternal hills"* of Joseph (Deut 33:15).

Shiloh could be covered by foot in about half a day. That her visits were not more frequent was due in large part to the conservative stay-at-home lifestyle of hill country villagers in the biblical period.

It was also through these same upper valleys of the Shiloh wadi system that Jesus and his disciples journeyed from Jerusalem back to Galilee prior to his encounter with the woman at the well (John 4:1–45). According to the Mishnah (Ma'aser Sheni 5:2), the New Testament-era village of Acrabeta, six miles (10 km) north of Shiloh, was one day's journey from Jerusalem; Josephus (*War* 3.51) mentions that Anuathu Borcaeus, a little more than two miles (3 km) beyond Shiloh at the northern end of the Lebonah Valley, was the last Judean village before one entered Samaria. We can assume that on his trip Jesus stayed overnight on Judean soil, perhaps in one of these two towns, before pushing into Samaria. He would naturally arrive at Sychar, home of the woman at the well, a little before noon the next day (cp. John 4:4–6).

In any case, it is just beyond the site of ancient Bethel (modern Beitin, a village northeast of Ramallah) that the famed Central *Ridge* Route technically ends, as travelers begin to weave their way instead through the tight wadi bottoms of the upper Shiloh wadi system. One of these tributaries is the Wadi Haramiyeh, "the Valley of the Robbers," a historic name that aptly betrays the challenges of travel in the region during the Ottoman Turkish period. Like the road between Jerusalem and Jericho, this would have made a good setting for the parable of the Good Samaritan (Luke 10:30–37). As it makes its way further north, the natural route then passes through the Lebonah Valley west of Shiloh.

Here we have one of the best "roadmaps" preserved in the biblical text: "*There's an annual festival to the Lord in Shiloh, which is north of Bethel, east of the highway that goes up from Bethel to Shechem, and south of Lebonah*" (Judg 21:19). That Shiloh is nearly due east of Lebonah by compass direction is irrelevant to the one giving these directions, as well as to the one taking them. The fork in the road from which a traveler takes the turnoff heading northeastward toward Shiloh is, by topographical necessity, south of Lebonah. Today the main paved highway takes this Shiloh fork to the right, while the historic through-route always took the left fork, to Shechem via Lebonah. In any case, because the natural route bypassed Shiloh, it left ancient Israel's first religious center a bit isolated from the main flow of traffic with the result that the term "sanctuary" in all of its meanings can apply nicely to the site. Shiloh's relative seclusion made it a natural choice for the location of the tent of meeting as Israel sought to gain an initial foothold in the land of Canaan (Josh 18:1). The yearly harvest festival of summer fruit that was held at Shiloh during the time of the judges, perhaps the festival of *Succot* (i.e., Booths or Tabernacles; Judg 21:19), is an indication of the pleasant productivity of the place.

The natural routes into and out of the Ephraim highlands from the west follow the tops of the ridges that define the southern and northern edges of the Shiloh wadi system. These ran from Bethel to Aphek and from Michmethah to Aphek, the approximate lines of modern Highways 465 and 505, respectively. To the east, the tortuous drop from Ephraim's watershed ridge into the Jordan Valley is absent a decent natural route.

A tumbledown watchtower on a spring day prompts images of a past that has all but disappeared from the Ephraim hills. From this tower in central Ephraim, peasant farmers once surveyed their vineyards and groves, living with their families among the crops during harvest time, the most critical season of the year. *"He built a tower in the middle of [his vineyard],"* said Isaiah (5:2), describing a profitable viticulturalist of the Iron Age. Jesus told a similar story as a parable: *"There was a landowner, who planted a vineyard, put a fence around it, dug a winepress in it, and built a watchtower"* (Matt 21:33). Both storytellers had in mind the age-old effort it takes to protect one's resources when surrounded by all manner of hostile or detrimental forces (cp. Isa 5:3–7; Matt 21:34–41).

(Israeli Highway 505, with dramatic switchbacks via the modern town of Ma'aleh Ephraim, "the Ascent of Ephraim," mocks the terrain.)

It is both remarkable and odd that among the city lists of the various Israelite tribes preserved in the book of Joshua, there are none for Ephraim or Manasseh, the largest and by all accounts most powerful of the northern tribes (Josh 16:1–17:13; cp. Josh 15:20–63; 18:21–28; 19:1–8,17–23,40–46). For this reason, we don't have as complete a picture for the settlement of the Hill Country of Ephraim as we do for many of the other regions of the land of ancient Israel. Other than Shiloh, which was well fortified during the second half of the Middle Bronze Age (ca. 1750–1550 BC), no large city rose within the remote interior of Ephraim in ancient times. Rather, this was a land of small, rural villages, nearly all of which were destined to be forever nameless in the scant written memories of time. We can assume that, as in Judah, topographical factors in Ephraim prompted its inhabitants to foster independent, conservative, and self-sufficient lifestyles. According to the biblical record, the Ephraimites were proud partisans, eager to lead the way into battle (Judg 7:24–8:3; 12:1; 2 Chr 25:10) or bend the bow for their own cause (2 Sam 20:21; 2 Chr 28:7; Ps 78:9–10), and—as highlanders often are—were known for their distinctive accent (Judg 12:5–6).

The absence of a city list for either Ephraim or Manasseh is particularly striking in light of the prominent role the region played in the early decades of Israel's settlement of the land. Key events mentioned in the Bible that were related to Israel's settlement process took place in the Hill Country of Ephraim and its environs. In addition, individuals who played key leadership roles in the early days of Israel's settlement were also connected to the tribal holdings of Ephraim. Of these, the most important relate to Shiloh, Israel's earliest tribal center. This was the place chosen to accommodate the tent of meeting as well as to host Joshua's distribution of the land (Josh 18:1–10; 21:1–8). Joshua himself was an Ephraimite, whose landed inheritance and burial place were at Timnath-serah, a terraced hilltop village perched high on the natural route between Bethel and Aphek (near modern Beir Zeit), with many springs in the vicinity (Josh 19:49–50; 24:29–31; Judg 2:8–9). Timnath-serah was a grand place to settle down, as different from the flat, irrigated fields of Egypt out of which Joshua had come as we could possibly imagine (Deut 11:10–12; Pss 78:54; 104:10–13). Eleazar, Aaron's son and successor, who was high priest during the time of the conquest, was also buried in the Ephraimite highlands, in the inheritance of his son, Phinehas (Josh 24:33; cp. Num 20:25–26). And, in an ongoing display of tribal dominance, it was specifically the house of Joseph (Ephraim and Manasseh) among all the tribes of ancient Israel that took special initiative to expand their holdings in the land by moving into the forested folds beyond the Shiloh wadi system: "'*If you have so many people,' Joshua replied to them, 'go to the forest and clear an area for yourselves there in the land of the Perizzites and the Rephaim, because Ephraim's hill country is too small for you. . . . It is a forest; clear it and its outlying areas will be yours*'" (Josh 17:15,18).

Current archaeological evidence has revealed a pattern of small villages with a shared horizon of material culture that appeared first in the drier, eastern hills of Ephraim and Manasseh during Iron Age I (1200–1000 BC). Israelite settlement then spread to the Hill Country of Judah and Galilee, finally dropping into the Jezreel Valley and coastal plain during the Israelite monarchy (Iron Age II).[1] This picture is consistent with the biblical emphasis on Ephraim and Manasseh as the focal point of tribal settlement during the period of the judges.

"A Levite staying in a remote part of the hill country of Ephraim acquired a woman from Bethlehem in Judah as his concubine. But she . . . left him for her father's house in Bethlehem in Judah. She was there for four months. Then her husband got up and followed her to speak kindly to her and bring her back" (Judg 19:1–3). Away from its larger, disturbing context, this would seem a homey story from a simple land, one far removed from the eyes of armies and kings. The path the Levite and his concubine traveled was likely no more than a line of trodden soil, largely unimproved, weaving along the edges of wadis and avoiding whatever large rocks might lie in the way. Folks got around in those days, but life moved slowly. It took four months for the man to decide to go fetch his concubine; what need was there for highways made for speed?

1 Israel Finkelstein, *The Archaeology of the Israelite Settlement* (Jerusalem: IES, 1988), 324–35. Finkelstein's conclusions were not made with a literal reading of the biblical account in mind. Nevertheless, it is interesting that, in broad outline, his presentation of the data related to the earliest archaeologically recoverable material culture of ancient Israel does support the priority of Ephraim and Manasseh among the early Israelite tribes as pictured in Joshua and Judges.

Luz, meaning "almond tree," was either an alternate Canaanite name for Bethel (Gen 28:19) or the name of a prominent place nearby (Josh 16:2). Though not one of the seven species of Deuteronomy 8:8, the almond tree is native to the Levant, and its fruit appears to have been first domesticated there. The first tree to blossom in the spring, the almond loves the highland climate of Ephraim and Judah, pushing out floral bursts of pink and white by early February. The writer of Ecclesiastes likened the certainty of the blossoming almond to the unending cycle of life: *"The almond tree blossoms, the grasshopper loses its spring, and the caper berry has no effect; for the mere mortal is headed to his eternal home"* (Eccl 12:5). It was sage advice for people who typically spent their entire lives in the predictable and contented folds of Ephraim.

Control over the southern part of Ephraim was contested when Jerusalem became the capital of ancient Israel. During the days of Solomon, strategic points along the tribe's southwestern border that had allowed Ephraim to forge connections with the northern part of the Judean Shephelah, namely through Upper Beth-horon and Gezer, were seized by Judah in order to secure Jerusalem's own access to the coast (1 Kgs 9:16–17). In the list of Solomon's district commissioners, the governor of Ephraim, Ben-hur, is listed first (1 Kgs 4:8). This perhaps reflects an official recognition that from Jerusalem's point of view, Ephraim's geographical location as the doorway to the north warranted special attention—and protection. Indeed, during the time of the monarchy, the northern gate in the wall of the city of Jerusalem was called the Ephraim Gate (2 Kgs 14:13; Neh 8:16)—a tacit acknowledgment of the essential unity of the central and southern regions of the land of ancient Israel.

After the fracture of the united kingdom, Solomon's grandson Abijah made a successful foray into Ephraimite territory as far as Jeshanah and Ephron, five miles north of Bethel (2 Chr 13:1–19). These Judean gains at Ephraim's expense were lost during the reign of Abijah's son, Asa (1 Kgs 15:16–22). As a result, Bethel remained firmly Ephraimite, attached to the Northern Kingdom.

By this time, Bethel ("house of God") had already carried a long tradition of being an important religious center in Canaan (cp. Gen 12:8; 28:10–22; 35:8–10; Judg 20:26–28). It is to be expected, then, that the first king of divided Israel, Jeroboam, would confirm that role when he made the city a border sanctuary marking the southern end of his breakaway kingdom (1 Kgs 12:28–33). Within half a century, Hiel from Bethel rebuilt Jericho, thereby claiming the Jordan Valley oasis as a launch pad for Israelite moves into Transjordan and in effect running Joshua's route of conquest backward (1 Kgs 16:34). In this way, the natural route from Aphek to Bethel to Jericho came to define the southernmost commercial corridor of the Northern Kingdom of Israel.

The biblical history of Ephraim traces the delicate line between blessing received and responsibility failed. On the one hand, the tribe's founding ancestor was the favored son of Joseph, who was in turn the favorite son of Jacob (Gen 37:3; 48:13–20). Jacob's blessing to Joseph anticipated the inherent beauty and productivity of the land in which the tribes of Ephraim and Manasseh would eventually live:

Joseph is a fruitful vine,
a fruitful vine beside a spring;
its branches climb over the wall....
The Almighty... blesses you
with blessings of the heavens above,
blessings of the deep that lies below,
and blessings of the breasts and the womb.
The blessings of your father excel
the blessings of my ancestors
and the bounty of the ancient hills.
(Gen 49:22,25–26)

Moses was of the same opinion, barely able to contain his excitement for the realization of Ephraim's place in their promised land:

May his land be blessed by the LORD
with the dew of heaven's bounty
and the watery depths that lie beneath;
with the bountiful harvest from the sun
and the abundant yield of the seasons;
with the best products of the ancient mountains
and the bounty of the eternal hills;
with the choice gifts of the land
and everything in it;
and with the favor of him
who appeared in the burning bush.
(Deut 33:13–16)

So how did "Ephraim" become the favored nickname for all Israel (Jer 31:9,20; Hos 6:4; 11:8; Zech 10:7)? Perhaps the equation *Ephraim = Israel* reflects the idea that small village Ephraimite life was somehow the most genuine lifestyle for ancient Israelites, just as the tent-dwelling Rechabites held that theirs was the most authentic lifestyle for those of Judah (cp. Jer 35:1–19).

Ephraim's proximity to Judah prompted the psalmist to declare twice that though *"Judah is my scepter," "Ephraim is my helmet"*—another rather important role that reflects the geographical shape and location of the Ephraimite highlands above Jerusalem (Pss 60:7; 108:8). Yet the relationship between Judah and Ephraim was more often than not rough-and-tumble, as persistent sibling rivalries tend to be (Isa 11:13). Shiloh's position as the earliest center of tribal activity did not last long. Archaeological evidence suggests that the site was destroyed by the Philistines in a follow-up campaign to the battle at Aphek in which the ark of the covenant was captured (1 Sam 4:1–22). After that, its location was largely forgotten (or ignored) by the biblical writers when the focus of political and religious activity switched to Jerusalem. The writer of Judges even had to give specific directions to the place, something that he would not have done if Shiloh still maintained its prior status within Israel (Judg 21:19; but cf. 1 Kgs 14:2). Indeed, the psalmist went to great lengths to explain how God had rejected Shiloh—and the Hill Country of Ephraim generally, in spite of its blessed geographical setting—in favor of rocky Mount Zion:

He abandoned the tabernacle at Shiloh,
the tent where he resided among mankind....
He rejected the tent of Joseph
and did not choose the tribe of Ephraim.
He chose instead the tribe of Judah,
Mount Zion, which he loved. (Ps 78:60,67–68)

Then, to counter the conviction that the divine blessing thus *automatically* resided in the hearts of the people of Jerusalem, the prophet Jeremiah intoned his fellow Judeans to make the journey up to the ruined sanctuary in Shiloh lest they forget that they, too, could be overrun by God's judgment (Jer 7:12–15; 26:1–6).

So Ephraim's position came full circle: a land that had fostered quiet living for centuries came to serve the biblical writers as a reminder that such life is secure only when grounded in the rock-solid hands of God.

"Joseph is a fruitful vine... its branches climb over the wall" (Gen 49:22). The traditional village farmers in the highlands of Ephraim have only recently begun to train their vines to climb on trellises. For millennia, vines throughout the region have simply run along the ground, then were lifted up on portable slabs of stone when the summer fruit appeared. But fortunate was the farmer whose vines climbed the sides of a watchtower, or extended over the wall of a terrace as seen here. Such was the sign of a well-cared-for land, as blessed as the people who called it home.

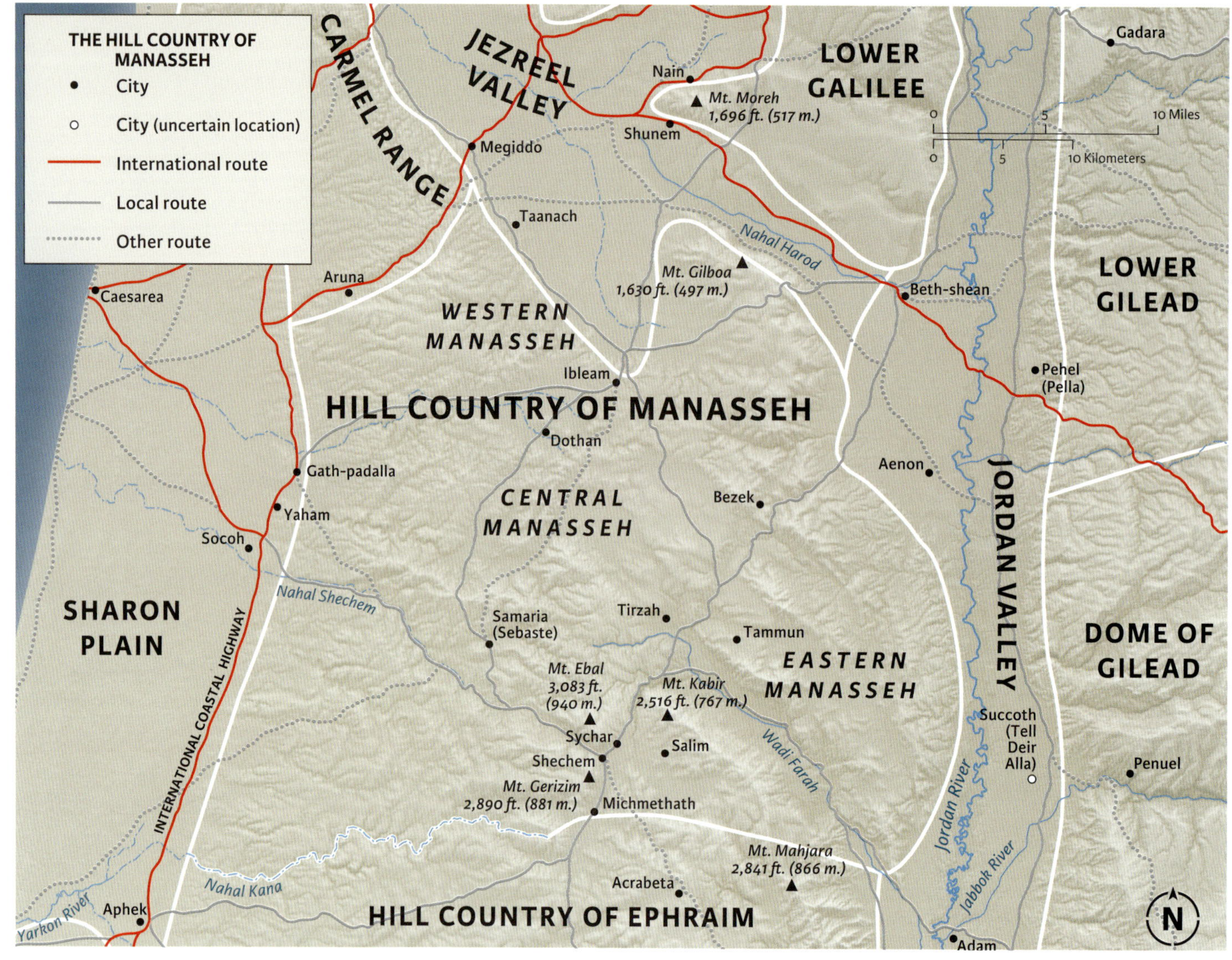

B. THE HILL COUNTRY OF MANASSEH

The ranges and valleys that make up the Hill Country of Manasseh cradle the southern edge of an area so geographically diverse that biblical geographer Denis Baly has labeled it the "Zone of Greater Complexity."[1] Here the north-northeast angle of the folded mountain range that forms the backbone of Judah and Ephraim sideswipes the north-south line of the Rift Valley fault; the collision is complete in Galilee. In the process, the Manasseh hills were fractured by side faults running off the Rift Valley to the northwest, carving out broad interior valleys at right angles to the fold. To complicate matters further, the straightforward geological sequence of the Judean hills (Eocene-Senonian-Cenomanian) is repeated here twice—three times, if its extension along the Mount Carmel Range is included. The result is a complex and interesting topography that offers a variety of living and travel opportunities, most of which are quite favorable for long-term settlement. The biblical writer sensed the inherent richness of the region when he spoke of Israel as "*a lush vine; it yields fruit for itself*" and "*a well-trained calf that loves to thresh*" (Hos 10:1,11); these images matched the people of Manasseh with their promising homeland.

The Hill Country of Manasseh divides evenly into three geological subregions; each is oriented on the south-southwest/north-northeast lay of the land, and each is about the size of the Judean Shephelah (a 10 by 20 mi./16 by 32 km rectangle). These subregions can be labeled Eastern, Central, and Western Manasseh, using the old tribal name for the entire region together with its inherited boundaries (Josh 17:7–10).

The backbone of **Eastern Manasseh** is the north-northeastward extension of the folded arch of the Ephraim range. Most of this subregion is composed of hard Cenomanian-Turonian limestone, though thin bands of Senonian chalk and Eocene limestone line the Rift Valley to the east. This is the most drastically uplifted part of Manasseh, having elevations soaring to 2,516 and 2,841 feet (767 and 866 m) on its stronger, western side (Mounts Kabir and Mahjara, respectively). Eastward, the hills of Eastern Manasseh cascade to below sea level in the Rift Valley. Three dramatic valleys slice across the region on right angles to the fold, running west-northwest to east-southeast. The southernmost, the Salim Valley, stretches five miles (8 km) southeastward from Shechem (modern Nablus) into a mountain-enclosed cul-de-sac defined by Mounts

1 Denis Baly, *The Geography of the Bible*, new and rev. ed. (New York: Harper & Row, 1974), 29.

Kabir and Mahjara; an alluvial floor as flat as the top of a table rests between. A little to the north, on the other side of Mount Kabir, the majestic cut of the Wadi Farah (also called the Tirzah wadi and, in some older atlases, the Wadi Fari'a[1]) slices completely through Eastern Manasseh in a gorge one-half to two miles (1 to 3 km) wide. A third, the Tammun Valley (in Arabic *el-Buqei'a*, "the little valley"), lies just to its north.

The Wadi Farah chasm and the Salim Valley were formed when double (parallel) fault lines angling off of the great fault of the Rift Valley caused the ground between to drop into steep, down-faulted basins. Each has cut into the water table (much of the Farah is below sea level), exposing many springs in the process. John baptized at "*Aenon* [meaning "springs"] *near Salim*," which some scholars[2] place in the Salim Valley for, as the Gospel explains, "*there was plenty of water there*" (John 3:23). For its part, the Farah Valley carries the natural route from the Manasseh highlands to the Adam crossing on the Jordan River (Tell ed-Damiya; Josh 3:16). This wide-open doorway helped to bind the people of the Hill Country of Manasseh to Transjordan. In this regard, it will be remembered that half of the tribe of Manasseh ended up settling in parts of Gilead and northern Transjordan (Num 32:33–42; Josh 22:7), and there was a "*forest of Ephraim*" in the Gilead highlands (2 Sam 18:6; cp. 17:26). The ancient city of Tirzah (Tell el-Farah) was located in a wonderfully pleasant setting at the Farah's upper, western end; it was fully worthy of the poetic couplet "*You are as beautiful as Tirzah, my darling, lovely as Jerusalem*" (Song 6:4). The route was no doubt busy, frequented by all sorts of folk looking for occasions to interact with their counterparts on the other side of the Rift Valley. The prophet

The dramatic double-faulted cut of the Wadi Farah (the Tirzah wadi) has opened a broad doorway through the dry hills of Eastern Manasseh, connecting the region of Tirzah (off to the left) to the Gilead hills of Transjordan (beyond to the right). The valley floor in this early springtime view, seen from Mount Kabir, is covered by a patchwork quilt of green and plastic-wrapped hothouses, visual evidence of the superior agricultural capacity of Manasseh's highland valleys. The Tammun Ridge rises beyond. Down south, Jerusalem's eastern connection was limited to a few high ridges twisting through the arid Judean Wilderness to Jericho. In sharp contrast, Manasseh's push eastward through the Wadi Farah was by nature inviting and easy.

1 Denis Baly and A. D. Tushingham, *Atlas of the Biblical World* (New York: The World Publishing Company, 1971), 97; note also Baly, *Geography of the Bible*, 11, 14, *passim*.

2 Following William Foxwell Albright, *The Archaeology of Palestine* (Gloucester, MA: Peter Smith, 1971), 247. Note that the next event in the narrative flow of John's Gospel is Jesus's encounter with the Samaritan woman at Sychar (the modern village of Askar) on the western end of the Salim Valley.

Hosea was astute enough to see that the opportunities of this vital Shechem-Adam-Gilead connection were not always good:

> *They, [as at] Adam,*[1] *have violated the covenant;*
> *there they have betrayed me.*
> *Gilead is a city of evildoers,*
> *tracked with bloody footprints.*
> *Like raiders who wait in ambush for someone,*
> *a band of priests murders on the road*
> *to Shechem.* (Hos 6:7–9)

Most of Eastern Manasseh is hilly steppe land. Its higher, westward slopes and the upper ends of its interior valleys are fertile, but the rest—especially the hills of the eastern declivity that tip toward the Jordan Valley—lie barren before the Rift Valley. This is a land with few permanent villages (Tirzah is an exception). It's a place where shepherds face the double threat of summertime heat and hungry hordes prowling out of the thickets of the Jordan below (Jer 49:19).

The prophets Hosea and Amos, drafted by God to speak against the injustices endemic to the Northern Kingdom of Israel, called the play as eastern desert imagery overwhelmed the highlands west of the Jordan. Hosea wrote, *"An east wind will come, a wind from the LORD rising up from the desert. His water source will fail, and his spring will run dry"* (Hos 13:15). Amos warned, *"The shepherd snatches two legs or a piece of an ear from the lion's mouth"* (Amos 3:12), and Hosea's writings clarify that the sheep in danger in this case are of the human rather than animal variety: *"For I [the Lord] am like a lion to Ephraim and like a young lion to the house of Judah. Yes, I will tear them to pieces and depart. I will carry them off, and no one can rescue them"* (Hos 5:14).

The block of Eocene hills constituting **Central Manasseh** forms the heartland of the tribal inheritance of Manasseh. Geologically, Central Manasseh is a continuation of the Eocene hills of the Judean Shephelah; it lies on the same north-northeastward angle.[2] It would be a mistake, though, to think of Central Manasseh and the Judean Shephelah as topographically similar. The entire subregion of Central Manasseh has been thrust upward to heights that rival those of the Judean hill country—so much so that it is not proper to speak of the region as a *shephelah* (lowland) at all. It is, rather, on average higher than the hard limestone subregions of Eastern and Western Manasseh. This is the geological reverse of Judah, where the Cenomanian-Turonian hills tower over the Eocene. Indeed, unlike the softer Eocene limestone of the Judean Shephelah, that of Central Manasseh is fairly hard, resisting the forces of erosion and giving it a look that feels more like the Hill Country of Judah than the relaxed forms of a Shephelah.

In terms of topography, the southern and northern ends of Central Manasseh are marked by prominent mountains. On the south, the twin peaks of Mount Ebal (3,083 ft; 940 m) and Mount Gerizim (2,890 ft; 881 m) dominate the skyline. The mound of Shechem (Tel Balata) lies in the tight valley between, once controlling the pass, now completely surrounded by the blocky shapes of the modern buildings of metro Nablus. The 360-degree view from the top of Mount Ebal cannot be rivaled. On a clear day, the eye can take in the waters of the Mediterranean, the spine of the Carmel Range, the hills of Upper Galilee, and Mount Hermon standing seventy-five miles to the northeast, as well as the rise of Gilead across the Jordan and, to the south, Ephraim to Nebi Samwil, five miles north of Jerusalem.[3] Because the summit of Ebal is now crowned by an Israeli army base, the view is restricted today to military eyes only. Fortunately, the panorama from the top of Gerizim is nearly as fine with the exception of the gaze to the north, partially blocked by Ebal. There is no view like these in Judah—certainly not from Mount Zion!—and we can almost sense that the lofty vantage point from Ebal and Gerizim gave Manasseh's Israelite and Samaritan inhabitants a sense of proprietorship over the sacred rights of the landscape below.

In the biblical narrative, Moses designated Mounts Gerizim and Ebal as the places to which all Israel should assemble to proclaim the blessings and curses of the covenant. Even though these mountains dominate the skyline of the central Hill Country of Manasseh, he felt that he had to give the Israelites specific directions: *"Aren't these mountains across the Jordan, beyond the western road [lit. "the sunset road"] in the land of the Canaanites, who live in the Arabah [i.e., the southern Jordan Valley], opposite Gilgal, near the oaks of Moreh?"* (Deut 11:30). Moses's roadmap evokes all sorts of sacred associations, past and yet to come: the place where Abram built his first altar in Canaan (Gen 12:6); the hallowed ground where Joshua would set up the twelve stones of testimony, circumcise Israel, and celebrate the Passover (Josh 4:19–24; 5:2–12); and the venerable locus where Samuel would offer sacrifices after anointing Saul king of Israel (1 Sam 10:8).

Central Manasseh's third mountain is Gilboa (1,630 ft; 497 m), its arched back defining the northern edge of the region. Because Gilboa is surrounded on three sides by the Jezreel and Harod Valleys, its historical associations are there, connected to battles and movements of people passing along the international highway that skirts Manasseh to the north (e.g., 1 Sam 31:1–8). When David was told that the bodies of Saul and Jonathan, Israel's king and crown prince, lay dead on Gilboa's slopes, he cursed the entire range: *"Mountains of Gilboa, let no dew or rain be on you"* (2 Sam 1:21; cp. Deut 11:17; 28:23–24). The implication, of course, is that Mount Gilboa, with a high northern exposure that faces the winter rains, is normally wet and green—as is, in fact, nearly all of Central Manasseh to the south.

It was precisely in a land as pleasant as this, where the cycle of rainfall and dew is more predictable than in Judah and where lofty hills command the scene, that

1 Reading Adam as a place name rather than a personal name, as *inclusio* with "the road to Shechem." Note, for instance, Francis I. Andersen and David Noel Freedman, *Hosea*, vol. 24 *The Anchor Bible* (Garden City, NY: Doubleday & Company, 1980), 438–39.

2 Note that the Eocene limestone once covered the western hills of Ephraim between Judah and Manasseh but has eroded completely away.

3 Note the view of George Adam Smith in *The Historical Geography of the Holy Land* (1894), 119–23. Says Smith, "No geography of Palestine can afford to dispense with the view from the top of Ebal," the "obvious centre" of the land (120).

In the 1970's, a member of Kibbutz Shamir found a small cast-bronze bull by chance among the rolling hills of northern Central Manasseh, east of Dothan. Subsequently called the "Bull Site," the place of the find was surveyed and excavated by archaeologist Amihai Mazar in 1978 and 1981.[1] Mazar identified the site as an open-air sanctuary dating to Iron Age I (1200–1000 BC), the time of the judges. The site, on a low rise, included remains of a crude stone perimeter wall, a standing stone (*matsevah*), a pavement for offerings, and pieces of broken pottery vessels. He interpreted the site as evidence of an active folk religion in which Israelites petitioned Baal, the Canaanite male deity of fertility, for rain so that his impregnated female consort, Asherah, could cause growth in the crops and herds. For the peasant farmers of ancient Israel, whose livelihood was directly linked to rainfall, this so-called "religion of the hearth and home" offered an immediate and compelling alternative to traveling all the way to the temple in Jerusalem. But, importantly, devotees of Baal and Asherah conceived of their gods as if they were in the image of men, and prophets like Hosea and Amos rightly condemned the practice as idolatry.

the temptation was ever at hand to build sanctuaries "*on every high hill and under every green tree*" (2 Kgs 17:10) to Baal and Asherah, the Canaanites' male and female deities of fertility. In condemning the practice, the prophet Hosea allows us a look at the practical advantage of the wooded growth that once covered the hills of Central Manasseh: "*They sacrifice on the mountaintops, and they burn offerings on the hills, and under oaks, poplars, and terebinths, because their shade is pleasant*" (Hos 4:13).

Religious sensibilities aside, life *was* pleasant in the hills and dales of Manasseh.

Between the Eocene highlands of Central Manasseh and the Cenomanian-Turonian core of Eastern Manasseh runs a thin trough of Senonian chalk. This trough is the extension of the chalk trough that separates the Judean Shephelah from the Judean Hill Country to the south-southwest. Like its associated band of Eocene limestone, the chalk has eroded completely off of the Ephraimite highlands between. The Manasseh extension of the trough points in a straight line from Michmethath (Josh 17:7) to Beth-shean, linking Shechem, Tirzah (with its side route through the Wadi

Tel Balata, the round mound of ancient Shechem, can be seen amidst the squared shapes of modern Nablus, just to the left (west) of the lowest part of the shadow in the middle of the picture. The view is from the summit of Mount Gerizim; Ebal rises to the left, while Mount Kabir frames the scene in the distance (center and right). The low ground between, fast being enveloped by urban sprawl, is the confluence of the Salim Valley (running off to the right), the Senonian chalk trough that separates Central from Eastern Manasseh (angling away between Mounts Ebal and Kabir, top center), and the valley of Nablus between Ebal and Gerizim, left. Abraham's first appearance in Canaan was at the oak of Moreh, somewhere here in the heart of the land of Manasseh (Gen 12:6). It began a string of historical associations that have energized claims to the valley ever since.

1 Amihai Mazar, "The 'Bull Site'—An Iron Age I Open Cult Place," *BASOR* 247 (1982): 27–42.

Farah), and Bezek (Khirbet Ibziq; 1 Sam 11:8) along the way. Filled with fertile alluvial soil, the trough carries a natural route that opens the heartland of Manasseh to an important international route crossing the northern Rift Valley.

The subregion of **Western Manasseh** is a geological depression of mixed limestones—primarily Cenomanian-Turonian—cut by several east-west faults. The whole thing slopes gradually to the coast, with the main drainage in its southern section following the outer run of the Nahal Shechem, the wadi that flows westward from the valley lying between Mounts Ebal and Gerizim. To the northwest, a V-shaped fault outlines the Vale of Dothan, a broad and convenient passage connecting the coastal plain with the Jezreel Valley.

The Vale of Dothan sits hard against the Manasseh highlands and historically has carried the tightest line of the international highway that skirts the hills between Transjordan and the coast. Caravans of camels heavily loaded with exotic trade goods have passed this way for centuries, on their way to eager customers along the Mediterranean. If we look closely, we can imagine "*a caravan of Ishmaelites coming from Gilead. Their camels were carrying aromatic gum, balsam, and resin, going down to Egypt*" (Gen 37:25), stopping in Dothan to pick up one more commodity—a young Joseph—on the way. So, too, the Arameans came this way and encamped at Dothan to capture Elisha—a prophet who knew too much (2 Kgs 6:11–12)—and put a choke-hold on Israel in the process (2 Kgs 6:13–20).

The mixed geological base of Western Manasseh provides a picturesque landscape well-suited for all kinds of livelihoods. Its broad, western exposure and wide valleys are watered by numerous lines of springs, which cluster wherever one type of limestone gives way to another. Rainfall is abundant and living conditions are nearly ideal for vine-and-fig-tree villagers, allowing the inhabitants of Manasseh to prosper. The main city in the region was Ahab's capital at Samaria (Hellenistic Sebaste; modern Sabastiya); the place was chosen by his father Omri for its ready access to the coast (1 Kgs 16:23–24). The city of Samaria became the type-site for the entire region: its "*houses of cut stone*" surrounded by "*lush vineyards*" and wagons "*full of grain*" (Amos 2:13; 5:11; cp. 9:14) represented the promise of the Northern Kingdom. Such symbolized "*the choice gifts of the land and everything in it*" (Deut 33:16). The name Samaria eventually came to designate the entire Northern Kingdom of Israel during the time of the Old Testament; it continued to serve as the name of the Manasseh hills in

The view southward from the top of Mount Kabir takes in the eastern flank of Mount Ebal (right) as well as the northeastern shoulder of Mount Gerizim beyond (center). Modern Nablus (ancient Shechem) lies tight in the valley between, exactly on the watershed ridge. (The parting of waters is the top of Ebal, the top of Gerizim, and the crest in the Nablus Valley now blanketed by buildings, shown just right of center here.) The Michmethath Valley stretches away to the south (back left), while the opening to the Salim Valley can be seen on the far left. The canyon running below Mount Ebal and off to the lower right of the picture (toward the northeast) carries the Wadi Beidah, which drains the entire valley system seen here through the Senonian chalk trough separating Eastern from Central Manasseh, then into the Wadi Farah, and out to the Jordan Valley. Shechem had what Jerusalem lacked—a ready base of soil and nice confluence of natural routes. Its advantage for kingdom-building was obvious.

the centuries that followed (2 Kgs 17:24; Amos 3:9; Ezra 4:10; Neh 4:2; Luke 17:11; Acts 9:31).

The Bible mentions several Manassite cities lining the edges of the Jezreel Valley (Beth-shean, Ibleam, En-dor, Taanach, and Megiddo; Josh 17:11; Judg 1:27), but, as is the case with Ephraim, it provides no comprehensive city list for the Manasseh highlands. It does, however, supply enough information to allow us to draw the border between the central and western parts of Manasseh on the one hand, and the slopes of Ephraim on the other. This was the region of heaviest settlement in the central hills. The line followed the bottom of the Kana wadi, leaving a few towns belonging to Ephraim north of the wadi and some from Manasseh to the south (Josh 17:7–10). This data suggests that while a wadi did not divide social groups in ancient Israel (indeed, the shared soil and water resources within a fertile wadi tended to bind people on either side together), lines drawn for administrative purposes did not always take into consideration the social dynamic of real life.[1]

Our look at the settlement patterns of the Hill Country of Manasseh is aided by the Samaria ostraca, a collection of more than sixty inscribed potsherds found in the ruins of the capital city of Samaria that date to the early eighth century BC. These ostraca bear notations regarding shipments of wine or oil sent from landed estates in western Manasseh to officials living in the capital. From these we can identify the names of several contemporary villages in the region, together with the clans to which their residents belonged. Among them are the Ophrah of the Abiezer clan, hometown of Gideon (Judg 6:11), tucked in the hilly slopes of Manasseh west of Shechem.[2] Thus, the Samaria ostraca provide a partial city list for Manasseh that somewhat offsets the lack of a Manasseh city list in the book of Joshua.

The biblical history of the Manasseh highlands is tied to the succession of capitals of the Northern Kingdom of Israel. Jeroboam, the first king of the Northern Kingdom of Israel, "*built Shechem in the hill country of Ephraim and lived there*" (1 Kgs 12:25). This was the obvious choice for his administrative center, for Shechem already had a long history as the largest city state in the region and was, in fact, the object of imperial attention during Egypt's New Kingdom (the sixteenth through fourteenth centuries BC).[3] Indeed, though on the watershed ridge and in the very heart of the Ephraim-Manasseh highlands, Shechem lies at a hub of valleys radiating in four directions, open and exposed and as different in its geographical setting from Jerusalem as any hill country capital could possibly be. The area is fertile, and the living conditions are comfortable. Mark Twain, who rode by the site on horseback in 1867, noted that "the narrow canyon in which Nablus, or Shechem, is situated is under high cultivation, and the soil is exceedingly black and fertile. It is well watered, and its affluent vegetation gains effect by contrast with the barren hills that tower on either side."[4]

When we consider Twain's normal penchant for irreverent comments about the rocky infertility of the Holy Land, his praise for the valleys surrounding Shechem is noteworthy. In any case, the north and northeastern slopes of Mount Gerizim, the sides of the mountain closest to Shechem, are dotted with springs, all flowing into the valley surrounding the city and making it, for Shechem, the blessed mountain. The slopes of Mount Ebal facing Shechem, on the other hand, are completely devoid of springs, giving it the reputation of

Under the watchful eye of a Palestinian farmer, a student of biblical geography puts her hand to the plow and doesn't look back (cp. Luke 9:62). Though stony by the standards of America's farm belt, the fields of Ephraim and Manasseh promised the good life to a people not long off the Sinai wilderness. The potential was even greater: *"Look,"* Amos declared on behalf of the Lord, *"the days are coming . . . when the plowman will overtake the reaper . . . [and] I will restore the fortunes of my people Israel"* (Amos 9:13–14).

1 We should note the comments by Anson Rainey on tribal and clan mobility and stability in *The Sacred Bridge*, 151–54. Three examples of towns identified with one tribe though being located within the borders of another are Shaaraim of Simeon within Judah (Josh 15:33–36; 1 Chr 4:31), Dibon of Gad within Reuben (Num 32:1–4,33–38; 33:45), and En-gannim of Issachar at Manesseh (if identified with Ginae) or within Naphtali (if identified with Kh. Beit Jann; Josh 19:21).

2 Anson F. Rainey and R. Steven Notley, *The Sacred Bridge: Carta's Atlas of the Biblical World*, 2nd. Emended & Enhanced Ed. (Jerusalem: Carta, 2014), 221–22; Anson Rainey, "Aspects of Life in Ancient Israel," in Richard E. Averbeck, Mark W. Chavalas, and David B. Weisberg, *Life and Culture in the Ancient Near East* (Bethesda, MD: CDL Press, 2003), 256–61. The Samaria ostraca mention the Abiezer clan but not the town of Ophrah by name.

3 G. Ernest Wright, *Shechem: The Biography of a Biblical City* (New York: McGraw-Hill Book Company, 1965).

4 Mark Twain, *The Innocents Abroad* (New York: New American Library Signet Classic, 1966), 393.

The orchards around Ahab's capital of Samaria are blanketed with a covering of wild mustard in late winter, a testament to the inherent fertility of the land. The prophet Hosea spoke of God's blessings for a renewed Israel in language that reflected the potential that the land itself had to offer: *"His new branches will spread, and his splendor will be like the olive tree. . . . The people will return and live beneath his shade. They will grow grain and blossom like the vine"* (Hos 14:6–7).

being a cursed mountain (cp. Deut 11:29).[1] This important detail was noted by Benjamin of Tudela, a Jewish traveler from what is now Spain who visited the region in the mid-twelfth century AD: "On Mount Gerizim there are fountains (i.e., springs) and gardens and plantations but Mount Ebal is rocky and barren, and between them in the valley lies the city of Shechem."[2]

Shechem's openness and natural fertility made it a religious center, and here we find a host of sacred spots and shrines to which people came to commune with the Lord—or the local deities of the land: the oak of Moreh near which Abraham built his altar (Gen 12:6); the "*oak near Shechem*" (Gen 35:4); the Diviner's Oak (Judg 9:37); the temple of Baal-berith ("lord of the covenant"; Judg 9:4); the "*large stone . . . under the oak at the sanctuary of the LORD*" (Josh 24:26); the mountains of the blessing and curse (Deut 11:29; Josh 8:33–34); a Samaritan temple on Mount Gerizim (John 4:20); and a temple to Zeus perched nearby, above the Roman city of Neapolis (modern Nablus).

Shechem's greatest advantage—its openness and fertility—made it difficult to defend, and the city's history is a litany of failed attempts to establish a viable kingdom beyond its city walls (e.g., Judg 9:1–57; 1 Kgs 12:25; and the notorious King Lab'ayu of the el-Amarna correspondence[3]). From Shechem, a site straddling the vale between Mounts Gerizim and Ebal, the view skyward takes in "*shadows of . . . mountains [that] look like men . . . coming down [in ambush] from the central part of the land*" (Judg 9:36–37)—a disconcerting thought for a city looking to protect its assets. Indeed, nearly a century ago the German biblical scholar Albrecht Alt called the place the "uncrowned queen of Palestine," an epithet recognizing Shechem's natural advantages as well as its most fatal flaw.[4]

Sensing trouble, Jeroboam moved his residence and capital city northward down the chalk trough to Tirzah (1 Kgs 14:17). From there he could focus on the wide-open Wadi Farah connection linking Manasseh to Gilead and his secondary capital at Penuel, in the cleft of the Jabbok River opposite the Jordan crossing at Adam (1 Kgs 12:25). The move to Tirzah allowed Jeroboam and his successors to concentrate their kingdom-building activities on the hills lining the Jordan, in the relative safety and security of the highlands of Gilead, Eastern Manasseh, and Ephraim (1 Kgs 15:21,33; 16:6–9,15). Before long, the ambitious general Omri seized the Israelite throne and moved the capital again, this time to the open hills of Western Manasseh facing the Mediterranean coast (1 Kgs 16:17–24). From the city of Samaria "*on the summit above the rich valley*" (Isa 28:1), Omri and his hardscrabble son Ahab forged a kingdom by conquest and marriage that stretched from Phoenicia to Moab. During those heady days, all roads met in Samaria; trade goods ranging from Moabite wool to African ivory found their way to the Israelite capital (1 Kgs 22:39; 2 Kgs 3:4; Amos 3:15; 6:4).

The post-kingdom history of Samaria—the name now designates the entire Hill Country of Manasseh—reflects its international connections: from the nations settled there by Assyria (2 Kgs 17:24), to the Macedonian colony founded on the grounds of Ahab's old capital after the conquest of Alexander the Great, to Herod's rebuilding of the place as the *polis* Sebaste (Gk for "Augustus") so soldiers and patrons loyal to the cause could live out their years in manorial ease (*Ant.* 15.246, 292, 342; *War* 1.403). When Jesus visited Jacob's well in Sychar, a village in the Salim Valley beneath Mount Gerizim a little east of the spot where the "uncrowned queen" already lay in ruins, his disciples and the woman at the well were all keenly aware that the people of Samaria had developed deeply rooted associations of foreignness, sown by millennia of keeping open contacts with the outside world. This was something the people of isolated Judah never could quite accept or understand (John 4:9,27).

1 Gilad J. Gevaryahu, "Why Was Mount Gerizim Chosen for the Blessing Ceremony?" *JBQ* 43:2 (2015): 122–25.

2 Marcus Nathan Adler, *The Itinerary of Benjamin of Tudela: Critical Text, Translation, and Commentary* 1907; repr., (Whitefish, MT: Kessinger Publishing, 2010, 21.

3 Wright, "Appendix 2: Shechem in the Amarna Archive," in *Shechem*, 191–207.

4 Cited without reference in Wright, *Shechem*, 9.

The biblical prophets, too, had things to say about Samaria, wrapping their comments about the moral failings of its people with the character of their land. Amos called the nations of the world to "*assemble on the mountains of Samaria, and see the great turmoil in the city*" (Amos 3:9). The scene is appropriate: Ahab's capital was on a rise surrounded by a plain with higher hills all around, like a stage in the middle of a coliseum (to borrow a later image, albeit apt); this geographical reality fit the situation of Amos's call to watch the show. The script was predictable, and at hand. This was a land that was particularly proud of its home-grown food supply; the region exported basic staples such as wheat, meal, and oil to the ports of Tyre and Sidon in order to keep the Phoenician economic motor running smoothly (Ezek 27:17). So it was precisely these resources that Amos attacked as he spoke of God's judgment, remembering the land-and-people blessings and curses that all Israel had so faithfully shouted from Mounts Gerizim and Ebal years before (cp. Deut 28:1–68; Josh 8:30–35):

I also withheld the rain from you
while there were still three months
until harvest. (Amos 4:7)
The locust devoured
your many gardens and vineyards,
your fig trees and olive trees. (Amos 4:9)
You will never drink the wine
from the lush vineyards
you have planted. (Amos 5:11)
The Lord God . . . was forming a swarm
of locusts at the time the spring crop
first began to sprout—after the cutting of the king's hay. (Amos 7:1)
I will send a famine through the land:
not a famine of bread or a thirst for water,
but of hearing the words of the Lord. (Amos 8:11)

Of course, Amos also saw a day when both land and people would be reborn, which he again expressed in the simple words of fertility.

Look, the days are coming—
this is the Lord's declaration—
when the plowman will overtake the reaper
and the one who treads grapes,
the sower of seed.
The mountains will drip with sweet wine,
and all the hills will flow with it.
I will restore the fortunes of my people Israel.
They will rebuild and occupy ruined cities,
plant vineyards and drink their wine,
make gardens and eat their produce.
I will plant them on their land,
and they will never again be uprooted
from the land I have given them.
The Lord your God has spoken. (Amos 9:13–15)

About 350 Samaritans—half their total population worldwide—live on the summit of Mount Gerizim today. Here Husney Wasef, a Samaritan priest, displays a scroll copy of their holy book, the Samaritan Pentateuch (the first five books of Moses). The Samaritan community takes seriously Moses's instructions to gather at Mount Gerizim and recite the blessings of the covenant (Deut 11:29–32; 27:12–13). They are quick to point out, when asked, that the word "Jerusalem" does not appear in the Pentateuch. So in the traditions of Samaritan spiritual geography, Mount Gerizim takes full precedence over Jerusalem, labeled by them as "that Jebusite city."[1] Gerizim, the Samaritans believe, is the oldest, most central, and highest mountain in the world. Adam, they hold, was made from dust there, and it was there that Noah's ark landed. This was Mount Moriah, where Abraham offered Isaac to God, and the Beth-el, "house of God," where Jacob slept next to the ladder ascending to heaven. It was on Mount Gerizim, the Samaritans insist, that Joshua set up the twelve memorial stones after crossing the Jordan (they will point them out if asked) and erected the tabernacle as the place of God's meeting. Stephen's assertion that it was in Shechem rather than Hebron that Abraham had purchased his family tomb may also have Samaritan overtones; perhaps Stephen was a Samaritan (Acts 7:16).[2] "*Our fathers worshiped on this mountain,*" the woman at the well noted to Jesus (John 4:20). Though the temple is long gone, the Samaritans still revere the mountain, which today they call Tura Berikha, "The Blessed Mountain."[3]

1 See, for instance, Husney Wasef, *The Israelite Journey through the Wilderness in the Sinai Peninsula* (Nablus: Centre of the Good Samaritan, 2012), 257–76; Ingrid Hjelm, *The Samaritans and Early Judaism: A Literary Analysis* (Sheffield: Sheffield Academic Press, 2000); R. J. Coggins, *Samaritans and Jews: The Origins of Samaritanism Reconsidered* (Oxford: Basil Blackwell, 1975); and Yitzhak Magen, *Mount Gerizim Excavations: A Temple City* (Jerusalem: IAA, 2008).

2 Various suggestions regarding this idea have been summarized and expanded by Elaine Phillips, "'The Tomb that Abraham Had Purchased' (Acts 7:16)," in Steve A. Hunt, ed., *Perspectives on Our Father Abraham* (Grand Rapids: Eerdmans, 2010), 110–25.

3 The name is Aramaic and appears in *Genesis Rabbah* 32:10.

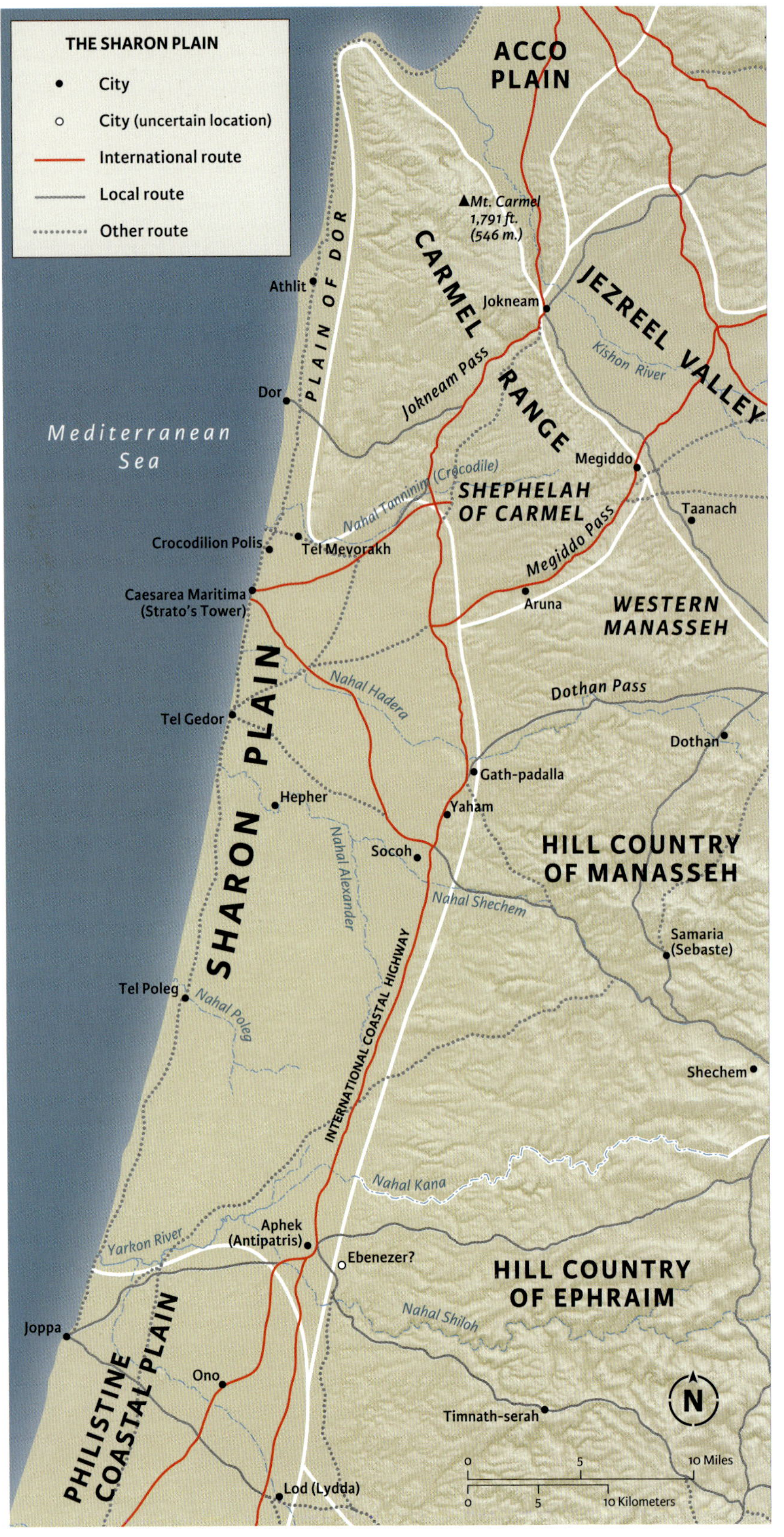

Jesus also saw a hopeful day, late one spring (cp. John 2:23), commenting to his disciples in the Salim Valley near Sychar on both the state of the surrounding crops and the spiritual ripeness of people: "*Open your eyes and look at the fields, because they are ready for harvest*" (John 4:35).

Here in the essential land of Manasseh, life always came down to the basics.

C. THE SHARON PLAIN

The Sharon Plain is that portion of Israel's Mediterranean coast that lies between Philistia and Mount Carmel. On topographical grounds, the Sharon's southern end is frequently drawn along the Yarkon River, though some ancient sources bring it south as far as the Soreq wadi in order to include the fertile band of Mousterian brown-red sands east of Joppa.[1] In the north, the natural border of the Sharon is the short and sluggish line of the Nahal Tanninim (Crocodile River), which flows to the Mediterranean from springs at the southwestern tip of Mount Carmel. The eastern line of the plain is marked by the rise of the hills of Ephraim and Manasseh, while the western limit is, of course, the sea. The shoreline of the Sharon Plain is quite straight, even more so than Philistia, and surrenders nothing that would serve as a decent natural harbor. This feature is consistent with the region's name: Sharon, which may come from the Hebrew verb *yashar*, "to be level or straight." By dimension, the Sharon Plain is about ten by thirty miles (16 by 48 km) in size.

North of the Tanninim River, the coastal plain narrows to no more than two miles (3 km) in width, where it is squeezed between the heights of Mount Carmel and the Mediterranean Sea. This thin stretch of coastline, the **Plain of Dor**, extends northward for twenty miles (32 km) to the point where Mount Carmel thrusts its nose into the Mediterranean. This northern extension of the Sharon Plain takes its local name from its elegant and effective natural harbor, Dor (Josh 12:23; Judg 1:27; 1 Chr 7:29).

The most distinctive geological feature of the Sharon Plain is its three parallel ridges of kurkar, a rough sandstone formed from calcified sand dunes. The remnants of one kurkar ridge can be traced exactly along the shoreline. Over time, wave action has broken this ridge in many places, allowing the sea to creep inward in dozens of shallow arcs. Today this first kurkar ridge is almost completely covered by beach sand and dunes, though portions of its jagged edge are exposed at the water line. A second kurkar ridge, the most intact of the three, runs parallel to the first, one half mile (1 km) inland. For the most part, the sand dunes of the Sharon Plain do not extend eastward beyond this ridge. (Recall that on the Philistine Coastal Plain to the south, the dunes extend up to three miles inland). A third ridge, the so-called "red ridge," lies two miles (3 km) further east and is, at 150 to 240 feet (45 to 75 m) in elevation, the highest of the three. This red ridge, as well as most of the remainder of the Sharon Plain, is covered by a blanket of coarse brown-red Mousterian sands, hence its name. Today the trough between the first and second kurkar ridges carries the line of Israel's coastal highway (Highway 2), while Israel's Highway 4 tracks just east of

1 For instance, both Eusebius and Jerome, in their *Onomasticon* 162:5-6; see G. S. P. Freeman-Grenville, Rupert L. Chapman III, and Joan E. Taylor, *The Onomasticon by Eusebius of Caesarea* (Jerusalem: Carta, 2003), 89. The evidence is summarized by Rainey and Notley, *The Sacred Bridge*, 37.

Waters of the firmament (the sky) and the deep meet at the coastline of Dor, the northern extension of the Sharon Plain. Here the beach is relatively narrow, with dune sand, stabilized by low growth, rising in lumps just a bit inland. A wave-battered natural breakwater of kurkar protects the shore but can wreak havoc on ships trying to make beachhead. The view is northward from the ruined mound of Dor, with the rise of Mount Carmel in the distance.

the third ridge. All three of these kurkar ridges extend as far south as Gaza, but they are less visible on the Philistine Coastal Plain because of the heavier covering of alluvial soil and dune sand there.

Elevations across the southern two-thirds of the Sharon Plain are quite stable, reaching at most 280 feet (85 m), an elevation somewhat lower than the hills of the northern Philistine plain behind Joppa and significantly lower than the hills inland of Ashkelon and Gaza. If the word "Sharon" indeed derives from the Hebrew word *yashar*, the reference may well be not to the shoreline but to the comparative levelness of the ground between the Yarkon and Tanninim Rivers, as compared to the somewhat rolling Philistine Coastal Plain.[1] In any case, a heavy mass of kurkar-reinforced Mousterian sands has forced the Shiloh and Kana wadis that exit the hills of Ephraim from the east to circle around this part of the plain southward, where their flow joins the Yarkon River's run to the sea. Over time, these wadis have deposited a large swath of alluvial soil in the vicinity of Aphek at the head of the Yarkon. Similarly, the Nahal Alexander, a smaller wadi system descending from the Manasseh hills further north, bends northward to join the Nahal Shechem rather than forcing its way directly west through the Mousterian sands of the southern Sharon Plain.

These three kurkar ridges also impede drainage *within* the mass of Mousterian sands that dominates the southern Sharon Plain. The entire region is by nature given over to large expanses of overgrown seasonal swamps which resist cultivation, impede travel, promote water-borne disease, and thwart permanent settlement. The contrast with the intrinsically favorable living conditions in Philistia cannot be more striking. We might describe the region as rustically, rather than usefully, rural.[2] The first largescale, successful attempt to cut through the kurkar ridges and improve the water flow was made during Roman times.

1 Hence translating *sharon* as "flat country," akin to Hebrew *mishor*, "tableland." See J. Simons, *The Geographical and Topographical Texts of the Old Testament* (Leiden: E. J. Brill, 1959), 83.

2 The description "rustic and rural" is that of Harry Weeks in David Noel Freedman, ed., *The Anchor Bible Dictionary*, vol. 5 (New York: Doubleday, 1992), s. v. "Sharon."

Kurkar is formed from solidified sand dunes in which individual grains of sand have been cemented together by solutions of calcium derived from dissolved seashells. Visually, the result is reminiscent of a high stack of thick sandpaper. If the calcium cement is strong, kurkar can be quite durable. Here a natural outcropping of kurkar along a gravely part of the Caesarea shore provides a stout foundation for a wall that was built to surround part of the palace complex of Herod the Great. These rounded building blocks, with a look of tanned pumice, were themselves cut from kurkar.

The entire area was not fully drained, however, until the rise of Jewish settlement in the Sharon a little more than a century ago. This monumental change to the region's natural ecosystem was born of necessity rather than convenience, in order to support the area of dense Jewish settlement that became the narrow "waist" of the modern state of Israel in 1948. Today, the Mousterian sands in the southern two-thirds of the Sharon Plain provide ideal growing conditions for all kinds of citrus and other orchard crops that came to dominate the region only after the water flow had been regulated. Indeed, visitors to the Sharon today see nothing but large cities surrounded by vast stretches of arable fields, getting little indication and scant appreciation of the intense human and mechanical effort it took to tame the land.

The northern third of the Sharon Plain is both lower and flatter (hence more *sharon*) than the rest, with ground levels not exceeding 160 feet (50 m) in elevation. Without a solid rise of Mousterian sands to block their flow, the wadis here are able to trace fairly direct, though sluggish, courses to the sea. Three, the Shechem, Hadera, and Tanninim wadis, have carried long stretches of alluvial soil out onto the plain, thereby vastly improving the northeastern Sharon's natural capacity for agriculture. Historically, the largest cluster of cities on the Sharon has been here, where arable soil is more plentiful and the water is relatively fresh compared to the swampier parts of the plain further south.

Rainfall across the Sharon Plain averages twenty-five inches (635 mm) annually. With mild winters and hot, noticeably humid summers, the region boasts perfect natural conditions to foster the stickiness of overgrown swamps. From the earliest periods, the Sharon's wetlands have produced large stands of scrub oak forests and a dense undergrowth of wildflowers, brush, and weeds. Indeed, the Sharon is called *drumos*, "forest," in the Greek translation of the Hebrew Bible (the Septuagint; Isa 65:10), prompting some to suggest that the primary meaning of the Hebrew word *sharon* might be "[oak] forest" rather than "level plain."[1] In the late first

1 So, for instance, Geoffrey W. Bromiley, ed., *The International Standard Bible Encyclopedia*, vol. 4 (Grand Rapids, MI: William B. Eerdmans, 1988), s.v. "Sharon," by A. F. Rainey.

century BC, the Greek geographer Strabo described the entire plain as "a large forest" (*Geog.* 16.2.27). In his writings, nearly one hundred years later, Josephus twice referred to a place called "Oak Thicket" near Mount Carmel (*War* 1.250; *Ant.* 14.334). The Sharon's forests were also mentioned by Richard I (the Lionheart) of the Third Crusade (the Crusaders called the Sharon *La Forêt*, "the forest") and by Napoleon, each of whom had trouble driving their armies along the coast. Only small and scattered remnants of these once-grand stands of oak[1] remain today.

The biblical description of the Sharon Plain is equally verdant. Well known is the Shulamite's contented glow: "*I am a wildflower [Hb* havatselet*] of Sharon, a lily of the valleys*" (Song 2:1). The plain's natural growth also figures prominently in prophetic speech imaging the blessings of God. The Sharon is one of four regions lining the heartland of ancient Israel that the prophet Isaiah labeled as being especially blessed: the other three are Mount Carmel, Lebanon (including Upper Galilee), and Bashan in Transjordan. Each claims at least two of the three criteria that define what is likely to be considered "wet" according to the land's rules of rainfall: they are high, north, and/or west. Moreover, each of these regions lies on ancient Israel's outer frontier, where together they form a verdant crown over the highlands of Ephraim and Manasseh. That each had fallen into the grip of the Assyrian kings in Isaiah's day adds to the immanence of the prophet's image. Indeed, Tiglath-Pileser III overran precisely these four regions a decade before he conquered the Northern Kingdom of Israel (cp. Isa 9:1). Knowing their verdant potential for sustaining life, Isaiah reversed the expected picture of the overgrown fertility of the Sharon Plain to portray something that never happens in nature; the goal was to create an on-land image that reflected the heart of the people of Israel. He said, "*The land mourns and withers; Lebanon is ashamed and wilted. Sharon is like a desert; Bashan and Carmel shake off their leaves*" (Isa 33:9).

Isaiah recognized that once the Sharon's God-given garland dried up, its sandy base would be exposed as nothing but open desert. But, of course, Isaiah also put the image back the way it was supposed to be, seeing a day when the wilderness itself would become like the Sharon naturally is:

> *The wilderness and the dry land will be glad;*
> *the desert will rejoice and blossom like*
> *a wildflower (Hb* havatselet*).*
> *It will blossom abundantly*
> *and will also rejoice with joy and singing.*
> *The glory of Lebanon will be given to it,*
> *the splendor of Carmel and Sharon.* (Isa 35:1–2)

The "wildflower of Sharon" (*havatselet*) is usually rendered by the English term "rose," perhaps prompting some Bible readers to picture garden roses (genus *Rosa*) behind a white picket fence. But the *havatselet* seems to be one of the wildflowers native to the region, though exactly which one is open to debate. Suggestions include the meadow saffron, crocus, narcissus (a marsh plant), white lily, anemone, and tulip. Each of these flowers indeed provides a splash of color that brightens the "*splendor of . . . Sharon*" (Isa 35:2). A somewhat different suggestion is that *havatselet* is derived from the Akkadian botanical term *habatsillatu*, a "fresh shoot of reed." If so, the plant provides an image that

This field of Mousterian brown-red sand (Arabic *hamra*) lies ready for fall planting. In their natural state, brown-red sands are completely devoid of lime and lack the capacity to hold water. But when mixed with the clayey alluvial soils washed down from the hills of Ephraim and Manasseh to the east, these sands gain minerals essential for plant growth. Properly drained and aerated fields of brown-red sand can be wondrously productive.

1 These consist primarily of Mount Tabor oak (*Quercus ithaburensis*) and Kermes oak (*Quercus calliprinos*); see Nili Liphschitz, Simcha Lev-Yadun, and Ram Gophna, "The Dominance of *Quercus Calliprinos* (Kermes Oak) in the Central Coastal Plain in Antiquity," *IEJ* 37 (1987): 43–50.

A dense mix of grasses, brush, and small trees overwhelm the sand dunes that line the Sharon's Mediterranean shore. Once carpeted with green, the dunes become stabilized, then act as longitudinal dams blocking the flow of runoff rainwater from easily reaching the sea. Functionally, this line of dunes marks the limits of the sea, as some biblical writers likely noted: *"[The Lord is] the one who set the sand as the boundary of the sea, an enduring barrier that it cannot cross."* (Jer 5:22)

specifically illustrates God's renewed favor on his people and his land.[1]

As a geographical region, the entirety of the "splendor of Sharon" was given by Joshua to the tribe of Manasseh (Josh 17:10; cp. Num 26:28,32; 27:1; Josh 17:2). There is corroborating archaeological evidence of small, unfortified (perhaps Manassite) settlements scattered throughout the region during the Iron Age I (the time of the judges). For practical purposes (i.e., to avoid perennially wet and tangled areas), significant permanent urban settlement didn't pass beyond the bays of alluvial soil on the plain's northeastern and southeastern ends until the Roman period. The four most important cities on the Sharon Plain throughout the biblical period, Aphek, Socoh, Yaham, and Gath-padalla, thus stood in a line along its fertile eastern edge, following the raised seam between the plain and the highlands of Ephraim and Manasseh. All were gateways linking the opportunities of the Sharon to the hills above.

In the southeast, adjacent to the powerful Yarkon springs and surrounded by a broad stretch of alluvial soil, is the strategic gateway city of Aphek (Josh 12:18). Aphek commanded full control of the southern Levant's main international land route as it squeezed its way through the narrow bottleneck between the Yarkon springs and the rise of the Ephraim hills. Appropriately, whenever Aphek is mentioned in the Bible, it is in the context of someone coming through, rather than settling down to call the place home. At the end of the period of the judges, for instance, the Philistines moved north to seize the Aphek pass, thereby threatening to expand their influence into the Ephraimite highlands beyond. Israel responded by a show of force at Ebenezer (possibly *Izbet Sarta*), losing the ark of the covenant in the process (1 Sam 4:1–2,10–11). Some years later, the Philistines again mustered their armies at Aphek before pushing northward into the Jezreel Valley, killing Israel's king and its crown-prince, Saul and Jonathan, in battle at Mount Gilboa in the process (1 Sam 29:1; 31:1–8). A thousand years later, Herod the Great renamed the city of Aphek: he called it Antipatris, in honor of his father Antipater (Josephus *Ant.* 16.143). The place main-

1 Note the commentary on the entry for *habatsillatu* in A. Leo Oppenheim, ed., *The Assyrian Dictionary* (*CAD*) vol. 6 (Chicago: The Oriental Institute, 1956); see also Bromley, *ISBE*, vol. 4, s.v. "Sharon," by Anson Rainey.

tained its role as an international juncture throughout the Roman period (Acts 23:31). Today's large Israeli city that sits squarely in the pass, adjacent to the spring and the ruins of ancient Aphek/Antipatris, is called, appropriately, Rosh haAyin, "Head of the Spring."

The other three cities that played an ongoing role in the ancient history of the Sharon stood in a south-north line in the northeastern corner of the plain. Each was fed by a separate fan-shaped deposit of alluvial soil carried out of the Manasseh hills by the Shechem and Hadera wadis. From south to north these are Socoh (Khirbet Shuweikah er-Ras), from which Solomon governed the region in the tenth century BC (1 Kgs 4:10 cp. 1 Kgs 4:22–23,27–28); Yaham (Khirbet Yamma), where the triumphalistic pharaoh Thutmose III held his famous war council prior to marching on Megiddo in the mid-fifteenth century BC;[1] and Gath-padalla (Jatt; 1 Chr 7:21), the object of regional expansion by the opportunistic Lab'ayu, king of Shechem during the fourteenth century BC (the Amarna Age).[2] The king of (La)sharon who was conquered by Joshua (Josh 12:18) may have been a king of Gath-padalla, which seems to have been the most important city on the plain at the time.

As we have seen, the historic track of the international coastal highway had to thread its way through the Aphek bottleneck, then keep to high ground along the edge of the Ephraim and Manasseh hills owing to the tight geographical constraints of the Sharon Plain. After running the Socoh–Yaham–Gath-padalla line, travelers on the route found their way through any of three interior passes of the Mount Carmel Range before entering the Jezreel Valley beyond. This is also essentially the line of Israel's first modern superhighway, Highway 6, built in the first decade of the twenty-first century AD. Historically, whoever dominated these four cities controlled the north-

A good supply of fresh water is hard to find out on the flats of the Sharon Plain. Herod the Great solved the problem for his new port city, Caesarea, by building this high-level aqueduct to carry fresh water into the city from springs feeding the Nahal Tanninim at the base of Mount Carmel, seven miles to the northeast. Though the length of this aqueduct is relatively modest compared to normal Herodian proportions, its southern end, the broken remains of which are shown here, is well-preserved and proudly carries the distinctive Roman architectural stamp that Herod so successfully introduced into the land. Today's beachgoers carry on the spirit of the seashore that must have indwelt Herod's port city in the time of the New Testament.

1 James B. Pritchard, ed., *Ancient Near Eastern Texts Relating to the Old Testament (ANET)* (Princeton: Princeton University Press, 1955), 235; William W. Hallo, ed., *The Context of Scripture*, Vol. II: *Monumental Inscriptions from the Biblical World* (Leiden: Brill, 2000), 9.

2 *EA* 250 in William L. Moran, *The Amarna Letters* (Baltimore: Johns Hopkins University Press, 1992), 303.

south orientation of the plain. The sweep of military history through the Levant necessarily flowed this way, and we can envision Thutmose III, Amenhotep II, Seti I, Rameses II, Shishak, Tiglath-pileser III, Sargon II, Sennacherib, Esarhaddon, Necho II, Nebuchadnezzar, Alexander the Great, Ptolemy, Antiochus III, his son the Epiphanes, Vespasian, and even Napoleon—a veritable Who's Who of Frightful Conquerors of the Holy Land—all driving their armies up or down its storied length.

So, too, for local military priorities. As the kings of the Northern Kingdom of Israel first sought to expand westward, their moves were not onto the Sharon itself but, like the flow of the wadis from the Ephraim and Manasseh hills, circled around toward the south or north. Nadab, Baasha, Zimri, and Omri all fought at Gibbethon south of Aphek to open a doorway to the routes and ports of Philistia (1 Kgs 15:27; 16:15–17), while both Omri and Ahab fostered trade connections with Phoenicia via routes through the passes of the Carmel Range (1 Kgs 16:31).

The bulk of the Sharon Plain, though, was a kind of frontier land with vast expanses of wetlands that were never quite tamed until modern times. At best, the area was suitable for grazing livestock (1 Chr 27:29). Isaiah was familiar with this situation and spoke of secure pasturage as the region's ideal value for Israel: "*Sharon will be a pasture for flocks*" (Isa 65:10). Yet that it was frontier land also made the Sharon a good locale for cattle rustling (1 Chr 7:21) and other illicit activities common to regions edging settled lands. Indeed, out on the plain, the Sharon's tangled undergrowth typically better served the needs of those seeking a quick escape from society than the populace at large. Toward the end of the Ottoman period, for instance, local Arabs habitually withdrew into the dense marshes of the Sharon to try to escape their tax obligations and conscription owed the Turkish government. And throughout history, the hinterland of the Sharon was the haunt of robbers who would prey on caravans along the international highway running its long eastern edge. For instance, the ancient Egyptian composition commonly known as "A Satirical Letter" details the difficulties of travel along the routes frequented by international travelers in Canaan during the second millennium BC. If the examples of dangerous travel conditions mentioned in the letter bear any relationship to an actual sequential travel itinerary, the paragraph prior to the phrase "Thou are come into Joppa" must describe conditions on the Sharon Plain. It is here that we read,

> The narrow valley is dangerous with Bedouin, hidden under the bushes. . . . Thy path is overgrown with reeds, thorns, brambles, and "wolf's-paw." . . . Thou startest to trot. [Finally] the sky is opened.[1]

We can sense throughout the uneasy anticipation of the traveler that danger really does lie in the undergrowth of every tree along the way. Throughout the time of the Old Testament, the view westward from the highlands of Ephraim and Manasseh simply ran right over the scrub forests and wetlands of the Sharon Plain out to the stiff, uninviting shoreline at water's edge. For ancient Israel, the shore was largely unknown and unknowable. This reality gave literal force to Hosea's call that "*the number of the Israelites will be like the sand of the sea,* which cannot be measured or counted" (Hos 1:10; emphasis added). Indeed, the Israelites never quite came to terms with the Mediterranean. (Interestingly, the sea's Canaanite reflection was *Yamm*, their god of chaos and death.[2]) Jacob's descendants preferred to leave the risks and rewards of maritime activities to others (Ps 107:23–30; Ezek 27:1–36).

But all this up and down the eastern seam of the Sharon Plain is not to ignore the ongoing flow of sea traffic that necessarily had to make its way along the shore. Ships from Egypt, Phoenicia, Cyprus, Greece, and Rome all plied the waters of the eastern Mediterranean, and the run between the ports of Philistia and Acco required at least one stop-over even though there was no obvious break in the Sharon's straight-line shore except at Dor. Yet necessity demanded what geography gave no thought to providing. George Adam Smith has summarized the dilemma nicely: "While the cruelty of many another wild coast is known by the wrecks of ships, the Syrian shore south of Carmel is strewn with the fiercer wreckage of harbors."[3]

There is archaeological evidence from the Middle Bronze II, Late Bronze, and Iron Ages (1550–586 BC) of a few small estuary harbors clinging to the kurkar ridges where the Sharon's streams have broken through to the sea. One is Tel Poleg on the second kurkar ridge one-half mile (1 km) up the Nahal Poleg, the small wadi that drains the interior of the mass of Mousterian Sands in the south-central Sharon Plain. Two more can be found further north at breaks in the red ridge, the easternmost of the kurkar ridges. These are Tell el-Ifshar (perhaps biblical Hepher) on the northern bank of the Nahal Alexander, and Tel Mevorakh on the southern bank of the Nahal Tanninim. These ports were more naturally associated with powers that plied the sea[4] than they were with the caravans that ran the inland routes east of the plain. Egyptian economic interests right along the coast, for instance, can be traced throughout the period; and by the time the Philistines were settling down between Joppa and Gaza, their Sea People cousins, the Tjekker, were making their home on the seaward side

1 *ANET*, 477–78.

2 Stolz, Fritz, "Sea," in Karel van der Toorn, Bob Becking, and Pieter W. van der Horst, *Dictionary of Deities and Demons in the Bible* (Leiden: E. J. Brill, 1995), 1,390–402. For an annotated list of primary sources that mention or allude to the Canaanite deity *Yamm* (or *Yammu*), see Alan Cooper, "Divine Names and Epithets in the Ugaritic Texts," in *Ras Shamra Parallels: The Texts from Ugarit and the Hebrew Bible*, vol. III, by Stan Rummel (Rome: Pontificio Instituto Biblico, 1981), 369–83.

3 Smith, *The Historical Geography of the Holy Land*, 131.

4 Archaeological evidence from Tel Mevorakh, for instance, shows intensive Cypriot connections in the region. See Ephraim Stern, *Excavations at Tel Mevorakh*, QEDEM 18 (Jerusalem: The Institute of Archaeology, The Hebrew University of Jerusalem, 1984).

"[T]he whole seaboard from Dora (Dor) to Joppa . . . was without a [decent sea] harbor, so that vessels bound for Egypt along the [Sharon] coast of Phoenicia had to ride at anchor in the open when menaced by the south-west wind; for even a moderate breeze from this quarter dashes the waves to such a height against the [sand] cliffs that their reflux spreads a wild commotion far out to sea" (Josephus, *War* 1.409).

of the Sharon Plain.[1] That Solomon's administrative district in the Sharon was given the name "*Socoh and the whole land of Hepher*" (1 Kgs 4:10) may reflect his attempt to bring the commercial opportunities of the port side of the plain under Israelite control.[2] But from the outset, the need for constant dredging limited the long-term growth of these ports, and the swamps and forests on their backside conspired to prevent easy inland access. In the long run, the relative isolation of the ports and villages of the Sharon's kurkar ridges resulted in a degree of freedom in regard to their control of sea-based commerce that was difficult for land-based powers such as Israel to root out. Solomon's notable attempt is the exception that proves the rule.

The only real harbors in the region that were located on the coastline were on the northern Dor extension of the Sharon Plain, that is, at the cities of Dor and, ten miles further north, Athlit. Both places were blessed by breaks in the kurkar, which formed isles and protected

The view is to the north-northeast from the highest point in the modern Arab village of Jatt, a place that properly preserves the first part of the ancient name Gath-padalla. The highlands of Western Manasseh rise in the distance (right), with the shallow gap just left of the center forming the natural pass via Dothan into the Jezreel Valley. The dense settlement in the region, today composed primarily of Arab villages, reflects the historic nature of this busy northeastern corner of the Sharon Plain. Here, in the seam between hills and open plain, the soil is good and the water fresh; that's an ideal recipe for prosperous settlement and growth.

1 The Egyptians and the Tjekker both play a prominent role in the eleventh century BC composition, "The Journey of Wen-Amon to Phoenicia," *ANET* 25–29; William W. Hallo, ed., *The Context of Scripture*, Vol. I: *Canonical Compositions from the Biblical World* (Leiden: Brill, 1997), 89–93.

2 Archaeological evidence shows that the Yarkon basin and Sharon Plain flourished during the tenth century BC, but not before or after. A likely scenario is that Solomon used Joppa as the port of Jerusalem, spurring growth in the region. With the later division of the kingdom, the kings of Israel reached the Mediterranean through Dor and Acco, while the kings of Judah were largely curtailed in their coastal activities. See Avraham Faust, "The Sharon and the Yarkon Basin in the Tenth Century BCE: Ecology, Settlement Patterns and Political Involvement," *IEJ* 57 (2007): 65–82.

inlets at which ships could anchor.[1] Dor was an important port from all ages (Josh 11:2; 12:23; Judg 1:27; and the Egyptian *Journey of Wen-Amon*[2])—but especially so from the Persian period onward. Though best known for the ruins of its Crusader castle (Château Pélerin), Athlit was also an effective port throughout the Iron Age. Historically, it is important to note that both sites have tended to be related more to Phoenician ports further north than to ports in Philistia or points inland.

When, with the march of Alexander the Great in the late fourth century BC, the pendulum of power in the ancient world swung from the land routes of the Fertile Crescent to the sea lanes of the Eastern Mediterranean, the locus of control of the land of ancient Israel shifted from its international highways to its ports. We can assume that a land route, running the length of the sandy shore, developed in proportion to the rise in importance of these ports.[3] This continental shift in geopolitics provided enough incentive for the Greek and then Roman rulers of the Sharon Plain to begin to cut through the kurkar ridges and dry out its wetland flats, thereby being able to establish additional new ports along the coast and bend the international highway their direction.[4] Two notable anchorages developed at breaks in the kurkar south of Dor during the Hellenistic period. These were Crocodilion Polis (at the outlet of, naturally, the Tanninim, or Crocodile, River) and Strato's Tower. It was at the latter, founded near the mouth of the Nahal Hadera on a relatively easy land connection to Yaham and Gath-padalla, that Herod the Great chose to build Caesarea Maritima, a place that would eventually become the largest port in the eastern Mediterranean (Acts 10:1–8; 23:23–24,31–33). Herod's penchant for overcoming the obstacles of nature was showcased with his man-made breakwater that circled for more than a third of a mile (500 m) into the sea (Josephus *Ant.* 15.331–339; *War* 1.408–415). By the Late Roman period (the second and third centuries AD), Caesarea's sea gates to the west were flung wide open, foreshadowing the modern reality in which Israeli cities on the Sharon are fueled by Western investment and flooded by corporate signs written in English.

It is helpful to draw the boundary line that separates the world of the ancient Near East from the world of the Mediterranean about two-thirds of the way across the Sharon Plain. The plain can thus be sliced into two longitudinal sections of unequal size, the first including the bays of alluvial soil and line of land-route cities on its eastern side. The other includes the remainder of the plain, with its wetlands and kurkar ridges, out to the ports of the sea. The flow of settlement history on the Sharon suggests that this larger, western section of the plain was not so much the western fringe of the land-based powers of the ancient Near East as it was the eastern margin of the maritime powers of the Mediterranean.[5] The Sharon is the West's gateway to an Asian population more at home among the dry limestone hills and rocky deserts of Palestine than the coast. So just by carrying the gospel out of the hills of Judea to Lydda (Lod) and Sharon (Acts 9:32–35), Peter the Galilean stepped boldly into "*the ends of the earth*" (Acts 1:8). The same Isaiah who viewed the Sharon as ideal pastureland for flocks of sheep and goats (Isa 65:10) envisioned Peter's day, and relished the sight:

> Herod's choice of Strato's Tower as the site of his magnificent new harbor city, Caesarea, makes sense on a number of historical-geographical grounds. First, Herod needed a port that would serve both Judea and Galilee, and a midpoint harbor met the needs of both without favoring one over the other. Second, the choice of a (near) virgin spot for his harbor meant that Herod would not be beholden to the established economic patterns of a local population but could call the shots from the ground up with fewer encumbrances. Third, and perhaps most visibly, the site of Caesarea fit Herod's ego and penchant for building in places thought impossible to tame. Said Josephus, "Notwithstanding the totally recalcitrant nature of the site, [Herod] grappled with the difficulties so successfully that the solidity of his masonry defied the sea, while its beauty was such as if no obstacle had existed" (Josephus, *War* 1.411).

This is my servant; I strengthen him,
this is my chosen one; I delight in him. . . .
He will not grow weak or be discouraged
until he has established justice on earth,
The coasts and islands will wait for
his instruction. (Isa 42:1,4)

D. THE CARMEL RANGE

The profile of the Carmel Range is one of the most prominent markers on the geographical landscape of ancient Israel. Its soaring, evergreen height, rising abruptly from both plain and sea, has conferred an aura of divine presence on the mountain for millennia. Thutmose III, Rameses II, and Rameses III, all pharaohs who sent military expeditions into the Levant during the period of Egypt's New Kingdom (the Late Bronze Age, 1550–1200 BC), called the mountain "The Holy Headland" (*rosh qudshi*[6]), using a Semitic term that suggests the mountain already had divine associations for the region's inhabitants. Conquerors from Mesopotamia also recognized Carmel's mystique. In 841 BC, Assyrian King Shalmaneser III reported that he had reached "a cape (jutting out into) the sea" called *Baali-ra'asi* (lit. "Baal of the Headlands"); he erected a royal statue there to commemorate his feat.[7] Not incidentally, this was just a few years after Elijah had confronted the prophets of Baal on the eastern slopes of the same mountain (1 Kgs 18:20–40). By the fourth century BC, as the Greco-Roman pantheon started to make headway into the Levant, we find Carmel called "the Holy Mountain of Zeus." (Zeus was the Hellenistic

1 Avner Raban, "Near Eastern Harbors: Thirteenth – Seventh Centuries B.C.E.," in *Mediterranean Peoples in Transition*, ed. Seymour Gitin, Amihai Mazar, and Ephraim Stern (Jerusalem: IES, 1998), 428–38.

2 *ANET*, 26; Hallo, *Context of Scripture* I, 89–93.

3 Yehuda Karmon, "Geographical Influences on the Historical Routes in the Sharon Plain," *PEQ* 93 (1961): 47–49, 53–57.

4 Karmon, "Geographical Influences," 53–57.

5 Yehuda Karmon, "Geographical Aspects in the History of the Coastal Plain of Israel," *IEJ* 6 (1956): 33–50.

6 *ANET*, 243.

7 A. Kirk Grayson, *Assyrian Rulers of the Early First Millennium BC II (858–745 BC)*, RIMA, vol. 3 (Toronto: University of Toronto Press, 1996), 48; cp. 54–55.

A Judean town on the steppe-land between Hebron and Arad was also called Carmel. This is where Nabal, a harsh man with an intelligent and beautiful wife, Abigail, pastured his large flocks of sheep and goats and ran afoul of David in the process (Josh 15:55; 1 Sam 25:2; 2 Sam 23:35; and likely 1 Sam 15:12). As a common noun, *carmel* can refer not only to "fertile land" but also "pastures" (Mic 7:14); it is in this sense that the name was attached to this otherwise semi-arid town. For shepherds coming out of the even drier Negev basin, the region of this Carmel certainly must have looked fertile by comparison!

equivalent of the Semitic god Baal.)[1] Of particular interest on that score is a story told by the early second century AD Roman historian Tacitus, which relates that while Vespasian was campaigning in Judea, Samaria, and Galilee in AD 67, "thinking over his secret hopes" to become emperor, he paid due homage to the gods of Mount Carmel. Tacitus notes, "Between Judea and Syria lies Carmel: this is the name given to both the mountain and the divinity. The god has no image or temple—such is the rule handed down by the fathers; there is only an altar and the worship of the god."[2] The notation "no image or temple" sounds like Yahwistic syncretism. In any case, a large carved limestone foot on display at the Stella Maris Carmelite Monastery above Haifa—perhaps the base of a statue dating to the second or third century AD—bears the name "Zeus Carmelus Heliopolitamus."[3] Zeus was the head of the Greek pantheon who blended with chief deities across the Mediterranean world. And finally, the Syrian philosopher Iamblichus, who in the fourth century AD wrote a biography of the sixth century BC mathematician Pythagoras, noted that Carmel is "a mountain holy above all and regarded as inaccessible to the vulgar."[4]

All of these names and their associated events reflect Mount Carmel's natural religious associations, but so does the Hebrew common noun *carmel.* While the popular etymology "vineyard (*kerem*) of God (*el*)" should be rejected as fanciful, the word is used in the Bible to refer to "*fertile lands*" (2 Chr 26:10; Jer 2:7), "*fertile field*" (Jer 4:26; 48:33), "*orchards*" (Isa 10:18; 29:17; 32:15), and the "*densest forests*" (Isa 37:24)—all of which, in their essence, are places associated with the divine blessing of rainfall. That is, the mountain's natural character was itself enough to prompt divine associations.

Other names for Mount Carmel are descriptive in different ways. Noting its proximity to the Plain of Dor, the biblical writers labeled the western face of Carmel "*the slopes of Dor*" (Josh 11:2; cp. 1 Kgs 4:11), a name that refers to the mountain's natural seaward associations. And perhaps most famously, in the late third millennium BC, the Egyptian general Weni claimed to have landed his sea-borne army behind the "Antelope's Nose,"[5] an apparent reference to Carmel's Mediterranean protrusion, the first prominent landmark seen by sailors tracing the otherwise straight coastline out of Egypt. Even today, local Arabs call the point anf el-Jebel, "the nose of the mountain."

Topographically, Carmel is a thirty-mile (48-km) long range of mountains that cuts sharply across the line of the coastal plain and hill country on a northwest to southeast angle. From its chiseled seaward tip, the familiar hooked profile of the coast, the range gradually widens to a breadth of more than twelve miles (19 km) before merging into the Manasseh hills. Its bulky mass blocks the route of the international coastal highway in the process, forcing travelers to find their way through three natural passes evenly spaced along its length. Geologically, the Carmel Range can be divided into three distinct subregions defined by rock type and details of topography: from northwest to southeast, these are Mount Carmel proper, the Shephelah of Carmel, and, doing double-duty with the Manasseh highlands, the northern part of Western Manasseh as far as Dothan.

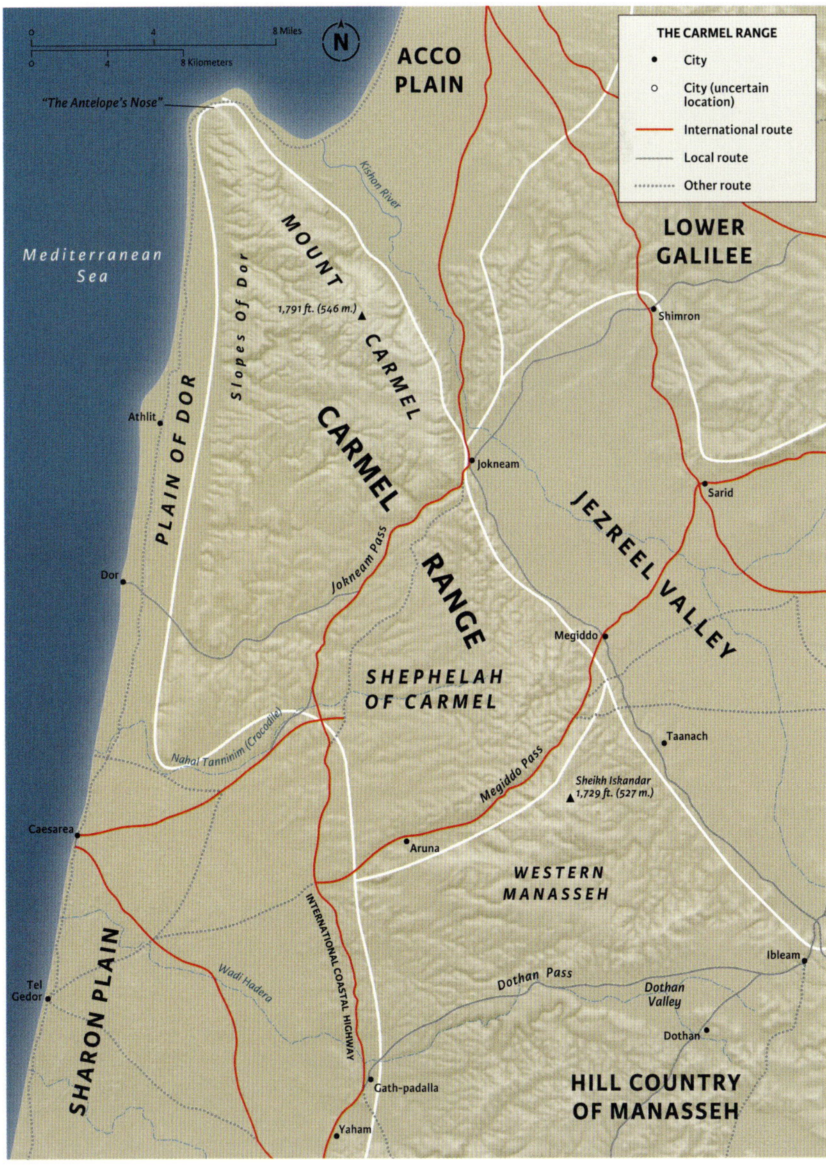

1 *Periplus of Scylax*; Charles Müller, *Geographi Graeci Minores*, vol. 1 (Paris: Editore Ambrosio Fimin Didot, 1882).

2 Tacitus, *Histories*, 2.78.

3 Michael Avi-Yonah, "Mount Carmel and the God of Baalbek," *IEJ* 2 (1952): 118–24.

4 Iamblichus, *The Life of Pythagoras*, trans. Thomas Taylor (Los Angeles, CA: Theosophical Publishing House, 1918), 3.14.

5 *ANET*, 228.

The first of these three subregions, **Mount Carmel** proper, is a triangular block of hard Cenomanian-Turonian limestone tilted up (and still rising) along its sharp, northeastern edge. Because its western and northeastern sides rise directly off the coast, the mountain, at an elevation of 1,791 feet (546 m), looks higher than it actually is. Mounts Ebal and Gerizim, the highlands of Ephraim and Judah, and nearly all of Upper Galilee are all higher; nevertheless, it is Mount Carmel's prominent position astride the international land and sea routes of the southern Levant that made it a signal mountain on the landscape of ancient Israel. Said Jeremiah, "*The king of Babylon will come like Tabor among the mountains and like Carmel by the sea*" (Jer 46:18). That passage was the prophet's warning to Egypt that like the famed mountain, the Babylonians would loom up from the north, then swoop down the flatland coast to the Nile. In fact, Carmel and Tabor are both signal mountains, their prominent shapes clearly visible to travelers from afar. A traveler coming out of Egypt need only be told, "Head for Carmel, the first mountain that touches the sea, then turn inland." Likewise, a foreigner coming into the Galilee from the north could see the distinctive rounded shape of Tabor from many vantage points, miles away: "Just keep heading for Tabor, and you'll find your way." That Tabor is visible across the flat Jezreel Valley from Carmel, and vice versa, allows the traveler to finish the journey heading the other direction.

The strength of Mount Carmel is perhaps best seen from its Jezreel Valley side. Here the view is from Megiddo, taking in the mountain's northeastern flank, its most dramatic rise. The line of trees in the foreground descends from the lower hills of Carmel's Shephelah; the Mediterranean Sea lies beyond the shoulder of Mount Carmel to the right.

Annual rainfall on Mount Carmel exceeds thirty-two inches (815 mm) on average, with heavy dew and predictably strong winds impacting the area for much of the year. Indeed, the mountain's western face and prominent proboscis are fully exposed to the force of the Mediterranean's winter storms; it drinks water from the rain of heaven in large gulps. The mountain is nearly completely covered with rich vegetation of all kinds—most places boast a dense growth of trees, some of which are scrub-like though many are majestic—and in its depressions, patches of rich terra rosa soil have collected so that summer fruit takes firm root and flocks can safely graze thereabouts (Jer 50:19). It is not without merit that the biblical writers properly speak of "*the splendor of Carmel*" (Isa 35:2) with words otherwise used to describe either the adornment of God himself (Job 40:10; Pss 96:6; 104:1) or the work of his hands (Pss 90:16; 111:3). When the protagonist in the Song of Songs portrayed his lady in a way that embodied the very best that the world of nature had to offer, the rich covering of Carmel came to mind: "*Your head crowns you like Mount Carmel, the hair of your head like purple cloth*" (Song 7:5). (Such cloth, interestingly, was made with the crimson-colored dye derived from spiraled murex shells found on the coast beneath Carmel's slopes.)

The "splendor of Carmel" is also seen in a reverse image that pictured God's disfavor with the world as a Mount Carmel that had lost all of its leaves (Isa 33:9; Nah 1:4). Most striking is Amos's opening salvo against the complacent court of Israel's privileged elite. He said, "*The* Lord *roars from Zion and makes his voice heard from Jerusalem; the pastures of the shepherds mourn, and [even] the summit of Carmel withers*" (Amos 1:2). It was one thing for the already marginal (southern) grazing lands to dry up when God opened his mouth, reversing as it were the life-giving word of creation. But when the always-green summit of Carmel also withered, the evidence was incontrovertible that it was the God of Jerusalem who called the shots—even in the northern homeland of Baal.

Owing to the mountain's sudden rise off the sea and the rugged outcroppings of hard limestone and forested growth on its slopes, natural routes go around, rather than over, Carmel's gnarled heights. Its slopes and summit hide no lack of places in which to escape from folks down below, giving a practical sense to the mountain's role as a sanctuary (cf. Amos 9:3). While the entire range fell within the inheritance of the populous tribe of Manasseh (Josh 17:7; 19:26), the soils and terrace lines of Mount Carmel remained underdeveloped; thus, it did not support large-scale settlement in ancient times. Even today, with the exception of the urban sprawl of Haifa that is steadily climbing the mountain's northern face, Carmel is only sparsely settled, and that by a scattering of mostly Druze villages. At the same time, its ridge line is readily visible from vantage points all around. From Carmel's summit, the eye takes in a considerable view on a clear day, from the southern extremity of the Sharon Plain to Transjordan and Mount Hermon in the northeast. This juxtaposition of inaccessibility + prominence helped to give Mount Carmel its widely recognized aura of divinity in the ancient world.

From Mount Carmel, the Carmel Range stretches southeastward into a down-warped, rectangular block of Eocene limestone having elevations of less than 1,000 feet (300 m). This is the **Shephelah of Carmel**, the second of the range's subregions and possibly the Shephelah adjacent to "*the Slopes of Dor*" and "*hill country of Israel*" mentioned in the account of Joshua's conquest (Josh 11:2,16). In terms of a horizon-line view, this Shephelah looks very much like the Shephelah of Judah, but

The summit of Mount Carmel is blanketed by a patchwork of exposed bedrock outcroppings interspersed with scrub wood and trees. The whole mountain carries a look of wild abandon, unbridled and free, reflecting a sense of an open-handed, divine blessing. The clouds in this view, seemingly in reach, carry just a hint of the kind of moisture that sent Ahab and Elijah running (cp. 1 Kgs 18:41–45). Here the view is to the northeast, with the hills of Lower Galilee filling the horizon.

without the wide intervening valleys that define that region's role as a gateway between the Judean hills and Philistia. The low, rolling hills of the Shephelah of Carmel are dull in color and lack character most of the year, taking on a green cast only during the months of late winter and early spring. The drop of the Shephelah of Carmel into the Jezreel Valley toward the northeast is rather sharp, and today it is covered by a refreshing stand of pine trees called the Manasseh Forest. Meanwhile, its coastward, southwestern flank is more gradual and sprinkled with a number of small springs. Unlike the heights of Mount Carmel, the Shephelah of Carmel was actually settled by the tribe of Manasseh, though with small villages rather than thriving cities. There are remarkably few tells in the area.

The southeastern tail of the Carmel Range, an arched block of Cenomanian-Turonian limestone, blends into the structurally complex region of Western Manasseh. This is the third subregion of the range, and it lacks a known biblical name. For this reason, modern geographers label it variously as the **Umm el-Fahm Upwarp**[1] (after the large Arab Israeli city on its northwestern flank), the **'Iron Hills**[2] (from the wadi that drains to the northwest), or the **Iskandar Uplift**[3] (based on its highest peak, Sheikh Iskandar, 1,729 ft/527 m in elevation). Like Mount Carmel, elevations here are generally high and together bookend the lower foothills of the Shephelah between. Rainfall amounts in this southeastern flank of the Carmel Range average twenty inches (510 mm) annually, which, while significantly less than those of Mount Carmel proper, are more than enough for productive agriculture. The whole block of hills drops into the broad Vale of Dothan, allowing the region to function as a transition zone between the cities of the Hill Country of Samaria and the routes of international highway.

The cities and towns most readily associated with the Carmel Range are not located on the range itself but in

1 Baly, *Geography of the Bible*, 172.

2 Yehuda Karmon, *Israel: A Regional Geography* (London: Wiley-Interscience, 1971), 202–4; and Efraim Orni and Elisha Efrat, *Geography of Israel*, 4th ed. (Jerusalem: Israel Universities Press, 1980), 71–72.

3 James M. Monson with Steven P. Lancaster, *Geobasics in the Land of the Bible* (Rockford, IL: Biblical Backgrounds, Inc., 2008), 4, 10.

The view is unmistakably "Shephelah": colorless, scraggly brown weeds and rounded scrub brush over low, chalk-white hills, with dull Mediterranean brown forest soil filling the flats below. Modern agricultural equipment has helped area farmers make a living in the region, though even with an above-average number of springs, the Shephelah of Carmel has never had a high population density. Sandwiched between the Sharon Plain and the Jezreel Valley, people realize that better living conditions lay elsewhere, close at hand.

the valleys and passes below. These include Dor on the Mediterranean coast (Josh 12:23; Judg 1:27), Megiddo and Jokneam-in-Carmel lining the edge of the Jezreel Valley (Josh 12:21–22; 19:11; 21:34, Judg 1:27), and Dothan in the Vale of Dothan to the southeast (Gen 37:17). All were perched on tells associated with the well-established network of Canaanite city-states and international routes traversing the land.

The three blocks of Cenomanian-Turonian and Eocene limestone that make up the Carmel Range are separated from one another by thin seams of soft Senonian chalk. These seams have eroded into natural passes that allow the International Coastal Highway to penetrate the range perpendicularly and enter the Jezreel Valley on a southwest-northeastern line. Were it not for these chalk troughs, travelers on the international route would be able to make their way over the Carmel Range only with difficulty. Each of these passes funnels traffic into a different part of the Jezreel Valley, and each can be named after the large Canaanite (and later, Israelite) city that protected its Jezreel Valley end. So the northwestern-most of these three passes, the Jokneam Pass, carries traffic between the Sharon Plain and the Plain of Acco, from one section of the coastal plain to another (Josh 12:22). The Megiddo Pass points travelers straight across the Jezreel Valley to Galilee and Damascus beyond (Judg 5:19; 2 Kgs 23:29–30; 2 Chr 35:22–24). And the Dothan Pass (also called the Gur Pass; 2 Kgs 9:27) allows traffic to cut the corner of the Manasseh hills by swinging through the city of Jezreel on the way to Transjordan (Gen 37:17,28; 2 Kgs 6:13–14).

The Carmel Range, then, lies between two distinct living spaces. On the one hand, the coastal plain, hills, and deserts to the south are connected most easily with Egypt and routes into the Arabian Peninsula. On the other, the hills and valleys of Galilee are oriented toward Phoenicia, Damascus, and points north. The Carmel Range provides a convenient marker between a southern economic zone that historically has been dominated by small villages, deserts, and shepherds, and a northern zone that is strengthened by broad, fertile valleys, viable ports, and a number of large urban centers. But because the Carmel Range is thrice pierced by the International Coastal Highway, it acts less as a barrier than a busy, contested frontier between the two.

The history of the Carmel Range has not been its own. Rather, its story has fallen to the nations large and small that swept across the routes encircling its heights and penetrating its passes. The options and opportunities of the parade of armies and caravans that have traversed the route between Egypt and Mesopotamia is perhaps best seen in the attack of Pharaoh Thutmose III on Megiddo in about 1457 BC. Thutmose held a war council with his generals at Yaham on the northeastern edge of the Sharon Plain in order to seek their advice as through which of the three passes that cross the range the Egyptian army should march. He was advised to take either the Dothan Pass or the Jokneam Pass because the most direct route, the Megiddo Pass (called by Thutmose the Aruna road), was too narrow for his army to traverse safely. Indeed, in recent times the northern end of the Megiddo Pass has had to be widened by construction equipment simply to accommodate the width of the modern highway, Number 65, that now runs its length. Refusing to bend to the threat of ambush, however, Thutmose drove his army up the Megiddo Pass and successfully attacked Megiddo headlong. His assessment of the battle? "Capturing Megiddo is like capturing a thousand cities!"[1]

During the biblical period, the towns and villages of the Shephelah of Carmel and the Umm el-Fahm Upwarp were well-enough connected to the international highway to participate in the living opportunities of both the coast and the Jezreel Valley. The heights of Mount Carmel proper, however, remained aloof. Its main role seems to have been as a sanctuary, a place of retreat either toward God (or, one's gods), or away from trouble. Amos referenced the latter:

None of those who flee will get away;
none of the fugitives will escape. . . .
If they hide
on the top of Carmel,
from there I will track them down
and seize them;
if they conceal themselves
from my sight on the sea floor,
from there I will command
the sea serpent to bite them. (Amos 9:1,3)

1 *ANET*, 235–37; Hallo, *Context of Scripture* II, 7–13.

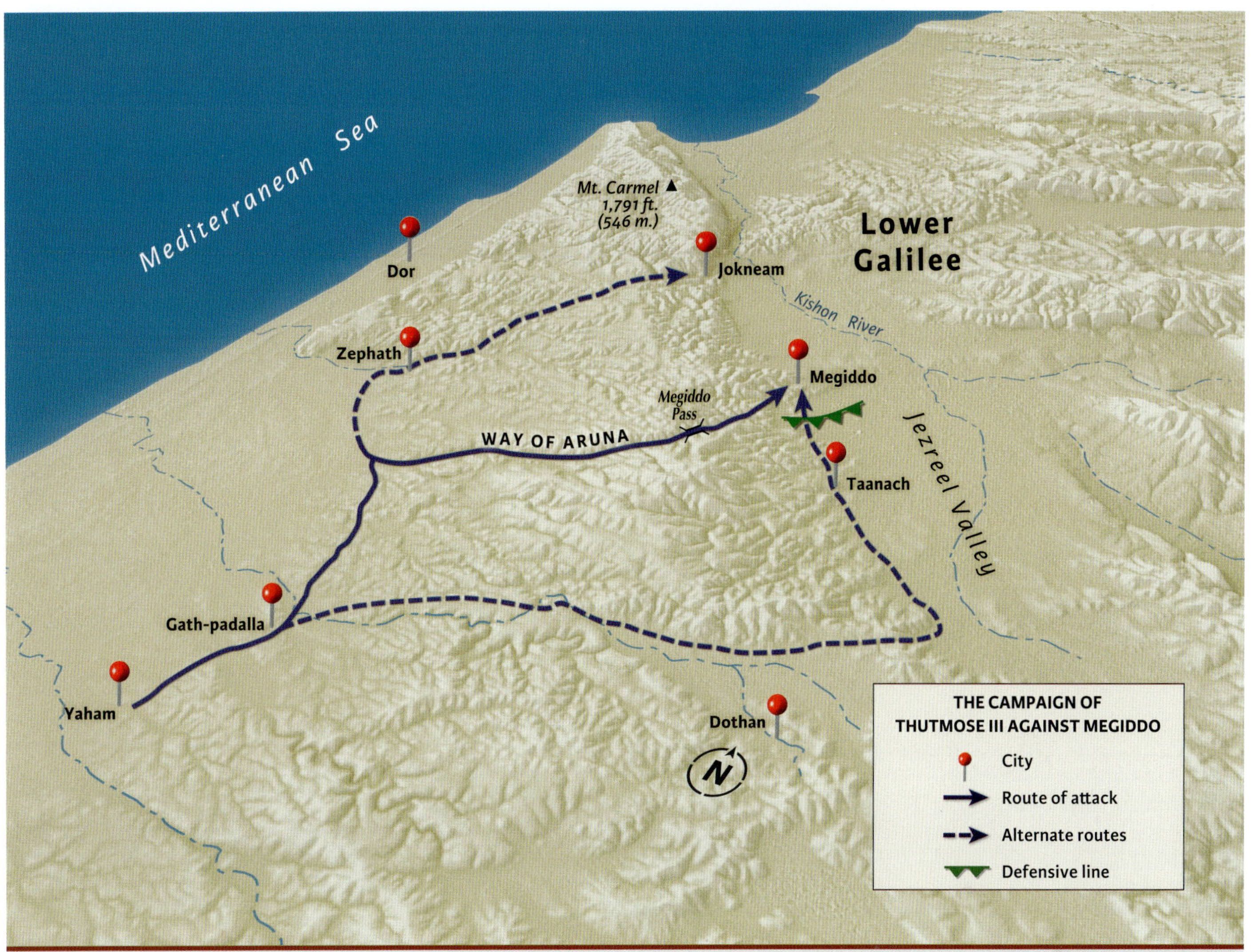

Thutmose III's written accounts provide the necessary geographical detail of his great victory at Megiddo:[1]

Year 23, 1st month of the third season, day 16. [The Egyptian army had traveled] as far as the town of Yaham. [His majesty Thutmose III] ordered a conference with his victorious army, speaking as follows:

"That [wretched] enemy of Kadesh [in the northern Levant] has come and has entered into Megiddo. He is [there] at this very moment. He has gathered to him the princes of [every] foreign country [that had been] loyal to Egypt. . . . Will you tell me [what is in your hearts that I should do?]"

[The Egyptian generals] said in the presence of his majesty, "What is it like to go [on] this [road directly to Megiddo] that becomes so narrow? It is [reported] that the foe is there, waiting and becoming more numerous. Will we not have to proceed horse after [horse, and the army] and the people similarly, [single-file]? . . . Now two [other] roads are here. One of the roads—behold, it is [to the east of] us so that it comes out at Taanach [near Dothan]. The other—behold, it is to the north side of Djefti and we will come out [at Jokneam] to the north[west] of Megiddo. Let our victorious lord proceed on the one of [them] that is [satisfactory to] his heart, [but] do not make us go on that difficult road! . . ."

[Thutmose answered,] "I [swear], as [my god] Re loves me . . . my majesty shall [indeed] proceed upon this [Megiddo] road! . . . Behold, [if I don't choose this route] these enemies whom Re abominates will say, 'Has his majesty [Thutmose III] set out on another road because he has become afraid of us' ['"]

Baal,[2] the Canaanite god of the thundercloud, lightning, and rain, had a natural home court advantage on Mount Carmel. High, west, and north—with its point to the sea from which winter storms burst onto the land, its northern edge facing Jezebel's Phoenician coast, and its southeastern flank merging into Ahab's Manasseh homeland—the mountain offered a particularly well-placed stage from which the priests and prophets of Baal could touch both the rising storm clouds and the mass of peasant farmers who looked to rain as their primary source of life. In the local imagery of the day, Baal was pictured as a man striding on the thundercloud, holding a lightning bolt in his hand and standing ready to hurl it down to earth. North Syrian texts from Ugarit called him "the Rider of the Clouds": "Seven years shall Baal fail, eight, the Rider of the Clouds. No dew, no rain, no welling-up of the deep, no sweetness of Baal's voice."[3]

Elijah's choice to challenge the prophets of Baal on Mount Carmel was aimed at emasculating both the would-be god and his prophets in the very place where Baal was most expected to be able to work at full strength (1 Kgs 18:18–46). The biblical writers went to great lengths to explain that rain, fertility, and life—the most essential commodities of the land of ancient

1 *ANET*, 235.

2 The West Semitic storm god was Hadad. The name Baal (lit. "owner" or "possessor") seems to have been a local title of Hadad in parts of the Levant, including at Ras Shamra (Ugarit on the north Syrian coast) and in much of Canaan.

3 AQHT C in *ANET*, 153; cp. Hallo, *Context of Scripture* I, 351.

The rolling hills of the Shephelah of Carmel are visible here from Mount Carmel's high southeastern point, below the Carmelite monastery of Muhraqa, traditional location of Elijah's challenge to the prophets of Baal. Bits of the modern city of Jokneam (left) can be seen in their folds, marking the narrow northern end of the Jokneam Pass. The heartland of Ahab's kingdom stretches to the hilly horizon beyond. If elevation meant anything in the region, it signaled a sense of divine proprietorship over everything below, and the prophets of Baal, most at home on Carmel's heights, knew their role as mediator between land and rain. In an image that Baal's followers would come to acknowledge, the challenge of Elijah the prophet—*"As the Lord God of Israel lives, in whose presence I stand, there will be no dew or rain during these years except by my command!"* (1 Kgs 17:1)—showed the Canaanite god of fertility to be impotent.

Israel—were actually the exclusive domain of the Lord God, Maker of heaven and earth. Said the psalmist,

> *Exalt him who rides on the clouds—*
> *his name is the Lord—and celebrate before him....*
> *You, God, showered abundant rain;*
> *you revived your inheritance*
> *when it languished.*
> *Your people settled in it;*
> *God, you provided for the poor by*
> *your goodness.* (Ps 68:4,9–10)

The writer of the book of Job said,

> *See how [God] spreads his lightning around him*
> *and covers the depths of the sea....*
> *He covers his hands with lightning*
> *and commands it to hit its mark.*
> *The thunder declares his presence;*
> *the cattle also, the approaching*
> *storm.* (Job 36:30,32–33)

So while Mount Carmel may have had a long history as the abode of the Canaanite and Greco-Roman gods of fertility, it was the Lord who co-opted both its location and attributes in the end. (He had, after all, created it.) Carmel became a dwelling place of Elisha, the prophetic successor to Elijah, and from its heights God brought healing and life to a thirsty world below (2 Kgs 2:25; 4:25). What was long considered the mountain of Baal had returned to its true destiny of being a mountain of God.

E. THE JORDAN VALLEY

The Jordan Valley is the portion of the Middle East's great linear rift that lies between the Sea of Galilee and the Dead Sea. In length, it extends some sixty-five miles (105 km) north to south. Its two lateral sides, formed by a series of roughly parallel and somewhat continuous fault lines, are irregular in shape, causing the valley to vary from two to fifteen miles (3 to 24 km) in width. From end to end, this is by far the deepest river valley on earth: its higher, northern end is already 690 feet (210 m) below sea level, over twice as low as California's Death Valley, while its outlet at the Dead Sea measures an oppressive 1,350 feet (412 m) below sea level. The Jordan River, for which the valley is named, flows for 135 miles (220 km) through a serpentine trough tracing the lowest line of the valley floor. The name "Jordan" likely derives from the Hebrew verb *yarad*, "to go down," which describes not only the angle of the water flow but the steep descent into the valley from the hills that tower along its long sides. In a summary statement that

At 505 feet (154 m) below sea level, the Turfan Depression in China is the second-lowest spot on the earth's exposed land surface. The broad Qattara Depression in Egypt's Western Desert, which bears the same name as a particularly arid slice of the Jordan Valley, is 436 feet (133 m) below sea level. Badwater Basin in California's Death Valley rings in at -282 feet (-86 m). The Bentley Subglacial Trench in Antarctica, at 8,327 feet (2,538 m) below sea level, wins the on-land negative elevation race hands-down—even though this claim is often considered "foul" because the trench is completely covered by ice.

also serves as an introduction to the region, historical geographer George Adam Smith noted that while "there may be something on the surface of another planet to match the Jordan Valley: there is nothing on this [one that does]."[1] (However, his observation didn't stop the National Geographic Society from comparing the Jordan Valley to Utah's Jordan River in their December, 1958 issue.)[2]

The southern end of the Jordan Valley ends at the harsh, salt-encrusted Lisan marl flats encircling the Dead Sea, what the Bible calls the **Arabah** (or, Aravah, "desert plain"; Josh 11:2; 12:1,3; 2 Sam 2:29).[3] To the east lay biblical Gilead, one of the greenest parts of the modern Hashemite Kingdom of Jordan, while to the west is the biblical Hill Country of Ephraim and Manasseh, the northern part of today's West Bank (which is aptly named). Other than the Jordan River itself, which runs too low to be used extensively for irrigation, most of the water that enters the valley flows in from the east, through the perennial Yarmuk and Jabbok wadis. These drain the westward-facing heights of Gilead and Bashan (the Golan), large catchments soaring nearly 4,000 feet (1,220 m) in elevation. By contrast, the lower, eastward slopes of Ephraim and Manasseh lie in the rain shadow and contribute little by way of runoff water or alluvium to the region's already-delicate ecosystem. The stronger erosive power from the Transjordanian hills has pushed the Jordan River bed into the western half of the valley, allowing a fine alluvial plain, which can be irrigated by the Yarmuk and Jabbok wadis, to form along the river's eastern bank.

With moderate to warm winter temperatures, the more fertile parts of the Jordan Valley allow for a growing season year-round. In spite of summertime temperatures that routinely reach well over 100 degrees Fahrenheit (38° C), a variety of crops and garden vegetables can be grown wherever the soil is kept moist by irrigation.

Though relatively small in total area, the Jordan Valley is a highly complex region with marked contrasts in water supply, soil quality, and living conditions along its length. To organize our discussion, it is helpful to divide the valley into three longitudinal zones based on its geography, and four horizontal zones to view its patterns of human settlement.

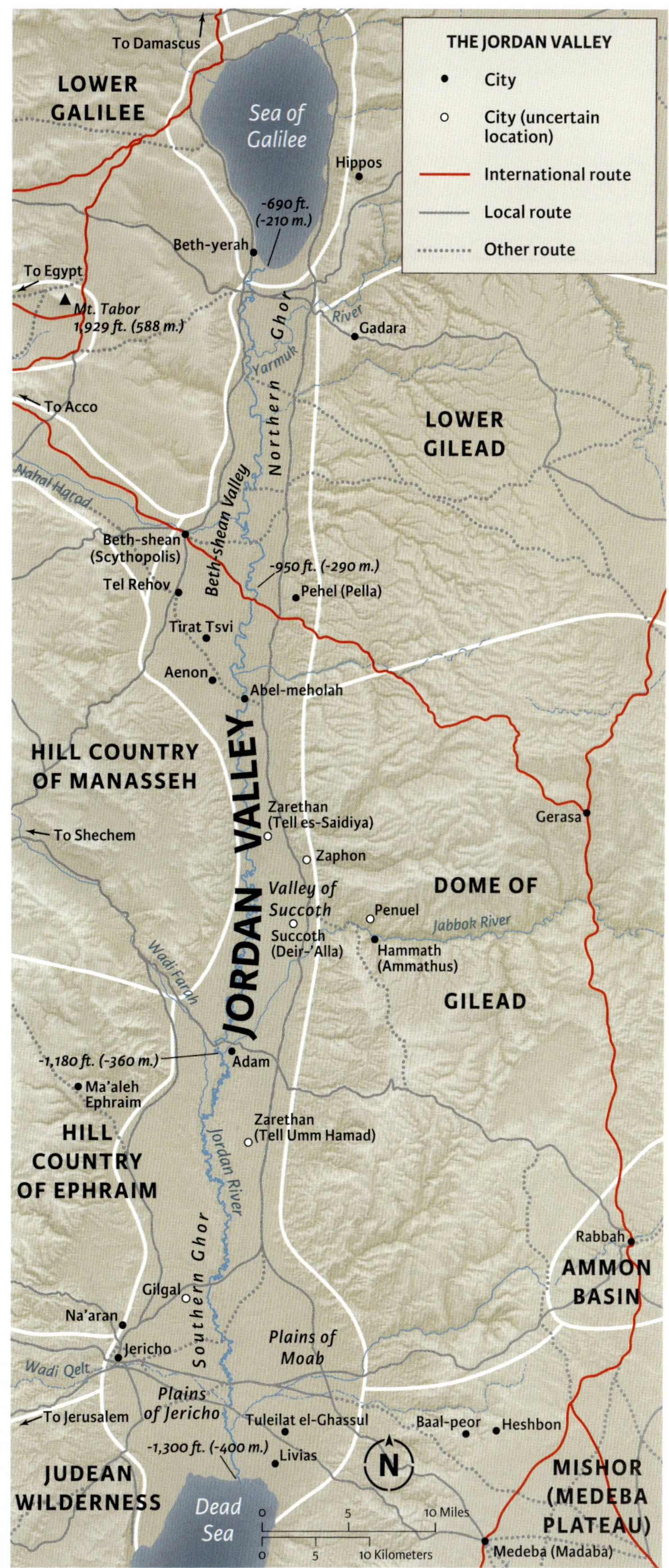

1 Smith, *Historical Geography of the Holy Land*, 468.

2 David Boyer, "Geographical Twins a World Apart," *The National Geographic Magazine* 114/6 (1958): 848–59.

3 Ze'ev Meshel, "Defining the Biblical 'Arabah," in Sidney White Crawford, ed., *"Up to the Gates of Ekron": Essays on the Archaeology and History of the Eastern Mediterranean in Honor of Seymour Gitin* (Jerusalem: IES, 2007): 423–35.

This eastward view across the *Ghor* takes in the stark contrast between living conditions on the Jordan Valley's western side and those across the way. In the foreground, the barren foothills of Eastern Manasseh give way to the *Ghor*, here generally flat and spotted by cultivation. Tell es-Saidiya, in the center, rises on the east bank of the Jordan; nearby, the river flows out of sight in a cut in front of the tell. Es-Saidiya is likely either biblical Zaphon (Josh 13:27; Judg 12:1) or Zarethan, near to the spot where Solomon's workmen cast bronze objects for temple use in the ground's fine clay (1 Kgs 7:45–46). Nicely arable land and a continuous line of modern villages lies beyond, at the base of the Gilead hills. The eastern side of the *Ghor* has always been the preferred side for living and travel.

The Jordan Valley's largest longitudinal zone is the **Ghor**, which is an Arabic term for "depression" or "rift." The *Ghor* is the gently sloping plain that levels out from the hills lining the valley's two long sides. This is an area of steppe pasturelands and scattered fields, where farmers and shepherds readily mix. The plain along the eastern side of the valley is wider, wetter, and more productive than its counterpart in the rain shadow of Ephraim and Manasseh. This is partly a result of the runoff from the Bashan and Gilead hills, and partly because of the large number of springs found on the valley's eastern slopes. As a result, the eastern side of the valley has always been the preferred location for settlement, boasting many ancient urban centers including Pella (Old Testament Pehel) opposite Beth-shean/Scythopolis, Succoth (Tell Deir 'Alla) at the mouth of the Jabbok, and Tuleilat el-Ghassul across the Jordan River from Jericho. Historically, the best natural route running the length of the Jordan Valley traced the line of springs and towns here, and we can assume that it was through Perea, "*beyond the Jordan*" (Matt 19:1; Mark 3:8; 10:1 NASB), that Jesus most often walked when he traveled between Galilee and Jerusalem. Today this Jordanian side of the valley boasts an almost continuous line of towns and villages, while the *Ghor* of the western, West Bank side of the valley remains largely empty save for the sites of historic towns at perennial streams or springs (e.g., Jericho and Beth-shean), or scattered modern Israeli settlements supplied by water piped in from the outside.

Toward the center of the Jordan Valley, the gently sloping floor of the *Ghor* suddenly drops away into a highly dissected band of badlands called the **Qattara**. The northern end of the *Qattara* can be seen at a point midway between Beth-shean and Pella, while its southern extremity reaches the Dead Sea. Travelers driving along the roadways on either side of the *Ghor* can easily recognize the *Qattara* by its ashen-grey color, broken topography, and surfaces devoid of vegetation. Composed of chalky marl mixed with clay and fine-grained gypsum, the *Qattara* resists water penetration and becomes slippery, crumbly, and virtually impossible to cross when wet. Runoff water has eroded the *Qattara* into a dense jumble of buttes, mesas, chimneys, and other wild forms, the steep sides of which sometimes collapse from earthquakes or flooding. In extreme cases, large landslides of the *Qattara* have even temporarily blocked the flow of the Jordan. Apparently, this happened as Joshua began to cross the Jordan opposite Jericho; it was the time of spring flooding (Josh 5:10), and the water flowing downstream stood still, rising up in a mass at Adam (see Josh 3:13,15–16; cp. 2 Kgs 2:8–14).

The Jordan River itself flows through the **Zor**, which is an Arabic word for "thicket." The *Zor* is a low trench running down the middle of the *Qattara*, one-quarter to two miles (.5 to 3 km) wide, with the river twisting and turning snake-like down its length. The width of the river channel itself is a relatively narrow eighty to one hundred feet (24 to 30 m), though the river "*overflows*

Several landslides are known to have temporarily dammed up the Jordan River at Adam, where the *Qattara* encroaches quite closely on the river. On December 8, 1267, a large mound of the *Qattara* near the Adam ford fell into the river and blocked the water flow for sixteen hours. Another landslide stopped the river's flow for two days in the year 1547, while a third was caused by the massive series of earthquakes that shook everything from Jerusalem to Gilead in July 1927 and again in January 1928. This last time, a large section of the 150-foot (46 m) high cliff lining the bank of the Jordan River at Adam fell completely across the river channel, stopping the water flow for more than twenty-one hours.[1]

its banks throughout the harvest season" (Josh 3:15), that is, during the springtime. In doing so, the flood waters replenish the *Zor* and even parts of the *Ghor* lying nearby with new layers of mineral-rich mud. Likely it was the Jordan's muddy flow that prompted Naaman's proud retort to Elisha's command that he wash himself in its waters seven times: "*Aren't Abana and Pharpar, the rivers of Damascus, better than all the waters of Israel?*" (2 Kgs 5:12). In any case, the Jordan River's tendency to flood made the *Zor* itself a kind of mini-Nile River valley, providing an annual gift of alluvium to folks farming along its banks who could sow their seed and irrigate it "*by hand [or foot] as in a vegetable garden*" (Deut 11:10; cp. Gen 13:10). The cut of the Jordan has always been too low to irrigate the *Ghor* except in flood season. Indeed, in ancient times cities located within the Jordan Valley tended to rely on the water of local springs rather than that of the river itself.[2]

Historically, the waters of the Jordan River have run three to ten feet (1 to 3 m) deep with, for all their meandering, a fairly steep gradient and a relatively strong flow. The estimated average discharge of the Jordan prior to modern times is 344 billion gallons (1.3 billion cubic meters) per year.[3] Yet because there are numerous spots with rocks, rapids, and even small waterfalls, the waterway has always been difficult to navigate by boat. The famed journey down the Jordan by the American explorer Lieutenant William F. Lynch in 1848, under the auspices of no less an institution than the United States Navy, was the first scientific exploration of the river. The

Neat rows of tomatoes poke from lines of plastic placed over their seedlings in a clever attempt to trap every drop of moisture that tries to evaporate from the arid soil of the southern *Ghor*. This Jericho field is one of hundreds that dot the lower Jordan Valley today, providing a constant stream of fresh vegetables to the markets of Jordan, the West Bank, and Israel.

1 As reported by John Garstang in his commentary *Joshua/Judges* (London: Constable & Co, 1931),136–37.

2 Yigal Levin, "The Jordan River in Biblical Geography: From Boundary to Allegory," *ARAM* 29 (2017): 222.

3 Micha Klein, "Water Balance of the Upper Jordan River Basin," *Water International* 23 (1998): 244–48.

The cold colors of winter grip the mid-Jordan Valley as an early-March storm blows through the region. Warmer air on the valley floor has condensed into a tight band of fog as it meets the colder, wet air sweeping down from the Ephraim hills. A thin line of snow crowns the Gilead hills in the distance.

Lynch team experienced eight days of high adventure and raw danger, partly due to difficult travel conditions, partly because of hostile inhabitants along the shore.[1] Today, because virtually all of the water capacity of the Jordan River is tapped for human use by the State of Israel and the Hashemite Kingdom of Jordan prior to it's entering the river channel, the Jordan's flow south of the Sea of Galilee has become both sluggish and narrow. The inevitable result is that the annual flood cycle of the *Zor*, with its agricultural benefit, has been broken.

But these same shallows make the river fairly easy to cross—at least in the drier summer months. Israeli geographer Menashe Har-el has counted as many as fifty-four fords that could be waded or easily swum along its length.[2] This number seems high, though Judges 3:28 and 12:5 mention fords (plural; *ma'aberot*; lit. "crossings") in the vicinity of Jericho and east of the Ephraim hills. On the other hand, Swiss traveler Johann Ludwig Burckhardt recorded in 1822 that "the few spots where [the river Jordan] may be crossed in the rainy season were known only to the Arabs."[3] The Egyptian scribe who in the late second millennium BC composed the so-called "Satirical Letter" in which he relentlessly prodded his students to learn the difficulties of travel in the Egyptian-controlled parts of the Levant posed this relevant question: "The stream of the Jordan: How is it crossed?"[4] Apparently the scribe expected his students to know, since the text doesn't provide an answer. More helpful is the Old Testament, which specifically mentions several of the Jordan's fords (Josh 2:7; Judg 3:28; 12:5–6; 2 Sam 17:16; 19:15–18). Each was a convenient spot for an army in flight to seize, thereby preventing passage by pursuing troops: "*The fords have been seized, the marshes set on fire, and the fighting men are terrified*" (Jer 51:32). Pressed in pitched battle at a place along the Jordan without fords, Jonathan the Maccabee and his army were once forced to swim the river channel in retreat (1 Macc 9:48).

American historical geographer Edward Robinson forded the Jordan River below Jericho on May 12, 1838. He said of the experience,

"We proceeded therefore to the place of the crossing where there was an opening through the canes and trees. Here the low banks of the channel were broken or worn away for the convenience of passing, and were now covered by the water. There was a still though very rapid current; the water was of a clayey color but sweet and delightfully refreshing. . . . [W]e estimated the breadth of the stream to be from eighty to one hundred feet [24 to 30 m]. The guides supposed it to be now ten or twelve feet [3 to 3.5 m] deep. I bathed in the river without going out into the deep channel; the bottom here (a hollow place in the bank) was clayey with mud and also blue clay. . . . [T]he current was so strong that even Komeh, a stout swimmer of the Nile, was carried down several yards in crossing. . . . The sand-hills which here form the upper banks [the *Qattara*] are of the same naked character as the desert we had passed over in coming to this spot."[5]

Archaeological evidence for bridges in ancient Israel dates only as early as the Roman period. (Herod the Great built one across the Wadi Qelt to service his palace in Jericho.) None are known from the time of the Old Testament (*gesher*, the Hb word for "bridge," occurs only in post-biblical texts). We can assume, then, that during biblical times innovative residents along the Jordan River rigged up ferries or rafts at various high-traffic crossing points, perhaps even using ballooned goatskins as floats to aid the buoyancy of persons or their cargo, as was the practice in ancient Babylon (cp. 2 Sam 19:18).[6]

Much of the *Zor's* marshy floodplain has grown into an impenetrable tangle of tamarisk oak, willow, poplar,

1 W. F. Lynch, *Narrative of the United States' Expedition to the River Jordan and the Dead Sea* (Philadelphia: Lea and Blanchard, 1849); Yehoshua Ben-Arieh, *The Rediscovery of the Holy Land in the Nineteenth Century*, 2nd. ed. (Jerusalem: The Magnes Press, 1983), 124–28.

2 Menasheh Har-el, "The Pride of the Jordan–:The Jungle of the Jordan," *BA* 41 (1978): 69.

3 Johann Ludwig Burckhardt, *Travels in Syria and the Holy Land* (London: J. Murray, 1822), 345.

4 *ANET*, 477.

5 Robinson gave a summary account of the challenges of crossing the Jordan River in the early nineteenth century AD, when it still possessed its naturally swift-flowing character; see Edward Robinson and Eli Smith, *Biblical Researches in Palestine, Mount Sinai and Arabia Petraea: A Journal of Travels in the Year 1838 by E. Robinson and E. Smith Undertaken in Reference to Biblical Geography*, vol. 1 (Boston: Crocker and Brewster, 1841), 536–39.

6 David A. Dorsey, *The Roads and Highways of Ancient Israel* (Baltimore: Johns Hopkins Press, 1991), 33–39.

oleander, cane, reeds, and tropical shrubs, with exposed roots, creepers, and vines crowding the river bank. This is the "jungle [or, thickets] of the Jordan" (lit. "swelling of the Jordan," Hb *ga'on ha-yarden;* Jer 12:5; cp. 1 Macc 9:45), where the combination of water and heat has created a tropical ecosystem that stands in sharp contrast to the parched places of the wilderness through which the water flows. The trees lining the river provided logs that were strong enough to construct houses for Elisha's prophets; lumber was a real prize in a land of mud brick, scrub brush, and stone (2 Kgs 6:1–4). We might fully expect the thickets of the *Zor* to have been a haven for wild animals, and indeed, nineteenth-century AD travelers mention wild boars, jackals, hyenas, leopards, gazelles, otters, poisonous reptiles, and an occasional bear lurking—though not always quietly—in the tangled mass. Indeed, the biblical writers speak of lions preying up into the wilderness above the *Ghor* in search of fast food snatched from an unsuspecting flock (1 Sam 17:34–35; 2 Kgs 17:25; Jer 4:7; Hos 5:14; Amos 3:12; Mic 5:8; Nah 2:11–12; Zech 11:3). Jeremiah turns it into an illustration: "*Look, [the coming invasion by Babylon] will be like a lion coming from the thickets of the Jordan to the watered grazing land*" (Jer 50:44).

The last lion in the Jordan Valley was reportedly seen at the time of the Crusades, although "hoped for" sightings persisted in travelers' accounts until quite recently.[1] Wild boars, the largest mammal that survives in Israel, still prefer the river's swamped thickets as home (cp. Ps 80:13), as does the fish-savoring jungle cat (*Felis chaus*) which, at three feet (1 m) long, can startle even the most seasoned hiker. So even if the waters of the Jordan were relatively easy to cross, its living jungle was not: "*If you stumble in a peaceful land, what will you do in the thickets of the Jordan?*" (Jer 12:5).

In its geopolitical role, the Jordan River traced the eastern boundary of Canaan (Num 34:2,12; Ezek 47:18). So, too, for practical purposes the Jordan functioned as the eastern border of biblical Israel (Num 32:1–42; 34:10–12; Deut 9:1; 11:31; Josh 22:9–10).[2] The Israelite tribes of Reuben, Gad, and half-Manasseh, which had settled east of the river, lay exposed to the whims of Syria, Ammon, Moab, and Edom and—as might be expected—had difficulty maintaining their independence (cp. 2 Kgs 10:32–33). The Jordan River is also an international border today, separating the Hashemite Kingdom of Jordan from the Palestinian territories of the West Bank and, further north, from Israel. These political realities, when combined with very real hindrances to traveling cross-wise through the Rift Valley, can easily give the impression that the Jordan Valley is first and foremost a barrier between nations, a force to divide rather than unite. And biblical history amply illustrates natural rivalries between people groups living on either side of it (Josh 22:1–34; Judg 3:12–14; 8:4–17; 12:1–6; 21:8–12; 2 Kgs 3:1–27). The differences of dialect expressed in Jephthah's *Shibboleth* (as it was pronounced east of the river) and *Sibboleth* (the western pronunciation)

The mosaic artists who composed the Madaba Map in the sixth century AD made sure to include a lion chasing a gazelle on the plains east of the Jordan River. Sometime later, the lion was erased, for unknown reasons; most of its mosaic cubes were scrambled. Unlike many other area mosaics from the Byzantine period, which depicted plant and animal life from around the known world, we can assume that the Madaba Map showed only flora and fauna native to the region.

1 See, in general, George Cansdale, *Animals of Bible Lands* (Devon: The Paternoster Press), 1970.

2 Yigal Levin, "The Jordan River in Biblical Geography," 221–34.

The plains of Jericho (left) and the plains of Moab (right) are separated by only the lower course of the Jordan River. Together their bulbous girth spans a width of fourteen miles (22 km). Soil and living conditions are generally better on the Moab side, shown here with Mount Nebo rising in the distance, than on the Jericho side to the west. It was somewhere below Nebo that *"Moses began to explain this law"* (i.e., the Torah; Deut 1:5), which, when written, became what we know as the book of Deuteronomy. Moses's last journey was to the top of Nebo; Israel's next greatest prophet, Elijah, rose to heaven with Nebo as his backdrop (Deut 1:1; 2 Kgs 2:1–12). Jesus passed the same way. All other journeys across these plains are by comparison rather mundane.

account is telling enough (Judg 12:4-6).[1] Also, in modern times, even though both banks of the river belonged to the Hashemite Kingdom of Jordan from 1946 to 1967, people living on either side saw those on the other as somehow distinct—as Palestinians rather than Jordanians. So, too, stories of individuals that tend to portray the river as a threshold to a different kind of life: Elijah crossed the Jordan to be taken to heaven; Moses wasn't allowed to cross (2 Kgs 2:1–12; Deut 34:1–6).

Yet the flow of history, when marked by the daily events of normal human activity, shows the Jordan Valley to have been quite permeable, with resources to be shared rather than divided. The Jordan Valley is, after all, the location of the most persistent sources of fresh water in the region year-around, and its role as a watering hole in attracting people and animals alike for normal daily sustenance cannot be underestimated. Ancient texts, the Bible included, seem to emphasize the movements and conflicts of people groups across the Jordan Valley; it is these, rightly or wrongly, that give the region its reputation as the Great Divide. But a closer look at geography counsels otherwise. When viewed horizontally, with the routes and settlements of its east-west highways in mind, the Jordan Valley suddenly appears as a unifier of peoples who share more than just a common view of the depths between. It should be noted that the same cannot be said for the portion of the Rift Valley that lies between the southern end of the Dead Sea and the Red Sea, where the soaring hills of Edom lining its eastern flank do tend to preclude ready passage east-west.

Of the many possible connectors that cross the Jordan River, four stand out. From south to north—and spaced rather equidistantly—are the Jericho/Moab routes, the Farah/Jabbok routes, the Beth-shean/Pella routes, and the Beth-yerah/Gadara routes.

The routes connecting Jericho with the Mishor (Medeba Plateau) and Moab cross the *Ghor* just north of the Dead Sea, at its widest point. Here both sides of the valley push outward in large arcs, with the semicircular **plains of Jericho** (the *aravah* of Jericho) lying west of the river (Josh 4:13; 2 Kgs 25:5) and their more pronounced counterpart, the **plains of**

1 *Shibboleth*, the password to cross the Jordan, is, appropriately, a geographical term that means "flowing stream" (cp. Ps 69:16; Isa 27:12).

Moab (the *aravah* of Moab), lying to the east (Num 22:1; 26:3; Deut 34:1). Together these plains form the driest section of the *Ghor*, averaging less than four inches (100 mm) of rainfall annually and having some of the valley's poorest soil and certainly its highest concentrations of salts. During the summer, the southwestern portion of the Jordan Valley is frequently blasted by afternoon winds that are superheated from passing over the Judean Wilderness.[1] Yet there are important sources of fresh water in the area. The springs of Jericho (including those of the Wadi Qelt and Na'aran near Gilgal/Khirbet el-Mafjar?) create a series of small oases at the base of the limestone cliffs on the western side of the *Ghor*, while the presence of several strong springs together with the effects of runoff rainfall from the westward-facing hills rising to the Medeba Plateau have enriched large areas of arable soil on the plains of Moab. The bulbous southern end of the Jordan Valley sometimes carries the specific geographical name *kikkar*, "the round area," a word often rendered simply as "valley" or "plain" (Gen 13:10; 19:17; Deut 34:3). Abraham's nephew Lot drove his flocks into the *kikkar* because it was "*well watered everywhere, like the Lord's garden and the land of Egypt*" (Gen 13:10). This description acknowledges the value of oasis-green in an otherwise arid-brown plain. Indeed, in the spirit of the writer of Genesis, it was quite possible to be reminded of the annual inundations of the Nile when viewing the effects of springtime flooding of the Jordan prior to modern times. The oasis of Jericho, with a cliff line of tan limestone rising behind, even looks like many places in Upper Egypt where the green line of the Nile Valley is backed by an almost identical rise of pallid limestone. On the strength of Genesis 13:3–13, which states that Abraham and Lot could see the *kikkar* from the region of Bethel and Ai, these plains of Moab may well have been the location of Sodom and Gomorrah.[2]

Because Judah and Moab are separated by the Dead Sea, the plains of Jericho and plains of Moab offer the most convenient and necessary crossing point between the two lands. Three natural routes descend from the Benjamin highlands eastward to Jericho, with everything crossing the river at various points along a two mile (3 km) stretch due east. These combined routes then climb either southeastward onto the Mishor and Moab plateaus, or northeastward into Gilead and Ammon. For most of recorded history, this southern crossing could generally be characterized as carrying local, rather than international, priorities since most of the time it carried traffic between the "mouse" powers of Judah, Israel, Ammon, or Moab. Here Israel crossed into Canaan under Joshua during the spring floods (Josh 3:1–17), only to be followed some time later by Eglon, who tried to establish a Moabite presence in the same region (Judg 3:12–30). David's general Joab, with Uriah, likely pushed across the Jordan opposite Jericho to establish a Judean hold on the Ammonites at Rabbah (modern Amman; 2 Sam 11:1). In the end, it was a combination of Moabite and Ammonite pressures that prompted Israel's Kings Omri and Ahab to seize Jericho (1 Kgs 16:29–34; cp. Judg 10:9) and extend Israelite control over Moab, while attempting to block the kings of Judah from the region in the process (cp. 2 Kgs 1:1; 3:4–5; and the Mesha Stela/Moabite Stone[3]).

The Judean monarchy collapsed when its last king, Zedekiah, fled Jerusalem in the face of the Babylonian onslaught and was captured on the plains of Jericho (2 Kgs 25:3–6). The era of the New Testament opened with John the Baptist preparing the way for a new kind of kingdom in the same vicinity (Matt 3:1; Luke 3:3; cp. John 1:28). John probably stationed himself adjacent to the ford that connects Jericho with Livias, capital of the district of Perea ("Beyond the Jordan"); the spot combined desert asceticism with the sophistication of commerce and trade. Here the wilderness of death met the Living Water of Life (John 7:38). Herod's elegant palace at Jericho was not far away. Today, churches on both banks of the Jordan mark the memory of the spot; the modern Allenby Bridge (recently renamed the King Hussein Bridge by the Hashemite Kingdom of Jordan) lies three miles (5 km) north.

The Farah-Jabbok routes bind the hills of Manasseh to the highlands of Gilead fifteen miles (24 km)—or a morning's hard march (2 Sam 2:29)—upstream from Jericho. The main crossing point is the ford at Adam[4] (Josh 3:13; cp. Judg 12:5), near the confluence of the Wadi Farah (Nahal Tirzah) and Jabbok River. The Farah's perennial stream drains Eastern Manasseh on a southeastward angle, while the Jabbok, a true river, flows westward out of the Gilead highlands before turning southwest to intersect the Jordan River at the Adam

The *Qattara's* badland cliffs frame the lower reaches of the thickets of the Jordan (cp. Jer 12:5) near the Dead Sea, seen here at the Allenby crossing east of Jericho. Though this crossing point is a natural ford used for centuries, a foot-journey across the Rift Valley is anything but easy. Travelers must go down the steep descent from the Judean Wilderness into the *Ghor*, across a large tract of salty, barren wasteland, through the impermeable *Qattara* and impenetrable thickets of the Jordan lining the *Zor*, then the river itself, followed by the same in reverse order on the other side. All of this is done under insufferable heat much of the year and without clean drinking water. Based on the itineraries given in the Gospel accounts, Jesus likely crossed this way more than once.

1 Snow was recorded only once in the long history of Jericho: flurries on February 5, 1950, a day on which Jerusalem received more than twenty-seven inches (70cm).

2 Steven Collins, "Where is Sodom? The Case for Tall el-Hammam," *BAR* 39/2 (2013): 32–41, 70–71.

3 For text, translation, notes, and commentary regarding the Moabite Stone/Mesha Stele, see Shmuel Ahituv, *Echoes from the Past* (Jerusalem: Carta, 2008), 389–418.

4 Note the play on words "*at Adam they crossed*" (Hos 6:7; author's translation). With the direct object "covenant" (*berith*), the Hebrew verb "to cross," '*avar*, has connotations of "crossing beyond" or "crossing over;" hence, "at Adam they crossed beyond (i.e., *violated*) the covenant."

crossing. This section of the mid-Jordan Valley, the **Valley (or Vale) of Succoth** (Ps 60:6), is blessed with plenty of fresh water and large tracts of fertile alluvial soil. As a result, the Vale of Succoth has boasted a relatively high population throughout history. Several tells can be spotted at the point where the Jabbok drops into the eastern *Ghor*. Two were the sites of biblical Succoth (Tell Deir 'Alla)—the main site in the region—and Zarethan (either Tell es-Saidiya or Tell Umm Hamad). It was in the firm clay lining the Jabbok's banks between them that Solomon's workmen cast bronze implements for the temple (1 Kgs 7:45–46). We might wonder whether the Philistines, who enjoyed a regional monopoly on metal-working during the time of the judges, had their eyes on this smelting site as they repeatedly tried to push eastward through the hills of Benjamin (1 Sam 13:19–31). In any case, the archaeology of Tell Deir 'Alla attests to important trade connections with the Philistines, Egyptians, and Myceneans during the late second millennium BC; it's adequate indication that the mid-Jordan Valley played a supporting role in the westward-focused international priorities of the day.

At the same time, the rugged heights of the hard Cenomanian-Turonian highlands of Gilead served to block eastward-bound traffic from easily penetrating Transjordan at this point, somewhat restricting the international horizon as a result. Most of the traffic moving through the Farah-Jabbok connector must have been local in character, between populations living in the hills on either side of the Jordan Valley. Both Gideon, a judge from Manasseh, and Jephthah, the rogue deliverer from Gilead, crossed the Jordan near Succoth in their struggles to secure the eastern tribal borders of Israel (Judg 7:24–8:9; 12:1–6). Jeroboam, the first king of the Northern Kingdom of Israel, built a secondary capital at Penuel on a secure bend in the fold of the Jabbok in Gilead, just a scoot down the Farah from Shechem (1 Kgs 12:25). With a formal base of operations in Penuel, Jeroboam hoped to ensure the loyalty of his independent-minded eastern subjects.

Twenty-five miles (40 km) north of Succoth, the Jordan Valley opens up dramatically to the west where it is joined on a northwestward angle by the Harod Valley, a broad, practically level connector to Galilee

The view northward from the top of the mound of Tell Deir 'Alla, biblical Succoth, takes in the Valley of Succoth, a large stretch of alluvial soil washed onto the *Ghor* from the Jabbok River. Today, as in the past, the region is intensely cultivated, making it a bit of an equivalent, for the Hashemite Kingdom of Jordan, to Israel's coastal plain. Secure in the middle of the Jordan Valley, the people of Succoth enjoyed a balance of connectedness and isolation; they could afford to be loyal to whomever they wished. Likely that factored in to the men of Succoth's refusal to supply Gideon and his men with bread when he was in hot pursuit of the Midianites. But upon returning, Gideon thrashed them with briars and thistles from the wilderness. Having chosen to collaborate with desert dwellers, the leaders of Succoth were made to feel wilderness pain (Judg 8:4–17).

In the third century AD, rabbi Simeon ben Lakish, a Torah scholar who had worked as a gladiator in his youth, commented, "If paradise is situated in the Land of Israel, its entrance is Beth-shean" (*Babylonian Talmud*, Eruvin 19a). The medieval rabbinic scholar Rashi added, "[Beth-shean's] fruits are the sweetest in all Palestine." And Ashtori ben Moshe Hafarhi, a resident of Beth-shean in the fourteenth century AD, said his city was "situated on rich waters, a blessed, beautiful land bearing fruit like the garden of God, a very entrance to Paradise."[1]

Students of biblical historical geography walk off Tel Rehov in the southern part of the Beth-shean Valley. The hills of Lower Gilead rise above a line of villages, including Tabaqat Fahl, ancient Pehel/Pella, that edge the eastern side of the *Ghor*. Rounded mounds of the *Qattara* are visible in the seam between the fields of Tel Rehov and those of Pella beyond. By acreage, Tel Rehov is the largest archaeological site in the region. Like Beth-shean, it hosted an Egyptian military garrison during the Late Bronze Age (ca. 1550–1200 BC). In the first year of his reign (ca. 1291 BC), Pharaoh Seti I led a well-documented campaign to the Beth-shean Valley in order to aid the Egyptian garrisons at Beth-shean and Rehov that had been attacked by the kings of Pehel and Hammath. The latter was a city at the southern tip of the valley.[2] Recent excavations have uncovered evidence of the Egyptian presence at Tel Rehov, as well as an Israelite city from the time of Solomon.

and the Mediterranean Sea. This section of the Rift Valley carries the local name the **Beth-shean Valley**, after its most prominent city. Perhaps nowhere else in the land of ancient Israel are the living conditions at the same time so harsh yet blessed. On the one hand, the powdery, bleached soil and arid, steppe-like climate of the Beth-shean Valley mitigate against easy agriculture. Summertime heat is particularly oppressive, though winters are pleasant. The official record high temperature for the continent of Asia, 129 degrees Fahrenheit (54° C), was set near Beth-shean. Without much of a watershed ridge to reap the prevailing westerly rains, the Beth-shean Valley receives twelve inches (300 mm) of rainfall annually, which is the minimum needed for a decent crop of wheat. Yet the water table here is high, producing many fresh-water surface springs. The Harod stream, on whose southern bank the tell of Beth-shean rose, flows perennially. Because both the topography and the water supply of the Beth-shean Valley foster irrigation, the region has always had a high population density. Indeed, more than forty tells have been identified in the vicinity, mostly clustered along the Harod stream and the Jordan River. The combination of warmth and water prompts a growing season that is early and long, and the rabbis equated the region with the gates of heaven.

The highest recorded official air temperature in all of Asia was 129 degrees Fahrenheit (54° C). That measurement was taken at Tirat Tsvi near Beth-shean on June 21, 1942, offering modern proof of Josephus's assertion that Beth-shean "is suffocatingly hot in the summer time" (*War* 3.413). Jericho's highest-ever temperature, recorded on May 24, 1999, was a balmy 121 degrees Fahrenheit (51° C) by comparison. (The author was on Mount Nebo, overlooking Jericho from the east, at the time.) The official world high temperature record is 134 degrees Fahrenheit (57° C), a number met at Furnace Creek Ranch in California's Death Valley on July 10, 1913. The former world record, 136 degrees Fahrenheit (58° C) that was set at el-Azizia, Libya in 1922, was decertified due to faulty recording. The World Meteorological Organization measures standard air temperature at points six feet (1.5 m) above ground and shielded from direct sunlight.

Of all the east-west routes through the Jordan Valley, the Beth-shean/Scythopolis—Pehel/Pella connector is the most international. To the northwest, the Harod Valley provides a wide-open doorway to the Jezreel Valley, the great imperial crossroads of the southern Levant. To the east, the hills of Gilead, here composed of soft Eocene limestone and Senonian chalk, have eroded to form a relatively smooth climb to the international routes on the Transjordanian highlands above. This crossing point connected Beth-shean with Pehel; these twin cities were important actors on the international stage throughout the biblical period. By the time of the New Testament, they had become the Decapolis cities of Scythopolis and Pella, respectively. Beth-shean appears in Egyptian historical texts as early as the reign of Pharaoh Thutmose III (the mid-fifteenth c. BC), and it maintained its importance as a fortified Egyptian garrison post throughout the Late Bronze Age (ca. 1550–1200 BC). The Philistines inherited the Egyptian presence at Beth-shean during the time of the judges and early Israelite monarchy. (They unceremoniously hung the bodies of Saul and his crown-prince, Jonathan, on the city wall.) Their "might makes right" approach kept Israel's attempts to control the valley at bay until the reigns of David and Solomon (Josh 17:11–12; Judg 1:27; 1 Sam 31:1–10). We read that in the days of Gideon, Midianites, Amalekites, and other camel-riding raiders from the east pushed through the Beth-shean Valley all the way to Gaza (Judg 6:1–6), foreshadowing the ongoing problem that ancient Israel would face in trying to secure this wide-open gateway against incursions from numerous directions. Today, this is the location of the busy Sheikh Hussein Bridge, the international crossing between the State of Israel and the Hashemite Kingdom of Jordan.

The northern end of the Jordan Valley touches the Sea of Galilee. Here the climate is of the Mediterranean type; it's similar to that of the Sharon Plain (and coastal southern California). With its eighteen inches (460 mm) of rainfall annually and a good base of alluvial

1 As cited in Alan Rowe, *The Topography and History of Beth-shan*, vol. 1 (Philadelphia: University Press, 1930), 3–5.
2 *ANET*, 253; Hallo, *Context of Scripture* II, 25–26.

In the time of the New Testament, the Jordan Valley was bordered on the northwest by the political district of Galilee and on the southeast by Perea, "beyond the Jordan" (cp. Mark 3:7–8). Both districts, shown here in pink, were governed by Herod Antipas, the son of Herod the Great. Both had large Jewish populations and were regions in which Jewish travelers could move around comfortably. Between Galilee and Perea lay the very Gentile region of the Decapolis, with cities such as Scythopolis, Pella, Gadara, and Hippos leading the way. Geographical logic would suggest that whenever Jesus walked from Capernaum to Jerusalem, he would stay in the district of Galilee west of the Jordan River, then cross to the eastern side somewhere between Scythopolis (Beth-shean) and Pella to continue his journey southward through Jewish-dominated Perea. Like other travelers, he then would have forded the river again opposite Jericho for the climb to Jerusalem.

soil, living conditions in this northernmost part of the Jordan Valley are nearly ideal. The entire width of the *Ghor* just south of the Sea of Galilee is, in fact, arable almost all the way to Beth-shean, making this the most favored region of the entire Jordan Valley. The large tell of Beth-yerah that sits just west of the Jordan River, together with the Decapolis city of Gadara (*Umm Qais*), high on the rise above the *Ghor* to the east, represent a type of prosperity grounded in the fusion of abundant local resources and active international trade. Because this northernmost end of the Jordan Valley is closely connected to the Sea of Galilee, its overall living dynamic will be discussed with that region, below.

Economics and politics aside, the most enduring imprint of the long, awe-filled arena of the Jordan Valley has been its prophetic associations. Elisha hailed from Abel-meholah (probably Tell Abu-Sus) south of Beth-shean (1 Kgs 19:16); his spirited mentor, Elijah of Gilead, necessarily crossed the *Ghor* in the same vicinity for his several rendezvous with Ahab (1 Kgs 17:1; 21:17–18; 2 Kgs 1:3). Succoth, in the valley's midsection, also lay within the prophetic circle: it was here that archaeologists found an Aramaic inscription from the eighth century BC that relates an account of a divine visit to Balaam son of Beor (the *Deir 'Alla Inscription*[1]). This Balaam was apparently the same seer who had cursed Moab in the days of Joshua, then caused Israel so much trouble at Baal-peor on the plains of Moab opposite Jericho (Num 22:1–25:18; 31:8,16; Deut 4:3; Hos 9:10; 2 Pet 2:15; Rev 2:14). And it was at the southern end of the valley—somewhere near the point of Moses's death, Joshua's crossing, and the fiery flight of Elijah—that John the Baptist, another prophet who "felt fiercely" (to borrow the words of Abraham Heschel[2]), came dressed like the wilderness, eating desert bugs (at least they were kosher; Lev 11:21–22), and preaching wrath, repentance, and fire (Matt 3:1–12). Out of the living waters of the Jordan, Jesus rose to bring life (Matt 3:13–17). The Jordan River has offered rich motifs for Christian art and hymnody for centuries, evoking especially the passage of earthly life into life eternal. It's a fitting legacy for a chasm that both in location and character snatches life from the otherwise clenched jaws of death.

SUMMARY

From the shore of the Mediterranean Sea to the far side of the Rift Valley, the five regions that make up the central section of the land of ancient Israel differ widely in character, shape, and population density. Taken together, they form a strategic core that allowed Israel to grow strong at home while taking advantage

1 Ahituv, *Echoes from the Past*, 432–65.

2 Abraham J. Heschel, *The Prophets*, vol. 1 (New York: Harper & Row, 1962), 5.

> "It was not because the Jordan was beautiful that John the Baptist chose it as the scene of his preaching and ministry, but because it was wild and rude, an emblem of violent and sudden change, of irrevocable parting, of death itself, and because in its one gift of copious and unfailing water, he found the necessary element for his deep baptism of repentance, in which the sinful past of the crowd who followed him was to be symbolically immersed and buried and washed away."—Henry van Dyke[1]

of opportunities that lay on the circle of routes and resources at its perimeter. This is a land of strength and splendor (Ps 78:61), and its history is full of talented leaders who sought to build kingdoms among the fertile hills and valleys surrounding Shiloh, Shechem, Tirzah, and Samaria. Several of ancient Israel's formative events took place on Ephraimite and Manassite soil; but in spite of this promising beginning, the focus of biblical history flowed down to Jerusalem or up to the Sea of Galilee. For the biblical story, the region of Samaria remained a land of great potential, unfulfilled.

1. *The Hill Country of Ephraim.* The hard limestone hills of Ephraim provided quiet living spaces for some of the earliest inhabitants of ancient Israel. Here life was both pleasant and secure, largely out of the way of the larger political and economic forces sweeping the land. Israel's first formal tribal center was at Shiloh. With its destruction by the Philistines, Israelite political and religious fortunes moved southward, eventually to Jerusalem.
2. *The Hill Country of Manasseh.* The strong hills and fertile valleys of Manasseh formed the heartland of the Northern Kingdom of Israel. Close to international routes yet rooted in relatively protective hills, the region of Manasseh was well situated to balance the needs of home with the opportunities next door. A network of open routes angled toward Shechem, the "uncrowned queen of Palestine." From Samaria—a city that eventually gave its name to the entire region—Israelite kings forged an economic alliance that stretched from Phoenicia to Moab. But with this natural tendency toward openness came a reputation of embracing things foreign, something that was never quite accepted by the more conservative folk down in Jerusalem.
3. *The Sharon Plain.* Though it was Israel's shortest connection to the Mediterranean, the Sharon Plain was largely underutilized throughout the biblical period because of its swampy ground and dense undergrowth. The international trunk route kept to the higher ground on the Sharon's eastern side, where the most viable line of cities developed. Eventually the swamps were sufficiently drained so as to allow large-scale ports along the coastline to interact with the hill country populations to the east.
4. *The Carmel Range.* One of the most prominent natural features on the landscape of ancient Israel, the Carmel Range rises suddenly from the coastal plain and Mediterranean Sea. The international trunk route, otherwise blocked by Carmel's height, has to find its way through any of three natural passes that pierce the range. This interplay of route + inaccessibility, crowned by an aura of divine blessing on Mount Carmel proper, combined to give the range a mixed history of opportunity and retreat.
5. *The Jordan Valley.* A place unlike any other on the face of the earth, the Jordan Valley is at the same time a great divider and an active unifier of the economic and political fortunes of people living on either side. The resource base of the northern half of the valley is pleasantly sufficient for human settlement, though conditions are decidedly spotty in the south where oases like Jericho provide relief in an otherwise unforgiving land. Inhabitants on both sides of the valley kept up a constant interaction with their neighbors across the way. A series of important routes were forged through the Jordan Valley's arid flats, tangled jungle, and rushing water. They bound its sides like laces on a tightened shoe.

QUESTIONS

1. Explain how the physical shape of the Hill Country of Ephraim helped to give the region a reputation of rugged independence and self-sufficiency in the time of the Bible.
2. Is there anything about the geographical character of the Hill Country of Ephraim that might have prompted the name "Ephraim" to become a nickname for all Israel?
3. Why was Shiloh a particularly appropriate place to become the first political and religious center of ancient Israel?
4. In terms of their geographical settings, compare Shechem, "the uncrowned queen of Palestine," with Hebron, the natural capital of the southern hills. Which might have won the title "most likely to succeed"?
5. Track the efforts of Jeroboam and Omri to move the capital of the Northern Kingdom of Israel from Shechem to Tirzah and then to Samaria. What policy shifts might we assume lay behind these moves?
6. How did the physical characteristics of the Hill Country of Manasseh reflect the supposed attributes of Baal and Asherah? In light of this, what images did Hosea and Amos, prophets to the Northern Kingdom, use to speak directly to the tendency of the people of Israel to follow these gods?
7. What geographical features hindered ancient Israel from settling on the Sharon Plain? How were these hindrances overcome?
8. Why was the international traffic flow of the Sharon Plain more "north-south" than "east-west?"

1 Henry van Dyke, *Out-of-Doors in the Holy Land: Impressions of Travel in Body and Spirit* (New York, Charles Scribner's Sons, 1908):145–46.

9. Describe the "splendor of Sharon." How did the biblical writers use geographical imagery that described the Sharon Plain to speak about the character and provision of God?
10. Justify or criticize the statement, "Mount Carmel is a divine mountain."
11. Describe and illustrate the role of the Senonian chalk valleys in the Carmel Range and the Hill Country of Manasseh.
12. Which was the more favorable border for ancient Israel, the Sharon Plain or the Jordan Valley? How and why?
13. Describe the types of water sources in the Jordan Valley. How usable is each for human activity?
14. Why is the eastern side of the Jordan Valley more suitable for human habitation than the western side? What biblical events support your answer?
15. Of the four main east-west crossing points in the Jordan Valley, which one or two were most essential for the Northern Kingdom of Israel to control? What biblical events support your answer?
16. Moses, Elijah, and John the Baptist were all associated with the southern Jordan Valley. How might the geographical features of the region have influenced or heightened the messages they came to tell?

THE LAND OF ANCIENT ISRAEL: THE NORTHERN REGIONS (GALILEE)

5

The northern regions of the land of ancient Israel are collectively known as Galilee (Hb *galil*). In its most basic sense, the noun *galil*, from the verbal root *gll* "to roll," refers to things that are circular or round in shape, such as the "rods" mentioned in Esther 1:6 and Song of Solomon 5:14. But by extension, *galil* also carries the geographical sense of "circuit," "region," or "district," and it is this use that is more common in the Old Testament (Josh 13:2; 20:7; 21:32; 22:10–11; 1 Kgs 9:11–13; 1 Chr 6:76; Joel 3:4). Because, as we have seen, proper names designating biblical regions often describe a local geographical characteristic of the region so named (e.g., *shephelah* = "lowland," *negev* = "dry land," *sharon* = "level" or "straight," and *mishor* = "flat land" or "tableland"), we might expect that an area of land designated as a *galil* would somehow be roundish or at least bounded in shape or surface form, similar to the word *kikkar* = "round." This is the suggestion of George Adam Smith, who translates *galil* as "ring" and notes that it was a region constantly pressed by foreigners on three sides.[1] Or, as has been noted by Simons, the term might have been used to designate smaller bounded areas only,[2] for which we have inadequate territorial information to allow us to define their shapes or character. Indeed, the Bible mentions "*districts*" or "*territories*" (*galilot*, pl.) of Philistia (Josh 13:2; Joel 3:4) and "*region* (*galilot*, pl.) *of the Jordan*" (Josh 22:10–11), providing two instances of *galil* being used as a common noun to designate specific territories within a larger region.

Yet when we consider the actual location of the districts mentioned in the Hebrew Bible that are called *galil*,[3] an interesting and perhaps significant geographical pattern emerges. Every use of *galil* for "district," "region," or "territory" in the Old Testament refers to a place that lay on the circumference, or outer circle, of the land of ancient Israel. This may be either coincidental or intentional. Specific to the data, the "territories (*galilot*) of Philistia" lined Judah's western frontier, while the "regions (*galilot*) of the Jordan Valley" edged Judah to the east. More importantly, we also find the name *galil* designating districts in the very northernmost part of the land of ancient Israel: "*Kedesh in* galil" (Josh 20:7; 21:32; 1 Chr 6:76) and "*twenty towns in the land of* galil" (i.e., Cabul; 1 Kgs 9:11–13). These two districts were on the far end of the much larger region that is typically called Galilee today, that is, at the very top of the circle, as it were, of the land of ancient Israel. We might suggest, then, that *galil*, when used territorially, was a technical term to designate in particular *perimeter* or *outlying* districts from the point of view of people living (and keeping administrative records) in the heartland center of any given region or nation state. In the case of the writers of the Bible, that center would have been the Hill Country of Israel and Judah, with districts lining its frontier found along the coast, in the Jordan Valley, and at the frontier of Lebanon. *Galil*, then, can be compared to the term *Shephelah*, which is "lowland" only when viewed from the vantage point of the higher Judean hills, or Negev, a place "south," again only for someone living in the Hill Country of Judah. If so, then Philistia and the Jordan Valley perhaps were labeled *galilot* to indicate that they were outlying, or perimeter, districts of Judah.

The first use of the term *galil*, Galilee, to designate a larger region, specifically the entire northern area of the land of ancient Israel and not just districts on its northern frontier, was Isaiah's evocative phrase "*Galilee of the gentiles*" or "*Galilee of the nations*" (*galil ha-goiim*; Isa 9:1 NASB, CSB; cp. 1 Macc 5:15; Matt 4:15). The prophet attached this label to everything north of the Manasseh hills late in the eighth century BC, after the Assyrian King Tiglath-pileser III had overrun and formally annexed the entire area lying between Damascus and Mount Carmel into the ravenous Assyrian Empire. Isaiah's phrase "Galilee of the nations" was the logical conclusion of a long history during which the "galilees" of Israel's northern frontier had been routinely overrun by enemies, as frontiers are wont to be (e.g., 2 Kgs 15:29). Indeed, the tag "Galilee of the nations" calls a spade a spade and reflects the need for the people of Isaiah's day to come to terms with the reality that their entire northland—a region that had once been home to all or part of fully half the tribes of Israel (cp. Josh 19:10–39; 22:7; Judg 18:27–29)—had in his day formally become a *foreign* district lying just beyond the frontier of a now-severely truncated Northern Kingdom.[4] The

> Common geographical terms that became the names of specific places in the land of ancient Israel often appear with the definite article *the* in their Hebrew forms. We find, for instance, "the hill" (Gibeah; 1 Sam 11:4), "the height" (Ramah; 1 Sam 1:19), "the heap" (Ai; Josh 7:2), "the white mountain" (Lebanon; Deut 1:7), "the river" (the Euphrates; Deut 1:7), "the Jordan" (Gen 13:10), "the Negev" (Gen 12:9), "the Shephelah" (Josh 10:40), "the Carmel" (Isa 35:2), "the Sharon" (Isa 35:2), and others. Galilee, too, occurs with the definite article in Hebrew: *ha-Galil*, "the Galilee." We might assume that each of these places, originally common nouns, became definite (i.e., proper names) when they were singled out for special reference by their local inhabitants or their neighbors, the details of which are lost.

1 George Adam Smith, *The Historical Geography of the Holy Land* (London: Hodder and Stoughton, 1894), 413–14.

2 J. Simons, *The Geographical and Topographical Texts of the Old Testament* (Leiden: E. J. Brill, 1959), 34, 50, 507.

3 The possible reference to a city or region in the topographical list of Thutmose III called Galilee is problematic. The Egyptian spelling of the place in question is *k-r-r*; neither the West Semitic nor Hebrew reading of the name, or its location, have been positively identified. See Yohanan Aharoni, *The Land of the Bible: A Historical Geography*, rev. and enlarged ed. (Philadelphia: Westminster Press, 1979), 162; Anson Rainey and R. Steven Notley, *The Sacred Bridge: Carta's Atlas of the Biblical World*, 2nd, emended and enhanced ed. (Jerusalem: Carta, 2014), 73; and Shmuel Aḥituv, *Canaanite Toponyms in Ancient Egyptian Documents* (Jerusalem: The Magnes Press, 1984), 94.

4 We might argue that the region had been by nature more foreign than Israelite from the beginning. On this point, see below.

prophet understood the uneasy dynamic of the region all too well!

Irrespective of possible etymological meanings of the word *galil*, the name *Galilee* at least offers appropriate imagery related to understanding certain persistent characteristics related to the living, historical-geographical dynamic of the northern regions of the land of ancient Israel. Galilee not only lies on the northern bend of the circumference of the tribal inheritances of ancient Israel, but is itself a region that can be understood as circular in function and form. When viewed schematically, Galilee is circumscribed on its three Israel-oriented sides (west, south, and east) by broad plains through which the all-important international highways of the southern Levant wrap around a central hilly core. That is, of Galilee's six main regions, two (Lower and Upper Galilee) form a relatively isolated interior around which the remaining four (the Acco Plain, Jezreel Valley, Sea of Galilee, and Huleh Basin) scribe an open and accessible "U" shape. Just as a traffic circle is designed to handle traffic moving in and out of an interchange in multiple directions, so this loop around the hills of Galilee allows travel in and out of the area on a number of compass angles. Biblical theologian Sean Freyne speaks of an active, living dynamic between Galilee's comparatively remote hilly central core and the flat and open international circle forming its periphery. He states, in summary,

> [We have] found that the name Galilee, meaning "circle," is not just an accurate ethnographical description [i.e., Galilee of the nations], as is generally assumed, but it also and perhaps originally [had] a suitable geographic one, too. The central hill country [of Upper and Lower Galilee], despite the internal differences between north and south, is still quite distinct from the surrounding plains and rift, and historically we know that such distinctions generated a very different culture and life style between the center and the periphery. Inevitably, social and cultural tensions were to emerge between coast [and the Jezreel Valley] and interior, but it should not be assumed that the older way of life had always to be the loser in such circumstances. On the other hand, commercial links can co-exist within such cultural diversity provided no attempt is made by the stronger partner to "take over" or totally dominate the weaker. If this does occur it is likely to be resisted fiercely, and so we find that the geographical diversity of coastal plain and interior gave rise to a fluctuating set of human relations between the two.[1]

Freyne's observations offer a handy schematic for understanding and organizing the motives, events, and

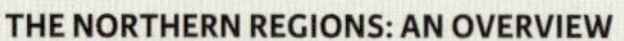

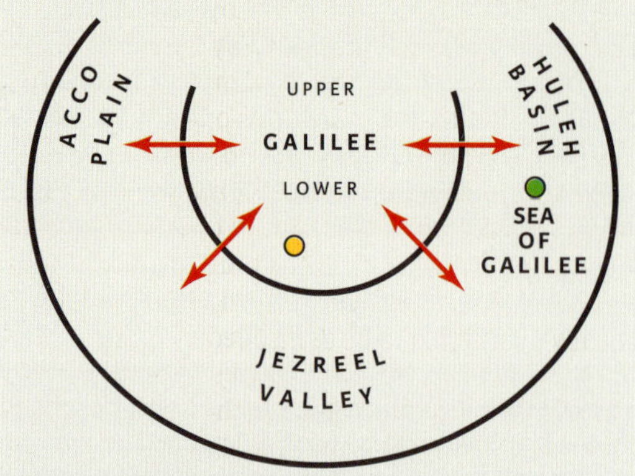

This schematic map provides an overview of the basic geographical character of Galilee. Red arrows show the major natural traffic points connecting an outer, international ring with a more isolated heartland core. Tracing the historical events of the Old and New Testaments on a schematic such as this allows a student of the Bible to better understand the issues and energy that informed decisions and shaped actions in the region. Jesus, for instance, grew up in Nazareth of Galilee (Mark 1:9; Luke 2:51; the yellow dot), on a ridge high on the seam between circle and core, where centripetal forces pulled residents inward. He then *"withdrew . . . to live in Capernaum by the sea"* (Matt 4:12–13; the green dot), a place whirled by centrifugal forces of internationalism and trade. The implications for the Gospel story are many.

consequences that played out on Galilee's well-ordered stage throughout the biblical period.

By this and nearly every other criterion, Galilee is the most complicated area of the land of ancient Israel. This is most obvious in its geological structure and surface topography. Biblical geographer Denis Baly has aptly called the entire region "the zone of greater complexity."[2] Here down-faulted basins cut across uplifted ranges on acute angles, and natural routes are forced to find their way through tight mountain passes, around swamps or canyons, and over rushing streams. Within this complexity lay a tangled network of "cat routes" and "mouse holes," all facing equal measures of opportunity and threat. We can expand Baly's intended referent—the zone of greater *geographical* complexity—to include the greater *social, cultural, political, and economic* complexity that as a result characterized the region in biblical times as well.

The southern half of Galilee is part of the Galilee-Bashan Depression, a broad geological trough that runs completely across the southern Levant on an east-west line. (See the map showing natural east-west corridors in the Levant referenced in chapter 3.D "The Negev," p. 98 above). This depression severs the spiny backbone that forms the hill country core of the southern Levant, in effect separating the hills of Judah and Ephraim/Manasseh from the higher mountains of Upper Galilee and Lebanon further north. As a result, Galilee as a whole is geographically more naturally connected to Phoenicia and Lebanon than it is to the heartland of

1 Sean Freyne, *Galilee from Alexander the Great to Hadrian: A Study of Second Temple Judaism*, (Edinburgh: T & T Clark, 1980), 15–16.
2 Denis Baly, *The Geography of the Bible*, new and rev. ed. (New York: Harper & Row 1974), 29–30.

Israel. The implications for settlement, economic influence, and political control throughout the biblical story are immense. An equally important observation is that while Phoenicia is characterized by seaports and the heartland of Israel is dominated by land routes, Galilee, by geographical nature, has ample access to both. This makes the southern sections of Galilee—namely the Jezreel Valley, Acco Plain, and to some extent Lower Galilee—an important corridor for international traffic flowing between the desert routes of Transjordan and the sea lanes of the coast. These southern parts of Galilee are a true Land Between, busy in their own right but critically positioned to be controlled by either Israel to the south, Phoenicia to the northwest, Aram-Damascus to the northeast, or, more likely in the end, by one of the cat empires lying just beyond Israel's frontier.

Overall, Galilee contains the most fertile regions in the land of ancient Israel. Abundant rain falls throughout (it's all high, west, and north, so to speak), and numerous alluvial plains foster strong economies where communities can thrive. The best resourced areas are found on the circle of Galilee (the Acco Plain, Jezreel Valley, and Huleh Basin and Sea of Galilee), but local opportunities are close at hand throughout the hilly center as well (in Upper and especially Lower Galilee). In the first century AD, Josephus summarized the character of Galilee nicely—though as a native of the region he must be excused for his obvious exaggeration and homeland pride:

> The land is everywhere so rich in soil and pasturage and produces such variety of trees that even the most indolent are tempted by these facilities to devote themselves to agriculture. In fact, every inch of the soil has been cultivated by the inhabitants; there is not a parcel of wasted land. The towns, too, are thickly distributed, and even the villages, thanks to the fertility of the soil, are all

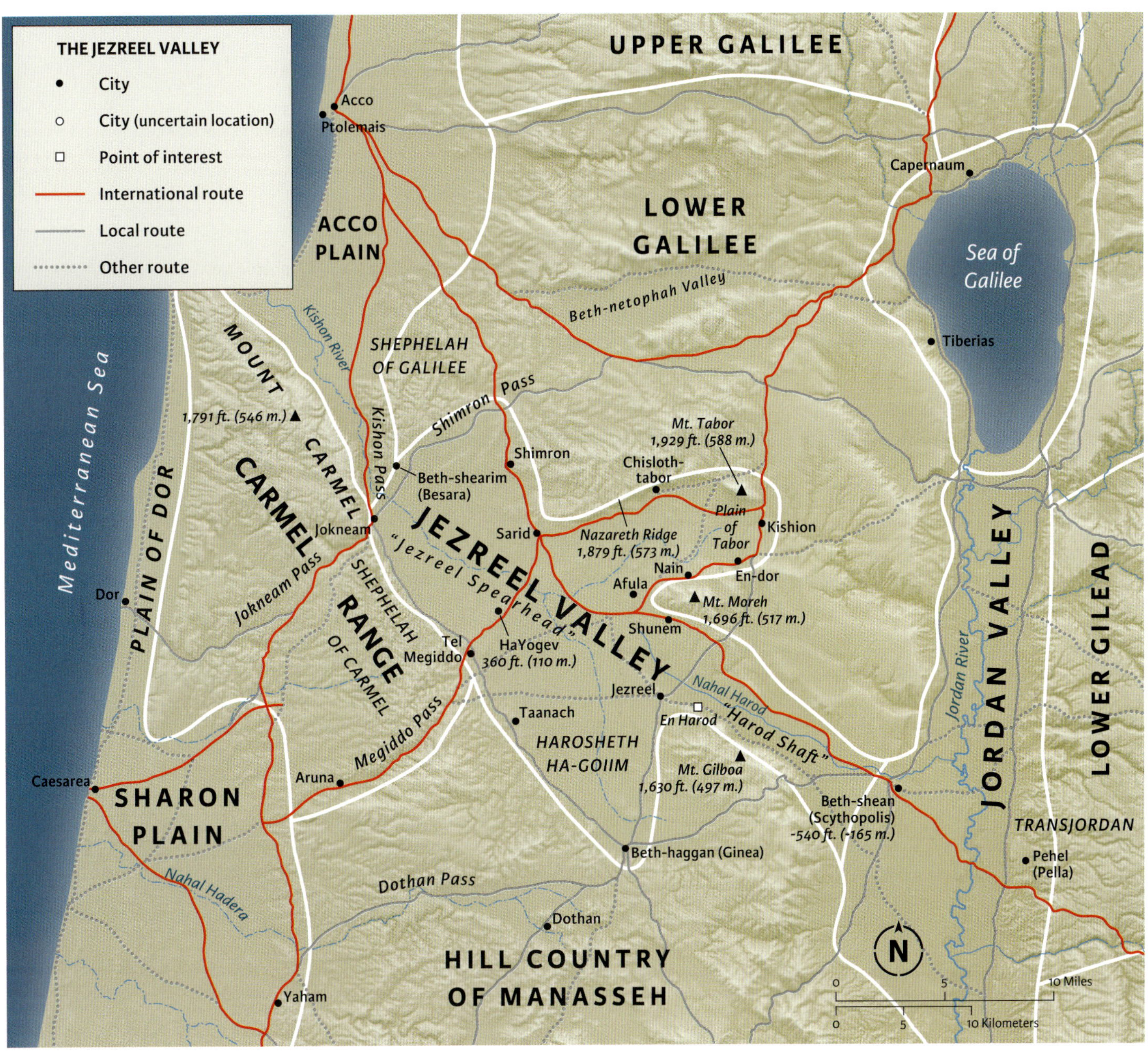

> so densely populated that the smallest of them contains more than fifteen thousand inhabitants. (*War* 3.42–43)

If we pull up to a bird's eye view, we can readily see that the "circle/core" schematic that works so well on the local human landscape of Galilee also applies to the entire land of ancient Israel. That is, with the bigger picture in mind, it is the international highways of Galilee that historically have been the economic center of the entire southern Levant, forming a hub that connects the shipping lanes of the Mediterranean Sea with the caravan routes of the eastern desert while skirting the central hilly spine of Judah/Ephraim/Manasseh in the process. Galilee as a whole thus lies at the center of the balance of regional powers (Phoenicia, Damascus, and Israel) and is on the crossroads (or in the crosshairs?) of stronger forces further afield (Egypt, Arabia, Mesopotamia, and the Aegean). And, if the opportunities of internationalism do indeed define Galilee as the center of the southern Levant, then a provincial hill city like Jerusalem, marginalized by its relative inaccessibility from the commercial interests of the world below, lies on the frontier.

But the circles shift as circles tend to do, and we also see that what is first considered circumference becomes core, and what was first core becomes circumference. So when we consider that the center of the land of ancient Israel was the city of Jerusalem, capital of the united monarchy and unbroken home to the spiritual and national aspirations of the Jews throughout the time of the New Testament and beyond—and this is the view of most of the biblical authors and many biblical readers as well—then the northern regions of Galilee become the periphery rather than core. Prone as it was to the constant incursions of Gentiles, Galilee for Jerusalem was a frontier to be tapped when conditions might permit, but a place that ultimately was not crucial for Judah's survival. On the geopolitical map of ancient Israel, "Us versus Them" circled both ways.

It is significant, then, that the gospel emerged in the converging circle of Galilee, a set of regions that lies open to both opportunity and threat and is at the same time center and frontier; then moved to Jerusalem, itself both periphery and core; before being launched into the world. Historically, the cultural, social, and religious matrix that made up the human dynamic of Galilee was equally complex over time, with ever-moving circles of influence and control. Indeed, the regions of Galilee are a true zone of greater complexity that demands to be viewed through multiple lenses. With geography in mind, the lay of the land is a good place to start.

A. THE JEZREEL VALLEY

The Jezreel Valley is the largest and most fertile of all of the valleys in the land of ancient Israel. It is also the only one that provides a flat, straight-line connection between the coastal plain and Transjordan. Though the valley (or its constituent parts) is known by several different names in ancient sources, it is the name "Jezreel Valley" (*emeq yizre'el*) that is most common in the Old Testament (Josh 17:16; Judg 6:33; Hos 1:5) and hence appears on modern Israeli roadmaps today. The name certainly derives from the valley's association with the city of Jezreel, a place at a prominent juncture on the valley's eastern side that became Israel's secondary capital in the ninth century BC, during the reigns of the expansionist Kings Omri and Ahab (1 Kgs 18:46; 21:1; 2 Kgs 9:30; 10:1). The well-known term *Esdraelon*, the Greek and Latin form of Jezreel, doesn't appear in literature until intertestamental times (e.g., Judith 1:8; 3:9; 4:6; 7:3). Writers from the Hellenistic, Roman, and Byzantine periods usually called the valley "the Great Plain," a rather obvious name that has the advantage of political and cultural neutrality (Judith 1:8; Josephus *Life* 115; *War* 2.188; Eusebius *Onomasticon* 108.12–14). A poetic name for the Jezreel Valley is "*the pasturelands of God*" (Ps 83:12 NIV), a phrase coined by the psalmist that says something not only about its fertility but also about the ultimate guardianship of the place. One name that *doesn't* appear in ancient sources is "the Valley of Armageddon." This is a wholly modern term popularized by the valley's role as a battlefield for the ages, combined with the idea that Armageddon (Rev 16:16) is connected with the tell of Megiddo.

The popular idea that the Greek word *Armageddon* reflects the Hebrew place name Har (Mount) Megiddo is countered by the fact that Megiddo is not a mountain but a tell. Tells and mountains are very different topographical forms, and the author of Revelation certainly knew the difference. It is possible that Har Megiddo may refer to the mountainous area to the south of tell Megiddo (the Manasseh Hill Country), but then why the emphasis in interpretive history on the Jezreel Valley to the north? Or, if the history of battles in the area somehow requires that "*the battle of the great day of God, the Almighty*" (Rev 16:14) be in the Jezreel Valley, then why didn't the author of Revelation coin a Greek term preserving the name of the place as "the plain of Megiddo" (Hb *biqa'at Megiddo*), a good biblical name (2 Chr 35:22; Zech 12:11 NASB), or even "Tel Megiddo"? An alternative suggestion posits that the Greek name Armageddon preserves the Hebrew place name Har Mo'ed, "Mount of Assembly," which Isaiah used to refer to the abode of the gods "*in the remotest parts of the North*" (Isa 14:13). This place was later equated by the psalmist with Zion, "*the city of the great King*" (Ps 48:1–2). Isaiah (29:1–3), Joel (3:2), and Zechariah (12:2,9; 14:2) all portray enemy armies assembling at Jerusalem for the world's last great battle. Because Revelation 16:14–16 also describes armies gathering together for that battle, it is tempting to suggest that Armageddon, the site of the battle in Revelation, is a code word for Jerusalem.[1]

Geologically, the Jezreel Valley is a complicated basin where two lines of faulting converge at an approximate 45-degree angle. One, ripping away from the Rift Valley in a northwestward direction, has formed the strong face of the Carmel Range. A parallel fault line shaped

1 This is the suggestion of Meredith G. Kline, "Har Magedon: The End of the Millennium," *JETS* 39:2 (1996): 210–13. Kline posits that the Greek letter *gamma* of Armageddon preserves the Hebrew letter *'ayin*, the middle consonant of *mo'ed*. However, while some proto-Hebrew *'ayins* do shift to a *gimel* in Hebrew or a *gamma* in Greek, the *'ayin* of *mo'ed* is not of that type, making Kline's suggestion problematic linguistically even though it is theologically interesting, or even compelling.

the prominent face of Mount Gilboa, the northern end of the block of Eocene limestone that comprises Central Manasseh. The other fault line, running generally east-west, marks the sudden rise of the Nazareth Ridge along the Jezreel Valley's northern side. The ground between has dropped into a broad triangle resembling the shape of a large spearhead (the **Jezreel Valley** proper), with a narrow handle shaft (the **Harod Valley**) attaching it to the Rift Valley. The Jezreel Valley is approximately twenty miles (32 km) long on each of its angled sides and seventeen miles (27 km) across its widened eastern end. The Harod "shaft" runs another ten miles (16 km) southeastward to Beth-shean and the Jordan River.

The Jezreel Valley can also be defined by the mountains lining its perimeter. Its southwestern edge, as already seen, is marked by the nearly straight-line back of the Carmel Range. Carmel's highest point, at 1,791 feet (546 m), lies off the valley's seaward tip. The straight-faced Nazareth Ridge, a rise of Cenomanian-Turonian limestone reaching 1,879 feet (573 m), together with the lower Eocene Shephelah of Galilee, defines the northern edge of the valley. Hanging just off the eastern end of the Nazareth Ridge is Mount Tabor, an oval mound of hard Cenomanian-Turonian limestone tightly circumscribed by a fault line running around its base. At 1,929 feet (588 m), Tabor is the highest of the mountains on the perimeter of the Jezreel Valley and, like Mount Carmel, bore ancient sacred associations (cp. Deut 33:18–19; Hos 5:1). Tabor's distinctive shape, highlighted because it "looms up" (words supplied in NASB at Jer 46:18), is visible from points throughout lower Galilee as well as from places in Bashan and Lower Gilead east of the Jordan River. Mount Moreh (1,696 ft; 517 m), our first view of the basalt that dominates eastern Galilee, punctuates the midpoint of the Jezreel's eastern line. Off Moreh's southern flank, and completing the valley's mountainous perimeter, lies the Eocene rise of Mount Gilboa (1,630 ft; 497 m). The mountains surrounding the Jezreel Valley all soar from the level floor below, providing the visual image of a vast triangular baseball field, with home plate at its western tip, the Tabor-Moreh-Gilboa line defining the outfield fence, and clean and ready grandstands all around. The splendid view from the peak of each of these mountains offers a distinct perspective on the directional traffic that since the dawn of recorded history has rutted the rich alluvial soil below.

From end to end, the Jezreel Valley is nearly table-top-flat, rising in elevation from 85 feet (26 m) at its seaward point to only 230 feet (70 m) above sea level twenty miles (32 km) to the southeast, with a nearly imperceptible crest to 360 feet (110 m) midway. This crest was formed by an underground swelling of basalt (a geological sill) that acts as a kind of dike impeding the valley's natural drainage to the Mediterranean Sea. Historically, this sill served as a natural causeway carrying traffic across the valley on an angle between Megiddo and Mount Tabor. Because it is blanketed by a thick layer of dark alluvial soil, the sill blends in nicely with the valley floor. It is best seen from Megiddo as the low rise on which the buildings of the Israeli *moshav* (agricultural settlement) HaYogev have been built.

Stretching eastward from Mount Carmel, the super-fertile Jezreel Valley opens to connections, routes, and trade on every side. Mounts Tabor, Moreh, and Gilboa (left to right) define the valley's far eastern horizon. The Jezreel's higher and drier northeastern bay (the Plain of Tabor) is to the far left; the somewhat lower and wetter southeastern bay (the area of Harosheth ha-Goiim or "Harosheth of the Nations") lies on the far right. The valley's flatness makes it difficult to notice any appreciable change in elevation. Twin runways of an Israeli air force base (center left) tempt the eye that views the valley as Armageddon since they don't appear on any map available to the public. Yet it is the Jezreel's many water reservoirs, albeit modern, that speak to its more essential role as an economic center of both ancient and modern Israel.

Eleven lanes of asphalt push past the expanding industrial zone at Jokneam, then head off toward the Kishon Pass in a vibrant modern version of the "circle" of Galilee. This view from the summit of Tel Jokneam is northwestward into the Kishon Pass; Mount Carmel rises to the left while the lower hills of the Shephelah of Galilee trace the horizon on the right. The largest city in the immediate vicinity is Jokneam, from which the Jokneam Pass cuts away toward the Sharon Plain. The modern highway, shown here, disappears into this pass, center left. Though lying against the southern, Manasseh side of the valley, ancient Jokneam belonged to the Israelite tribe of Zebulun, whose holdings stretched northeastward across the valley and beyond the Nazareth Ridge. Zebulun, oddly enough, thus guarded a vital Manasseh route coming from the Mediterranean (Josh 12:22; 19:11; 21:34; cp. Gen 49:13). The Kishon Pass itself was assigned to the tribe of Asher, adding further allegiances to the already crowded mix. Ahab must have come this way in his dealings with the Phoenicians, and Elijah killed the prophets of Baal at the Kishon stream somewhere nearby (1 Kgs 18:40).

The highest part of the Jezreel Valley is its northeastern bay, the Plain of Tabor, a kind of foothill plateau embraced by mounts Tabor, Moreh, and the Nazareth Ridge. Here, in line with the valley's basalt sill, elevations step up to a consistent 360 to 460 feet (110 to 140 m) above sea level as they start to merge with those of Lower Galilee. The view back toward the Jezreel Valley from deep within the Plain of Tabor hides the rest of the valley floor below, giving this corner a sense of its own place.

The Jezreel's southeastern bay, slumped between the hills of Manasseh and the hook of Mount Gilboa, is lower, topping out at only 230 feet (70 m) above sea level. This part of the Jezreel Valley is especially given over to swampy conditions, as the water that drains the western face of Gilboa backs up behind the valley's basalt sill. Near Taanach on its southern edge were the "waters of Megiddo," the staging ground for Sisera's force of 900 chariots that became trapped in a morass of mud and mire when in a thunderstorm "*the stars fought [against them] from the heavens*" (Judg 4:3; 5:19–21). Ahab's deluge-dodging chariot dash from Mount Carmel to his capital at Jezreel crossed the same sloppy ground (1 Kgs 18:45–46).

Gertrude Bell, an eccentric British adventure traveler and self-styled diplomat during the years prior to the First World War, tried to cross the Jezreel Valley from Haifa to Jenin on February 1, 1905, over approximately the same line that Ahab raced his chariot from Mount Carmel to the city of Jezreel twenty-seven centuries before (1 Kgs 18:45–46). She was somewhat less successful than the king:

"I had a ride full of vicissitudes from Haifa. The first day was extremely and unavoidably long, thirty-one miles [50 km] which is more than one can comfortably take one's animals. Moreover the road lay all across the Plain of Esdraelon . . . and the mud was incredible. We waded sometimes for an hour at a time knee deep in clinging mud, the mules fell down, the donkeys almost disappeared . . . you could see nothing but his ears! And the horses grew wearier and wearier. I got in to camp after dark, at a place called Jenin [south of Jezreel city], feeling very tired and head-achy and wondering why."[1]

The Jezreel Valley floor, together with the slopes of its perimeter mountains, drains into the Kishon River (Judg 4:7,13; 5:21; 1 Kgs 18:40), making it the largest of the catchment basins between the Negev and Lebanon that flow into the Mediterranean Sea. Rainfall totals in the valley reach approximately 20 inches (510 mm) annually, a good though not particularly plentiful amount. The mountains around, though, receive up to 30 inches (760 mm) or more of rain on average per year, and the total, all flowing inward, can quickly overwhelm the Kishon's ability to drain the valley's flat expanse. The upper, eastern streams of the Kishon pierce the Jezreel's basalt sill at a single point in the middle of the valley floor, midway between the modern towns of Afula and HaYogev. From here the river is joined by the Kishon's lower streams, and everything funnels into the narrow gap between Mount Carmel and the rise of western Galilee's Shephelah hills at the valley's western tip. Hindered by these two pinch-points, the slight gradient of the valley floor simply cannot drain the winter rains fast enough. Until recent times, the valley's open center remained soggy for much of the year. With the wave of Jewish agricultural settlement in the region during the 1920s and 1930s, the winter swamps of both the Jezreel and Harod Valleys were eventually mechanically drained, their waters collected into pools. Today, dozens of large reservoirs and fish ponds dot the valley's floor, especially in the lower Harod Valley near Beth-shean.

The lowest point of the Jezreel Valley lies between Mounts Gilboa and Moreh at the midpoint of the valley's eastern side, where the Jezreel "spearhead" con-

1 Gertrude Bell, *The Letters of Gertrude Bell*, vol. 1 (Harmondsworth, Middlesex, UK: Penguin Books, 1987), 76.

nects to its Harod "shaft." Here, in the gap between the towns of Shunem and Jezreel, elevations drop to sea level, then continue downward on a gradual slope to Beth-shean/Scythopolis (at 540 feet; 165 m) and to the Rift Valley beyond. Because the entire Harod Valley lies below sea level, its floor has cut into the water table, exposing numerous springs along its southern, Gilboa side. These springs are like holes in the bottom of a water barrel, flowing strong due to the water pressure above. One of these is En Harod, the spring famed as the place where Gideon's men lapped water "*like a dog*" (Judg 7:5) and from which the valley receives its modern name.

The entire floor of the Jezreel Valley, as well as its Harod extension, is covered with dark, rich alluvial soils that sometimes reach up to 330 feet (100 m) deep. These soils hold water well—too well, in fact—but usually dry out nicely during the hot months of summer. Jezreel means "God sows"; it's a perfect name for the place that no doubt prompted the psalmist's sobriquet, "*the pasturelands of God*" (Ps 83:12 NIV). Until the swamps of the Jezreel were drained in recent times, the best agricultural land lay along the valley's perimeter; in fact, it is here that the largest and best-resourced cities took root. All were on trade routes; some were especially known for the fertility of their adjacent fields. One of these was Shunem, on the southern slope of Mount Moreh, where Elisha made friends with a successful farmer and his wife (2 Kgs 4:8,18; cp. 8:6). Shunem's fields were important enough to be co-opted and cultivated by Biridiya, king of Megiddo, in the fourteenth century BC (*EA* 365).[1]

So too we have evidence of the fertility of the northwestern part of the Jezreel Valley: Josephus mentions that when he was appointed general for the Jewish Revolt in Galilee in AD 66, he expropriated grain from the region of Besara (Beth-shearim) in order to support his war effort (*Life*, 118–19). Much of this grain belonged to Bernice, queen of Herod Agrippa II. Thutmose III did the same to the wheat fields around Megiddo after conquering that city in the mid-fifteenth century BC.[2] In a similar theme, the El-Amarna letter 224 speaks of an ongoing arrangement by which Shum-Adda, king of a city called Shamhuna—likely biblical Shimron near Beth-shearim (cp. Josh 11:1)—supplied grain to Egypt during the fifteenth and fourteenth centuries BC.[3] Harosheth ha-Goiim, meaning "the cultivated fields of the Nations,"[4] was located near Taanach and Megiddo (= "*the Waters of Megiddo*"; Judg 5:19). The name says something about the area's natural fertility but also its tendency to be seized (Judg 4:2–3). It is not without merit that the historic Arabic name for the Jezreel Valley is *Marj ibn-Amir*, meaning "the Valley of the Son of the Prince," an ongoing confirmation of its privileged place in the economy of the region. Jesus once opened a parable with the words, "*A rich man's land was very productive.*" Then he continued, "*He thought to himself, 'What should I do, since I don't have anywhere to store up my crops? I will do this,' he said. 'I'll tear down my barns and build bigger ones and store all my grain and my goods there'*" (Luke 12:16–18). The setting for this story could have been many places in Galilee, but the reputation of the Jezreel Valley in particular, fertile yet vulnerable and usually in the

Nearly flooded by rolling swells of rich alluvial soil, residents of the modern Israeli Arab village of Sulam enjoy nearly perfect growing conditions all around—indeed, some of the best in the entire Jezreel Valley system. The northern profile of Mount Gilboa rises in the distance. Sulam preserves the name of the ancient city Shunem, where Elisha made his home-away-from-home with a prosperous yet childless farming couple (2 Kgs 4:8–37; 8:1–6). A document from Egypt's El-Amarna archive (fourteenth c. BC) also mentions the city's productive fields (EA 365; cp. EA 250). Remains of the ancient site lie beneath the houses and gardens of the modern village.

1 William L. Moran, *The Amarna Letters* (Baltimore: Johns Hopkins University Press, 1992), 363.

2 James B. Pritchard, ed., *ANET* (Princeton: Princeton University Press, 1955), 238.

3 Moran, *Amarna Letters*, 287; cp. EA 225 (pg. 288), which mentions that Shum-Adda is the ruler of Shamhuna.

4 From Akkadian *erištu*, "cultivated land." On the name and location of *Harosheth ha-Goiim*, note especially Anson Rainey and R. Steven Notley, *The Sacred Bridge*, 150–51. This is contrary to Aharoni, *Land of the Bible*, 221, 223, and others who relate the word *harosheth* to the biblical Hebrew word *horesh*, "forest."

hands of a strong outsider, gives special punch to Jesus's tagline: "*You fool! This very night your life is demanded of you*" (Luke 12:20).

Forced to share its resources by the steady hand of practicality, the Jezreel Valley's largest cities were evenly spaced around its higher, drier perimeter, above the disease-ridden swamps that filled the lower parts of the valley much of the year and separated into their own living spaces. Most of these cities (Jokneam, Shimron, Sarid, Chisloth-tabor, Kishion, Nain, Shunem, Jezreel, and Beth-haggan/Ginea) were located at a point where the valley edge takes a sharp turn or pulls back into a bay. Except for Megiddo, none were able to see—or control—the entire valley, though each claimed an arc of adjacent arable soil and tapped into the routes that came its way. For this reason, area names such as "*Jokneam with its pasturelands*" (Josh 21:34), "*the plain of Megiddo*" (2 Chr 35:22; Zech 12:11 NASB), and even "*Jezreel Valley*" (Judg 6:33; cf. Judg 7:1; Josh 17:16; Hos 1:4–5) must have originally been local terms for the particular portion of the larger valley system that lay adjacent to the city named.[1]

The best known of all the cities of the Jezreel Valley is, of course, Megiddo. The tell of Megiddo is located not only at the midpoint of the valley's most exposed (southwestern) side, but at a place where the Manasseh hills project a little onto the valley floor. From this privileged position alone, the entire Jezreel Valley lies visible and open. This made Megiddo the city most front and center in the valley. Megiddo also guarded the most direct pass to the coast through the Carmel Range, as well as the end of the basalt sill running the width of the valley to Mount Tabor. All of these geographical factors clinched its reputation as chief among equals, prompting the victory whoop of the Egyptian Pharaoh Thutmose III: "Capturing Megiddo is like capturing a thousand cities!"[2]

There is no recorded name for the entire Jezreel Valley system in either Egyptian or Assyrian sources. This suggests that in its earliest history, the valley functioned less as a single unit than as a series of local, connected bays, each somewhat separated from the others by the seasonal area of swamps between. The idea is also supported by the city lists and boundary descriptions of the northern tribes of Israel recorded in Joshua 17 and 19: the territories of Manasseh, Asher, Zebulun, and Issachar all met around the edge of the valley. The list of conquered cities in Judges 1:27 shows that the main population centers of the Canaanites, too, hugged the valley's perimeter line. We should not assume, however, that the Jezreel Valley's floor lay unclaimed: Joshua 17:11; 19:11; and 21:34 all indicate that the Israelite tribes lining its northern edge—Asher, Zebulun, and Issachar—established rights reaching across the valley floor. This reality suggests that the Jezreel Valley belonged more to Galilee than to the Manasseh hills to the south. That Jabin, king of Hazor, a city north of the Sea of Galilee, stationed his general Sisera at Taanach and Megiddo, on the southern rim of the Jezreel Valley, suggests the same (Judg 4:2; 5:19). As confirmation, in the first century AD the Jezreel Valley (by then called the Great Plain) was under the political control of the district of Galilee governed by Herod Antipas, not Samaria to the south.

Coming the other way, from the south, Kings Omri and Ahab pushed through the city of Jezreel to Phoenicia and Transjordan, giving us a textbook example of how the valley's disparate parts could be united around larger political and economic ends. The use of the term "Jezreel Valley" to designate the entire valley likely dates to their dynasty, when the city of Jezreel became an administrative center for the Northern Kingdom of Israel that was second only to the city of Samaria. The valley also functioned as a single unit whenever the cats prowled through town—during the time of Assyria, Babylon, and Persia, as well as throughout the era of the New Testament when the political and economic forces of Hellenism and then Rome unified the whole under the name the Great Plain.

As valuable as the fields of the Jezreel Valley were, the major unifying force of the region was the great highways that met there. On the principle that natural routes tend to follow paths of least resistance, we rightly find that travelers on the imperial highways connecting Africa, Europe, Asia, and Arabia preferred to find their way between desert and sea by crossing the widest and most level gap in the hilly backbone of the southern Levant possible—and what a set of open doorways and broad corridors the Jezreel Valley is! Indeed, the Jezreel can be likened to a great traffic circle, or, in the dramatic imagery of George Adam Smith, a military theatre-in-the-round, an amphitheater of focused battle:

> With our eyes on [its] entrances and remembering that they are not merely glens into neighboring provinces but passes to sea and to the desert—gates

The massive girth of Megiddo's Iron Age grain silo bears ample testimony to the productivity of the plain of Megiddo (2 Chr 35:22–23) that encircles the excavated tell. The silo was located next to the Israelite governor's palace and near the famed stables (which were more likely storehouses) on the protected southern end of the city. Access to its rooms must have been under direct governmental control. The silo dates to the reign of Jeroboam II (mid-eighth c. BC), a king who orchestrated an age of economic expansion and great national prosperity. Called to confront abuses characteristic of a top-heavy economy, the prophet Amos blasted Israel's echelons of power: *"Because you trample on the poor and exact a grain tax from him, you will never live in the houses of cut stone you have built"* (Amos 5:11). The long, low buildings in the valley beyond belong to HaYogev, the Israeli farming village that sits on the slight basalt rise bisecting the valley floor on a line from Megiddo to the Plain of Tabor north of Mount Moreh.

1 Simons, *Geographical and Topographical Texts*, 32.

2 *ANET*, 237.

> on the great road between the empires of Euphrates and Nile, between the continents of Asia and Africa—we are ready for the arrival of those armies of all nations whose almost ceaseless contests have rendered this plain the classic battle-ground of Scripture. Was ever [an] arena so simple, so regulated for the spectacle of war? Esdraelon is a vast theatre, with its clearly-defined stage, with its proper exits and entrances.[1]

One might think of a coliseum with multiple entrances through which the lions would come, and no way to block them all.

Together, seven main passageways carry traffic into or out of the Jezreel Valley, each finding its way through a natural gap between the mountains that surround the valley's well-defined perimeter.

- Three of these passageways, the Senonian chalk passes of Jokneam, Megiddo, and Dothan, pierce the Carmel Range from the southwest, connecting the Jezreel Valley with the Sharon and Philistine plains and Egypt beyond. The Dothan Pass has the added advantage of giving direct connection to the Hill Country of Manasseh and Ephraim, thus serving as ancient Israel's primary access point into the valley. Israel's two capitals, Samaria and Jezreel, lie on a straight line beyond the southern and northern ends of the Dothan Pass, respectively.
- To the northwest an international route follows the flow of the Kishon Wadi through the Kishon Pass, then bends northward across the Acco Plain to Acco (New Testament-era Ptolemais). Acco/Ptolemais is the only truly natural port in the entire land of ancient Israel. Phoenicia lies beyond.
- The Shimron Pass, following the trough between the Cenomanian-Turonian highlands and Eocene foothills of the Nazareth Ridge, carries traffic directly north into the Beth-netophah Valley and the heart of Lower Galilee.
- To the northeast, the Plain of Tabor guides the international route around the eastern side of Mount Tabor and then on to the Sea of Galilee, Damascus, and eventually Mesopotamia beyond. In moving off the Sharon Plain and across the Jezreel Valley, the International Coastal Highway loses, as it were, its middle name.
- The seventh natural route traces the northern, drier edge of the Harod Valley, the "shaft" which connects to the Jezreel Valley's "spearhead," from Shunem to Beth-shean (New Testament-era Scythopolis). It then climbs out of the Rift Valley through Lower Gilead to the Transjordanian watershed where the King's Highway (Num 20:17; 21:22) links the kingdoms of Aram-damascus, Ammon, Moab, and Edom with the Spice Route of Arabia. The route from Megiddo to Beth-shean through the Harod Valley was an established Egyptian imperial route during the Late Bronze Age (1550–1200 BC). It was co-opted by the Philistines in the following centuries (cp. 1 Sam 31:1–10).

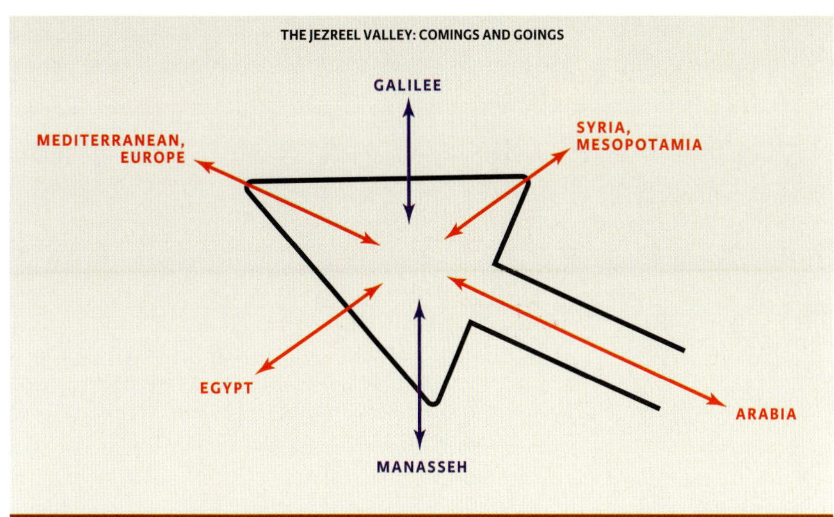

This schematic of the Jezreel Valley system shows the basic international "X" (in red) and the local "I" (in blue) traffic patterns that cross the valley.

The schematic, then, is that of a large X, the angled arms of which carry international traffic to the four corners of the world. The northwest-southeast angle of the X links the land's only natural port (Acco/Ptolemais) with Transjordan, while its southwest-northeast angle channels the flow of traffic between Africa and Asia through the valley's wide gap in the otherwise hilly backbone of the southern Levant. Bisecting this is a north-south regional "I" connecting the Hill Country of Manasseh to Galilee. The foot traveler can easily spot the access points into the Jezreel Valley along the NW-SE angle since the Kishon Pass from the Acco Plain and the Harod Valley from Beth-shean are clear gaps in the hills. More difficult is identifying the entrances into the valley following the Mesopotamia-to-Egypt connector northeast to southwest. Here a poetic couplet of the prophet Jeremiah offers a practical clue: "*[The king of Babylon] will come like Tabor among the mountains and like Carmel by the sea*" (Jer 46:18 ; author's translation).

When a traveler from the north swings around the shoulder of Mount Hermon and the land of ancient Israel first comes into view, he is greeted by the gradual drop of the Golan into the Rift Valley, then by a mass of hills forming Upper and Lower Galilee and Manasseh bounding away beyond. The most distinctive shape among all of these hills is Mount Tabor—and it is to that signal mountain that the traveler directs his feet in order to drop into the great international crossroads of the southern Levant at its base. Similarly, when a traveler first pushes into Asia from the Sinai, he follows the coastal corridor between hills and sea until he reaches the looming shape of Mount Carmel dead-ahead. Only then does he bend his path inward, finding the Jezreel Valley straight away.

Once in the Jezreel Valley, each of these routes hugs its higher, drier perimeter, where together they trace a "spearhead and shaft" outline using the valley's main cities as dot-to-dot points. The convenient exception is the track of the imperial route connecting Egypt

1 George Adam Smith, *The Historical Geography of the Holy Land* (London: Hodder and Stoughton, 1894), 391.

with Mesopotamia, which makes a beeline across the valley on the basalt sill linking Megiddo with the Plain of Tabor.

Initially, Egypt's primary route through the valley would have hugged the eastern perimeter of Mount Carmel by pushing through the Jokneam and Kishon passes. This is because Egypt's primary interest in the southern Levant during their Old and Middle Kingdoms (the Early and Middle Bronze Ages) was controlling the ports along the eastern Mediterranean seaboard and gaining access to the big timber resources of Lebanon. To do so, they plied the coastline's parallel water and land routes. With the rise of Egypt's New Kingdom at the beginning of the Late Bronze Age, Pharaoh Thutmose III seems to have permanently bent Egyptian imperial interests in the southern Levant inward, favoring the land route through the Jezreel Valley to Mesopotamia via Megiddo instead. By establishing a permanent military garrison at Megiddo, Egypt fronted the importance of the Megiddo Pass for the "cats" in subsequent military history.

Locally, the mousy Israelite Kings Omri and Ahab seized the route along the valley's southern perimeter by turning the site of Jezreel into the chariot headquarters of their kingdom.[1] In doing so, they were able to cut this international arena at its narrowest point, eclipse the historic Egyptian power bases in Megiddo and Beth-shean, and tie the hills of Manasseh to Galilee in the process. As a result, Israel was able to control the valley's access channels to the resources and routes of Phoenicia (an alliance sealed by marrying Jezebel helped!) and Transjordan.

Herein lies the paradox. For all of its strategic value as being front and center, the Jezreel Valley was primarily a place not *within*, but a place *between* the established regional power centers of the day: Israel to the south, Phoenicia to the northwest, and Syria (Aram-Damascus) to the northeast, with interested empires lying further afield. The valley seems to have never been the home base, or center, of a nation state, but rather a valuable base of resources lying between. It functioned mostly as a point of friction between the major players of the southern Levant, and the locals felt the heat of the action in the process. In general, such lands between tend not to be unified internally, but rather are pulled under the priorities of an outside power far or near, a power with

With springtime moisture in the air, the Harod Valley is filled with shades of green; it's a welcome doorway for *"a caravan of Ishmaelites coming from Gilead . . . carrying aromatic gum, balsam, and resin, going down to Egypt"* (Gen 37:25) or hungry Midianite hordes from the east *"with their cattle and their tents like a great swarm of locusts"* in number (Judg 6:5). This was ancient Israel's greatest international connection to Transjordan and Arabia, and the highways of the Harod saw an endless parade of traffic seeking economic gain through trade or conquest. The view is from the tell of Jezreel, Ahab's northern capital, from which he kept a ready eye on the opportunities and threats that were part and parcel of his desire to maintain control of "Galilee of the nations." And it was into this view, over the area of Naboth's vineyard on the near slope, that Ahab's son Joram spied his general Jehu driving furiously to Jezreel to usurp the Israelite throne (2 Kgs 9:16–29). For effect, compare this view eastward to Transjordan with the view eastward into the Judean Wilderness from Jerusalem.

1 Shawn Zelig Aster, "The Function of the City of Jezreel and the Symbolism of Jezreel in Hosea 1–2," *JNES* 71/1 (2012): 38.

From high atop the limestone Nazareth Ridge, students of biblical historical geography take in the same view over which Jesus's own eyes must have gazed whenever he wandered just a half-mile south of his boyhood home. From here Jesus could recall a long litany of great acts of God on behalf of his people. This particular view takes in the Plain of Tabor on which Deborah and Barak's troops confronted the chariot forces of Sisera (Judg 4:14–15; Ps 83:9–10). The site of the village of En-dor lies far left, where a desperate King Saul ("God's anointed one" David kept calling him) slipped away to conjure up advice from his rejected prophetic mentor Samuel, then died on the battlefield the next day behind Mount Moreh, the rise in the distance (right; 1 Sam 28:1–25; 31:1–13). The New Testament-era village of Nain lies on the near slope of Moreh, where Jesus himself raised a dead boy to life (Luke 7:11–17). It was in Shunem, an Old Testament town on the same mountain, that Elisha had done the same (2 Kgs 4:8–37), prompting Gospel readers to look for geographical as well as theological intentionality in the words and actions of Jesus. *"A great prophet has risen among us [again!]"* (Luke 7:16).

the eyes and the energy to exploit the region's resources or its position as a land bridge. While the Judean Shephelah, Biblical Negev, Jordan Valley, and Sharon Plain all provide good examples of this pattern, it is the Jezreel Valley—and, in a larger sense, Galilee as a whole—that formed the template by which the rule was forged. Isaiah's moniker "*Galilee of the nations*" (Isa 9:1) fits the Jezreel Valley perfectly, as does his poetic commentary on the economic and military priorities of the region:

You [the Lord] have enlarged
the nation [of Israel]
and increased its joy.
The people have rejoiced before you
as they rejoice at harvest time
and as they rejoice when dividing spoils.
For you have shattered their oppressive yoke
and the rod on their shoulders,
the staff of their oppressor,
just as you did on the day [when
Gideon routed] Midian.
For every trampling boot of battle
and the bloodied garments of war
will be burned as fuel for the fire. (Isa 9:3–5)

From the point of view of Isaiah (and Ahab), the harvest-and-spoils advantage of the Jezreel Valley should have been oriented southward, toward Israel and Judah, with the stronger agendas of the nations round about tipped on end. Yet plenty of biblical examples seem to indicate that the Jezreel Valley's more natural orientation was to the north: from Jabin's stationing of Sisera in Harosheth ha-Goiim (Harosheth of the nations; Judg 4:2; 5:19), to Issachar and Asher's claim over the valley's southern

THE ACCO PLAIN
City
City (uncertain location)
International route
Local route
Other route
0 5 10 Miles
0 5 10 Kilometers
N
Tyre
To Sidon, Beirut, Byblos, Arvad
Rosh ha-Niqra (Ladder of Tyre)
Hanita Ridge
UPPER GALILEE
Achzib
Nahal Keziv
Mediterranean Sea
85 ft. (25 m.)
Mt. Meron 3964 ft. (1208 m.)
ACCO PLAIN
Acco
Ptolemais
Beth-haccherem Valley
Nahal Na'aman
Cabul
LOWER GALILEE
Haifa
Aphek
Cana
Beth-netophah Valley
Hannathon
Kishon River
MOUNT CARMEL
Achshaph
SHEPHELAH OF GALILEE
Sepphoris
1,791 ft. (546 m.)
Kishon Pass
CARMEL
Nazareth
PLAIN OF DOR
Mt. Tabor 1,929 ft. (588 m.)
Jokneam
JEZREEL VALLEY
Jokneam Pass
SHEPHELAH
RANGE
OF CARMEL
Dor
Mt. Moreh 1,696 ft. (517 m.)
Megiddo
Nahal Harod
HAROSHETH HA-GOIIM
Megiddo Pass
SHARON PLAIN
Mt. Gilboa 1,630 ft. (497 m.)

line (Josh 17:11), to the way that Syrian King Ben-hadad repeatedly marched through the Jezreel Valley to contain Israel in the Manasseh hills (1 Kgs 20:1–3; 2 Kgs 6:8–14,24–25). With the conquests of Tiglath-pileser III in 734–732 BC, the Jezreel Valley was administratively attached to the rest of Galilee and became the Assyrian province of Megiddo, separating it from the now-rump state of Israel to the south. This formalized the valley's natural connection to Galilee and the Lebanese hills to the north, rather than to Manasseh. In the time of the New Testament, the valley maintained its northward orientation, based on Josephus's statement that Carmel and Samaria lay on the southern frontier of Galilee (*War* iii.35–36).

From high atop the Nazareth Ridge, the mount where he "*grew up and became strong, filled with wisdom, and God's grace was on him*" (Luke 2:40; cp. 2:52), Jesus's view into the Jezreel Valley took in the broad sweep of Israel's already ancient history.[1] From the victories of Deborah, Barak, and Gideon (Jdg 4–8), to the crushing defeat of Saul and then Josiah (1 Sam 28, 31; 2 Kgs 23:28–30), as well as the lone prophetic voices of Elijah and Elisha, who went about towns and villages doing good (cp. Acts 10:38), Jesus was able to confirm God's ongoing redemptive activity by an eye-witness view into the arena of his own people's past (cp. Isa 9:1–7; Matt 4:15–16). With it, the center of so much divine-human effort in the land of ancient Israel brought together not just north and south, but past and present, and God and man.

B. THE ACCO PLAIN

The Acco Plain is one of the smallest of Israel's coastal plains but arguably the most important, for it is here that we find the land's only truly natural seaport, Acco/Ptolemais. The plain is isolated from the Philistine, Sharon, and Dor Plains further south by the protrusion of the Carmel Range, and from Phoenicia by Rosh ha-Niqra, a sheer white cliff rising out of the Mediterranean on a right angle to the sea. Both are formidable blocks to easy coastline travel and have created a distinct settlement area that, though localized, has a clear international character. Further north, the mountains of the Lebanese Range (Phoenicia) run right down into the sea, forming tight inlets and islands that from earliest times have served as the best harbors of the eastern Mediterranean. From north to south, these Phonecian cities are Arvad, Byblos, Beirut, Sidon, and Tyre. The site of Acco/Ptolemais can rightfully take its place as the next and southernmost port in this list. All are deep water ports, as opposed to the shallow water ports that characterize the flatter, sand-based shorelines south of Mount Carmel. It is this natural connection to Phoenicia that orients the Acco Plain more toward the Mediterranean Sea and Phoenicia than to the hilly interior of the Levant.

A small fishing boat trawls the waters of Haifa Bay, its belly hungry for the catch of the day. Choices are plentiful along the Mediterranean coast and seldom disappoint.

Though small, the Acco Plain easily divides into two sections based on distinct characteristics of its geography, with the Acco/Ptolemais port exactly between.

The southern half of the Acco Plain is nine and one-half miles (15 km) long and just over six miles (10 km) wide, with pointed valleys running eastward up into the wadis of Lower Galilee. The coastline along this section of the plain forms a pleasant concave bay, bowing inward from the promontory of Mount Carmel up to the Acco/Ptolemais port. Offshore, the Carmel headland directs the northbound Mediterranean current out to sea, while eastward-driven waves wash water-suspended sand toward the coast, filling the relatively shallow bay floor below and forming a shoreline dune one mile (1.5 km) wide.

The geographical features of this southern part of the Acco Plain resemble those of the Sharon Plain to the south, though in miniature. Like the Sharon Plain, the

1 Smith, *The Historical Geography of the Holy Land* (1894), 433, speaks of the view into the Jezreel Valley from the Nazareth Ridge as "a map of Old Testament history."

Israel's northern coast ends at Rosh ha-Niqra, "head of the grottos," the seaward end of a ridge of Cenomanian-Turonian limestone that marks its modern border with Lebanon. Weathering action of wind and waves has exposed a band of brilliant white chalk at the shoreline that the Roman historian Pliny called "the White Cape."[1] The cliff line is pocked by some of the longest sea grottos in the world. Here the waves heave and boom in an impressive display of the power of the "depths" that the biblical writers knew lay beyond their understanding or grasp (Gen 1:2; Job 38:16).

Acco Plain's broad shoreline dune is backed by a kurkar ridge covered with a band of brown-red (*hamra*) sands, here reaching only fifty feet (15 m) in elevation. Behind, the plain drops to just twenty feet (6 m) above sea level, then slowly rises to the east until it meets the hills of Lower Galilee. The Kishon River, carrying a seasonably large flow of water from as far east as the mountains of Tabor and Gilboa, cuts a sluggish line northwestward at the base of Mount Carmel, then pokes through a gap between promontory and dunes to the sea. Five miles (8 km) north, in the center of the southern section of the plain, large springs surface at Aphek (Tel Kurdaneh; Josh 19:30). These are the source of the Na'aman Wadi, which flows around the northern end of the dunes and enters the sea just south of the tell of Acco. The word Aphek means "enclosure," with special reference to a channel that contains water. It will be remembered that the Aphek lying at the head of the Yarkon River separating the Philistine from the Sharon plains also lay beside large springs.

The beds of the Kishon and Na'aman Wadis are too small to carry the seasonal influx of water that flows into them from the tributaries draining Lower Galilee and the Jezreel Valley. For this reason, broad swamps have formed on the flats behind the Acco Plain's kurkar-reinforced dunes, similar to those that dominated the Sharon Plain prior to modern times. Elevations in the eastern third of the Acco Plain, however, rise enough to allow its soil to drain nicely. It is here, along the Shephelah foothills of western Lower Galilee, that long-term cultivation and real settlement in the area took root. One of the cities in the eastern Acco Plain was Achshaph (Tel Regev) at the mouth of the Kishon Pass, a place strategically valuable enough to be included in Jabin's northern coalition force against Joshua (Josh 11:1–3; cp. Josh 12:20; 19:25).

Because the southernmost part of the Acco Plain is isolated between the heights of Mount Carmel and the swamps of the Kishon, conditions there never favored large settlement until fairly recently. Today this southern half of the plain is dominated by the large industrial port city of Haifa, which rises like a wave over the seaward end of the Carmel Range, its suburbs flooding the plain below with the urban sprawl of asphalt and concrete. This growth was fostered when the swamps of the Acco Plain were drained by Jewish settlers in the 1920s and 1930s; the lowest lying land was converted to reservoirs and fish ponds. Haifa's natural advantage is that the northern face of Carmel plunges into a trough under the sea, making the water offshore deeper than anywhere else along the Acco coast and thus able to handle modern ocean-going vessels easily. With a modern breakwater blocking the effect of winter storms, Haifa now serves as one of Israel's three heavy-freight ports (the others are Ashdod and Eilat). It's also the base in the eastern Mediterranean for the U.S. Sixth Fleet.

The northern half of the Acco Plain, twelve miles (19 km) long but less than four miles (6 km) wide, covers the run from the port of Acco/Ptolemais to Rosh ha-Niqra, the seaward end of the strong east-west ridge of Cenomanian-Turonian limestone that today marks the international border between Israel and Lebanon. Josephus noted that in his day local inhabitants called this ridge the "Ladder of the Tyrians" (*War* 2.188), probably because by then passage up its steep sides had been improved by artificial terraces or slopes. The Babylonian Talmud adds that the cliff was considered the northern border of ancient Israel.[2]

The same three kurkar ridges that line the Sharon Plain are visible north of Acco. The westernmost breaks the surface of the waves as a line of tiny islets one-half to one mile (1 to 1.5 km) out to sea. The middle ridge extends as a low, rough platform just offshore and is alternately exposed and covered by sea swell and waves. Both are picturesque but wreak havoc on boats venturing too closely to land. The apostle Paul sailed safely along this coastline and stopped in Ptolemais, in what must have been a glorious springtime journey from Macedonian Philippi to Caesarea in AD 57 (Acts 21:7–8). The easternmost kurkar ridge lies one-half to one mile (1 to 1.5 km) inland, rising to 120 feet (36 m) in height. Unlike the southern part of the Acco Plain, there is hardly any dune sand here, though in the first century AD the Greek geographer Strabo mentioned that "between Acco and Tyre is a sandy beach which produces the sand used in making glass."[3]

The northern half of the Acco Plain is backed by the sharp rise of the hills of Upper Galilee. Six wadis de-

1 Pliny, *Natural History* v.76.

2 *Babylonian Talmud*, Eruvim 22b.

3 Strabo, *Geography* 16.2.25. Pliny, *Natural History* 5.75 mentions the beach as lying between Acco and Carmel. The description of the same location by Josephus (*War* 2.190-191) is clearly fanciful.

scend onto the plain from their western slopes, with enough force to have cut through the inland kurkar ridge and channeled their water directly to the sea. The main one is the Nahal Keziv, above which the famed Crusader castle of Monfort looks down onto the plain. These wadis have carried large quantities of rich terra rosa soil out toward the coast. The alluvium has filled the level ground behind the kurkar ridge, adding rich organic material to the brown-red *hamra* sands along the shore. Elevations behind the ridge reach to only eighty-five feet (25 m). But because the wadis flow on through, the soil here is well drained and provides excellent growing conditions—among the best of all the coastal areas in the land of ancient Israel. An average annual rainfall of 30 inches (760 mm), the most for Israel's coastal plains, is an added blessing.

As expected, and conforming to the pattern of the Sharon Plain to the south, the historic line of towns follows the eastern rise of the Acco Plain at the edge of the Upper Galilee hills. A second, newer line of Israeli towns has sprouted on the top of the inland kurkar ridge. One port of note, Achzib (Judg 1:31), clung to the shoreline outcroppings of kurkar just south of the mouth of the Nahal Keziv. Achzib was active from at least the Middle Bronze Age and benefited from small rocky coves that project from the shoreline both north and south of the tell. These formed harbors that sheltered ships whichever direction the wind blew. One biblical term for such harbors is, literally, "breaking out places" (*miphrats*; Judg 5:17), a nice description of the interplay between kurkar and sea.

With virtually no coastal plain of its own, the city of Tyre, twelve miles (19 km) north of Rosh ha-Niqra, coveted the fields lying between Acco and Achzib. We can rightly assume a long-standing economic relationship between that Phoenician city in particular, and this plain (cp. Judg 1:31–32; Ezra 3:7; Ezek 27:1–3; 17). The patriarchal blessing of Asher, the Israelite tribe that settled on the Acco Plain, speaks of treasures that passed through these ports, but also of the riches that sprang from the land itself. It's a place much better suited for royal estates than, say, were the tracts and terraces of landlocked Judah: "*Asher's food will be rich, and he will produce royal delicacies*" (Gen 49:20).

The Acco/Ptolemais port best represented the opportunities of the far-flung Mediterranean world for ancient Israel. The Bronze and Iron Ages site of Acco was Tell el-Fukhkhar, just north of the outlet of the Na'aman Wadi, its source of fresh water, and a mile east of the coastal "hook" that in later periods became the port city of Ptolemais. The actual port of Old Testament-era Acco was likely somewhere at the mouth of the Na'aman Wadi, where boats could pull a bit inland for protection from the waves. This was the pattern of nearly all of the coastal cities of the southern Levant during the Bronze and Iron Ages.

In the late third century BC, a new port was constructed on the coast in the small kurkar hook directly west of the tell of ancient Acco—this, thanks to developments in breakwater technology. The new port became the

The run of the shoreline of the northern half of the Acco Plain, from Rosh ha-Niqra to Acco/Ptolemais, enjoys the warmth of a pleasant midwinter morning. The long rise of Mount Carmel, marking the Acco Plain's far southern end, can be seen in the distance. A small ship sails between the coast and three tiny kurkar islets offshore. (Their names translate as Seagull, Wagtail, and Light Blue.) This is all that can be seen of the first kurkar ridge that otherwise lines the shore of the Sharon Plain on the other side of Mount Carmel. The second kurkar ridge forms the rocky shoreline. Prior to modern times, travel by land or sea via this northern end of the Acco Plain was difficult, and most boats still seek anchorage elsewhere.

The view eastward from the rise of Aphek (Tel Kurdaneh), the midpoint of the southern portion of the Acco Plain, takes in the hills of Lower Galilee's Shephelah. This is the land of Cabul that Solomon ceded to Hiram of Tyre (1 Kgs 9:10–14). The higher hills of Upper Galilee form the horizon line on the left, with the wedge of the ash-Shagur fault between. The stand of trees at the base of the tell (front) surrounds the Aphek spring. Rich alluvial fields fill the gap behind. With blessings to spare, the Aphek of the Acco Plain understandably withstood initial attempts by the tribe of Asher to bring the region into the orbit of ancient Israelite control (Judg 1:31).

Hellenistic and Roman-Byzantine city of Ptolemais, as well as Crusader Acre; the modern city of Acco envelopes both hook and tell. Ptolemais was shielded from the relentless effects of the sea: the promontory of Carmel blocks the current from the southwest, while the rocky hook breaks the effect of the prevailing northwestern storms. As the only truly natural port in the entire land of ancient Israel, Acco/Ptolemais is a magnet that helped pull all of Galilee into the Mediterranean's international arena. An added benefit is that it lies on the western end of the great *ash-Shaghur* fault that marks the division between Upper and Lower Galilee and separates the northern section of the Acco Plain from its counterpart to the south. Of importance for the economic viability of the region, this fault carries a natural route due east into the hills of Galilee.

It was through the port of Acco/Ptolemais that the land-based centers of the hill country of the southern Levant came into contact with the world of the Mediterranean, primarily via the Phoenicians who dominated the sea lanes in ancient times. The main sea route that put in at Acco hugged the coast, with stops at every port along the way (cp. Acts 21:3,7–8; 27:2). A parallel land route also followed the shore but had difficulty with the headlands of Carmel and especially Rosh ha-Niqra (the Ladder of Tyre). Egyptian and Assyrian documents mention this coastal land route in connection with trade and military expeditions.[1] Both routes were active on an ongoing basis as Tyre sought to feed its own people from foodstuffs produced in Israel (1 Kgs 5:11; Ezra 3:7; Ezek 27:17; Acts 12:20). The British cut a tunnel through the Rosh ha-Niqra cliff in 1942 to carry the Cairo-Istanbul rail line; today that cut is sealed at its midpoint, on the exact border between the modern states of Israel and Lebanon. In any case, this coastal land route should be seen as one that supported the offshore shipping lane rather than as a major north-south land corridor in itself. *That* route remained the Megiddo-to-Damascus international highway further east.

The main route heading inland toward Galilee from Acco/Ptolemais skirts the swamps of the Acco Plain by running southward along the edge of the Shephelah hills of Lower Galilee, then scoots through the Kishon Pass to the Jezreel Valley and its many option-points beyond. Josephus recognized the primary importance of this route when he noted that Ptolemais was "a maritime town in Galilee built at the entrance to the Great Plain" (i.e., the Jezreel Valley; *War* 2.188). A second natural route, less important for the larger picture but vital for the economic health of Lower Galilee, angles southeastward from Acco and crosses Lower Galilee via Hannathon and Sepphoris before touching the Sea of Galilee. A third climbs straight east through the high trough of the *ash-Shaghur* fault dividing Upper from Lower Galilee, toward the Huleh Basin.

Acco/Ptolemais, then, sat on the corner of an L-shaped economic corridor: away to the north stretched a long line of viable Phoenician ports, while off to the east ran a string of land terminals tying together the highways of Africa, Arabia, and Asia. We should not be surprised that the earliest text recounting an Egyptian military expedition into Asia (ca. 2350 BC) relates a successful campaign in which Pharaoh Pepi I landed his ships "to the rear of the heights of the mountain range on the north of the land of the Sand-Dwellers" at a place called "Antelope's Nose," almost certainly a reference to the Acco Plain north of the Carmel protrusion.[2] By taking the angle of the "L," Pepi was able to assert control over the whole. Acco remained an important anchor point for Egyptian military and commercial interests throughout the New Kingdom (the Late Bronze Age, ca. 1550–1200 BC) as pharaoh after pharaoh sought to extend and maintain control over the land and sea routes of the southern Levant, this in the face of Mittanian, Hittite, Canaanite, Philistine, and, eventually, Israelite efforts to control the same.[3]

Israel's settlement history on the Acco Plain, first undertaken during a bit of a lull in Egyptian imperial interests at the beginning of the Iron Age, reflects the

1 Note, for instance, the so-called "Letter of the Satirical Scribe," *ANET* 477; and the itineraries of Sennacherib and Esarhaddon, *ANET* 287, 291; William W. Hallo, ed., *The Context of Scripture*, vol. II: *Monumental Inscriptions from the Biblical World* (Leiden: Brill, 2000), 302–3.

2 *ANET*, 228.

3 Note, for instance, Amarna texts 88 and 234 which mention the loyalty of the king of Acco to Egypt in the fourteenth century BC; Moran, *Amarna Letters*, 160–61, 292–93.

pull between circle and center that characterizes, to a greater or lesser extent, all of Galilee. The plain was given to the tribe of Asher, though all indications suggest that it was not permanently settled by them. Of the towns in the city list of Asher that can be identified (Josh 19:24–31), most were located within the Shephelah of Lower Galilee or at the point where the hills gave way to the plain, rather than out on the exposed flats. This is consistent with the tenor of the tribal blessing in Deuteronomy: "*May Asher... dip his foot in olive oil*," a reference to olive trees that mainly lined the slopes above the plain (Deut 33:24). The tribe was unable to dislodge the indigenous Canaanite population from its strong seaward positions (Judg 1:31–32). Consequently, Asher ended up playing a negligible role in Israel's recorded history. As long as Jerusalem and Samaria were the center of the biblical narrative, the imperial hub of Acco remained the frontier.

In fact, the sources seem to indicate that for most of their history, the Israelites likely would not have known what to do with the Acco Plain even if they had obtained it. Sean Freyne rightly notes that Israel harbored "a grudging admiration for the opulence of Tyre,"[1] and this sentiment surely spilled over to the lifestyle opportunities of the city and townsfolk living out on the Acco Plain. All evidence points to the plain being a place that more naturally fell within the orbit of Phoenicia than Israel (Isa 23:1–18; Jer 25:22; Ezek 26:1–29:26; Joel 3:4–8; Amos 1:9–10; Zech 9:2–3). Of note is an inscription of the Assyrian King Shalmaneser III from the mid-ninth century BC indicating that the plain adjacent to Mount Carmel was Tyrian: "I marched to Mount Ba'ali-ra'asi,

Everything is seaward from the pleasant grassy rise of the tell of ancient Acco, including the stout Turkish and Crusader buildings of Acre, ancient Ptolemais, on the point along the shore. A modern breakwater shelters small fishing and pleasure craft under a bright October sky, promising nothing but clear sailing as far as the eye can see. The sea knows no boundaries, save for the skill and resolve of those who *"went to sea in ships, conducting trade on the vast water"* (Ps 107:23). This gave whoever held the plain and its ports an economic advantage in the southern Levant not shared by the hill people to the east.

1 Sean Freyne, *Jesus a Jewish Galilean* (London: T&T Clark, 2004), 84–8.

A woman takes a stick to an olive tree on the Acco Plain; its fruit is ripe for harvest. Her husband uses a closer approach up and in. With mechanical harvesters amounting to little more than rods with attached spinners, many olive growers in Israel and Palestine prefer traditional methods of harvest: beating the tree, then collecting the fruit off the ground (Isa 17:6). The olive is the symbol of prosperity in the hills, and the tribe of Asher, who *"remained at the seashore"* (Judg 5:17), enjoyed the benefits of both worlds: *"May Asher be the most blessed of the sons; may he be the most favored among his brothers and dip his foot in olive oil"* (Deut 33:24).

which is a cape [jutting out into] the sea before the land of Tyre."[1] So, too, Josephus mentions that by the first century AD, Mount Carmel and the plain to its north belonged to Tyre: "[Lower Galilee's] western frontiers are the outlying territory of Ptolemais and Carmel, a mountain once belonging to Galilee and now to Tyre" (*War*, iii.35). As well, note the entry for Mount Carmel in Eusebius's *Onomasticon* from the fourth century AD: "Karmelos. A mountain on the Phoenician Sea which divides Palestine from Phoenicia. Here Elijah dwelt."[2]

Indeed, with Asher's boundary touching (or falling within) the orbit of Tyre (Josh 19:24,28; cp. 2 Sam 24:5–7) but separated from the heartland of Israel by Mount Carmel and the Jezreel Valley, we would expect on geographical grounds alone that the loyalties of its inhabitants even in the time of the Old Testament would bend toward Phoenicia. This reputation seems to have been codified in the Song of Deborah, a kind of camp-fire song from the time of the judges: "*Asher remained at the seashore and stayed in his harbors*" (Judg 5:17).

The Acco Plain was briefly incorporated into Solomon's administrative districts (1 Kgs 4:7–8,16). When the cities and towns of Cabul—eastern Asher in the foothills of Galilee—were given to Tyre in exchange for materials and aid to build the temple in Jerusalem, the coast surely fell to Phoenicia as well (1 Kgs 9:10–14). This was good news for residents of Tyre, who, as already seen, coveted the plain and its routes as a base for importing foodstuffs from Israel that fueled their seaborne ventures (cp. 1 Kgs 5:11; Ezek 27:17; Acts 12:20). It is possible to posit a cooperative effort during the Iron Age between ancient Israel and at least the Tyrian Phoenicians, if not those from Sidon, on the eastern Mediterranean's sea lanes, though there is no direct evidence to corroborate the extent to which Israelites might have become mariners in their own right.[3] At

1 A. Kirk Grayson, *Assyrian Rulers of the Early First Millennium BC II (858-745 BC)*, The Royal Inscriptions of Mesopotamia: Assyrian Periods, vol. 3 (Toronto: University of Toronto Press, 1966), 54.

2 *Onomasticon* 118:8-9; G.S.P. Freeman-Grenville, Rupert L. Chapman III, and Joan E. Taylor, *The Onomasticon by Eusebius of Caesarea* (Jerusalem: Carta, 2003), 66.

3 Barry J. Beitzel, "Was There a Joint Nautical Venture on the Mediterranean Sea by Tyrian Phoenicians and Early Israelites?," *BASOR* 360 (2010): 37–66.

In condemning Tyre, the prophet Ezekiel gives us the blueprint for a seaworthy Mediterranean vessel of the sixth century BC. Not only did Phoenician ships carry products into Tyre from across the known world, but they were themselves constructed from the finest of imported materials:

Your realm was in the heart of the sea;
your builders perfected your beauty.
They constructed all your planking
with pine trees from Senir [Mount Hermon].
They took a cedar from Lebanon
to make a mast for you.
They made your oars of oaks from Bashan.
They made your deck of cypress wood
from the coasts of Cyprus,
inlaid with ivory.
Your sail was made of
fine embroidered linen from Egypt,
and served as your banner.
Your awning was of blue and purple fabric
from the coasts of Elishah [likely Cyprus]. (Ezek 27:4–7)

the very least we should assume that while Israel's contribution to Tyre's trade network was foodstuffs, Israel must have received any number of exotic goods via routes passing through the Acco Plain in return (cp. Ezek 27:12–24). But in the end, the reality that only a few men from Asher bothered to go to Jerusalem for Passover at the expressed invitation of Josiah (2 Chr 30:10–11) signaled that centrifugal forces had pulled the frontier away from the center by the late seventh century BC.

Like Dor to the south, Acco flourished under Persian and Greek control as the economic pendulum of the ancient world swung from Mesopotamia to the eastern Mediterranean. The Phoenician ports, with Acco, played a sustained role in this coming together of East and West; they also represented the new world order of Hellenism that eventually flooded the conventional Semitic highlands of the Levant. The pace was intensified with the march of Alexander the Great down the Levantine coast in 332 BC; his regional successors, the Ptolemies of Egypt, promptly changed the name of Acco to Ptolemais. This was the only city on the coastline given a new name by the Greeks, suggesting its chosen importance as *the* gateway into Galilee for things Hellenized. Ptolemais and the Acco Plain were never fully incorporated into either the Jewish Hasmonean (Maccabean) kingdom or the kingdom of Herod the Great; rather, they remained the symbol and reality of things foreign. It is reasonable to suppose that on his trip to "*the area of Tyre and Sidon*" (Matt 15:21; Mark 7:24; cp. 1 Kgs 17:8–9) Jesus may have kept to the Upper Galilee hills above the Acco Plain rather than descending onto the exposed parts of the coast. Though corridors of Hellenism pierced Galilee during the time of the New Testament, the Gospel writers fail to mention that Jesus ever actually entered any of the larger Greek cities of the region.

But in regard to the Plain of Acco, Luke was more forthright. He mentions that Anna, who waited a lifetime to see the Messiah, was from the tribe of Asher (Luke 2:36–38). Anna's quiet persistence was indication enough that in spite of the centrifugal forces of the Acco Plain, there were still among its rightful residents a remnant who could be counted among the pious faithful of Jerusalem.

As the chief economic gateway into the land of Israel, Acco/Ptolemais had a long and storied history of military conquest. Herod the Great landed here in 39 BC after the Roman Senate granted him the right to conquer all the lands formerly held by the Maccabees, which were in open revolt against Caesar. Ptolemais thus became the launch pad of the emergent Herodian kingdom. The Crusaders took the site a thousand years later, in AD 1110, losing it to the great Saladin in 1187. Saladin strengthened the city's fortresses, and it was only with gallant (and savage) effort that Richard I (the Lionhart) took the city in 1191. The Knights of St. John, given custody of the city, renamed it St. Jean d'Acre. Under the protection of the Crusaders, the Acre became a place to meet emissaries or launch far-flung expeditions and saw visits by St. Francis of Assisi and Marco Polo. Falling to the Saracens in 1291, Acre was the last stronghold of the Latin Kingdom of Jerusalem. The Turkish fortifications of Acco, rebuilt in the eighteenth century, were strong enough with British help to withstand the assault of Napoleon in 1799. Today the walled remains of the Crusader city offer a picturesque stop for Israelis and tourists alike who want to wander the corridors of the land's storied—and bloodied—past.

C. LOWER GALILEE

If the Jezreel Valley and the Acco Plain define the circumference of Galilee, the hills of Upper and Lower Galilee—the heartland of the north and cradle of the Gospel story—are its core.

Writers both ancient and modern are quick to note the natural division between Upper and Lower Galilee. The ever-practical Mishnah, for instance, states that Lower Galilee is where sycamore trees can grow, while Upper Galilee is where they don't.[1] Indeed, all elevations of Lower Galilee are under 2,000 feet (610 m), offering a suitable habitat for the sycamore. This neat topographical division coincides with the *ash-Shagur* fault, a clean incision that has ripped a spectacular trough eastward from Acco to a point five miles northwest of the Sea of Galilee. Part of the trough is called the Beth-haccherem, ("Vineyard House") Valley today; modern Highway 85 runs its length. The topography north of the *ash-Shagur* fault, in Upper Galilee, is jumbled and tight. By contrast, south of the fault the landforms are generally open and inviting, the result of the down-faulted Galilee-Bashan Depression, which, it is recalled, also helped to form the Jezreel Valley further south.

Based on rock type and the overall direction of its local topography, Lower Galilee can be divided into two subregions. One, Western Lower Galilee, opens to the Acco Plain; the other, Eastern Lower Galilee, tips into the Rift Valley.

Geologically, **Western Lower Galilee** is a stack of four ridges of mostly Cenomanian-Turonian limestone, each running on an east-west line and each with wide, flat valleys of fertile terra rosa soil between. Like the Hill Country of Judah and Ephraim, Western Lower Galilee began as a broad up-warp of hard limestone. In stark

1 Mishnah Shevi'it 9:2

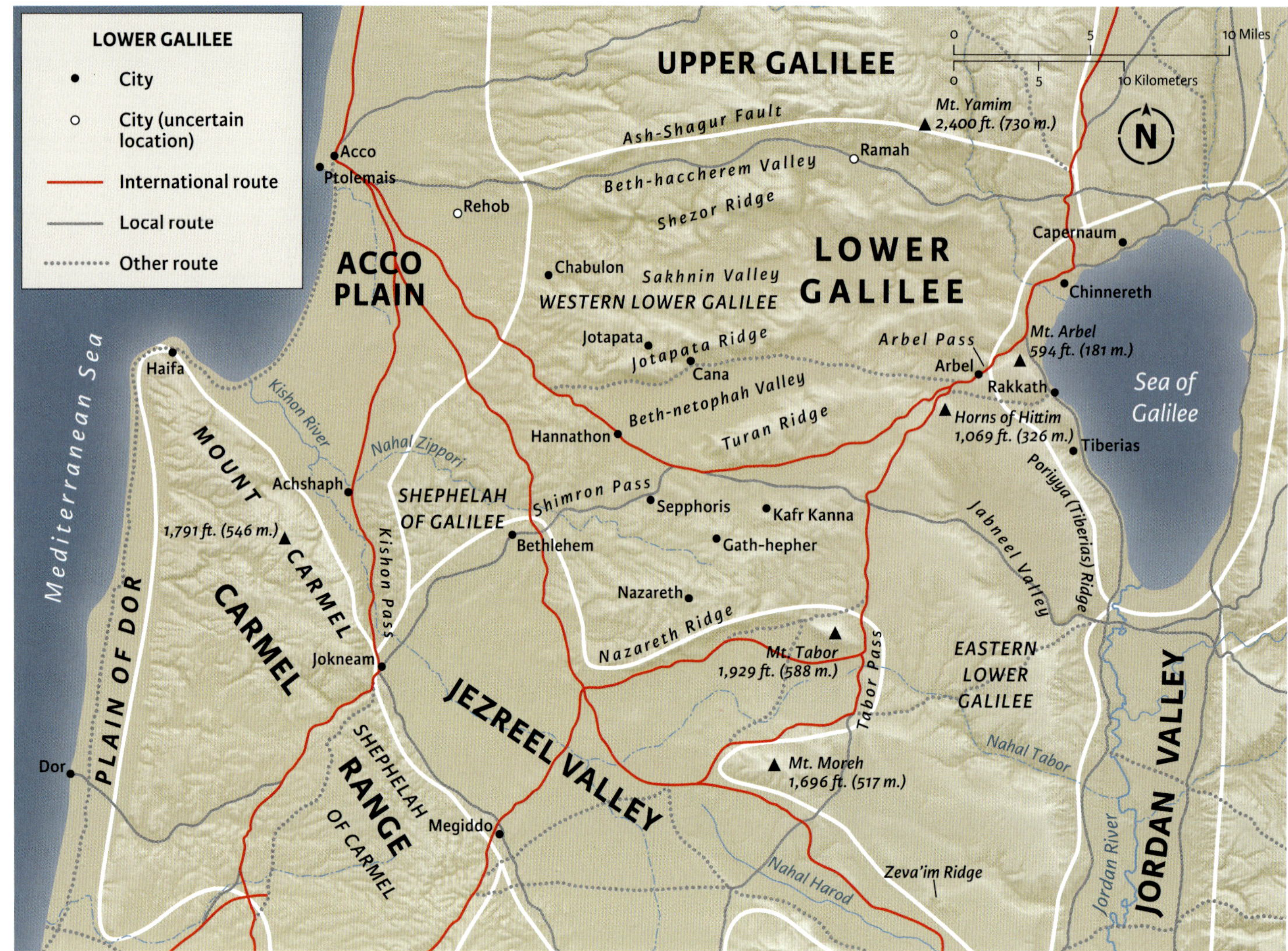

contrast, though, it was subsequently shattered by an intricate mesh of fault lines, mostly running east-west, which sculpted its up-and-down forms. Because the overall elevation of Galilee rises toward Lebanon, the crest of each of these ridges is higher than the one to its immediate south. Adding to the geological drama, the ridges of Western Lower Galilee were also shoved by tectonic pressure from the north, causing them to have sharp southern faces but relatively gentle northern slopes. Moreover, each is naturally highest on its eastern end where it attaches to the watershed, tapering gradually westward toward the sea. The result is a kind of tipped stair-step look that carries our view toward heights of Upper Galilee, while at the same time allowing sideways glances to the Mediterranean and Sea of Galilee.

The ridges and valleys of Western Lower Galilee offer wonderful conditions for secure agricultural village life.[1] With an agreeable climate, twenty-five inches (635 mm) of rainfall annually on average, ample springs, seasonal pools of water, rich alluvial soil, and delightful views throughout, Western Lower Galilee offers a mix of resources that fosters pleasant living. The region is especially noted for its wide fields of grain and groves of olive trees. When Josephus boasted of Galilee's fertility (*War* iii.42–43, quoted above), he had in mind the heartland of the political district that was called Galilee during the time of the New Testament.

Of the ridge-valley sequences that comprise Western Lower Galilee, the most important is the Nazareth Ridge and Beth-netophah Valley to its north. The southern, sharp face of the Nazareth Ridge—the edge facing the Jezreel Valley—is composed of hard Cenomanian-Turonian limestone. Its top and northern slopes are a mixture of softer Eocene limestone and Senonian chalk. The crest of the Nazareth Ridge has eroded into typical chalky forms, with an elongated basin. There, in the first century AD, the houses of the unpretentious village of Nazareth clustered around a small spring. With fertile though chalky rendzina soils, relatively soft natural building material, a water supply that was adequate but not particularly plentiful, and a bottom-of-the-bowl-though-on-top-of-the-ridge horizon line, the inhabitants of ancient Nazareth were never going to get rich on the resources at hand. The economic bases in the better connected Jezreel and Beth-netophah Valleys down slope were far superior. By comparison, residents of towns and cities in these advantaged valleys, such as Nathanael of Cana, understandably fostered the backwater stigma, "*Can* anything *good come out of Nazareth?*" (John 1:46, emphasis added;

1 B. Golomb and Y. Kedar, "Ancient Agriculture in the Galilee Mountains," *IEJ* 21 (1971): 136–40.

21:2).[1] It should be noted that the situation today, by which Nazareth has become the largest urban center in the Galilee hills, owes much to the city's historical associations as a pilgrimage site and little to its intrinsic geographical setting.

In contrast, the broad, gently angled northern slopes of the Nazareth Ridge lay open and inviting. With towns like Gath-hepher, home of the nationalistic prophet Jonah (2 Kgs 14:25), and Sepphoris, the first Herodian capital of the Roman district of Galilee, nestled among its folds, these Beth-netophah-oriented slopes have always been the preferred location for prosperous cities and villages in the region.

The Beth-netophah Valley cradles the largest expanse of well-watered soil in the interior of Western Lower Galilee. The name is appropriate—it means "drippings": of water, dew, honey, or the juice of ripe fruit. The eastern end of the valley is split by the sudden rise of the Turan Ridge, leaving a broad arm to the north and a narrower twin, pinched by the Nazareth Ridge, to the south. Historically, this southern arm of the Beth-netophah Valley has carried the preferred track of the Acco/Ptolemais–Tiberias highway (modern Highway 79 and a portion of Highway 77). The large tell of ancient Hannathon (Tell el-Bedawiya) dominates the valley's wetter, western end (Josh 19:14; *EA* 8, 245); its role in Canaanite and Israelite history is not well documented but must have been significant if geographical factors alone are any indication. Along the midpoint of the northern edge of the Beth-netophah Valley stands the rocky mound of Khirbet Qanah, certainly the Cana of Galilee visited by both Jesus and Josephus (John 2:1,11; 4:46; 21:2; *Life*, 86). Recent historical and archaeological evidence suggests Cana was home to a prosperous community of religiously minded Jews in the first century AD, and that the city should perhaps be seen as a Jewish counterpoint to the vibrant and more Hellenized city of Sepphoris within sight on the opposite edge of the valley.[2]

"Tenacious yet productive" is a good description of Western Lower Galilee. The words define the covering of terra rosa soil that has been painstakingly collected into hundreds of narrow basins scattered among the area's ridges and hills over the centuries. They speak of gnarled olive trees whose roots are wrapped around a never-ending scattering of surface rock. And they describe the generations of peasant farmers who love the soil and have expended enormous efforts in wresting a good life from the land.

1 Paul H. Wright, "The Size and Makeup of Nazareth at the Time of Jesus," in *Lexham Geographic Commentary on the Gospels*, ed. Barry J. Beitzel (Bellingham, WA: Lexham, 2017), 30–41.

2 Peter Richardson, *Building Jewish in the Roman East* (Waco: Baylor University Press, 2004), 55–71, 81, 91–107.

"Listen! Consider the sower who went out to sow" (Mark 4:3). Figuratively speaking, Jesus's hearers had their ears to the ground, which in their case was the fertile soil of Lower Galilee. Here a proud farmer walks his windrows of winter wheat under a bright late-April sky, providing a visual witness that the Beth-netophah Valley between Nazareth and Cana still speaks the language of parables. The gentle northern slope of the Nazareth Ridge rises in the distance.

In the process of matching events with X's on the ground, early church traditions tended to lock memories in place by collecting events that were historically or theologically related, then collapsing them to a single site, or a close confluence of sites, in the vicinity. The result was the development of devotional itineraries by which pilgrims could make day trips by foot from places like Jerusalem and Nazareth to the believed location of various events related to the life of Jesus. In this way Cana of Galilee became associated with the Byzantine, medieval, and modern Arab city of Kafr Kanna, an hour's walk from Nazareth, rather than its actual location at Khirbet Qanah, a five- to six-hour walk on the opposite side of the Beth-netophah Valley. The location of the Transfiguration was similarly moved from its likely location on the slopes of Mount Hermon to Mount Tabor (Matt 17:1–9; cp. 16:13), making it a Nazareth-oriented event as well.

The entire floor of the Beth-netophah Valley drains through the upper end of the Shimron Pass (the Valley of Iphtah-el; Josh 19:14,27). But rather than flowing all the way through the pass and out into the Jezreel Valley, the water course, here called Nahal Zippori (Wadi el-Melek), veers directly west, slicing a narrow, rocky gorge laterally through the Eocene limestone that edges Western Lower Galilee. Its run drops 450 feet (137 m) in ten miles (16 km) before joining the Kishon River out on the Acco Plain for a final sluggish push to the sea. The Beth-netophah Valley's drain-exit is tight enough to restrict the valley's runoff; historically, seasonal swamps typically formed behind the pinch-point. We might imagine that nearby Tell el-Bedawiya, "Mound of the Lady Bedouin," was a camping spot for tented herders seeking reliable seasonal water sources for their flocks of sheep and goats. In the mid-twentieth century, Israel's National Water Company, *Mekorot*, transformed the area into two large purification and sedimentation reservoirs which, as part of the National Water Carrier, provide drinking water channeled from the Sea of Galilee for the rest of the country.

The alternating series of ridges and valleys north of the Beth-netophah Valley carries a more isolated

Initial plans drawn up during the years of the British Mandate for what would become Israel's National Water Carrier called for the headwaters of the Jordan River to be diverted into a mammoth reservoir in the Beth-netophah Valley. This would have caused the level of the Sea of Galilee to drop dramatically, an unwelcome change accompanied by a sharp rise in its salinity. These preliminary plans were scrapped for several reasons, the most important of which were cost related. In any case, it was found that the Cenomanian-Turonian bedrock along the edges of the Beth-netophah Valley is so porous that much of the diverted water would have leaked into the ground and been lost, and it was deemed impractical to seal all of the cracks with concrete. The idea that the Sea of Galilee had to be protected because of its historical associations played little role in the discussion.[1]

feel. From south to north, these are the Jotapata Ridge (above Khirbet Qanah/Cana of Galilee), the Sakhnin Valley, the Shezor Ridge, and—in the *ash-Shagur* fault bordering Upper Galilee—the high and picturesque Beth-haccherem Valley. All share a typical hard limestone hill country look characterized by terraced slopes and tight ridgelines. All also drain through a narrow opening on their western end. Historically, each of these parallel valleys has tended to function somewhat independently from the others, with the best natural lines of communication following the direction of the topography east-west rather than cutting up and over the ridges, south to north. Indeed, in his description of Galilee Josephus notes that "Lower Galilee extends *in length* from Tiberias to Chabulon which is not far from Ptolemais on the coast" (*War* 3.38). This is an indication that in the first-century orientation of its human geography, Galilee looked east-west, from sea to shining sea, not north-south as modern compass directions might prefer.

The western end of the Nazareth Ridge and the hills separating the Beth-netophah Valley from the Acco Plain stand somewhat apart from the rest of Western Lower Galilee in that they are composed of softer Eocene limestone and hence carry the look of a Shephelah. Indeed, this **Shephelah of Galilee** is a continuation of the Shephelah of Carmel to the south, though separated from it by the western end of the Jezreel Valley. Its hard nari surface, given over to a rather dense covering of scrub oak forests, hindered easy settlement prior to modern times. Even though the Shephelah of Galilee provides gentle slopes that in principle might be used to facilitate travel onto the Nazareth Ridge from the west, natural routes tended to avoid the region. All of this made the Shephelah of Galilee more an area of refuge than permanent settlement in the historic past.

Traffic into the Beth-netophah Valley from the coast instead tended to follow two natural passes. One is the Shimron Pass carrying traffic to Hannathon and Sepphoris via the Jezreel Valley, passing Bethlehem of Zebulun (Josh 19:15) on the way. (A portion of the route is followed by modern Highway 77.) A more direct route connecting Acco/Ptolemais with both Hannathon and Sepphoris follows a shallow pass of eroded Senonian chalk at the valley's northwestern corner (modern Highway 79). These natural routes join (as Highway 77) in the vicinity of Sepphoris, directing traffic through the southern arm of the Beth-netophah Valley eastward, toward the Sea of Galilee. Largely for this reason, the heartland of Western Lower Galilee has always been pierced by international priorities, merging circumference with center like spokes on a wheel.

The Beth-netophah Valley, together with the Nazareth, Turan, and Jotapata Ridges that define its perimeter, formed the heartland of the tribal territory of Zebulun during the Iron Age (Josh 19:10–16). The tribe of Naphtali was given the ridges and valleys of Western Lower Galilee that lay to the north, as well as a large part of Upper Galilee beyond that (Josh 19:32–39). In a theme common to ancient Israel's settlement process, the people of Zebulun had trouble settling the

A dirt path carries the line of the Israel Trail through the hard limestone folds of Western Lower Galilee. Mount Mitzpe Yamim, at 2,400 feet (734 m), one of the hills bordering Upper Galilee, rises in the distance. The mount is aptly named "Lookout of the Seas": from its summit, the Mediterranean and Sea of Galilee are both visible on a clear day. This is the far northeastern corner of Western Lower Galilee, east of the Beth-haccherem Valley, where the topography becomes particularly jumbled and tight. These northeastern regions belonged to the tribe of Naphtali, *"a doe set free that bears beautiful fawns"* (Gen 49:21).

Josephus described the geographical situation of Jotapata, a fortified town on the Jotapata Ridge above Cana, this way:

"Jotapata is almost entirely built on precipitous cliffs, being surrounded on three sides by ravines so deep that sight fails in the attempt to fathom the abyss. On the north side alone, where the town has straggled sideways up a descending spur of the mountains, it is accessible. . . . Concealed by other mountains surrounding it, the town was quite invisible until one came right up to it" (*War* iii.158–60).

Jotapata was the location of Josephus's last stand as general of the Jewish forces in Galilee during the Great Revolt against Rome in the summer of AD 67. While his role as defending general required that he portray the site as virtually impregnable to his Roman audience for whom his book *Wars of the Jews* was written, Josephus's words, though exaggerated, still fairly represent the tight living spaces within the northern ridges and valleys of Western Lower Galilee.

1 Yehuda Karmon, *Israel: A Regional Geography* (London: Wiley-Interscience, 1971), 122–23.

Beth-netophah Valley floor due to a strong Canaanite presence there (Judg 1:30). Eventually they managed to put down roots and become well-connected to the comings and goings in the area. Moses's short blessing to the tribe of Zebulun, though poetic, is geographically instructive: "*Rejoice, Zebulun, in your journeys* [lit. 'in your going out']" (Deut 33:18).

The most significant characteristic of Western Lower Galilee in terms of its historical geography is its openness to traffic due to the east-west corridors formed by its sequence of valleys. The region offered a certain protectiveness that was lacking in the wide open Jezreel Valley or out on the Acco Plain, yet was easily connected to them. Indeed, because the Phoenicians on Zebulun's northwestern flank maintained *de facto* control over the Acco Plain throughout much of the biblical period, it is helpful to view the western slopes of the land of Zebulun (the Shephelah of Galilee) as a kind of inland port or gateway for maritime trade entering Israel. This role may lie behind the otherwise geographically odd description of Zebulun in Genesis 49:13: "*Zebulun will live by the seashore and will be a harbor for ships, and his territory will be next to Sidon.*"

It is interesting, and perhaps telling, that the description of the land-locked tribal inheritance of Zebulun emphasized its role as a harbor, while the related blessings of Asher, the tribe that actually did touch the coast, spoke instead of its agricultural produce, specifically olive oil (cp. Deut 33:24). Rather than arguing that these two blessings were somehow switched or mixed up by the author of Genesis and Deuteronomy, we must consider that they both represent the tug between promise and reality that Israel faced on its frontier. Knowing that the harbors of the Acco Plain lay outside Israel's natural reach, the biblical writers chose instead to emphasize the benefits of the territory of Asher that were most consistent with Israel's own subsistence base, namely olive oil. At the same time, they recognized the need for Israel to participate in the seaward economy of their successful maritime neighbors, but from the safety of the inland corridors of Zebulun. In any case, the people who were able to make their home within the tribal inheritance of Zebulun had the double advantage of protection and connection. This, as will be seen, provided a setting for the early chapters of the gospel story that was at the very least evocative of great opportunities that would later arise in the Mediterranean world on behalf of the kingdom of God.

The biblical account is otherwise essentially silent on subsequent events in Zebulun save for allusions to the requisite litany of invasions that poured through Galilee from the north (e.g., 1 Kgs 15:20; 2 Kgs 15:29). The attack route of Assyrian King Tiglath-pileser III in the eighth century BC cut through the Beth-netophah Valley, the heart of Western Lower Galilee, then dropped to Megiddo.[1] This seems to have been a deliberate line of march. In taking the Beth-netophah Valley, the Assyrians were able to establish a solid foothold in Galilee while avoiding initial confrontations on the corridor through which Egypt historically had penetrated the land, namely the line of march through the Tabor Pass. When all of Lower Galilee subsequently became part of the Assyrian province of Megiddo, Assyrians were able to consolidate their gains before continuing southward to challenge Egypt directly. The region's short history under Israelite control took a long hiatus until the rise of the Maccabean (Hasmonean) kingdom nearly six hundred years later.

Like Western Lower Galilee, the surface topography of **Eastern Lower Galilee** is defined by a stack of four parallel ridges and their intervening valleys, but in every other way is a negative image of its western counterpart. The region is a down-warped zone of Eocene limestone, the long and narrow continuation of the hills of Central Manasseh though severed from them by the Harod Valley. Geologically, both Eastern Lower Galilee and Central Manasseh are an extension of the Eocene hills that we first saw as the Shephelah of Judah. This entire band of Eocene runs on a SSW-NNE line following the direction of the coast, and in Eastern Lower Galilee sideswipes then crashes into the Rift Valley and the Sea of Galilee. Or, since the deposition of the limestone preceded the formation of the Rift Valley in geological time, it is more accurate to say that here the rift ripped the end off of the Eocene hills. Then, in doing so, it released volcanic pressure from deep beneath the surface of the earth that covered the Eocene with a thick layer of basalt. At the same time, stress from the formation of the rift tore a number of side-faults into Eastern Lower Galilee on the same northwestern angle as the Carmel Range. Tectonic pressure from the southwest, rather than from the north as in Western Lower Galilee, caused the sharper edges of the ridges of Eastern Lower Galilee to face northeast, toward the Sea of Galilee. (The ridges themselves run on a northwest-southeast line.) The result is an angled, basalt region that tips toward the Rift Valley. Protrusions of Eocene and other soft limestones can be seen around the perimeter, such as at the cliffs of Arbel, atop Mount Moreh, and in the wide cut of the Tabor Wadi that dissects the region's midsection.

The leveling effect of basalt on the softer underlying Eocene limestone has created a region significantly smoother in appearance than is Western Lower Galilee. Its high point, Mount Moreh (1,690 ft/515 m), hangs on the western end of the Zeva'im Ridge, the otherwise low northern edge of the Harod Valley. The only other easily distinguished feature of Eastern Lower Galilee is the Horns of Hittim (Hb *Qarne Hittim*; sometimes spelled in Aramaic, *Hittin*, or even *Hattin*), the eroded cone of a long-extinct volcano above Tiberias that marks the northern edge of the basalt expanse. Extending southeastward from the Horns of Hittim, the Poriyya (or, Tiberias) Ridge lines the southwestern edge of the Sea of Galilee; its long, level face standing proudly over the waters. The beautiful Yabneel Valley hides behind (southwest), cradling a wide expanse of alluvial soil. Its floor scoops down to 250 feet (76 m) below sea level (nearly the depth of California's Death Valley), but because it cuts into a sizeable underground water table, the valley offers the best agricultural conditions of the entire region. Everywhere else the black basaltic soil of Eastern Lower Galilee is rocky and relatively difficult to cultivate. With higher air and soil temperatures than Western Lower Galilee and rainfall that is highly

1 Anson F. Rainey and R. Steven Notley, *The Sacred Bridge*, 231.

irregular, everything here has a rather burned-off look much of the year. Local Arabs call it *Bilad al-Hawa*, "the windy lands."

Natural communication lines within Eastern Lower Galilee follow the same northwest-southeast direction as its valleys and ridges, parallel to the Harod Valley and the southwestern angle of the Sea of Galilee. The steepness of the Poriyya slope cuts off natural communication with the sea, and although connections with the Harod and Jezreel Valleys are gradual and therefore promising for traffic, the barren landscape and unpredictable climate of Eastern Lower Galilee did nothing to attract permanent and useful settlement from that direction until modern times.

Indeed, archaeological evidence suggests that the entire area of Eastern Lower Galilee was largely empty prior to ancient Israel's settlement in the land. It appears that even the tribe of Issachar, given the southern and central part of the region in the narrative of the book of Joshua (19:17–23),[1] wasn't able to put down permanent roots until the rise of the united monarchy in the tenth century BC.[2] Language in the blessings of Jacob ("*Issachar is a strong donkey*"; Gen 49:14) and Moses ("*Rejoice . . . Issachar, in your tents*"; Deut 33:18) reflects the arduous task of gaining a foothold in the region. The whole was, rather, better suited as an area of refuge where Heber the Kenite found a campsite far from his tribal home and to which Jotham fled from the bloody hands of Abimelech his brother (Judg 4:11; 9:21)—or a place out of which tenacious fighters arose (cp. Judg 5:15; 1 Kgs 15:27; 1 Chr 7:5).

The cut of the Tabor Wadi drains the interior of Eastern Lower Galilee southeastward, toward the Rift Valley. The narrow, eastern end of Mount Tabor is perched at the wadi's upper end (center, in the distance). Here the water flow has cut through the region's basalt covering and into the softer Eocene limestone below, creating a surface topography that is more relaxed than the steep, rugged slopes of Western Lower Galilee's Cenomanian highlands on the other side of Mount Tabor. Due to its rocky basalt covering, the region has always had a low population density and the open feel of grazing land. This is the burnt view of mid-summer.

1 The fertile Jabneel Valley fell to the tribe of Naphtali (Josh 19:32–33).

2 Zvi Gal, "The Settlement of Issachar: Some New Observations," *TA* 9 (1982): 79–86.

A healthy crop of young wheat fills the Jabneel Valley beneath the Horns of Hittim, the most fertile area of Eastern Lower Galilee. Hittim's "horns" are the now rounded, raised edges of the rim of a volcanic cone, long extinct, at the northern end of the valley (center, back). Its ancient lava flow eventually broke down into the rich black basaltic soil that covers the valley's sloping floor. Hittim, appropriately, means "wheat" in Hebrew, the rich staple of the region. (Hittin, the historic name of the nearby Arab village, is "wheat" in Aramaic; cp. Ezek 4:9.) The view is in January, when rain and moderate temperatures maximize growth.

Wedged in the seam between Western and Eastern Lower Galilee is a trough of Senonian chalk that traces a northeastward line connecting Mount Tabor with the Huleh Basin. This trough marks the hinge joining the two subregions of Lower Galilee. From it the Cenomanian-Turonian ridges of Western Lower Galilee run straight west, while the Basalt-covered Eocene ridges of Eastern Lower Galilee angle down and away toward the southeast. The watershed lies just off the seam to the west. The trough carried the historic route of the international highway from the Jezreel Valley to Hazor, serving as Israel's all-important corridor to or from the north; it is essentially the route of modern Highway 65 today. An important spur, also international in character, angled eastward from this chalk trough past the Horns of Hittim, then either dropped into the Arbel Pass on the way to the northern end of the Sea of Galilee or ran the sloped plain just south of Arbel to Rakkath just north of Tiberias. The juncture of modern Highways 65 and 77, the so-named "Golani Junction,"[1] is where the Acco/Ptolemais–Tiberias international route crosses the Megiddo–Hazor international route. We might think that a major city would have sprung up here, but neither in ancient times nor today was that the case. Still, the empires of the ancient Near East all passed this way, within eyesight of places that by the first century AD would become the towns of Nazareth and Capernaum. In doing so, they forced the inhabitants of an otherwise geographically diverse land to recognize its natural demographic diversity as well.

The interior ridges and valleys of Lower Galilee thus had a natural connection to the priorities of the larg-

1 All of the major highway junctions in the modern State of Israel have names that serve as direction points for travelers. The names come from nearby towns, historic personages, natural features, military units (e.g., "Golani"), or other items noteworthy to modern Israeli society.

er world that lay on its perimeter. This was especially evident during the time of the New Testament, when cities such as Ptolemais, Sepphoris, and Tiberias carried a decidedly Greco-Roman stamp. It was, indeed, this west-east route through the Beth-netophah Valley that became one of the busier corridors of Hellenism in the southern Levant. The Shimron and Tabor passes, with links southward into the Jezreel Valley, provided international options for those living in Lower Galilee, but also led directly to the Manasseh hills. This fact on the ground reminded everyone that for all of its "*of the nations*" (Isa 9:1) character, Galilee also maintained a natural connection to the heartland of ancient Israel. The region was well connected: Jesus often spoke of wealthy, though sometimes absentee, landowners and people going off on business journeys (Matt 21:33–46; 25:14–30; cp. Deut 33:18). Yet there were always enough small villages tucked into the fractured folds of Lower Galilee to foster a conservative partisanship that was as tenacious as the gnarled olive trees clinging to its stubborn ridgelines. That virtually no Old Testament-era events are recorded as having taken place on the hills of Lower Galilee—events of note can instead be traced in the circle of the valleys on its circumference—does nothing to erase the reality of the region's native roots.

But the narrative line that Lower Galilee lacked in the Old Testament was more than compensated for in the Gospels and the works of Josephus. By the end of the first century BC, Galilee had coalesced into a main center of Jewish settlement, rivaling Judea in its economic base if not intellectual energy. Galilee's economy was given a sharp boost by Rome's penetration to the wheat fields of Bashan and to the imperial highways in Transjordan via the corridors of the Jezreel and Beth-netophah Valleys. The entire region had become an important eastern terminus for the emerging Mediterranean world by the end of the first century AD. This both prompted, and was prompted by, the international shift in demographics and world markets from a Levantine line that had been oriented primarily north-south during the Bronze and Iron Ages, to one that now ran basically east-west, to and from Rome. Locally, Sepphoris, for instance, just downslope from Nazareth, was a vibrant city that combined elements of traditional Jewish life with Hellenistic and Roman culture during, and especially following, the time of the New Testament. By the first century AD, "Galilee" had become a technical term for the political district governed by Antipas, son of Herod the Great, which enclosed the hills of Lower Galilee. It is largely in this sense that the name appears in the Gospels (Luke 3:1; cp. Matt 2:22; 3:13; 4:23; Mark 3:7–8; Luke 23:6; John 4:3; Josephus, *Ant.* 17.188; *War* 3.35–39). It was, on the whole, a stimulating environment in which Jesus began to preach news about the emergent kingdom of God (Luke 4:14–15).

Throughout the time of the New Testament, the hills and dales of Lower Galilee, well suited to a small-village, peasant lifestyle, were never far from corridors of Hellenism that leapt out of the circle of the Jezreel Valley and Acco Plain and into their profitable center. The fields and villages of Lower Galilee were full of an earthy reality that lent itself to the imagery of parables. Although the timelessness of the genre doesn't allow us to pinpoint the exact location where any of Jesus's parables might first have been spoken, all continue to resonate with those whose feet have pressed Galilee's promising sod (cp. Matt 13:1–53; 21:28–32; 22:1–14; Luke 15:1–16:31). The focus of Jesus's earliest ministry lay on the circuit between Nazareth and Cana, then spread northward and east, toward Capernaum (Matt 4:12–13; Luke 4:14–21; John 2:1–12). The prophet Isaiah had foreseen that "*the gloom of the distressed land . . . of Zebulun and . . . Naphtali*," its inhabitants being figurative road-kill on the imperial routes running right through, would someday see "*a great light*" (Isa 9:1–2). His words were not lost on Matthew, for whom Jesus embraced the past, present, and future of the land of Galilee (Matt 4:12–17).

"Observe how the wildflowers of the field grow: They don't labor or spin thread. Yet I tell you that not even Solomon in all his splendor was adorned like one of these" (Matt 6:28–29). King Solomon was all about tapping the international markets of his day, either through the Acco Plain to the rim of the Mediterranean Sea, or by way of the Negev to Egypt and the land of Sheba (1 Kgs 9:26–28; 10:21–29). Such things circled around: Jesus reminded his hearers that greater beauty lay right at home.

D. UPPER GALILEE

The land of ancient Israel finds its natural northern limit in the majestic heights of Upper Galilee. Here the hills really begin to soar, eventually blending into the long line of snowcapped mountains that form the Lebanese Range. As a place name, Galilee is mentioned only six times in the Old Testament—usually in association with sites in Upper Galilee (Josh 20:7; 21:32; 1 Kgs 9:11; 2 Kgs 15:29; 1 Chr 6:76; cp. Isa 9:1)—but the name Lebanon, also a geographical term, occurs frequently. Lebanon means "the whitest one," surely in reference to the snow-capped mountains of the far north, and it is this association that gave Upper Galilee its identity of freshness and majesty. It is a place most invigorated by the moistured blessings of God.

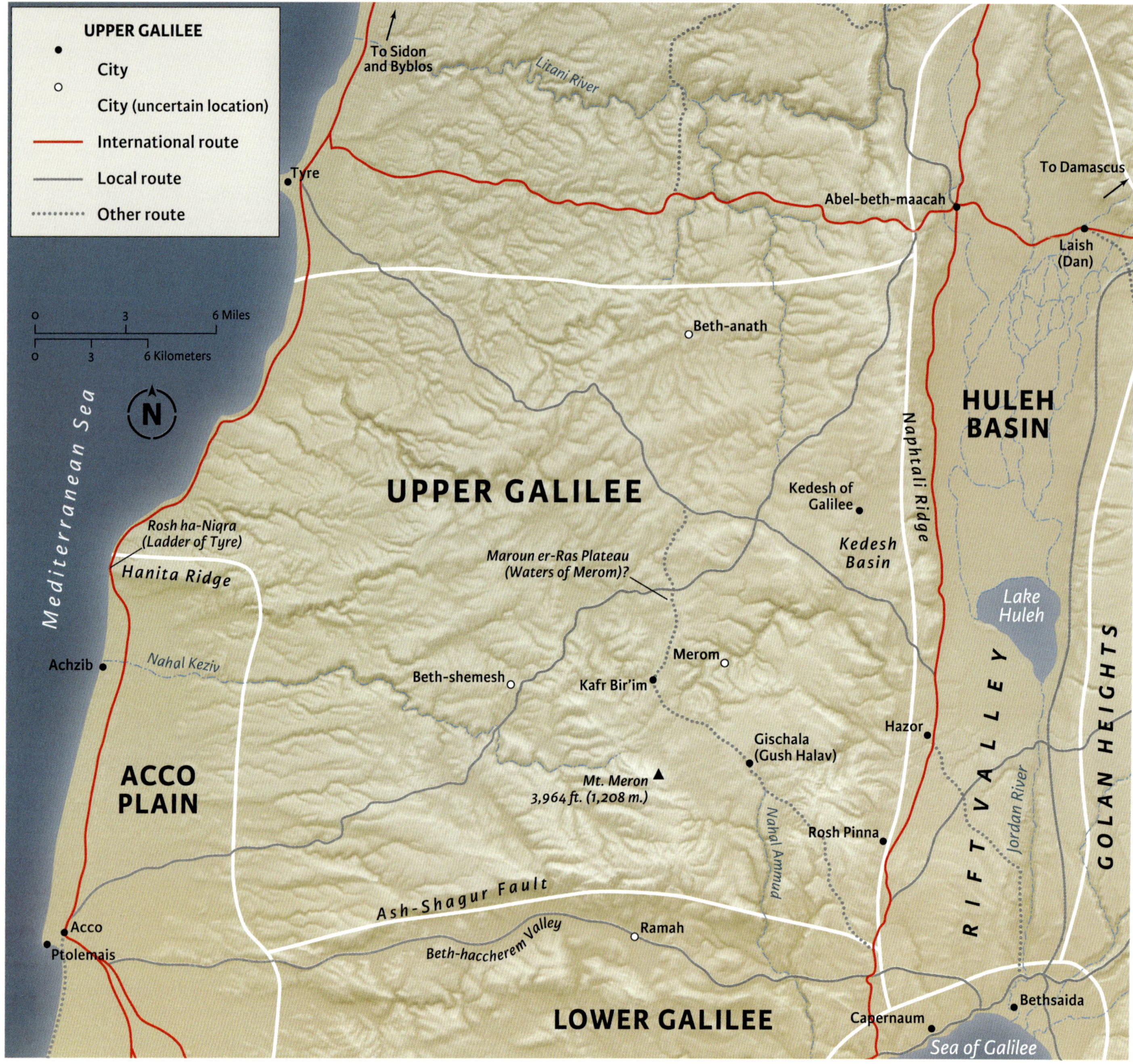

Geographically, the region of Upper Galilee can be easily defined on its eastern, southern, and western sides. On the east, the straight-backed Naphtali Ridge drops 2,600 feet (790 m) into the Huleh Basin, which is the extension of the Rift Valley north of the Sea of Galilee. To the south, Upper Galilee's natural limit is the steep scarp that rises 1,500 feet (460 m) out of Lower Galilee's Beth-haccherem Valley, the dramatic northern face of the *ash-Shagur* fault. The modern Israeli town located at the right angle where the Naphtali Ridge meets the *ash-Shagur* fault is called Rosh Pinna, "head of the corner" or "*cornerstone*" (Ps 118:22). Upper Galilee's western limits are also quite clear: the northern Acco Plain and, north of Rosh ha-Niqra, the Mediterranean Sea itself.

But the northern border of Upper Galilee is more difficult to mark. The dramatic gorge of the Litani River, which cleaves the comparatively lower mountains of Galilee from the towering Lebanese heights beyond, is a clear topographical marker. In the fourth century AD, Eusebuis noted that the ridge marking the southern line of the Litani was "the boundary of Judaea,"[1] an interesting observation in that Tyre, a place universally recognized as Phoenician in all ancient sources, lies south of the Litani. The gorge of the Litani also was the northern limit of the work of the Survey of Western Palestine. On the other hand, the Babylonian Talmud, preserving a memory roughly contemporary with Eusebius, stated that the northern boundary of the land of Israel was the Ladder of Tyre (Rosh ha-Niqra).[2]

1 *Onomasticon* 76:6; Freeman-Grenville, Chapman, and Taylor, *The Onomasticon by Eusebius*, 46.

2 *Babylonian Talmud*, Eruvim, 22b.

In the Bible and ancient texts, the place name Lebanon usually occurs with the definite article, i.e., "the Lebanon," literally "the whitest one." The name refers to the forested, snow-capped mountain range that runs along the Mediterranean Sea for one hundred miles north of Galilee (Josh 9:1; Judg 3:3). The hills of Upper Galilee form Mount Lebanon's lower, southern end. North of the Litani River, where the range is higher, the peaks reach 10,000 feet (3,050 m). Today, the word *Lebanon* is a political name that designates a country that lies within borders that approximate the ancient geographical term. The political names for some of the people groups who inhabited Mount Lebanon during the biblical period—or, more properly its narrow Mediterranean coast—include Tyre, Sidon, and, more generally, both Canaan and Phoenicia (Gen 10:19; Josh 13:4,6; Judg 3:3; 1 Kgs 5:6; Ps 83:7; Mark 3:8; Luke 6:17; Acts 11:19).

The current international border between Israel and Lebanon, which follows the top of the Hanita Ridge from Rosh ha-Niqra eastward and then snakes its way from hill to dale toward the Huleh Basin, essentially mirrors this line—though it owes its presence more to the random vagaries of a modern cease-fire line than geopolitical precedent. A third option finds the natural northern limit of Upper Galilee to be the point where Galilee's Cenomanian-Turonian limestone mass gives way to softer Senonian and Eocene forms, approximately midway between Rosh ha-Niqra and Tyre. This line approximates the northernmost settlement of the tribe of Naphtali (Josh 19:32–38), though it lay significantly beyond the border of the political district of Galilee in the time of the New Testament.[1] Marking the northern extent of Upper Galilee on geological rather than strict topological grounds has the advantage of following the principle that contiguous zones of limestone within the land of ancient Israel tended to develop cohesive identities as settlement areas which transcended the specific details of any given period of history. It also supports the notion that Upper Galilee—and indeed all of Galilee down to the Jezreel Valley—was by nature more closely associated with the mountains of Lebanon than the hills of Manasseh.

In any case, it is only the western two-thirds of Upper Galilee that is actually an upwarped block of Cenomanian-Turonian limestone; the eastern third is a syncline of Eocene that extends up into Lebanon. This Cenomanian-Turonian block is the most rugged part of the region, and some of its highest points are thrust even further upward due to seismic activity and faulting. Several of the mountains in this part of Upper Galilee reach more than 3,500 feet (1,066 m), with the summit of Mount Meron (lit. "Mount Peak"), 3,964 feet (1,208 m) above sea level, being the highest point in the modern State of Israel west of the Rift Valley.

Mount Meron dominates the southeastern quadrant of Upper Galilee; from its height, the entire Cenomanian-Turonian limestone block tips toward the northwest. Rugged wadis flow off Mount Meron in every direction. Most notable are Nahal Keziv, which heads northwest and then west to Achzib on the coast, and Nahal Ammud, flowing the opposite direction, southeastward into the Sea of Galilee. Both of these defiles are made all the more dramatic by a tangled maze of fault lines that radiate around Mount Meron. The slope to the west is more gradual, with fault lines conspiring to form a number of tight ridge lines pointing toward the Acco Plain. On one, above Nahal Keziv, Crusader lords built the strong Monfort castle in the twelfth century AD, a sentinel holding the westward defiles for the Latin Kingdom of Jerusalem. The drop southeastward through the Ammud canyon is shorter but more rugged, with sheer canyon walls lining parts of the wadi. Both wadis are typical of an Upper Galilee surface topography that is highly dissected, with abrupt peaks, gorges, basins, canyons, and rushing streams.

The eastern third of Upper Galilee is a down-warped syncline of softer Eocene limestone. This is the geological extension of Eastern Lower Galilee and Central Manasseh, though bent back from its otherwise north-northeastward line. Harder Cenomanian-Turonian limestone again appears along its easternmost edge (the Naphtali Ridge), with a thin band of Senonian chalk running the seam between. Because this part of Upper Galilee is only nine miles (14 km) wide, the drop from the Meron highlands into the Rift Valley, especially down the cascade of the Naphtali Ridge, is quite abrupt.

The softer forms of the Eocene limestone and Senonian chalk portions of Upper Galilee have eroded into a series of three plateaus east of Mount Meron. Heading

Winter rain clouds blow over the hills of Upper Galilee, a visible reminder of the rule of rainfall that north, west, and high are wet. Upper Galilee has in abundance what most of the rest of the land of ancient Israel lacked: a nearly always predictable supply of rainwater and even snow, and, as a result, a hedge against famine. Ancient Israel's political and cultural control seldom reached into Lebanon beyond, where Baal and Asherah, the old-time Canaanite fertility deities, continued to roam, as it were, at will. Upper Galilee, within Israel's fold, was a constant reminder of a greater reality: that the *"land of mountains and valleys, watered by rain from the sky"* was *"a land the LORD your God cares for"* (Deut 11:11–12)—and that, by itself, was enough.

1 Josephus (*War* 3.39-40) notes that Upper Galilee ended at the village of Baca (probably modern Peqiin), "the frontier of Tyrian territory."

It's tight going for these intrepid hikers in the Upper Ammud canyon, where everything is either up, down, or sideways. It is terrain like this that tends to separate villages in Upper Galilee from each other, and everything from wheeled traffic seeking to stick to imperial through-routes elsewhere in the land of ancient Israel. Such are the *"side roads"* (lit. "roundabout" or "really crooked" paths) of the Song of Deborah (Judg 5:6) that Israel used in order to avoid the chariot forces of Jabin king of Hazor during the time of the judges. The fight to clean out Jabin's men was eventually taken by Deborah and her general Barak into the circle of the Jezreel Valley; partisans from Naphtali joined *"on the heights (*merom*) of the battlefield"* (Judg 5:18), thus relieving Canaanite pressure on their tribal homeland core.

eastward, each is lower than the next, and all provide pleasant, self-contained places for settlement. Of these, the best defined is the easternmost, the alluvial Kedesh Basin, where one of the three cities of refuge west of the Jordan River was located (Josh 20:7; 21:32; 1 Chr 6:76).

Upper Galilee proves the rule of thumb for rainfall in the land of ancient Israel: north, west, and high are wet. Annual rainfall amounts exceed twenty-eight inches (710 mm) on every slope facing the Mediterranean, with up to forty inches (1,016 mm) at the higher elevations and a decrease to only twenty-four inches (610 mm)—equal to the rainfall of Jerusalem—in the drier east. Snow falls on Mount Meron nearly every year. Upper Galilee's hard limestone core, nearly as rugged underground as above, is filled with karstic (water dissolution) chambers, caves, sinkholes, chimneys, seepage channels, and the like, many holding reservoirs of fresh, cool water. Springs of living water are plentiful wherever these aquifers are exposed by the jagged surface above. Some streams, like Nahal Ammud, are perennial, and it is not unusual to find surface ponds tucked among the crevices of the Upper Galilee hills that hold water throughout the year. But while water resources are plentiful in Upper Galilee, broad expanses of soil suitable for agriculture are not, except among the softer topographical forms in the east. It is here that the larger villages have tended to congregate. The bulk of the region was covered with a dense natural blanket of Mediterranean scrub forest (*maquis*) well into the Iron Age, the time of the Israelite monarchy. By the first century, these forests gradually had been cleared so that many of the hillsides and narrow wadi bottoms were able to be cultivated. In recent decades, the Jewish National Fund reforested Upper Galilee, and today the land carries a look that is both pristine and tamed.

For a traveler from the south, the hills of Upper Galilee offer the first view of the reality of Lebanon and indicate that the marginal desert lands of Judea and even Samaria are actually a pretty tough place to make a living by comparison. Linked with Mount Carmel and Gilead in biblical texts, the glory of Lebanon—as represented by Upper Galilee—eagerly stood as the preeminent biblical image of the tangible blessings of God (Ps 92:12; Isa 35:2; Jer 22:6; cp. Isa 33:9). Its water and stately groves of cedar, the *"fragrance of Lebanon"* (Song 4:11), were something to sing to one's sweetheart about: *"You are a garden spring, a well of flowing water streaming from Lebanon"* (Song 4:15). The prophet Ezekiel apparently appreciated its poetic potential too when he wrote about *"a cedar in Lebanon, with beautiful branches and shady foliage and of lofty height. Its top was among*

Psalm 29 pictures the coming of the glory of the Lord as a powerful thunderstorm, sweeping off the Mediterranean Sea, smashing into the mountains of Lebanon, shattering the cedars and bending the trees so much that they resemble calves gamboling up the mountainside (Ps 29:3–6). The storm then blows across the Rift Valley, up and over Mount Senir (Mount Hermon), and out into the open desert beyond (Ps 29:6–9). This theophany, viewed by Israel from over the high, west and north hills of Upper Galilee, uses imagery that for the indigenous Canaanites described Baal, god of the lightning storm and rain. The psalmist co-opted these images to describe the Lord, the God of Israel, as a way of not only portraying the awe-inspiring majesty of God, but showing that he, not Baal, controls the life-giving blessing of rain.

the clouds" (Ezek 31:3). And Hosea incorporated similarly poetic language about the area in his own writings:

> *I [the Lord] will be like the dew to Israel;*
> *he will blossom like the lily*
> *and take root like the cedars of Lebanon.*
> *His new branches will spread,*
> *and his splendor will be like the olive tree,*
> *his fragrance, like the forest of*
> *Lebanon.* (Hos 14:5–6)

Already prized in the ancient world for its big timber, Lebanon was Solomon's source for logs of cedar, cypress, pine, and fir to build important national buildings in Jerusalem. These include the royal palace and Solomon's throne room, the armory, and, of course, the temple (1 Kgs 5:6–10; 6:9–10,14–18; 7:1–12; Isa 22:8; 60:13). Using the majesty of Lebanon (cp. Isa 10:34) as a building material gave tangible shape to the idea that the Jerusalem temple was at the very least a physical representation of the primal garden of Eden, where God first flourished with his people. The rugged Judean Wilderness, crouching at Jerusalem's back door, offered ancient Israel the notion of refuge and escape, but it was the stately hills of Upper Galilee and Lebanon, blanketed in the blessings of God, that embodied sanctuary as the goal of retreat.

The softer Eocene limestone of the eastern third of Upper Galilee provides topographical forms that encourage the growth of strong, profitable villages. Here, the neat oval of the Kedesh Basin (= *"Kedesh in Galilee and its pasturelands"*; 1 Chr 6:76) sits above the rim of the Huleh Basin. Further beyond, over the drop of the Huleh, is the rise of the Golan Heights (Bashan), its flat horizon marked by the rise of several extinct volcanic cones. The Kedesh Basin offers a strategic foothold into Galilee for armies sweeping into the land from the northeast (2 Kgs 15:29). It was also close enough to main routes so as to qualify as home to one of the six cities of refuge designated in the book of Joshua to which persons guilty of unintentional manslaughter could flee (Josh 20:7–9; 21:32; 1 Chr 6:76).

Upper Galilee was also valued for resources beyond timber, enough so that we can assume that the villages scattered among its mountain folds were more than self-sufficient for their daily needs. The quality of the vineyards throughout Lebanon and Upper Galilee, in fact, was renowned (Hos 14:7). Josephus speaks of imperial granaries in various Upper Galilee villages that were worth raiding to support the Jewish revolt against Rome (*Life* 71); perhaps it was farmers in these villages that helped to supply grain to the northern coastal cities of Tyre and Sidon in the first century AD (Acts 12:20; cp. 1 Kgs 5:11; Ezek 27:17). The towns of Gischala and Meron have been major centers of olive oil production since Roman times, and likely before. Gischala (modern *el-Jish*) appears with the productive name Gush Halav, "fat clod" or "milk clod" in ancient Jewish sources;[1] the same is its Hebrew name today. Enjoying lives of quiet isolation, Upper Galilee's farmers and horticulturalists were devoted first and foremost to their ancestral soil. Josephus notes that rather than join the revolt against Rome in AD 67, the inhabitants of "Gischala, a small town in Galilee . . . were inclined to peace, being mainly agricultural laborers, whose whole attention was devoted to the prospects of the crops" (*War* 4.84).

Though Upper Galilee's rugged beauty attracted small village settlement, through-routes, especially of the international variety, tended to avoid the region. The anchor points on its perimeter—Tyre and Acco/Ptolemais to the west and Damascus and Hazor on the east—coveted the level passes that ran through the Jezreel and Beth-netophah Valleys instead. Indeed, one of the motives for Aramean (Syrian) moves against Israel in the ninth and eighth centuries BC was to secure control of the passages that circle around to the Mediterranean Sea via Lower Galilee and the Jezreel Valley, thus avoiding the direct but more difficult routes over Upper Galilee (cp. 1 Kgs 15:20; 2 Kgs 6:24).

As expected, the natural routes within Upper Galilee make for rather difficult travel throughout. With no clear watershed ridge, it is impossible for a route to cross the region without travelers having to navigate steep slopes and tight passes around Mount Meron. Historically, the better routes (none could be called "best") have crossed the spring-fed Maroun er-Ras Plateau, a likely candidate for the "*Waters of Merom*" (Josh 11:5,7) north of the mountain. One, cutting northwestward from Hazor, skirts the Kedesh Basin on its way to Phoenicia. This was likely the route traveled by Jesus when he "*withdrew to the area of Tyre and Sidon*" during his Galilean ministry (Matt 15:21). Passing through many small Jewish towns and villages on the way, Jesus knew that his travels would take him toward the northwestern edge of the district of Galilee, where the pull of a Hellenized Canaanite culture was strong. A perpendicular route, cutting diagonally across Upper Galilee between Dan, Kedesh, and Acco, carries traffic from Damascus to the coast. A more direct route from Damascus traces the spine of the ridge south of the Litani River to Tyre.[2] With the advent of sophisticated Roman road building techniques, this road was graded, paved, curbed, marked, and incorporated into the Roman Road network in the second century AD.[3]

One might expect, then, that the grand events of biblical history tended to avoid the mountainous mass of Upper Galilee, and in large measure this is correct. The archaeological and historic record indicates that the population density of the region increased significantly during the beginning of the Iron Age. This was likely largely due to processes by which the tribe of Naphtali sought areas for settlement that were at a safe distance from neighboring Canaanite city-states, though some sites in the region must have been established by eastward-penetrating Phoenicians from Tyre.[4] The density of villages in Upper Galilee also spiked in the second century AD, after the destruction of the Jerusalem temple when Jews endeavored to reconstitute their communities in places within the historic borders of ancient Israel, but not so directly under the eye of Rome. Overall, population numbers in Upper Galilee

The lumber of Lebanon was used not only for constructing temples and palaces in the ancient world, but also for building large ships. From at least as early as the third millennium BC, the Egyptian pharaohs imported cedar logs through the Phoenician port of Byblos to build vessels to sail the Nile. The best lumber was likely reserved for the Solar Boat, a special ship made only to ferry a pharaoh's mummified remains to their final resting place on the west bank of the Nile. This trip represented the daily journey taken by Pharaoh for all eternity across the arc of the heavens. The Solar Boat of Cheops, the pharaoh who built the largest pyramid, is shown here, on display in a small museum next to his pyramid in Giza, Egypt. Two thousand years later, the prophet Ezekiel gave a materials list for Mediterranean boat builders who used trees felled in the vicinity of Upper Galilee or hauled across its hills: "*Your realm was in the heart of the sea; . . . pine trees from Senir* [Mount Hermon] *. . . cedar from Lebanon . . . oaks from Bashan . . . cypress wood from the coasts of Cyprus*" (Ezek 27:4-6).

1 For example, in the the Mishnah Arakhin 9:6 and the Tosefta Shevi'it 7:15. The name Gischala does not appear in the Bible.

2 Anson Rainey has proposed that this Damascus- to -Tyre route across Upper Galilee is the Way of the Sea mentioned in Isa 9:1; Anson Rainey, "Toponymic Problems (cont.), The Way of the Sea, Shim'on—Shimron Once Again," *TA* 8 (1981): 146–51; Rainey and Notley, *The Sacred Bridge*, 12, 230.

3 *Onomasticon* 76:6-8; Freeman-Grenville, Chapman, and Taylor, *The Onomasticon by Eusebius*, 46.

4 Israel Finkelstein, *The Archaeology of the Israelite Settlement* (Jerusalem: IES, 1988), 97–110.

Ruins of the Maronite (Lebanese) Christian village of Kafr Bir'im can be seen among the scrub forest (maquis) and undergrowth of the Maroun er-Ras plateau north of Mount Meron, the peak on the right. Before it was abandoned during the Israeli War of Independence in November 1948, and its buildings leveled by the Israeli army in 1953, Kafr Bir'im was home to more than 700 people living in approximately 150 houses. Supported by a mixed agricultural economy, the residents of Kafr Bir'im placed approximately 920 acres (372 ha.) under grain cultivation, with another 275 acres (111 ha.) dedicated to orchards and irrigated crops. There are two springs nearby. These living conditions are typical for the historic villages of Upper Galilee and reflect deep peasant roots in the land. Remains of two ancient synagogues have been found within the abandoned Arab village. The site, which does not appear in sources prior to medieval times, is called Bar'am on modern Israeli maps; its grounds are part of the Israeli National Park system today.

have remained fairly stable throughout the centuries, a reflection of the rural, conservative, and generally separatist character of its hilly living spaces. Jacob's blessing, "*Naphtali is a doe set free*" (Gen 49:21), fits the scene nicely.

In spite of its rural character, we should not conclude that Upper Galilee stood alone. It was, after all, a border region with an indigenous Canaanite population that looked not only toward Tyre and Sidon but also Hazor and Laish (Dan). Here the Canaanite cities that Naphtali was unable to dispossess, Beth-shemesh (possibly Khirbet Tell el-Ruweisa) and Beth-anath (perhaps Safad el-Battikh), were *not* located on the plain. Naphtali's inheritance filled mostly the eastern, southern, and central parts of the region (Josh 19:32,37–38), in addition to the cities that the tribe controlled in Lower Galilee (Josh 19:35–36). The tribe of Asher originally claimed a portion of the western slopes of Upper Galilee above the northern Acco Plain, but it was these that Solomon turned over to Hiram of Tyre to settle the negative balance of trade spurred by his import of Lebanese timber (Josh 19:24–31; 1 Kgs 9:10–13). Hellenistic influences pressured the villages of Upper Galilee throughout the time of the New Testament, as the coastal cities of Phoenicia opened their mountainous hinterland to the glories of Greece and Rome. In the time of the New

A loose-block wall preserves a tantalizing memory of the Roman temple at Kedesh, dedicated to the god Baal-shamin, "the lord of heaven," the Syrian equivalent of Zeus (above). This temple, built in the Corinthian style, was the religious center of a thriving Rome-oriented community in Upper Galilee's Kedesh Basin in the second and third centuries AD. The building was likely destroyed by the earthquake of 363 AD; it makes for wonderful exploring today. In the first century AD, Josephus noted that "Cydasa [Kedesh] was a strong inland village of the Tyrians, always at feud and strife with the Galileans, having its large population and stout defenses as resources behind it in its quarrel with the [Jewish] nation" (*War* 4.105). Josephus's assessment was keen and hints at the tension between forces of confrontation and those of assimilation that residents of Galilee have faced for millennia. The much-better preserved façade of the contemporary synagogue at Bar'am (below), located seven miles west of the Kedesh temple, betrays similar elements of style that suggest that it, too, was originally constructed as a Roman temple.

Testament, Tyre's orb of political control stretched all the way to Kedesh in southeastern Upper Galilee and to just above the Huleh Basin Josephus, (*War* 4.105). By implication, when Jesus traveled to "*the area of Tyre and Sidon*" (Matt 15:21; Mark 3:8), he likely stayed somewhere within the folds of the Upper Galilee hills rather than dropping to the Phoenician plain below. In any case, it is clear that the Jewish population of Upper Galilee continued to thrive among the region's hills in the centuries following the destruction of thc temple. By the fifteenth century AD, Zefat (Safed), southeast of Mount Meron, had developed into a major center of Jewish (mainly kabbalistic) learning; this is the closest to becoming an urban center that any town in the region was at the time.

Over the succeeding centuries and up until the last several decades of the twentieth century AD, the population of Upper Galilee, like that of the other regions of the land of ancient Israel, was mostly Arab. Today, Upper Galilee's Arab population remains among the highest, percentage-wise, of the regions of the modern State of Israel, though with a significant Jewish mix. While the secluded topography of Upper Galilee has always given its residents a sense of enclosed identity, the region's mixed demographic base is a constant reminder that in Galilee, the circle indeed continues to swirl around, and even penetrate, the core.

E. THE HULEH BASIN

North of the Sea of Galilee, the Rift Valley rolls up and over a broad dike of basalt called the Rosh Pinna Sill, then drops into the Huleh Basin, a neatly defined valley that marked the northernmost living space of the land of ancient Israel. Although the Huleh Basin has played a pivotal role throughout the history of the southern Levant, it is not mentioned by name in either the Old or New Testaments. The word *Huleh* likely comes from *Ulatha*, the valley's Greek name that was known to Josephus (*Ant.* 15.360).

In dimension, the Huleh Basin stretches fifteen miles (24 km) north-south and up to six miles (10 km) east to west. Its borders are clean and easy to define. To the west, the firm Cenomanian-Turonian line of Upper Galilee's Naphtali Ridge rises an abrupt 2,600 feet (790 m), its strong face shaped by an arrow-straight fault line. Opposite, the gentle basalt slopes of the Upper Golan pull up more gradually to a string of extinct volcanic cones seven to ten miles (11 to 16 km) east of the valley. These were responsible for the large flow of lava north and east of the Sea of Galilee. The northern end of the Huleh Basin is drawn on a line even with the southern end of Mount Hermon, where the foothills of the massive Anti-Lebanese Range encroach into the Rift Valley. The basin's southern end is marked by the rounded rise of the Rosh Pinna Sill, a thick protrusion of basalt that has flowed southwestward off the Golan and blocked the width of the rift just above the Sea of Galilee. The whole thing resembles a thumbprint in modeling clay. Within its raised edges the floor of the Huleh Basin lies almost completely flat, with an elevation of 280 feet (85 m) above sea level in the north and an imperceptible drop to 225 feet (68 m) in elevation at its swampy southern end.

Because the Huleh Basin functioned as the all-important northern gateway for the land of ancient Israel, facing Damascus but giving access to Mesopotamia, it is appropriate to take a quick look further north, beyond the imperial frontier, before focusing on the basin itself.

The northern end of the Huleh Basin rises to what was called the Land of Mizpah, "Lookout Land," in Joshua 11:3,8. Whether intentional or not, this name reflects the reality of the favored view from the lower slopes of Mount Hermon, but also the historic pattern that the northern end of the Huleh Basin is a natural seam between Israel and various Aramean nation-states to the north. Damascus is the closest of these, and the Aramean and Israelite kings kept a constant eye on each other in the region. Their modern counterparts still do. Here the Anti-Lebanese Range, of which Mount Hermon is the southern end, almost touches the seaward Lebanese Range, effectively blocking the Rift Valley northward for a distance of about twenty-five miles (40 km). This mountainous juncture, the **Bir ed-Dahr blockage**, rises to elevations of more than 4,000 feet (1,220 m), then drops into the high Beqa'a Valley in the interior of Lebanon between the Lebanese and Anti-Lebanese Ranges. The Beqa'a is perhaps what Joshua 11:17; 12:7 calls the Valley of Lebanon. Lebo-hamath (lit. "the entering in of Hamath"), the point beyond which Moses's spies didn't go, lies on the Orontes River at the Beqa'a's far end (Num 13:21; cp. 1 Kgs 8:65). The Bir ed-Dahr blockage constricts easy movement of northbound traffic in the Rift Valley beyond the Huleh Basin, prompting most travelers to swing around Mount Hermon northeastward to Damascus instead.

For travelers pushing northward through the Huleh Basin, the dominant view has always been toward **Mount Hermon**. The entire southern end of the Anti-Lebanese Range, including all of Hermon, is composed of hard, bedded Jurassic limestone, formed earlier, and hence originally lying deeper, than the limestone sequence visible throughout the rest of the land of ancient Israel. Here, though, the pressures of mountain-building have lifted this huge Jurassic block far above everything else. The peak of Hermon, at 9,232 feet (2,814 m) above sea level, is the highest in the Anti-Lebanese Range. On clear winter days, the heights of Hermon can be seen from points throughout Israel, including from Mounts Ebal and Carmel, the Nazareth Ridge, and the surface of the Sea of Galilee. Turning the view, from the Israeli military base on the highest point of Mount Hermon that lies within the modern State of Israel (7,297 ft; 2,224 m), high-powered binoculars can pick up the skyscrapers in Tel Aviv as well as the license plate numbers of vehicles in Damascus.

The Bir ed-Dahr blockage and the western slopes of Mount Hermon were heavily forested with oak and wild fruit trees in antiquity, much more so than today, providing a long exclamation mark on the "*glory of Lebanon*" for which the mountain was famed (Isa 35:2; 60:13). A stately grove of large, old oak trees, a stubborn vestige of this earlier covering, still stands at Horshat Tal southwest of Tel Dan, on the northern fringe of the Huleh Basin. Nowadays the timber line on Hermon is quite low for a mountain of its height, lying at only 4,600 feet (1,400 m) elevation. The vast upper elevations of the

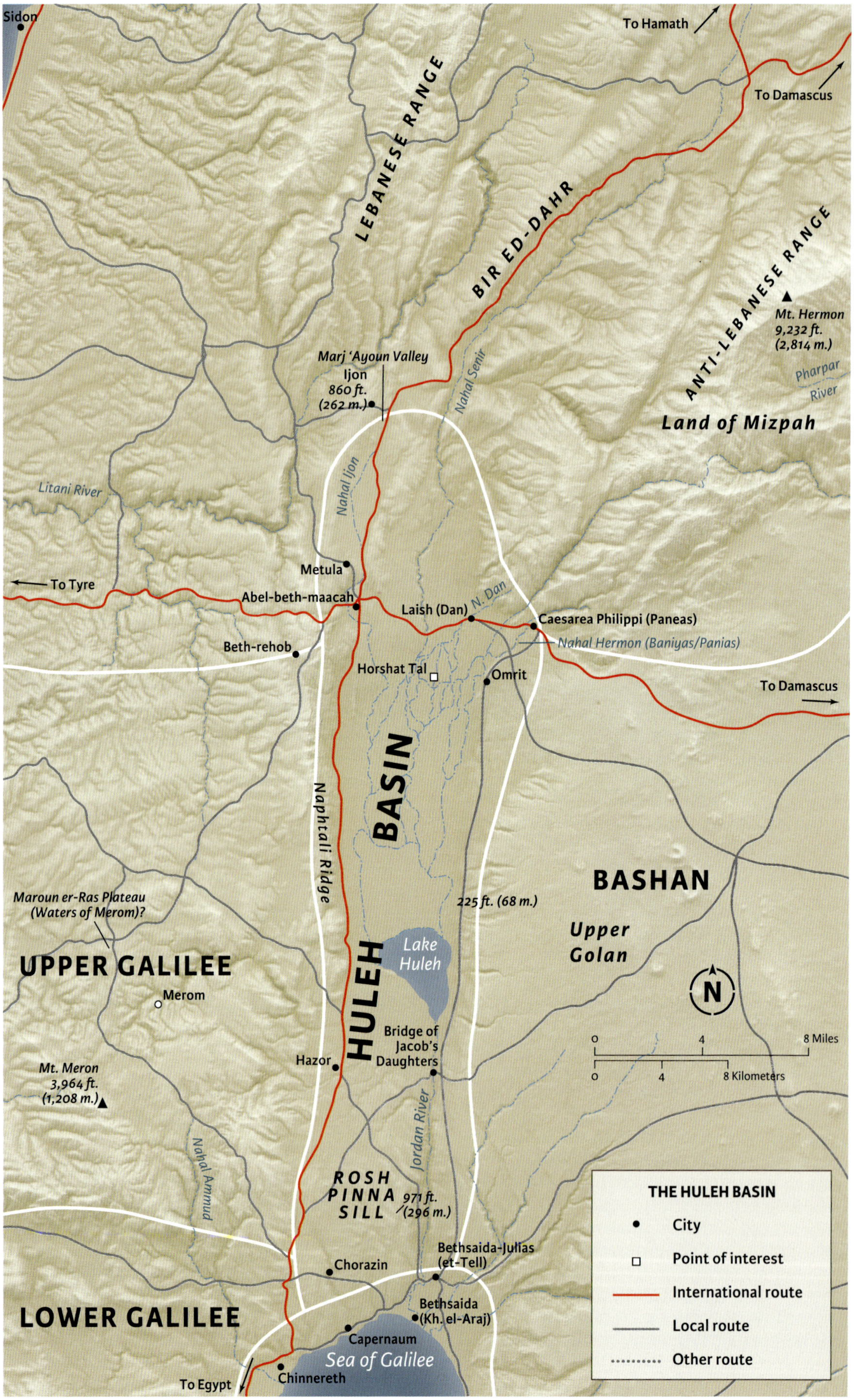

Sidon
To Hamath
To Damascus
LEBANESE RANGE
BIR ED-DAHR
ANTI-LEBANESE RANGE
Mt. Hermon 9,232 ft. (2,814 m.)
Pharpar River
Land of Mizpah
Marj 'Ayoun Valley
Ijon 860 ft. (262 m.)
Nahal Senir
Nahal Ijon
Litani River
Metula
To Tyre
Abel-beth-maacah
Laish (Dan)
N. Dan
Caesarea Philippi (Paneas)
Nahal Hermon (Baniyas/Panias)
Beth-rehob
Horshat Tal
Omrit
To Damascus
HULEH BASIN
Naphtali Ridge
BASHAN
225 ft. (68 m.)
Maroun er-Ras Plateau (Waters of Merom)?
UPPER GALILEE
Lake Huleh
Upper Golan
Merom
Bridge of Jacob's Daughters
Hazor
Mt. Meron 3,964 ft. (1,208 m.)
Jordan River
Nahal Ammud
ROSH PINNA SILL
971 ft. (296 m.)
Bethsaida-Julias (et-Tell)
Chorazin
Bethsaida (Kh. el-Araj)
LOWER GALILEE
Capernaum
Sea of Galilee
Chinnereth
To Egypt
N
0 4 8 Miles
0 4 8 Kilometers

THE HULEH BASIN

•	City
□	Point of interest
red line	International route
gray line	Local route
dotted line	Other route

mountain have virtually no soil cover and as a result very little vegetation. All of this makes the peak appear higher than it actually is.

Mount Hermon was called Senir in the annals of Assyrian King Shalmaneser III,[1] as well as by the local Amorite population generally (Deut 3:8–9; 1 Chr 5:23). To the Sidonians the mountain was Sirion or Sion (Deut 3:8–9; 4:48), while today Arabs refer to its heights as Jebel al-Talj ("Snow Mountain") or Jebel esh-Sheikh (loosely "Old Man Mountain," on account of its white pate). Indeed, heavy snows fall on Hermon every year, and in its highest crevices, north of the border of the modern State of Israel, some snow nearly always remains throughout the heat of summer. The result is a mountain whose huge aquifers are full of cold spring water, much of which spills out as the headwaters of the Jordan River and Abana and Pharpar Rivers of Damascus (2 Kgs 5:12). *"Does the snow of Lebanon ever leave the highland crags?"* Jeremiah once asked an audience that needed to be reminded that God was still active, then added, *"Or does cold water flowing from a distance ever fail?"* (Jer 18:14). The rhetorical answer was, of course, no!

For the indigenous inhabitants of Canaan, Hermon was a divine mountain, its head wrapped in moisture and its sides spilling out the blessings of stored rainfall. Indeed, the name *Hermon* (or, more properly, *Baal-hermon*; Judg 3:3; 1 Chr 5:23) comes from a Semitic root that means "to devote" and references in particular the mountain's ancient sacral associations. Biblical writers, too, spoke of the mountain with elevated language, recognizing its divine reputation but transferring imagery that was typically associated with Canaanite Hermon to Mount Zion instead (e.g., Pss 48:1–2; 89:12–13; 133:3; Song 4:8).

The waters that drain from Mount Hermon and into the Huleh Basin join to form the main headwaters of the Jordan River. There they are bolstered by a number of springs lining the lower slopes of the Naphtali Ridge and Upper Golan.[2] The total flow into the Huleh Basin is estimated to be 740 million cubic meters of water per year, or, on a straight average, a little more than 6,000 gallons—the capacity of a semi-trailer tanker found on US or Canadian highways—per second. Added to this is rainfall that averages twenty-five inches (635 mm) per

The majestic heights of the Anti-Lebanese Range peak at Mount Hermon, here with a springtime crown of snow. The view is from the outskirts of modern Israel's northernmost town, Metula, on the eastern slope of the Lebanese Range. The Rift Valley lies between the two rises, constricted at the point where the Huleh Basin (the northern end of which is just visible in the bottom of the valley, right) starts to give way to the Bir ed-Dahr blockage. A historic international route ran the length of the valley floor, from Abel-beth-maacah to Ijon and eventually the entrance of Hamath in the Beqa'a far to the north (Num 13:21; Josh 13:5; 2 Sam 20:14–15; 1 Kgs 15:20; 2 Kgs 14:25; 15:29). The favored route, however, passed on the other side of Hermon eastward, joining Galilee with Damascus and the Euphrates River beyond.

1 *ANET*, 280. Shalmeneser III mentions that Hazael, the Aramean king of Damascus (cp. 1 Kgs 19:15), made "the mountain Senir, a mountain facing the Lebanon, his fortress."

2 The *Survey of Western Palestine* lists dozens of natural water sources in and around the valley; C. R. Conder and H. H. Kitchener, *The Survey of Western Palestine: Memoirs of the Topography, Orography, Hydrography, and Archaeology*, vol. I: *Galilee* (London: The Committee of the PEF, 1881), 98–105.

Nearly 250 Tabor oak trees stand in a spreading grove at Horshat Tal, an Israeli National Park in the northern Huleh Basin. The source of the Jordan River that begins at the mighty Dan springs flows through the park, where it is channeled into large, frigid pools that are popular swimming holes in the heat of an Israeli summer. Some of the oaks in the grove are more than 400 years old, remnants of much larger stands of Tabor oak that once covered the slopes of the Hermon Range. Horshat Tal means "dewy grove," finding inspiration for its name in *"the dew of Hermon falling on the mountains of Zion"* mentioned in Psalm 133:3.

year in the northern part of the basin and a modest sixteen inches (406 mm) in the southern, the Rosh Pinna Sill end of the basin fifteen miles (24 km) south. Hermon itself enjoys more than seventy inches (1,780 mm) of rain (or its equivalent in melted snowfall) each year. As a result, the Huleh Basin is the wettest region in the entire land of ancient Israel, holding far more water than is actually useful. As a result, much of the basin floor was given over to swamps, and accompanying malaria-plagued living conditions, throughout recorded history.

> Roman naturalist and historian Pliny the Elder (AD 23–79) described the Jordan River this way:
> "The source of the river Jordan is the spring of Panias from which Caesarea . . . takes its second name. It is a delightful stream, winding about so far as the conformation of the locality allows, and putting itself at the service of the people who dwell on its banks, as though moving with reluctance towards that gloomy lake, the Dead Sea, which ultimately swallows it up, its much-praised waters mingling with the pestilential waters of the lake and being lost."[1]

Of the many sources of the Jordan River that enter the Huleh Basin, the four that arise out of Mount Hermon and Bir ed-Dahr blockage provide most of the river's water. The easternmost, Nahal Hermon (the *Banyasi* wadi), is the only Jordan spring that flows directly out of the exposed rock of Mount Hermon. The Arabic name of the spot is Baniyas, preserving the Greek name Panias, site of fervent cultic activity devoted to the Greco-Roman nature god Pan during the Hellenistic and Roman periods.

From here the stream flows down a steep, rocky gorge to a double waterfall, the most dramatic in the entire land of ancient Israel. The Baniyas stream's cascade rushes downward at the rate of 200 feet (60 m) per mile for its first four miles (6 km), with more than enough force to power several profitable flourmills during the Ottoman Turkish period. American Bible scholar Edward Robinson, who visited the place in the spring of 1852, said the Baniyas stream looked "like a small mountain brook, tumbling, foaming and roaring along its steep rocky bed."[2] It was "small" perhaps for Robinson's part of the world in New England; but for residents of the arid land of ancient Israel, this churning flow and its sudden waterfalls may well have been the "*deep [that] calls to deep in the roar of your waterfalls*" by which the psalmist recalled God's works "*from the land of [the] Jordan and the peaks of Hermon, from Mount Mizar*" (Ps 42:6–7).

> Josephus considered the Baniyas stream to be the apparent source of the Jordan. "Apparent" only, for he told a story that suggested that the actual source was a circular pool called Philae (modern Birkat Ram) high on Mount Hermon's slopes, which he thought might be connected to the Baniyas spring by an underground channel. According to Josephus, Philip the Tetrarch, son of Herod the Great and governor of the region during the time of Jesus (Luke 3:1), had chaff thrown into the Philae pool and saw it exit at the Baniyas springs below (*War* 3.510-513). A subterranean connection between the pool and the springs does not exist. This didn't stop Philip's royal engineers from making sure that their tetrarch saw the evidence he wanted to see. Loyal to a fault, they apparently threw similar chaff into the Baniyas spring to provide evidence of the passage!

A second source of the Jordan, cutting a clear course over a low rise west of the Baniyas stream, is Nahal Dan (aka *Liddani* wadi, not to be confused with the much larger Litani River in Lebanon). This is the largest karstic spring in the Middle East, producing 2,000 gallons (7.5 m3) of water per second, fully one-third of the Jordan's total source flow. The major outlet of the Dan spring arises rather limpidly into a large, crystal-clear pool at the northwestern base of the tell of ancient Dan (Canaanite Laish), cascades downward for the first mile (1.5 km), and then slogs over flat ground into the Huleh Basin. It, too, was used to turn mills during the Turkish period. In length, this is the shortest of the Jordan's source streams (Josephus called it the "so-called little Jordan"; *War* iv.3), but it is the most popular for visitors to the region today.

Just over a mile (1.5 km) to the west of the tell of ancient Dan, Nahal Senir (the *Hatsbani* wadi) flows into the Huleh Basin from a number of springs issuing from the southwestern tip of Mount Hermon. Like the Hermon and Dan streams, the Senir stream is a perennial flow, with much of its volume sustained by runoff from Hermon's southwestern flank. The Senir is the longest

1 *Natural History* 5.71.

2 Edward Robinson and Eli Smith, *Later Biblical Researches in Palestine and in the Adjacent Regions: A Journal of Travels in the Year 1852* (Boston: Crocker and Brewster, 1856), 386.

of the headwater sources of the Jordan River. Its quick springtime flow makes it a popular spot for rubber rafting and other river sports today.

The fourth major source of the Jordan River is Nahal Ijon (the *Bareigheti* wadi). The Ijon stream collects its water from springs in the narrow Marj 'Ayoun Valley (biblical Ijon; 1 Kgs 15:20; 2 Kgs 15:29) west of Nahal Senir, then crosses the modern border between Lebanon and Israel and drops through a series of waterfalls near Metula before flowing into the Huleh Basin. Today the Ijon's springs are tapped for human use quite close to their source, making its stream bed seasonal and dependent on surface runoff. The Ijon flows into the swamps at the southern end of the Huleh Basin by itself, while the eastern three streams (the Hermon, Dan, and Senir) join into a common channel early on, then split back into two before flowing into the same marshy ground at the opposite end of the Huleh.

Historically, the swamp water in the southern end of the Huleh Basin backed up against the rise of the Rosh Pinna Sill where it collected into a lake that, on maps drawn prior to 1960, was labeled, appropriately, Lake Huleh. Josephus called the lake Semechonitis (*Ant.* 5.190; *War* 3.515; 4.2–4); in the Talmud, the name appears as the

Though not the highest waterfall in the land of ancient Israel, the double falls at Baniyas are the largest in volume and arguably the most dramatic. A large oriental plane tree (*Platanus orientalis*), old, persistent and defiant, divides the flow: *"Deep calls to deep in the roar of your waterfalls; all your breakers and your billows have swept over me"* (Ps 42:7).

The Dan stream starts its run toward the Huleh Basin on a quick pace, here just a few hundred feet from the place where it exits the ground at the base of Tel Dan. Such are the *"fountain[s] of living water"* and *"streams of living water [that] flow from deep within"* that become tangible images of God's grace in the lives of the faithful (Jer 2:13; John 7:38).

The Mill Falls, so named because of the ruin of an Ottoman Turkish-era flour mill at its base, plunges seventy feet (21 m) down a wide cliff face in the Iyyon (Ijon) Nature Reserve in the northern Huleh Basin. The reserve, which lies on the border of the modern States of Israel and Lebanon, offers fresh vistas and a hiking experience that cannot be found in other, more conveniently located areas of the country.

Lake of Sibkay.[1] On toponymic grounds, the Waters of Merom mentioned in Joshua 11:5, sometimes identified with Lake Huleh,[2] are perhaps better located on the Maroun er-Ras Plateau in Upper Galilee.[3] Ancient sources, as well as the accounts of early travelers, speak of the Huleh's marshes and lagoons, with water lilies, papyrus, and water birds common to the Nile Delta.[4] Some travelers to the Huleh Basin in the nineteenth and early twentieth centuries AD left colorful accounts of the indigenous inhabitants of the region, stating that they lived in huts made from tough, fibrous swamp reeds, raised water buffalo—and were infected with malaria.[5] Others, taking a more comprehensive view, noted that large swaths of the basin were under cultivation right up to the edge of the swamps.[6] The area of the northern Huleh Basin was controlled by the tribe of Dan during the Israelite monarchy, and Dan's tribal images— "*a viper beside the path*" and "*a young lion, leaping out of Bashan*" (Gen 49:16–17; Deut 33:22)—betray a frontier land that was a haven for wildlife.

Prior to being drained in the 1950s, Lake Huleh's waters covered an area of five square miles (13 km2), reaching a maximum depth of eighteen feet (5 m). The swamp extending from its northern side covered an area three times as large, with shallow, plant-entangled waters no more than six feet (2 m) deep. Evidence from the deposition of silt shows that throughout time, the water level of the lake and its swamps fluctuated year by year, with longer wet or dry cycles raising and lowering its overall level over time. Alluvium brought into the center of the basin by the streams of the Jordan actually formed banks that raised the water channels above the valley floor, with the result that when the channels spilled over their banks in seasons of high rainfall, much of the valley became flooded. As might be expected, permanent settlement tended to keep to higher ground at the Huleh Basin's northern and southwestern ends. In any case, between 1951 and 1958 an ambitious land-reclamation project by the Israelis channeled and regulated the water of the Huleh Basin,

1 Bava Batra 74b.

2 Scholars generally following Edward Robinson and Eli Smith, *Biblical Researches in Palestine, Mount Sinai and Arabia Petraea: A Journal of Travels in the Year 1838 by E. Robinson and E. Smith Undertaken in Reference to Biblical Geography*, vol. 2 (Boston: Crocker and Brewster, 1841), 440.

3 Rainey and Notley, *The Sacred Bridge*, 129.

4 See, for instance, Yehoshua Ben-Arieh, *The Rediscovery of the Holy Land in the Nineteenth Century*, 2nd. ed. (Jerusalem: The Magnes Press, 1983), 129, 198, 222–23.

5 Henry van Dyke, *Out-of-Doors in the Holy Land* (New York: Charles Scribner's Sons, 1909), 267–73.

6 For example, Robinson and Smith, *Later Biblical Researches in Palestine* III, 370; and Conder and Kitchener, *The Survey of Western Palestine* I, 97.

leveling the valley floor and bringing tens of thousands of acres under annual cultivation. Although Lake Huleh has now essentially disappeared, an area of water ponds and marshes remains as a protected nature reserve. This reserve maintains primal habitat for a wide variety of flora and fauna, both indigenous and migratory, which continue to make the swamps their home.

Today, the resources of the Huleh Basin are nearly ideal for agriculture. The soil is a healthy mixture of terra rosa and black basaltic alluvium, with some peat under and around the swamps. The southern end of the basin acts as a kind of filtration pool for the Jordan's flow, trapping large amounts of rich organic material before the river's run to the Sea of Galilee. Daytime winter temperatures on the valley floor are pleasant due to the colder winds from Upper Galilee staying high as they blow over the basin from the top of the Naphtali Ridge to Upper Golan. Yet frost sometimes forms at night when cool air from the heights of Mount Hermon sweeps into the valley; this allows the cultivation of apple trees. All-in-all, the combination of sun, warmth, ample groundwater, and high humidity creates a kind of greenhouse effect in the Huleh, without a noticeable gap in the growing season.

The Huleh Basin is separated from the Sea of Galilee by the **Rosh Pinna** ("Cornerstone") **Sill**, a massive dike of basalt ten miles (16 km) long and five miles (8 km) wide. Alternating layers of peat and chalk beneath the Huleh's swamps suggest that the dike was built up in layers as basalt spilled into the Rift Valley from the east on at least three separate occasions. Each time, the outlet of Lake Huleh (or its geological predecessor) became blocked, with the backed-up water eventually forcing a fresh exit cut along the eastern edge of the dike. The Jordan River drops through the current cut in dramatic fashion, tumbling down 900 feet (275 m) in ten miles (16 km). In places, narrow canyon walls rise 1,000 feet (300 m) above the river. In the springtime, when the flow is especially strong, rapids cascading through the cut can reach Class 5. These portions of the Jordan River are not readily accessible by most vehicles, but visitors who

The remnant of Lake Huleh and its swamps still harbors a wide variety of plant and animal life, which drink deeply from its still waters. White and yellow lilies, lake rush, blue lotus, and papyrus are among the species found in the region, as well as yellow Jussiaea, whose air-filled roots allow the plant to walk on the surface of the water. Herbivorous and carnivorous fish lurk below (giant catfish can reach 45 lbs or 20 kg), as do shellfish and water turtles. Mosquitoes, now largely under control, once filled the air above. The lake and swamps have trapped a vast amount of rich organic material behind them, much of which has now been plowed into fields.

make the effort are rewarded by a landscape not seen elsewhere in the land of ancient Israel.

The surface of the Rosh Pinna Sill is covered with basalt boulders and rough, thorny vegetation. Its topography is smoother in the north, where several springs are found, but highly dissected on the drier, southern exposures facing the Sea of Galilee. Because the scattering of rocks is too extensive to encourage large plots of agriculture, it seems the population density of the sill was never very high. At least there is good grazing land for cattle, sheep, and goats. Still, it was on the sill's seaward southern flank that we find the living spaces of much of the Gospel account: Capernaum, Chorazin, and "deserted places" between (cp. Mark 1:35).

In its larger human dynamic, the Huleh Basin functions as the very busy eastern segment of the "circle" that loops around the hills of Galilee. Through its corridors, empires and city-states large and small launched ventures of commerce, conquest, and control along the great imperial routes of Syria and Mesopotamia. At the same time, like-minded traffic from the north funneled back down through the basin toward the heartland of ancient Israel and the coast. During the time of the Old Testament, the international highway ran along the western edge of the Huleh Basin, above the swampy valley floor, connecting Hazor with Abel-beth-maacah and Dan before swinging eastward around the southern slopes of Mount Hermon to Damascus and points beyond. Or, the route ran through Abel-beth-maacah northward, up and over the Bir ed-Dahr blockage and into the great Beqa'a Valley between the Lebanese and Anti-Lebanese Ranges. In the time of the New Testament, following the principle that main routes connected main cities, the highway shifted to the eastern side of the basin. There it joined Bethsaida-Julias on the northeastern corner of the Sea of Galilee to Caesarea Philippi at the Jordan's Baniyas source. A spur line to Damascus crossed the Jordan between Lake Huleh and the rise of the Rosh Pinna Sill, climbing the Upper Golan on a northeastward angle. This crossing spot is called the Bridge of Jacob's Daughters (*Gesher benot Ya'aqov*), after the Daughters of St. James who kept a convent there during the time of the Crusades. Ruins of the picturesque castle Chastellet, site of a crucial victory by Saladin over the forces of Baldwin in 1179, are perched above the bend in the river that commanded this spot.

This is a tranquil spot of the Jordan River as it makes its way between the rise of the Rosh Pinna Sill (left) and the Upper Golan (right). Here geographical drama is traded for economic usefulness, as cattle drink and graze along the Jordan's evergreen banks. It's a part of the land of ancient Israel that is a bit tucked away, yet pleasant to behold.

Whoever held the corridors of power that channeled through the Huleh Basin had good cause to lay claim to the international priorities of the day. Hazor, secure on a healthy rise above the southwestern corner of the Huleh Basin, was, at two hundred acres, the largest city in the southern Levant during the second half of the second millennium BC (the Middle and Late Bronze Ages); the biblical moniker "Hazor, the head of all those kingdoms" (see Josh 11:10) fit that situation well. If the Huleh Basin can be pictured as a kind of funnel channeling traffic from the north into the land of ancient Israel, Hazor was the city that blocked the opening at the bottom of the spout: nothing poured through without its consent. This made Abel-beth-maacah and Laish/Dan, two cities which marked the natural northern end of the kingdom of Israel (2 Sam 3:10; 1 Kgs 4:25; cp. Gen 14:14; Josh 12:1; Judg 18:27–29; 1 Kgs 12:29), a kind of early warning system for threats from the north. The archaeological remains at Dan show both Israelite and Aramean influences during the time of the Old Testament; those at Abel-beth-maacah indicate influence from Phoenicia as well. Like the east-west valleys of the Judean Shephelah, the Huleh Basin, together with the cities on its northern and southern ends, saw a brisk movement of two-way traffic, comprising both friend and foe, throughout the biblical period. It was to the credit of the kings of ancient Israel that they were able to keep the valley within their fold as long as they did.

One might ask the question, "To whom does the Huleh corridor belong?" and get several viable answers. On the one hand, the natural border between Israel and Syria is the southern tip of Mount Hermon, which rises above the northern end of the Huleh Basin. From Dan, the soaring range runs away to the north while water from its massive aquifers drains to the south. But archaeology provides a more nuanced answer. Looking internationally, the archaeological evidence at Hazor and Dan dating to the Middle and Late Bronze Ages has revealed building plans and objects of art with a decidedly northern (north Aramean and even Hittite) stamp. Archival cuneiform documents from the eighteenth century BC and found at the city-state of Mari on the great bend of the Euphrates in far northeast Syria mention both Laish (Dan) and Hazor in contexts that imply that these Huleh cities were important commercial centers on the great trade routes of the Fertile Crescent.[1] The growing number of

1 Note, for instance, the discussion in the works of Abraham Malamat, *Mari and the Early Israelite Experience: The Schweich Lectures of the British Academy, 1984* (Oxford: Oxford University Press, 1989), 55–66; and *Mari and the Bible* (Leiden: Brill, 1998), 33–55.

A warm spring day embraces the Huleh Basin beyond the tell of Hazor, with the snowy peak of Mount Hermon in the distance. Here the remains of a large pillared storeroom from the Iron Age anticipate another bumper crop from the fields that lie beyond. The city of Hazor lay astride the imperial highway that penetrated ancient Israel from the shoulder of Mount Hermon, offering a land connection to the markets of Asia and Europe while making good use of the natural resources in the immediate vicinity as a resupply center for travelers. During the time of ancient Israel's settlement, Hazor also lay claim to the routes and cities circling the Jezreel Valley (Josh 11:1–2; Judg 4:1–2; 5:19). All of this was justification for the city's famed rubric, *"head of all these kingdoms"* (Josh 11:10 NIV).

cuneiform documents found at Hazor itself confirms this reputation.[1] These pointers are consistent with the note in Judges 18:28 that "[Laish/Dan] *was in a valley that belonged to Beth-rehob,*" a city in north Syria. We can conclude that Hazor and Dan look northward, much as Acco/Ptolemais looks toward Tyre and the Mediterranean Sea. At the same time, Hazor, Laish, Abel (-beth-maacah), and Ijon also appear in Egyptian administrative and military documents dating to the Middle and Late Bronze Ages (e.g., the Execration Texts[2] and Thutmose III's city list[3]). This suggests that the pharaohs saw the Huleh Basin as a necessary launch pad for points beyond those which they already more comfortably held in Canaan, such as Megiddo and Beth-shean.

Looking further afield, the empires of the eastern Mediterranean waged the same kind of struggle for control of the Huleh Basin at the end of the first millennium BC as the powers of the ancient Near East did during the Bronze and Iron Ages. This culminated in the Battle of Panias (198 BC), which saw the entire land of ancient Israel pass from the Egyptian Ptolemies to the Syrian Seleucids, both heirs of the kingdom of Alexander the Great. Similarly, strategic points in and around the Huleh Basin became a focal point of fortification for parry and thrust between the Latin Kingdom of Jerusalem and the Muslim forces of Damascus during the Crusades.[4] Throughout the recorded history of the region, the cities, water sources, and routes of the Huleh Basin remained a prized frontier worth seizing by international centers that lay far beyond the Galilee hills.

But the history of the Huleh Basin during the time of the Israelite monarchy was a litany of tug-and-pull between the local powers as well. Here Israel, Phoenicia, and the Aramean city-state of Damascus (Syria) played the major roles. In the biblical narrative, Moses's spies made an early claim on the valley when they walked the length of the land all the way to the entrance of Hamath in the northern Beqa'a (Num 13:21). Although ancient Israel's ideal northern boundary thus reached into the Beqa'a (Josh 13:5; Ezek 47:15–17) and David, Solomon, and Jeroboam II were all able to push their influence into that region (2 Sam 8:9–10; 1 Kgs 4:21; 2 Kgs 14:25), Joshua's claim, which stretched only from Hazor to "*the foot of Hermon in the land of Mizpah*" (Josh 11:3), was more realistic. Indeed, land given to the tribe of Naphtali didn't extend much beyond Hazor (Josh 19:32–39), and

1 Wayne Horowitz and Takayoshi Oshima, *Cuneiform in Canaan: *The Next Generation* [italicized], 2nd. ed. (University Park, PA, Eisenbrauns, 2018), 10–24, 63–88.*

2 Rainey and Notley, *The Sacred Bridge*, 58; Yohanan Aharoni, *The Land of the Bible* (Philadelphia: Westminster Press, 1979), 145–46.

3 Rainey and Notley, *The Sacred Bridge*, 72–7; Aharoni, *Land of the Bible*, 160.

4 Joshua Prawer, *The Latin Kingdom of Jerusalem: European Colonialism in the Middle Ages* (London: Weidenfeld and Nicolson, 1972), 265–66, 284–88.

Dan's move to Laish, though renegade in motive (Judg 17:1—18:31), sealed Israel's northernmost claim on the land at the northern end of the Huleh Basin. When Solomon fortified Hazor together with Megiddo and Gezer, he meant to ensure that the most strategic junctures of the great trunk road of the southern Levant remained firmly in Israelite hands (1 Kgs 9:15). These included Hazor's all-important northern gateway, Megiddo's great crossroads in the Jezreel Valley, and Gezer's spur line to Jerusalem.

Subsequent banter on the battlefield pushed the Israelite-Aramean border from one end of the Huleh Basin to the other. Two notable attempts at border shifting are Ben-hadad's move to attack "*Ijon, Dan, Abel-beth-maacah, all Chinneroth, and the whole land of Naphtali*" in the early ninth century BC (1 Kgs 15:20), and Hazael's boast to have killed the kings of Israel and the House of David as reported in a victory stela he erected at Dan half a century later.[1] And, in a now-familiar litany, the Assyrians (2 Kgs 15:29), followed by the Babylonians and then the Persians, eventually just took it all as a staging ground for their moves toward Egypt:

From Dan, the snorting of horses is heard.
At the sound of the neighing of mighty steeds,
the whole land quakes.
They come to devour the land
and everything in it,
the city and all its residents. (Jer 8:16)

Toward the end of the first millennium BC, Jews who remembered their roots in the vicinity of the Huleh Basin attempted to reestablish a viable presence there (Josephus, *Life* 74–75; *War* 2.592). By then the base of international power had shifted from Egypt and Assyria to Greece and Rome, and the one-two punch of Hellenistic culture + Roman might ensured that for those who preferred to be oriented toward Jerusalem, the Huleh Basin remained a frontier. This was perhaps no more apparent than in Caesarea Philippi, where with Rome's patronage the Herodian family had settled in quite nicely. Here, in a place that was both physically and culturally as distant from Jerusalem as Jesus would travel, he asked his disciples, "*Who do* you *say that I am?*" (cp. Matt 16:13–15; emphasis added).

As an eager participant in the emperor cult that swept the Roman world in the first century BC to the first century AD, Herod the Great built temples in honor of the divine Caesar Augustus in Sebaste, Caesarea Maritima, and "near the place called Paneion" (Josephus, *Ant.* 15.296-298, 339-340, 363-364). With the recent discovery of a temple at Omrit, just south of Baniyas on the northeastern corner of the Huleh Basin, it is likely that all three of Herod's shrines to Augustus have now been discovered. The Omrit temple underwent three dramatic building phases, each with a temple larger than the previous. Herod's temple, which according to Josephus was "a beautiful temple of white stone" (*Ant.* 15.363), was apparently the second of the three phases. The archaeological remains that project from the wide-mouthed cave at Baniyas (Caesarea Philippi), long thought to be Herod's Augusteum at Paneion, were more likely associated with cultic activity dedicated to the god Pan.

1 Rainey and Notley, *The Sacred Bridge*, 212–13.

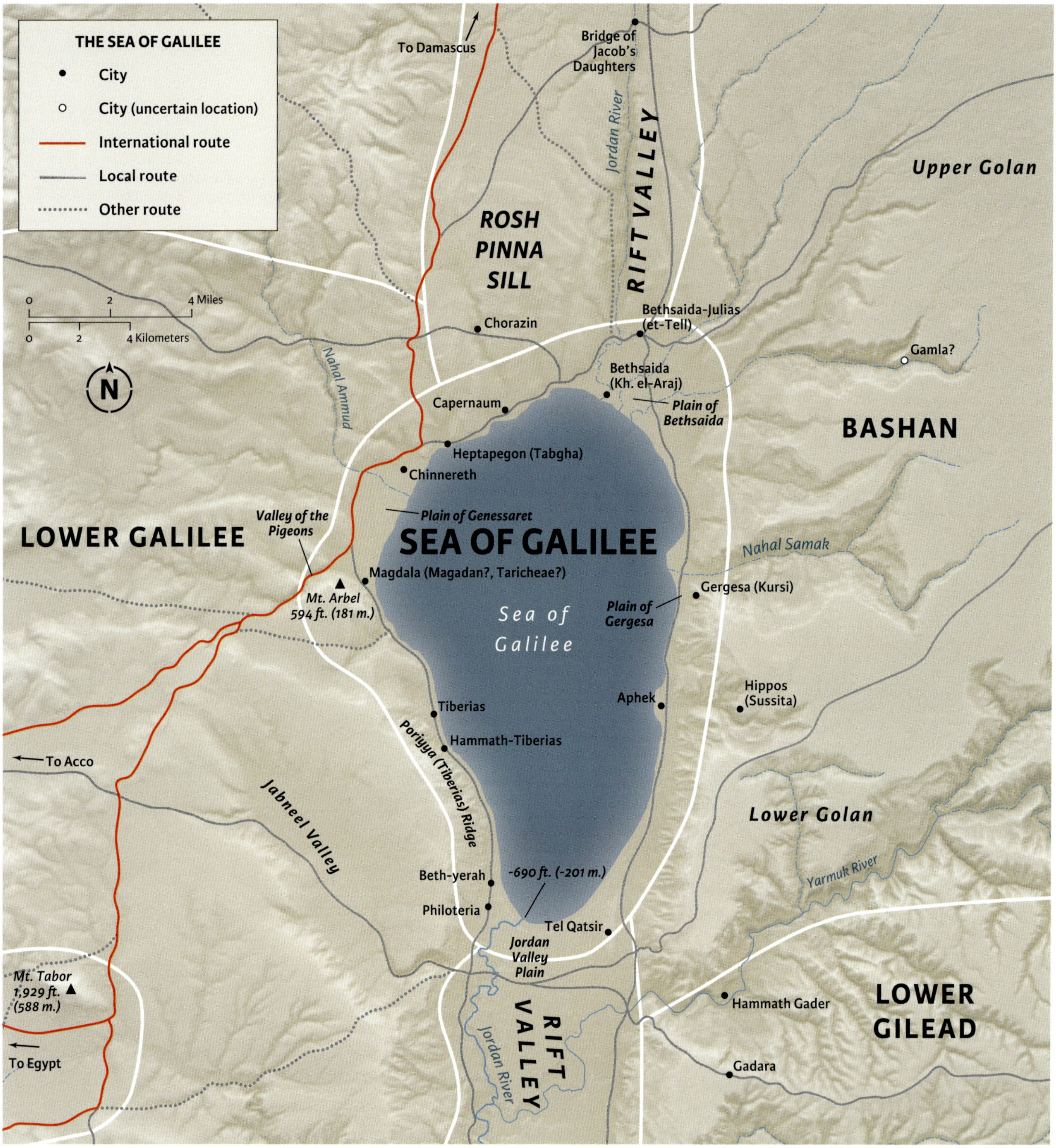

F. THE SEA OF GALILEE

The Sea of Galilee is the only sizeable natural body of fresh water on the Mediterranean's eastern seaboard, yet it played only a minor role in the recorded history of the Old Testament—even in a world whose desert tracts and rocky hillside villages never seemed to have water enough. But in the first century AD, the sea burst to center stage. This was due in part to Josephus's fondness for Galilee and his detailed account of the Galileans' response to the Great Revolt against Rome in AD 66–67, but also because Jesus chose Capernaum, a bustling village on the sea's northern shore, as his adoptive home (Matt 4:13).

Though it is only thirteen by seven and one-half miles (21 by 12 km) in its largest dimensions, the Sea of Galilee is often called a *sea*, rather than a *lake*, by English speakers. For this reason, first-time visitors are often surprised by its small size. Hebrew speakers, at home in the dry lands and deserts of the southeastern Levant, had only one word for "large body of water": *yam*. In the Bible, *yam* is used equally to designate the Mediterranean Sea (Num 13:29; Jonah 1:4), the Red Sea

(Exod 13:18; 15:1), the Dead Sea (Josh 3:16; Ezek 47:18), the Sea of Galilee (Josh 12:3), and even the bronze water reservoir that stood within the confines of the temple complex in Jerusalem—a structure perhaps meant to represent the cosmic sea out of which the dry land of creation arose (1 Kgs 7:23). Greek, though, a language borne on the water, distinguishes between *limon*, typically a freshwater lake, and *thalassa*, a saltwater sea. Thus Josephus, writing in Greek, called the Sea of Galilee a lake (*limon*; *Life* 96, 153; *War* 2.635 etc.). Still, the Gospel writers, certainly knowing the same word, preferred *thalassa*, sea (Matt 8:24; Mark 9:42; Luke 17:2). So why this preference?

Did the writers of the Gospel prefer to preserve the concepts of Hebrew, their native language, as a way of reinforcing their ancient identity in a newly Hellenized land (hence the use of *thalassa* as a Hebraism in the text)? Or did they want to somehow signal that there was an essential connection between what was happening in the Gospel story around Lake Galilee and what would happen when the Gospel spread to the Mediterranean, a kind of literary foreshadowing of what the church might become? Indeed, Jesus's actions around the culturally diverse and ever-challenging smaller Sea of Galilee *did* anticipate the actions of his disciples around the Mediterranean, the latter a zone of opportunities larger in size yet essentially no greater in cultural composition than was Lake Galilee in the first century AD. This point can prove helpful to those seeking to follow the flow of the Gospel in its early years.

In any case, the Old Testament term for the lake is the Sea of Chinnereth (*yam kinnereth*; Num 34:11; Josh 12:3; 13:27); it was named after the large Bronze and Iron Ages city on its northwestern shore (Deut 3:17; Josh 19:35). Preserving that name, Israelis today simply call the sea "the Kinneret." In 1 Maccabees 11:67 we have "the waters of Gennesaret"; and in Luke 5:1 we read "*Lake Gennesaret*": both names were borrowed from the plain adjacent to Chinneroth which, by the end of the first millennium BC, was called Gennesar (cp. Josephus, *War* 3.506). The Gospel of John calls the lake the Sea of Tiberias after what was by the late first century AD the largest city on its western shore (John 6:1; 21:1). Matthew (4:18; 15:29) and Mark (1:16; 7:31) prefer the name Sea of Galilee, taking that name from the first-century AD political district that bordered the western side of the lake. In these cases, the body of water was named after a city or region adjacent to the lake on the west, certainly a reflection of the Galilee-orientation of our sources. For lack of additional sources, we might posit that in the first century AD people who lived on the other side of the lake might have used the term "the lake of Hippos" or the "lake of Gadara" instead, after the two prominent Decapolis cities whose landed holdings touched its eastern and southern shores, respectively.

Defined geologically, the Sea of Galilee fills a low spot in the Rift Valley where the valley is crossed perpendicularly by the same Bashan Depression that helped to shape the open topography of Western Lower Galilee. It is, in essence, a wide spot of the Jordan River. The Jordan enters the sea from the northeast, after slicing through the seam between the Rosh Pinna Sill and the Golan Heights and tracing the western edge of the Plain of Bethsaida, its river delta. The Jordan exits the Sea of Galilee at its southwestern end opposite the lake, heading first due west, then quickly bending southward to begin a twisted run to the Dead Sea. There is sedimentary evidence to suggest that the Jordan River once exited the sea a few hundred feet north of its current channel, on the northern side of the third millennium BC site of Beth-yerah (Khirbet el-Kerak). Modern Highway 90 cuts through the middle of that tell and crosses the Jordan just to the south, at Yardenit, a popular modern (and very commercialized) site for Christian baptism.

Slung between the hills of Galilee and Transjordan, the Sea of Galilee is the largest above-ground reservoir of fresh water on the 400-mile (645-km) eastern seaboard of the Mediterranean. The next closest similar lake is in south-central Turkey. This view is from atop ruins of the Decapolis city of Gadara (modern Umm Qais, Jordan), high above the southeastern corner of the lake. The city of Tiberias can be seen opposite, with the hills of Upper Galilee rising beyond. The view emphasizes the interconnectedness of lands on either side of the Rift Valley.

A popular folk tradition holds that the name *Kinneret*, the modern Hebrew name of the sea, comes from the Hebrew word *kinor*, "harp," so-named because the shape of the sea resembles a harp. The Babylonian Talmud (Megillah 6a) adds the following musings, prompted by the fertility of the Kinneret's shore: "Why was it called Kinneret? Because its fruits are sweet like the music of a harp."

The Sea of Galilee covers sixty-four square miles (166 km2) in surface area. It is up to 150 feet (48 m) deep in the north, but noticeably shallower at its southern end where a muddy islet sometimes appears a little offshore. The normal capacity of the lake is nearly 800 billion gallons (3 billion m3) of water. A small dam near Degania (the first Israeli Kibbutz, founded in 1910) at the outlet of the Jordan River regulates the level of the lake to keep the water no higher than 690 feet (210 m) below sea level. There are certainly yearly fluctuations, and in

A bit muddy and its banks overgrown, the Jordan River makes its final push here, through the Plain of Bethsaida and into the Sea of Galilee. Slowed by the flat run of its delta, the waters of the Jordan move with a serene confidence that brings life to those who can read its mood. Bethsaida, the hometown of Peter, Andrew, and Philip (John 1:44)—and perhaps James and John—lies nearby. Jesus's band of disciples must have been skilled river men. Jesus said, *"The one who believes in me, as the Scripture has said, will have streams of living water flow from deep within him"* (John 7:38). For his disciples, such was an image from home.

drought years the surface of the sea can drop 25 feet (7.5 m) or more. While the volume of water in the Sea of Galilee over time can be ascertained by the thickness of sedimentary deposits along its shore, a better indication of its natural level may be the archaeological remains of ancient piers and nearby villages. For instance, the level of the sea during the time of the New Testament can be determined by plotting the location of the foundations of ancient anchorages and harbors that circled the lake at the turn of the first millennium. These can still be seen whenever water levels drop significantly below the 690- foot (210 m) level. That the foundations of the first-century AD harbors are at or close to the current shoreline suggests the level of the sea has not changed appreciably in the last two millennia.

The Sea of Galilee is fed by a number of fresh water streams in addition to the Jordan; most of these enter off the hills of Upper Galilee from the northwest, or off the Golan from the northeast. Not all of these springs are perennial. Other water sources lie closer at hand, but these tend to be less fresh. Seven springs, slightly salty, once entered the sea at Heptapegon (modern Tabgha) on the northwestern shore; some still do. Hot mineral springs at Hammath-Tiberias flow into the sea at the midpoint of its western shore; these were used in Roman and Ottoman Turkish times for their medicinal qualities. In the first century AD, the Roman naturalist Pliny called the Hammath-Tiberius springs "salubrious."[1] More hot mineral springs enter the lake from its bottom, some arising from fissures nearly 10,000 feet (more than 3,000 m) deep and causing the lake to be slightly saline, though it's not noticeable to human taste. These salt springs, however, become a concern whenever the level of the lake drops significantly because the rate of their salty flow increases with the lessened weight of the water above. Nevertheless, the sea's reputation for fresh water is secure. Notes Josephus,

> Its water is sweet to the taste and excellent to drink, clearer than marsh water with its thick sediment. It is perfectly pure, the lake everywhere ending in pebbly or sandy beaches. Moreover, when drawn [the water] has an agreeable temperature, more pleasant than that of river or spring water, yet invariably cooler than the great expanse of the lake would lead one to expect. It becomes cold as snow when one has exposed it to the air, as the people of the country are in the habit of doing during the summer nights. (*War* 3.506–509)

Hills rising as much as 1,300 feet (400 m) from the surface of the water surround the Sea of Galilee on nearly every side, giving people living at water's edge a bit of a hemmed-in, protected feel. In some places the hills come quite close to the shore, leaving scarcely a level place by which to pass. From any point on the water except the southern end of the sea where the Rift Valley opens to the Jordan Valley, our view has to rise upward: to the Poriyya (or Tiberias) Ridge tracing the lake's southwestern shore; eastward to the Lower Golan; north to the Rosh Pinna Sill; or, rising in the distance beyond, to Upper Galilee northwest and snowy Mount Hermon far to the north.

Nearly all of the hills forming the close perimeter of the Sea of Galilee are composed of black or grey volcanic basalt. The local soil is rich black basaltic, fortified by alluvium that has washed down by streams entering the sea. The fertility of the soils around the southern end of the sea is somewhat negatively offset by the higher concentration of Lisan marls typical of the Jordan Valley. The local building material for villages is also basalt, giving them a rough, darkened look. In contrast, the material used to construct the white limestone synagogue that graced Capernaum in the late Roman and early Byzantine periods had to be brought in from the limestone hills of Lower Galilee. Local basalt was also used for manufacturing heavy agricultural implements such as olive presses, grindstones, and millstones.

Josephus commented on the region of Capernaum: "Skirting the lake of Gennesar, and also bearing that name, lies a region whose natural properties and beauty are very remarkable. There is not a plant which its fertile soil refuses to produce, and its cultivators in fact grow every species. The air is so well-tempered that it suits the most opposite varieties. The walnut, a tree which delights in the most wintry climate, here grows luxuriantly beside palm trees that thrive on heat, and figs and olives that require a milder atmosphere. One might say that nature had taken pride in thus assembling, by a tour de force, the most discordant species in a single spot, and that, by a happy rivalry, each of the seasons wished to claim this region for her own. For not only has the country this surprising merit of producing such diverse fruits, but it also preserves them. For ten months without intermission it supplies those kings of fruits, the grape and the fig; the rest mature on the trees the whole year round. Besides being favored by its genial air, the country is watered by a highly fertilizing spring, called by the inhabitants Capernaum" (*War* 3.516–19).

1 Pliny, *Natural History*, 5.72.

Besides the water of the sea, the fertility of the basaltic soil produced by these perimeter hills is the greatest gift to the region. Four plains, spaced somewhat equidistantly, touch the sea; each is quite flat and very fertile. The largest is the **Jordan Valley Plain** on the lake's southern end; it has a narrow but productive arm reaching half way up the eastern shore to what are today the fields of kibbutz En Gev (Khirbet el-Asheq, perhaps the Aphek of 1 Kgs 20:30). Three miles north is the **Plain of Gergesa** (modern Kursi), a small alluvial fan formed from the Samakh (which is Arabic for "fish") Wadi's seasonal flow off the Lower Golan. Another three miles further north, at the northeastern bend of the sea, is the **Plain of Bethsaida**, a broad rectangle of alluvial soil and small rock that has been swept off the Upper and Lower Golan by its several streams or carried out of the Huleh Basin by the Jordan River. Opposite, and lining the northwestern corner of the Sea of Galilee, is the narrow **Plain of Gennesaret** (1 Macc 11:67; Matt 14:34). Its southern end feeds into the V-shaped Valley of the Pigeons (or, Valley of the Doves; Wadi Hamam) beneath the pock-faced cliffs of Arbel. The alluvial flow of the Ammud Wadi and other streams dropping out of Upper Galilee has pushed the shoreline edge of the Plain of Gennesaret a little into the lake, causing the slightly flattened shape of the sea's northwestern corner. The much larger, harp-shaped indent on the sea's southwestern side was caused as the Rift Valley dropped away from the rise of Eastern Lower Galilee's Poriyya Ridge.

Nearly every plant that is native to the land of ancient Israel can grow on these plains, though most species have vanished due to centuries of neglect, followed by recent decades of intensive, planned cultivation. Early photographs and contemporary travelers' accounts witness a rocky, bare shoreline in the nineteenth century AD[1] where date palms and banana plants dominate shoreline fields today. The first-century AD geographer Strabo mentions that in his day aromatic rush, reed, and balsam grew around the lake (*Geography* 16.2.16), and Josephus reports that diverse fruits ripened in the warm sea-lined soil all year round, without a significant break in the growing season (*War* 3.516–19).

This growth is favored by the weather. Because the Sea of Galilee lies so far below sea level (it's surface is two and a half times lower than California's Death Valley), rainfall is not particularly high (16 in or 406 mm on average annually). This, however, is of little consequence due to the plentiful supply of ground water. Though the sea itself is relatively small, its surface area in relation to the total cultivable acreage of the shoreline plains moderates wintertime temperatures. At the same time, the excessive evaporation rate during the long, hot summer months claims more than five feet (1.5 m) of surface water annually. This evaporated moisture hangs between the hills lining the Rift Valley, giving a nearly perpetual haze to the air that is cleared only when strong winds blow across the lake.

Locally, the Sea of Galilee creates winds of its own. During the late hours of the night, weak winds often blow from the shore toward the center of the sea. As the land-water temperature ratios moderate early in the morning, the direction of the winds is reversed. This rhythm is disrupted most afternoons when strong Mediterranean winds sweep into the sea's basin from the west. Their force is bolstered by a wind-tunnel effect caused by air funneling through the west-east valleys of Western Lower Galilee. When these strong westerly winds drop over the Poriyya Ridge, they scoop along the sea's basin before finding their way up and over the eastern rise of the Lower Golan. The effect is particularly strong in the winter, and during the spring and fall transitional seasons when the weather can change with little warning. The same phenomenon takes place, though in reverse direction and with stronger effect, whenever eastern desert winds blow off the Transjordanian heights. This, too, is most noticeable in the fall and spring. In both cases the result is the same: the waters of the sea stir up quickly (cp. Matt 16:1–3; Mark 4:35–41; 6:47–52). Local fishermen report that the highest waves they have experienced reach six feet (nearly 2 m), creating walls of water plenty high enough to swamp the low-slung fishing boats of the first century AD.

A consistent resource base, a familiar climate, and a tight horizon line all make for a shared living space around the lake. Historically, the Sea of Galilee's main population centers have been located on, or closely associated with, its four major plains. Profiting jointly from the wealth of the water between, each was invariably drawn toward the others for social and economic interaction.

The largest of the plains around the sea, that formed by the Jordan Valley at its southern end, was likely always the most heavily populated. Sites such as Beth-yerah at the outlet of the Jordan, Tel Qatsir at the sea's southeastern end, and the double site of Aphek (on the southeastern shore) and Sussita-Hippos (on a prominent rise just above Aphek) attest to its busyness. The Roman-era site of Gadara, high on the plateau to the

Houses around the Sea of Galilee, as well as food processing machines used in their courtyards, were made of dark grey basalt, the local building material in the region. This collection is at Gamla, a first-century AD city on the Golan Heights above the northeastern corner of the sea, though it could be just about anywhere in the vicinity. The basalt houses of common folk were made with rough-hewn stones, chinked together for support. More care was given to grain mills. The lower millstone (right) is cone-shaped and grooved; the upper millstone (seen at left, on top of its lower mate) is shaped as a concave sleeve and fitted over the top of the lower cone. A basalt mortar and pestle rests between. Wooden bars once protruded from the square holes, from which the top millstone was turned by brute strength. In the first century, this was women's work, but it took two (Matt 24:41). The mill operator poured whole grain into the round opening up top. The grain was ground as it fell between the moving upper stone and its stationary lower pair. The sound of the grindstone was familiar and homey in villages throughout ancient Israel (cp. Rev 18:22).

1 Mark Twain, for instance, who visited the Sea of Galilee in 1867, had a grand and irreverent time comparing its shoreline of "low, shaven, yellow hillocks of rocks and sand, so devoid of perspective," to the "grand peaks . . . clad with stately pines" that compass Lake Tahoe in California. *The Innocents Abroad* (New York: New American Library Signet Classic, 1966), 364–65.

southeast, with its hot springs at Hammath Gader near the outlet of the Yarmuk River, maintained a cultural and economic hold on the Jordan Valley Plain throughout the time of the New Testament. The confluence of the Yarmuk and Jordan Rivers five miles (8 km) south of the sea has been an important resource base and crossing point for millennia. It was here, at a site called Naharayim ("Two Rivers"), that a hydroelectric power plant was built in 1932 to provide electricity for most of British Mandate Palestine.

The Plain of Gennesaret to the northwest was book-ended by two prominent cities, Chinnereth and Magdala. Chinnereth was a Bronze and Iron Ages city on a rise above the northern end of the plain. Magdala (for which there are many variants of spelling in the ancient sources, with some reading Magadan) dominated the southern shore of the Gennesaret plain; it was the bustling and profitable home to Mary Magdalene (Matt 15:39; 27:56). Scholars generally have long assumed that Magdala; Magadan (Matt 15:39); Migdal-Nunia, "fish tower" (*Babylonian Talmud,* Pesahim 46b); Taricheae, "salted fish" (*Babylonian Talmud,* Pesahim 64a; Josephus, *Life*, 188); and Dalmanutha (Mark 8:10) are variant names for the same location. The problem is complex, and in principle we might assume that a plain as fertile and well located as this would have supported a number of cities and villages.[1] Taricheae in particular seems to have been a real center of economy and trade, as Strabo has noted: "[A]t the place called Taricheae the lake supplies excellent fish for pickling."[2] Josephus adds that in the first century AD Taricheae had plenty of construction materials—and, by implication, expert hands—for boat building (*War* 3.505).[3]

The flat and fertile Plain of Bethsaida stretches from the site of et-Tell, "the ruin," to the Sea of Galilee, two miles distant. This view is to the southwest, with the cut of the Arbel Pass on the opposite shore. The excavators of et-Tell, a sizeable Iron Age mound, suggest that this was also the site of the first-century AD town of Bethsaida, meaning "house of the fishermen," mentioned in the Gospels. They posit that et-Tell sat on the shoreline in the time of the New Testament, and that in the centuries following, seismic-induced landslides pushed the shoreline of the sea southward. Archaeological remains from the time of Jesus atop the mound are sparse. An alternative and more likely site for the Bethsaida of the Gospels is Khirbet el-Araj, down at the water's edge. That site has rich finds from the time of Jesus and the Byzantine period, which is to be expected given that Philip the Tetrarch, son of Herod the Great, raised the village to the status of a Greco-Roman polis in the early first century AD (Josephus, *Ant.* 18.26-28; *War* 2.168). Philip renamed the city Julias, after the daughter of Caesar Augustus and mother of Caesar Tiberius; local Jews certainly chose to retain the name Bethsaida.

1 Joan E. Taylor, "Missing Magdala and the Name of Mary 'Magdalene'," *PEQ* 146/3 (2014): 205–23; K. R. Dark; "Archaeological Evidence for a Previously Unrecognized Roman Town Near the Sea of Galilee," *PEQ* 145/3 (2013): 185–202.

2 *Geography* 16.2.45.

3 Nikos Kokkinos has suggested that, based on a close reading of distances given by Josephus, Taricheae was more likely located on the southwestern shore of the Sea of Galilee, near Tel Bet Yerah. Nikos Kokkinos, "The Location of Tarichaea: North or South of Tiberius?," *PEQ* 142/1 (2010): 7–23.

The main population center on the Plain of Bethsaida was Bethsaida, "house of the fisherman," on the northeastern corner of the sea. The site of et-Tell, which its excavator identifies as the ancient site of Bethsaida, lies about two miles north of the shore.[1] Archaeological evidence suggests that the mound may have been the capital of the regional Old Testament-era kingdom of Geshur, which was connected to the house of David by marriage (2 Sam 3:3; 13:38). Bethsaida's role in the New Testament was gained by its being home to Jesus's disciples Peter, Andrew, and Philip, and perhaps also James and John (John 1:44; cp. Luke 5:9–10). An alternative site for Bethsaida, which better fits the geography, the narrative line of the Gospels, and the archaeological record, is Khirbet el-Araj, closer to the shoreline.[2]

Around to the east, the small Plain of Gergesa, home to the village of Gergesa (modern Kursi) in the Roman period, is remembered chiefly for its role in the healing of the demon-possessed man (Mark 5:1–20).

This spot makes nearly everyone's list of "Top Ten Views in Galilee." It's the Plain of Gennesaret and northwestern corner of the Sea of Galilee as seen on a hike down the cliffs of Arbel. The cliffs gained fame from Josephus's story of a mop-up campaign fought by Herod the Great in which his opponents, Jewish nationalists, chose to jump from its sheer-faced caves rather than submit to puppet rule under Rome (*Ant.* xiv.420–30). Many visitors like to think that Jesus pondered his own call to a kingdom from a point on or near the top of the cliff, although the Gospels are mute on the suggestion.

The story of the healing of the demon-possessed man (the so-called "Miracle of the Swine"; Matt 8:28–34; Mark 5:1–20; Luke 8:26–39) has three early claimants for place. Some early Greek New Testament manuscripts record that the man and pigs were in "the region of the Gerasenes," others have the reading "the region of the Gadarenes," while still others say "the region of the Gergesenes." All three were in the Decapolis, a region of unbridled Hellenism lying south and east of the Sea of Galilee. If the correct reading is "Gerasenes," the event would have been in Gerasa, modern Jerash, fifty miles (80 km) southeast of the Sea of Galilee and at an elevation of 3,000 feet (915 m) in the hills—clearly a geographical impossibility. The region of the Gadarenes, on the other hand, is possible since the city of Gadara controlled the sea's Jordan Valley shoreline during the time of the New Testament. Yet this would require the disciples to make a thirteen-mile (21-km) storm-tossed journey by boat, an unlikely and very unpleasant voyage (cp. Mark 4:35–41). Geographical logic best supports the reading Gergesenes, with Jesus's boat being blown to the Plain of Gergesa on the eastern shore of the sea, just slightly south of its likely intended destination of somewhere in Philip's territory. All three sites boast the requisite remains of Byzantine churches memorializing the event.

The remains of other cities and villages from the biblical periods can be found up on the rocky slopes lining the Sea of Galilee, or where the slopes meet water's edge. These relatively infertile shorelines were populated especially in times of economic expansion, such as the first century AD. Examples are Chorazin and Capernaum on the Rosh Pinna Sill north of the sea (Matt 11:21–24), and Rakkath (Tel Raqqat; Josh 19:35) and Tiberias at the base of the Poriyya Ridge to the west.

Because it contains such an important mix of natural and human resources, the Sea of Galilee has always been a magnet for travel and trade. The primary east-west route through Galilee, running between Acco/Ptolemais and Tiberias, linked the sea directly with the Mediterranean. Although not featured in the biblical story, a major international route also swung around the southern end of the Sea of Galilee through the Jordan Valley Plain. This route must have been active during the decades when Kings Omri and Ahab struggled for economic and political control of Galilee with the kings of Aram-Damascus (cp. 1 Kgs 20:1,22–30), but also as Rome sought to push its influence up into Transjordan. The international route connecting Egypt with Asia during the Bronze and Iron Ages also touched the sea, at Chinnereth, on its run between the Jezreel Valley, Hazor, and Dan. The line of this route shifted eastward by the time of the New Testament, as Bethsaida and Caesarea Philippi replaced Chinnereth, Hazor, and Dan as the major economic centers in the region. This put Capernaum squarely on the international route during the time of Jesus, setting the stage for a Gospel story that is more cosmopolitan than provincial. Indeed, the Gospel accounts portray a lively mix of people at Capernaum: religious leaders, Roman soldiers, a tax collector, fishermen[3], and laborers, most with families. Archaeological evidence suggests Capernaum was also a place of manufacturing mill stones, and Josephus adds that there was a doctor in town (*Life*, 72). We might with some justification call Capernaum Jesus's chosen second home (Matt 4:13), a microcosm of all of Galilee.[4]

The double witness of archaeology and geography portrays an active settlement dynamic in and around the Sea of Galilee throughout the time of the Bible. The

1 Rami Arav, Richard A. Freund, and John F. Shroder, "Bethsaida Rediscovered," *BAR* 26/1 (Jan-Feb 2000): 44–56.
2 Mendel Nun, "Has Bethsaida Finally Been Found?," *JP* 54 (July-Sept 1998): 12–31; see also Rainey and Notley, *The Sacred Bridge*, 356–59.
3 Facundo D. Troche, "Ancient Fishing Methods and Fishing Grounds in the Lake of Galilee," *PEQ* 148 (2016): 281–93.
4 Paul H. Wright, *Rose Then and Now Bible Map Atlas with Biblical Background and Culture* (Torrence, CA: Rose Publishing, 2012), 191–92.

additional witness of documents contemporary to the Bible adds important—though never quite enough—detail. Epic literature (e.g., the *Aqht* story) from Ugarit (*Ras Shamrah*) on the north Syrian coast suggests that the sea fell within a north-Aramean horizon in the late second millennium BC,[1] while Egyptian texts from the Late Bronze Age bring the area into the Egyptian orbit. The west-east dynamic between the Mediterranean Sea and Transjordan is best illustrated by Rome's incessant eastward push.

The Sea of Galilee also hung in the balance between local powers such as Damascus, Hazor, Megiddo, and Beth-shean; it is a true Land Between (in the words of James Monson[2]) whose resources were co-opted by all sides. Jabin, king of Hazor, for instance, brought "*the Arabah south of Chinnereth*" (the Jordan Valley Plain) into his northern coalition (Josh 11:1–2), necessarily claiming the resources of the sea in the process. But by the time of David, the entire area became enclosed within the expanding territory of ancient Israel to the south. The tribal boundaries as demarcated in the book of Joshua recognized the sea's multifaced orientation: Naphtali received the northern and western shores, Manasseh the east, and Gad the Jordan Valley on the south (Josh 13:24–31; 19:32–34). So during the biblical period—indeed, during all periods—the region settled into the uneasy paradox of being blessed with everything necessary for a good life, yet always under the shadow of the economic and military priorities of others. It shared, in this sense, the living dynamic of the Jezreel Valley, or the Judean Shephelah.

A first-century view may best illustrate the dynamic of the overall living-spaces of the Sea of Galilee. During the ministry of Jesus, the shoreline of the sea was divided among three distinct political districts: Galilee proper under the political control of Herod Antipas on the west; Gaulanitis under Philip the Tetrarch on the northeast (both were sons of Herod the Great); and, to the south and east, the Decapolis, a region of Hellenistic cities that, though functioning largely independently, were under the general administrative control of the Roman legate in Damascus. Each of these districts had

Peter and Andrew; James and John. Working in pairs, the men of the sea pull up the net from an early morning's work on Lake Galilee. Modern technology aids these fishermen; their tenacity and patience are timeless. The best fishing spots around the lake are along the northern shore, where an influx of organic material brought in by the Jordan River and from streams flowing off the Lower Golan supplies an ever-renewed source of fish food. There are eighteen species of fish native to the Sea of Galilee, most of which are kosher according to Jewish rabbinic law. Josephus Flavius reports the idea that the sea might have been fed by an underground branch of the Nile because of the similarity of fish found in both places (*War* 3.520). Though wrong in his geographical supposition, he was rewarded in the end: the scientific classification of one of the species indigenous to the sea is *Astatotilapia flaviijosephi*.

1 Baruch Margalit, "The Geographical Setting of the *AQHT* Story and Its Ramifications," in *Ugarit in Retrospect: Fifty Years of Ugarit and Ugaritic*, ed. Gordon D. Young (Winona Lake, IN: Eisenbrauns, 1981), 131–58.

2 James M. Monson, *The Land Between: A Regional Study Guide to the Land of the Bible* (Jerusalem: James M. Monson, 1983); *Regions on the Run* (Rockford, IL: Biblical Backgrounds, 1998), 6.

roughly equal access to the lake's rich resource base, controlling the Plain of Gennesaret, the Plain of Bethsaida, and the Jordan Valley Plain, respectively. Moreover, each profited from a thriving economic center on or near the lake that enjoyed the formal status of a Greco-Roman *polis*: the newly built Tiberias in Galilee, the newly elevated Bethsaida-Julias in Gaulanitis, and, in the Decapolis, Hippos and Gadara. Life was diverse, shared, cosmopolitan, and full. It is likely that the closeness of the horizon-line formed by the rise of hills encircling the lake worked more to pull people together than set them apart. Likely the phrase "*Let's cross over to the other side*" (Mark 4:35; cp. Matt 8:18; Mark 5:1,21; 6:45; 8:13; John 6:22) was as much related to sailing from one of these political districts into another as it was a strict directional reference *per se*.[1]

The traditional site of the Sermon on the Mount (Matthew 5–7) is on a rise of the Rosh Pinna Sill above Capernaum, on the northern side of the Sea of Galilee. While proof of the spot remains elusive, all reasonable evidence suggests the bulk of Jesus's Galilee teachings were given somewhere in the vicinity, within the triangle enclosed by Capernaum, Bethsaida, and Chorazin (cp. Matt 11:20–24; Luke 10:13–16). From here it is possible to see the Hellenized Decapolis city of Hippos, in Jesus's day the largest city around the lake, that was set high on a hill. Jesus and his disciples must have seen its lights almost every evening, beckoning the call of a Rome away from home. "It is you who are the light of the world," Jesus told his disciples in effect. *"A city situated on a hill cannot be hidden. . . . In the same way, [you, too, should] let your light shine before others, so that they may see your good works and give glory to your Father in heaven"* (Matt 5:14–16). Byzantine memory identified "the city on a hill" as Jerusalem, even though Jerusalem is hidden among the hills rather than prominently visible on one. Geographical common sense suggests instead that because Jesus referred to an unhidden city on a hill while he was in Galilee, to a Galilee audience, that we should look there rather than to Jerusalem for his on-the-ground referent.

Yet the various people groups inhabiting each of these three districts maintained important social distinctives. Living in a world oriented toward Jerusalem, the first-century district of Galilee was a place where Jews—its majority population—could feel comfortable, and this in spite of the obvious corridors of Hellenism (Ptolemais to Sepphoris to Tiberias) running through. The population of Gaulanitis, on Galilee's northeastern frontier, was more diverse, with Jews and Gentiles fairly evenly mixed. Jesus's sea-based ministry, triangulating between Capernaum, Chorazin, and Bethsaida (Matt 11:20–24; Luke 10:13–16), was focused on both districts. The Decapolis, of course, had a majority Gentile population, even though Jesus's ministry also spread there (the Plain of Gergesa lay just within the northernmost jurisdiction of Hippos; Mark 5:1–20; 7:31). We might conclude, in fact, that the Sea of Galilee served as a model in microcosm of the opportunities that awaited Jesus's disciples around a much larger sea, the Mediterranean. If so, it was the best of all possible arenas for the birth of the Gospel message.

SUMMARY

By every criterion, Galilee is the most complex area in the land of ancient Israel west of the Rift Valley. From its underlying geological structure to its surface topography to the patterns of human settlement that unfolded among its hills, valleys, and sources of water, Galilee is unique among places in the ancient Near East. We might justly speak of Galilee's colorful personality or time-honored distinctions, borrowing phrases from the human endeavor in an effort to feel the essential character of a place that was at the same time Israel's "Galilee of the nations" and God's chosen arena for life with us. Galilee also provides one of the greatest examples of what happens when the priorities of international players tracing the circle of the world's stage meet the tenacity of local partisans who will not be moved from their homeland core. The six regions of Galilee set the scene:

1. *The Jezreel Valley.* The broad expanse of the Jezreel Valley offers the easiest travel access between the Mediterranean coast and Transjordan, and as such served as the greatest international crossroads of the southern Levant. With rich soil and ample sources of water, this was also the largest agricultural breadbasket in the land of ancient Israel. The region was an ongoing zone of conflict between international players who sought to control the imperial highways connecting Egypt, Arabia, Mesopotamia, and the Mediterranean, but also by local players such as Israel and Aram-Damascus (Syria) who struggled to expand their own much smaller spheres of influence in the process. That the Jezreel Valley separates the hills of Manasseh from Galilee heightened Israel's desire to control its routes—and their vulnerability in trying to do so.
2. *The Acco Plain.* While the smallest of the coastal plains in the land of ancient Israel, the Acco Plain is arguably the most important. Acco/Ptolemais is the best natural port along the coast of the southern Levant, and it enjoys direct highway connections to the routes of the Jezreel Valley. The plain was closely tied to the commercial opportunities of Phoenicia, and though coveted by ancient Israel, was difficult to keep within Israelite control.
3. *Lower Galilee.* The parallel ridges and valleys of Western and Eastern Lower Galilee offer perhaps the best mix of living conditions to be had in all of Galilee. With fertile soil, adequate water sources, good highway access to three sides of the international "circle," pleasant vistas, and plenty of living space, this was the heartland of Galilee. But Lower Galilee also lay too close to the international highway not to be overrun, and it offers a geographical storyline where insiders versus outsiders struggle for identity and control.

---

1 Cyndi Parker, "Crossing to 'The Other Side' of the Sea of Galilee," in Barry J. Beitzel, ed., *Lexham Geographic Commentary on the Gospels* (Bellingham, WA: Lexham Press, 2017), 157–64.

4. *Upper Galilee*. The high and jumbled hills of Upper Galilee double as the southern extremity of Lebanon. They offered ancient Israel not only a place to settle in relative isolation from the swirl of internationalism moving through the rest of Galilee, but also rich images of the blessings of God in the process. This was ancient Israel's northernmost frontier, and it had a population base that was independently minded, never very large, and decidedly provincial.
5. *The Huleh Basin*. The value of the Huleh Basin is twofold: here are the sources of the Jordan River, and here the international highways of the southern Levant all funnel on their run between Israel and Aram-Damascus. Brisk commercial and military traffic moved north-south along the drier edges of the basin throughout the biblical period, and its cities were among the most important land gateways into and out of ancient Israel.
6. *The Sea of Galilee*. The Sea of Galilee is the main water reservoir for the southern Levant, and control of its shoreline has always been critical for regional powers. The agricultural landscape of the sea is relatively small, but adequate to maintain a population dedicated not only to harvesting the lake's fish, but securing and controlling its centers of trade. Historic sources indicate that the shoreline of the sea was inhabited by a mixed population throughout the biblical period. Its geographical position was well-suited to the birth and early spread of the gospel.

QUESTIONS

1. Trace the idea of "international circle" versus "local core" on a map of Galilee. What kind of Bible story took place in each arena? Give examples.
2. Explain the term "Galilee of the nations" in light of the physical settings of Galilee and its role in the history of the region.
3. What geographical features made the Jezreel Valley an international area?
4. Why is the phrase "the pasturelands of God" (Ps 83:12 NIV) an especially apt description of the Jezreel Valley?
5. What role did Megiddo play in the history of the Jezreel Valley? Speaking geographically, how was its position more privileged than that of other cities of the valley?
6. How successful was ancient Israel in claiming the Jezreel Valley? What areas of the valley were easier to hold than others? Why?
7. Explain the significance of the Jezreel Valley as a historic arena into which Jesus could gaze during his formative years.
8. Geographically, what is the most significant way in which the Acco Plain differs from the Sharon and Philistine Plains to the south?
9. What makes the port of Acco/Ptolemais more favorable than other ports of ancient Israel such as Ashkelon, Joppa, or even Caesarea?
10. Is the Acco Plain oriented more toward land or sea? Israel or Phoenicia? Support your answers by points of geography and history.
11. What advantages did the tribe of Asher have in its land inheritance? What were its disadvantages? How did Asher's location affect its tribal history?
12. How was Western Lower Galilee similar to the Hill Country of Ephraim, Manasseh, and Judah? What made it different?
13. Which was more favorable for settlement, Western or Eastern Lower Galilee? Why? Give examples.
14. Describe the physical living situation of Nazareth. In your opinion, were Mary and Joseph doing Jesus a favor by raising him there? Why or why not?
15. Find and describe five specific examples of parable imagery typical to Western Lower Galilee.
16. For the Jews of the first century AD, was Western Lower Galilee more "circle" or "core"? Why?
17. Geographically, how does Upper Galilee differ from Lower Galilee?
18. Describe the biblical images of Lebanon. What geographical realities do these images emphasize? How are they appropriate illustrations for God and people?
19. Why was the eastern third of Upper Galilee more favorable for settlement than the western two-thirds of the region?
20. What was the actual living dynamic of Upper Galilee; was it open or closed? Was it an area of connection or refuge?
21. How does the Huleh Basin, as part of the Great Rift Valley, differ from the Jordan Valley further south?
22. What might make Mount Hermon a more appropriate "divine mountain" than Mount Zion? How did the biblical writers describe Zion in light of Hermon? Why might they have done this?
23. What is the Huleh Basin's more valuable resource: its water (the sources of the Jordan) or its routes (the northern international gateway into the land of ancient Israel)? Explain and illustrate your answer by historic events.
24. How successful was ancient Israel in controlling the Huleh Basin? Why?
25. Describe the resource base of the Sea of Galilee and its surroundings. What made it favored in comparison to other regions in the land of ancient Israel?
26. How might a town built in a region of basalt differ from a town built in a region of limestone?
27. Is the Sea of Galilee more of a center or a border for people of the region? Does it more naturally belong to one people group or many?
28. Why might Jesus have chosen to live in Capernaum, as opposed to somewhere else (especially Nazareth), during his adult ministry?
29. Which region of Galilee looks most like home to you? On this basis, what biblical stories and images most resonate with you?

TRANSJORDAN

6

Because most of the events recorded in the Old Testament and the Gospels took place in lands that lie west of the Jordan River, many Bible readers and Holy Land visitors tend to associate the land of the Bible with the land of ancient Israel, not Transjordan. This inclination is reinforced by the biblical authors' focus on people and events related to Jerusalem, and the belief that ancient Syria (Aram-Damascus), Ammon, Moab, and Edom were hostile to Israel and Judah by nature. Modern political considerations do little to alter the view: the State of Israel and the Palestinian territories, together encompassing the "Dan to Beer-sheba" core of the land of ancient Israel (cp. 1 Kgs 4:25), lie opposite the Hashemite Kingdom of Jordan in a kind of territorial face-off on either side of the Rift Valley. Indeed, as we have seen, when viewed from just about anywhere in the land of ancient Israel, the unbroken ridgeline of Transjordan seems a straight-armed barrier, a horizon standing aloof even though it actually lies quite near. To be fair, the view from the other direction, from Jordan to Israel, can give the same impression. The tendency to give priority to things west of the **Rift Valley** is also inherent in the name **Perea**, "beyond [the Jordan]," the "over yonder" designation for much of Gilead and the Medeba[1] Plateau during the centuries that Rome penetrated the Levant (Matt 4:25; Mark 3:8; *War* 2.57). Similarly, the Crusaders used the term Oultre-Jourdain, "Across the Jordan [River]," to designate Frankish holdings in Gilead, Moab, and Edom.[2] The Neo-Latin terms **Transjordan** (lit., "across the Jordan [River]") and **Cisjordan** ("on this side of the Jordan [River]") indicate the same.[3] These latter two names gained favor in the wake of emerging European priorities for the Middle East following the First World War. Yet all-in-all, the "us versus them" disposition of a Mediterranean-based perception of the region is rather artificial, inasmuch as a comprehensive reading of the historical data shows that the chasm of the Rift Valley has more often tended to be a meeting place, rather than a separator, of peoples. Thus, instead of focusing on its role as a border (political divisions, after all, shift over time), it is more helpful to consider the Rift Valley as a meeting place, a confluence of highways bringing people down to its well-watered resources, and then carrying them on to places beyond.

Our overall purpose is to focus on the human dimension of the landscape and resources of Transjordan during the time of the Bible, especially as it relates to the land of ancient Israel. With this aim in view, we must pay careful attention to geographical and cultural factors that unite the lands lying on opposite sides of the Rift Valley. This is seldom the starting point. Speaking with the majority, prominent biblical geographer Denis Baly emphasizes Transjordan's "otherness":

> If one goes there, snaking down between the barren hills of Jeshimon and across the muddy Jordan, he goes to another type of country. This is immediately apparent on leaving the hot and dusty lowlands of the Ghor to climb up beside the waters of Nimrin [identified by Baly as the wadi draining the eastern plateau opposite Jericho, along which the modern highway rises to Amman]. The frowning honey-colored cliffs, the rushing stream, and the glorious pink oleanders in the valley bottom all proclaim a different landscape. This impression of "otherness" is heightened when at last the road toils up onto the plateau and the vast, unlimited steppes open out toward the east.[4]

While not wanting to minimize the significance of the oft-cited differences between the landscapes of Cisjordan and Transjordan as pointed out by Baly and many others, we prefer to give priority to their historical and geographical connectedness instead. Yehuda Karmon and Gideon Biger have pointed out that it was the great eastern desert and not the Rift Valley that habitually formed the natural border of settlement in the Levant (just as, we might add, the Mediterranean Sea does to the west). As a result, Transjordan always had political and economic connections with Cisjordan to the west.[5] Indeed, the continuity of the human story west and east of the rift, including many events described in the Bible, is justification enough to seek out similar living spaces, shared interests, and familiar cultural adaptations between them.

For all its soaring vastness and "unlimited steppes [that] open out toward the east,"[6] many of the geographical features of Transjordan are similar to the landforms, climate, and settlement patterns of Cisjordan. For instance, we find the same sequence of limestone strata throughout the highlands of Gilead, Medeba, Ammon, Moab, and Edom that characterizes Israel and Judah.

1 Medeba is the spelling in the Hebrew Bible (e.g., Num 21:30; Josh 13:9; Isa 15:2). The Arabic spelling, Madaba, refers to the modern city of the same name and its adjacent region in Jordan.

2 Joshua Prawer, *The Latin Kingdom of Jerusalem: European Colonialism in the Middle Ages* (London: Weidenfeld and Nicolson, 1972), 44.

3 Note that the Hebrew phrase *'eber hayyarden*, "beyond the Jordan," refers to lands both east (Deut 3:8; Josh 12:1) and west of the Jordan (Deut 3:20; 11:30; Josh 9:1; 12:7) depending on the position of the narrator of the action. A related phrase, *'eber nāri*, "across the river," is attested in Assyrian documents as early as the late eighth century BC, referring to land that lay west of the upper reaches of the Euphrates. In the late sixth century BC, the Persians used the phrase, usually translated in English as "Beyond the [Euphrates] River," to designate their expansive satrapy that contained the entire Levant. R. Borger, *Die Inschriften Asarhaddons Königs von Assyrien*, Archiv für Orientforschung, Beiheft 9 (Berlin: E. Weidner, 1956), 60; and Anson Rainey, "The Satrapy 'Beyond the River,' *AJBA* 1 (1969): 51–78.

4 Denis Baly, *The Geography of the Bible*, new and rev. ed. (New York: Harper & Row, 1974), 210.

5 Yehuda Karmon, *Israel: A Regional Geography* (London: Wiley-Interscience, 1971), 6; Gideon Biger, "The Names and Boundaries of Eretz-Israel (Palestine) as Reflections of Stages in Its History," in Ruth Kark, ed., *The Land that Became Israel* (New Haven: Yale University Press, 1989), 4.

6 Baly, *Geography of the Bible*, 210.

Moreover, the basic factors of land formation that we met in our discussion of the geological foundations of Cisjordan (tectonic pressure, folding, faulting, and erosion) also shaped the rocky face of the east. Some important differences lie in the fact that in Transjordan there is a large mass of basalt in the north (Bashan) and vast areas of exposed sandstone far to the south, particularly along the Rift Valley and in Wadi Rum.

The overall pattern of Cisjordan's interior longitudinal zones is also similar to those of Transjordan, though of course differing in detail. Here we should note first that because the limestone and sandstone deposits of the southern Levant were laid and folded prior to the formation of the Rift Valley, the Transjordanian watershed was the original watershed in the southern Levant. A single westward slope once reached all the way from what is now western Transjordan to the Tethys Sea, the ancient forerunner of the Mediterranean. The subsequent formation of the rift sliced this slope severely. One result is that Transjordan has a western plain lining the east bank of the Jordan River. This plain is similar to Israel's coastal plain in the sense that much of it enjoys a rich covering of alluvial soil washed down from the hills above, though it is of course much more modest in scope. From here the hills rise eastward, as they do in Cisjordan, though quite suddenly and without the foothills of a shephelah between. Because the Transjordanian uplands are generally higher than the hills of Cisjordan—and in southern Moab and Edom *much* higher—their westward slopes often receive more rain and snow in any given winter than do the hills at the same latitude west of the rift. Here the "high is wet" rule of rainfall overrides "east is dry." When rain clouds cover the hills of Judah, Ephraim, and Galilee in the wintertime, it is common to see heavier clouds blanketing the highlands of Gilead or the Mishor/Medeba Plateau to the east, with an open band of blue hovering above the cut of the rift. The higher elevations of Transjordan translate into colder temperatures and stronger winds in the winter as well. When combined with the hotter, drier summertime temperatures that dominate the Arabian Desert, it seems as though Transjordan experiences a more bracing year-round climate than does Cisjordan. Perhaps, we might argue, it has bred hardier souls as a result.

The spine of the Transjordanian watershed is not nearly as sharp as is that of the Hill Country of Judah, and it lies quite close to the Rift Valley. The uplift of the Transjordanian hills is strongest (and steepest) along this western rim, with the result that by far the larger, though less inhabited, portion of Transjordan's land mass tips toward the east. The exception is in the north in Bashan and, to a lesser extent, in Lower Gilead, where the orientation is reversed and the larger land surface opens to the west. As would be expected, the zone of viable rainfall and hence permanent settlement in Transjordan narrows considerably as we proceed southward, away from the moisture of the Mediterranean Sea and toward the Arabian Peninsula. It also diminishes quickly east of the watershed, where the settled areas of Transjordan back onto a relatively narrow band of open steppe land. Here rainfall is unpredictable, highly irregular, and never quite enough for agriculture. The much smaller Cisjordan equivalent to this steppeland is the Judean Wilderness. Beyond furls the largely uninhabitable North Arabian Desert, open to nothingness except for a few coveted oases connected by tracks known only to those skilled in the ways of the camel. This eastern wasteland is Transjordan's most dominant feature, one that finds a wilderness parallel in Cisjordan only in the Sinai Desert to the south and southwest, and to a much lesser extent in the arid Ghor on the western side of the Jordan Valley.

On the other hand, the vast eastern desert does have a functional parallel in Cisjordan, and that is the Mediterranean Sea. Desert and sea are both zones with endless horizon lines, where life lived within the safety and security of field and plow is impossible. Both embrace a scattering of far-flung outposts that offer refuge, fresh water, and a confluence of routes (oases in the desert and islands in the sea). Both can be crossed safely only by specialized means of transport commanded by men able to read the stars or trained to look for the right bump on the sea's horizon while on camel back or aboard ship. Both are avenues to the wealth of far-off lands (e.g., Isa 60:6), venues of interaction between widely differing cultures, or frightful boundaries out of which agents of destruction sweep ashore, "*like a great swarm of locusts*" (Judg 6:5). And both become useful by means of cities functioning as ports or trailheads, where sea or desert meets arable land: places such as Gaza, Ashkelon, Jaffa, Caesarea, and Acco/Ptolemais along the Mediterranean Sea, but also Bozrah, Rabbath-Ammon, and Damascus fronting the North Arabian Desert. The functional dynamic linking seaport to desert port, Gaza to Bozrah, for instance, is a large part of the story of kingdom-building and empire-controlling that makes up so much of the political and economic history of the southern Levant.

There are, of course, also some significant differences in landforms east and west of the Rift Valley as well. The most outstanding has to do with water flow. Unlike the land of ancient Israel, where the surface of the land is scored by dozens of separate wadi systems, most of which lie dry for much of the year, the highlands of Transjordan are deeply sliced by the incisions of four huge canyon-like watercourses. More properly understood as rivers instead of wadis due to their size and constant flow, from north to south these are the Yarmuk (Wadi Yarmuk), the Jabbok (Wadi az-Zarqa), the Arnon (Wadi al-Mujib), and the Zered (Wadi al-Hasa). These four rivers are fed by numerous springs and tributaries as well as plentiful winter rains and snow. Indeed, the four watercourses of Transjordan are so large that the erosive power of each actually has cut through the watershed to capture the courses of numerous smaller wadis that originally flowed eastward, out toward the open desert. It is important to note that as a result, travelers on the King's Highway (Num 20:17; 21:22), Transjordan's watershed ridge route, have to descend into, then climb out of these canyons when traveling longitudinally through the country. In any case, by bending and redirecting the watershed's eastward surface runoff into their larger, westward-flowing courses, the Yarmuk, Jabbok, Arnon, and Zered Rivers provide reliable, perennial water sources at regular intervals throughout Transjordan.

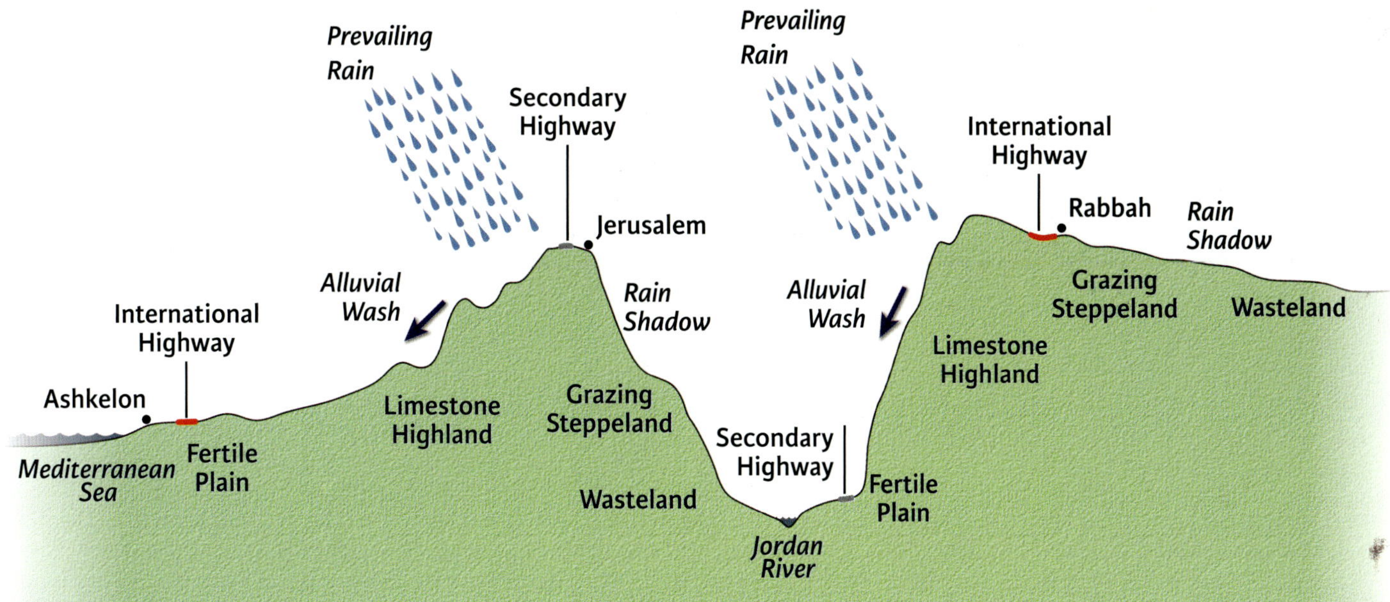

This schematic shows a cross section of Cisjordan and Transjordan from Ashkelon on the Mediterranean Sea to the open desert east of Rabbah (modern Amman). Note the overall similarity of land forms in spite of regional differences in area, elevation, and angle of the watershed ridge.

The human dynamic that makes use of the resources and living spaces of the hills and valleys of Transjordan is also largely similar to that found in the lands lying west of the Rift Valley. The weathering effect of climate on rock has produced a similar soil cover. Such is the case in areas dominated by limestone, which supports the same basic types of flora and fauna found in the land of ancient Israel. This, in turn, provides a familiar subsistence base: shepherding in the drier areas to the east and south (Ammon, Moab, and Edom); tending vines and orchards producing summer fruit in the higher, terraced areas of Cenomanian-Turonian limestone and terra rosa soil (the Dome of Gilead); and growing winter grain in the wide valleys and flat tablelands of rendzina soils that cover a base of Eocene limestone and Senonian chalk (Lower Gilead and the Mishor/Medeba Plateau). Springtime grasses are able to support large flocks of sheep and goats throughout; note the assessment of the pastoral tribes of Reuben and Gad about Gilead and the Mishor: this land "*is good land for livestock*" (Num 32:4). All in all, Transjordan is surprisingly fertile for a land that backs onto the vastness of the eastern desert.

We find a familiar pattern of communication via natural routes as well, with north-south corridors dominating the direction of the traffic flow. Here, however, the international trunk route (the King's Highway) follows the watershed ridge rather than the Jordan Valley, Transjordan's topographical equivalent of the coastal plain. This echoes an economic expediency: one north-south corridor linked ports of call on the Mediterranean coastal plain while the other did the same along the eastern desert watershed. The latter, the route of the King's Highway from Bostra in southern Bashan to Aila (Aqaba) on the Red Sea, was incorporated into the network of Roman roads known as the *Via Nova Traiana*, "Trajan's New Way," after the emperor folded the Nabatean kingdom into the Roman Empire in AD 106.[1]

Today a second international route, the Desert Highway, swings around the eastern extremities of the Yarmuk, Jabbok, Arnon, and Zered Rivers. This Desert Highway has become Jordan's main six-lane expressway, carrying a massive amount of heavy truck traffic between the Gulf of Aqaba and Saudi Peninsula on the one hand and Amman, Damascus, and Baghdad on the other. It doubles as the Darb al-Shami, the "Northern Way" pilgrimage route linking Damascus and the northern Levant to Mecca via Amman, and it is not unusual to see buses from central Asia tracking southward on its long asphalt ribbon for the Hajj. This international route also approximates the line of the famed Hejaz Railway, the narrow-gauge track built by the Ottoman Turks at the beginning of the twentieth century AD to link Damascus with Aqaba and Medina via Amman. Lawrence of Arabia gained fame by disrupting rail freight on the Hejaz Railway during the First World War.

All of this makes for a familiar pattern of interaction between the shepherd and the farmer, the mobile inhabitant of marginal lands and the stable resident of the village. The symbiotic melding of desert and arable land in Transjordan fostered political and economic structures that worked to repulse threats, protect mutual interests, and expand the influence of city states along an intricate network of local, regional, and international routes. These principles are quite similar to those we tracked west of the Rift Valley. Indeed, we witness the same tendency for city states located in arable, resourced lands to develop into kingdoms (Aram-Damascus, Ammon, Moab, and Edom), then expand into the buffer zones, or mini-lands between, that separate one

1 David F. Graf, "The *Via Nova Traiana* in Arabia Petraea," *JRA* 14 (1995): 141–67.

A shepherd drives his flock down the thorny slope of the traditional site of Mount Nebo, the peak from which Moses gazed into the promised land (Deut 34:1). It's thin grazing here—at least in late fall before the early rains green the land. This is a familiar scene on both sides of the Rift Valley, where Israel, Ammon, Moab, and Edom all shared a common base of landed life. Shepherd imagery overrides imagery of all other occupations on the pages of the Bible, and it offers points of connectedness between people and land that work equally well in both Cisjordan and Transjordan.

from the other (Bashan, Gilead, and the Mishor/Medeba Plateau). But here in Transjordan, the risks and rewards inherent to a successful life are somehow heightened since favorable living conditions are found in such close proximity to the open desert. George Adam Smith has rightly labeled this feature of Transjordan a "strange combination of opulence and insecurity."[1]

Although the narrative line of the biblical story may favor events of the land of ancient Israel over those of Transjordan, there is a clear and persistent awareness on its pages that not only do both sides of the Rift Valley share a similar essence of function and form, but their peoples were related as well (e.g., Gen 19:36–38; 36:1–8). Perhaps more importantly, the Bible notes that Israel itself experienced self-defining moments in the hills and deserts of Transjordan (e.g., Gen 32:24–32; Deut 1:19–3:29; 33:2; Hab 3:3). Archaeological and linguistic data now suggest the same.[2]

The canyons of Transjordan's four great rivers, the Yarmuk, the Jabbok, the Arnon, and the Zered, form the natural topographical divisions of the land. They also tended to serve as administrative, ethnic, or political boundaries, though the details were in constant flux.[3] Around them it is possible to identify seven distinct regions, based in part on aspects of geology but also (and more importantly) on specific characteristics of topography, economy, and settlement patterns that derive from the bedrock beneath. From north to south these are Bashan, Lower Gilead, the Dome of Gilead, the Ammon Basin, the Mishor/Medeba Plateau, the Moab Plateau, and the Highlands of Edom; to the last we can attach Wadi Rum in the far south. Ammon, Moab, and Edom are best known as nation-states that interacted—usually competitively—with one another and with Israel and Judah to the west throughout their shared history. The other four regions, though certainly with their own story to tell, more often than not functioned as lands between, with shifting ethnic, political, and administrative borders. These tended to be dominated by the various mouse-states in the vicinity, or, when empires were on the prowl, Assyria, Babylon, Persia, Greece, and Rome. Cats and mice alike took turns penetrating the buffer zones of Bashan, Gilead, and/or the Mishor/Medeba Plateau in their varied attempts to gain staging grounds so as to better check the aspirations of each other, but also to claim additional resources at hand. The plot line echoes that of the land

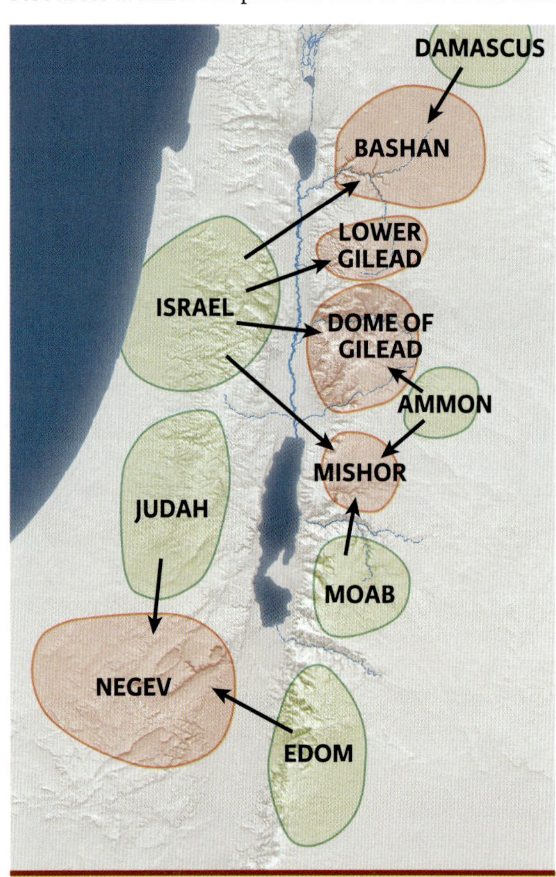

This map provides a schematic overview of the seven regions of Transjordan, highlighting some of the natural interaction points between them. The green ovals represent the heartlands of important Transjordanian nation-states during the time of the Old Testament, while the orange-red ovals are contested lands-between into which these nations tended to expand. Specific historic examples that illustrate these pressure points are mentioned in the text below.[4]

1 George Adam Smith, *The Historical Geography of the Holy Land* (London: Hodder and Staughton, 1894), 529.

2 See, for instance, Avraham Faust, *Israel's Ethnogenesis: Settlement, Interaction, Expansion and Resistance* (London: Equinox, 2006), 221–26; and Anson Rainey, "Redefining Hebrew—a Transjordanian Language," *MAARAV* 14/2 (2007): 67–81, and "Whence Came the Israelites and Their Language?," *IES* 57 (2007): 41–64.

3 Aharoni, *Land of the Bible*, 37.

4 The brilliantly simple idea of representing patterns of interaction between natural regions in the southern Levant schematically, with ovals and arrows, is that of James M. Monson, *Regions on the Run* (Rockford, IL: Biblical Backgrounds, 1998).

of ancient Israel. So with this familiar stage and these well-known actors standing before us in the east, it is time to enter the regions of Transjordan.

A. BASHAN

Used most precisely, the name Bashan refers to a high basaltic plateau in northern Transjordan lying north, east, and southeast of the Yarmuk River. In practical usage, however, the term also includes several neighboring regions that are likewise covered with basalt: The Golan (Jaulan), the Leja Flow ("the Refuge"), Hauran, and Jebel Druze (Mountain of the Druze). The word *Bashan* probably means "smooth ground," a reflection of the relative flatness of its plateau, with particular reference to the region's suitability for fields of grain. The overall smoothness of Bashan's topography allows the region to be easily distinguished on relief and satellite maps from areas of rougher limestone all around. The ancients didn't need modern technology to appreciate this uniqueness: they knew Bashan's flatland heights as a vast, windswept breadbasket, but also as an open staging ground from which to control a confluence of international routes joining the land of ancient Israel with Damascus, or both with the Arabian Peninsula.

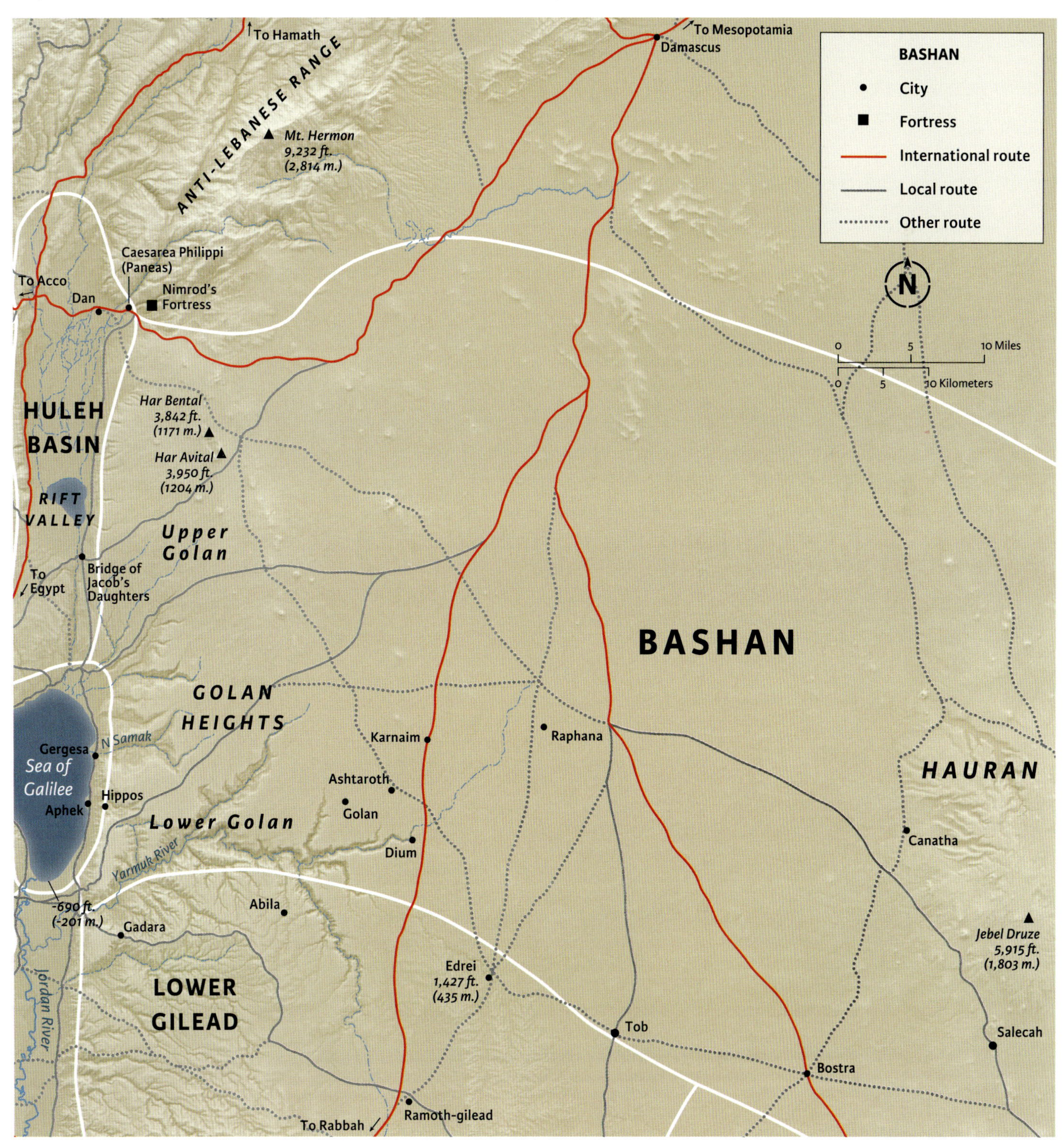

Though the heartland of Bashan is comparatively smooth, it is not exactly *level*; the whole mass tilts upward from southwest to northeast. Unlike the rest of Transjordan, which rises quite suddenly out of the Rift Valley, Bashan lifts relatively unobtrusively off the eastern side of the Huleh Basin, though dramatically from the Sea of Galilee which lies at 690 feet (210 m) below sea level, then pulls up gradually to the east and north. This opens a much larger surface area to the prevailing westward rains than is found in the other regions of Transjordan. The flatness of much of Bashan is due in no small measure to several basalt (lava) flows which took place during the relatively recent geologic past and leveled the surface of the Eocene hills once dominating the area. Altogether there are more than one hundred extinct volcanic cones scattered across the region. What's left are vast lava lands of large, dark boulders and wild surface forms interspersed with wide tracts of rich, basaltic soil. The favorable consequences for agriculture are obvious. Under the influence of soil and rain, the edge of the desert has retreated eastward for seventy miles (112 km), a distance twice as far as Galilee is wide.

Bashan's western end, including its drop into the Rift Valley and the landforms lying on both sides of the Raqqad stream, the major northern tributary of the Yarmuk River, is the **Golan (Jaulan)**. Today the westernmost portion of the Golan is known as the Golan Heights, a region that is ten miles (16 km) east-west by thirty miles (48 km) north-south that falls within the borders of the modern State of Israel. In the time of the New Testament, the Golan was known as Gaulanitis (Latin for Golan; cp. Josephus, *Ant.*17.189), a name derived from "*Golan in Bashan*," one of the places designated as a city of refuge by Moses (Deut 4:41–43; Josh 20:8–9). Ironically, *that* town actually lay further east, at *Sahm el-Jaulan* in modern Syria, on the northern bank of the Yarmuk. In the time of the New Testament, the region of Ituraea (Luke 3:1) bordered Gaulanitis to the north.

Topographically, the Golan divides into two distinct subregions, a smaller Lower Golan in the south and a larger Upper Golan to the north. **Lower Golan** lies within the eastern extension of the Galilee-Bashan Depression, immediately east of the Sea of Galilee and just north of the great cut of the Yarmuk River. The corner of Bashan that faces the land of ancient Israel is thus part of the same geological depression responsible for forming the open, level topography of Lower Galilee. Although the region of Lower Golan rises abruptly from the Sea of Galilee and the canyons of the lower Yarmuk, its top generally lies quite flat, leveling out at between 1,200 and 1,400 feet (365 and 425 m) above sea level. Here, covered by a thick layer of black basaltic soil, can be found some of the best, though certainly not largest, fields in the entire southern Levant. Springs, ponds, and perennial streams abound, giving the region a plentiful supply of water. Some of the wadis of Lower Golan, in particular those of the Raqqad tributary of the Yarmuk and the Samak, which flow into the Sea of Galilee at ancient Gergesa, have cut deeply through the surface basalt overlay and into the softer, lighter Eocene limestone below. Dramatic waterfalls are common amidst their dark grey and buffed white defiles. The division between Upper and Lower Golan is marked by the wadis Meshushim, Yehudiyah, and Daliyyot, all of which flow from the heights into the Plain of Bethsaida on the northeastern corner of the Sea of Galilee. The courses of these wadis are generally in line with the *ash-Shaghur* fault separating Lower from Upper Galilee. Lower Golan's routes, like its wadis, flow southwestward, off Bashan and toward the Sea of Galilee. The main cities of the region trace the seam between Galilee and Bashan: Aphek (Khirbet el-Asheq, modern En Gev; 1 Kgs 20:26) at water's edge, the stately Decapolis city of Hippos (Aramaic, Sussita) perched on the tongue of the scarp above, and Gamla.[1]

Farther north, filling the gap between the northern end of the Sea of Galilee and the foothills of Mount Hermon, is **Upper Golan.** The eastern edge of Upper Golan is marked by a dramatic and very visible line of extinct volcanic cones running on a south-southeast angle away from the southern tip of Mount Hermon. The higher of these cones rise an abrupt 1,500 feet (460 m) from the ground: Mount Bental, "Son of the Dew," tops out at 3,842 feet (1,171 m) above sea level; its twin, Mount Avital, "Father of the Dew," reaches an elevation of 3,950 feet (1,204 m). These cones trace the Bashan watershed beyond which the gradual pull of Upper Golan gives way to the largely level terrain of the Bashan Plateau further east. They also mark the border between the Golan Heights (Israel) and the Syrian Arab Republic today.

The surface of Upper and Lower Golan was covered by two major lava flows in the fairly recent geologic past. The more recent formed the hard basalt shield that covers most of the region. Over time, the forces of erosion have cut craters, cavities, and canyons into the rocky surface of the ground; some remain visible and provide challenging venues for adventure-seeking hikers today. Others were filled by later lava flows. The western and southwestern edges of Upper Golan in particular are highly dissected by the cuts of steep wadis. Several of these have exposed walls of hexagonally-shaped columns that stand as a dramatic reminder of hot lava flows that once cooled and crystallized on the surface of the Eocene limestone rise beneath. Abundant rainfall—more than forty inches (1,016 mm) annually on the northeastern heights—has scoured much of the soil from these dramatic lava forms, though abundant grasses grow within the cuts of the

1 The location of Gamla at Khirbet es-Salam northeast of the Sea of Galilee is nearly universally accepted, even though the evidence for that location is at best inconclusive. An alternate site is Tell el-Ahdab, "humpback hill," in lower Golan (Josephus, *War* iv.2) east of the sea and adjacent to the Syrian village of Jamleh, which sits in the Raqqad branch of the Yarmouk River. Josephus's description of the site of Gamla fits both sites equally well: "From a lofty mountain there descends a rugged spur rising in the middle to a hump, the declivity from the summit of which is the same length before as behind, so that in form the ridge resembles a camel . . . its sides and face are cleft all round by inaccessible ravines, but at the tail end, where it hangs on to the mountain, it is somewhat easier of approach" (*War* iv.5-4). Tell el-Ahdab has not been excavated (it is just on the Syrian side of the boundary between Syria and Israel's Golan Heights), but it does have visible remains on the surface. Toponymy favors the equation Gamla = this site near Jamleh, while Khirbet es-Salam more likely preserves the name of the first-century village Solyma, which Josephus says also revolted against Rome (*Life* 187). See G. Schumacher, *The Jaulân* (London: Richard Bentley and Son, 1888), 34–35, 229; and G. Schumacher, *Across the Jordan: Being an Exploration and Survey of Part of Hauran and Jaulan* (London: Alexander P. Watt, 1889): 84–85.

wadis. This makes Upper Golan a region better suited to grazing than farming.[1] Throughout the long summers, the yellowed, dry grasses and grey-black surface boulders give the entire area a scorched-earth look.

As has already been mentioned, Bashan proper, the **Bashan Plateau**, lies northeast, east, and southeast of the Yarmuk River and its Raqqad tributary, an area that is largely within the borders of the Syrian Arab Republic today. The Aramaic form of the name Bashan, Batanea, was used to designate this region in the time of the New Testament (Josephus, *Ant.* 15.343; 17.25). In the late second millennium BC, the area just north of the eastern reaches of the Yarmuk, homeland of the kingdom of Og, king of Bashan (Num 21:33), was called the "*region of Argob*" (Deut 3:13–14; 1 Kgs 4:13). This seems to have been the most fertile area of the Bashan Plateau and might justifiably be considered the heartland of the entire region, hence it's likely the place from which the name Bashan originated (Deut 3:13). It should be noted that some biblical texts reflect a historic reality in which the term *Bashan* included parts of Lower Gilead south of the Yarmuk, even though this is a distinct region geologically. Note, for instance, the Bashan settlements of Havvoth-jair (Jair's Villages) lying primarily south of the river (Deut 3:14; cf. Num 32:40–42; Judg 10:14).

The far northern border of the Bashan Plateau is marked by the Wa'arah Flow, a rocky basalt wasteland that touches the southeastern corner of Mount Hermon. This part of the plateau is so rough that natural routes to and from Damascus tend to avoid it altogether. The plateau's southern border is less well defined although it can be drawn geologically on a line tracing the broad curve of the Yarmuk River, essentially following the line where the basalt gives way to the Eocene hills of Lower Gilead. Indeed, the main course of the Yarmuk is where it is precisely for this reason—the mass of water flowing off of the hard, basalt-covered Golan was able to carve such a canyon only when it hit the softer exposed Eocene hills lining its southern edge.

The Bashan Plateau rises gradually from an elevation of 1,600 feet (490 m) above sea level in the south to more than 3,500 feet (1,070 m) just below the Hermon Range. A great many surface features betray the region's violent, volcanic past: gigantic basalt boulders, tuffs, and explosion craters, and numerous extinct volcanic cones. Whereas the drainage of Upper and Lower Golan is to the west and southwest, that of the Bashan Plateau is south-southeast, lying as it does east of the Transjordanian watershed ridge. The courses of these eastern-flowing wadis have been captured by the erosive power of the Yarmuk and redirected southwestward back through the watershed ridge and into the Jordan Valley. Rainfall throughout the Bashan Plateau is an irregular twelve to twenty-four inches (300 to 610 mm) annually. With cold, windswept winters and hot, sunny summers, the thick cover of black basaltic soil made this some of the most coveted wheat-growing country in the Roman Empire. The most important cities of the Bashan Plateau lay within the eastern tributaries of the Yarmuk: Ashtaroth (Tell Ashtarah) and Edrei (Dar'a) of the Og story (Deut 1:4; cp. 1 Chr 6:71), Karnaim (Sheikh Sa'd; Gen 14:5; Amos 6:13; 1 Macc 5:43–44), and the Decapolis city of Dium.

The view here is eastward out onto the Bashan Plateau, taken from the top of Har Bental, one of the extinct volcanic cones separating the plateau from Upper Golan. The tree-lined fields in the foreground are within the border of Israel's Golan Heights, while the blue water pond and low volcanic hills on the horizon lie across the modern political border in the Syrian Arab Republic. The flatlands stretching to the horizon are perfectly suited for growing wheat but also for waging pitched chariot battles (2 Sam 10:17–18). In a modern equivalent of the latter, these fields saw intense tank battles between Syrian and Israeli forces in the Six Day War of June 1967, and again in the Yom Kippur War of October 1973.

Further east, twenty-five miles (40 km) beyond the line of volcanic cones separating Upper Golan from the Bashan Plateau, is a broad band of sharp lava extrusions called the **Leja Flow**. This saw-toothed expanse covers an area of twenty by twenty-five miles (32 by 40 km). The word *leja* is Arabic for "refuge" and such it is, for the Leja's ruggedness prompts travelers to circumvent the entire mass, leaving a history of only the disenfranchised or outlaws to find cover among its jagged folds. George Adam Smith has correctly described the Leja Flow as "a tempest in stone."[2] Here we find vast areas of angular, calloused basalt rock with long crisscrossed features and jumbled masses of sharp protrusions that cut the feet of any camel that hopes to trace a short-cut to the other side. With little arable soil and water nearly nonexistent, the Leja was practically uninhabited throughout history except for people needing to disappear. This, and the adjacent area even further east which was at least habitable, was called Trachonitis, "torn-up land," in the time of the New Testament (Luke 3:1; Josephus, *Ant.* 15.344-348; and Strabo, *Geography* 16.2.16).

The rougher landscape south of the Leja Flow, southeast of the Bashan Plateau and east of the limestone rise of Gilead is known as **Hauran** (Ezek 47:16,18). While many geographers have traditionally used the term *Hauran* to include everything that lies between Damascus and the northern border of the Hashemite Kingdom of Jordan,[3]

1 Schumacher noted that local Arabs called Jaulan "the grazing country" (*Belad er-Rabi'ah*) in contrast to the flatter lands of Hauran, "the wheat country" (*Belad el-Kameh*), up above. Schumacher, *Across the Jordan*, 25.

2 Smith, *Historical Geography of the Holy Land*, 624.

3 Schumacher, *Across the Jordan*, 1–2; Samantha Eams, "Between 'The Desert and the Sown': The Hauran as a Frontier Zone in the Middle Bronze Age," *PEQ* 135/2 (2003): 88.

its referent here is to the largely empty basaltic middle of Bashan. The Hellenized form of the name Hauran, Auranitis, appears in the writings of Josephus (*Ant.* xvii.319). Here successive lava flows have sculpted an irregular, wild landscape, the "ragged edge of civilization" in the poetics of George Adam Smith.[1] The basalt of Hauran is very tough, though torn in many places; some crevices conceal entrances to cavities filled with groundwater below. In the southeastern part of Hauran, it is still possible to find open places of basaltic soil that allow grain farming to remain an important part of the local economy. Viable agriculture starts to vanish, however, as we head eastward toward the slopes of Jebel Druze. The western part of Hauran was the land of Tob, Jephthah's Gilead getaway, which suited his role as a traveling outlaw perfectly (Judg 11:1–3). The city of Bostra marks the southern fringe of Hauran; it was an important stop on the Arabia- to -Damascus route during the Roman period.

The relative smoothness of Bashan gives way as Hauran rises eastward to **Jebel Druze** (the "Druze massif"), a massive block of basalt ruggedness in which many peaks exceed 5,600 feet (1,700 m). The highest is Tell al-Jennah, an extinct volcanic cone ringing in at 5,905 feet (1,800 m) above sea level. (Here the Arabic word *tell* labels cones as well as mounds of ancient cities.) For lying so far to the east, rainfall is rather heavy on Jebel Druze: up to thirty inches (762 mm) annually come down on its western slopes, and snow covers the tops of its peaks most winters. This, rather than Mount Hermon, is likely the psalmist's "*Mount Bashan is God's towering mountain . . . of many peaks*" (Ps 68:15), which historically served as an area of refuge for people seeking to flee settled society (cp. Ps 68:22). Area villages, today mostly inhabited by Druze (hence the name), cling to the western foothills of Jebel Druze, where the last bit of grain and grapes can still be grown. Among these is biblical Salecah (Salkhad), marking the far southeastern border of greater Bashan, a place located about as far to the east as someone at home in the land of ancient Israel could possibly conceive of going. (Note the phrase "*as far as Salecah*" in Deut 3:10 and 1 Chr 5:11.)

For folks living down in the nation-states of the land of ancient Israel, greater Bashan was a true frontier: untamed, largely unknown—and coveted by all. This political reality found expression in Bashan's reputation as a place of wild energy: a land of stout forests, large animals, and giant men. That the region centers on a high, open plateau, is windswept by winter storms and seared by summer heat, adds to the aura of the nature-bred toughness of the place. The biblical prophets recognized the majesty of Bashan, likening its fertility to that of Lebanon and Mount Carmel (Isa 33:9; Nah 1:4; cp. Jer 22:20). The oaks of Bashan were especially renowned and compared favorably to the cedars of Lebanon (Isa 2:13); their hardwood was used to make oars for the seagoing ships of Tyre (Ezek 27:6). The "*stately* (or impenetrable) *forest*" of Bashan mentioned in Zechariah 11:2 likely refers to stands of Tabor oak once found on the western slopes of Upper Golan, the part of Bashan most closely connected to Israel and Phoenicia. Unfortunately, little of the forest covering of the past remains; today the entirety of Bashan is almost completely treeless.

Bashan's proximity to Mount Hermon, a stronghold for "*dens of the lions [and] mountains of the leopards*" (Song 4:8), bolstered its reputation as a place where only the stout-hearted could survive. The "*young lion, leaping out of Bashan*" (Deut 33:22) might weigh in as the Golan's heraldic symbol, as could the "*strong [bulls] of Bashan*" (Ps 22:12), which were necessary to plow its heavy, boulder-encased soil. For his part, Amos compared the large females of the species ("*you cows of Bashan*"; Amos 4:1) with the wealth- and privilege-engorged royal wom-

Bulls and cows of Bashan crowd for shade under two eucalyptus trees on the summer-burnt flats of Upper Golan. Eucalyptus trees are a recent import in the region. Tumble-down walls of basaltic stone, behind, still retain some of the dignity they had when they were first erected as a home during the Byzantine period sixteen centuries ago. A scattering of basalt boulders which were once used to construct neighboring houses fills the ground all around. This and similar parts of Bashan remain more suitable for large animal grazing than plowing for grain fields.

1 Smith, *Historical Geography of the Holy Land*, 624.

en of Samaria; his observation was not meant to be a compliment. In any case, the boulder-strewn landscape that stretched eastward from the Huleh Basin and Sea of Galilee was well suited for raising "*rams, lambs, male goats, and all the fattened bulls of Bashan*" (Ezek 39:18; cp. Deut 32:14; Josh 22:7–8; 1 Chr 6:71; Jer 50:19; Mic 7:14); this natural resource rivaled the region's stock in winter wheat.

As for Bashan's reputation of being home to big, tough people, we need only note the Bible's description of the Rephaim, one of its aboriginal populations (Gen 14:4; 15:20; Deut 2:10,20; 3:13).[1] The last surviving remnant of the giant-sized Rephaim was apparently Og, king of Bashan, whose bedstead of iron measured six by thirteen feet (2 by 4 m; Deut 3:11; Josh 12:4; 13:12). Og and his ancestors were viewed by the biblical writers as somehow larger than life, carrying a reputation that was typical of people who lived out on the raw, bouldery frontier. We might almost posit the word *rephaim* as an adjective to describe the entire untamed region. A recent endorsement of similar notoriety is found in the folksy name "Nimrod's Fortress" for the medieval castle *Qala'at al-Subeiba,* which commands the slopes of Upper Golan beneath Mount Hermon. In a defensive move consistent with Bashan's role as a frontier, the castle was built in the thirteenth century AD by the Ayyubid governor al-Aziz Uthman in a successful attempt to keep the knights of the Sixth Crusade out of Damascus. Popular tradition, however, claims that the castle was home to Nimrod, "*a powerful hunter in the sight of the Lord*" (Gen 10:9).

The Crusader-era castle of *Qala'at al-Subeiba* (Nimrod's Fortress) stands guard over the Upper Golan (below), adjacent to the international route connecting Damascus with the powerful Jordan River springs at Baniyas (Caesarea Philippi) and Dan. Untold armies passed this way, seeking either to extend Syria's influence in Galilee or, conversely, to prevent Damascus from penetrating southwestward beyond Mount Hermon. Now part of the Israel National Park system, Nimrod's Fortress offers intrepid visitors hours of exploration opportunities. They may go into an octagonal tower, through a secret passage, up to its keep (secure tower), or down dark spiral staircases to the bowels below.

Mount Hermon was the natural northern political boundary of the land of ancient Israel, although the apogee of Israel's economic orbit reached to Damascus beyond. This made the flatlands of Bashan that lie below Hermon's southeastern flank a wide-open buffer between Aram-Damascus and Israel (by way of Galilee), or between Aram-Damascus and Ammon (via Gilead). Throughout history, Bashan has also been a staging ground for the merchants of Damascus who have sought to push their way to ports on the Mediterranean, such as Tyre and Acco/Ptolemais, or, coming the other way, for seaborne trade to gain a foothold in Transjordan. Merchants from Israel, too, crossed Bashan in search of eastern markets. And to the victor belonged the spoils: the right to favored trading status in the other's capital city (1 Kgs 20:34).

An overview of historic events in the northeastern quadrant of the land of ancient Israel shows that the drive for profit and political connectedness overcame the harsh living conditions of Bashan, prompting a continued ebb and flow of economic and military action across its storied stage. Indeed, that there are so many historic names for Bashan and its several subregions is witness enough of the multiple waves of peoples who have swept over its rocky plateau. Most sought to control either the great trunk route that connected Asia to Egypt as it swung around Mount Hermon, or the lucrative Spice Route coming out of the Arabian Peninsula via Bostra. Bashan is where these two imperial routes meet; spur routes radiating from them link local people groups in Amman, Gilead, and Upper and Lower Galilee. For Israel, the primary local routes into Bashan were two: one crossed the Bridge of Jacob's Daughters at the southern end of the Huleh Basin, the other climbed

Nearly everyone who invaded the southern Levant from the north first took Damascus, then faced a choice for further advance: either through Bashan southward to the kingdoms of Transjordan and Arabia, or southwestward through Bashan to Israel, the Mediterranean, and eventually Egypt. The prophet Ezekiel drew the roadmap:

The word of the Lord came to me: "Now you, son of man, mark out two roads that the sword of Babylon's king can take. Both of them should originate from the same land [i.e., Damascus]. And make a signpost at the fork in the road to each city. Mark out a road that the sword can take to Rabbah of the Ammonites and to Judah into fortified Jerusalem. For the king of Babylon stands [in Bashan] at the split in the road, at the fork of the two roads." (Ezek 21:18–21)

---

1 For the suggestion that the Rephaim were a kind of super-skilled warrior, see C. E. L'Heureux, "The Ugaritic and Biblical Rephaim," *HTR* 67 (1974): 265–74 and "The *yelîdê hārāpā'*—a Cultic Association of Warriors," *BASOR* 221 (1976): 83–85. For a possible connection of the biblical *Rephaim* with Ugaritic *rp'u*, the ponderous yet ephemeral "healer-god" or "long-departed ancestor" who lived in Ashtaroth and Edrei, see Marvin H. Pope, "The Cult of the Dead at Ugarit," in *Ugarit in Retrospect: Fifty Years of Ugarit and Ugaritic*, ed. Gordon D. Young (Winona Lake, IN: Eisenbrauns, 1981), 159–79.

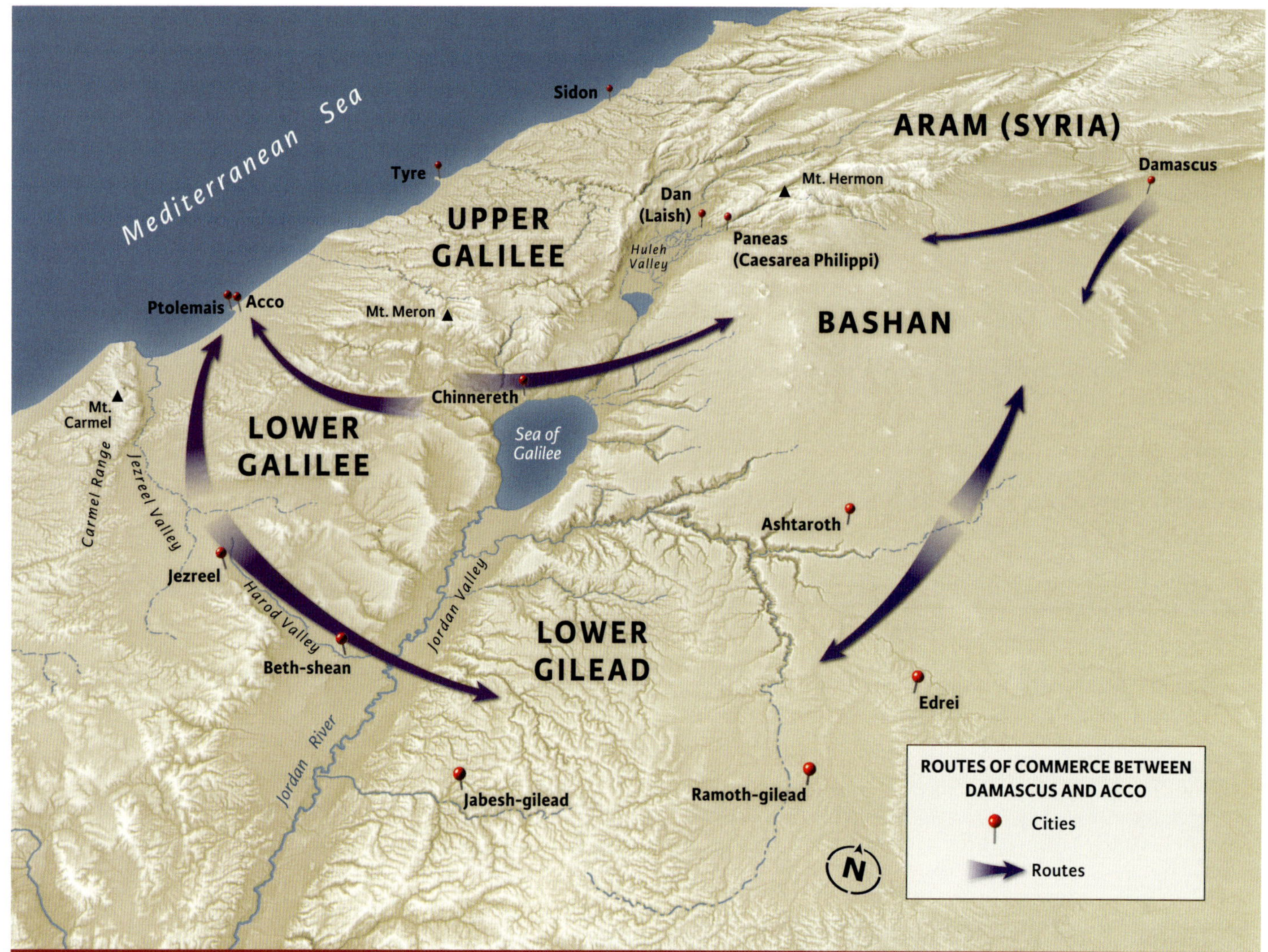

The shortest route from Damascus to the Phoenician ports was the most difficult, taking the traveler or ware-laden merchant up and over the towering Anti-Lebanese and Lebanese Ranges. Much easier was to push across Bashan, then swing through the open valleys of Galilee. Rome's penetration into the southern Levant simply reversed the direction of flow. In either case, control of these routes by outsiders posed a direct threat to the economic and national aspirations of peoples living in the hills of Israel or Gilead. By marrying into the royal house of Sidon and claiming rights to Ramoth-gilead just south of Bashan, Israel's King Ahab hoped to siphon the entire revenue flow his way.

onto its heights from Aphek and Sussita/Hippos on the eastern edge of the Sea of Galilee.

These are some of the plot options; the reality is that in the storyline of Bashan, Aram-Damascus was nearly always first among equals. Although the biblical narrative emphasizes Israel's view of the matter, historically Aram-Damascus has always been the main player in the region. Simply put, Bashan's flatlands were better accessed by a short chariot-ride from nearby Damascus than by the long up-and-down journey through the Rift Valley from the land of ancient Israel. The kings of Damascus took this fact-on-the-ground seriously, but they were not above justifying their success in Bashan on divine favor: "*[Israel's] gods are gods of the hill country. That's why they were stronger than we were [when we fought them on Israelite land]. Instead, we should fight with them on the plain; then we will certainly be stronger than they*" (1 Kgs 20:23).

Every time a king of Damascus appeared in the land of ancient Israel or pushed down to Ramoth-gilead—and during the time of the Israelite monarchy this was often—we can assume that Bashan was already firmly in Syrian hands (1 Kgs 15:20; 20:1,26; 22:3; 2 Kgs 6:8,13–14,24; 9:14–15; 10:32–33; 13:3; Amos 1:3; 6:13 and the Tel Dan Inscription[1]). Indeed, the only recorded battle story between Aram-Damascus and Israel that was actually waged in Bashan itself was all the way down at Aphek. Even here the rest of Bashan must have already fallen to the Aramean king since the battle site lay on the eastern shore of the Sea of Galilee (1 Kgs 20:26–30). We can sense Israel's frustration by not being able to check the Arameans in Bashan, and their glee whenever they could make inroads up on the plateau: "*Don't you know that Ramoth-gilead is ours, but we're doing nothing to take it from the king of Aram?*" (1 Kgs 22:3). "*Didn't we capture Karnaim for ourselves by our own strength?*" (Amos 6:13).

1 Shmuel Ahituv, *Echoes from the Past* (Jerusalem: Carta, 2008), 466–73; Anson F. Rainey and R. Steven Notley, *The Sacred Bridge: Carta's Atlas of the Biblical World*, 2nd emended and enhanced ed. (Jerusalem: Carta, 2014), 212–13.

Rarely do we get a glimpse in the historic sources of an independent kingdom in Bashan, one not under the direct control of either Aram-Damascus or Israel, or subject to a larger power further afield. Two examples that are recorded in texts are the early Iron Age Aramean city-states of Geshur and Maacah in Lower and Upper Golan, respectively (Deut 3:14; Josh 12:5; 13:11,13). The most storied instance of an independent state in Bashan, however, was a bit earlier, during the Late Bronze Age, when from the region of Argob, King Og of Bashan controlled cities from Ashtaroth and Edrei to Salecah (Num 21:33; Deut 3:1–11; Josh 12:5). Geshur, Maacah, and the kingdom of Og were remnants of the pattern of semi-independent city-states that thrived in the land of Canaan during the late second millennium BC. Perhaps these Bashan-based kingdoms survived longer than many of the others precisely because they lay on an open frontier, between the emerging monarchies of Israel and Damascus and just beyond the reach of Egypt's waning New Kingdom empire.

In his pre-Canaan conquests, Moses took this area from Og and assigned it to the up-and-coming tribe of Manasseh (Num 32:33; Deut 3:13–14; Josh 13:12–13; 17:1; 1 Chr 5:23). Initially, the local Manassite clan of Jair replaced Og as the dominate player in the region. Jair's territory, which stretched into Lower Gilead, became known as Havvoth-jair, "Jair's Villages." The writer of Kings later described the inheritance as "*sixty great cities with walls and bronze bars*"—an appropriate defensive development for a region constantly subject to the onslaught of outsiders (1 Kgs 4:13; cp. Deut 3:14; Josh 13:30). David married into the royal house of the kingdom of Geshur in order to gain a loyal ally on his border facing the region. The son of that union was Absalom (2 Sam 3:3). David also took the kingdom of Maacah further north (in Upper Golan) in an attempt to contain Aram-Damascus (2 Sam 8:3–12; 10:6–19). All of this early activity gave the kings of Israel and Judah a certain claim to the region. Yet Israel had a hard time holding onto these gains during the monarchy, and it was only in the mid-eighth century BC that Jeroboam II managed to reassert Israelite control over Bashan and Damascus (2 Kgs 14:28). The region's open, windswept plateau was too easily scoured by Syrian blows.

This is the gradual rise from the Sea of Galilee onto the Golan Heights. The twin volcanic cones of Mount Shiphon stand as sentinels over the view. Ancient Israel's climb to Damascus began here; Syria's downward swoop came the other way.

From a decommissioned military post on the top of the extinct volcanic cone of Har Bental in Upper Golan, Israeli soldiers—and now a multitude of civilian visitors—can take in the sweep of the shoulder of Mount Hermon toward Damascus. Some of the greatest campaigns for human gain passed this way. And it was somewhere out here, on the road to Damascus, that Saul of Tarsus testified that he *"saw a light from heaven brighter than the sun"* and heard the voice of Jesus (Acts 26:13–15).

Bashan became a happy hunting ground as the empires of the ancient Near East started to pour into the southern Levant in the eighth century BC. First up was the Assyrian Shalmaneser III who, as we have seen, pushed through Bashan all the way to Mount Carmel in the mid-eighth century BC.[1] A century later and after the temporary foray northward by Jeroboam II, Assyrian King Tiglath-pileser III conquered Damascus, Ashtaroth, and *"the land east of the Jordan"* (1 Chr 5:26; Isa 9:1). He converted Bashan into two Assyrian provinces, Karnaim on the plateau between Gilead and Damascus, and Hauran further east. Then followed the Babylonians, Persians, Ptolemaic Egyptians, Greek Seleucids, and finally—and most decisively—Rome. Bashan was, by proof of invasive history, ancient Israel's most porous frontier.

When the pendulum of power in the ancient world swung from Mesopotamia out to the Mediterranean basin in the late first millennium BC, the age-old north-south corridors of the Levant started to give way to new doorways opening from the west. With this shift, the main axis of world trade bent ninety degrees, toward the Aegean and then Rome, to which all roads eventually led. To service this new economic reality, the most promising port in the southern Levant became Acco/Ptolemais. (Eventually that honor would fall to Caesarea.) Unlike the port cities of Tyre and Sidon, which backed up against the towering Lebanese and Anti-Lebanese Ranges, Acco/Ptolemais funneled traffic directly into Galilee via the down-warped valleys of the Galilee-Bashan Depression. From there the smooth topography and relatively gentle rise of the Lower and Upper Golan invited Greek and Roman control over the all-important staging ground of Bashan. The land's potential for raising wheat and controlling the routes of a fast-growing world economy kept them there. Indeed, Marcus Terentius Varro, a Roman scholar writing on agriculture in the mid-first century BC, noted that while the normal yield for grain fields across the Roman Empire was ten- to fifteenfold, at Gadara just south of the Yarmuk it was a hundredfold (cp. Matt 13:3–9).[2]

The New Testament-era story of Bashan is the story of Rome's penetration into the East. The Herodian kingdom, Rome's client state in the area, included Gaulanitis, Batanea, Trachonitis, and Auranitis, first under the control of Herod the Great and then under that of his son Philip the Tetrarch (Josephus, *Ant.* 15.217, 343; *War* 2.95; Luke 3:1). Bashan was also the gateway into the Decapolis, a loose confederation of cities planted in and just south of the region during the centuries between the Testaments to foster and disseminate a set of Mediterranean-based loyalties in an otherwise Semitic world.[3] In Bashan these included Hippos, Dium, Canatha, and Raphana.

Demographically, Bashan was a decidedly mixed region in the first century AD. Here a seductive and op-

---

1 A. Kirk Grayson, *Assyrian Rulers of the Early First Millennium BC II (858–745 BC)*, RIMA, vol. 3. (Toronto: University of Toronto Press, 1996), 48; cp. 54–55.

2 Marcus Terentius Varro, *On Agriculture* (*de Re Rustica*) 1:44:1-2.

3 See, for instance, David F. Graf, "Hellenisation and the Decapolis," *ARAM* 4 (1994): 1–48.

portunistic Greco-Roman culture took deep root in a fertile soil that for centuries had been claimed—though not always successfully—by Israel. But by then winds of change were again sweeping this highland plateau. Somewhere on its open heights, on the road from Galilee to Damascus, a scrupulous rabbi from a Hellenized city on the northeastern bend of the Mediterranean Sea, Saul of Tarsus, met the risen Jesus (Acts 9:1–9). An early church tradition voiced by Eusebius, though it is a minority view, places the Transfiguration of Jesus on Mount Hermon[1] (cp. Matt 17:1–4). If that location is correct—and it is theologically tempting—Jesus of Nazareth and Saul of Tarsus both saw the Light and heard the Word at a place where Jew and Gentile were forever entwined by the juncture of place and time. Like the young lion of Deuteronomy 33:22, the Christian movement leapt into the world from the crossroads of Bashan.

B. LOWER GILEAD

As a place name, Gilead refers generally to the limestone hills east of the Jordan River that lie between the basalt Bashan Plateau in the north and the chalky Mishor/Medeba Plateau in the south. We say "generally" because the borders of Gilead as a political unit changed in response to varying land claims made by surrounding city and nation-states over time. Indeed, the Bible's many references to Gilead present a complicated picture of territorial conflict throughout the biblical period and beyond. Similar to other regional names (e.g., Philistia, Samaria, Jezreel, Galilee, and Bashan), the name Gilead likely first designated a relatively small area, then was expanded to include neighboring regions as political conditions warranted. Denis Baly has suggested that the original Gilead lay within the upper, encircling arm of the Jabbok River northwest of Rabbah (modern Amman), where the Arabic place name *Jal'ad* is firmly affixed.[2] These fertile hills south of the main cut of the Jabbok River would indeed make a good heartland for an emerging regional identity. On the other hand, some of the territorial and genealogical language in the Bible describing Moses's apportionment of Transjordan among the Israelite tribes associates Gilead specifically with the inheritance of Manasseh in the north, the region of Lower Gilead (Deut 3:15–16; Josh 17:1–6). These texts suggest the name Gilead

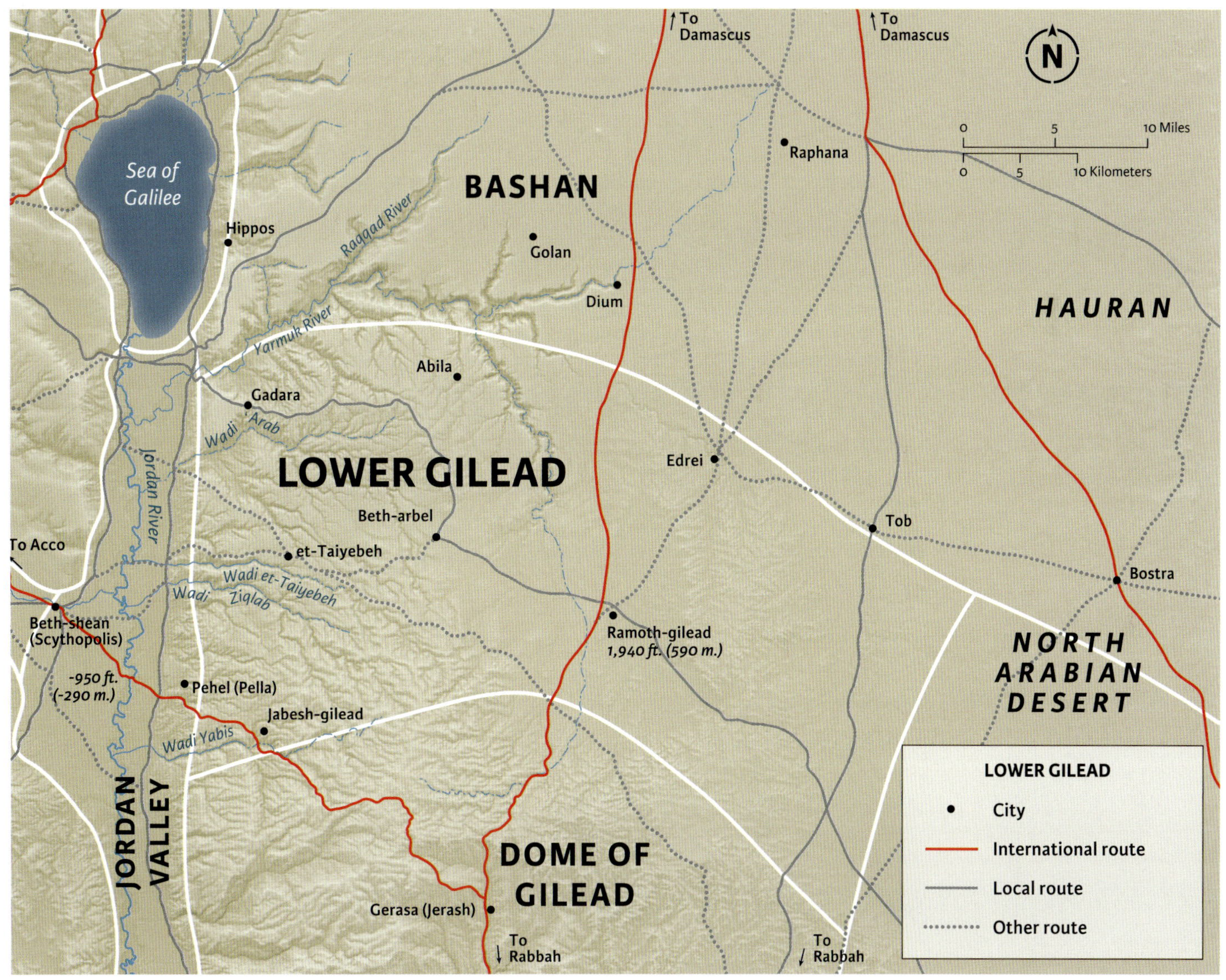

1 Eusebius, *Commentary on the Psalms* 88:13.

2 Baly, *Geography of the Bible*, 219.

may have originated somewhere in that vicinity. Eventually Gilead became a generic term referring to all of the areas claimed by Israel in Transjordan, that is, to the regions assigned to the tribes of Manasseh, Gad, and Reuben, which included all or parts of Bashan and the Mishor (e.g., Josh 22:9,13,15; Judg 20:1; 2 Kgs 10:33; 1 Macc 5:24–27). We have seen above that the biblical writers came to use the name Ephraim, which originally designated the heartland of Israel's earliest settlement west of the Jordan, to refer to the entire central hill country (e.g., 1 Kgs 12:25; 1 Chr 6:67; cp. Hos 5:3; 12:13–14). We might similarly conclude that the name Gilead became the default term for Israel's entire territorial claim across the Jordan precisely because their heartland there was the Gilead hills. Said Jeremiah, "*[Israel's desire] will be satisfied in the hill country of Ephraim and of Gilead*" (Jer 50:19)—that is, both west and east of the Jordan. At the very least, we can assume that the name Gilead reflects centuries of geographical and political ebb and flow.

The origin and meaning of the word *Gilead* is uncertain. Jacob's Galeed, "mound of witness," seems to be a folk etymology or pun on the word *Gilead*, which was certainly already known as a regional name before Jacob's time (Gen 31:45–47).

We have also seen that a regional study of the land of ancient Israel is less concerned with the movement of political boundaries *per se* than it is with defining regions by geographical characteristics that outlast individual attempts at kingdom building. If we chose to define the region of Gilead politically, we might conclude that the mighty cut of the Jabbok that cleaves the Dome of Gilead was foremost a divider since it separated Gad from Manasseh (Num 32:22–42; Deut 3:12–17) and the kingdom of Sihon from that of Og (Josh 12:2,5). But a political division, even if repeated from time to time, is not always a natural one. It will be recalled that while the Kana wadi may have been the official political border between Ephraim and Manasseh during the Iron Age, actual tribal settlement was blurred along the seam as villages belonging to each shared the resources in the bottom of the wadi (Josh 17:7–10). The same holds true for the living dynamic of the Jordan Valley. Indeed, wadi beds that are fertile tend to function more naturally as shared economic zones, pulling people who live on opposite banks together rather than serving as political boundaries splitting them apart. Since on-the-ground patterns of land use tend to be conservative while political borders are liable to shift, we prefer to make a division in Gilead based on elements of geology and topography, that is, on differences in living conditions and economic activities that result from specific characteristics of geography, thus letting the ebb and flow of political and military activity find its own level across the terrain as specific conditions permit.

Defined primarily by its topography and geology, then, Gilead is composed of two natural regions, Lower Gilead in the north and the Dome of (or, Upper) Gilead in the center and south.

As a distinct geologic unit, Lower Gilead is a rainbow-shaped band of soft limestone that stretches southwestward and southeastward, about twenty-five miles (40 km) in each direction, from the bend of the Yarmuk River. The outer edges of Lower Gilead on the west, north, and east are composed of Eocene limestone, a continuation of the same Eocene mass that underlies Bashan, though here it is not covered by lava flow. It will be recalled that the course of the Yarmuk River, the clear topographical marker dividing Lower Gilead from Bashan, is where it is precisely because the water that flows off the basalt surface of the Bashan Plateau cut deeply into the bedrock only when it reached the softer exposed Eocene to the south. The inner part of Lower Gilead, its central and southern core that wraps around the northern bulge of the Dome of Gilead, consists of softer Senonian chalk. There is a splash of basalt on a small plateau in Lower Gilead's far northwestern corner, just west of Gadara (modern *Umm*

The wide cut of the lower Yarmuk River winds its way between the soft Eocene limestone edge of Lower Golan (right) and the rise of the hills of Lower Gilead (left). This is a late autumn view, prior to the onset of the early rains, with the slopes still shouldering the burn of summer. Yet the river valley bottom is ever green, living testimony that while the Yarmuk may mark the formal boundary between two distinct geographical regions, it must have served as a shared meeting place for peoples who lived on either side of the cut.

Ruins of the Decapolis city of Pella (Khirbet Fahl) surround the copious spring of water in the green depression in the middle of this view, climbing the hills on either side. The older Bronze and Iron Ages mound of Pehel (Tell al-Husn) rises to the left. The ridge of Mount Gilboa lines the far horizon, with one of the most fertile parts of the Jordan Valley filling the space between.

Qais), and another to the east between Abila (Tell Abila) and Ramoth-gilead (Tell er-Rumeith).

Persistent rainfall has caused the surface of Lower Gilead's relatively soft limestone base to erode into a mass of rounded hills and valleys. Lower Gilead's western slope, its Rift Valley-facing façade, is cut by a number of equally rounded canyons, none of which form a particularly difficult obstacle to incoming traffic. The most prominent of these canyons are Wadi 'Arab, which parallels the Yarmuk just to its south, the wadis et-Taiyebeh and Ziqlab at the region's midpoint, and Wadi Yabis; it traces the northern edge of the Dome of Gilead. None of these are mentioned in the Bible by name, though Wadi et-Taiyebeh could preserve an echo of the name of "*the land of Tob*" (Judg 11:3).[1] One of these, or a smaller wadi in the vicinity, may have been the Cherith "*which is east of the Jordan*" to which Elijah, whose homeland was Gilead, fled after his initial confrontation with Ahab (1 Kgs 17:1,5 NASB). East of the watershed, the topography of Lower Gilead has not been as severely cut by erosion; the land levels out considerably between Beth-arbel (modern Irbid; Hos 10:14) and Ramoth-gilead ("the heights of [Lower] Gilead"). Because Lower Gilead lies directly east of the down-faulted Jezreel and Harod Valley system and just south of the Galilee-Bashan Depression, its elevations are relatively low, topping out on the Ramoth-gilead plateau at just under 2,000 feet (610 m). This combination of lower elevations and rounded topographical forms conspires to open Lower Gilead to commerce and travel. Yet the main factor that makes Lower Gilead Transjordan's prime international T-junction for traffic oriented to the west is that it lies opposite the Jezreel corridor, thus having a straight-line and level connection to the markets of the coast. The tribal holdings of Gad (in Lower Gilead) and Asher (on the Acco Plain), who were full brothers in Jacob's genealogy (Gen 35:26), controlled the termini of this route.

If Bashan is Transjordan's granary, Lower Gilead is the open barn door. While the Jordan River can be forded at several places east of Beth-shean, the most active crossing led southeast to Pehel (Roman Pella), a city that was built on a series of mounds around a generous spring just above the Rift Valley floor. Beth-shean/Scythopolis and Pehel/Pella are within easy sight of each other, and each dominated its own side of this most fertile segment of the Jordan Valley. The two were twin cities in every way, and their joined history speaks of the impact that this double front door made on the political and economic landscape of northern Transjordan throughout recorded history.

From Pehel/Pella the main natural route into Gilead climbs southeastward to Jabesh-gilead (Tell el-Maqlub), a mound perched above a prominent fork in the Wadi Yabis where the chalk of Lower Gilead gives way to the Cenomanian-Turonian highlands of the Dome of

1 Smith, *Historical Geography of the Holy Land* (1966), 393.

Scant remains of the Damascus-facing gate of the fortress at Ramoth-gilead (Tell er-Rumeith) are sufficient to reconstruct in the mind's eye the chariot battles between Israelite and Aramean forces in the mid-ninth century BC. The flatland plateau stretching away from the site was well suited for chariot warfare. The Arameans generally proved adept on the battlefield of Ramoth-gilead, where they repeatedly checked Israelite advances toward Damascus.

Gilead. Jabesh-gilead's natural connection to Beth-shean helped its residents sneak through Philistine lines to claim the bodies of Saul and Jonathan for burial, while its position up in the hills helped ensure that the conquering Philistines could not easily snatch back the remains of the fallen king and crown prince of Israel (1 Sam 31:8–13; cp. 2 Sam 21:11–14 and Judg 21:8–14; 1 Sam 11:1–15 for Saul's previous ties to the city). From Jabesh-gilead the natural route climbs onto the Dome of Gilead, where at Gerasa (modern Jerash) it joins the international highway connecting Damascus with Rabbah of the Ammonites.

In his *Historia Ecclesiastica* (111.5; cp. Matt 24:15–22), Eusebius mentions that Christians from Jerusalem fled to Pella when Rome destroyed the city in AD 70. We might ask, "Why to Pella of all possible places?" Rome's army was intent on stamping out the Jewish rebellion across all of the lands that had been under the control of the Herodian dynasty. The region of the Decapolis was the closest political district to Jerusalem that had not been under Herod's control and hence lay outside of Rome's wrath. Of the Decapolis cities, Pella offered the most convenient place to which a Jerusalemite might flee, being the first city one encountered when running straight up the Jordan Valley on its eastern, more easily traveled side.

A second natural route heading eastward from Beth-shean/Scythopolis enters Lower Gilead somewhat north of Pehel/Pella, then climbs to either the Decapolis city of Gadara on the small basalt plateau above the southeastern end of the Sea of Galilee or traces the ridge south of the Wadi 'Arab to Beth-arbel and Ramoth-gilead on Lower Gilead's far eastern plateau. Here, too, traffic joins the Damascus-Rabbah international route that traces the heights behind the canyons scarring Gilead's western face. During the Iron Age, Ramoth-gilead was the key to military strategy in the entire region, witnessing a series of chariot-battles between the armies of Israel and the forces of Aram-Damascus. Today, appropriately, the site is adjacent to a Jordanian air force monument and just east of the intersection where the major modern highway connecting Damascus with Amman (Jordanian Highway 25) joins the direct route to Baghdad (Jordanian Highway 10).

During the Turkish Ottoman Period (sixteenth through early twentieth centuries AD) the *Darb el-Harwana*, "Road of the Hauranites," connected Hauran in eastern Bashan with the port of Acco/Ptolemais. This grain route circled south of the Sea of Galilee through the gateway of Lower Gilead rather than tracing the basaltic terrain of Bashan into and out of the Huleh Basin further north.

Moses designated three cities of refuge in Transjordan to which those who had shed innocent blood could flee: Bezer on the Medeba Plateau, Ramoth-gilead in Gilead, and Golan in Bashan (Josh 20:8–9). All three were on major highways and likely represent subregions where early Israelite tribal populations were concentrated in Transjordan during the Iron Age.

Always a throughway, Lower Gilead was also valued for the resources of its own. Rendzina soils dominate throughout. While not as heavy or rich as the basaltic soils of Bashan, the soils of Lower Gilead are easily plowed and are also well-suited for fields of grain. Rainfall in Lower Gilead reaches twenty-four inches a year, about the same as the Hill Country of Judah and Ephraim, diminishing as expected beyond the watershed to the east. The width of arable land that formed the seventy-mile (112 km) bulge up in Bashan here drops to no more than thirty miles (48 km); it will taper to scarcely five miles (8 km) wide in Edom far to the south. In any case, the shared homeland economy in Bashan and Lower Gilead—both regions are based in grain farming and long-distance commerce—may have led to the historic connection between the two.

The prophet Amos chastised Damascus *"because they threshed Gilead with iron sledges"* (Amos 1:3). Threshing sledges common to the Iron Age were typically made of heavy oaken slabs into which sharp stones were set as teeth. When the sledge was pulled over sheaves of grain strewn across the threshing floor, the teeth knocked the heads of grain from their stalks. In Amos's image, teeth of iron replaced the sledge's stones, making it a tool sharp enough to do real damage as it knocked Gilead—by implication its people—to pieces. In crafting the image, Amos likely had in mind the conquests of Hazael, king of Damascus in the late ninth century BC, or other, unrecorded Syrian attacks of a similar nature. (There must have been many.) In any case, his use of imagery specific to the process of harvesting grain suggests that the Syrian conquests to which Amos alluded were concentrated in the wheat-growing region of Ramoth-gilead.

The natural connection of Lower Gilead to Bashan is strengthened by the role of Ramoth-gilead during the Iron Age. The plateau around Ramoth-gilead is a southern protrusion of the flatlands of Bashan into Lower Gilead, an easy fifty-mile (80 km) chariot ride due south of Damascus and the closest open field for chariot battles to the Dome of Gilead. *"Don't you know that Ramoth-gilead is ours, but we're doing nothing to take it from the king of Aram?"* (1 Kgs 22:3), asked Israel's King Ahab of Judah's King Jehoshaphat in the mid-ninth century BC. The question presupposes the cold political realities of Lower Gilead's easy connection to Bashan (and hence Damascus), as well as the need for Israel to seize the region as a foothold to control the routes and markets of Bashan. We sense that Ahab and Jehu felt distended and exposed in battles here, while the Syrian kings were right at home. In fact, the armies of Damascus were almost always more successful than those of Israel whenever battle was joined on the open Ramoth-gilead plateau (1 Kgs 22:1–40; 2 Kgs 8:28–9:13; 10:33; 15:29). The same could be said of the Assyrians: their first successful invasion of the southern Levant, under Shalmaneser III, reached Beth-arbel in 841 BC.

Indeed, the plateau forming Lower Gilead's northeastern corner seems to have been more tightly bound to Bashan than it was to the Dome of Gilead—not only in its local economy, but also in the narrative line of the Bible. The biblical record of ancient Israel's early tribal inheritances, together with related genealogical material, is the first to establish the point. The Manassite territory of Havvoth-jair seems to have enveloped as much land south of the Yarmuk, in Lower Gilead, as it did to the north (Num 32:39–42; Deut 3:14–15; Judg 10:3–5). Og's territory, which the clan of Jair inherited, also stretched south of the Yarmuk, by some accounts as far as the Jabbok (Deut 3:13; Josh 12:2,5; 13:30). When Solomon divided Israel into twelve administrative districts, he recognized this connection to Bashan, placing the higher, eastern two-thirds of Lower Gilead with Bashan under the authority of Ben-geber, his commissioner in Ramoth-gilead (1 Kgs 4:13). The western third of Lower Gilead, its Rift Valley slopes and southern rise toward the Dome of Gilead, tended to remain associated with the tribe of Gad whose heartland was the dome (Deut 3:16–17; 1 Kgs 4:14).

Lower Gilead's connection to Bashan is further reinforced by the role of the Decapolis cities within the Roman Empire. Most were located in southern Bashan and Lower Gilead: Hippos, Dium, Raphana, Canatha, Gadara, Abila, and Pella, with Scythopolis west of the Jordan serving as their natural gateway to the Mediterranean Sea. These cities represent Rome's most important inland hold on the southern Levant, an anchor cast inward to lash the routes and resources of Transjordan to the markets of the sea. Ever the political strategist, Rome also used the Decapolis cities to separate the historic power base of Damascus from the wealth of the Nabateans further south, hoping to neutralize the local priorities of each and funnel the resources of the region down through the natural routes of Lower Gilead to the coast. The international T-junction of Lower Gilead never worked better than it did for Rome.[1]

All in all, Lower Gilead can perhaps best be seen as a land lying between lands between. The heartlands of the strongest area nation-states—Israel, Syria, and Ammon—are separated one from the other by three buffer zones: Galilee, Bashan, and the Dome of Gilead. In

1 The earliest known Roman road milestones in the southern Levant date to AD 56 and mark a coastal road running from Syrian Antioch to Ptolemais. The earliest evidence of a Roman road heading inland from Ptolemais to Scythopolis dates to AD 69. Milestones dating to AD 112 mention the restoration of the extension of this road between Pella and Gerasa. These early milestones point to an imperial Roman policy of tapping into the resources of Gilead via the international connector of the Jezreel Valley. For a summary of data, see David Graf, Benjamin Isaac, and Israel Roll, "Roads and Highways (Roman)," in David Noel Freedman, ed., *ABD* vol. 5 (New York: Doubleday, 1992) 782–87.

The flatlands on the plateau around Ramoth-gilead have always supported a mixed economy. Here rendzina soils sprout an ample—though far from uniform—crop of winter wheat, while camels, hardy denizens of heavy lifting and long-distance travel, enjoy down-time and a snack. A family of Bedouin and flock of sheep always seem to be nearby. We can sense the draw of a well-supplied life in the land of opportunities that is Lower Gilead.

the midst of these is Lower Gilead, a bull's eye that, like the better-known Jezreel Valley to which it is connected to the west, is a real junction of routes, of doorways, and of opportunities. But for all of their good intentions, the efforts of Israel's kings to seize and hold the area were never quite enough to define the region as "theirs."

C. THE DOME OF GILEAD

While an important part of the land of Gilead encompasses the low region of soft limestone and chalky hills south of the Yarmuk River, the term *Gilead*, as it is most often used in the Bible, refers to the broad, rounded, uplifted dome of Cenomanian-Turonian limestone that lies directly across the Rift Valley from the Hill Country of Ephraim and Manasseh. Geologically, this dome is the northeastern continuation of the Judean Arch; the limestone was deposited when the ancient Tethys Sea inundated the region before the formation of the rift. The eastern end of the Dome of Gilead pushes the desert backward to some forty miles (65 km) east of the rift, significantly less than the eastern frontier of Bashan but still enough to provide a large block of contiguous living spaces with adequate supplies of soil and water. The northeastern angle of the dome actually touches the basalt of the Hauran (Lower Gilead is wedged to the west), forming a continuity of living space with Bashan out toward the ragged edge of the desert. The

Bertha Spafford Vester, of Jerusalem's American Colony, gives this account of her visit to the Ajlun Castle in 1914:

"Our next camp was at Ajlun, beside a lovely stream. From Qalat ar-Rabad majestically surmounting the village of Ajlun we had a perfect view of the surrounding country. A sharp east wind was blowing from the desert, making visibility sharp and clear. Standing on the ramparts of the Saracen castle begun in AD 1184 on the site of a still older foundation, we enjoyed the most perfect view of Palestine it has ever been my good fortune to see. Snow-capped Mount Hermon rose to the north representing Dan, and we could see the seashore south of Gaza—representing the complete area from' Dan to Beersheba.'"[1]

Vester could see the Mediterranean Sea from the hills around Ajlun partly because the spot where she was standing was significantly higher than the crest of the watershed west of the Rift Valley, partly because that watershed takes a dip at the Central Benjamin Plateau—which was precisely on her line of sight to Gaza, and partly because the Philistine coastline takes a southwestward sweep, allowing her to see the outer part of the plain over the top of the Cisjordan watershed ridge. Perhaps Moses gazed into Canaan *"as far as the Mediterranean [Western] Sea"* (Deut 34:2) from the same spot, then remembered the view when God showed him the land from a less lofty Mount Nebo (Deut 34:1).

1 Bertha Spafford Vester, *Our Jerusalem: An American Family in the Holy City, 1881–1949* (Jerusalem: Ariel Publishing House, 1988), 245.

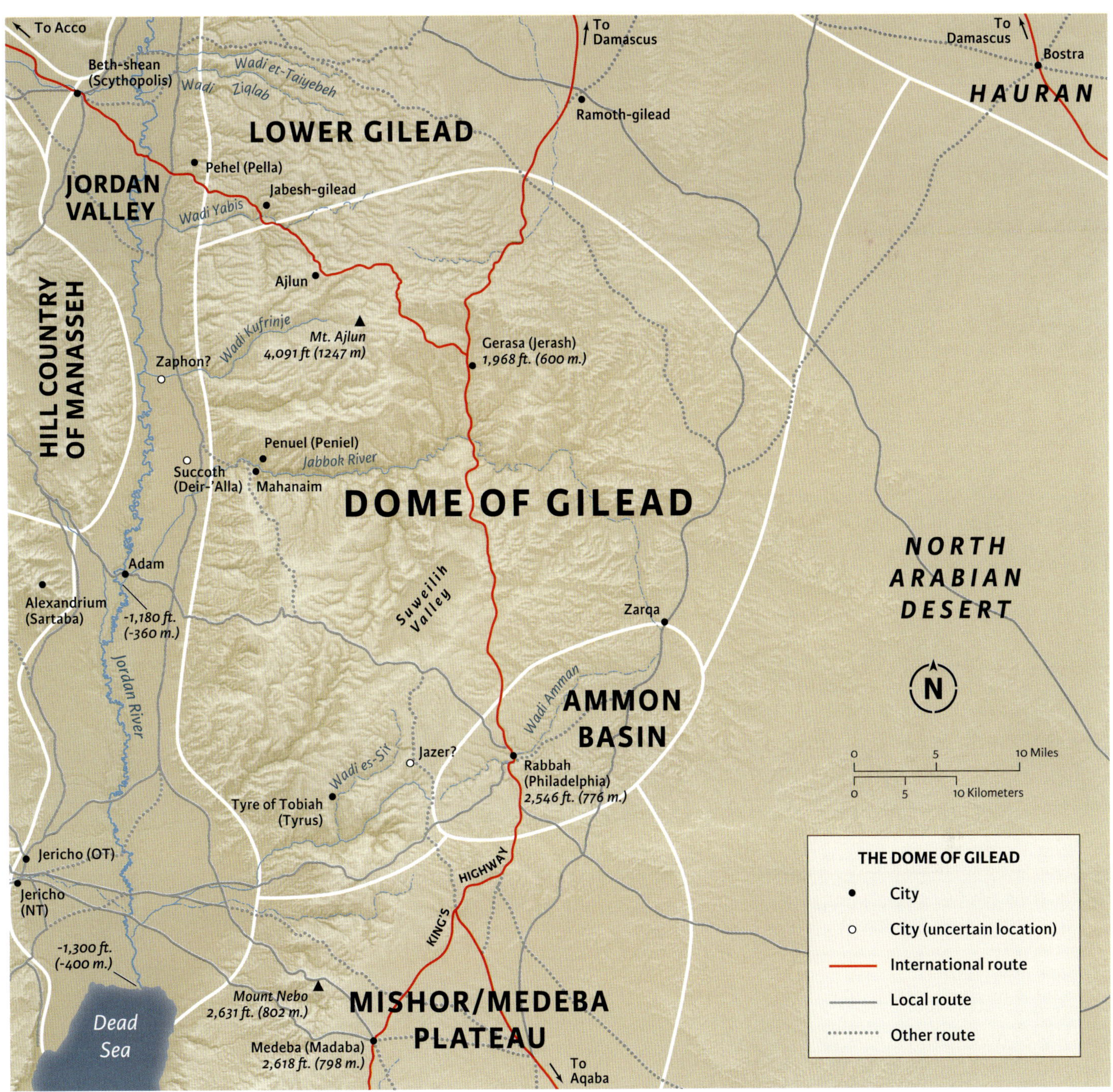

dome gives way to the high, flat Mishor/Medeba Plateau on the south, with the chalky Ammon Basin on its desert-oriented, southeastern fringe. The western edge of the Dome of Gilead is, of course, the Jordan Valley, while its northern curve, as we have seen, merges into the softer hills of Lower Gilead. The Dome of Gilead, then, has natural connections with every other region in northern Transjordan as well as with the central hill country west of the Rift Valley. As a result, it played a critical role in economic and political interactions of all of the major nation-states in the region.

The bulging crest of the Dome of Gilead has been sliced so deeply by the Jabbok (*az-Zarqa*) River that at first glance we might think that this part of Gilead comprises two smaller domes, one lying to the north of the Jabbok and the other to the south. They are, in fact, halves of the same. The dome's inner, Jabbok-facing slopes are steeper than its outer, perimeter slopes, and the cut exposes vast stretches of Jurassic limestone and Nubian sandstones beneath the Cenomanian-Turonian core. The major tributaries of the Jabbok River arise in the Senonian chalk (Ammonite) basin on the southeastern edge of the dome (primarily the Wadi Amman), and with the tributaries of the Golden River amid the hills around Jerash, ancient Gerasa, further north. Like the Yarmuk, the Jabbok has captured wadis that originally flowed eastward from the watershed ridge, bending the erosive power of their flow westward instead. Once its tributaries join into the main body of the Jabbok, their combined waters flow due west to the edge of the Rift Valley, then angle southwestward through the alluvial plain of Succoth to join the Jordan River at the Adam fords. All told, the incised course of the Jabbok, from its Ammonite source to the Jordan River, traces a great oval bend more than sixty miles long, not counting its many twists and turns.

The elevation of the northern half of the Dome of Gilead soars to 4,091 feet (1,247 m) at Mount Ajlun (Jebel Umm ed-Daraj), three miles southeast of the Crusader castle at Ajlun (Qala'at ar-Rabadh). Elevations here are more than 1,000 feet (305 m) higher than the highest hills in Ephraim and Manasseh west of the Jordan River. The southern half of the dome is slightly lower, topping out at a relatively modest 3,652 feet (1,113 m). The overall topography of the Dome of Gilead is similar to that found in the hill country west of the Rift Valley thanks to a shared limestone base, but the dome is much grander in scale. As expected, the dome has been highly eroded by rainfall on its incised western face. Particular mention should be made of the rugged Wadi Kufrinje, which drains the high hills of Ajlun into the Rift Valley. But the top of the dome, unlike the spiny backbone of the watershed west of the Jordan River, is here rounded and broad. South of the Jabbok River, the uppermost surface of the Dome of Gilead flattens out into a very fertile valley called the Suweilih or Baqa'a ("Wide") Valley. To the east, the Cenomanian-Turonian hills gradually give way to a narrow tableland suitable for grazing, eventually merging into the arid Senonian flats of the open desert.

The Dome of Gilead is the part of Transjordan that most closely resembles the highland core of the land of ancient Israel. In landscape, climate, vegetation, and living conditions, an Israelite would have felt right at home on the Dome of Gilead, as would a Gileadite in the Judean and Ephramite hills west of the Rift Valley. For the Old Testament period, we might justifiably speak of a "West Israel" and an "East Israel"—just as in the mid-twentieth century, the Hashemite Kingdom of Jordan included territory on both the west and east banks of the Jordan River.[1] Because of Gilead's elevation, rainfall amounts here are actually higher, and snows more frequent, than they are west of the Rift Valley. (The "high is wet" rule of rainfall overrides "east is dry.") Many strong springs can be found on Gilead's western slopes, and dew is heavy throughout. Blessed with an abundance of terra rosa soil, terraced hillsides, and, on the watershed, landforms that flatten out into broad highland valleys, the advantages for agriculture in the Dome of Gilead are obvious. Josephus described the agricultural benefits of Perea, the northern end of which covered the western slopes of the Dome of Gilead:

> [T]here are tracts of finer soil which are productive of every species of crop; and the plains are covered with a variety of trees, olive, vine and palm being those principally cultivated. The country is watered by torrents descending from the mountains and by springs which never dry up and provide sufficient moisture when the torrents dwindle in the dog-days. (*War* 3.44-47)

Here the economic base is not grain farming as in Bashan and Lower Gilead but the same mix of summer fruit that wraps the terraced hillsides of Judah, Ephraim, and Manasseh. Gilead's olives and grapes are especially rich, and its figs, pomegranates, and almonds are prized. In the biblical period, the region's most famed product, however, was the balm of Gilead, a plant resin (of exactly which plant is unknown); it was valued for its medicinal qualities and in demand as a commodity of export (Gen 37:25; Jer 8:22; 46:11; Ezek 27:11). The horticulturalists of Gilead's highlands enjoy an attractive package of resources that is desired especially by people living in the less-fertile regions on

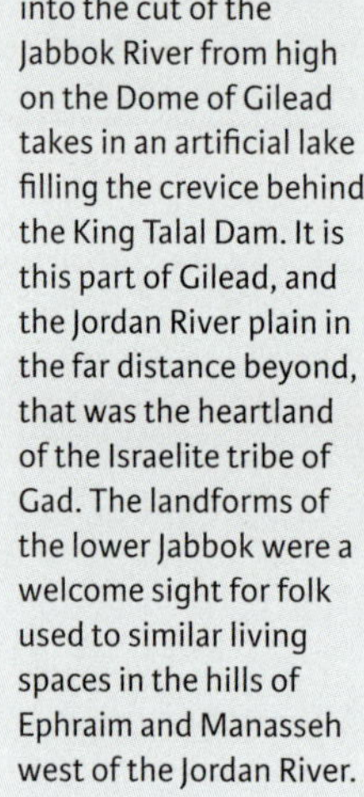

This view westward into the cut of the Jabbok River from high on the Dome of Gilead takes in an artificial lake filling the crevice behind the King Talal Dam. It is this part of Gilead, and the Jordan River plain in the far distance beyond, that was the heartland of the Israelite tribe of Gad. The landforms of the lower Jabbok were a welcome sight for folk used to similar living spaces in the hills of Ephraim and Manasseh west of the Jordan River.

1 Thus, the geo-political term *West Bank* for the largest area of the Palestinian territories.

This view toward the northeast takes in the upper reaches of the Jabbok canyon as it tops out on the crest of the Dome of Gilead's hard limestone core. The perennial water flow is visible in the lower left. Areas such as this lay within easy striking distance of Rabbah of the Ammonites. They witnessed the brunt of the constant push and pull between Ammon and Israel in the time of the Old Testament.

its frontier such as those in the Ammon Basin, in the Mishor/Medeba Plateau, or out on the eastern desert. This prompted the Gileadites (or whatever nation had a controlling interest in Gilead at the time) to be always on their toes, since encroachment or outright invasion was a persistent threat from all sides. Fortunately, the defiles of Gilead's westward-flowing wadis provide natural hiding places and strongholds against would-be raiders swooping by.

Gilead is also famed for its natural wooded cover. Jeremiah likened Gilead's forests to the ones that crown the summit of Lebanon (Jer 22:6; cp. Zech 10:10) and its pastoral grazing land to the woodland heights of Carmel, Bashan, and Ephraim (Jer 50:19; cp. Mic 7:14). The folksy image of the Shulammite's hair reflects Gilead's quiet fortitude: *"How beautiful you are, my darling. How very beautiful!... Your hair is like a flock of goats streaming down Mount Gilead"* (Song 4:1; 6:5).

One particularly rugged Gilead woodland was called the Forest of Ephraim. This name not only hints at regional connections to landscapes west of the Jordan River, but it may well reflect a historical reality in which ancient Israel's earliest settlement activity took place in precisely these two areas. The growth of the Forest of Ephraim was overhung enough that Absalom got tangled up in the branches of a large oak tree there (2 Sam 18:6–9). George Adam Smith, a native of sylvan Scotland, was duly impressed with the forests that still clung to Gilead's slopes in the late nineteenth century AD. Smith spoke of "ridges covered by forests under which you may march for the whole day in breezy and fragrant shade," and he cited Western travelers who favorably compared its natural vegetation to the forests of Europe.[1] As in most of the rest of the Middle East, the trend toward deforestation has been advancing in Gilead for centuries, though stands of scrub oak, carob, and pine can still be found among the more prevalent groves of olives and other orchard trees.

The three main crossing points of the Jordan River all carry routes that lead up into the Dome of Gilead. In terms of international traffic, the heaviest-traveled of these was certainly the road from Beth-shean/Scythopolis and Pehel/Pella to Gerasa, via Jabesh-gilead. This is likely the desert-to-Dothan connector over which *"a caravan of Ishmaelites coming from Gilead... carrying aromatic gum, balsam, and resin"* traveled before picking up Joseph on their way to Egypt (Gen 37:25). Desert caravans must have frequented this route when the Decapolis cities funneled the wealth of the East to Rome.

A second natural route traces the southern arc of the Dome of Gilead from the Jordan River crossings east of Jericho to Rabbah, capital of the Ammonite kingdom and later known as the Decapolis city of Philadelphia. This route follows the high ridge above the southern bank of the massive Wadi Kufrein through the region of Jazer (Khirbet as-Sar?; Num 32:1; Josh 13:25; 1 Chr 26:31). This is the Judah-Ammon connector, which witnessed brisk trade and military activity from the Iron Age through the Roman period (e.g., 2 Sam 10:1–4; 11:1; 1 Kgs 14:31; 2 Chr 27:5; Jer 40:11–14; 1 Macc 5:6–7). These two east-west routes joined the international Damascus-to-Arabia Desert Highway as it pushed southward

1 Smith, *Historical Geography of the Holy Land*, 522.

The view here is due east from the top of the mound of Tell Deir 'Alla, biblical Succoth, into the opening of the Jabbok River. The alluvial plain of the Jabbok sweeps around the tell on its way into the Rift Valley. Jeroboam came this way to set up his eastern capital at Penuel (1 Kgs 12:25), as did Gideon chasing the Midianite princes out to the eastern desert (Judg 7:19–8:12).

from Ramoth-gilead to Gerasa up on the eastern heights of the dome. The most important cities of the Dome of Gilead could nearly always be found along these circumference routes.

The third natural crossing point on the Jordan River is at the fords of Adam. This route connects the heartland of Manasseh with the interior of Gilead via Succoth (Deir 'Alla) in "*the Valley of Succoth*" (Ps 60:6), a local name for the eastern side of the mid-Jordan Valley. There are wonderful living spaces around Succoth and in the higher areas of the Dome of Gilead, and the entire region was dotted with settlements in the Middle and Late Bronze Ages. The Adam crossing connector tends to dead-end as this route pushes further up the Jabbok toward the east. For this reason, the twin cities of Mahanaim (Tell edh-Dhahab el-Garbi; Gen 32:2) and Penuel (Tell edh-Dhahab esh-Sherqiya; 1 Kgs 12:25; cp. Gen 32:30–31), which command opposite sides of a tight S-bend about three miles (5 km) up the Jabbok River, were historically westward focused, connecting more with Israel's aspirations in Gilead than with the international priorities high on the dome above. Otherwise, the eroded middle of the Dome of Gilead is given to small village horticulture and quiet vine-and-fig-tree living (cp. 1 Kgs 4:25). It all provided great places for refuge (or getting lost) throughout the biblical period; it was also good for trying to (re)establish a kingdom while in hiding (cp. 1 Sam 13:7; 2 Sam 2:8–9,24–29; 17:24–29).

The westward slopes of the Dome of Gilead, including the interior of the Jabbok Valley as well as the region of Jazer at the top of the watershed ridge west of the Ammon Basin, are the only areas of Transjordan that were effectively brought under Israelite control during the Iron Age. The connection was natural, partly because Gilead lay in close, visible proximity to Israel's central hill country and partly because both shared access to the resources of the Jordan Valley between. We must also keep in mind that of all the regions of Transjordan, it is the hard limestone living spaces of the Dome of Gilead that best mirror those of the hilly heartland of ancient Israel, thus giving a practical side to their proximity. People from one region felt at home in the other. With language that is inclusive, the psalmist revealed that he understood the connection: "*Gilead is mine, Manasseh is mine, and Ephraim is my helmet; Judah is my scepter*" (Ps 60:7). The imagery is essential: Gilead was part of Israel's heartland core. According to the contrast offered by the psalmist, Transjordan's other regions were utilitarian and mundane, better fit for servitude: "*Moab is my washbasin. I throw my sandal on Edom*" (Ps 60:8).

In a prophetic view, Hosea was as concerned with the failings of the inhabitants of Gilead as he was with those of Ephraim and Manasseh. His criticisms were sharp ("*Gilead is a city of evildoers*"), but of the kind that showed concern for the redemption of his own people rather than the condemnation reserved for Gentiles living across the border (Hos 6:7–11; 12:9–11).

Indeed, in the historical narrative of the founding events of ancient Israel, the region of Gilead is actually given priority over the hill country west of the Jordan River. The first mention of the name Israel was at Peniel (probably = Penuel) in the cleft of the Jabbok, the site of Jacob's divine wrestling match (Gen 32:24–30; Hos 12:4). It is only afterward that Jacob-renamed-Israel moved westward in stages to Succoth at the mouth of the Jabbok River, then on to Shechem (Gen 33:15–20), immigrating into the land of ancient Israel from the east. The Israel-Gilead tie grew stronger as the biblical storyline progressed, though with all due competitive rivalries (e.g., Judg 12:4–6). Saul's son Ish-bosheth, his general Abner, and the shepherd David all used the western, interior crevices of Gilead around Mahanaim to rally support for their kingdom-building efforts west of the Jordan (2 Sam 2:8–9,24–29; 17:24–29). Solomon followed up by making Mahanaim the administrative center of his Gilead district (1 Kgs 4:14). Jeroboam gave the connection formal political weight when he chose Penuel and Shechem as twin capitals of the Northern Kingdom of Israel (1 Kgs 12:25).

Yet in spite of this natural bond, the Dome of Gilead was still a bit removed from the line of events west of the Jordan. The connection seems to have been an uneasy one as relations between hill country-based populations often are; it bred mutual suspicion, a recurrent unwillingness to bend to the common good, and was certainly disrupted by differences in dialect and custom (Num 32:1–42; Josh 22:1–34; Judg 5:17; 8:4–17; 12:1–6; 21:8–12). The heated dialogue between Jephthah and the Ephraimites, neither of whom was native to the region, over who had the better right to protect the citizens of Gilead from Ammonite incursions is one of the better examples (Judg 12:1–6).

In terms of regional demographics, the cut of the Jabbok River through the Dome of Gilead sometimes functioned as a political border between Ammon and Israel (Num 21:24; Deut 2:37), or between Gad and the half-tribe of Manasseh (Deut 3:16). The data is difficult to sort out given the constant ebb and flow over the dome by all parties concerned as well as the tendency of the Jabbok canyon to be a meeting place for all comers due to its soil and water resources. Certainly,

Israel's claim to the western slopes of the dome was held by the tribe of Gad. The actual borders of Gad are difficult to pin down and certainly varied over time, as apparent inconsistencies in the data seem to indicate (Num 32:2–3,34-36; Deut 3:16–17; Josh 13:24–28; *Mesha Stela* 10–11[1]). Gadites can be found in southern Bashan and deep on the Medeba Plateau, making them Israel's most expansive Transjordanian tribe—but at the same time the one most vulnerable to encroachment by others. Jacob's blessing to Gad reflects the uneasy living situation that characterized the outlying edges of the land assigned to the tribe, areas up and out of the safety of the Jabbok crevice: "*Gad will be attacked by raiders, but he will attack their heels*" (Gen 49:19). The blessing by Moses enlarges the idea, adding in anticipation details of Gad's own historical narrative:

> *The one who enlarges Gad's territory*
> *will be blessed.*
> *He lies down like a lion*
> *and tears off an arm or even a head.*
> *He chose the best part for himself,*
> *because a ruler's portion was*
> *assigned there for him.*
> *He came with the leaders of the people;*
> *he carried out the* Lord*'s justice*
> *and his ordinances for Israel.* (Deut 33:20–21)

The reflections of these landed blessings onto Ephraim are obvious (Gen 49:22–26; Deut 33:13–17).

Repeated incursions into the Dome of Gilead by the Ammonites, whose own homeland was tucked in a less-fertile, chalky basin just to the southeast, as well as by Moabites and Arameans, kept Israel on the ready. Their kings took their losses in Gilead personally (Judg 10:6–12:7; 1 Sam 11:1–2; 2 Kgs 10:32–33; 15:25; Jer 49:1; Amos 1:13). Eventually Gilead went the way of the rest of the southern Levant, falling first to the Assyrians under Tiglath-pileser III (Isa 9:1), then to Babylon, Persia, and the Seleucid forces of Hellenism. In the meantime, the Ammonite Tobiad clan, which had made a habit of trying to extend its influence to the kingdoms west of the Jordan, carved out homeland space in the Gilead hills west of Rabbah (Neh 2:10,19; 13:4–9; cp. Isa 7:6).

Gilead fell back under Jewish control when Hasmonean Kings Jonathan and Alexander Jannaeus drove the Seleucids out in the late second and early first centuries BC. By the time of the New Testament, Israel's old Gilead homeland—the westward slopes of the Dome of Gilead and regions south onto the Mishor/Medeba Plateau—had become the district of Perea, "the country across" (the Jordan), and boasted a renewed and vibrant Jewish community (John 1:28; Mark 10:1–33; John 10:40; 11:54). In the end, the benediction of Deuteronomy 33:20 proved to be the stronger biblical theme: "*The one who*

The reconstructed remains of an early second-century BC pleasure palace at Iraq el-Amir command a pleasant bend of the Wadi es-Sir in southwestern Gilead. The palace was originally constructed by an undercut Jerusalem powerbroker from the Tobiad clan named Hyrcanus, who had failed in his attempt to rally local support for control of the Jewish capital city (Josephus, *Ant.* 12.228–34). Withdrawing in exile across the Jordan to the protected slopes of western Gilead, Hyrcanus decided to ride out his fate in self-created splendor, providing one of the best examples of Gilead's role as a refuge for the dispossessed.

1 Shmuel Ahituv, *Echoes from the Past: Hebrew and Cognate Inscriptions from the Biblical Period* (Jerusalem: Carta, 2008), 389–95, 403–5.

By the Byzantine period, the highlands of Gilead had been securely enveloped by Rome. Remains of the monumental Decapolis city of Gerasa (modern Jerash) sprout among springtime growth. The ancients nicknamed the city Antioch ad Chrysorhoas, "Antioch on the Golden River"; it is fondly called "City of One Thousand Columns" today. In the poetically understated phrase of Henry van Dyke, these are indeed "satisfactory ruins."[1]

enlarges Gad's territory will be blessed." With Jerusalem in view, the prophet Obadiah foresaw that the enlarger would be the tribe of Benjamin (Obad 19), a region that itself was an encroached-upon-yet-someday-to-be-restored land between.

D. THE AMMON BASIN

Ammon, or, more frequently *benê-Ammon*, meaning "the sons of Ammon," is an ethnic term for a people group whose origins the author of Genesis traces to Lot, the nephew of Abraham (Gen 19:38). The tenor of the story of the birth of Ammon reflects the back-and-forth relationship that the nation of Israel experienced with the Ammonites throughout the Iron Age. What made headlines in the biblical text was competition between Israel and Ammon over the resources of the Dome of Gilead, the Jordan Valley, and the Mishor/Medeba Plateau. In the fine print we can assume a complex mix of relationships as each sought to make use of the fertile living spaces that lay between their respective homelands.

Geologically, the Ammon Basin is a wide band of Senonian chalk that lies on a southwest-northeast angle tracing the southeastern, desert side of the Dome of Gilead. It is separated from the eastern desert by a low, narrow upfold of Cenomanian-Turonian limestone running the length of its long outer side, and opens directly to the desert at its narrow, northeastern end. At five by twenty miles (8 by 32 km) in size, this is the smallest of all of the natural regions of Transjordan and, with the exception of the shoreline plains encircling the Sea of Galilee, it's also smaller than any of the regions of the land of ancient Israel.

Topographically, the Ammon Basin is best defined as the area circumscribed by the local watershed that encloses the upper tributaries of the Jabbok River. The Jabbok's headwater streams flow east-northeast for most of the length of the Ammon Basin, then bend north and northwest through the modern city of az-Zarqa before entering the Dome of Gilead from the east. In an early description of the natural line marking the easternmost extent of Israel's settlement on the Medeba Plateau (Deut 2:37), the uppermost, outstretched fingers of the Jabbok River—those lying nearest the seam between the Dome of Gilead and the Medeba Plateau—are called the *yad nahal Jabbok*, literally "the hand of the Jabbok wadi."[2] Other biblical texts relate that the territory of the Israelite tribes of Reuben and Gad extended "*up to the Jabbok River, the border of the Ammonites*" (Deut 3:16; Josh 12:2). Surely these references have in mind the watershed defining the tributaries of the upper Jabbok (i.e., "up to the [beginning of] the Jabbok"), rather than the more prominent cut of the Jabbok deep within the Dome of Gilead. The heartland of Ammon, then, lay east and northeast of this upper Jabbok watershed, among the low, rounded, and rather barren hills and within the broad flowing valleys (cf. Jer 49:4) that fill the Ammon Basin. Even though it is noticeably lower than the soaring heights of the Dome of Gilead, this Ammonite homeland is still relatively high, with elevations varying from 2,600 to 3,300 feet (800 to 1,000 m) above sea level. For comparative purposes, this is somewhat higher on average than the hill country around Jerusalem.

Although we can define the Ammon Basin geographically by reference to its rock type and patterns of surface drainage, its natural border with the Dome of Gilead is difficult to trace today. This is largely because many distinctive surface features in and around the basin have been obscured by the unbridled westward

The disproportionately large size of the modern city of Amman, capital of the Hashemite Kingdom of Jordan, is a product of relatively recent actions played out on the world political and economic stage rather than a reflection of the indigenous resource base of the Ammon Basin. As recently as the 1940s, Amman was a small village of mostly stone and mud brick houses huddled in the valleys surrounding the ancient site of Rabbah on the Amman Citadel. For centuries prior, the main city of central Jordan had been as-Salt, the regional Ottoman Turkish administrative center located within the more productive western slopes of the Dome of Gilead. When Beirut imploded as the West's economic gateway to the Middle East during the prolonged Lebanese Civil War in the 1970s and 1980s, many foreign governments and investors relocated their regional interests to Amman. The Hashemite Kingdom of Jordan gained favored trading status with the United States when it signed a peace treaty with Israel in 1994, spurring further economic development in the city. Amman continues to grow at a furious pace, spurred most recently by a huge influx of Iraqi and Syrian refugees, pushing its economic zone well beyond the natural borders of the Ammon Basin.

1 Henry van Dyke, *Out-of-Doors in the Holy Land* (New York: Charles Scribner's Sons, 1909), 153.

2 See Steven P. Lancaster and James M. Monson, *Geobasics Study Guide* (Rockford, IL: Biblical Backgrounds, Inc., 2009), 95–96, for discussion.

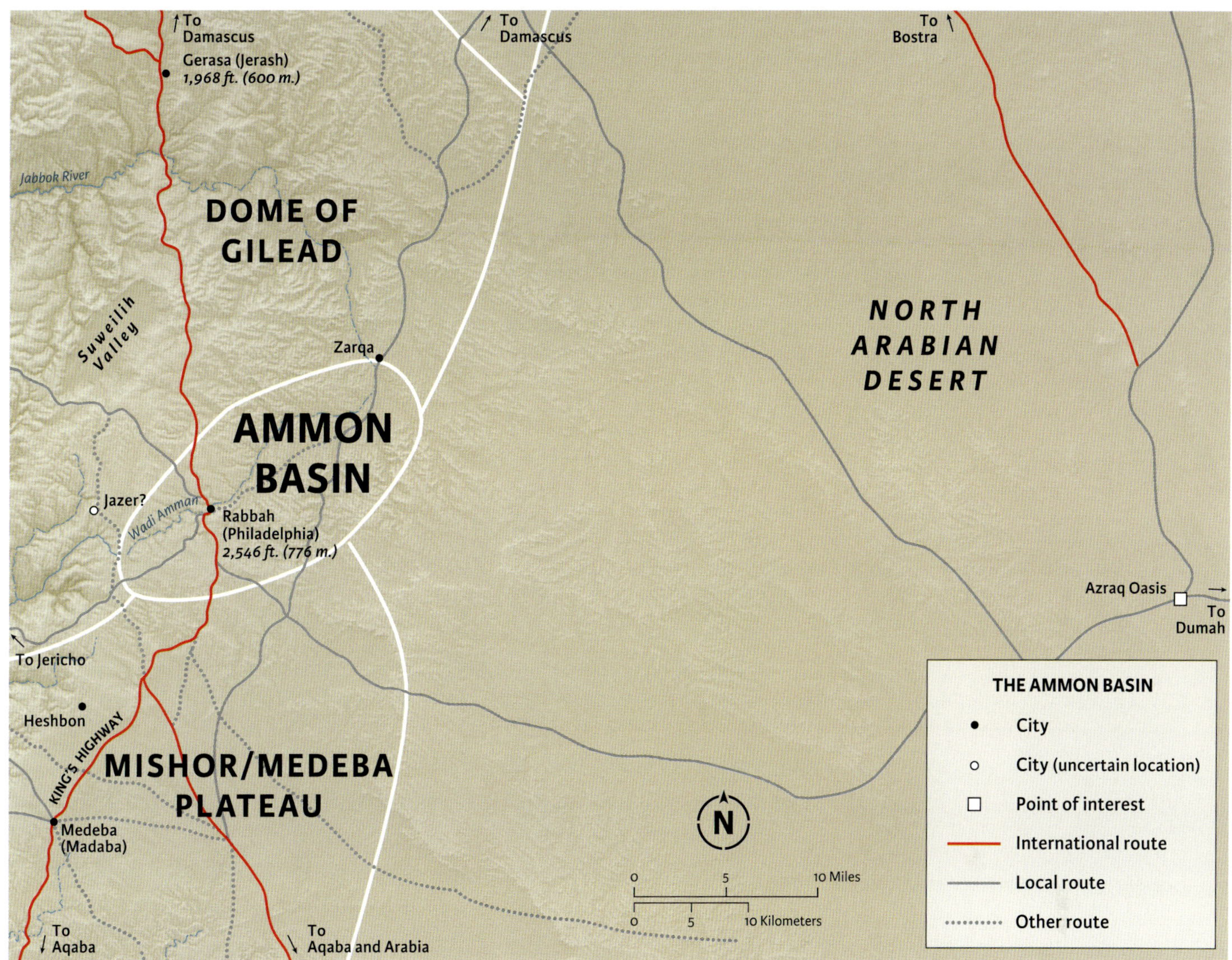

growth of Amman, the capital of the Hashemite Kingdom of Jordan. Modern Amman's cascading urban sprawl also blankets the low Cenomanian-Turonian rise separating the Ammon Basin from the Mishor/Medeba Plateau. That the Ammon Basin and the Mishor are both composed of Senonian chalk further blurs their regional distinctiveness on the geographical principle that shared landscapes and similar living conditions tend to make for shared economic aspirations. This principle is shown to be valid by the political history of the Ammonites, which includes an expected litany of attempts to expand their control over the Mishor.

To summarize: tucked behind the watershed ridge and clinging to the trailing edge of the arable land at the extremity of the Dome of Gilead, the entire Ammon Basin tips northeastward, toward the limitless expanse of the North Arabian Desert (cf. Ezek 25:4). The more productive land is out of sight, over the watershed to the west. There are a number of practical ramifications.

First, because the Ammon Basin lies on the wide seam between "the desert and the sown,"[1] the market base of its residents is a mixed package containing products from both "milk" and "honey" economies. High summertime temperatures and marginal rainfall make shepherding a necessary lifestyle, yet productive fields abound. The best agricultural lands within the basin are found in the broad, flowing valleys that carry the upper tributaries of the Jabbok River. Here the rendzina soils are worked easily, absorbing enough runoff rainfall to allow subsistence farming. Rainfall throughout is ten to twelve inches (250 to 300 mm) annually, half that of Jerusalem, and prone to come in unexpectedly heavy amounts at sporadic intervals. This is characteristic of moisture patterns more typical of the desert than the sea, though rain and dew are sufficient to coax annual crops of wheat and barley without irrigation. All told, the overall agricultural productivity of the Ammon Basin, though nothing spectacular, was sufficiently high so as to have prompted the attention of the prophet Jeremiah: "*Why do you boast about your valleys, your flowing valley, you faithless daughter—you who trust in your treasures and say, 'Who can attack me?'*" (Jer 49:4).

When David entered Gilead because of drama with his rebellious son, Absalom, he and his hungry army were fed by Shobi, son of Nahash the Ammonite king. On the menu were "*wheat, barley, flour, roasted grain, beans, lentils, honey, curds, sheep, goats and cheese from the herd*" (2 Sam 17:28–29). A display of such home-

1 Gertrude Bell, *The Desert and the Sown: Travels in Palestine and Syria* (London: W. Heinemann, 1907).

Israel and Ammon each played the role of antagonist-protagonist in the historical records of the Late Bronze and Iron Ages. Yet facts on the ground suggest that there was also a great deal of cooperative interaction between them. Jeremiah 40:11 speaks rather casually of *"Judeans . . . among the Ammonites"* as if a mixed population were quite normal, and of course it must have been. Archaeological excavations in Iron Age strata have uncovered distinctive architectural forms in Rabbah, the Ammonite capital, that are similar or even identical to structural elements of royal palaces found at Israelite and Judean sites such as Dan, Hazor, Megiddo, Shechem, Jerusalem, and Ramat Rachel. These include walls constructed in the header-stretcher technique (left) and capitals in the Proto-Ionic or (Proto-Aeolic) style (below).[1]

grown products typical of a mixed shepherding and farming economy are exactly what would be expected of someone living in the Ammon Basin and hosting a visiting royal. A similar bill of fare could be had in Bethlehem, another town hugging the desert seam (1 Sam 17:17–18). Similarly, in a kind of reversed imagery of Israel's possession of the land of milk and honey, Ezekiel announced that the Ammonites would be overrun by raiders off the eastern desert: "*I am about to give you to the people of the east as a possession. They will set up their encampments and pitch their tents among you. They will eat your fruit and drink your milk*" (Ezek 25:4).

A second ramification of the geographical orientation of the Ammon Basin is that its most natural highway connection was, for better or worse, eastward—even though the Ammonites were often pulled by economic necessity up and over the watershed ridge to the routes and resources of Gilead. Ammon's eastward orientation had both benefits and drawbacks. On the minus side was potential for invasion. We can assume that whenever "peoples of the east" (to use the Bible's generic term for Arabs from the desert) swept into lands west of the Jordan, as they did "*like a great swarm of locusts*" in the days of Gideon (Judg 6:1–6), the region of the Ammonites likely had first already been overrun. The metaphor is fed by reality. The Ammon Basin offers the first swath of green for whomever or whatever comes off the North Arabian Desert, placing it within easy grazing range of real locusts: the devouring, swarming, and destroying kinds (Joel 1:4). Throughout history, these "teeth of the wind"[2] have all too often clouded the Levant's southeastern sky with a flurry of yellow wings, turning springtime fields to stubble in an instant. The Middle East's locust wars lasted well into the middle of the twentieth century AD, when they were finally checked by another kind of invasion, that of pesticides spread by airplanes.[3]

The positive side of Ammon's eastward position is its role in desert trade. Here the Transjordanian Highway, reaching Rabbah from Damascus and Bashan (Ezek 21:19–20), forks into two branches: the King's Highway (Num 20:17) and the Desert Highway, which is locally called the Way to the Wilderness of Moab (Deut 2:8). The former traces the watershed southward from Rabbah to link Ammon with the chief cities of Moab and Edom. This was Transjordan's main north-south artery of regional correspondence and economy throughout the biblical periods. Today the paved route of the King's Highway is winding and relatively narrow—

1 Kay Prag, "Decorative Architecture in Ammon, Moab, and Judah," *Levant* 19 (1987): 121–27.

2 The phrase comes from an unnamed Sudanese village farmer. Robert A. M. Conley, "Locusts: 'Teeth of the Wind,'" *National Geographic* 119 (1969): 202.

3 For a first-hand account, see Tony Chapelle and Dickey Chapelle, "Report from the Locust Wars," *National Geographic* 103 (1953): 545–62.

though in the process of being improved—and carries slow-moving, local traffic. The latter route, the Desert Highway, pushes southward from Rabbah around the upper reaches of the Arnon and Zered wadis on its way to the Red Sea and the Hejaz mountain region of the Arabian Peninsula. This has been a camel caravan route for millennia; with the rise of Islam, it doubles as the Pilgrim Road to Mecca. It is also the Hashemite kingdom's primary corridor for fast, heavy truck traffic moving between Amman and Aqaba on the Red Sea.

Historically, the Ammon Basin has also served as one of the Transjordanian Highway's main T-junctions for routes heading east. That is, it has the characteristics of a port, though of the desert fringe rather than seashore kind. From here—Rabbah in particular—ancient caravan routes traced two lines of oases. One heads southeastward to Bayir (east of Petra), Kilwa (east of Wadi Rum), and the great oasis of Tema (Isa 21:12; Job 6:19) at the entrance to the interior of the Saudi Peninsula. This is a northern branch of the Spice Route that originates in the mountains and crevices of Yemen deep in the Saudi Peninsula and at seaports beyond. This corridor supplied the Mediterranean world with exotic goods such as gold, frankincense, and myrrh throughout the biblical period (Isa 60:6; cp. Ezek 27:20–23; Matt 2:1,11). The other caravan route heads due east from Rabbah via the Azraq Oasis to Karkor and the Dumah Oasis (*el-Jauf*) three hundred miles out into the North Arabian Desert (Isa 21:11). From Dumah difficult but direct connections can be made to Babylon and Assyria, cutting off the great bend of the Fertile Crescent. The Azraq Oasis (*Qa' al-Azraq*), the first stop on this route, lies at the center of a large stony basin fifty miles (80 km) east of Rabbah. Into its center, a 360-degree splay of wadis carry their seasonal flow from distances as far as Bashan and Edom. The confluence forms a muddy, reedy lake that fills to up to five feet (1.5 m) deep in the winter, then evaporates into a silt flat under the dry heat of summer. The Azraq Oasis has been a meeting place for caravans, camels, flocks, and migrating birds for millennia. Recent human intervention keeps the oasis a wetland year round. It—or similar geographical phenomena on a smaller scale further south—provides the imagery describing Job's deceptive friends:

> *My brothers are as treacherous as a wadi,*
> *as seasonal streams that overflow*
> *and become darkened because of ice,*
> *and the snow melts into them.*
> *The wadis evaporate in warm weather;*
> *they disappear from their*
> *channels in hot weather.*
> *Caravans turn away from their routes,*
> *go up into the desert, and perish.*
> *The caravans of Tema look for these streams.*
> *The traveling merchants of*
> *Sheba hope for them.*
> *They are ashamed because they had*
> *been confident of finding water.*
> *When they arrive there, they are*
> *disappointed.* (Job 6:15–20)

With such routes in mind, we might recall the "*large quantity of plunder*," including gold, that fell to David upon capturing Rabbah from the Ammonites (2 Sam 12:29–30), or the one hundred talents (approximately 7,500 pounds or 3,400 kg) of silver taken from the Ammonites by Judah's King Jotham, together with huge quantities of wheat and barley, in the mid-eighth century BC (2 Chr 27:5). While these totals have the aura of standard literary fare meant to impress the reader with the military effectiveness of the Iron Age Judean kings, they also accurately reflect the reality of the richness of Rabbah's role as a desert port. In the middle of the third century BC, Rabbah was established as the Hellenistic *polis* Philadelphia, eventually becoming the southernmost of the Decapolis cities and that confederation's gateway to the Nabateans, proprietors of the Spice Route in the time of the New Testament. Rome's eyes grew large at the possibilities.

The geographical setting of the Ammonite capital is worth special attention. The city's full name, *Rabbath-benê-'Ammon*, means "the Great [One] of the Ammonites" (Deut 3:11; Josh 13:25). The word *Rabbath* is grammatically feminine and most likely refers to the city's female deity; we don't know her personal name, so the appellation "the Lady" will have to do.[1] The imposing geographical setting of the city, coupled with its role as the chief and apparently only major city of the Ammonites, makes the name doubly appropriate.

Ancient Rabbah occupies an L-shaped hill (the Citadel) in the middle of the oldest part of modern Amman, now the capital of the Hashemite Kingdom of Jordan. The short upright of the "L," which formed the narrow end of Rabbah, is connected by a shallow saddle to Jebel el-Hussein (Hussein Mountain) rising north-northwestward from the site toward the watershed ridge. This was the logical direction of attack (cp. 2 Sam 11:15–17), and the saddle seems to have been artificially lowered and widened at some point in antiquity—perhaps as early as the Iron Age—to help protect the Ammonite capital. The much longer horizontal base of the "L," which runs for half a mile (1 km) from west to east, drops steeply along its southern side into the Wadi 'Amman 300 feet (90 m) below. It is recalled that Wadi 'Amman is one of the more prominent upper fingers of the Jabbok. The inner bend of the "L" falls northward into Wadi Abu er-Rauk, which, though not as deep as the Wadi 'Amman, is still a formidable moat protecting the ancient city from the north. A circle of hills rises beyond—all of which are higher than the Citadel and together which form a rather tight horizon line around the site. The only break on the horizon line is eastward, the direction of the natural drainage flow. Sometime in antiquity the surface of the Citadel hill was leveled to

1 Note the twin cities Ashtaroth and Karnaim (Gen 14:5; Deut 1:4; Amos 6:13) on the international highway in eastern Bashan, north of Ramoth-gilead. Ashtaroth the place must have been a center of worship of the Ashtaroth, the plural form of Ashtoreth, the Canaanite goddess of fertility. Karnaim, "double horns," is surely an appellation of Baal, the Canaanite god of fertility who was pictured in both texts and iconography as a horned bull. Ashtaroth became a Levitical city (Josh 21:27; 1 Chr 6:71), its nature as a place of divinity intact though redeemed.

The open, flat expanse of the Ammonite Citadel—site of the Iron Age city of Rabbah and the acropolis of its Greco-Roman successor Philadelphia—is easily appreciated by visitors who throng the site today. Two of the three terraces that leveled the site in antiquity are visible here. A small but well-preserved Byzantine church (fifth–sixth c. AD) fills the foreground, evidence of ongoing settlement at the site. The surface of the Citadel drops abruptly into the Wadi 'Amman (right and center) and Wadi Abu-er-Rauk (top left). A higher circle of hills surrounds the scene, with the overall slant tipping away toward the east, in the distance. Unlike Jerusalem, which is blocked from the east by the Mount of Olives, the city of Rabbah, crowned no doubt by the temple to the Ammonite national deity (or its feminine counterpart), must have been clearly visible to anyone approaching the city via the Ammonite Basin from the east.

form three artificial terraces, each a little lower than the previous as one heads eastward. The leveling was perhaps begun as early as the Iron Age, but certainly was expanded later to give the hill a proper acropolis shape for the temples of Greco-Roman Philadelphia.

In its overall geographical situation, then, ancient Rabbah resembled Jerusalem but was noticeably loftier and in some ways more secure than its Judean counterpart. Like the oldest part of the walled city of Jerusalem, the hill of Rabbah was surrounded by valleys on all but its narrow north-northwestern side, though the valleys surrounding Rabbah are deeper, and the hills beyond are a little further away, than those of ancient Jerusalem. The appearance of the Citadel today gives indication that even before it was artificially leveled, its surface was broader and more level—and hence better suited as a building site—than the narrow, plunging hill of David's city. Archaeological evidence corroborating the actual size of the walled city of Rabbah is almost entirely lacking. What is sure is that both it and Jerusalem were most vulnerable on their northern sides, and it is likely that it is this part of Rabbah, in the same location as the corresponding fortifications of Jerusalem, that the strong "*walls of Rabbah, and . . . its citadels*" (Amos 1:14) were to be found.

Unlike ancient Jerusalem's Gihon Spring, however, the spring of Rabbah lay at some distance from the city. There is a small spring on the southern side of the Wadi 'Amman a half mile (1 km) south of the southwest corner of the Citadel (the angle of its "L") and another, larger spring, 'Ain 'Amman ("the spring of Amman") a little over one mile (1.5 km) up the wadi to the west. In October of 1881, the Survey of Eastern Palestine reported this latter spring to be "perennial, of clear fresh water and full of small fish."[1] The spring no longer flows freely, but it did in recent memory; old-timers still recall that water was available for public consumption at the source and even flowed beneath the Citadel. Today, Amman's city hall is built on the site. The lack of a perennial source of fresh water within the walls of the city of Rabbah eventually prompted its residents to dig cisterns into the surface of the site and into the saddle at the base of the wall protecting the northern end of the ancient city. But in the tenth century BC, the source of the city's water was apparently only springs. Leading the Israelite assault on Rabbah, Joab reported to David that he had captured both "*the royal fortress*" and "*its water supply*," prompting us to think that one or both of the springs lying outside the city were also fortified (2 Sam 12:26–27). Most likely the royal fortress was located at the northern end of the city although nothing has been found yet dating to that time by archaeology. The rest of the Ammonite city was walled, and attacked, separately (2 Sam 12:28).

During the Iron Age, a fairly dense scattering of smaller towns, villages, and well-planned farmsteads filled the Ammon Basin to the east. Their presence attests to the economic potential of the area which, though not as large as that of other regions of the southern Levant, was sufficient to support an independent, though rel-

1 C. R. Conder, *The Survey of Eastern Palestine*, vol. 1, *The 'Adwân Country* (London: The Committee of the PEF, 1889), 52.

The Amman Citadel Inscription (its name refers to the location where it was found) is a fragment of a monumental stela (an engraved standing stone) dating to the late ninth or early eighth century BC. The text, written in Ammonite, says,

[The Ammonite god Mi]lkom [said to me] build for yourself entrances round about [. . .]

[. . .] that all who surround you may surely die [. . .]

[. . .] I will surely destroy them and every one who enters [. . .]

[. . .] and in every colonnade the righteous will dwell [. . .]

[. . . you shall lo]ck the door in the inner doorway [. . .]

[. . .Be]hold you shall fear the son(s) of the gods [. . .]

[. . .] (?) peace to you and pea[ce to your house][1]

The inscription may speak of palaces and fortresses within the walls of Rabbah, or of fortifications and/or a defensible terrain surrounding the city. In either case, the Ammonite capital was well fortified in the late Iron Age. Its defenses, however, were a sign of contempt for God, according to the prophet Amos: *"I will set fire to the walls of Rabbah, and it will consume its citadels"* (Amos 1:14).

atively small, kingdom. Many of these sites are known archaeologically, but their historic names are likely lost forever because of a lack of written sources. Also of note is a line of towers built of rough-hewn stones that seems to define a defensive line on the western side of the Amman Basin, facing the areas of Jazer, Gilead (1 Chr 26:31), and the Mishor. Many of these towers were constructed on wadi scarps, allowing a view into its respective wadi as well as line of sight to the next tower. Some seem to have been built as early as the Iron Age and can reasonably be related to Ammonite interests lying in the Dome of Gilead to the west. In what could be either an anachronistic reference to this line of towers or an acknowledgement of other unknown fortifications, the Hebrew text of Numbers 21:24 notes that Moses took the territory of Sihon (i.e., the Mishor) *"to the Jabbok, but only up to the Ammonite border, because it was fortified."*[2]

As we have seen, the Ammon Basin lies east by nature but pushed north, west, and south by economic necessity. Ammon was the smallest and, arguably, the weakest of the four main Transjordanian kingdoms in the Iron Age. But because it was the kingdom that lay closest to Jerusalem and Israelite interests in Gilead, Ammon received considerable attention on the part of the biblical writers. Even though it was a desert port, the resource base of the Ammon Basin was not particularly strong nor were its natural borders necessarily well-defined or easily protected. Ammonite history is a cycle of attempts to push for viable living space out onto the Dome of Gilead and/or the Mishor/Medeba Plateau, followed invariably by counterthrusts driving the Ammonites back east of the watershed and into the uppermost tributaries of the Jabbok (Hb *yad nahal Jabbok*; lit. "fingers of the Jabbok wadi"). And, as was the case with Gilead,

Neither the Judeans nor the Israelites made pictures or images of themselves, likely because of the prohibition against human likenesses contained in the commandment (Exod 20:4; Deut 5:8). The Ammonites had no such compunctions. This small limestone statue portrays Yerah-'Azar, who reigned in Rabbah at the end of the eighth century BC. It is the only known likeness of an Ammonite king. The statue contains the inscription "'Azar son of Zakir son of Sanipu." 'Azar's grandfather was the Ammonite king conquered by the Assyrian Tiglath-pileser III in 733 BC. Yerah-'Azar was thus a contemporary of Hezekiah, king of Judah. Because archaeological evidence shows that the royal capitals of Rabbah and Jerusalem shared architectural features in the late Iron Age, we can assume that kings' royal dress was also similar. In any case, the Old Testament gives the Hebrew names of each part of these royal garments; it wouldn't do so unless the Judean kings were dressed similarly.

1 Aḥituv, *Echoes from the Past*, 357–59.

2 The Septuagint says, "to the Jabbok [but only up] to the Ammonite border which was Jazer." The location of the city of Jazer is not certain, but a frequent suggestion is Khirbet es-Sar just west of the watershed in southern Gilead. It's a logical location for a border town between Israelite and Ammonite interests in the area.

we again see the difficulty of defining a region by its political borders when the textual evidence shows boundaries to have been fluid.

The Ammonites seem not to have been able to support sustained incursions alone, and more often than not their most effective thrusts to the west were made with the help of others: the Philistines (Judg 10:17), Moab (Judg 3:13; 2 Chr 20:1), or Aram-Damascus (2 Sam 10:6). Notable was the push across the Jordan and all the way into the eastern hills of Judah, Benjamin, and Ephraim in the days of the judges, when Israel's holdings throughout the land were still rather tenuous. In response, the opportunistic warrior Jephthah scattered the Ammonites back eastward, up and over the Transjordanian watershed (Judg 10:7–9; 11:29–33). Somewhat later, in a move that clearly threatened Israel's interests throughout Gilead, Ammonite King Nahash (whose name means "snake," which is rather fitting for someone from the desert fringe) pushed to Jabesh-gilead on the leading edge of Lower Gilead. In *his* finest hour, King Saul drove them back (1 Sam 11:1–11). David took the fight directly to Rabbah, temporarily checking Ammonite interests within the basin itself (2 Sam 11:1; 12:26–31). But the Ammonites remained understandably intent on carving out living space in the better resourced lands of Gilead and the Mishor. Thus it was, for Israel, a rough frontier, where Ammonites "*ripped open the pregnant women of Gilead in order to enlarge their territory*" (Amos 1:13) and "*taunted [God's] people and threatened their territory*" (Zeph 2:8). In the end, the usual succession of empires (Assyria, Babylon, and Persia) put the Israelite-Ammonite competition on hold, though Tobiah's attempts to gain ascendancy over Jerusalem after the Jews' return from exile (Neh 2:10; 4:3,7; 13:1) prove that nationalistic rivalries died hard. When incorporated into the Roman Empire as the Decapolis city Philadelphia, the economic corridors of Rabbah and the Ammon Basin finally worked in harmony with the interests of the other regions of the southern Levant—but only to the music conducted by Rome.

E. THE MISHOR (MEDEBA PLATEAU)

South of the Dome of Gilead and just beyond the southern angle of the hard limestone ridge that cradles the Ammon Basin, the landscape of Transjordan flattens out onto a high Senonian chalk plateau. The generic label *mishor*, "tableland" or "plateau," is so appropriate here that the biblical writers called the region *ha-Mishor*, "*the* plateau," as if this plateau defined the name (Deut 3:10; 4:43; Josh 13:9,16–17,21; 20:8; Jer 48:8,21). The term *mishor* is not only geographically accurate but politically neutral; Mishor became the region's preferred name even though the writer of Deuteronomy, in an apparent nod to Moab's persistent claim on the region, sometimes called the area "*the land of Moab*" (Deut 1:5; 29:1; 34:5). The popular name for the Mishor today is the Medeba, or Madaba, Plateau (Josh 13:9) after the largest city in the region, once an Iron Age town and now the center of a vibrant Christian population that traces its roots to the Byzantine period. The Arabic spelling, Madaba, is proper when referencing the modern town, while the Hebrew spelling, Medeba, is better when speaking of the Iron Age city mentioned in the Bible (e.g., Isa 15:2).[1]

The Mishor is framed by clear topographical forms on every side but east. To the north, tapered foothills rise to the hard limestone Dome of Gilead. Twenty-five miles (40 km) south, the Arnon gorge (Wadi al-Mujib) forms a deep chasm separating the Mishor from Moab proper. On the west, everything drops through a ten-mile (16-km) tumble of broken edges and cascading forms into the Dead Sea. But to the east, after a fifteen-mile (24-km) run of nearly level tableland, the Mishor simply gives way to the open desert. There is no discernable line here, certainly no real barrier, prompting George Adam Smith to comment: "[The plateau] rolls away unbroken, unvaried, save by the shadows of a few clouds on the featureless hillocks, into the infinite East."[2] Elevations on the Mishor level out at between 2,300 and 2,600 feet (700 to 800 m) above sea level, with some of the flattest sight lines from the cities of Heshbon and Medeba eastward.

The middle of the Mishor is scored by two major wadi systems. Each has cut completely through the plateau's chalk surface and into the bed of hard Cenomanian-Turonian limestone below. The overall directional flow of these wadis is northeast to southwest, following geological structure lines. The northernmost, the Zarqa Ma'in, gently drains the plain around the city of Medeba south and southwest, then bends due west where it begins a rapid descent to the Dead Sea. Its outlet cuts the cliff line just north of the hot springs at Callirrhoe where Herod the Great stayed briefly during his dying days (Josephus, *Ant.* 17.171; *War* 1.657). The larger and southernmost of these two wadi systems, the al-Heidan, begins on the tableland east of the upper reaches of the Zarqa Ma'in, then pulls drainage from the broad middle of the Mishor to the south and southwest, joining the Arnon canyon two miles before the Arnon makes its final, dramatic cut through the cliffs edging the Dead Sea. The most important upper tributary of the Wadi al-Heidan is the Wadi al-Wala, a wet and picturesque stream over which the King's Highway had to navigate its run between Medeba and Dibon. The al-Heidan/al-Wala wadi system separates the southernmost edge of the Mishor, the area around Dibon (the Dibon Plateau), from the rest of the Mishor. As we will see, this made the Dibon Plateau Moab's principal foothold in the region. In fact, a cogent argument could be made that the Dibon Plateau south of the Wadi al-Wala is more properly Moab than Mishor, and that the Mishor should be limited to the area north, in particular the flat tableland surrounding the town of Medeba. While this minimalistic understanding of the Mishor was likely correct at least during the reign of Mesha, king of Moab in the ninth century BC, the Dibon Plateau seems to have been functionally part of the Mishor more often than not due to the much deeper cut of the Arnon further south.

1 Note the spelling *Mehēdebā'in* the Mesha Inscription. Ahituv, *Echoes from the Past*, 402.

2 Smith, *Historical Geography of the Holy Land*, 563.

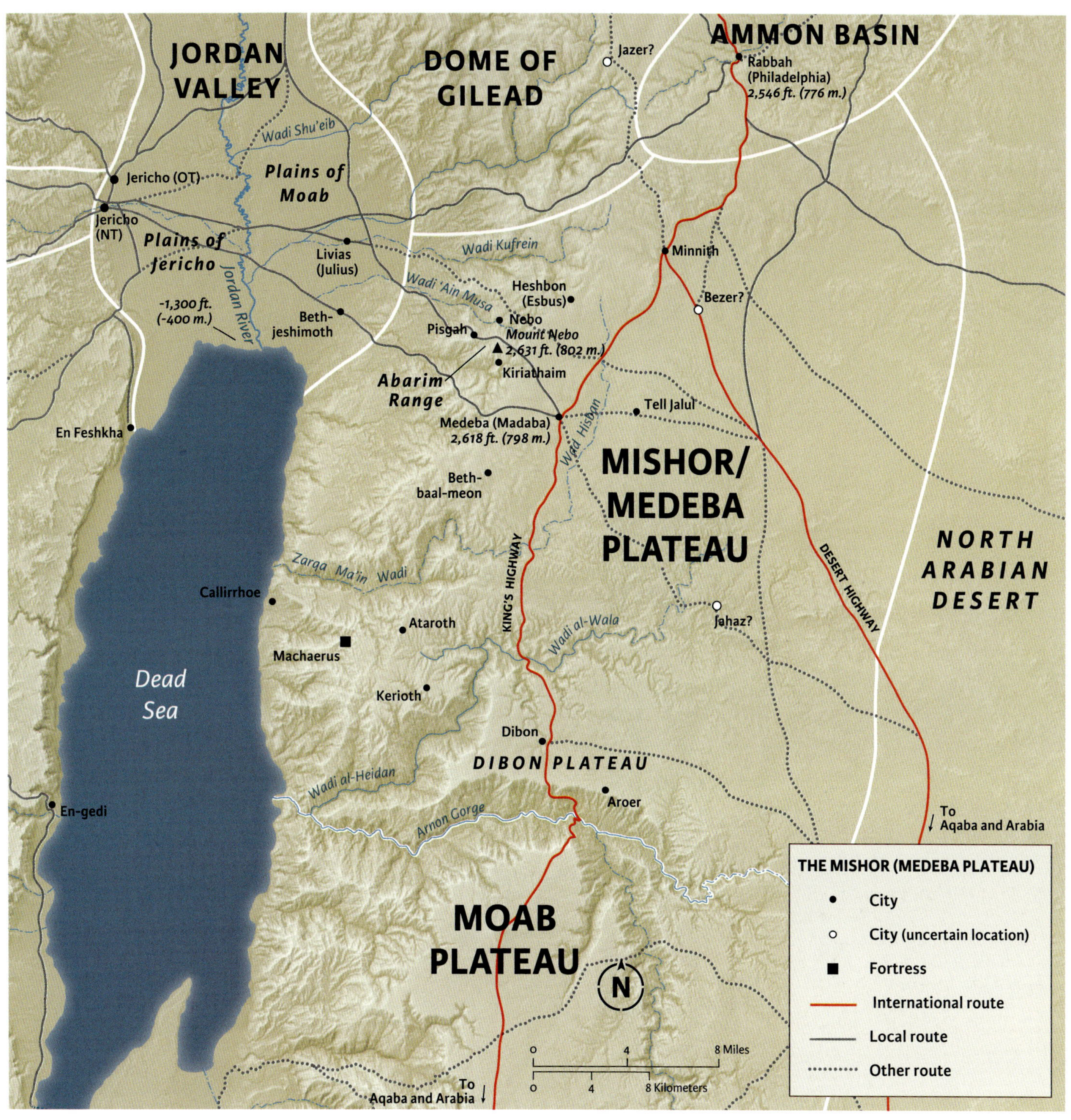

The Zarqa Ma'in and al-Heidan/al-Wala wadi systems are dwarfed by the great Arnon (Wadi al-Mujib), which cuts a massive wedge between the Mishor and the Moab Plateau (Num 21:13; 22:36; Deut 2:24; Josh 13:9; Judg 11:18). Though its shallow headwaters lie far to the south where they trace the eastern line of Moab proper, the Arnon here flows due east-west, following the line of the most severe structural weakness of the Mishor. The angle of structural weakness shifts from northeast-southwest to east-west and, eventually, to southeast-northwest south of the Arnon. The erosive force of the Arnon through the Senonian tableland has opened a gaping tear that's three miles (5 km) wide. Slicing 2,300 feet (700 m) deep, its cut exposes dramatic cliffs of Cenomanian-Turonian limestone, with colorful Nubian sandstones deep in the wedge below. The Arnon gorge is, arguably, the most dramatic physical feature of Transjordan north of Wadi Rum. The grandeur of the Arnon's chasms was celebrated in the hoary *Book of the LORD's Wars*, as noted in Numbers 21:14–15: "*Waheb in Suphah and the ravines of the Arnon, even the slopes of the ravines that extend to the site of Ar and lie along the border of Moab.*" Waheb and Suphah were certainly place names, now of unknown location. Their inclusion in this geographical couplet reminds us that every nook and cranny of this ancient land has an identity that is meaningful to its local inhabitants.

The cuts of the Mishor's wadis are particularly impressive once they drop off the western edge of the tableland and gash through the broken landscape that tumbles into the Dead Sea. Each ends its course between a tight rise of sheer cliffs lining the eastern side of the sea. This west-facing, wrinkled, grey-to-purple brow is the part of the Mishor that is most visible—and hence most recognizable—to people living in Judah, opposite the Rift Valley. These slopes are composed primarily of reddish or purplish Nubian sandstones, with lines of ancient Triassic sandstone and some relatively recent intrusions of basalt adding texture and color to the mix. Similar rocks are exposed on the western side of the Rift Valley only far to the south, near the Red Sea. This points to the possibility that the rift was formed by a pronounced northward slide of an eastern, Arabian geological plate against a more stable African geological plate edging it on the west. The hills along the eastern shore of the Dead Sea are also significantly higher than are those lining the Judean shore. It is, moreover, frequently interrupted by long, heavy masses of cliffs, some quite precipitous, that drop right into the sea.

The furrowed, crumbly slopes on the angle of the Mishor just above the northern end of the Dead Sea form the plateau's most open face toward the land of ancient Israel. Falling away from the table-flat northwestern ridgeline of the Mishor with sudden majesty, these slopes are perhaps best described as scarp lands. It is probably because this part of the Mishor was, for Judah, such an active doorway into Transjordan that the Bible preserves its specific name: it was called, appropriately, Mount Abarim, the "Over-Yonder Mountain," from the point of view of those living west of the Rift Valley (Num 27:12; 33:47–48; Deut 32:49; Jer 22:20). Alternatively, Jeremiah called these slopes "*Moab's forehead*" (lit., "corner"; Jer 48:45), while Ezekiel labeled them "*Moab's flank*" (Ezek 25:9). The broad, eastward arc of the floor of the Jordan Valley below is labeled "*the plains of Moab*" (lit. the *aravah* of Moab) in the biblical text (Num 26:3,63; 31:12; 33:48,50; 35:1; 36:15; Deut 34:1). These are all border terms, with Moabite claims on the entire Mishor in mind.

The chasm of the Arnon (Wadi al-Mujib) cuts deeply into hard Cenomanian-Turonian limestone, its horizontal, layered forms visible in the middle part of the picture. The rounded shapes of the upper layer of Senonian chalk are visible above. The surface of the ground on the far side of the canyon (left) forms part of the northern edge of the table-flat Moab Plateau. In a generous assessment of the Arnon's dramatic drop, Jordanians call this view, taken from the edge of the Mishor south of Dibon, "the Grand Canyon of Jordan." All drainage flows toward the Dead Sea (right). In spite of this massive obstacle to traffic, the Moabites routinely claimed both rims of the canyon in their ongoing attempt to claim control of the King's Highway that snaked into and out of its depths.

The eastern shoreline of the Dead Sea looks dramatically different from the western, Israeli side. Not only are there longer sections of cliff lines that drop directly into the water, but the rock is primarily red sandstone and granite rather than the tan limestones of the Judean Wilderness. The shoreline becomes encrusted with salts as the heavy seawater evaporates.

The northwestern lip of the Mishor, that facing the Abarim slopes and the plains (*aravah*) of Moab, ends in a slight rise of hills that helps hide the view down into the Rift Valley. One of these is the traditional site of Mount Nebo (Deut 32:49; 34:1). At 2,631 feet (800 m), the rise is slightly higher than the plateau and rather inconspicuous if we try to pick it out among the Abarim bumps from down below. The jumbled slopes of Pisgah ("the Cleft") form the particular section of the Abarim hills that have broken apart exactly below Mount Nebo (Deut 34:1; cp. Num 21:20; Deut 3:16–17). Other knolls lining the northwestern rim of the Mishor must have been places on which Balaam son of Beor built altars with the intention of cursing Israel at the behest of Balak king of Moab, though the exact spots of these cannot be known (Num 22:41; 23:3,14,28).

Wadis draining Mount Abarim include Wadi Shu'eib (with its headwaters in southern Gilead), Wadi Kufrein, Wadi Hisban (Heshbon), and Wadi 'Ain Musa (Moses's Spring), the last dropping along the northern side of Mount Nebo. The continuous ridges between each pair of wadis lift routes from the plains of Moab up onto Gilead, Ammon, and the Mishor. The floor of Wadi 'Ain Musa also provides a gentle access between the plains and the Mishor, making a nice setting, in the memory of tradition, for Moses's final ascent (Deut 34:1,6).

In terms of resources, rainfall is sufficiently high up on the Mishor for grain, though at twelve to fourteen inches (300 to 355 mm) per year, often only marginally so. Moreover, natural, sustainable sources of groundwater are relatively scarce. Appropriately, the book of Numbers preserves a song that praises the digging of a well out on the Mishor's eastern expanse: "*Spring up, well—sing to it! The princes dug the well; the nobles of the people hollowed it out with a scepter and with their staffs*" (Num 21:17–18).

The soils of the Mishor are mostly mature Senonian-based rendzinas. Those west of the city of Medeba are noticeably richer in color than are the soils to the south and east, where rainfall amounts taper off. The fields are flat to gently rolling and fertile, and grain does well nearly everywhere, though yields are comparatively thin by North American standards. Still, this is Jordan's great grain producing region today, and we can be sure that wheat and barley sprouted on the Mishor throughout the biblical period as well. Are these the fields of Moab (*sadē Moab*) to which the family of Elimelech and Naomi fled to avoid famine in Judah during the days of the judges (Ruth 1:1)? Perhaps, since the hills rising to the Mishor stood close on Naomi's eastern horizon, directly opposite Bethlehem.

The view northwestward from the traditional site of Mount Nebo is impressive even when the visibility is not as clear as it must have been for Moses. Here the tumbled slopes of Mount Abarim fall away into the Rift Valley, giving way to the plains of Moab below. The green color of the plains is due partly to modern irrigation, partly to natural runoff from the slopes above. The dark line center left is the course of the Jordan River, edged by dense undergrowth that the prophet Jeremiah called the *"thickets of the Jordan"* (Jer 12:5). Everything else is pretty desolate, including the rise of hills of the wilderness above Jericho to the west (left). All told, it was a foreboding view of the land of promise even for those eager to cross.

The population of the Mishor has tended always to be mixed, and Israelites (such as the family of Elimelech) and Moabites (such as the family of Ruth) could find ample opportunities there to interact. The fine "*wheat from Minnith*" that Judah and Israel supplied in abundance to feed Tyre in the sixth century BC (Ezek 27:17; cp. Judg 11:33) may have been grown in the vicinity of Heshbon. This is suggested by a notation in Eusebius's *Onomasticon* that "the village of Maanith (perhaps Minnith?) [was] four milestones from Esbos (Heshbon) for those going to Philadelphia (Rabbah)."[1] The edge of the Mishor that fronts the hard limestone Dome of Gilead between Heshbon and Jazer (Khirbet es-Sar?) was renowned for vineyards and orchards of summer fruit (Isa 16:8–10; Jer 48:31–33).

Down below in the Jordan Valley, the plains (*aravah*) of Moab are also quite fertile, benefiting from plentiful springs and surface runoff together with the displacement of alluvial soil from the westward-facing, rain-catching hills above. Here the water table is high and accessible, in stark contrast to the much dryer plains of Jericho that lie in the rain shadow of the Judean Wilderness across the Jordan River. This may have been the region of Sodom and Gomorrah, on the strength of Genesis 13:10, which notes that from the hills between Bethel and Ai, Abraham and Lot could see that "*the entire plain of the Jordan as far as Zoar was well-watered everywhere like the Lord's garden and the land of Egypt*" (cp. Gen 13:11–12).

Edward Robinson reported that when he explored the southern Jordan Valley on May 14, 1838, his search for a point on the nearly flat eastern horizon that might have been the Mount Nebo of his imagination was in vain.[2] Because the traditional site of Mount Nebo is but a minor rise on the tableland edge of the Mishor, many who try to replicate Robinson's view today feel the same way.

"To Nebo, again, the sacred story brings Moses to close his life—again to that long platform where the host, which he had guided through the desert for forty years, first lost their desert horizon, and saw the Promised Land open before them. And somewhere below the platform the Lord buried Moses. . . . Between the streams that in these valley bottoms spring full-born from the rocks, and the merry [wheat] fields on the Plateau of Moab above, there are some thousand feet of slopes and gullies, where no foot comes, the rock is crumbling, and utter silence reigns, save for the west wind moaning through the thistles. Here Moses was laid. Who would wish to know the exact spot? The whole region is a sepulcher"—George Adam Smith.[3]

Yet in spite of the Mishor's potential for grain, most of the region up top was better suited for flocks of sheep and goats. Biblical writers called the part of the plateau around Bezer (possibly *Umm el-Amad* east of Heshbon) *midbar bamishor*, "*the wilderness on the plateau land*" (i.e., the Mishor) (Deut 4:43; cp. Josh 20:8), in contrast to the term "*fields* (Hb *tsadē*) *of Moab*" in Ruth 1:2. The tribe of Reuben, which settled on the Mishor, found the land to be "*a good one for livestock*" (Num 32:1–5), a place particularly suitable for a lifestyle "*among the sheep pens listening to the playing of pipes for the flocks*" (Judg 5:16). Mesha, king of Moab in the mid-ninth century BC,

1 *Onomasticon* 132; G.S.P. Freeman-Grenville, Rupert L. Chapman III, and Joan E. Taylor, *The Onomasticon by Eusebius of Caesarea* (Jerusalem: Carta, 2003), 73.

2 Edward Robinson and Eli Smith, *Biblical Researches in Palestine, Mount Sinai and Arabia Petraea: A Journal of Travels in the Year 1838 by E. Robinson and E. Smith Undertaken in Reference to Biblical Geography*, vol. I (Boston: Crocker and Brewster, 1841), 569.

3 Smith, *Historical Geography of the Holy Land*, 565.

was by heritage a successful sheep breeder from Dibon; in the modern world, he would be someone analogous to a Bedouin *sheik*. From the land that he controlled, in Moab proper as well as on the Mishor, Mesha had to supply a vast number of lambs and rams as annual tax revenue to Israel's King Ahab (2 Kgs 3:4); grain is not mentioned in the passage.

In terms of settlement, the Mishor has always presented a mixed picture of living spaces interspersed with cities, villages, and goat-hair tents. The density of villages on the northern part of the plateau, within a radius of ten to twenty miles (16 to 32 km) around the modern city of Madaba (Num 21:30), is particularly high. Here, archaeologically recoverable material suggests a dynamic, connected living environment since at least the Iron Age.[1] Many towns significant to the biblical story lay along or quite close to the edge of the western scarp, or above the gorge of the Arnon. The majority were on or adjacent to the band of Cenomanian-Turonian limestone visible just below the top of the tableland. As such, they enjoyed the benefits of a mixed economy bolstered by varied conditions of soil and topography. Following a counter-clockwise direction starting in the north, these cities include Heshbon (Hisban; Num 21:25–26; 32:37; Isa 15:4; 16:8–9), Nebo (Khirbet Ayun Musa?: Num 32:28; 1 Chr 5:8; Jer 48:1,22), Kiriathaim (Qaryat al-Mekhaiyat; Num 32:37), Beth-baal-meon (Main; Num 32:28; 1 Chr 5:8), Ataroth (Khirbet Ataruz; Num 32:3,34), Kerioth (al-Qereiyat; Jer 48:24,41), Dibon (Dibhan; Num 21:30; 32:34; Jer 48:22), and Aroer (Khirbet Arair; Deut 2:36; 1 Chr 5:8; Jer 48:18–20). Most are mentioned in the Mesha Stela (Moabite Stone) as having been taken from Israel by Mesha king of Moab in the mid-ninth century BC, after the death of Ahab (2 Kgs 1:1; 3:4).[2] Ezekiel called Baal-Maon, Kiriathaim, and Beth-jeshimoth (Tell al-Azeima, on the plains of Moab at the base of the Abarim scarp) "*the splendor of the land*" (Ezek 25:9), apparently referring to the strategic value they held for Moab over against Israel. Other cities such as Medeba, Bezer (Umm el-Amad?; Deut 4:43; Josh 20:8; 21:36), Jahaz (Khirbet Medeiyina?; Num 21:23; Deut 2:32; Judg 11:20; Isa 15:4; Jer 48:34), and Tell Jalul (also a candidate for Bezer) can be found somewhat back on the eastern expanse of the tableland itself.

Flocks of sheep and goats are still at home on Dibon, the one-time capital of Moab and home of Mesha, its sheep-breeding king (2 Kgs 3:4). Fertile fields roll out to the horizon, current evidence of the mixed economic base that has blessed the Mishor for millennia. As can be implied from the Mesha Stele (Moabite Stone), Mesha and his father, Chemosh-yatti, had established the Moabite capital at Dibon, north of the Arnon gorge, giving them the opportunity to expand their influence to the routes and resources of the Mishor.

The Mishor is open in the sense that, lacking major topographical obstacles, traffic up on the plateau can go just about anywhere.[3] The Mishor's flatlands seem to have always been a place for all kinds of comings and goings: from seasonal grazing patterns to local traffic moving among its many towns and villages to international commerce or military activity that crosses Transjordan via the northern end of the Dead Sea. Historically, east-west traffic through the region has focused on Medeba and Heshbon, hubs collecting and directing routes to or from the oasis of Jericho, while north-south traffic has tended to move along the King's Highway linking Rabbah with Heshbon, Medeba, Dibon, and/or Aroer. The King's Highway tracks more or less along the watershed ridge, connecting these (and other) towns on as direct a line as possible, though this means dropping into and climbing out of the Wadi al-Wala and the gorge of the Arnon. The Old Testament prophets (Isa 16:2; Jer 48:19) and the Mesha Stela (line 26)[4] speak of passageways across the Arnon. These are corroborated by archaeological evidence, though in the form of milestones of a Roman road that descended into the defile from Aroer, then up to Moab proper on the southern side. This route is majestic if not determined, and remains the approximate line of the paved highway (Jordan Highway 35) today. Far to the east, the Desert Highway (Jordan Highway 15, a portion of which is called "*the road to the Wilderness of Moab*" in Deut 2:8) tracks a north-south line beyond the headwater streams of the Arnon. In doing so, it largely bypasses the towns of the Mishor in favor of running the track of the caravan route connecting Rabbah with the Arabian Peninsula.

On the one hand, the Mishor looks more like the Moab Plateau than it does the Ammon Basin or the Hill Country of Judah and Israel. On environmental criteria alone, this tended to connect the Mishor with the Moabites, who would have known best how to make a living off a land that was most suitable to their own. We recall that for the same reason the Gilead hills are associated with the hills of Ephraim and Manasseh. On balance, then, the Mishor was more Moabite than it was Ammonite, Israelite, or something else. Still, a review of history shows that the sweep of

1 Douglas R. Clark, Larry G. Herr, Øysten S. LaBianca, et al., *The Madaba Plains Project: Forty Years of Archaeological Research into Jordan's Past* (Sheffield: Equinox Publishing, 2011).

2 Ahituv, *Echoes from the Past*, 389–418.

3 Amman's Queen Alia International Airport, spread over the table-flat plateau east of Medeba, represents this historic reality in modern conveyance.

4 Ahituv, *Echoes from the Past*, 395: "I [Mesha] made the highway in the 'Arnôn."

events across the windswept stage of the Mishor is as open as its landscape might suggest. The region is a classic Land Between.[1] Its fertile fields and confluence of routes serve nicely as a buffer (or battleground) in a triangle of local powers: Moab, Ammon, and Israel/Judah. In addition, pressure from Gilead and threats from the ever-encroaching hordes off the eastern desert made this a very busy place. By analogy, we might think of a pentagon-shaped sports field with five teams aiming at five goals rather than just two, all fighting to control the same ball. If natural strongholds are defined by their surrounding topography—for example, by steep perimeter valleys or defensively controlled approach routes—then no individual city or town on the Mishor tableland qualifies as such, although Dibon may come the closest. Once one city of the Mishor falls, the rest tend to go the way of dominoes. The invasions of Moses (from the east), Ahab (from the northwest), and Mesha (from the south) are enough to illustrate the point. The story of the Mishor, then, was seldom its own.

An exception to the rule was Sihon king of the Amorites. (Here "Amorite" is a generic term for indigenous inhabitants of the region.) In the Late Bronze Age and at the expense of both Moab and Ammon, he was able to carve out a petty kingdom centered on the city of Heshbon (Num 21:26; Judg 11:13; cp. 1 Kgs 4:19). Under Moses, Israel took Sihon out, having swept off the open desert from the southeast (Num 21:13–31; Deut 2:24–27). In the eyes of Sihon, Israel was certainly just another example of the ever-encroaching desert hordes that had to be repulsed from settled lands. Sihon met Israel at Jahaz out at the edge of the desert, hoping—and failing—to stop them before they could reach the more fertile areas around Heshbon. The decisive battle came as Israel took the hills of Jazer (Num 21:32) on the watershed ridge west of the Ammon Basin. In so doing, Israel not only strangled Sihon but contained the Ammonites in the process. By settling the tribes of Reuben and Gad on the Mishor, Moses was able to stake a settlement claim in Transjordan, drive a wedge between Moab and Ammon, and prevent either from easy access to Jericho, the vital eastern gateway into the hill country of Cisjordan. The textual data detailing the subsequent settlement history of Reuben and Gad on the Mishor presents a mixed territorial picture. Reuben was concentrated around Heshbon, while Gad, the more dominant of the two Israelite tribes, settled in western Gilead, the Jordan Valley, and as far south on the Mishor as Ataroth and Dibon (Num 32:34–38; Josh 13:15–28; *Mesha Stela* lines 10–11). Both groups were tent dwellers, at least in the early stages of their recorded history, which not only explains their suitability to the physical settings of the Mishor but proximal intermingling as well.

The Chronicler preserves genealogical data that suggests that the Benjaminites also had territorial claims in the Mishor (1 Chr 8:1,8). Indeed, it is possible to posit the same sort of natural interaction between the land of Benjamin and the Mishor as can be traced further north between Ephraim/Manasseh and Gilead. We have already suggested that the story of Ruth indicates similar ties between the populations of the Mishor and Judah. In the mid-ninth century BC, Israel's King Omri, in a kind of reverse-Joshua move, was able to use Jericho as a gateway to conquer the entire Mishor from Moab except for its southwestern corner around Dibon, south of Wadi al-Wala (1 Kgs 16:33–34; 2 Kgs 1:1; 3:4-5; cp. *Mesha Stele*[2]). Playing the role of a well-positioned middleman, Omri and his more notorious, though politically astute, son Ahab suctioned off the resources of the Mishor in the amount of "*one hundred thousand lambs and the wool of one hundred thousand rams* [every year]" (2 Kgs 3:4). Ahab maximized his gain by shipping wool for manufacture through the ports of Phoenicia to which he had access by virtue of his marriage alliance with Jezebel (1 Kgs 16:31). This Mishor-Israel-Phoenicia economic axis was operative throughout the Iron Age (Ezek 27:17), though the products that moved—and the identity of the one who most benefited—changed with the shifting political fortunes and priorities of the particular nation-states involved.

Geographical logic suggests that the Ammonites must have also eyed the resources of the open Mishor from the narrow confines of their chalk basin behind the Gilead watershed, but textual data to reconstruct anything more than a bare outline of their story is lacking. We can assume that David's siege of Rabbah checked Ammonite claims on the region (2 Sam 11:1; 1 Chr 19:1–15), just as Moses's conquest of the Mishor had curtailed prior Ammonite claims to the same. Seldom acting alone, the Ammonites allied with Moab at the time of the judges (Judg 3:13) and again during the reign of Jehoshaphat to press across the Rift Valley (2 Chr 20:1–13); in both instances, we can assume a measure of prior control over at least the northwestern Mishor (at Heshbon and Medeba). We can also infer the same from the vehemence with which Ezra and Nehemiah forbade intermarriage between Jews and Ammonites (as well as Moabites) after the return from exile. The Mishor must have been a fertile Land Between for individual, as well as national, aspirations throughout the biblical period (Ezra 9:1–3; Neh 13:23–31).

But Israel's claims on the Mishor during the time of the monarchy were most effectively countered by Moab. Moabite King Eglon, with the assistance of the Ammonites, was able to advance as far as Jericho and in the process give a wake-up call to the precarious nature of Israel's tribal settlement east of the Jordan (Judg 3:12–30). And, of course, it was Mesha who, after the death of Ahab, was able to sweep across the entire plateau from Dibon and bring it back under the political and economic control of Moab. His victory stela mentions first the conquest of Medeba (*Mesha Stela* lines 7-9), a strategic deep-strike to seize the hub of economic corridors that cross the Mishor's tableland. The prophets, as we have seen, considered Heshbon and the surrounding area to be Moabite (Isa 15:4; 16:8-9; Jer 48:2,45; Ezek 25:9), while at the same time speaking quite naturally of "all the Judeans in Moab" as if a mixed population on the Mishor was both natural and expected. Throughout, the ability of the prophets of ancient Israel to describe the physical geography of the region and name Moabite cities almost as if looking at a map (Isa 15–16; Jer 48) is one of the best pieces of evidence we have to suggest an ongoing interaction of peoples whose respective homelands lay on either side of the Rift Valley.

---

1 James M. Monson, *Regions on the Run* (Rockford, IL: Biblical Backgrounds, 1998), 20–27.

2 Ahituv, *Echoes from the Past*, 389–418.

One of the most wonderful contributions to the discipline of biblical historical geography is the Madaba Map. The map is a depiction in colorful mosaic of the world of the Bible as it was remembered in the sixth century AD. It can be seen in situ, as part of the floor of the Greek Orthodox Church of St. George in Madaba, Jordan. While large portions of the mosaic map are damaged or missing, the sections that remain—including portions of the Mishor, Moab, the southern Jordan Valley and Dead Sea, the Hill Country of Judah, the Negev, and Jerusalem—offer a pictorial commentary on the geographical and theological priorities of its Byzantine-era artists. The map's detailed depiction of Byzantine-era Jerusalem is shown here.

National aspirations in, or over, the Mishor took a back seat during the Age of Empires (that is, from the Assyrian conquest in the late eighth century BC onward), though we have seen hints of an Ammonite-Moabite-Judean tug for control over the Mishor during the days of Ezra and Nehemiah (the fifth century BC). Jewish Hasmonean King John Hyrcanus was able to restore Jerusalem's suzerainty over the Mishor when he conquered Medeba in the late second century BC (*Ant.* xiii.254-255). But by the time of the New Testament, the Mishor, like the rest of the southern Levant, was in the process of being incorporated into the Roman Empire, initially as part of the district of Perea ("across [the Jordan]") under the control of Herod the Great and his son, Herod Antipas. Herod the Great built a palace fortress at Machaerus (*Mukawer*) on a prominent spur among the slopes above the Dead Sea south of the outlet of the *Zarqa Ma'in.* From there his boss, Caesar Augustus, gained a secure foothold facing the Nabateans, the coveted purveyors of wealth in this most critical corner of the Roman Empire. Josephus adds the detail that it was at Machaerus, which doubled as a prison, that Herod Antipas executed John the Baptist (*Ant.* xviii.116-119). Archaeological evidence suggests there was a harbor at Callirrhoe below Machaerus during the Roman period, receiving ships from En Gedi and En Feshkha on the western shore of the Dead Sea.[1]

Israel's aspirations for the Mishor are perhaps best expressed in the two blessings of Reuben: the first was spoken by Jacob, the second by Moses. As full brothers (Gen 29:31–35) who possessed landed inheritances that shared the shoreline of the Dead Sea, the respective histories of Reuben and Judah are things we might expect to have been intertwined, and so they were. But Reuben's tribal history did not reflect his position as the *oldest* son of Jacob. Likened first to turbulent water (Gen 49:4), the tribe of Reuben indeed soon ebbed away, replaced on the high Mishor stage by any number of eager players round about, including Judah, his youngest full brother. Moses's blessing understood the precarious reality that the Reubenite tent dwellers would face on the open plateau around Medeba and Heshbon, and urged their survival: "*Let Reuben live and not die though his people become few*" (Deut 33:6). Words aptly spoken for inhabitants of the contested tableland that is the Mishor.

F. THE MOAB PLATEAU

In its geological composition, surface topography, patterns of climate, and mix of natural resources, the Moab Plateau resembles the tableland of the Mishor. Yet the Moab Plateau is a distinct geographical unit, indeed the most easily defined of all the regions of Transjordan, because of its obvious topographical borders on three sides: the sudden drop of the Arnon (Wadi al-Mujib) to the north (Num 21:3; Judg 11:18), the equally dramatic gorge of the Zered (Wadi al-Hasa) on the south, and the chasm of the Dead Sea to the west. In size, the Moab Plateau runs thirty miles (48 km) north-south and less than twenty miles (32 km) west-east. Like the Mishor, it gives way gradually to open desert further to the east.

If we look for a natural eastern border for the Moab Plateau, it is to be found in the upper streams of the Arnon. Some of the multiple headwaters of the Arnon River begin just north of the eastern reaches of the Zered River, deep in the plateau's southeastern corner. They flow northward in a gradually deepening depression the entire length of Moab, each joining in turn to form

1 Gideon Hadas, "Dead Sea Anchorages," *RB* 118/2 (2011): 161–79.

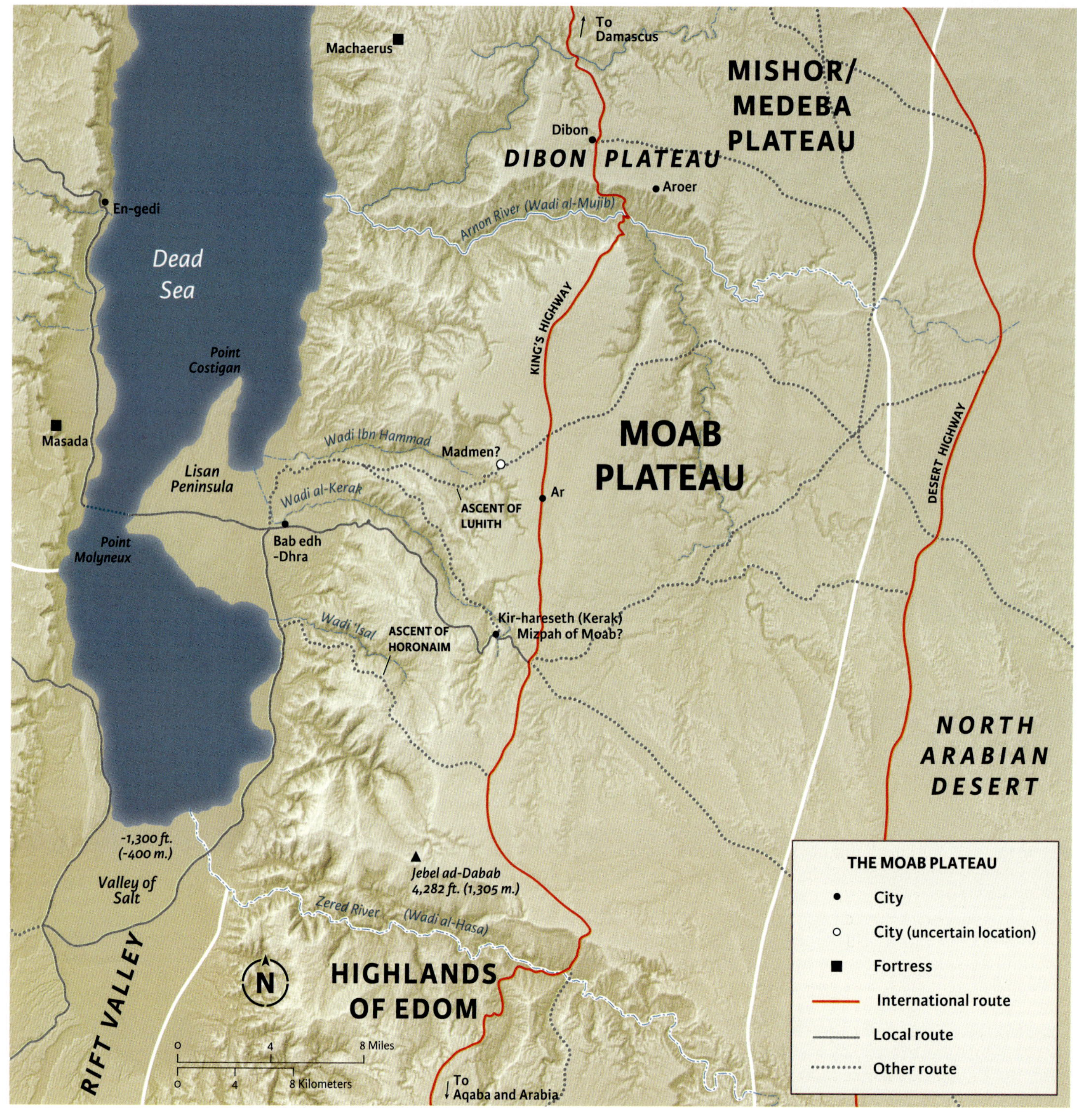

a single stream. Other headwaters flow off the open desert from the east. The sites of the ancient place names "*Waheb in Suphah and the ravines of the Arnon*" (Num 21:14) likely can be found somewhere along one or the other of these outer courses, at the edge of the desert through which Moses led the Israelites on their climactic journey toward the Mishor (Num 21:12–20). All of these streams combine at a point that defines the northeastern corner of the Moab Plateau. Here they become caught in, and follow, a structural weakness in the limestone that has eroded into the magnificent chasm of the Arnon, directing everything straight west to the Dead Sea.

The western slopes of the Moab Plateau are nearly identical to the corresponding slopes of the Mishor north of the Arnon River. That is, the Senonian chalk surface on the Moab tableland above gives way to harder shapes of Cenomanian-Turonian limestone mid-slope, then red-purple Nubian sandstones below. While the slopes of the Mishor tend to drop right into the Dead Sea, those south of the Arnon level out onto a shoreline plain. This plain projects westward into the Dead Sea, forming the Lisan ("Tongue") Peninsula, a large, level mass of marl stretching to within two miles of the Judean shore opposite Masada. This peninsula gives the Dead Sea its familiar, hooked shape. The northern tip of the peninsula has been christened Point Costigan, while the point furthest west has the name Point Molyneux. Costigan (in 1835) and Molyneux (in 1847) were

A crumbly base of Eocene limestone is crowned by a solid cap of basalt on the Moab Plateau. As is typical for basalt, the once-molten rock cooled along vertical lines that break off as thin columns under the forces of erosion. The basalt covering is nearly devoid of vegetation; a determined flock of sheep and goats grazes scant fare along the point of the soft limestone seam.

two of the earliest Western adventure-travelers who dared to explore the surface and shoreline of the Dead Sea. Tragically, the heat and lack of fresh water killed Costigan; Molyneux died of fever six months after his travels.[1] Their fate is unsurprising: the Lisan Peninsula is hyper-arid and laden with salt. It is totally devoid of anything that would attract or support plant or animal life, is without shade, bakes under insufferable heat, is surrounded on three sides by the Dead Sea, and is arguably the most inhospitable acreage on earth. Yet in stark contrast, much of its eastern end, where the peninsula joins the Moab shore, is quite habitable due to a line of copious springs and alluvium washed down from the westward-facing hills above.

We have seen that the structural lines and the courses of the interior wadis of the Mishor north of the Arnon run generally on a northeast-southwest line. Here, south of the Arnon, the direction is reversed to southeast-northwest; it is easily traced in the orientation of the wadis and fault lines that scour the surface of the plateau. Together, the Mishor and the Moab Plateau both drain toward the middle of the eastern shoreline of the Dead Sea, in the general direction of the outlet of the Arnon. The main wadi draining the interior of the Moab Plateau is the Wadi al-Kerak, named after the largest city on the plateau. Its upper tributaries penetrate the modern town of Kerak, nearly encircling the mound of Kir-hareseth (2 Kgs 2:25), its ancient site. The Wadi al-Karak flows on a nearly straight line to the northwest, exiting into the Dead Sea at the northern end of the Lisan Peninsula. The Ibn Hammad and 'Isal wadis trace similar, though less impressive, lines north and south of the Kerak wadi, respectively.

The highest elevations of the Moab Plateau are nearly all located on the edge of the scarp that overlooks the Dead Sea. These increase gradually from north to south, from 3,494 feet (1,065 m) just south of the Arnon River canyon to the 4,282 foot (1,305 m) Jebel ad-Dabab on the northern bank of the Zered canyon. If we add to this the elevation of the shoreline of the Dead Sea, which is another 1,200 feet (366 m) below sea level, this highest point of Moab is a rise of more than one mile (1.5 km) over a horizontal west-east run of just five miles (8 km). Strong winds always seem to push up these slopes from out of the Rift Valley, cresting the Moab scarp with noticeable force and bringing blustery, cold winters to towns perched on its edge. Technically this scarp line is the Transjordanian watershed ridge, though it is broken by multiple wadis that have their headwaters further east. Elevations east of the scarp typically settle in at between 2,800 and 3,200 feet (850 and 975 m) above sea level. The shallow depression that directs the upper tributaries of the Arnon along the eastern edge of the Moab Plateau is only 100 to 200 feet (30 to 60 m) lower, a change in elevation that is barely noticeable to travelers and offers no obstacle to traffic. Further east, a second low watershed directs everything beyond into the stony, open desert, draining northeastward to the Azraq Oasis east of Amman.

Though most of the surface of the Moab Plateau is composed of soft Senonian chalk, large expanses in the center and east are covered with sheets of hard, black flint and broken fields of basalt. Everything is broken into small fragments and strewn helter-skelter across the landscape. The eastern half of the plateau in particular has the appearance of seared callousness. At least the covering of basalt and flint gives structural

1 Yehoshua Ben-Arieh, *The Rediscovery of the Holy Land in the Nineteenth Century*, 2nd ed. (Jerusalem: The Magnes Press, 1983), 76, 123–24, 150.

"For kilometers on end the landscape is black with myriads of lava and flint pieces glistening in the sunshine with a brilliance that blinds the unaccustomed or unprotected eye. Driving over these stone carpeted areas makes an automobile sound like the proverbial bull in the china shop. Once while driving through a long stretch of this black, forbidding area, we saw ahead of us in the distance a large patch of green, a welcome sight for sore eyes. Surely a small oasis! Soon we reached the patch of green and it began to hop all over us. It was composed of a tremendous swarm of locusts."[1]

strength to the upper layers of the topography, though with "brimstone scattered over the sheepfolds" (Job 18:15; author's translation), settled life here is nearly impossible: *"His roots below dry up, and his branches above wither away. All memory of [anyone who tries to live here] perishes from the earth"* (Job 18:16–17).

When standing in the depths of the Judean rain shadow on the western shore of the Dead Sea and gazing over the Lisan Peninsula to the barren heights of Moab on the other side, one can be excused for being underwhelmed with the impression that land further east could not possibly support viable life. The most familiar view of Moab for travelers to the land of ancient Israel is that from Masada, where the view takes in the stark rise above the Dead Sea's Lisan Peninsula, or from Ein Gedi, opposite of which the Arnon canyon cuts through the sandstone cliffs lining the eastern side of the sea. When the air is clear, the scene is dramatic for its rugged beauty of purples, blues, and grays—totally devoid of the least hint of green that might portend that some kind of life inhabits the opposite shore or its highlands above. A popular suggestion holds that the plain along the shore of the Dead Sea opposite Masada is the location of the Cities of the Plain: Sodom, Gomorrah, Admah, Zeboiim, and Bela/Zoar (Gen 14:2–3). Certainly, it's a landscape worthy of the reputation of having once hosted fire and brimstone (Gen 19:23–24). Yet our view must be tempered: the wadis draining the western slopes of the Moab Plateau provide fresh water and pleasant growing spaces at intervals all along the eastern shore of the Dead Sea with the exception of out on the Lisan Peninsula itself. We might rightly label any number of these spots of green with the term "oasis" and expect to find a wide variety of fruits and vegetables thriving under the blistering heat of the Rift Valley. Archaeological evidence at *Bab edh-Dhra*, the largest ancient site in the region and perhaps one of the Cities of the Plain, shows a prosperous settlement and, by implication, that living conditions in the area were favorable for much of the Early Bronze Age (the third millennium BC). The thin line between green and brown, life and death, blessing and destruction, is nowhere more fragile than here. One Old Testament-era prophet, who knew the view, commented rightly: *"Moab will be like Sodom and the Ammonites like Gomorrah: a place overgrown with weeds, a salt pit, and a perpetual wasteland"* (Zeph 2:9).

Climate and landforms preclude the development of towns in the canyons of the Arnon and Zered Rivers, and permanent settlement along the eastern shore of the Dead Sea is limited to its several oases. In contrast, living conditions on top of the Moab Plateau and within the folds of its interior wadis are much more favorable. The three main wadis draining the interior of the Moab Plateau, Wadi Ibn Hammad, Wadi al-Kerak, and Wadi 'Isal, form a large, westward-facing embayment dominated by a large expanse of exposed Cenomanian-Turonian limestone. This, and the chalky plateau immediately above, make up the heartland of ancient Moab. The main cities were located on or just below the scarp within the arc of the embayment. Of these, two enjoyed prime location by virtue of being at the head of separate wadis. These were Kir-hareseth (Kerak), capital of the Iron Age kingdom of Moab (2 Kgs 3:25) high in the upper reaches of the Wadi al-Kerak, and Madmen (Jer 48:2; Khirbet Dimna?) in the upper folds of Wadi Ibn Hammad.

Rainfall on the Moab heights averages a marginal twelve to sixteen inches (300–400 mm) per year, just scant enough to ensure that the primary resource base will be shepherding (2 Kgs 3:4–5). But the flatter areas of rendzina soil along the Kings Highway between Kir-hareseth and the Arnon have always also been valuable grain producing areas, resembling those of the Mishor though they are more limited in size. This was the vicinity of Ar, the viable northern portion of Moab that Moses took care to bypass on his way to the Mishor (Num 21:13–15,28; Deut 2:18). Perhaps we should also look for the fields of Moab that belonged to the family of Ruth here, rather than north of the Arnon. Summer fruit does very well on the upper elevations of the westward scarps of Moab, particularly in the hills cradling the sources of the al-Kerak and 'Isal wadis. The raisin cakes of Kir-hareseth were especially renowned, comparable to similar commod-

In addition to the plain adjacent to the Lisan Peninsula, at least three other suggestions have been made for the location of the Cities of the Plain and the Valley of Siddim mentioned in Genesis 14:2–3.[2] One is on either the Plains of Jericho or the Plains of Moab north of the Dead Sea, a proposal based on the evidence that Lot saw the region of Sodom and Gomorrah from the hills east of Bethel (Gen 13:3–13). A second locates the Cities of the Plain beneath the shallow waters of the southernmost section of the Dead Sea, where the water has sometimes receded to expose the dry marl bed below. Here the salt concentrations along the shoreline are heaviest, letting us more fully imagine the caustic nature of the destruction of Sodom and Gomorrah (Gen 19:23–28). A third suggestion places the cities on (or under) the muddy salt flats that extend for ten miles southward from the Dead Sea, at the outlet of the Zered Wadi. A Byzantine memory codified by the Madaba Map locates here the cave to which Lot fled to escape the rain of fire and brimstone. Convincing archaeological evidence for any of these suggestions is lacking.

1 Nelson Glueck, *The Other Side of the Jordan* (Cambridge: ASOR, 1970), 41.

2 For a summary of views, see J. Simons, *The Geographical and Topographical Texts of the Old Testament* (Leiden: E. J. Brill, 1959), 222–29; Steven Collins, "Where Is Sodom? The Case for Tall el-Hammam," *BAR* 39/2 (2013): 32–41, 70–71.

Much of the shoreline of Moab in the vicinity of the Lisan Peninsula is well served by its reputation as a land of fire and brimstone (left). But in other places, near springs or where wadis carry fresh water down from the scarps above, oases have formed. Here locally grown eggplant, squash, and tomatoes (right) replace marl, flint, and salt-encrusted stone—proof that life can flourish.

ities produced on the northwestern Mishor (Isa 16:7; cp. Isa 16:8–9 and Jer 48:32–33). Moab's suitability for grain production was recognized by the prophet Isaiah, though in a way that was anything but complimentary: "*Moab will be trampled in his place as straw is trampled in a dung pile*" (Isa 25:10). The Hebrew word for "dung pile," *madmena*, must be a reflection of the Moabite city Madmen, which took its place among other Moabite cities under the withering prophetic voice (Jer 48:2). The arable portion of the Moab Plateau starts to taper off noticeably as one heads east, with the wheat becoming thinner and the fields patchy and sparse. Eight to ten miles (13–16 km) beyond the watershed scarp, even before the line of the Desert Highway, the possibilities for farming give way to the land of the shepherd altogether. In years when the winter and spring rains are good, the eastern reaches of Moab sprout a thin covering of grass, though the soils are rocky, immature, and often covered with shards of basalt and flint. Water collects everywhere in hollows and depressions of all kinds, and Bedouin flocks come to graze until every last bit of grass and water is gone. We might expect that Moses's journey around the eastern end of Edom and Moab took place in the wintertime and that it was during the summer months that he camped deep in the Zered and the Arnon canyons, where perennial sources of water are more plentiful (Num 21:12–13; Judg 11:18).

The overall isolation of the Moab Plateau, when combined with the relatively low carrying capacity of its land, suggests that the population of the region was never very large. Indeed, many more towns both ancient and modern can be found on the Mishor than the Moab Plateau, though by comparison permanent settlement in Edom, south of the Zered, is even more difficult. In its Arnon-to-Zered heartland Moab is, to an important degree, comparable to the Ammon Basin—a region built around a single major city. Kir-hareseth (2 Kgs 3:25–27), also called Kir-Moab (Isa 15:1) or Kir-heres (Isa 16:11; Jer 48:31,36), was the capital of the Moabite kingdom. The city was well located: it sat on the fresh and wet western scarp overlooking the Dead Sea yet in the geographical center of Moab. It was at the head of a fertile wadi (al-Kerak) that could support a mixed grain and summer fruit economy; and, like ancient Jerusalem, Rabbah, and Bozrah, it was on a prominent defensible spur surrounded on three sides by natural moats or valleys.

Kir-hareseth sits just west of the watershed ridge, where its residents enjoy easy access to the north-south route of the King's Highway. Perpendicular natural routes follow the continuous ridges tracing the top of the northern and southern rims of the Wadi al-Karak. Baly has suggested that the "*descent of Horonaim*" (Jer 48:5; cp. Isa 15:5; Jer 48:34) can be found in the wadi itself,[1] though it and the "*Ascent of Luhith*" (Isa 15:5; Jer 48:5) may be associated with the rim ridges above with equal conviction.[2] In any case, these routes all drop onto the Lisan Peninsula from which, it is supposed, travelers could cross the shallow part of the Dead Sea to the vicinity of Masada, then make their way to Ein-gedi and points beyond. The trip across the sea must have been both inconvenient and uncomfortable, but possible when water levels were low and necessary when political conditions demanded. It is likely that this was the attack route of the coalition of Moabites, Ammonites, and Meunites that invaded eastern Judah during the days of Jehoshaphat (2 Chr 20:1–2). Kir-hareseth thus sits at an important T-junction connecting Judah and Jerusalem with Transjordan, the importance of which

1 Baly, *Geography of the Bible*, 231.

2 Lancaster and Monson, *Geobasics Study Guide*, 107.

The table-flat portions of the Moab Plateau are especially suitable for fields of wheat and barley, which are planted in early winter, green in mid-spring, and harvested from late spring to early summer. The fields are still marked by rows of stones interspersed by cairns that served as boundary markers, the ancient equivalent of a fence line (cp. Deut 27:17).

was heightened when Jericho and the Mishor came under the control of the Northern Kingdom of Israel in the ninth century BC. The narrow waist of the Dead Sea was certainly forded (or sailed) during the time of the New Testament, since the Masada-Nabatean connection was as important for the Herodian royal family (Herod's mother was Nabatean; Josephus, *War* 1.181) as it was for Roman political priorities on this, their southeastern frontier.

The same chasms that so clearly define the edges of the Moab Plateau on the north, west, and south were by necessity crossed by these highways, though not easily. Reading the terrain makes it possible to posit the most likely lines of travel. But to the east, with no real barrier to mark the edge of the desert, the exact network of natural routes is harder to trace. In part, this is because the eastern lands lie relatively flat and open; thus, routes were not always restricted by factors of topography. But we must also keep in mind that the lack of permanent settlements beyond the narrow zone of arable land on the western half of the plateau hinders our ability to identify the location of eastern termini and hence the road network connecting them. Everything heading east eventually joined with the Desert Highway. The Moabites, unlike the Ammonites, established no known port city on their portion of that international route except up on the Mishor, and the caravans, for the most part, seem to have passed on by—or so our written and archaeological sources seem to suggest. The east was, rather, a direction of forays and raids (cp. 1 Chr 1:46), and Moses's approach to the Mishor from the desert must have portended to the Moabites more of the same (Num 21:11–13; Judg 11:18; cp. Num 22:3–4).

Like the place name *Ammon*, the name *Moab* defines a geographical region as well as a people group. The biblical account traces the origins of both to half brothers, ancestors with the eponymous names of Moab and Ben-ammi. The story of these siblings anticipates the eventual struggle of their descendants over the Mishor (Gen 19:30–38). But the Moab Plateau and Ammon Basin share an additional defining characteristic: they are regions which, by themselves, are unable to fully support or contain the national aspirations of their respective peoples. And so the story of the Moab Plateau, like that of the Ammon Basin, is basically a narrative of the struggle of its people to expand beyond its natural borders, with most of the recorded action taking place on the Mishor between. Moab, secure behind its canyon moats and living on an adequate though precarious base of home-grown resources, was drawn onto the Mishor, since the chalk base, rendzina soils, and landforms of the Mishor were as familiar to the Moabites as the Dome of Gilead was to the Israelites. So, though their heartland lay south of the Arnon (Judg 11:18), Moab's landed identity took deep root on the Mishor. The evidence for their push northward is persistent in all available written sources. We have seen, for instance, the ease by which Eglon king of Moab moved into Jericho during the time of the judges (Judg 3:12–13) and how, during the days of Kings Omri and Ahab in the ninth century BC, Mesha and his father pushed northward at least as far as Nebo. Place names verify the reality: early on in Israel's settlement

The black iris (*Iris nigricans*), the national flower of the Hashemite Kingdom of Jordan, grows in the chalky, rendzina soils of the Moab Plateau. Stands of the flower can be found along the King's Highway just south of the Arnon.

history, the Bible called the southeastern corner of the Rift Valley the plains of *Moab*; as late as the sixth century BC, the prophet Ezekiel labeled cities on the Abarim slopes "*Moab's flank . . . its frontier cities, the splendor of the land*" (Ezek 25:9).

On the other hand, recorded events that are specific to the Moabite heartland are few. A rare example comes from an account about David, a fellow who shows up nearly everywhere in the southern Levant and who left his family in Mizpah of Moab ("Moab's Lookout") when being chased by Saul. David then went down to "*the stronghold*," perhaps Masada (1 Sam 22:3–4). Mizpah of Moab is not yet identified, but it is interesting that there is line-of-sight connection between several points lining the Moabite scarp high in the folds of the al-Kerak wadi and Masada. David followed up by bringing Moab under the political control of his emerging Israelite state (2 Sam 8:2,12; 1 Chr 18:2). In the mid-ninth century BC, after the death of King Ahab, an Israel-Judah coalition was able to take the battle all the way to the Moabite capital, Kir-hareseth, by attacking Moab via the southern end of the Dead Sea rather than through the Mishor (2 Kgs 3:4–27). These were favors that for all of their ambition neither Mesha nor any of the kings of Moab were ever quite able to repay. The Mishor easily and repeatedly fell into Moabite hands; attempts by Moab to take anything beyond, based on what we know from the biblical record, typically stalled (e.g., Judg 3:15–30; 2 Chr 20:1–23). Moabite national aspirations were eventually extinguished during the Age of Empires in the second half of the first millennium BC through the prolonged effect of Assyria, Babylon, Persia, Greece, the Hasmoneans, and Rome. In the first century AD, the canyon of the Arnon played well its role as a border: Rome ruled the Mishor through the Herodian Dynasty while the Moab Plateau fell within the orbit of the Nabateans. By the time of the New Testament, Roman international priorities called the shots, and what was once the heartland of a viable nation-state became the frontier of a far-flung empire. In the ebb and flow of the southern Levant, heartland once again became land between.

Late season rain clouds push up the Wadi al-Kerak, bringing the *"blessings of the heavens above"* (Gen 49:25)—and a good winter chill—to Moab. With plenty of dewy nights throughout the year, this is the part of the Moab Plateau that supports summer fruit. When the air is clear, the view down the wadi from atop the remains of the Crusader castle of Kerak (foreground) takes in the flat blue of the Dead Sea, the blanched rise of the Judean Wilderness, and even Masada—living spaces vastly different from those on the Moab Plateau above.

G. THE HIGHLANDS OF EDOM

Like the homelands of Moab and Ammon, the Highlands of Edom form a distinct geographical region associated with a particular ethnic group, in this case the Edomites, descendants of Esau (Gen 36:1,8,19,21). As a place name, *Edom* is derived from the general Semitic word for "[brownish] red-" or "blood-colored" (Hb *'ādom*). The term evokes both the color of the sandstone mountains that rise out of the Rift Valley southeast of the Dead Sea and ruddy Esau, whose descendants inhabited the area (Gen 25:25; 32:3; 33:16; Josh 24:4). Equally evocative is the name *Seir* (or, Mount Seir; Ezek 35:15), which is often—though not exclusively—associated with the northern part of the Highlands of Edom, the Edomite heartland during the Iron Age. According to the biblical record, Seir was the name of an indigenous Horite patriarch who lived in the hills on either side of the Arabah south of the Dead Sea before Esau arrived in the area (Gen 36:20–21). As a place name, *Seir* predates *Edom* with reference to the hills that lie both east and west of the southern part of the Rift Valley (Deut 1:44; 2:1,8,12,21–22; Josh 24:4; 1 Chr 4:42). *Seir* also seems to be a wordplay on the Hebrew word *sa'ir*, "hairy," a term for male goats and, by implication, the place where goat herding (and not much else) is viable. Alternatively, a persistently popular suggestion holds that the Highlands of Edom were called Mount Seir (Hairy Mountain) because the tree line up top, prior to deforestation in the early twentieth century AD, gave the scarp a bristled appearance resembling Esau himself (Gen 25:30)—though it must be noted that the look was also characteristic of other parts of the Transjordanian highlands and not unique to the rim of the Rift Valley south of the Dead Sea. Such place name associations, whatever their original points of reference, form convenient connections with the biblical narrative, merging the identity of people and land here as securely as Jacob, Esau's twin, has been identified with the Gilead hills as well as the highlands west of the Jordan River. We should note that associating the Edomites with a red scarp crowned by bristly "hair" works best when the region is viewed from the west, from the direction of Israel, whose point of view, it seems, has come to influence the historical record.

A third name associated with the mountain of Esau is Teman, which was either an important district within the Highlands of Edom, an alternate name for Bozrah, capital of Edom during the Iron Age, or, like the name Samaria, both (Jer 49:7,20; Amos 1:12; Obad 9). Teman seems to have been first a personal name (Gen 36:11; Job 2:11) and may have been connected, through etymology, genealogy, or geography, to the great oasis of Tema on the desert road to Babylon and Arabia (Job 6:19; Isa 21:14). If so, the name hints at Edom's desert-ward role as a gateway for Transjordan's international caravan traffic. Indeed, a safe assumption would allow for many of the regional names associated with the Highlands of Edom to have been ethnic names first, and only later names of places. This idea is certainly consistent with the depiction of Esau in Genesis 36:1–43 and the pattern of settlement in tribal lands generally.

The Highlands of Edom, in fact, are the largest of the regions of Transjordan and the most complex geographically. They divide naturally into three distinct parts: two high limestone plateaus edged by a western

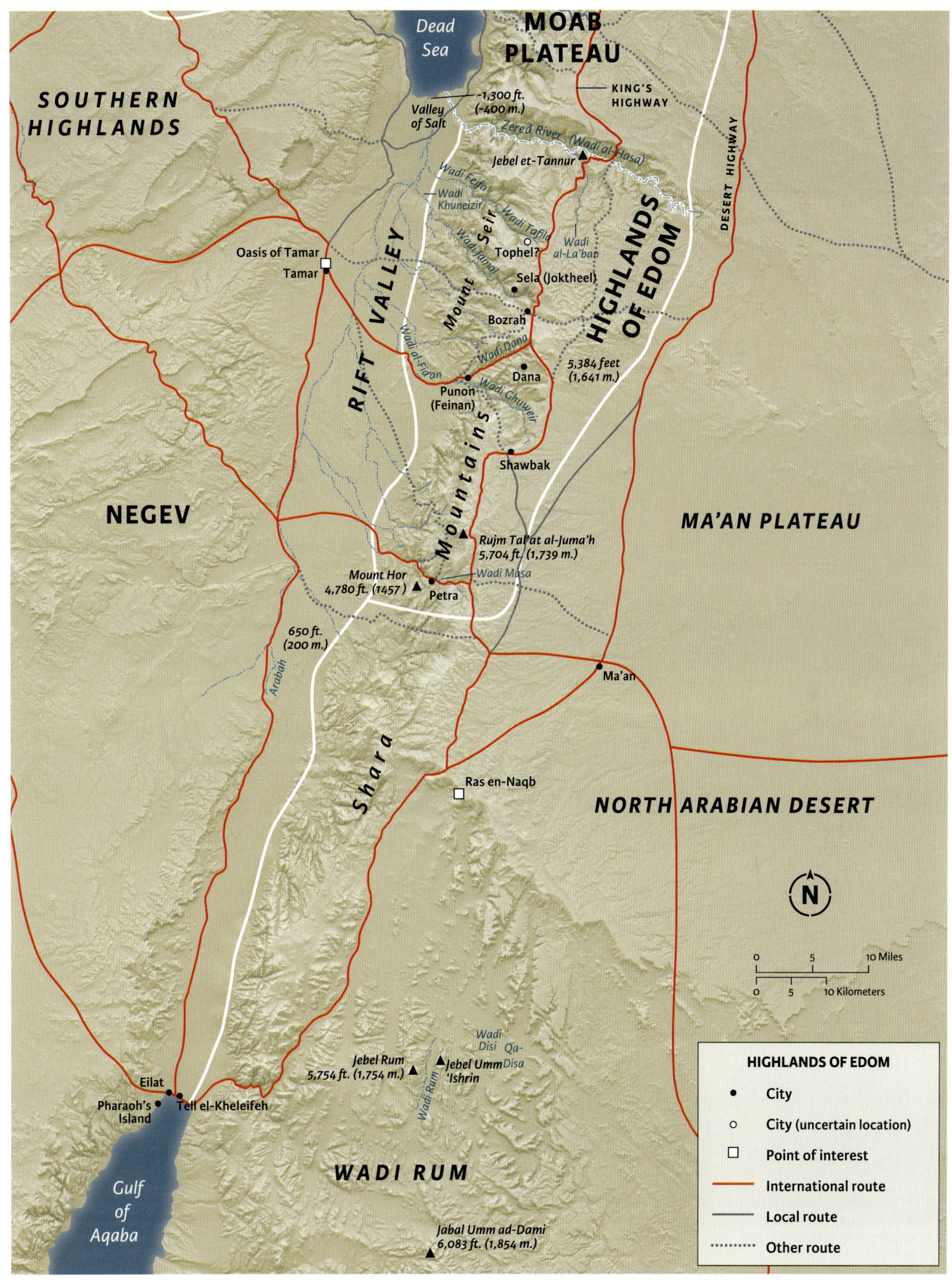
Dead Sea
MOAB PLATEAU
SOUTHERN HIGHLANDS
-1,300 ft. (-400 m.)
Valley of Salt
KING'S HIGHWAY
Zered River (Wadi al-Hasa)
Jebel et-Tannur
DESERT HIGHWAY
Wadi Feifa
Wadi Khuneizir
Wadi Tafila
Seir
Wadi Jamal
Tophel?
Wadi al-La'ban
HIGHLANDS OF EDOM
Oasis of Tamar
Tamar
RIFT VALLEY
Sela (Joktheel)
Mount
Bozrah
Wadi al-Fidan
Wadi Dana
Dana
5,384 feet (1,641 m.)
Punon (Feinan)
Wadi Ghuweir
Mountains
Shawbak
NEGEV
MA'AN PLATEAU
Rujm Tal'at al-Juma'h 5,704 ft. (1,739 m.)
Mount Hor 4,780 ft. (1457)
Wadi Musa
Petra
650 ft. (200 m.)
Arabah
Ma'an
Shara
Ras en-Naqb
NORTH ARABIAN DESERT
N
0 5 10 Miles
0 5 10 Kilometers
Wadi Disi
Qa-Disa
Jebel Rum 5,754 ft. (1,754 m.)
Jebel Umm 'Ishrin
Wadi Rum
Eilat
Pharaoh's Island
Tell el-Kheleifeh
WADI RUM
Gulf of Aqaba
Jabal Umm ad-Dami 6,083 ft. (1,854 m.)
HIGHLANDS OF EDOM
City
City (uncertain location)
Point of interest
International route
Local route
Other route

When the Dana Nature Reserve was established in 1993, it was the first area to be so protected by the government of the Hashemite Kingdom of Jordan. The reserve encloses 115 square miles (300 km²), centered on the er-Rummana ridge and the Dana wadi, which descends from Edom's limestone plateau to the Feinan copper mines in the Arabah more than a mile (1.5 km) in elevation below. The Dana Reserve includes a vast display of botanic diversity within its borders, much of which is specific to local ecosystems found at distinct elevations. The old stone houses of the Dana village have also been incorporated into the reserve; there visitors can learn about traditional patterns of life in the region. Local residents speak passionately about the need to preserve and protect their heritage. Designated hiking trails and official campsites with strict regulations limiting noise and supplies allow visitors a chance to participate in a way of life that is fast being swallowed up by the more hectic pace common to much of the Middle East.

escarpment of exposed sandstone and granite (Mount Seir, which we have already mentioned, and the Ma'an Plateau), and a majestic expanse of sandstone opening into the Arabian Peninsula further south (Wadi Rum). This is the most severely uplifted portion of Transjordan, with elevations consistently mile-high or higher, three times the height above sea level of the Negev highlands west of the Rift Valley. The tough, untamed strength of the Edomite highlands, with a bracing climate to boot, was not lost on the ancient Israelites, who considered its inhabitants, like Edom's hairy eponymous ancestor Esau, to be fit only for the edges of civilization: "*Look, your dwelling place will be away from the richness of the land, away from the dew of the sky above*" (Gen 27:39) and "*I throw my sandal on Edom*" (Pss 60:8; 108:9).

Mount Seir, the northernmost section of the Edomite Highlands, stretches from the Zered Wadi (Wadi al-Hasa) southward for thirty miles (48 km) to the town of Shawbak, just below the Wadi al-Fidan embayment. Its striking topography is the result of two conflicting geological forces: an especially strong uplift of the plateau coupled with a complex fracturing of the western escarpment by some extraordinary fault lines. These fault lines, running southeastward out of the Rift Valley, have splintered along odd angles in their eastern extremities to form a number of isolated mini-plateaus that trace the line of limestone just below the rim of the scarp. Each mini-plateau functions as a separate and relatively independent living space. Historically, some of these mini-plateaus have supported a single small town or village; on a line from north to south, these include Tafila (ancient Tophel?; Deut 1:1), Sil' (Sela = Joktheel; 2 Kgs 14:7; Isa 16:1), Buseira (Bozrah; Gen 36:33; Isa 34:6; Amos 1:11–12), Dana, and Shawbak. A few other mini-plateaus lining the western scarp of the Edomite highlands, such as the prominent er-Rummana ridge between Buseira and Dana, remain too rugged or isolated to support viable permanent village life.

Three major wadi systems drain Mount Seir to the west. Each has carved a majestic network of canyons along various fault lines angling northwestward into the Rift Valley. The northernmost and smallest is the Wadi Feifa, with its main tributary, the Wadi Tafila, draining the town of Tafila. Next comes Wadi Khuneizir, exposing deposits of fine, bright white silica sand at various bends along its length. One of its upper tributaries, Wadi Jamal, drains Sela and Bozrah, capitals of the Iron Age kingdom of Edom. The southernmost of the wadi systems of Mount Seir is the great Wadi al-Fidan, the largest of the three. Its two main tributaries are the Wadi Dana and the Wadi Ghuweir. The Dana wadi follows a perpendicular fault that runs on an absolutely straight line southwestward from the village of Dana, while the Ghuweir wadi traces a wet, winding course northwestward from Shawbak. Both are scored by modern hiking trails that lead to vistas and passageways that are nothing short of majestic. They merge into the Wadi Feinan near the ancient copper mines of Punon (Num 33:42–43; modern Feinan), ten miles (16 km) below the rim of the Edomite scarp. The Feinan wadi in turn becomes the Wadi al-Fidan as it widens out into the Arabah, then bends northwestward toward the Dead Sea. Together these wadi systems have carved a stunning eastward embayment into the Edomite scarp from Tafila to Shawbak. The Ghuweir wadi has cut a noticeably deep bulge in the arc of this embayment southeastward, pinching the Mount Seir plateau, the heartland of ancient Edom, from the Ma'an Plateau that lies beyond Shawbak to the south.

A fairly hefty band of Cenomanian-Turonian limestone is visible along the upper reaches of Mount Seir's western scarp, just below the point where everything begins to drop away from the featureless cap of Senonian chalk above. This line of hard limestone contains the best springs in the Edomite highlands, and it is here that the region's most important towns, both ancient and modern, are found. The limestone is more dominant around Bozrah and Sela than it is in the vicinity of Tafila up north or southward around Shawbak. On this account alone we might find grounds for the choice of Bozrah as the capital of ancient Edom. The bulk of the mass of majestic rock that comprises Mount Seir's westward defiles, in contrast, is composed of white and then red-purple Nubian sandstones and Precambrian granites, all in a wild tumble of dramatic features and forms. Elevations along the rim of the scarp from Tafila to Shawbak generally top out above 5,000 feet (1,525 m), rising to a height of 5,384 feet (1,641 m) midway along its length three miles (5 km) east of Dana village. When the depth of the Arabah is factored in, the difference in height becomes 6,500 feet (1,980 m) in just over ten to thirteen horizontal miles (16 to 21 km). Denis Baly has described the view from spots where the modern road approaches the scarp's sharp rim: "The traveler peers dizzily down into a bizarre world of dark, gigantic cliffs and deep, terrifying gorges... a region altogether apart, forbidding and inaccessible."[1]

From down below, on the mud-caked salt flats of the Arabah south of the Dead Sea, the view upward is equally awe-inspiring. The serrated rise from this Valley of Salt (2 Sam 8:13; 2 Kgs 14:7) was the first up-close view of Edom for a Judean making his way into the Rift Valley by way of the Negev (cp. 2 Kgs 3:9–20). David described the fissured scene after facing Edom in pitched battle in the Valley of Salt: "*You [God] have shaken the land and split it open. Heal its fissures, for it shudders*" (Ps 60:2).

The prophets Jeremiah and Obadiah also encountered Mount Seir with an upward view, their necks craned toward foes "*who live in the clefts of the rock... seem to soar like an eagle, and make [their] nest among the stars*" (Jer 49:16; Obad 3–4) in strongholds pocked with "secret places" to hide in (Jer 49:10). God alone could conquer terrain like this: "'*Even from there I will bring you down!' This is the* LORD*'s declaration*" (Jer 49:16; Obad 4).

For the Nabateans, the sandstone mountains of Edom, with their hidden crevices and inaccessible heights stretching southward beyond Petra, touched the world of the divine. The Nabateans called these the Shara Mountains; they were the sacred home of Dushara, "the lord of the Shara Mountains," the head of their pantheon and a deity whom the Greeks identified with the Olympian Zeus.[2]

This western escarpment is the most dramatic feature of Mount Seir. Yet like Moab across the Zered Wadi to the north, the heartland of the Edomite kingdom lay on the arable portions of the limestone plateau above. The watershed crests along a narrow band of Cenomanian-Turonian limestone just behind the scarp, and from there the Senonian chalk surface, free of fault lines, slants eastward into the open desert to level off at around 3,500 to 4,000 feet (1,070 to 1,220 m) above sea level. A dozen or so splotches of basalt, some fairly large and many covering rises that crest above 5,000 feet (1,525 m), can be found east of Shawbak, along the seam that separates Mount Seir from the Ma'an Plateau. These dark bumps on an otherwise nondescript and barely undulating surface drain in all directions, their normally scant moisture

Of all of the capital cities of the nation-states of the southern Levant, it was Bozrah, chief city of the kingdom of Edom, that was the most dramatically situated. Like Jerusalem, Samaria, Rabbah, Dibon, and Kir-hareseth, the site of Bozrah was surrounded by wadis on three sides, but here the fingers of Wadi Jamal, an upper tributary of Wadi Khuneizir, are extremely steep, neatly isolating the plateau on which the city was built with only a very narrow pinch point, or saddle, connecting it to the ridge beyond (left). Moreover, unlike the ridge on which the City of David, the oldest part of Jerusalem, was built, the plateau of Bozrah is broad and relatively flat, providing a firm foundation on which to erect strong citadels and construct a thriving urban center (cp. Amos 1:12). The only drawback to Bozrah's position is that its spring is deep in the wadi off the northeastern point of the plateau. The site has not been excavated sufficiently to determine how the residents of Bozrah provided water for the city during times of siege.

1 Baly, *Geography of the Bible*, 235.

2 Jane Taylor, *Petra and the Lost Kingdom of the Nabateans* (London: I.B. Tauris, 2001), 122–45; Udi Levy, *The Lost Civilization of Petra* (London: Floris Books, 1996), 76–81.

The prophet Jeremiah must have been familiar with the imposing geographical position of the Edomite highlands, for he painted the image of the setting well: *"You who live in the clefts of the rock, you who occupy the mountain summit, though you elevate your nest like the eagles, even from there I [that is, the Lord] will bring you down"* (Jer 49:16). He then reversed the image to call down God's judgment on Judah's southeastern neighbor: *"At the sound of their fall the earth will quake; the sound of her cry will be heard at the Red Sea. Look! It will be like an eagle soaring upward, then swooping down and spreading its wings over Bozrah"* (Jer 49:21–22).

eventually flowing into either the outer tributaries of the Zered or the main course of the great wadi itself. Mention should be made of Wadi al-La'ban, the most dramatic of the tributaries of the Zered and a canyon in its own right. The modern road tracing the King's Highway northward out of Edom runs parallel to, then drops into the La'ban, joining its parent beneath Jebel et-Tannur ("Oven Mountain"), a huge mound of dark basalt nestled deep in the otherwise bland crevice of the Zered.

Dushara, the national god of the Nabateans, is typically depicted as a carved, upright rectangle of stone with large, square eyes and a straight nose between. Here the depiction of Dushara is found within a niche topped by a Doric frieze, likely meant to be his temple or shrine. The whole was carved into a freestanding rock of red sandstone within the mighty siq, or narrow canyon, that leads visitors to Petra. What is striking is that depictions of Dushara, a god associated with the high mountains of the southeastern desert, are essentially iconoclastic, with minimal carvings, quite unlike the full human forms typically associated with images of deities in most other places of the ancient Near East.

The western scarp of Mount Seir continues on a fairly straight line south of Shawbak for about forty miles (65 km), then makes a broad sweeping arc toward the southeast for another thirty miles (48 km), eventually running eastward and blending into the Midian mountains in the north Arabian Desert. This great bend defines the perimeter of the **Ma'an Plateau**, Edom south of Mount Seir. The plateau is named after the modern town of Ma'an, the commercial center of the region today that's located out on the Desert Highway east-southeast of Petra. The sudden, cliffy drop of the southern edge of the Ma'an Plateau, at *Ras en-Naqb* ("Head of the Dry Land"), also marks the end of the limestone in Transjordan.

The Transjordanian watershed ridge, with elevations generally above 5,000 feet (1,525 m) on Mount Seir and the Ma'an Plateau, bends with this arc. Its highest point, the 5,704-foot (1,739-m) *Rujm Tal'at al-Juma'h*, is in a thin band of Cenomanian-Turian limestone in the Shara Mountains halfway between Shawbak and Petra. Everything behind this watershed ridge levels off to around 3,500 to 4,000 feet (1,070 to 1,220 m), elevations similar to those in the flatter, eastern parts of Mount Seir. And, as in the northern part of Edom, the surface of the Ma'an Plateau is almost entirely composed of low monotonous swells of stony, pallid Senonian chalk. Here, though, basalt is completely absent. The Ma'an Plateau lies south of the southernmost reaches of the Zered, and all of its eastern-lying wadis run out into the open desert where they disappear in dry lake beds.

Some of the most dramatic theophanies, or appearances, of God in the Bible involve acts of nature that are absolutely magnificent, numbingly awe-inspiring, and even terrible. These include the sunrise, violent earthquakes (Exod 19:18; Judg 5:5), and powerful thunderstorms (Ps 29:3–11). The Highlands of Edom may have been home to one of Judah's most persistent enemies during the time of the Old Testament, but it was from the open desert beyond the land of Esau that God made some of his most dramatic appearances to his people:

The Lord came from Sinai
and appeared to them from Seir;
he shone on them from Mount Paran
and came with ten thousand holy ones,
with lightning from his right hand for them. (Deut 33:2)

Lord, when you came from Seir,
when you marched from the fields of Edom,
the earth trembled,
the skies poured rain,
and the clouds poured water. (Judg 5:4)

God comes from Teman,
the Holy One from Mount Paran. Selah.
His splendor covers the heavens,
and the earth is full of his praise.
His brilliance is like light;
rays are flashing from his hand.
This is where his power is hidden. . . .
He stands and shakes the earth;
he looks and startles the nations.
The age-old mountains break apart;
the ancient hills sink down. . . .
You split the earth with rivers.
The mountains see you and shudder;
a downpour of water sweeps by. (Hab 3:3–4,6,9–10)

Wisps of sandstone carved by the winds of time decorate the surface of the western escarpment of the Ma'an Plateau. Far beyond the capacities of the paintbrush or chisel, the mountains themselves speak of the skilled hand of God, as creative and faithful as the rhythm that he placed in the seasons below and skies above.

In noticeable contrast to the direction of the fault lines in Mount Seir, those in the scarp south of Shawbak generally run parallel to the Rift Valley. As a result, the face of the western escarpment of the Ma'an Plateau is largely closed to easy human penetration. At its lower levels, the underlying band of Precambrian granite becomes more visible beneath the red sandstone than it is in Mount Seir. Adding variety to the mix, a diverse pattern of dolomite and crystalline rocks are intermixed with limestone, chalk, and sandstones of various colors at different stages of the escarpment. The most familiar views, of course, are those in and around Petra, the "rose-red city half as old as Time."[1]

The Petra platform stands at 3,500 to 4,000 feet (1,070 to 1,220 m) above sea level, about the same elevation as most of the expanse of the Ma'an Plateau though more than 1,000 feet (300 m) below the top of the limestone watershed just to its east. The view from the modern highway that descends off the Ma'an Plateau and into Wadi Musa, the name of the wadi system that drains through the various canyons of Petra as well as the town at its upper end, takes in both, in a wild landscape that is often a tourist's first glimpse of the majesty of south Edom. A popular tradition conveniently places Mount Hor, the peak upon which Aaron the brother of Moses died, at Jebel Haroun, the highest point (4,430 ft/1,350 m) within the mountains of Petra (Num 33:37–38).

South of the great scarp line of the Ma'an Plateau and free of the limestone cap that either has eroded completely away or never existed this far to the southeast, the sandstone and crystalline rocks of the Rift Valley are given free range to wander and merge with the Midian mountains of the north Arabian Peninsula. This vast and mysterious moonscape of rugged peaks of sandstone and granite, each surrounded and partially buried by an endless sea of sand, is **Wadi Rum**. Here great masses of colored rock—in reds and purples mostly, but also violets, oranges, and yellows in wild and romantic shapes—form towering canyons with gnarled walls soaring skyward up to 4,000 feet (1,220 m) from the level surface of the sand. Though significantly lower than the Ma'an Plateau, this is still by all criteria high desert; its sandy surface is about the same elevation as the hills around Jerusalem. Wadi Rum's highest peak, which is also the highest in the Hashemite Kingdom of Jordan, is Jabal Umm ad-Dami on the Saudi border,

1 John William Burgeon, *Petra, a Poem* (Oxford: F. MacPherson, 1846).

6,083 feet (1,854 m) above sea level. Its peak is snow covered most winters.

The mountains of Wadi Rum are nearly all elongated in shape. Most of these stand in parallel lines extending southward off the great limestone scarp that defines the southern edge of the Ma'an Plateau. From high in the sky, the look is like that of massive tapered icicles dripping off a limestone eave, then breaking into small fragments that fall toward the Arabian Peninsula. Some of the mountains of Wadi Rum are very hard, their edges rounded and surfaces furrowed by eons of wind or water erosion; others break into rocks that, if dropped from a height of only a few feet, explode into powder. All have the worn look of great age. The sandy floor between serves as perpetual evidence that creation still has time for building up and tearing down:

As a mountain collapses and crumbles
and a rock is dislodged from its place,
as water wears away stones
and torrents wash away the soil from the land,
so you destroy a man's hope. (Job 14:18–19)

Wadi Rum proper, from which the region gets its name, is a relatively short, normally dry watercourse that runs northward between two towering sandstone mountains, Jebel Rum (5,754 ft/1,754 m) and Jebel Umm 'Ishrin (5,751 ft/1,753 m), in the center of the region. It joins the course of the much larger Disi wadi system, which flows generally east to west. This and numerous other sandy flows all form the great Wadi Yutem, a magnificent canyon angling southwestward and down through the scarp of the Rift Valley into the Arabah just north of the Gulf of Aqaba (Gulf of Eilat). Low spots in the Wadi Disi such as Qa-Disi form shallow lakes after rare winter cloudbursts; these are identifiable most of the year as broad, caked sand flats good for camel—and now auto-sport—racing. Such areas may be referenced in Job 14:11–12: "*As water disappears from a lake and a river becomes parched and dry, so people lie down never to rise again.*"

The hues of Wadi Rum are as subtle as the sandstone mountains and goat-hair tents for which the region is known—subtle, striking, ephemeral, and enduring.

In their setting and imagery, the harsh lands of southern Transjordan seem to be a good geographical fit for the book of Job, with Wadi Rum in particular being one of the few places in the Levant that touches arable grazing land (the limestone plateaus to the north; Job 1:14–16; 5:10), desert caravan routes (Job 6:16–19), and the open sea (the Gulf of Aqaba/Gulf of Eilat; Job 9:8; 11:9; 41:1).

Far back up on the Mishor, arable land can be found twenty miles (32 km) east of the watershed scarp, with towns and villages scattered across much of the region. In Moab proper, between the Arnon and Zered Wadis, this zone of permanent settlement is cut in half and supports only a double line of sites that trace the watershed ridge and the King's Highway. South of the Zered, the width of arable land is reduced even more, to a scarp-tracing taper that's less than five miles (8 km) wide that trails off into scattered basins south of Shawbak then disappears altogether just beyond Petra. This leaves room for only a single line of viable towns on Mount Seir and the Ma'an Plateau (Tafila to Wadi Musa above Petra), with a mere scattering of seasonal or relatively short-lived villages elsewhere. The distance between these towns increases as the available resource base decreases the further south and east we penetrate into the land. Indeed, if the phrase "*the tents of Edom and the Ishmaelites*" (Ps 83:6) is not simply formulaic, it is perhaps the most apt description of settlement patterns in Edom. So is Bildad's resigned assessment of life in an uncertain land:

His roots are intertwined around a pile of rocks.
He looks for a home among the stones.
If he is uprooted from his place,
it will deny knowing him,
saying, "I never saw you." (Job 8:17–18)

There are a number of perennial springs in the exposed band of Cenomanian-Turonian limestone that lies between Tafila and Dana, just west of and below the top of the Mount Seir scarp. Several of these springs line the bend carved by the uppermost tributaries of the Wadi Khuneizir between Sela and Bozrah. It is here that we should look for the heartland of the Iron Age kingdom of Edom. Out on Mount Seir's eastern expanse, as well as on the Ma'an Plateau to the south, there is virtually no surface water except for seasonal pools. The town of Wadi Musa above Petra has a strong spring, but Ma'an lacks perennial water. Ma'an instead owes its existence to the good fortune of straddling a junction of caravan routes and as such, fifteen miles (24 km) east of the scarp, stands as an anomaly to the settlement pattern found elsewhere in the Edomite highlands. The sandstone portions of the scarp are also largely devoid of water except for seasonal runoff. Further below, in the Valley of Salt, a combined army of men from Israel, Judah, and Edom ran out of water as they

pushed to attack Moab from the south via the "*route of the Wilderness of Edom*" (2 Kgs 3:8–9). A rainstorm in the Highlands of Edom above filled the wadis of the scarp and revived the attacking triumvirate, while the reddish color of the sandstone made the water appear as blood to the Moabites above. Weather patterns such as this are typical to the Rift Valley, though the timing was certainly mapped out by God (2 Kgs 3:13–24).

Rainfall is marginal to submarginal throughout the Highlands of Edom, with twelve to fifteen inches (300 to 380 mm) at best wetting the narrow arable portions of Mount Seir but only six to ten inches annually coming in the corresponding sections of the Ma'an Plateau further south. Rainfall decreases very quickly everywhere east of the watershed ridge. This is consistent with weather patterns found throughout southern Transjordan, though it is perhaps more pronounced here. Yet sudden and unexpected lightning storms can strike anywhere:

> *Who cuts a channel for the flooding rain*
> *or clears the way for lightning,*
> *to bring rain on an uninhabited land,*
> *on a desert with no human life,*
> *to satisfy the parched wasteland*
> *and cause the grass to sprout?* (Job 38:25–27)

Though surface water in Edom is scarce, massive aquifers below the ground hold reserves sufficient to meet all of the water needs of the Hashemite Kingdom of Jordan for nearly a century. These aquifers were filled from millennia of rain and snowfall east of the watershed. The surface water evaporates here in the eastern desert, while most sinks underground, leaving none to form permanent lakes in the broad depressions that characterize the open landscape. As Job said, "*Dry ground and heat snatch away the melted snow*" (Job 24:19).

High elevations result in extreme temperatures, and this, more than the lack of predictable rainfall, is what makes living conditions throughout the region difficult. Winters are icy cold with "*weight [to] the wind*" (cp. Job 28:25), when savage storms blow up and over the western scarp and "*water becomes as hard as stone*" (Job 38:30). Job, in fact, caught the image well: "*Without clothing, they spend the night naked, having no covering against the cold. Drenched by mountain rains, they huddle against the rocks, shelterless*" (Job 24:7–8).

Snowfall is surprisingly frequent in the higher, western elevations and can be quite heavy, even closing roads, sometimes for days. As Job said millennia ago, "*[The wadis] become darkened because of ice, and the snow melts into them*" (Job 6:16). By contrast, summer days are often very hot even at the higher elevations, though such height brings with it refreshingly cool and even chilly nights well into late summer.

All in all, the yearly rain that falls on the heights of Mount Seir is just enough for the inhabitants of the region to tough out a rather Spartan existence. Fortunately,

Ma'an's primary virtue is its location. The town sprang up at the first juncture of routes on Edom's limestone plateau for travelers heading northward out of the Arabian Peninsula. As such, it was the first rallying point for Abdullah I, a native of the Arabian Peninsula who sought to carve out an independent Arab kingdom in Transjordan and Syria following the First World War. Abdullah was unsuccessful in gaining power in Syria but, with the blessing of the British, became the first king of the Hashemite Kingdom of Jordan. The borders of his kingdom were a convenience of colonial interests, establishing an important buffer between historic powers in Arabia, Damascus, Baghdad, Phoenicia, Palestine, and Egypt.

Grain farming is a thin but necessary way of life along the watershed scarp of the Highlands of Edom. The job is never easy, and local farmers are nowhere near able to approach the kind of bumper crop production of the fertile valleys of Galilee or the Philistine Coastal Plain. The barley in this late spring scene lags weeks behind that found in other parts of Transjordan or the land of ancient Israel. Here the still-proud remains of the Crusader castle of Montreal at Shawbak maintain a silent vigil over scrappy fields that provide the staff of life for a resilient band of Bedouin who are but one generation removed from the desert, seeking a more predictable way of life than they have had for centuries.

the extreme elevations result in a number of heavy dew nights throughout the year, and in the winter months the towns lining the western scarp are often enveloped by clouds of moisture that push their way up and over its watershed ridge. It is perhaps this dew, its presence more faithful than rain (Deut 32:2), that gives what crops there are in Edom a real chance to survive: "*My roots will have access to water, and the dew will rest on my branches all night. My whole being will be refreshed within me, and my bow will be renewed in my hand*" (Job 29:19–20).

The economic base of the Edomite highlands is, by necessity, mixed: orchard crops, very thin fields of grain, some large cattle, and flocks of mostly goats. No one element is guaranteed in a land where "*wadis evaporate in warm weather*" and "*roots are intertwined around . . . rocks*" (Job 6:17; 8:17). By all accounts, a fairly dense though narrow tree line covered much of the scarp of Mount Seir up until a century ago, including stands of oak, juniper, hawthorn, almond, and carob. The forested areas of Edom were reportedly decimated for rail ties and railroad engine fuel during and after the First World War, though with great effort some are being replanted. A few very old Atlantic Pistachios—gnarled, tough, and resilient—remain in the vicinity of Shawbak. The prophets even spoke of grape harvesters[1] in Edom (Jer 49:9; Obad 5), gathering a product that surely benefited from the highland's heavy dew nights. And they made reference to garments of one coming from Edom that were reddened "*like [those of] one who treads a winepress*" (Isa 63:2). The remains of a large winery at the Crusader-era castle of Montreal in Shawbak lends to the persistence of the idea that summer fruit could be coaxed from Edom's hills. But the winter grain, scattered like patches of grass throughout the highlands, is short, thin, and planted only in tiny hollows where a slight covering of soil hides the rocks just below. What matures ripens very late in the season. As for livestock, shepherds find that conditions on the Ma'an Plateau and throughout Wadi Rum are too thin for sheep, though not for goats. Isaiah spoke of "*young bulls with the mighty bulls*" in Edom—these can be found up on Mount Seir but not south of Shawbak; such animals were especially fat, a sign of health in an otherwise severe land (Isa 34:6–7). We are reminded of the sturdy livestock bred in similar conditions up on the Bashan (Ps 22:12; Amos 4:1).

Small isolated stands of Atlantic Pistachio trees (*Pistacia atlantica*) are found in nearly all areas of modern Israel and Jordan, scattered evidence of larger forested tracts that once covered much of the mountainous and marginal areas of the southern Levant. Many, like this one on the King's Highway just north of Shawbak, have very wide trunks relative to their height, attesting to great age. Each speaks of the kind of resiliency that all living beings have had to learn in order to survive in the Highlands of Edom.

Down below, areas of enriched alluvial soil can be found at the outlet of the Zered wadi, where the northwestern corner of the Highlands of Edom touches the southeastern corner of the Dead Sea. Like similar patches of arable soil that have collected at the mouths of the wadis draining the Medeba and Moab plateaus, there is enough alluvium here to support a local population. Yet the region is far from available markets, and traffic moving in and out of the Valley of Salt has to deal with difficult terrain and, for most of the year, heat that is nothing short of oppressive. Tracts of arable soil can also be found in the cleft of the Zered and its larger tributaries, though archaeologically attestable permanent settlements within these folds are rare. Indeed, the cut of the Zered seems to have been a real border between political aspirations in Moab and those in Edom, posing a formidable challenge to their economic connectedness, this in marked contrast to the Yarmuk and Jabbok canyons and even the Arnon, which more easily bound together peoples living on either side of their banks. The wet bottomlands of the Zered, on the other hand, are certainly a place of seasonal encampment, and we are reminded of Moses and the Israelites who camped in the eastern Zered while skirting Edom and Moab on the desert side (Num 21:12; Deut 2:13).

Everything off the arable portions of the scarp—east, west, and south—is described in the Bible as a land of "*fiery serpents*" (Num 21:6–9, NASB), adding another element to the dangers of the place. Conditions out on the desert side of the Ma'an Plateau and throughout Wadi Rum resemble those around Masada in the deepest part of the Judean rain shadow. The Rum mountains lie barren and stark throughout the year, though their wadi bottoms and sand plains contain a variety of hardy desert shrubs suitable for grazing goats. The local Bedouin have become experts at practical botany, harvesting a rich repertoire of herbs, medicines, and potions from their scanty fare. If wisdom is defined as skill in living,[2] the inhabitants of the desert fringe, where security is defined by formulae that lack large populations and

1 The Hebrew word for "grape harvesters" used in Jer 49:9 and Obad 5 is *botsrim*, from the same root as the name of Edom's capital, Bozrah. The basic meaning of the root word *batsar* is "cut off," which describes both the action of grape gatherers working their vines and the inaccessible position of Bozrah among the rugged scarps of Edom.

2 Elmer A. Martens, *God's Design: A Focus on Old Testament Theology* (Grand Rapids, MI: Baker Book House 1981), 166.

predictable resources, have developed the reputation in abundance (Jer 49:7; Obad 8).

Considering its diverse but severely limited local resource base, we might justifiably conclude that on natural conditions alone the inhabitants of the Highlands of Edom had to become survivalists; indeed, they learned to preserve and protect whatever they could. By geographical opportunity and economic necessity, the Edomites in the time of the Old Testament and Nabateans in the centuries surrounding the New came to look outward; thus, they played the role of international traders. There was money to be made in Edom, if not from the land itself then certainly from controlling the lucrative trade routes coming off the Arabian Desert and up from the Red Sea. This made Edom's main advantage among the regions of Transjordan its role as a desert terminal, or port. Situated on the harsh southeastern corner of the Southern Levant, the land was protected enough—and its people tenacious enough—to make it work.

The overall geographical setting of the Highlands of Edom is somewhat analogous to that of Phoenicia: a narrow band of arable terrain sits on a corner of the land of ancient Israel. Its single line of cities faced a wide open and inhospitable "sea," though in this case the role of the watery deep is played by the desert and its shipping lanes traversed by caravans of camels rather than fleets of ships. The skills of navigation, risks of travel, opportunities for competitive internationalism, and potential for economic reward are not dissimilar for those wanting to tame these otherwise very different geographical settings. Also necessary was the cultivation and possession of a set of aptitudes and tools not needed by those who kept to the familiar limestone hills back home.

We might expect the Phoenicians and Edomites (or the Nabateans) to have pursued common economic interests, with ancient Israel the middleman between. The prophet Amos notes that in the eighth century BC, Tyre "*handed over a whole community of exiles to Edom and broke a treaty of brotherhood*" (Amos 1:9)—a pronouncement of judgment that presupposes a habit of shared, exploitative interests. For his part, Ezekiel took care to juxtapose mirrored oracles of judgment against Edom and Sidon (Ezek 32:29–30). The specifics of these prophetic invectives are lost, but our ability to reconstruct motives and suggest opportunities by which they wished to maintain a corner-to-corner pattern of interaction in the economic arena of the Southern Levant is clear enough.[1] Ezekiel provides a commodity list of products moving to Tyre from off the eastern desert:

> *Dedan was your merchant in saddlecloths for riding. Arabia and all the princes of Kedar were your business partners, trading with you in lambs, rams, and goats. The merchants of Sheba and Raamah traded with you. For your merchandise they exchanged the best of all spices and all kinds of precious stones as well as gold. Haran, Canneh, Eden, the merchants of Sheba, Asshur, and Chilmad traded with you. They were your merchants in choice garments, cloaks of blue and embroidered materials, and multicolored carpets, which were bound and secured with cords in your marketplace.* (Ezek 27:20–24)

Goats are hardy enough to forage a meal among the rocks and harsh desert shrubs of southern Jordan; sheep are not. The rock-hewn façade of the Palace Tomb (left) and Corinthian Tomb (right) in the necropolis of Petra form a fitting backdrop to their efforts. Like local grazing patterns, everything here is timeworn yet wears the grandeur of age.

These exotic goods evoke images of the one in the "*crimson-stained garments from Bozrah . . . splendid in his apparel*," their color "*like one who treads a winepress*" (Isa 63:1–2). This cloth from Edom is reminiscent of fabrics dyed in the famed Phoenician purple. Many of the commodities mentioned by Ezekiel certainly moved through other desert ports in Transjordan as well, such as Damascus, Bostra in southern Bashan, or Rabbah of the Ammonites. But of all these desert ports, the dynamic is heightened in the Highlands of Edom, on the Arabian corner of the Southern Levant, where the local resource base, like that of Phoenicia, is just large enough to keep a line of ports going and where other options for expansion are limited.

In function, then, the southeastern (Edomite) and northwestern (Phoenician) corners of the southern Levant are similar, their connections and corridors characterized more by the priorities of merchants than by marching generals, and their movement of commodities related more directly to patterns of trade than conquest. All this stands perpendicular to the action that dominates the other corners of the southern Levant, namely the ends of the southwestern (Egyptian) to northeastern (Aramean) diagonal. This latter line carries the great

1 Monson, *Regions on the Run*, 8–9, 12–13, 21–22.

All sorts of strange and beautiful creatures lurk in the rocky nooks and crannies of the Edomite highlands. The Sinai Agama lizard (upper left) is one of the most striking. Males are blue but turn yellow-brown, the color of the females, for camouflage. One of the most dangerous is the yellow scorpion, nicknamed the "Death-stalker" (upper right). This scorpion injects venom of powerful neurotoxins that can kill humans. Local guides offer the following advice, only partly in jest: "If you see one, just start digging your own grave." Of the thirty-six species of snakes known to the Hashemite Kingdom of Jordan, several are vipers (bottom) with venom of hemotoxin that quickly attacks a victim's red blood cells. At least locusts and grasshoppers (center right), of which there is a wide variety of species (this one is a *Poekilocerus* grasshopper), aren't deadly to humans. Nevertheless, they can devastate crops with a vengeance when they decide to swarm.

trunk route linking Africa with Asia and over time has borne the brunt of the empire-based military action in the Levant. The priorities that have dominated each of these two intersecting diagonals are, of course, related; they make for an intricate dance where the overall flow of the choreography is clear enough although the particular steps varied with the times.

Moses's offer to take the Israelite masses up the King's Highway and not *"travel through any field or vineyard, or drink any well water"* (Num 20:17) was the opening salvo of a time-honed pattern of hospitality: honor is maintained when, in an initial encounter, a traveler refuses to impose his needs on a prospective host, while the host reciprocates generously in turn. But the Edomite king, rather than offering hospitality to his long-lost ethnic brothers (ancestors Jacob and Esau were twins), chose to relate to Moses as he would to any invasive horde leader off the desert (Num 20:18–21). As the head of a people who themselves were trying to eke out a living on a resource-thin plateau, the actions of the king of Edom are fully understandable; from the point of view of ancient Israel, however, it was a terrible breach of etiquette.

As for routes, the King's Highway cuts through the Highlands of Edom longitudinally, following the edge of the western scarp just above the line of permanent towns that define the heartland of the Edomite kingdom. After circling around the bend of the great Fidan embayment from Tafila to Shawbak, north to south, the route continues south-southeastward to Ma'an, where it joins the Desert Highway that has dropped down from the north. From there the Desert Highway heads into the Arabian Peninsula along the eastern side of the great Midian, or Hejaz, mountain range. It continues to the oases of Dedan (Gen 25:1–3; Isa 21:13; Ezek 38:13) and Tema (Isa 21:13–14; Jer 25:23), then on to Medina and eventually Yemen, one of the possible locations for Sheba. This is the ancient world's great Spice Route, supplier of things medicinal, cosmetic, and ritual to a world starving for aromatics:

> *Caravans of camels will cover your land—*
> *young camels of Midian and Ephah—*
> *all of them will come from Sheba.*
> *They will carry gold and frankincense*
> *and proclaim the praises of the LORD.* (Isa 60:6)

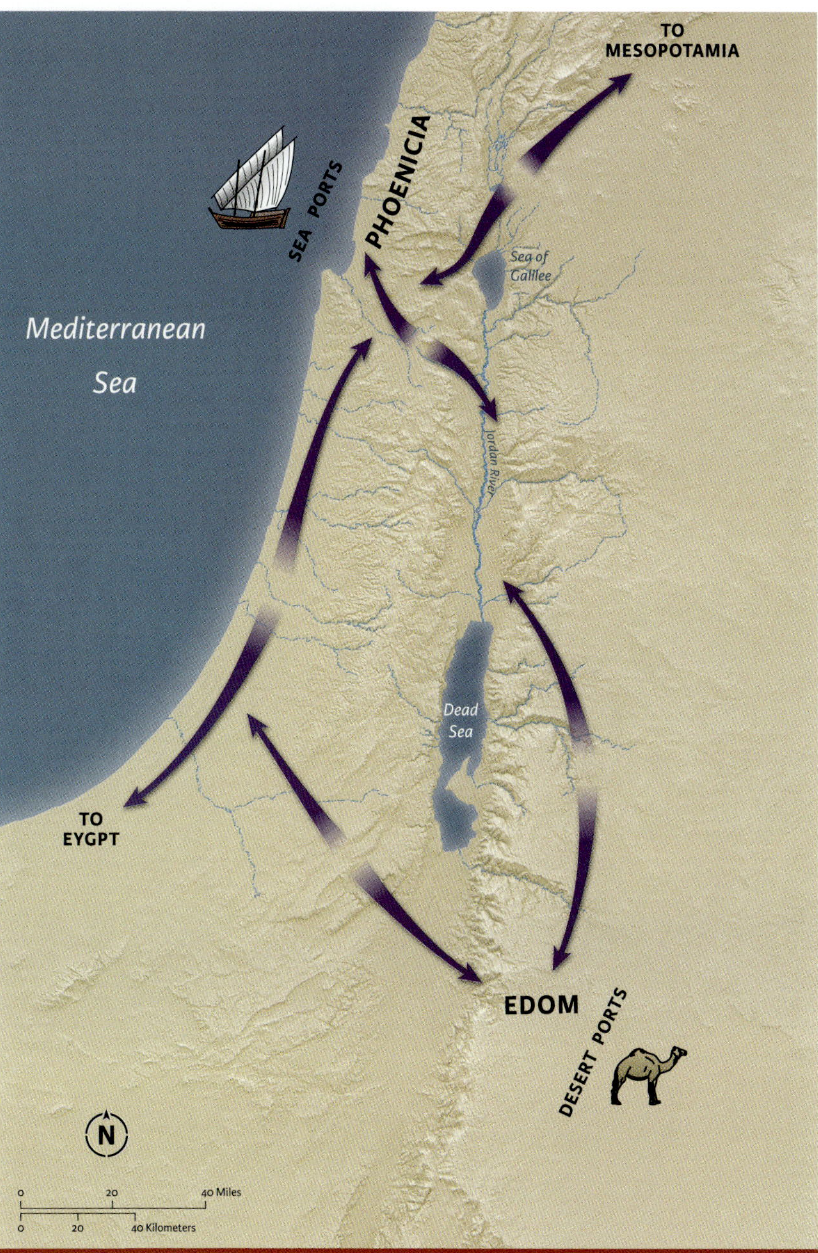

Sweeping X's dominate the pattern of imperial highways on a map of the southern Levant. In terms of big money to be made, the land was most active from its corners, with ancient Israel and Judah well positioned to be either profitable middlemen or road kill.

If the magi of Matthew 2 were Nabateans, we can track them on routes such as this. If, on the other hand, they hailed from Babylon or Persia,[1] their gifts to the Christ child were still typical of commodities that moved out of the Arabian Peninsula and via the Highlands of Edom to a waiting Mediterranean world.

For its part, the route of the King's Highway continues southward from Ma'an into Wadi Rum via the great descent at Ras en-Naqb, then down through the magnificent Wadi Yutem, and into the Arabah just north of Aqaba on the Red Sea. Great paved highways follow both routes today, as corridors for heavy trucks that preserve millennia-old pathways of camel caravans. A spur off the Ma'an-Aqaba route in Wadi Rum allows traffic to circle the northern end of the Midian mountains from the Gulf of Aqaba to Medina without climbing onto the Ma'an Plateau.

Heading the other way, once travelers on the Spice Route reached the northern end of the Gulf of Aqaba, they had to find a way across the Rift Valley and through the Greater Negev to markets in Egypt or the Mediterranean. One connector used by the Nabateans dropped through Petra and Wadi Musa to Moa (Moje 'Awad) on the western edge of the Arabah, where there are remains of a Roman-era caravanserai but no immediate source of water.[2] From there the route crossed the rugged ridges of the Greater Negev to Gaza or points in Egypt. A second east-west connector left the Mount Seir scarp at Bozrah

1 For a synopsis of views, see Raymond E. Brown, *The Birth of the Messiah* (Garden City, NY: Doubleday, 1977), 167–70, 197–200.

2 Rudolph Cohen, "New Light on the Date of the Petra-Gaza Road," *BA* 45 (1982): 240–47.

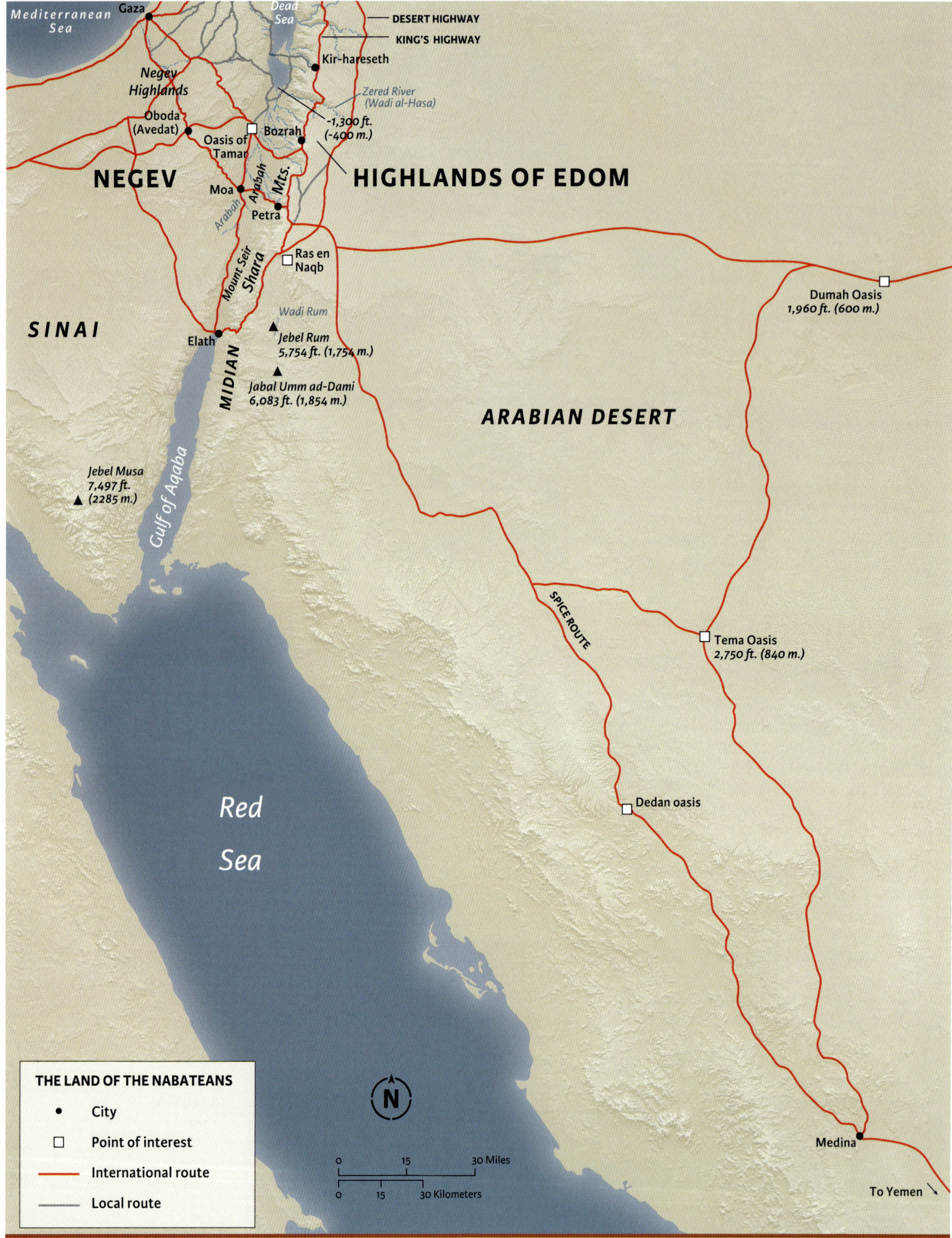

By the time of the New Testament, the Nabateans controlled the great Spice Route of antiquity. The main land line of the route tracked just east of the Hejaz Mountains from the southern Arabian Peninsula (modern Yemen) to ports on the Mediterranean via the oases of Dedan and Tema. The Nabateans also controlled a spur line through the Dumah oasis to the Persian Gulf.

A Bedouin makes his way through a camp of resting camels deep in the sandy canyons of Wadi Rum. By such conveyance, the route from the source of spices in Yemen to the Mediterranean once took four months to travel. Nowadays trucks and airplanes have largely relegated camel caravans to tourist traffic only; the Bedouin, fiercely proud of their roots to the desert, are having to adapt to more mundane kinds of loads as a result.

following either the ridge south of the Wadi Khuneizir or the course of the Wadi Dana: both point to the oasis of Tamar (En Hatzevah) opposite the Rift Valley with its connections to international markets further west. These routes to Bozrah, via Beer-sheba and Arad, were active locally during the Iron Age as the kings of Judah and Israel contended with the kings of Edom and Moab for economic and military supremacy in the region (2 Sam 8:13; 1 Chr 18:12; 2 Kgs 3:7–27; 8:20–22).

The overall dynamic of the Edomite highlands is perhaps best illustrated by the struggles of the Kingdom of Edom to carve out viable living space on the heights and not only survive, but thrive. Everything is contested in a land where resources of water and soil are scarce and imperial through-routes prevail—even more so when the habitable portions of the land are heavily dissected by topography and numerous rival powers want to take root. Perhaps the greatest accomplishment of the Edomite kingdom—a nation that the Bible indicates had a head start on Israel and Judah in kingdom-building[1] (Gen 36:31; Exod 15:15–16; 1 Chr 1:43)—was that it was able to forge a common authority over Mount Seir from its fortified capitals of Bozrah and Sela and hold on long enough to witness the destruction of its rivals across the Rift Valley by Assyria and Babylon. There is strong textual and archaeological evidence—not to mention plain geo-political common sense—to support the idea that the Edomite kings were engaged in a continued struggle with their counterparts in Jerusalem to control the routes and trading centers of the eastern Greater Negev. A prior Edomite claim on lands west of the Rift Valley can be seen in the early use of the name Mount Seir for the hills of the Greater Negev (Deut 1:2,44; 2:1; 33:2; 1 Chr 4:42–43). For its part, Israel's claim on the Greater Negev was forged by Solomon, who followed up David's subjugation of Edom by establishing a trading center at Ezion-geber/Eloth (Eilat) on the Red Sea (1 Kgs 9:26–28). That Solomon was aided by the Phoenicians adds strength to the idea that there is a natural economic connection between powers making use of the gateways opening from the northwestern and southeastern corners of the southern Levant. It is possible to make a reasonable case for Solomonic interest in mining activity at Feinan, the closest source of copper to Jerusalem. (Note that Solomon's workmen cast bronze furnishings for the Jerusalem temple in the mid-Jordan Valley, up the Rift Valley from Feinan; 1 Kgs 7:45–47.) In the mid-ninth century BC, Jehoshaphat was also able to reduce Edom to deputy status, though he failed in his attempt to revive Judean trade connections through the Red Sea (1 Kgs 22:47–49). We should note as well a historic pattern of Egyptian economic interests in both the Greater Negev (via the Sinai) and Midian, with a

1 Archaeological evidence shows settlement at scores of small sites on the northern Edomite Plateau in Iron Age I (1200–1000 BC). This supports the idea that the Edomite kingdom developed at least as early as that of Israel and Judah, if not before. Israel Finkelstein, "Edom in the Iron I," *Levant* 24 (1992): 159–66.

Wide swaths of blue-green copper ore decorate the surface of the sandstone at Feinan (ancient Punon) in the Arabah below Mount Seir. Here are remains of one of the largest copper mining and smelting centers in the ancient Near East. Horizontal mines and shaft mines at Feinan date from the Early Bronze Age through the Roman period.[1] The episode of the wilderness wanderings in which Moses made a bronze snake as a symbol of healing for those bitten by deadly vipers took place somewhere in the vicinity (Num 21:4–10; cp. 33:42–43).

motive as strong as that of the kings of Judah to keep the Edomites in check (cp. 1 Kgs 11:14–22).

But whenever they could, the Edomites reasserted their independence behind the natural fortifications of their rugged highlands. Jerusalem's supply lines through the Greater Negev were too long to protect over time, and the Judean songs of triumph (Pss 60:8; 108:9) gave way to the repeated refrain of Edomite pressure, flowing out of the protected crevices of their highlands to envelop the lucrative trade routes in the Rift Valley below (2 Kgs 8:20–22; 16:5–6; 2 Chr 20:1–37; Amos 1:11–12). In the end, the Edomites found a willing and rather natural partner in the Babylonians, whose traders tracked the north Arabian Desert to the oasis of Tema and forged an alliance with the Edomites based on mutual economic interests. The Edomites reaped the benefits of Babylonian control over Judah, filling the local power void in the Negev all the way up to the southern Shephelah, where we meet them as Idumeans in the time of the New Testament (Ps 137:7; Obad 10–13). The prophet Obadiah longed for the reverse: "*People from the Negev [again, someday,] will possess the hill country of Esau*" (Obad 19).

Emperor Trajan (AD 98–117) worked to secure Rome's annexation of Nabatea in AD 106 by constructing the *Via Nova Traiana*, a formal Roman road running the length of Transjordan. Numerous milestones and remains of curbing and paving stones here and there along the route allow scholars to reconstruct the line of the highway, which ran some 260 miles (420 km) from the northern provincial capital of Bostra in the Hauran to Aila (Aqaba) on the Red Sea. The route generally followed the well-established path of the King's Highway, though deviating somewhat in its drop into the Arnon and Zered wadis. At least two spur lines connected the main route of the *Via Nova Traiana* with Petra. Trajan secured the route with forts and watchtowers. In the following centuries, Rome's Arabian frontier was further strengthened by the *Limes Arabicus*, a line of fortifications further east. The *Limes* was never completed and by the sixth century AD had fallen into disrepair, opening the critical southeastern corner of the Roman Empire to Muslim incursions that overran Transjordan and the land of ancient Israel by the middle of the seventh century AD.

We have already seen that this dynamic continued into the time of the New Testament, although the main players were now of imperial (cat) rather than local (mouse) stature. Indeed, we can make a credible case that the Caesars of Rome wanted to control Judaea for the express purpose of establishing a base by which to take over the lucrative Nabatean trade routes of the Arabian Peninsula, bending the revenue flow through the Highlands of Edom to the vast Rome-controlled markets of the Mediterranean. Rome eventually constructed a line of forts east of Edom, the *Limes Arabicus*, to seal this corner of their empire from the incursions of not-so-cooperative Arabian tribes. This effort complemented the *Via Nova Traiana*, Rome's second-century AD modernization of the old route of the King's Highway, to gather and then channel the wealth of the east westward where all roads led to Rome.[2]

SUMMARY

In some important ways, the seven regions that make up Transjordan reflect living conditions found in the regions of ancient Israel lying west of the Rift Valley. The patterns of climate, types of vegetation and animal life, variety of building materials, and possibilities for water and permanent settlement would have seemed familiar to an Israelite or a Judean—especially in areas that did not actually front the eastern desert. It is Transjordan's proximity to the open desert that is its most distinct and challenging feature, but one that provides the kind of valuable economic incentives that are part and parcel of living on a frontier that functions as an open trading door. Although the narrative line of the biblical account emphasizes periods of political, military, and spiritual conflict between Israel and its eastern neighbors, it is important and relatively easy to trace avenues of connectedness joining the two—in spite of the chasm of the Rift Valley that lies between.

1. *Bashan*. The broad and relatively flat lava lands that are Bashan serve a dual purpose for the nation-states of the southern Levant. On the one hand, the rich basaltic soil of the region provides vast fields suitable for growing wheat and barley,

1 Thomas E. Levy, "Pastoral Nomads and Iron Age Metal Production in Ancient Edom," in *Nomads, Tribes and the State in the Ancient Near East: Cross-Disciplinary Perspectives*, ed. Jeffrey Szuchman (Chicago: University of Chicago Press, 2009), 147–76.

2 David F. Graf, "The Saracens and the Defense of the Arabian Frontier," *BASOR* 229 (1978): 1–26; and "The *Via Nova Traiana* in Arabia Petraea," *JRA* 14 (1995): 1–33.

the staples of life in the agricultural world of the ancient Near East. On the other, Bashan was a clearly demarcated buffer zone between Aramean states to the north and the land of Canaan—then ancient Israel—south and southwest. Battles for control of Bashan stretched from the world of Mesopotamia to that of Rome, though the biblical story focuses on the priorities of the Israelite and Syrian (Aram-Damascus) kings.

2. *Lower Gilead.* The soft limestone hills of Lower Gilead provide relatively gentle access points into Transjordan from the west. That the area lies on a straight line to the Jezreel Valley and Acco Plain heightens its importance as a gateway into the region. This was one of ancient Israel's natural penetration points east, though their efforts to hold and control the area were never consistently successful.
3. *The Dome of Gilead.* Of all the regions of Transjordan, it is the Dome of Gilead that is most similar to the Hill Country of Judah, Ephraim, and Manasseh west of the Rift Valley. A hard-limestone lifestyle arising from its terraced hillsides, summer orchard crops, spring water, small villages, and fresh, airy heights characterizes the entire region. International routes bypass the interior of the area, though they do traverse its eastern heights through Gerasa. It is no wonder that in the biblical account the hills of Gilead, rising close on the other side of the Jordan Valley, played an important role in the settlement of ancient Israel during both the Old and New Testament eras.
4. *The Ammon Basin.* Though the smallest of the regions of Transjordan, the chalky Ammon Basin was home to an important people group in the biblical period. From here the Ammonites controlled a key trade route coming off the north Arabian Desert, funneling traffic up and down the King's Highway. The tightness of the basin and corresponding lack of large tracts of available resources at home prompted the Ammonites to expand into the Dome of Gilead and the Mishor, where they came into natural conflict with Moab, Israel, and other people groups intent on doing the same.
5. *The Mishor/Medeba Plateau.* Like Bashan, the high tableland (Mishor) forming the Medeba Plateau is a true land between. Here profitable rendzina soils and adequate rainfall provide a base of agriculture and herding that historically has supported a relatively large population scattered across the entire region. At the same time, the plateau is located amid natural power centers in Ammon, Israel, and Moab. As a result, it has borne the brunt of incursion after incursion and invasion after invasion throughout recorded history.
6. *The Moab Plateau.* The Moab Plateau is protected by steep ravines on the north, west, and south and the open desert on the east. The area is blessed with decent soils and favored by adequate, though not extensive, supplies of water. As such, it is a natural home for a people group seeking to carve out its own national identity. Though supporting an economy that favors shepherding more than farming, the plateau offers living spaces that are relatively isolated and self-sufficient. The opportunities afforded the Moabites when they pushed out of their homeland and up on the Mishor brought them into natural and persistent conflict with the kings of Israel and Judah, who were intent on doing the same.
7. *The Highlands of Edom.* The largest of the regions of Transjordan, the Highlands of Edom are also the most diverse. Historically, permanent settlement has been concentrated along the watershed scarp in the northwestern sector of the region, while a persistent scattering of clans and tribes that follow shepherding and/or semi-nomadic (Bedouin) lifestyles fills the rugged, open, and utterly majestic terrain south and east. The economic motor of the Highlands of Edom is fueled less by local resources than by international trade from the Arabian Peninsula and Red Sea, making its way through Edom to waiting markets further north or west, out on the Mediterranean.

QUESTIONS

1. Explain the point of view of terms such as Transjordan, Cisjordan, and Perea. What implications do terms such as these have on how much attention we pay to certain events described in the Bible as opposed to others?
2. What geographical factors tend to make the Rift Valley a barrier to travel between Cisjordan and Transjordan? Which parts of the rift (e.g., the Huleh Basin, the Jordan Valley, or the Arabah) are more barrierlike than others? Why? Give historical examples that support your answer.
3. What geographical factors within the Rift Valley tend to bind Cisjordan to Transjordan? Give historical examples that support your answer.
4. What are the main geographical differences of the lands that lie east of the Rift Valley, as opposed to those that lie to the west? What are some significant similarities? Which is more striking: the way that these differences divide peoples living on either side of the Rift Valley, or the way that these similarities pull them together?
5. In terms of its impact on human history, which is Transjordan's most dominant geographic feature: its four canyonlike rivers, its proximity to the desert, or its areas of exposed sandstone?
6. What adjectives describe the lava lands of Bashan? How do elevation and weather patterns in the region intensify the force of these adjectives?
7. What characteristics of Bashan make that land attractive for human settlement? What tends to make settlement in the region difficult?
8. What features made the Golan an especially critical region for the political, economic, and military priorities of ancient Israel?
9. Why would a power based in Damascus want to control the western and southern edges of Bashan?
10. Summarize three or four biblical events that took place in Bashan. In terms of strategic interest for the region, what do these events have in common?
11. Why was Bashan a particularly suitable location for the apostle Paul's "Damascus Road" conversion experience?

12. Though Lower Gilead is composed of soft limestone and Bashan is basalt, both are prime grain growing areas. How so? How did this tend to unite the two regions in the flow of biblical history?
13. Using examples from the time of the Old Testament and that of the New Testament, explain the concept that Lower Gilead was Transjordan's prime international T-junction for traffic oriented to the west.
14. Describe the role of Ramoth-gilead in the struggle between ancient Israel and Aram-Damascus for control of northern Transjordan.
15. What geographical features may have prompted Lower Gilead to become the center of the Greco-Roman confederation called the Decapolis?
16. In terms of living spaces, how do the Yarmuk and Jabbok Rivers differ from the Arnon and Zered? How might regional settlement patterns differ as a result?
17. Compared to Lower Gilead, how closed is the Dome of Gilead to through traffic? Why? How might this characteristic have shaped the overall flow of biblical events in each region?
18. Compare the economy and living spaces of the Dome of Gilead with those of the Hill Country of Ephraim and Manasseh. What role does the limestone base and topographical shape of these regions play in shared patterns of human settlement?
19. Trace ancient Israel's interaction with the region of the Dome of Gilead from the time of the patriarchs (Jacob at Penuel) to the New Testament (Jesus in Perea). Overall, did these interactions tend to be favorable or adversarial? In what ways?
20. What made the Dome of Gilead attractive for Aram-Damascus? For the Ammonites of Rabbah?
21. Describe the geographical position of the Ammon Basin. What geological and topographical features distinguish it from the Dome of Gilead and the Mishor/Medeba Plateau?
22. What factors make the Ammon Basin a viable, independent region even though it is much smaller than the other regions of Transjordan?
23. What historical and geographical evidence is there that makes the local economic base of the Ammon Basin a textbook case for understanding cooperation between the shepherd ("milk") and the farmer ("honey")?
24. Given that the Ammon Basin was one of the Transjordanian Highway's prime international T-junctions for traffic oriented to the east, what might David have hoped to gain by controlling Rabbah?
25. Compare the geographical setting of Rabbah with that of Jerusalem. Taking into account only natural features, which was the better location? Why?
26. Describe the geographical seam between Israel and the Mishor/Medeba Plateau in the southern Jordan Valley. Why might Jeremiah have called this corner of the plateau "*Moab's forehead*" (Jer 48:45)? Which biblical characters moved this way, either up to the plateau from the plains of Moab, or down from its heights toward Jericho?
27. Describe the land-between-ness of the Mishor/Medeba Plateau. Why might it have been so difficult to establish a local independent power base in the region?
28. Why might the kings of Ammon and Moab have wanted to establish a permanent presence on the Mishor? What might have motivated the kings of ancient Israel and Judah to try to do the same? Give specific examples of how each tried to take and hold the plateau. What tended to happen in the end?
29. Compare and contrast the historical fortunes of the tribes of Reuben (on the Mishor), Gad (in Gilead), and Manasseh (up on Bashan). How might the unique characteristics of these respective homelands have shaped the historic viability of these tribes in that they were otherwise connected to an Israel that lay west of the Rift Valley?
30. What might have prompted Moses to approach the land of Canaan by way of the Mishor?
31. Why can the area around Dibon be considered a distinct part of the Mishor? What ramifications did this have for kingdom building in the ninth century BC (the days of Mesha and Ahab)?
32. Describe the natural borders of the Moab Plateau. How do they make Moab the best-defined region of Transjordan?
33. What parts of the eastern shore of the Dead Sea have viable living spaces for towns or cities? Why?
34. Trace the natural routes into and out of the Moab Plateau. Compared to other routes in other parts of Transjordan, how "natural" are they?
35. Why is the amount of arable land in Moab significantly less than that of the Mishor? What ramifications does this have for settlement?
36. Is Moab more a land of the shepherd or the farmer? Why?
37. Why might the interactions with Israel and Judah with Moab have taken place more often on the Mishor than on the Moab Plateau itself?
38. Why is the name *Edom* particularly appropriate for the land the Edomites called home? How appropriate is the name *Seir*?
39. Compare and contrast the basic geographical features of Mount Seir, the Ma'an Plateau, and Wadi Rum.
40. Where are the majority of the towns and cities of Edom located? Why there?
41. Why might a king in Jerusalem have wanted to control the Highlands of Edom? What specific gains could Judah get that would outweigh the difficulty of taking and holding the region?
42. Explain how the biblical writers' descriptions of Edom (especially those of judgment) were geographically appropriate for that region.
43. Trace the international highways to, from, and through the Highlands of Edom. What products moved along these routes? Which international powers were most interested in controlling these highways?
44. To the extent that a people's homeland can shape their national character, how might the Edomites (descended from Esau) have differed from their brothers the Israelites (descended from Jacob)?

AFTERWORD: GEOGRAPHY OF THE HEART

7

Land is a substantial reality in the world of the Bible. While it is first and foremost a geographical concept, it has connotations that transcend time and place. As noted in the introduction, the Hebrew word *eretz*, land, is the fifth most frequently used noun in the Old Testament, after *YHWH* (LORD), *ben* (son), *elohim* (God), and *melek* (king). Even with no other data, this combination of nouns is instructive: it suggests there is an essential "trinity" (to borrow a word) comprising God, progeny, and land that somehow forms the basis of a life that is both earthly and spiritual, something made for the here and the hereafter. And although *eretz* is most often used in the Bible in connection with a particular, bounded area that was the homeland of the people of ancient Israel (e.g., Gen 15:18), its sweep is much larger, eventually encompassing that of "*all the nations of the earth* (*eretz*)" (Gen 18:18). Land is certainly a theological concept, but it is first a geographical one; for many writers of the Bible, these two realities can hardly be separated.

As an academic discipline, geography stands in the intersection of people and land. It is a practical study, with its various aspects (physical geography, human geography, environmental geography, and the like) finding their methodologies in the physical sciences as well as in the social sciences. Its goals are wrapped around nothing less than the complex task of understanding planet earth and how we should live responsibly on it.[1] We are tempted to think of this as largely a modern concern, yet interest in matters of geography is by all accounts quite old. Geographical thinking played an important role in the ancient Near East and Mediterranean worlds. By thinking geographically, our intellectual ancestors in Mesopotamia, Egypt, and the Mediterranean basin delineated property lines, traced the movement of celestial bodies so as to calculate time or navigate land and sea, and developed a system of usable roads. In addition to such practical applications of understanding the world geographically, the ancients realized that geography was also an art; they explained their expanding world in colorful terms that were a combination of fact and fancy. The authors of the Bible, for whom the basic data of geography—earth, sky, and water—were first and foremost things made by God, recognized the realities of land as well; they developed from them a whole host of meaningful symbols. Theirs was *eretz hatzvi*, "*the beautiful land*" (Dan 11:16,41), which might also be translated "the land of the antelope," nimble and free.

Although the world and its physical elements are not divine (*contrary to* the worldview of Israel's neighbors, who failed to draw a clear distinction between Creator and creation),[2] they are not simply mundane either: everything is God-made and God-directed and as such is an integral part of the experience of us all. From the very beginning, the biblical storyline has been grounded in the specifics of time and place. This aspect of the divine-human relationship is reflected throughout the Bible in terms and attitudes that are land, or geographically, based.

For the people of ancient Israel—and indeed, for their compatriots throughout the ancient world—land was *place*, something that defined their personal and corporate identity, and on which they could find protection, provision, and security (1 Kgs 4:25). A family lived in a particular place, in an unbroken line of generations reaching back to their ancestors and forward to their descendants. But homeland was not just a place to live as much as it was a place to belong to;[3] the land owned its people as surely as they owned it. Family names became the names of places—Israel, Judah, Ammon, Moab, Shechem, Dan—with a personal identity that was as unbroken as it was shared. One's place on one's ancestral land was essential, in fact, and a person or

Life from a rock? Springtime cyclamen burst into bloom, their roots sunk into a seam of stratified Cenomanian-Turonian limestone, drawing all the moisture they need from its hollowed recess while also enjoying warmth from the reflected sun and protection from passers-by. Here the transient meets the eternal and finds everything it needs to live. Interestingly, Old Testament writers likened God to a rock, and people to flowers and grass (Pss 18:1–2; 71:3; 90:1–6; Isa 40:6–8). Then Jesus developed the theme: *"If that's how God clothes the grass of the field, which is here today and thrown into the furnace tomorrow, won't he do much more for you. . .?"* (Matt 6:30).

1 Paul H. Wright, *Understanding the Ecology of the Bible: An Introductory Atlas* (Jerusalem: Carta, 2018).

2 A helpful discussion of the foundational differences between the worldview of the biblical authors and those of all other ancient writers can be found in John N. Oswalt, *The Bible Among the Myths* (Grand Rapids: Zondervan, 2009).

3 Jeff Malpas, *Place and Experience: A Philosophical Topography* (Cambridge: Cambridge University Press, 1999), 15–16; and Cynthia Parker, "Deuteronomy's Place: An Analysis of the Placial Structure of Deuteronomy" (unpublished Ph.D. dissertation, University of Gloucestershire, 2014), 1.

family was not complete as long as they or their relatives lived elsewhere. The worst thing in the ancient Near East was not to die, but to die and be buried away from one's ancestral land, with the sacred triad of God-people-land broken. "*How can we sing the Lord's song on foreign soil,*" lamented the psalmist, exiled from his place and speaking of his homeland as if it were a living being like he:

> *If I forget you, Jerusalem,*
> *may my right hand forget its skill;*
> *may my tongue stick to the roof of my mouth*
> *if I do not remember you,*
> *if I do not exalt Jerusalem as my*
> *greatest joy!*" (Ps 137:5–6)

In the biblical world, land carried the connotation of both identity and security. An ancient Israelite or Judean felt safe in his ancestral home, where his right-to-be was recognized and his skills at making a living off whatever resources his small plot of ground had to offer were honed beyond the point of mere survival. But herein lay a paradox: the same land that promised security lay vulnerable to the whims of climate, to conquest, or to rapacious judges and kings. Of all the viable places to live in the southern Levant, it was the land of ancient Israel that perhaps most witnessed this paradox, wedged as it is between opportunities and threats, between blessing and curse. Like God, land gives and takes away. In the end, security had to find a way to live with vulnerability. For ancient Israel, this meant coming to terms with the blessings as well as the curses of their homeland. Thus, we return to the reassurance that was both stanza and refrain: "*It is a land the* LORD *your God cares for. He is always watching over it from the beginning to the end of the year*" (Deut 11:12).

Aware of their place, we should expect that the biblical authors would draw upon a never-ending supply of the elements of geography to describe themselves, their neighbors, and God. *Emmanu-el*, "God with us," is a concept as earthy as it is divine.

Mount Zion, Jerusalem
November, 2018

WORKS CITED

In a topic as large as the historical geography of the land of the Bible, the relevant bibliography is immense. The works listed below are those cited in the text above and must not be construed to represent an adequate bibliography for the subject. The interested student is encouraged to read widely.

Adler, Marcus Nathan. *The Itinerary of Benjamin of Tudela: Critical Text, Translation and Commentary*. Whitefish, MT: Kessinger, 2010, reprint of 1907 edition.

Aharoni, Yohanan. *Arad Inscriptions*. Jerusalem: IES, 1981.

————. "Forerunners of the Limes: Iron Age Fortresses in the Negev." *IEJ* 17 (1967): 1–17.

————. *The Land of the Bible: A Historical Geography*. Revised and enlarged edition. Translated and edited by A. F. Rainey. Philadelphia: Westminster, 1979.

Aharoni, Yohanan, Michael Avi-Yonah, Anson F. Rainey, Ze'ev Safrai, and R. Steven Notley. *The Carta Bible Atlas*. 5th edition. Jerusalem: Carta, 2011.

Ahituv, Shmuel. *Canaanite Toponyms in Ancient Egyptian Documents*. Jerusalem: The Magnes Press, 1984.

————. *Echoes from the Past: Hebrew and Cognate Inscriptions from the Biblical Period*. Jerusalem: Carta, 2008.

Albright, William Foxwell. *The Archaeology of Palestine*. Gloucester, MA: Peter Smith, 1971.

Alt, Albrecht. *Die Landnahme der Israeliten in Palästina*. Leipzig: Reformations Program der Universitäat Leipzig, 1925.

————. *Essays on Old Testament History and Religion*. Translated by R. A. Wilson. Oxford: Basil Blackwell, 1966.

Amiran, D. H. K. "A Revised Earthquake-Catalogue of Palestine." *IEJ* 2 (1952): 48–65.

Andersen, Francis I., and David Noel Freedman. *Hosea*. Vol. 24. *The Anchor Bible*. Garden City, NY: Doubleday & Company, 1980.

Arav, Rami, Richard A. Freund, and John F. Shroder. "Bethsaida Rediscovered." *BAR* 26/1 (Jan–Feb 2000): 44–56.

Aster, Shawn Zelig. "The Function of the City of Jezreel and the Symbolism of Jezreel in Hosea 1–2." *JNES* 71/1 (2012): 31–46.

Avi-Yonah, Michael. *The Madaba Mosaic Map*. Jerusalem: IES, 1954.

————. "Mount Carmel and the God of Baalbek." *IEJ* 2 (1952): 118-24.

Avigad, Nahman. *Discovering Jerusalem*. Nashville: Thomas Nelson, 1983.

Babylonian Talmud. Translated by Rabbi Dr. I. Epstein. London: Soncino, 1935–52.

Bahat, Dan. *The Carta Jerusalem Atlas*. 3rd revised edition. Jerusalem: Carta, 2011.

Baly, Denis. *The Geography of the Bible*. New and revised edition. New York: Harper & Row, 1974.

Baly, Denis, and A. D. Tushingham. *Atlas of the Biblical World*. New York: The World Publishing Company, 1971.

Bar-Deroma, H. "The River of Egypt (Na al Mizraim)." *PEQ* 92 (1960): 37–56.

Beck, John A. *God as Storyteller: Seeking Meaning in Biblical Narrative*. St. Louis: Chalice Press, 2008.

————. *Discovery House Bible Atlas*. Grand Rapids: Discovery House, 2015.

Beck, John A., general editor *Zondervan Dictionary of Biblical Imagery*. Grand Rapids: Zondervan, 2011.

Beitzel, Barry J. "The *Via Maris* in Literary and Cartographic Sources." *BA* 54 (June 1991): 65–76.

————. "Was There a Joint Nautical Venture on the Mediterranean Sea by Tyrian Phoenicians and Early Israelites?" *BASOR* 360 (2010): 37–66.

Bell, Gertrude. *The Letters of Gertrude Bell*. Vol. 1. Harmondsworth, Middlesex: Penguin Books, 1987. Reprint edition.

————. *The Desert and the Sown*. London: William Heinemann, 1907.

Ben-Arieh, Yehoshua. *Jerusalem in the Nineteenth Century: The Old City*. Jerusalem: Yad Izhak Ben Zvi Institute, 1984.

————. *The Rediscovery of the Holy Land in the Nineteenth Century*. Second edition. Jerusalem: The Magnes Press, 1983.

Biger, Gideon. "The Names and Boundaries of Eretz-Israel (Palestine) as Reflections of Stages in Its History". In *The Land that Became Israel*, edited by Ruth Kark, 1–22. New Haven: Yale University Press, 1989.

Bin Muhammad, Ghazi. *The Tribes of Jordan at the Beginning of the Twenty-First Century*. Amman: Atalla Design, 1999.

Birkerts, Sven. *The Gutenberg Elegies: The Fate of Reading in an Electronic Age*. New York: Fawcett Columbine, 1994.

Blank, Amy K. *The Spoken Choice*. Cincinnati: HUC Press, 1959.

Borger, R. *Die Inschriften Asarhaddons Königs von Assyrien*. *AfO* Beiheft 9. Berlin: E. Weidner, 1956.

Boyer, David S. "Geographical Twins a World Apart." *The National Geographic Magazine* 114/6 (December 1958): 848–59.

Brisco, Thomas. *Holman Bible Atlas*. Nashville: Broadman & Holman, 1998.

Brown, Raymond E. *The Birth of the Messiah*. Garden City, NY: Doubleday, 1977.

Brueggemann, Walter. *The Land*. Philadelphia: Fortress, 1977.

Burgeon, John William. *Petra, a Poem*. Oxford: F. MacPherson, 1846.

Burckhardt, Johann Ludwig. *Travels in Syria and the Holy Land*. London: J. Murray, 1822.

Cansdale, George. *Animals of the Bible*. Devon: Paternoster, 1970.

Chapelle, Tony, and Dickey Chapelle. "Report from the Locust Wars." *The National Geographic Magazine* 103/4 (April 1953): 545–62.

Clark, Douglas R., Larry G. Herr, Øysten S. LaBianca, et al. *The Madaba Plains Project: Forty Years of Archaeological Research into Jordan's Past*. Sheffield: Equinox, 2011.

Cohen, Rudolph. "New Light on the Date of the Petra-Gaza Road." *BA* 45 (1982): 240–47.

Coggins, R. J. *Samaritans and Jews: The Origins of Samaritanism Reconsidered*. Oxford: Basil Blackwell, 1975.

Cohen, Rudolph. "The Iron Age Fortresses in the Central Negev." *BASOR* 236 (1979): 61–79.

Collins, Steven. "Where Is Sodom? The Case for Tall el-Hammam." *BAR* 39/2 (2013): 32–41, 70–71.

Conder, C. R., and H. H. Kitchener. *The Survey of Western Palestine: Memoirs of the Topography, Orography, Hydrography, and Archaeology*. 3 volumes: *Galilee, Samaria, Judaea*. London: The Committee of the Palestine Exploration Fund, 1881–1883.

Conley, Robert A. M. "Locusts: 'Teeth of the Wind.'" *National Geographic* 119 (1969): 202–27.

Cooper, Alan. "Divine Names and Epithets in the Ugaritic Texts." In *Ras Shamra Parallels: The Texts from Ugarit and the Hebrew Bible*, edited by Stan Rummel, Volume 3, 335–469. Rome: Pontificio Instituto Biblico, 1981.

Dark, K. R. "Archaeological Evidence for a Previously Unrecognized Roman Town Near the Sea of Galilee." *PEQ* 145/3 (2013): 185–202.

Denin, Avinoam. "Paleoclimates in Israel: Evidence from Weathering Patterns of Stones in and Near Archaeological Sites." *BASOR* 259 (1985): 33–43.

Dorsey, David. *The Roads and Highways of Ancient Israel*. Baltimore: Johns Hopkins University, 1991.

Eames, Samantha. "Between 'The Desert and the Sown'; The Hauran as a Frontier Zone in the Middle Bronze Age." *PEQ* 135/2 (2003): 88–107.

Elitzur, Yoel. *Ancient Place Names in the Holy Land: Preservation and History*. Jerusalem: The Hebrew University-Magnes Press, 2004.

Faust, Abraham. *Israel's Ethnogenesis: Settlement, Interaction, Expansion and Resistance*. London: Equinox, 2006.

———. "The Sharon and the Yarkon Basin in the Tenth Century B.C.E. Ecology, Settlement Patterns and Political Involvement." *IEJ* 57 (2007): 65–82.

———. "The Shephelah in the Iron Age: A New Look on the Settlement of Judah." *PEQ* 145/3 (2013): 203–19.

Finkelstein, Israel. *The Archaeology of the Israelite Settlement*. Jerusalem: IES, 1988.

———. "Edom in the Iron I." *Levant* 24 (1992): 159–66.

Freeman-Grenville, G. S. P., Rupert L. Chapman III, and Joan E. Taylor. *The Onomasticon by Eusebius of Caesarea*. Jerusalem: Carta, 2003.

Freyne, Sean. *Galilee from Alexander the Great to Hadrian: A Study of Second Temple Judaism*. Edinburgh: T&T Clark, 1980.

———. *Jesus a Jewish Galilean*. London: T&T Clark, 2004.

Gal, Zvi. "The Settlement of Issachar: Some New Observations." *TA* 9 (1982): 79–86.

Garstang, John. *Joshua/Judges*. London: Constable & Co., 1931.

Geva, Hillel, ed. *Ancient Jerusalem Revealed*. Jerusalem: IES, 2000.

Gevaryahu, Gilad J. "Why Was Mount Gerizim Chosen for the Blessing Ceremony?" *JBQ* 43:2 (2015): 122–25.

Glueck, Nelson. *The Other Side of the Jordan*. Cambridge: ASOR, 1970.

Golomb, B., and Y. Kedar. "Ancient Agriculture in the Galilee Mountains." *IEJ* 21 (1971): 136–40.

Graf, David F. "Hellenization and the Decapolis." *ARAM* 4 (1994): 1–48.

————. "The Saracens and the Defense of the Arabian Frontier." *BASOR* 229 (1978): 1–26.

————. "The Via Nova Traiana in Arabia Petraea." *JRA* 14 (1995): 1–33.

Graf, David, Benjamin Isaac, and Israel Roll. "Roads and Highways (Roman)." In *ABD*, edited by David Noel Freedman, Volume 5, 782–87. New York: Doubleday, 1992.

Grayson, A. Kirk. *Assyrian Rulers of the Early First Millennium BC II (858–745 BC).* RIMA 3. Toronto: University of Toronto, 1996.

Hadas, Gideon. "Dead Sea Anchorages." *RB* 118 (2011): 161–79.

Hallo, William W., ed. *The Context of Scripture.* Vol. I: *Canonical Compositions from the Biblical World.* Leiden: Brill, 1997.

————. *The Context of Scripture.* Vol. II: *Monumental Inscriptions from the Biblical World.* Leiden: Brill, 2000.

Har-el, Menasheh. "The Pride of the Jordan – the Jungle of the Jordan." *BA* 41 (1978): 69.

Herodotus. *Histories.* Translated by A. D. Godley. Revised edition. LCL. Cambridge: Harvard University, 1938.

Heschel, Abraham J. *The Prophets.* Volume 1. New York: Harper & Row, 1962.

Hjelm, Ingrid. *The Samaritans and Early Judaism: A Literary Analysis.* Sheffield: Sheffield Academic, 2000.

Hobbs, Joseph J. *Bedouin Life in the Egyptian Wilderness.* Cairo: American University, 1989.

Horowitz, Wayne, Takayoshi Oshima, and Seth Sanders. *Cuneiform in Canaan: The Next Generation.* Second edition. University Park, PA: Eisenbrauns, 2018.

Iamblichus. *The Life of Pythagoras.* Translated by Thomas Taylor. Los Angeles: Theosophical Publishing House, 1918.

Josephus. *Jewish Antiquities.* Translated by H. St. J. Thackeray. LCL. Cambridge: Harvard University, 1930.

————. *The Jewish War.* Translated by H. St. J. Thackeray. LCL. Cambridge: Harvard University, 1927.

Kallai, Zecharia. "Remains of the Roman Road Along the Mevo-Beitar Highway." *IEJ* 15 (1965): 195.203.

Kallner-Amiran, D. H. "A Revised Earthquake-Catalogue of Palestine." *IEJ* 1 (1950–51): 223–46.

Karmon, Yehuda. "Geographical Aspects in the History of the Coastal Plain of Israel." *IEJ* 6 (1956): 33–50.

————. "Geographical Influences on the Historical Routes in the Sharon Plain." *PEQ* 93 (1961): 43–60.

————. *Israel: A Regional Geography.* London: Wiley-Interscience, 1971.

Kitchen, K. A. *On the Reliability of the Old Testament.* Grand Rapids: William B. Eerdmans, 2003.

Klein, Micha. "Water Balance of the Upper Jordan River Basin." *Water International* 23 (1998): 224–48.

Kline, Meredith G. "Har Magedon: The End of the Milennium." *JETS* 39:2 (1996): 207–22.

Kokkinos, Nikos. "The Location of Tarichaea: North or South of Tiberius?" *PEQ* 142/1 (2010): 7–23.

Lancaster, Steven P., and James M. Monson. *Geobasics Study Guide.* Rockford, IL: Biblical Backgrounds, 2009.

Lehmann, Gunnar. "The United Monarchy in the Countryside: Jerusalem, Judah and the Shephelah during the Tenth Century B.C.E." In *Jerusalem in Bible and Archaeology: The First Temple Period*, edited by Andrew G. Vaughn and Ann E. Killebrew, 136–56. Atlanta: SBL, 2003.

Levin, Yigal. "The Identification of Khirbet Qeiyafa: A New Suggestion." *BASOR* 367 (2012): 73–86.

————. "The Jordan River in Biblical Geography: From Boundary to Allegory." *ARAM* 29 (2017): 221–34.

Levy, Thomas E. "Pastoral Nomads and Iron Age Metal Production in Ancient Edom." In *Nomads, Tribes and the State in the Ancient Near East: Cross-Disciplinary Perspectives*, edited Jeffrey Szuchman, 147–76. Chicago: University of Chicago, 2009.

Levy, Udi. *The Lost Civilization of Petra.* London: Floris Books, 1996.

L'Heureux, C. E. "The Ugaritic and Biblical Rephaim." *HTR* 67 (1974): 265–74.

————. "The *yelîdê hārāpā'*—a Cultic Association of Warriors." *BASOR* 221 (1976): 83–85.

Lipschitz, Nili, and Yoav Waisel. "Dendroarchaeological Investigations in Israel (Taanach)." *IEJ* 30 (1980): 132–36.

Lipschitz, Nili, Simcha Lev-Yadun, and Ram Gophna. "The Dominance of *Quercus Calliprinos* (Kermes Oak) in the Central Coastal Plain in Antiquity." *IEJ* 37 (1987): 43–50.

Lipschits, Oded, and Aren M. Maeir, eds. *The Shephelah during the Iron Age: Recent*

Archaeological Studies. Winona Lake, IN: Eisenbrauns, 2017.

Lynch, W. F. *Narrative of the United States' Expedition to the River Jordan and the Dead Sea*. Philadelphia: Lea and Blanchard, 1849.

Magen, Yitzhak. *Mount Gerizim Excavations: A Temple City*. Jerusalem: IAA, 2008.

———. "Nebi Samwil: Whence Samuel Crowned Israel's First King." *BAR* 34/3 (2009): 36–45, 78–79.

———. *The Stone Vessel Industry in the Second Temple Period: Excavations at Hizma and the Jerusalem Temple Mount*. Jerusalem: IES, 2002.

Maisler [Mazar], Benjamin. "Canaan and the Canaanites." *BASOR* 102 (April 1946): 7–12.

Malamat, Abraham. *Mari and the Bible*. Leiden: Brill, 1998.

———. *Mari and the Early Israelite Experience: The Schweich Lectures of the British Academy, 1984*. Oxford: Oxford University, 1989.

Malpas, Jeff. *Place and Experience: A Philosophical Topography*. Cambridge: Cambridge University Press, 1999.

Margalit, Baruch. "The Geographical Setting of the AQHT Story and Its Ramifications." In *Ugarit in Retrospect: Fifty Years of Ugarit and Ugaritic*, edited by Gordon D. Young, 131–58. Winona Lake, IN: Eisenbrauns, 1981.

Martens, Elmer. *God's Design: A Focus on Old Testament Theology*. Grand Rapids: Baker, 1981.

Martin, James C., John A. Beck, and David G. Hansen. *A Visual Guide to Bible Events*. Grand Rapids: Baker, 2009.

Master, Daniel M. "Trade and Politics: Ashkelon's Balancing Act in the Seventh Century B.C.E." *BASOR* 330 (2003): 47–64.

Mazar, Amihai. "The 'Bull Site'—an Iron Age I Open Cult Place." *BASOR* 247 (1982): 27–42.

———. "Iron Age Fortresses in the Judean Hills." *PEQ* 114 (July–December 1982): 87–109.

Mazar, Amihai, Dvory Namdar, Nava Panitz-Cohen, Ronny Neumann, and Steve Weiner. "The Iron Age II Beehives at Tel Rehov in the Jordan Valley: Archaeological and Analytical Aspects." *Antiquity* 82 (2008): 629–39.

Meshel, Ze'ev. "Defining the Biblical 'Arabah." In *"Up to the Gates of Ekron": Essays on the Archaeology and History of the Eastern Mediterranean in Honor of Seymour Gitin*, edited by Sidney White Crawford, 423–35. Jerusalem: IES, 2007.

———. "Wilderness Wanderings: Ethnographic Lessons from Modern Bedouin." *BAR* 34/4 (2008): 32–39.

Meyer, Karl E., and Shareen Blair Brysac. *Kingmakers: The Invention of the Modern Middle East*. New York: W. W. Norton, 2008.

Melville, Herman. *Journals*. Edited by Howard C. Horsford with Lynn Horth. Evanston and Chicago: Northwestern University and Newberry Library, 1989. Reprint edition.

Miller, Fergus. *The Roman Near East, 31 B.C.–A.D. 337*. Cambridge: Harvard University, 1993.

Mishnah. Translated by Herbert Danby. Oxford: Oxford University Press, 1933.

Moldenke, Harold N., and Alma L. Moldenke. *Plants of the Bible*. New York: Dover, 1952.

Monson, James M. *The Land Between: A Regional Study Guide to the Land of the Bible*. Jerusalem: James M. Monson, 1983.

Monson, James M., with Steven P. Lancaster. *Regions on the Run*. Rockford, IL: Biblical Backgrounds, 2014.

———. *Geobasics in the Land of the Bible*. Rockford, IL: Biblical Backgrounds, 2008.

Moran, William L. *The Amarna Letters*. Baltimore: Johns Hopkins University, 1992.

Notley, R. Steven, and Ze'ev Safrai. *Eusebuis, Onomasticon: A Triglot Edition with Notes and Commentary*. Leiden: Brill, 2005.

Nun, Mendel. "Has Bethsaida Finally Been Found?" *JP* 544 (July–Sept 1998): 12–31.

Obenzinger, Hilton. *American Palestine: Melville, Twain and the Holy Land*. Princeton: Princeton University, 1999.

Oppenheim, A. Leo, ed. *The Assyrian Dictionary (CAD)*. Chicago: The Oriental Institute, 1956–2010.

Orni, Efraim, and Elisha Efrat. *Geography of Israel*. 4th edition. Jerusalem: Israel Universities Press, 1980.

Oswalt, John N. *The Bible Among the Myths*. Grand Rapids: Zondervan, 2009.

Ottosson, Magnus. *Gilead: Tradition and History*. Lund: CWK Gleerup, 1969.

Palmer, Carol. "'Following the Plough': The Agricultural Environment of Northern Jordan." *Levant* 30 (1998): 129–65.

Parker, Cynthia. "Deuteronomy's Place: An Analysis of the Placial Structure of Deuteronomy". Unpublished Ph.D. dissertation, University of Gloucestershire, 2014.

———. "Crossing to 'The Other Side' of the Sea of Galilee." In *Lexham Geographical Commentary on the Gospels*, edited by Barry J. Beitzel, 157–64. Bellingham, WA: Lexham Press, 2017.

Periplus of Scylax. Charles Müller. *Geographi Graeci Minores*. Volume 1. Paris: Editore Ambrosio Fimin Didot, 1882.

Phillips, Elaine. "'The Tomb that Abraham Had Purchased' (Acts 7:16)." In *Perspectives on Our Father Abraham*, edited by Steve A. Hunt, 110–25. Grand Rapids: Eerdmans, 2010.

Piccirillo, Michele, and Eugenio Alliata, eds. *The Madaba Map Centenary, 1897–1997*. Jerusalem: Studium Biblicum Franciscanum, 1998.

Pliny. *Natural History*. With an English translation by H. Rackham. LCL. Cambridge: Harvard University, 1942.

Pope, Marvin H. "The Cult of the Dead at Ugarit." In *Ugarit in Retrospect: Fifty Year of Ugarit and Ugaritic*, edited by Gordon D. Young, 159–79. Winona Lake, IN: Eisenbrauns, 1981.

Prag, Kay. "Bethlehem: A Site Assessment." *PEQ* 132 (2000): 169–81.

————. "Decorative Architecture in Ammon, Moab, and Judah." *Levant* 19 (1987): 121–27.

Prawer, Joshua. *The Latin Kingdom of Jerusalem: European Colonialism in the Middle Ages*. London: Weidenfeld and Nicolson, 1972.

Pritchard, James B., ed. *Ancient Near Eastern Texts Relating to the Old Testament* (*ANET*). Princeton: Princeton University, 1955.

Raban, Avner. "Near Eastern Harbors: Thirteenth–Seventh Centuries B.C.E." In *Mediterranean Peoples in Transition*, edited by Seymour Gitin, Amihai Mazar, and Ephraim Stern, 428–38. Jerusalem: Israel Exploration Society, 1998.

Rainey, Anson F. "Aspects of Life in Ancient Israel." In *Life and Culture in the Ancient Near East*, edited by Richard E. Averbeck, Mark W. Chavalas, and David B. Weisberg, 256–61. Bethesda, MD: CDL, 2003.

————. "The Biblical Shephelah of Judah." *BASOR* 251 (1983): 1–10.

————. *Canaanite in the Amarna Tablets: A Linguistic Analysis of the Mixed Dialect Used by the Scribes from Canaan*. Volume 1: *Orthography, Phonology, Morphosyntactic Analysis of the Pronouns, Nouns, Numerals*. Leiden: Brill, 1996.

————. "Early Historical Geography of the Negeb." In *Beer-Sheba II: The Early Iron Age Settlements*, by Ze'ev Herzog, 88–104. Tel Aviv: Institute of Archaeology, 1984.

————. "Redefining Hebrew—a Transjordanian Language." *MAARAV* 14/2 (2007): 67–81.

————. "The Satrapy 'Beyond the River." *AJBA* 1 (1969): 51–78.

————. "Sharon." In *The International Standard Bible Encyclopedia*, edited by Geoffrey W. Bromiley. Vol. 5, 451–53. Grand Rapids: Eerdmans, 1988.

————. "Whence Came the Israelites and Their Language?" *IEJ* 57 (2007): 41–64.

Rainey, Anson F., and R. Steven Notley. *The Sacred Bridge: Carta's Atlas of the Biblical World*. Second emended & enhanced edition. Jerusalem: Carta, 2014.

Rasmussen, Carl G. *Zondervan Atlas of the Bible*. Revised edition. Grand Rapids: Zondervan, 2010.

Reich, Ronny. *Excavating the City of David: Where Jerusalem's History Began*. Jerusalem: Israel Exploration Society, 2011.

Richardson, Peter. *Building Jewish in the Roman East*. Waco: Baylor University, 2004.

Robinson, Edward. *Biblical Researches in Palestine and the Adjacent Regions: A Journal of Travels in the Years 1838 & 1852*. 3 volumes. Jerusalem: Universitas Booksellers, 1970. Reprint edition.

Robinson, Edward, and Eli Smith. *Biblical Researches in Palestine, Mount Sinai and Arabia Petraea: A Journal of Travels in the Year 1838 by E. Robinson and E. Smith Undertaken in Reference to Biblical Geography*. 2 volumes. Boston: Crocker and Brewster, 1841.

————. *Later Biblical Researches in Palestine and in the Adjacent Regions: A Journal of Travels in the Year 1852, Drawn up from the Original Diaries, with Historical Illustrations, with New Maps and Plans*. Boston: Crocker and Brewster, 1856.

Roll, Israel. "The Roman Road System in Judea." In *The Jerusalem Cathedra*, vol.3, edited by Lee I. Levine, 136–61. Jerusalem: Yad Izhak Ben-Zvi Institute, 1983.

————. "Roman Roads in Western Samaria." *PEQ* 118 (1986): 113–43.

Rosenan, Naftali, and Mordechai H. Gilead, "Annual Rainfall, 1932/33–1975/76," sheet 13 in *Atlas of Israel: Cartography, Physical and Human Geography*. 3rd edition. Tel Aviv: Survey of Israel, 1985.

Rowe, Alan. *The Topography and History of Beth-shan*. Volume 1. Philadelphia: University Press, 1930.

Rowton, Michael B. "Autonomy and Nomadism in Western Asia." *Orientalis NS* 42 (1973): 247–58.

————. "Dimorphic Structure and Topology." *Oriens Antiquus* 15 (1976): 17–31.

Sailhamer, John H. *The Pentateuch as Narrative*. Grand Rapids: Zondervan, 1992.

Sauer, Carl Ortwin. "Forward to Historical Geography." In *Land and Life: A Selection from the Writings of Carl*

Ortwin Sauer, edited by John Leighly, 351–79. Berkeley: University of California, 1963.

———. "The Education of a Geographer." In *Land and Life: A Selection from the Writings of Carl Ortwin Sauer*, edited by John Leighly, 389–404. Berkeley: University of California, 1963.

Schumacher, Gottlieb. *The Jaulân*. London: Richard Bentley and Son, 1888.

———. *Across the Jordan: Being an Exploration and Survey of Part of Hauran and Jaulan*. London: Alexander P. Watt, 1889.

Siliotti, Alberto. *Guide to the Valley of the Kings and to the Thebian Necropolises and Temples*. Vercelli, Italy: White Star, 2000.

Simons, J. *The Geographical and Topographical Texts of the Old Testament*. Leiden: Brill, 1959.

Smith, George Adam. *The Historical Geography of the Holy Land*. London: Hodder and Stoughton, 1894.

———. *The Historical Geography of the Holy Land*. 13th edition. Jerusalem: Ariel, 1966. Reprint edition.

Stager, Lawrence. "Farming in the Judean Desert during the Iron Age." *BASOR* 221 (1976): 145–58.

Stager, Lawrence E., J. David Schloen, and Daniel M. Master. *Ashkelon 1: Introduction and Overview (1985–2006)*. Winona Lake, IN: Eisenbrauns, 2008.

Stern, Ephraim. *Excavations at Tel Mevorakh*. QEDEM 18. Jerusalem: The Institute of Archaeology, The Hebrew University of Jerusalem. 1984.

Stern, Ephraim, ed. *The New Encyclopedia of Archaeological Excavations in the Holy Land (NEAEHL)*. 4 vols. New York: Simon & Shuster, 1993. Supplementary volume 5. Jerusalem: IES, 2008.

Stewardson, Henry C, compiler. *The Survey of Western Palestine: A General Index*. London: The Committee of the PEF, 1888.

Stolz, Fritz. "Sea." In *Dictionary of Deities and Demons in the Bible*, edited by Karel van der Toorn, Bob Becking, and Pieter W. van der Horst, 1390–1402. Leiden: E. J. Brill, 1995.

Strabo. *The Geography of Strabo*. Translated by Horace Leonard Jones. LCL. Cambridge: Harvard University, 1917.

Stutzman, Linford. *Sailing Acts: Following an Ancient Voyage*. Intercourse, PA: Good Books, 2006.

Tacitus. *Histories*. Translated by Clifford H. Moore. LCL. Cambridge: Harvard University, 1925.

Tappy, Ron E. "East of Ashkelon: The Setting and Settling of the Judean Lowlands in the Iron Age IIA." In *Exploring the Longue Durée: Essays in Honor of Lawrence E. Stager*, edited by J. David Schloen, 449–63. Winona Lake, IN: Eisenbrauns, 2009.

———. "The Archaeology and History of Tel Zayit: A Record of Liminal Life." In *The Shephelah during the Iron Age: Recent Archaeological Studies*, edited by Oded Lipschits and Aren M. Maeir, 155–79. Winona Lake, IN: Eisenbrauns, 2017.

Taylor, Jane. *Petra and the Lost Kingdom of the Nabateans*. London: I. B. Tauris, 2001.

———. "Missing Magdala and the Name of Mary 'Magdalene.'" *PEQ* 146/3 (2014): 205–23.

Troche, Facundo D. "Ancient Fishing Methods and Fishing Grounds in the Lake of Galilee." *PEQ* 148 (2016): 281–93.

Twain, Mark. *The Innocents Abroad*. Signet Classic Edition. New York: New American Library, 1966.

Van der Steen, Eveline. "Bedouin Poetry and Landscape." In *The Land of Israel in Bible, History and Theology: Studies in Honor of Ed Noort*, edited by Jacques van Ruiten and J. Cornelis de Vos, 415–29. Leiden: Brill, 2009.

———. *Near Eastern Tribal Societies during the Nineteenth Century: Economy, Society and Politics between Tent and Town*. Sheffield: Equinox, 2013.

Van Dyke, Henry. *Out-of-Doors in the Holy Land*. New York: Charles Scribner's Sons, 1908.

Varro, Marcus Terentius. *On Agriculture*. Translated by William Davis Hooper, revised by Harrison Boyd Ash. LCL. Cambridge: Harvard University Press, 1934.

Vester, Bertha Spafford. *Our Jerusalem: An American Family in the Holy City, 1881–1949*. Jerusalem: Ariel, 1988.

Warren, Sir Charles, and Claude Reignier Conder. *The Survey of Western Palestine: Jerusalem*. London: The Committee of the Palestine Exploration Fund, 1884.

Wasef, Husney. *The Israelite Journey through the Wilderness in the Sinai Peninsula*. Nablus: Centre of the Good Samaritan, 2012.

Wazana, Nili. *All the Boundaries of the Land: The Promised Land in Biblical Thought in Light of the Ancient Near East*. Translated by Liat Qeren. Winona Lake, IN: Eisenbrauns, 2013.

Weeks, Harry. "Sharon." In *ABD* vol. 5 edited by David Noel Freedman, 1161–63. New York: Doubleday, 1992.

Wilkin, Robert L. *The Land Called Holy: Palestine in Christian History and Thought*. New Haven: Yale University Press, 1992.

Wise, Michael, Martin G. Abegg, and Edward Cook. *The Dead Sea Scrolls: A New Translation*. San Francisco: Harper, 1996.

Wright, G. Ernest. *Shechem: The Biography of a Biblical City.* New York: McGraw-Hill, 1965.

Wright, P. H. "Ezion-geber." In *Dictionary of the Old Testament: Historical Books*, edited by Bill T. Arnold and H. G. M. Williamson, 274–77. Downers Grove, IL: InterVarsity, 2005.

———. *Understanding Biblical Kingdoms & Empires: An Introductory Atlas & Comparative View.* Jerusalem: Carta, 2010.

———. *Rose Then and Now Bible Map Atlas with Biblical Background and Culture.* Torrance, CA: Rose Publishing, 2011.

———. "The Size and Makeup of Nazareth at the Time of Jesus." In *Lexham Geographic Commentary on the Gospels*, edited by Barry J. Beitzel, 30–41. Bellingham, WA: Lexham Press, 2017.

———. *Understanding the Ecology of the Bible: An Introductory Atlas.* Jerusalem: Carta, 2018.

———. "Introduction to Historical Geography." In *Behind the Scenes of the Old Testament: Cultural, Social, and Historical Contexts,* edited by Jonathan S. Greer, John W. Hilber, and John H. Walton, 5–11. Grand Rapids, MI: Baker, 2018.

Zohary, Michael. *Plants of the Bible.* Cambridge: Cambridge University, 1982.

SCRIPTURE INDEX

2 SAMUEL

1 KINGS

2 KINGS

GENERAL INDEX

Numbers in **bold** type refer to pages on which places pertinent to topics are shown on maps.

PLACE NAME INDEX

Numbers in regular type refer to pages on which places are mentioned in the text; numbers in **bold** type refer to pages on which places are shown on maps. The definite article is ignored when alphabetizing Arabic names. All ascents, highways, passes, roads, and ways are indexed under "routes."